PUBLIC AND PRIVATE FAMILIES

A Reader

SIXTH EDITION

Andrew J. Cherlin

Johns Hopkins University

Connect
Learn
Succeed™

Published by McGraw-Hill, an imprint of The McGraw-Hill Companies, Inc., 1221 Avenue of the Americas, New York, NY, 10020. Copyright © 2010, 2008, 2005, 2001, 1998. All rights reserved. No part of this publication may be reproduced or distributed in any form or by any means, or stored in a database or retrieval system, without the prior written consent of The McGraw-Hill Companies, Inc., including, but not limited to, in any network or other electronic storage or transmission, or broadcast for distance learning.

This book is printed on acid-free paper.

1 2 3 4 5 6 7 8 9 0 DOC/DOC 0 9

ISBN: 978-0-07-340436-3
MHID: 0-07-340436-5

Vice President, Editorial: *Michael Ryan*
Sponsoring Editor: *Gina Boedeker*
Managing Editor: *Nicole Bridge*
Marketing Manager: *Pamela Cooper*
Developmental Editor: *Phillip Butcher*
Production Editor: *Holly Paulsen*
Manuscript Editor: *Margaret Moore*
Design Manager: *Allister Fein*
Cover Designer: *Asylum Studios*
Production Supervisor: *Laura Fuller*
Composition: *10.5/12 Times Roman, Laserwords Private Limited*
Printing: *45# Publishers Matte, R. R. Donnelley & Sons*

Cover: Farinaz Taghavi/Getty Images

Library of Congress Cataloging-in-Publication Data has been applied for.

The Internet addresses listed in the text were accurate at the time of publication. The inclusion of a Web site does not indicate an endorsement by the authors or McGraw-Hill, and McGraw-Hill does not guarantee the accuracy of the information presented at these sites.

www.mhhe.com

ABOUT THE AUTHOR

(Courtesy of Will Kirk,
Johns Hopkins University)

ANDREW J. CHERLIN is Benjamin H. Griswold III Professor of Public Policy in the Department of Sociology at Johns Hopkins University. He received a B.S. from Yale University in 1970 and a Ph.D. in sociology from the University of California at Los Angeles in 1976. His books include *The Marriage-Go-Round: The State of Marriage and the Family in America Today* (2009), *Marriage, Divorce, Remarriage* (revised and enlarged edition, 1992), *Divided Families: What Happens to Children when Parents Part* (with Frank F. Furstenberg Jr., 1991), and *The New American Grandparent: A Place in the Family, A Life Apart* (with Frank F. Furstenberg Jr., 1986). In 1989–1990, he was Chair of the Family Section of the American Sociological Association. In 1999, he was President of the Population Association of America, the scholarly organization for demographic research.

In 2003, Professor Cherlin received the Distinguished Career Award from the Family Section of the American Sociological Association. In 2009, he received the Irene B. Taeuber Award from the Population Association of America for "an accumulated record of exceptionally sound and innovative research." He also has received the Olivia S. Nordberg Award for Excellence in Writing in the Population Sciences and a MERIT (Method to Extend Research in Time) Award from the National Institutes of Health for his research on the effects of family structure on children. In 2005–2006, he was a recipient of a John Simon Guggenheim Memorial Foundation Fellowship. His articles include "The Deinstitutionalization of American Marriage," in the *Journal of Marriage and Family* (2004);

"American Marriage in the Early Twenty-First Century," in *The Future of Children* (2005); and "The Influence of Physical and Sexual Abuse on Marriage and Cohabitation," in *American Sociological Review* (2004). He also has written many short articles for *The New York Times, The Washington Post, The Nation, Newsweek,* and other periodicals. He has been interviewed on *ABC News Nightline,* the *Today Show,* network evening news programs, National Public Radio's *All Things Considered,* the BBC, and other news programs and documentaries.

CONTENTS

v

PREFACE

The metaphor of public and private families in the title of this Reader reflects my sense that families matter in two senses. First, they perform activities of great importance to the public interest—most notably raising the next generation and caring for the frail elderly. Second, as the main site of our personal lives, they provide the private satisfactions of love, intimacy, and companionship. Many textbooks and readers focus more on the private family; they mainly describe how people manage their personal relationships as they proceed through their life course. I include this perspective, too; but I attempt to balance it with a consideration of the important public issues raised by the great recent changes in family life. Indeed, hardly a week goes by without some family issue—gay marriage, government programs to promote marriage, teenage childbearing, child care, domestic violence, and so forth—appearing on the front page of the newspapers. Consequently, it's crucial that students studying the sociology of the family encounter not just studies of the individual life course but also of the ways that family life affects our society. I have attempted to provide both the public and private perspectives on the family in this Reader.

ORGANIZATION

This book consists of 28 readings that are keyed to the 14 chapters of the sixth edition of the textbook that I have written for courses in the Sociology of the Family, *Public and Private Families: An Introduction*. Two readings are presented for each chapter. Nevertheless, this book can be used with other textbooks or no textbook at all. The readings represent a broad sampling of new ideas and older insights from the literature on families. After introductory and historical material, I introduce readings on gender, class, race, and ethnicity. I then turn to readings on sexuality, cohabitation, marriage, the work of caring for others, children, and older people. After that, the readings cover issues of conflict, disruption, and reconstitution such as domestic violence, divorce, and remarriage. The volume concludes with readings on family policy.

NEW TO THE SIXTH EDITION

Eight of the 28 readings are new to this edition. Here is a guide to what's new:

- *Chapter 1.* I have replaced a reading on demographic change with a more recent article by Claude Fischer and Michael Hout that covers the entire twentieth century. It summarizes some of the findings from their book-length treatment, *Century of Difference: How America Changed in the Last One Hundred Years.*
- *Chapter 2.* The readings are unchanged from the previous edition.
- *Chapter 3.* I have included an excerpt from Andrea Doucet's book, *Do Men Mother? Fathering, Care, and Domestic Responsibility,* in which she studied fathers who were full-time caregivers to their children. The 1991 article by DeVault on "feeding as women's work" has been deleted.
- *Chapters 4, 5, 6, and 7.* The readings are unchanged from the previous edition.
- *Chapter 8.* I have included an article from *Contexts* by Kathleen Gerson and Jerry A. Jacobs on trends in the hours of paid work that family members do. It covers some of the findings from their book, *The Time Divide: Work, Gender, and Gender Inequality.*
- *Chapter 9.* I have replaced a short article on fathers in Evangelical Protestant families with a longer treatment of the same topic by one of the authors, W. Bradford Wilcox, that appeared in *Contexts.*
- *Chapter 10.* The readings are unchanged from the previous edition.
- *Chapter 11.* The previous edition included an excerpt from a book chapter by Michael P. Johnson on his distinction between different kinds of intimate partner violence. I have replaced it with a newer, and I think clearer, treatment of the same topic drawn from Johnson's book, *A Typology of Domestic Violence.* In addition, I have included an article by Amy Leisenring on the controversial question of whether mandatory arrest policies, under which the police must arrest an alleged perpetrator if they are

called to a home because of an incident of violence, are effective. I have deleted an article on the long-term consequences of childhood abuse for later family patterns.

- *Chapter 12.* I have included a reading from two psychologists who urge that, when considering the effects of divorce on children, we differentiate between pain (sad, painful memories of one's parents' divorce) and pathology (effects that cause problems in a child's later life, such as not graduating from high school). I have deleted an article on examining divorce from the child's perspective.
- *Chapter 13.* I have included an article that examines how children are doing not only in conventional stepfamilies formed by marriage but also in the growing numbers of families in which a parent and her (occasionally, his) biological child are cohabiting with a romantic partner but are not married. I have deleted an article on overlooked aspects of stepparenting.
- *Chapter 14.* The readings are unchanged from the previous edition.
- *Chapter 15.* Because Chapter 15 of my textbook, *Public and Private Families: An Introduction,* has been deleted in the sixth edition, I have deleted this chapter of the reader.

ACKNOWLEDGMENTS

To write a book this comprehensive requires the help of many people. At McGraw-Hill, sponsoring editor Gina Boedeker provided initial support, freelance development editor Phil Butcher provided valuable editorial guidance, and Holly Paulsen smoothly managed the production process. In addition, the following people read the fifth edition and provided me with helpful suggestions for this revision:

Jennifer Meehan Brennom, Kirkwood Community College
Jerry Cook, California State University, Sacramento
Jeanine Pfahlert, Millersville University
Margaret L. Usdansky, Syracuse University
Michelle Wolkomir, Centenary College of Louisiana

Andrew J. Cherlin

Part One

Introduction

CHAPTER 1

Public and Private Families

The state of the American family—indeed, the state of the family in all industrialized nations—is a controversial issue, much debated by social commentators, politicians, and academic experts. A half century ago, few observers seemed concerned. But since the 1960s, family life has changed greatly. Many users of this reader will have experienced these changes in their own families. Divorce is much more common; at current rates, nearly one in two marriages would end in divorce. Young adults are postponing marriage and often living with a partner prior to marrying. A growing number of children—currently about 40 percent—are born to mothers who are not married (but who may be cohabiting). And many more married women are working outside the home.

These trends aren't necessarily negative. For instance, married women's jobs often give them an improved sense of self-worth and boost their families' standards of living. Young adults may use living with a partner as a way to search for a more compatible spouse. In fact, some commentators hail the decline of the 1950s middle-class family in which wives usually stayed home and specialized in housework and child care. These breadwinner-homemaker families, it is alleged, restricted the lives of women and supported the continuation of conflict-ridden marriages that may have been worse for children than a parental divorce would have been. But the overall tone of the public commentary on family change has been one of concern.

To develop your own views on the subject, you first need to know the basic facts about changes in American families. In the first selection, sociologists Claude S. Fischer and Michael Hout present a series of charts that show the demographic changes that occurred in the American family in the twentieth century. Their information comes mainly from the U.S. Census of Population, which the Constitution requires the federal government to conduct every ten years. Scholars now have access to Census records going back a century or more. Taking a long view, the authors find that, in some respects, the most unusual and distinctive period of family life occurred in the middle of the twentieth century rather than at the end. They examine the extent to which trends during the century support the widespread belief that "family troubles" have increased.[1]

But more than the demographics of family life changed during the twentieth century. At midcentury marriage was a partnership in which fulfilling one's roles—being a good homemaker, earning the family's income—provided the highest satisfactions. Much of a person's gratifications, then, occurred through activities external to the self. But after the 1950s, marriages, and the rising numbers of heterosexual and homosexual nonmarital partnerships, came to be defined more in terms of individual growth and development than in terms of fulfilling prescribed roles. Sociologist Francesca Cancian, in a selection from her book *Love in America: Gender and Self-Development,* calls this a transition "from role to self" in the focus of personal rewards in marriages and partnerships.

Cancian maintains that love itself was "feminized" under the older kinds of marriage because emotion was seen as the domain of women. Now, love is more "androgynous," meaning that both women and men are concerned about expressing love and emotional support. Correspondingly, autonomy and self-development were emphasized more for men, whereas now these goals are put forth for both genders. To provide evidence for her view of the evolution of marriage, she studied articles on marriage in popular magazines between 1900 and 1979. Their shifting content, she argues, demonstrates the shift from role to self.

---

[1]The authors presented a more thorough examination of changes during the century in their book, *Century of Difference: How America Changed in the Last One Hundred Years* (New York: Russell Sage Foundation, 2006).

The Family in Trouble

Since When? For Whom?

Claude S. Fischer

Michael Hout

OVERVIEW OF FAMILY CHANGES

American family life changed in many ways in the twentieth century, but the severity of a change and the severity of the conversations about that change

did not often match. As we shall see, some of the greatest changes involved the demography of the family and affected the elderly, while the much-discussed matters, such as family dissolution and family intimacy, were much more stable.

Major Changes

Let us highlight the "big" changes in the American family over the century. The first one to note is basic and critical: Americans live a lot longer than they used to.[1] Figure 1.1 shows the average life expectancy of white women and men who had already made it to the age of twenty.[2] A twenty-year-old white woman in 2000 could expect seventeen more years of life than could her ancestor in 1900; a twenty-year-old white man today could expect thirteen years more than a twenty-year-old man a century ago. (In addition to this change, there was an even greater expansion in the life expectancy of infants.) There are, as we shall see, profound implications to this greater longevity.

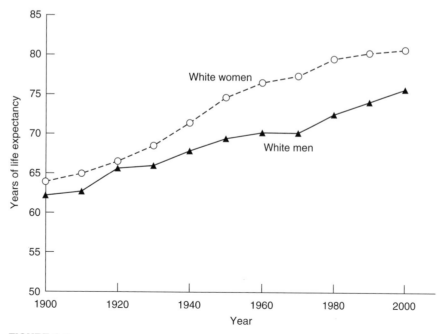

FIGURE 1.1

Years of life expected at age 20, white men and women, 1900–2000. (*Source:* National Center for Health Statistics via http://www.infoplease.com/ipa/A0005140.html.)

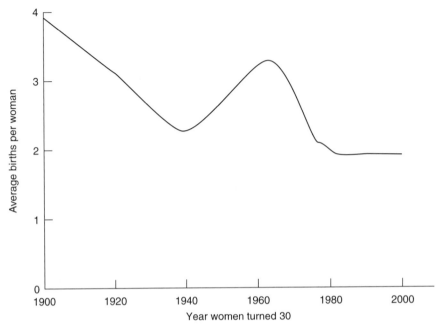

FIGURE 1.2

Number of births over a woman's lifetime by year of her 30th birthday, for women born 1870–1970. (*Source:* Steven Ruggles, Matthew Sobek, Trent Alexander, Catherine A. Fitch, Ronald Goeken, Patricia Kelly Hall, Miriam King, and Chad Ronnander, *Integrated Public Use Microdata Series: Version 3,* machine-readable database [Minneapolis: Minnesota Population Center, 2004], available at http://www.ipums.umn.edu/usa/.)

Add to this another major change—the reduction in the birthrate. The average number of births per woman, dated at the age she turned thirty, dropped steeply from 1900 to the 1940s, as shown in Figure 1.2; if we could push back the view here to 1800, we would see a tilted line starting from about seven or eight births per woman in 1800 down to about two in 1940.[3] The 1950s and early 1960s were unusual. Take out the anomalies—the drop in births during the Depression and World War II and the Baby Boom afterward—and we would see a smoothly declining curve from 1800 on; the last thirty years are right on track. Women who were thirty years old around 1900 averaged four children apiece; women who were thirty years old around 2000 averaged two children apiece.

Extensions of life and reductions in births drove two other major changes: A large increase in the proportion of people fifty and older living in an "empty nest" (with just a spouse) and an increasing proportion of elderly Americans living alone. In 1900, about one in four of the elderly lived in one of these two circumstances; in 2000, more than three in four elderly people did so. These are enormous reversals in family life, shown in Figure 1.3. Note that the biggest changes in family life, in Americans' living arrangements, during the twentieth century occurred for the elderly. The elderly today end their parenting much earlier in life, they have fewer children, and they live longer than the elderly a few generations ago. They also have more money and better health. They may also cherish their independence more than did the elderly of earlier eras.[4] Consequently, the elderly now live on their own instead of with their children. Ironically, during the past thirty years,

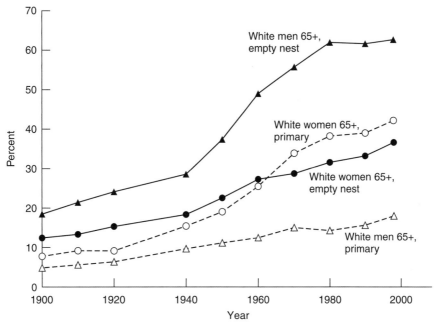

FIGURE 1.3

Percent of elderly who live either as "primary individuals" [alone or with nonrelatives only] (dashed lines) or in an "empty nest" (solid lines), for white men (triangles) and white women (circles), 1900–98. (*Source:* Steven Ruggles, Matthew Sobek, Trent Alexander, Catherine A. Fitch, Ronald Goeken, Patricia Kelly Hall, Miriam King, and Chad Ronnander, *Integrated Public Use Microdata Series: Version 3,* machine-readable database [Minneapolis: Minnesota Population Center, 2004], available at http://www.ipums.umn.edu/usa/; Current Population Survey.)

Americans have increasingly told pollsters that they think the aged should not live independently but should live with their children, but that trend emerged only because younger generations, not the elderly themselves, endorsed co-living.[5]

The next big change is the enormous increase in the proportion of married women, and the proportion of mothers with children under six, working outside the home, shown in Figure 1.4. In 1920, about 10 percent of married women officially worked; in 2000, more than 60 percent did. Note that the low percentages in the early part of the century are serious underestimates.[6] Nonetheless, the "real" trend is still a fundamental and sharp change. This trend, by the way, accelerated through the 1950s without pause. This transformation, too, had immense ramifications for our families, our children, and our culture—ramifications we have not yet fully absorbed.

These family changes, we submit, were the greatest in scale and probably in consequence. But there were also other noteworthy changes.

Modest Changes

One such change is the fluctuation in the age at which Americans married. First it dropped. American women marrying around 1900 tended to be about twenty-two years old; those marrying around 1950 tended to be about twenty, meaning that in the 1950s, about half of all brides were teenagers. This helps to explain the baby boom. Those marrying at the end of the century averaged twenty-four years of age on their wedding day, and a growing subgroup was marrying in their thirties.

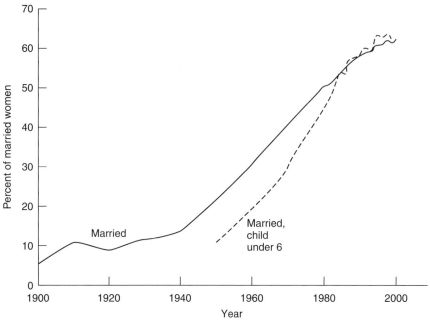

FIGURE 1.4

Percent of married women (and married women with a child under 6) in the labor force, 1900–2000. (*Sources:* U.S. Bureau of the Census, *Historical Statistics* and *Statistical Abstracts.*)

Also, of course, the divorce rate increased. At the beginning of the century, there was roughly one divorce issued for every ten marriages performed. By the early 1990s, it was about one for every two, although the divorce rate has been dropping since roughly 1980.[7] This is a fivefold increase in divorce, but we do not call it a "big change." One reason is that rates of marriage dissolution did not change nearly as much. Early in the century, marriages broke up because a spouse died. If one combines dissolution by death with dissolution by divorce, the total stayed pretty constant to 1970, as rising divorce balanced out declining mortality. By 1980, rising divorce pushed the total dissolution rate about one-fourth over its historical level, but it has subsided some since then.[8] Another reason we do not stress divorce is that most divorced people remarry. The proportion of adults living unmarried did not increase nearly as much as the

dramatic rise in the divorce rate would suggest. Many of those who do not remarry, it turns out, cohabit instead.

The increasing delay of marriage, in turn, contributed to higher rates of premarital sex. So, for example, about half of women who were teenagers in the 1950s were virgins at marriage, compared with under one-third of women who were teens in the 1970s.[9] The drop in virgin brides is, in part, simply the result of a longer time between puberty, which is now arriving earlier, and marriage, which is now arriving later. This change, by the way, also stopped or reversed in the 1990s.

Cohabitation, both before and after the first marriage, has increased significantly in the last few decades, as has popular tolerance of it. The proportion of American households at any one time with a cohabiting couple rose from under 1 percent in 1960 to a still low 5 percent in 2000.

More important, half of married couples now begin their conjugal lives by cohabiting.[10]

A consequence of both delaying marriage and increasing divorce is the increase in children living with a single parent. We shall look more closely at this below, but the simple fact is that for the first half of the century, about 5 percent of American children were recorded as living with only a single parent, and more than 20 percent were doing so in 2000.

Finally in this list, survey data, which do not go back further than about 1960, show that Americans became in recent decades increasingly tolerant of these and related changes—of smaller families, of women working, of premarital sex, of cohabitation, and of single-parent families. That is, Americans increasingly accepted wider ranges of individual choices in how to form a family.

Minor or Minimal Changes

Many other aspects of the family changed little, as far as we can tell. Both marriage and children continue to be valued. Americans still say they want to marry. For example, in a 2001 Gallup survey, more than nine in ten teenagers said that they wanted to marry and to have children, an increase over a generation.[11] Single adults age twenty through twenty-nine fully endorsed marriage; 78 percent said that being married was a very important life goal, 88 percent said that they were confident of finding a suitable spouse when they are ready to marry, and 88 percent answered yes when asked if there was a unique "soul mate" for them "out there."[12]

Moreover, Americans do get married. The latest estimates are that 90 percent of women now about forty years old have married or will eventually marry, even if later in life. This is a marriage rate notably higher than that in the early part of the twentieth century or, for that matter, the mid–nineteenth century.[13] Another indicator of how Americans value marriage is that, despite increasingly tolerating premarital sex, Americans in recent decades have become less tolerant of extramarital sex. The thread connecting

American attitudes on these subjects seems to be an increasing emphasis on freedom of choice combined with insistence on personal responsibility: Have premarital sex as you wish, marry as you wish, but if you marry, stay faithful.[14]

Finally, sociologists and historians have perused as many tea leaves as possible to see if they can spot a trend in familial intimacy, affection, and commitment. We can make no solid case one way or the other. What scholars can say with some confidence is that the standards and expectations for intimacy, affection, and commitment have increased. Whether in responses to survey data or in the complaints people list when filing for divorce, Americans during the twentieth century demanded more companionship, warmth, and happiness in marriage.

What can we generalize about family change over the century? Here are a few defensible statements:

- Americans always preferred the household of a married couple with children.
- During the twentieth century, it became increasingly possible to have such a nuclear family. In the earlier years, many external events blocked that goal: premature death, ill health, economic dislocation, unplanned pregnancies, and infertility. These disturbances became less important. People have more control now. So more people spend more of their lives in marriage than was true a few generations ago.
- The second choice after a married-couple household has changed. In the first half of the century, people who could not—because they were spinsters or widows or orphans—be in a married-couple household lived instead with other relatives, or in institutional settings like poorhouses and orphanages. In recent decades, this has changed. People have been more able and perhaps more willing to choose other alternatives—if the married-couple arrangement was not available—to live alone, cohabit, or be a single parent.
- Other values such as personal attainment and independence, especially for women, increasingly

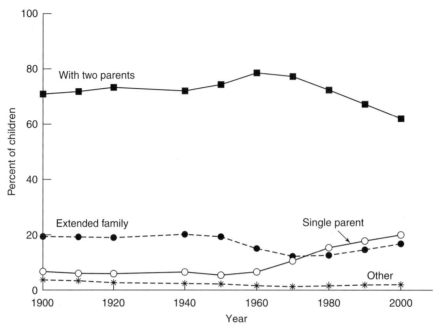

FIGURE 1.5
Percent of children (birth to age 17), by living arrangement, 1900–2000. (*Source:* Steven Ruggles, Matthew Sobek, Trent Alexander, Catherine A. Fitch, Ronald Goeken, Patricia Kelly Hall, Miriam King, and Chad Ronnander, *Integrated Public Use Microdata Series: Version 3,* machine-readable database [Minneapolis: Minnesota Population Center, 2004], available at http://www.ipums.umn.edu/usa/.)

competed with the goal of the married-couple household. Women's alternatives have expanded. Standards for a good marriage rose, and escapes from bad ones became easier. As a result, marriages are increasingly delayed or broken by choice rather than by external disruptions.

One consequence of these decisions can be trouble for the children. Children increasingly are living with a single parent outside a nuclear or an extended household. This is what we will look at more closely now.

FAMILY TROUBLE: THE SINGLE-PARENTED CHILD

It is generally understood that children have easier lives and do somewhat better when they live with two parents instead of one.[15] Figure 1.5

shows the distribution of children, age birth to seventeen years, by their living arrangements across the century.[16] On top, we see the percentage who lived just with two parents and siblings (if any), the ideal nuclear family. In 1900, about 70 percent of children lived that way; another roughly 20 percent lived in an extended family that often included both parents.[17] The proportion in the nuclear family then rose to 78 percent by 1960 and then dropped down to 64 percent at the end of the century, a bit lower than it was 100 years before. (If we add cohabiting parents to married parents, then the 2000 figure is 66 percent.) These numbers unfortunately do not distinguish between children living with their original parents from those living in a stepfamily, and some literature suggests that stepparent families are less conducive to child welfare than having both original parents.[18] The long-term data we draw upon cannot distinguish biological from stepparents, but stepparents surely formed a larger portion of two-parent households recently than they did in the 1950s; whether stepparents were more common recently than in the early part of the century is not clear.

Until thirty years ago, children who were not in a nuclear family were likely to be in extended-family households, perhaps with a grandparent, uncle, or cousins—shown in Figure 1.5 by a dashed line. Most of those households included both the child's two parents, at least early in the century, or one parent, more often now. Whether the extended household experience was better, the same, or worse than the two-parent household can be argued. The category of "other," shown at the bottom, refers to children living on their own or in some kind of group setting. Finally, we see—along a line connecting circles—the rise since 1960 in the proportion of children living with only one parent and no other relatives besides siblings. It had been under 10 percent for most of the century, took off in 1970, and reached 20 percent in 2000. This group and this last period is the subject of greatest public concern.[19]

The first question we have been raising is "Since when?" And we see here that the "when" is the 1950s. Indeed, if we were to push our view before 1900 back into the nineteenth century, we would quite likely see the bottom line, "other," keep going up and up as we move backward—backward into the era when children under eighteen, even many under twelve, were sent out of their homes to be farmhands, apprentices, and servants in other people's homes and thus lived with neither parent nor extended kin but with "others." The 1950s may have been the decade with the least disruption to Victorian ideals of childhood in American history.

If comparing a couple of centuries is too long a period to make the point that we need to be specific about "when," then consider the last decade alone. The proportion of children living

with fewer than two parents topped out at 32 percent in the mid-1990s (67 percent in 1995 for blacks) and dropped to 31 percent in 2002 (61 percent for blacks).[20] Other data also point to a recent decline in the behaviors that produce single-parent families, such as teen pregnancy and divorce, suggesting that we may have already seen the peak of one-parent households. So, again, we need to ask what we are using as historical comparisons and what is a reasonable comparison. Since when?

The other question we have been asking is "For whom?" Figure 1.6 focuses on the category of children living with only a single parent only or in one of those anomalous "other" settings. Then Figure 1.7 shows us that the rise in such children is disproportionately among black children. The black/white differential opened up in 1940 and then widened. Before 1940, white children were about 60 percent as likely as black children to be in a single-parent household; by the 1990s, they were about 40 percent as likely.[21] Single parenting has become disproportionately a "trouble" of the black community.

Sociologists believe that the trouble for black children, which accelerated in the 1950s and 1960s, coincides with increasing difficulties of black men in northern cities, which began with the loss of well-paying blue-collar jobs and then were compounded by rising drug use and crime. The result is that, though blacks and whites equally value the aspiration of getting married, blacks have become more disappointed with or even cynical about marriage.[22] That response may have taken on a life of its own, although there were signs in the late 1990s of marriage starting to rebound among African Americans. . . .

CONCLUSION

The effort we have gone through to look at who was affected when by family troubles is more than an accounting exercise. The numbers help us understand why these changes occurred and, potentially, what levers of influence exist. For

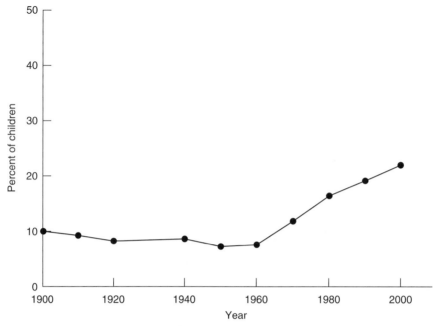

FIGURE 1.6

Percent of children (birth to age 17) living with one parent only or in "other" nonfamily arrangement, 1900–2000. (*Source:* Steven Ruggles, Matthew Sobek, Trent Alexander, Catherine A. Finch, Ronald Goeken, Patricia Kelly Hall, Miriam King, and Chad Ronnander, *Integrated Public Use Microdata Series: Version 3,* machine-readable database [Minneapolis: Minnesota Population Center, 2004], available at http://www.ipums.umn.edu/usa/.)

example, the historical data going back to the early part of the twentieth century make it difficult to explain family change as a linear consequence of "modernity." Classic sociological theories of the family, notably those of the 1950s, claim that the family lost its functions to the state and other institutions and therefore became weaker. But the nonlinear changes in the family cast doubt on such an explanation; for example, people are as or more likely to marry now as they were a century ago. The internal variations we have tracked also lead us to question such explanations. It is, after all, the most advantaged among us who have most embraced nonfamilial opportunities, sending children off to college and purchasing family services such as food, cleaning, child care, and parenting advice.

Yet the most advantaged have been the least affected by family troubles. The data also cast doubt on simple economic explanations of family patterns. For example, the notion that people have children to serve as their old-age insurance runs up against the contradiction that Americans indulged in a huge baby boom just after the U.S. government set up public old-age insurance.[23] History speaks to us.

When we put "family troubles" in historical perspective, we learn a few broad lessons. One is that troubles with marriage and parenting are concentrated among Americans with disadvantages. These Americans would live the 1950s ideal if they could, but they often cannot. In this way, they are like many Americans a century ago, whose family aspirations were blocked by death, disease,

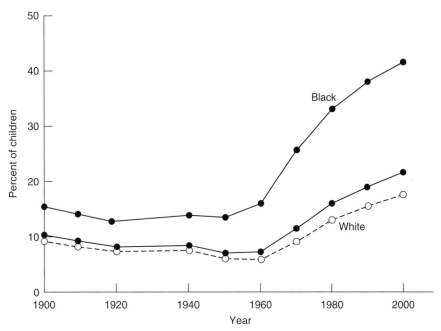

FIGURE 1.7

Percent of children (birth to age 17) living with one parent only or in "other" nonfamily arrangement, by race, 1900–2000. (*Source:* Steven Ruggles, Matthew Sobek, Trent Alexander, Catherine A. Fitch, Ronald Goeken, Patricia Kelly Hall, Miriam King, and Chad Ronnander, *Integrated Public Use Microdata Series: Version 3,* machine-readable database [Minneapolis: Minnesota Population Center, 2004], available at http://www.ipums.umn.edu/usa/.)

and disaster. Not many advantaged Americans have such problems. In 2000, only one in ten white children with a college-educated parent as head of household lived in a single-parent home.

Another lesson is that, for more advantaged Americans, being unwed, childless, or divorced is less a matter of malign fate and more a matter of new opportunities. Increasing affluence and improving health have made more choices more available to more people. These people choose to delay marriage, to have fewer children, and to live apart from those children when they age. These choices are not "family troubles," except insofar as one assumes that people not living in a nuclear family are ipso facto troubled. To be sure, trouble in the form of divorce or single parenting does occasionally visit such people these days. We might best understand

the family troubles that some of the advantaged face as a by-product of cultural shifts, such as the increasing freedom that individuals have to make personal, self-expressive choices in sex, marriage, and the family. And these are cultural shifts we typically approve. For example, vastly more wives work than before and vastly more Americans approve. In 1938, about one in four Americans said that it was okay for a wife to work if her husband could support her; by the 1990s, more than three in four did.[24] Yet such expansions of personal autonomy for the well-off can carry costs, one of which is increasing divorce and another is increasing numbers of children being single parented. Our moral burden, then, is to deal with the side effects, such as single parenting, of the changes we desire, such as more options for women.

Finally, we learn that America's social history is more complex and nuanced than many a simple gloss would have it. For example, every year the Bureau of the Census announces and newspapers report that a smaller percentage of American homes are occupied by nuclear families. True, but what does that mean? It largely means that more homes are occupied by still-vibrant older couples or singles whose youngest child left home before the parents turned fifty and who have thirty years of life to go. Increasing life spans have also meant that Americans spend more years knowing their aging parents, watching their children grow up, and sharing the company of a spouse.[25] So with regard to family troubles, we do need to ask "Since when?" and "For whom?"

■ Review Questions

1. Why do the authors consider the rise in divorce during the twentieth century not to be a major change?
2. Why do the authors say that people have more control over their family lives than they did a century ago?

ENDNOTES

1. Our data largely come from the U.S. censuses for 1900 through 2000—except for 1930, which has only just been released. These raw files have been compiled and made available as the Integrated Public Use Microdata Series; see Steven Ruggles, Matthew Sobek, Trent Alexander, Catherine A. Fitch, Ronald Goeken, Patricia Kelly Hall, Miriam King, and Chad Ronnander, *Integrated Public Use Microdata Series: Version 3,* machine-readable database (Minneapolis: Minnesota Population Center, 2004), available at http://www.ipums.umn.edu/usa/.
2. These numbers are from the National Center for Health Statistics, available at http://www.infoplease.com/ipa/A0005140.html.
3. That longer line is unavailable because earlier data use the number of children under five per the number of women age fifteen to forty-four. See U.S. Census Bureau, *Historical Statistics of the United States* (Washington, D.C.: U.S. Government Printing Office, 1977), 54; and subsequent *Statistical Abstracts.*
4. Frances E. Kobrin, "The Fall in Household Size and the Rise of the Primary Individual in the United States since 1940," *Journal of Marriage and the Family* 38 (May 1976): 233–39.
5. Authors' analysis of the General Social Survey (GSS) item "AGED," http://csa.berkeley.edu:7502/archive.htm.
6. For one, many wives worked informally in family businesses—farms, in particular. Others "took in" work, such as laundry, that they may not have reported. Also, we have reason to suspect that "respectable" families underreported the wives' work.
7. The gross divorce rate in 1979 was 5.3 per 1,000 Americans; it was 4.1 in 2000 (http://www.cdc.gov/nchs). Joshua R. Goldstein, "The Leveling of Divorce in the United States," *Demography* 36 (August 1999): 409–14, finds that this was a meaningful social change, not a statistical fluke.
8. These calculations are summarized in Andrew J. Cherlin, *Marriage, Divorce, Remarriage,* rev. ed. (Cambridge, Mass.: Harvard University Press, 1992), 25. The rate of dissolution from the 1860s through 1970 was about 33 to 34 dissolutions per 1,000 marriages; it rose to a peak of 41 around 1980 and declined to 39 by 1989.
9. Edward Laumann, John H. Gagnon, Robert T. Michael, and Stuart Michaels, *The Social Organization of Sexuality* (Chicago: University of Chicago Press, 1994), 197–99, 213–14; see also Sandra L. Hofferth, Joan R. Kahn, and Wendy Baldwin, "Premarital Sexual Activity among American Teenage Women over the Past Three Decades," *Family Planning Perspectives* 19 (March 1987): 46–53. On early-twentieth-century premarital sexuality, see, e.g., Daniel Scott Smith, "The Dating of the American Sexual Revolution" in *The American Family in*

Social-Historical Perspective, 2nd edition, ed. Micahel Gordon (New York: St. Martin's Press, 1978), 426–38; Amara Bachu, "Trends in Marital Status of U.S. Women at First Birth: 1930 to 1994," *Current Population Reports,* Special Studies (Washington, D.C.: U.S. Bureau of the Census, 1999), 23–197; and Stuart N. Seidman and Ronald O. Rieder, "A Review of Sexual Behavior in the United States," *American Journal of Psychiatry* 151 (March 1994): 330–41.

10. Lynne M. Casper and Suzanne M. Bianchi, *Continuity and Change in the American Family* (Thousand Oaks, Calif.: Sage Publications, 2002), chap. 1.

11. Linda Lyons, "Kids and Divorce," Gallup Online, http://www.gallup.com.

12. Kelley Maybury, "I Do? Marriage in Uncertain Times," Gallup Online, http://www.gallup.com.

13. Joshua R. Goldstein and Catherine T. Kenny, "Marriage Delayed or Marriage Forgone? New Cohort Forecasts of First Marriage for U.S. Women," *American Sociological Review* 66 (August 2001): 506–19. Goldstein and Kenny project current women's experiences into the twenty-first century. On longer historical comparisons, see Catherine A. Fitch and Steven Ruggles, "Historical Trends in Marriage Formation: The United States 1850–1990," in *The Ties That Bind: Perspectives on Marriage and Cohabitation,* ed. Linda J. Waite (New York: Aldine de Gruyter, 2000), 59–89. The percentage of never-married women in Charleston and Boston circa 1845 was higher than now; see Jane H. Pease and William H. Pease, *Ladies, Women, and Wenches: Choice and Constraint in Antebellum Charleston and Boston* (Chapel Hill: University of North Carolina Press, 1990).

14. On this and other attitude items, see Arland Thornton and Linda Young-Demarco, "Four Decades of Trends in Attitudes toward Family Issues in the United States," *Journal of Marriage and the Family* 63 (November 2001): 1009–38.

15. Sara McLanahan, "Life without Father: What Happens to the Children?" *Contexts* 1 (spring 2002): 35–44, provides an overview. The literature is large and controversial, but we assume that, other things being equal, a one-parent family is less desirable for children.

16. The numbers exclude from the base the few zero- to seventeen-year-olds who were in married couples with no children households—i.e., young brides and grooms. "Other" includes the very tiny fraction who were on their own and a small percentage who were in some form of "shared quarters."

17. Census data show that 84 percent of children in 1900 lived with two parents, suggesting that most of the children in extended households (seven of ten) had both parents there. U.S. Bureau of the Census, "Historical Living Arrangements of Children," http://www.census.gov/population/socdemo/child/p70-74/tab02.xls.

18. E.g., Andrew J. Cherlin and Frank F. Furstenberg Jr., "Stepfamilies in the United States: A Reconsideration," *Annual Review of Sociology* 20 (1994): 359–81, McLanahan, "Life without Father."

19. Census Bureau calculations show that the percentage of children living with one or neither parent was 13 to 17 percent from 1900 through 1970, then rose to 31 percent by 2000. U.S. Bureau of the Census, "Historical Living Arrangements of Children"; plus 2000 Current Population Survey.

20. These figures are based on slightly different data, "Table CH-1: Living Arrangements of Children under 18 Years Old: 1960 to Present," http://www.census.gov, drawn from the *Current Population Survey* and more recent data from the same source. These data count children living in extended households with a parent or two as living with a parent or both.

21. On this point, see also Fitch and Ruggles, "Historical Trends," 65.

22. This summary statement is supported by the many ethnographies of poor African Americans. It also shows up in survey data. The GSS asked unmarried people in the 1990s, "If the right person came along, would you like to be married?" There was no difference between blacks and whites (either a raw difference, or after statistical controls). Blacks were even slightly more likely to say that a bad marriage was better than no marriage. But on questions such as whether married people were happier than unmarried people, whether personal freedom was more important than marriage, whether people who want children should wait to get married, and whether single mothers can raise children as well as married couples, blacks were noticeably more skeptical about the marriage option. Authors' analysis of the GSS.

23. Similarly, scholars of the fertility decline that began in the nineteenth century have found simple economic explanations insufficient.
24. The GSS asked Americans whether the women's movement had improved, worsened, or not affected the lives of particular groups. Moderate pluralities to large majorities said "improved" in answers referring to questions about effects on "homemakers," working-class women, professional women, and even children. People were evenly split as to whether men benefited or lost from the women's movement (authors' analysis).
25. Susan Cotts Watkins, Jane A. Menken, and John Bongaarts, "Demographic Foundations of Family Change," *American Sociological Review* 52 (June 1987): 346–58.

READING 1-2

From Role to Self: The Emergence of Androgynous Love in the 20th Century

Francesca M. Cancian

In the long run, the social changes that began in the 19th century destroyed Victorian family patterns. The ideal of masculine independence spread to women and the private sphere, undermining people's willingness to be restricted by narrow family and gender roles. Wives became less subordinate and absorbed by mothering, as they had fewer children and increasingly joined the labor force, and many husbands became less consumed by their work as leisure time expanded and jobs became bureaucratized. Through most of the 20th century, there has been a trend toward more fluid, androgynous family roles and more involvement in self-development and personal life. Americans have become more concerned with individual happiness and pleasure, more tolerant of alternative lifestyles, more committed to equality for women and men, and more prone to divorce.

The trend to androgynous love has been discontinuous. In eras that emphasized personal liberation like the 20s and the late 60s, the trend accelerated, while in the 50s the long-range trend reversed as gender roles became more rigid and tolerance declined. These discontinuities can be used to identify different periods in the social organization of marriage, each dominated by a different family blueprint, or a different mix of blueprints.[1] Each blueprint combines a cultural image of the ideal marriage with expectations for daily life that guide behavior.

Figure 1.8 presents the major blueprints of marriage since the 19th century. First is the Victorian blueprint of family duty in which love is the woman's responsibility. Then come the three blueprints that dominate contemporary marriage: the more traditional companionship blueprint that first evolved in the 20s, and the newer blueprints of independence and interdependence in which the woman and the man share the obligation to work on their relationship, and the goal of self-development replaces conformity to roles. This reading gives a general description of these changes in blueprints of marriage, and then presents quantitative data on the major trends.

Francesca M. Cancian, "From Role to Self: The Emergence of Androgynous Love in the 20th Century," from *Love in America: Gender and Self-Development,* pp. 30–45. Copyright © 1987 by Cambridge University Press. Reprinted with the permission of Cambridge University Press.

	Who is responsible for love?	What is love?
Feminized love		
Family duty (19th century)	woman	fulfill duty to family
Companionship (1920–)	woman	intimacy in marriage
Androgynous love		
Independence (1970–)	woman and man	individual self-development and intimacy
Interdependence (1970–)	woman and man	mutual self-development, intimacy, and support

FIGURE 1.8
Blueprints of Love

THE DECLINE OF THE FAMILY DUTY BLUEPRINT

The family duty blueprint was the first solution to the problem of maintaining family bonds in an increasingly individualistic society. According to this image of family life, as we have seen, the ideal family was a nuclear household consisting of a father who left home every day to make the money to support the family, a loving mother who was the center of family life, and the children. Marriage was forever, and a man had considerable authority over his wife and children. The relation between husband and wife began with falling in love and might develop into companionship, although intimacy and sexual relations between spouses were not central and both spouses had important ties with relatives and friends of their own sex. The key relation was an intense, emotional tie between mothers and children, and raising moral, respectable, and healthy children was a woman's major task.

This ideal dominated in the United States from about 1840 to 1880 and then began to show signs of decline.[2] The divorce rate was increasing at the end of the century, and it doubled between 1900 and 1920. The proportion of women remaining single was rising, and so many affluent women were childless that some social critics raised the spectre of "race suicide" and "race sterility." Others criticized the family as an oppressive institution that deprived Americans of freedom and equality. Feminists attacked the tyranny of husbands over wives; plays like Ibsen's *A Doll's House* attacked the childlike position of women; advocates of free love protested against sexual repression; and sociologists viewed the difficulty of divorce as an unnecessary impediment to self-development.

By the turn of the century there was widespread debate in government, churches, and the mass media on the future of the family, the decline of sexual morality, and especially divorce. Opponents of divorce believed that it would destroy the family, which they saw as the basis of civilization. Divorce was attributed to "dangerous individualism," especially individualism in women, and women were charged with being spoiled, romantic, "jealous of men and usurpers of the male's time-honored functions." But by 1910, the opposition was overwhelmed and divorce was accepted.[3]

The 1920s witnessed the dissolution of Victorian family patterns. Social commentators believed that a "revolution in manners and morals" was sweeping the country, and, according to William Chafe, "almost all agreed that the age was one of unprecedented personal liberation."[4] The historian of the family, Arthur Calhoun, writing in 1917, believed he was witnessing the passing of patriarchy and devotion to the family, as people became more and more individualistic.

In the Roaring Twenties, college students and other young people cast aside Victorian clothes and pursued sexual liberation and exciting personal experiences.[5] The institution of dating developed—the pattern of young men and women seeing each other without chaperones, and without any intention of marriage, to "have a good time." High school students in Muncie, Indiana, in 1924 went to necking and petting parties and only with difficulty could be persuaded to be home for dinner three nights a week. On college campuses, dedication to social reform gave way to social activities organized by sororities and fraternities.[6] Women from respectable families smoked in public, wore short skirts and cosmetics, worked as secretaries before they married, and modeled the new image of a woman with an expensive wardrobe and sex appeal. The response of many older, more conservative Americans to all this was horror at the decline of morality and the sexual orgies (real and imagined) of the young.[7]

The causes of the decline of the family duty blueprint include changes in the sexual division of labor and an increasing value placed on self-fulfillment. Women's daily activities shifted away from motherhood and toward more participation in the public sphere. The ideal of the free, self-made man was spreading, and women were beginning to be seen as similar and equal to men, as persons who should develop themselves. The declining birthrate reduced the burdens of motherhood, although many housewives were busier than ever as standards for a clean and attractive home rose. Employment opportunities for women expanded through the growth of respectable jobs such as being a secretary or a saleswoman. "Nowadays," said suffragist Frances Willard in 1897, "a girl may be anything from a college president down to a seamstress or a cash girl. It depends only upon the girl what rank she shall take in her chosen calling."[8] In fact, most working women were segregated in a few low-paying jobs, and it remained shameful for married women to work, but being a single career woman was becoming a respected way of life.[9]

The Victorian ideal that woman's place was in the home was also challenged by women's participation in the temperance movement and in other social reform movements of the early 20th century. The movement for women's suffrage, which obtained the vote for women in 1920 and involved an estimated two million women, most directly undermined the family duty blueprint.[10] The suffragists used the rhetoric of separate spheres and argued that women needed the vote because they were more moral and altruistic than men, but women's suffrage removed a major barrier to women's participation in public life.[11]

Men's lives also changed as routine white-collar jobs expanded with the growth of large corporations, and the 40-hour workweek became more common. Men's work became more sedentary and regimented, and less heroic. According to several social historians, as many men found less validation for their masculinity in work, their personal identification with their jobs diminished and they became more involved with their personal lives, their families, and leisure activities.[12] Work probably continued to be the center of life for men pursuing challenging and prestigious careers, but personal life became increasingly important for men as the 20th century advanced.[13]

The increasing focus on personal life and self-development and decreasing commitment to traditional roles was fueled by several changes. Security—experiencing the world as safe and abundant—seems to promote a concern with self-development, and the average person's sense of security probably rose in the early 20th century because of gradual improvements in the standard of living and the widespread economic boom during the early 20s.[14] The growth of consumerism and advertising also encouraged people to develop new personal needs and try to fulfill them. "The American citizen's first importance to his country," editorialized the Muncie newspaper in the 1920s, is "that of consumer."[15] Valuing self-development and independence over conformity to roles was also encouraged by public education, which expanded enormously for both sexes.[16] In 1924, high-school diplomas were awarded to 213,000 men and 281,000 women, an increase since 1900 of about 500 percent for both sexes, while the population had only increased by 50 percent.[17] Finally, the social reform movements of the Progressive Era challenged traditional roles and political institutions, and the unpopularity of World War I further undermined established authority, leading people to seek direction and meaning in their own personal lives.[18]

THE COMPANIONSHIP BLUEPRINT

As the Victorian blueprint of duty to family roles was disintegrating, a new ideal was being articulated in academia and the mass media: the companionship family. This blueprint identified the family with marriage, not parenthood, and emphasized emotional and sexual intimacy between husband and wife.

Sociologists proposed a new family ideal focused on affection and supporting each other's personalities, now that families had lost their traditional economic and social functions. The modern family was "a unity of interacting personalities" in the famous phrase of sociologist Ernest Burgess, and had evolved "from institution to companionship."[19] The first principles of family life, according to Burgess, are "that the highest personal happiness comes from marriage based on romantic love" and "that love and marriage are essentially personal and private and are, perhaps, even more than other aspects of life to be controlled by the individual himself."[20] Marriage, in this view, is a private arena of self-fulfillment, not duty. With the spread of the companionship blueprint, affective individualism and a more androgynous self became part of mainstream American culture.

For the first time, popular advice books suggested that having children might weaken a family, and in 1931, for the first time, there were more advertisements for cosmetics than for food in the *Ladies' Home Journal*. Being an attractive companion was becoming more important

than being a competent homemaker. Dorothy Dix, in her syndicated newspaper column for women, advised: "The old idea used to be that the way for a woman to help her husband was by being thrifty and industrious . . . but a domestic drudge is not a help to her husband, she is a hindrance. . . . The woman who cultivates a circle of worthwhile people, who belongs to clubs, who makes herself interesting and agreeable . . . is a help to her husband."[21]

The companionship family blueprint emphasized the similarity of husband and wife much more than the family duty blueprint. Both partners were expected to need and to give affection and understanding, and increasingly, both were expected to enjoy sexual intimacy. But love was still feminized, and wives were still expected to be economically dependent and submissive to their husbands. Marriage was to be all of a woman's life but only part of a man's. There was no column by Dorothy Dix instructing a man on how to be a help to his wife, and the magazines of the period consistently told women that it was their responsibility to create successful marriages.[22] Despite some changes towards androgyny, gender roles remained fairly polarized in the companionship blueprint.

The reality of family life in the 20s, according to Robert and Helen Lynd's study of Muncie, is more similar to the family duty blueprint than to the world of companionship marriage and libertine flappers. In the business class (the top 30 percent of the families), wives did not work, and the social status of the family was a primary concern to both husband and wife. Most couples did not place a very high value on companionship in marriage, and frankness between spouses was not encouraged. Husbands described wives as purer, morally better, and more emotional and impractical than men, and their wives agreed. The motto of one of the women's clubs was "Men are God's trees; Women are his flowers."[23] Social life was organized primarily around couples, although men and women were also active in sex-segregated clubs and friendships were important to the women. Wives were very child-centered, while husbands had little contact with their children beyond meals and family auto trips. Husbands were, however, beginning to share in the housework. In the working class, a substantial minority of the wives worked, but marital relations were even farther from the companionship ideal. Husbands and wives rarely talked, and in the absence of other methods of birth control wives kept away from their husbands sexually. Only the beginnings of the companionship family were observable in Muncie; an intimate emotional and sexual bond between two developing personalities was seldom achieved or even strongly desired. Contrary to what many historians have suggested, marital intimacy was rare, as late as the 20s.

The Great Depression from 1929 to 1941 was probably the major force in reversing the trend towards individual freedom of the 20s. As the economy collapsed, people faced an insecure, hostile environment, and adopted a rigid version of the companionship ideal that emphasized traditional family and gender roles more than personal development. Although domestic politics became more radical in the 30s, with the growing power of labor unions and the social programs of the New Deal, family life became more conservative.

College students in the early 30s expressed less approval of divorce and extramarital sex than in the 20s, and there was a rise in the proportion of students who intended to marry and have children.[24] Opposition to women's entering the labor force reappeared as more and more men lost their jobs, and employers increasingly denied married women the right to work. A survey of 1,500 school systems in 1930 reported that 77 percent refused to hire wives and 63 percent fired women teachers if they married. When the Gallup Poll asked Americans in 1936 whether wives should work if their husbands were employed, 82 percent said "no."[25] Women's magazines "urged their readers to return to femininity and constructed an elaborate

ideology in support of the home and marriage to facilitate the process," according to historian William Chafe.[26] The *Ladies' Home Journal* told its readers that "the creation and fulfillment of a successful home is a bit of craftsmanship that compares favorably with building a beautiful cathedral," while *McCall's* observed that only as a wife and mother could the American woman "arrive at her true eminence."[27]

The effects of economic insecurity on commitment to traditional family roles is documented by Glen Elder's study of people who grew up during the Depression. Compared with people whose families had not suffered economically, men and women from families that had suffered substantial economic losses in the Depression placed a greater value on family life as opposed to work and leisure, and were more interested in raising children and less interested in husband–wife companionship. The deprived men actually had a larger number of children, on the average, than men from nondeprived backgrounds. Another finding that supports the link between economic deprivation and traditionalism is that working-class people have more traditional attitudes about family and gender than middle-class people.[28]

World War II ended the Depression and interrupted normal life for many families as men went off to war and women to work. Between 1940 and 1944, the proportion of married women in the labor force rose from 17 percent to 20 percent.[29] Although there was an effort to push women workers back into the home after the war, married women continued to enter the workforce in growing numbers, radically changing the division of labor between husbands and wives that had persisted since the 19th century.

The postwar decades were a period of extreme commitment to the family and to split gender roles. People married earlier, had more children, and avoided childlessness, causing the famous baby boom. The divorce rate stayed unusually steady,[30] and new suburban tracts provided a setting for a family-centered way of life. There was a resurgence of antifeminism and a revival of the 19th-century theme of separate spheres. Thus the head of one women's college advocated that preparing women for "the task of creating a good home and raising good children" be made the primary purposes of women's colleges.[31] Women's magazines described the joys of femininity and togetherness, and public opinion, which had supported wives working during the war, once again opposed their working if their husbands could support them. Most people also supported a traditional division of labor in which men determined where a family lived and how it spent its money.[32] Yet all the while, more and more wives were working.

The blueprint for family life was a revised version of the companionship family of the 20s and 30s.[33] The companionship ideal of the 50s was based on intimate affection between husband and wife. Although the relation between mother and children was vitally important, a woman was warned not to let motherhood weaken her relation with her husband or to smother her children with too much attention. The couple was expected to lead an active social life but not to have close ties outside the nuclear family. The Victorian ideology of separate spheres was still partly intact; it was the husband's job to support the family, while the wife was the center of home life. But the authority of the husband had declined—he was to be more of a pal to his children and more of a companion to his wife. The concept of family togetherness—of mom, dad, and the kids barbecuing dinner together in the backyard—softened the separation of men's and women's spheres. Marriage began with falling in love and developed into companionship; but if love died, divorce might be the best solution.

This family ideal was endorsed by most intellectuals and social scientists in the postwar era. Talcott Parsons provided a theoretical justification with his argument that a well-functioning family required an instrumental father and an expressive mother. Other sociologists obscured the gender differentiation in the companionship

model by emphasizing its equality and flexibility in comparison with the patriarchal Victorian family or the marriages of conservative Americans. Few observers noted that as long as marriage was defined as the wife's responsibility and love was feminized, emphasizing companionship increased her dependency on her husband.[34] The Victorian wife at least had her separate sphere of children and women friends. For the wife in a companionship marriage, her husband was her sphere, and her life was focused on getting the right emotional response from him. The price of companionship marriage was high, especially for the educated, middle-class women who valued their independence the most.[35]

The strong commitment to traditional family roles throughout the 50s and early 60s is somewhat puzzling since many social conditions encouraged androgyny and self-development. A growing number of wives had jobs and became less economically dependent on their husbands. By 1965, 45 percent of married women with school-age children worked, compared with 26 percent in 1948. There was an unprecedented economic prosperity in the postwar era, and a very large expansion of public higher education. One would expect these conditions to accelerate the trend from role to self, but this did not happen until the late 60s, when a wave of protest movements and the Vietnam War produced a counterculture that rejected traditional roles and beliefs, including the companionship family blueprint.[36]

THE DECLINE OF THE COMPANIONSHIP BLUEPRINT

Another period of personal liberation began in the sixties. This time many observers felt that a major boundary of social organization had been crossed—that we had passed from an era in which people's private lives were regulated by the obligations of family roles into a new era of the self.[37] There was a rapid reversal of the familism of the 50s. Divorces accelerated sharply and fertility declined to an all-time low. The rate of couples living together without being married doubled between 1970 and 1979, and there was a large increase in the number of persons living alone. Premarital sexual experience, which had been increasing since the 20s, became much more frequent; for example, the percentage of single 17-year-old girls who had experienced sex rose from 27 to 41 percent between 1971 and 1976.[38]

The trend toward wives working for money was probably the underlying cause of the decline of the companionship family. But the immediate cause was the antiestablishment social movements of the 60s and 70s. The 60s began a period of "revolution in manners and morals" similar to the twenties, literally a "counterculture."[39] The civil rights movement, the antiwar movement, and the women's movement involved a large minority of Americans in demonstrations, drug trips, petition campaigns and consciousness-raising groups, all of which undermined the patriotism and devotion to family of the postwar era.

The women's movement, in particular, attacked the companionship family blueprint. Conservative feminists endorsed the "two-career family," in which both husband and wife were equally committed to glamorous careers and to childrearing and homemaking. Radical feminists rejected the family as the preferred living arrangement and developed images of homosexual households or socialist collectives. By the early 70s, ideas about gender equality diffused throughout the nation as the women's movement received a great deal of media coverage and achieved a rapid series of legislative victories supporting expanded opportunities for women in the labor force and in education.[40]

Once again, a strong women's movement had undermined traditional family roles. As long as family blueprints emphasized self-sacrifice and polarized gender roles, women's freedom conflicted with family bonds. Thus Carl Degler concludes his history of women and the family in America by observing that "the great values

for which the family stands are at odds . . . with those of the women's movement."[41]

Companionship family roles were also attacked by the human potential movement. Popular psychology books like Gail Sheehy's *Passages* rejected the role of successful provider and cheerful housewife as hypocritical and deadening. They urged people to free themselves from restrictive obligations, get in touch with their feelings, and experience their full potential. New therapies and growth centers sprung up—encounter groups, Esalen, Primal Scream, EST—all of them encouraging adult men and women to develop themselves and reject traditional roles. In contrast to the orthodox therapies of previous decades that had urged patients to adjust to traditional family and gender roles, the new therapies preached androgyny, and urged men and women to reject the expectations of others and develop their own true selves.[42]

The decline of the companionship blueprint was welcomed by some groups and opposed by others. Not surprisingly, women supported the new flexibility in gender roles more than men, especially highly educated professional women.[43] These women valued independence the most and could benefit the most from improved career opportunities. Thus, in the political struggle over abortion, the "pro-choice" activists were mostly well-educated, career-oriented women who placed a high value on individual freedom and self-development. The "pro-life" women were primarily less educated housewives with a deep commitment to religion and to the traditional roles of the loving housewife and the strong husband who provides for her.[44] For these women and for many other Americans, the companionship family continued to be their ideal.

THE NEW BLUEPRINTS: INDEPENDENCE AND INTERDEPENDENCE

By the middle of the 70s, new androgynous images of close relationships were beginning to crystallize. A prolonged economic recession dampened people's aspirations for freedom, and academics and the mass media began to criticize the human potential movement as selfish and narcissistic.[45] The need for intimacy began to seem more pressing than the need to combat oppressive family and gender roles.

The new blueprints emphasize three sets of qualities that I label *self-fulfillment, flexible roles,* and *intimacy and open communication.* First, in the new images of love, both partners are expected to develop a fulfilled and independent self, instead of sacrificing themselves for the other person. Second, family and gender roles are flexible and are continually renegotiated. Third, the relationship centers on intimate communication of needs and feelings, and on openly confronting problems. Self-development and love are integrated in these blueprints, and love is the responsibility of the man as well as the woman. The independence and the interdependence blueprints both emphasize these qualities; they differ on the issue of self-sufficiency and independence versus mutual support and commitment.

The new blueprints of relationships began to emerge in the middle of the 60s, according to a study of women's magazines. Women were advised that they must develop an independent self in order to be loving, and they were told to build a vital, spontaneous relationship without fixed rules, by communicating openly about feelings and working through conflicts. In contrast, in the 50s, "putting aside of self was defined as loving behavior," and women were advised to sacrifice themselves for their families, follow traditional sex roles, and strive for harmony and togetherness.[46]

When Ann Swidler interviewed 60 residents of an affluent California suburb around 1980, she found that most of them emphasized self-fulfillment and accepted the "therapeutic ideal" of love promoted by psychologists and the human potential movement. They believed that love is partly expressed by sharing oneself and one's feelings; therefore, a person must develop a somewhat independent self in order to be

loving. For example, a young wife explained that she had had problems with her husband, Thomas, because "I was doing things just for him and ignoring things for myself." Now, since her therapy, she feels more independent and self-confident. "The better I feel about myself, I feel I have a whole lot that I can contribute to Thomas."[47]

Good communication is crucial in the new blueprints, both to express one's self, and to negotiate a unique, flexible relationship in the absence of definite family and gender roles. Verbal communication is also part of being intimate and working on the relationship. As a college man commented, "You have to work at your marriage, it's like a job." A poll conducted for *Playboy* magazine in 1976 indicates the importance of communication to contemporary American men. "Someone to be totally open and honest with" was the most frequently mentioned quality for an ideal lover.[48]

The new blueprints are radically androgynous and anti-institutional. The themes of self-fulfillment and intimate communication resemble the companionship blueprint, and its concern with personality development and marital interaction. But unlike the companionship ideal, the new blueprints do not legitimate predetermined roles or a sexual division of labor; they are blueprints for relationships, not marriages. Both partners are expected to work on the relationship, communicate openly and develop themselves. Wives are advised to cultivate independent interests and goals, while husbands are encouraged to express their feelings. Love is no longer part of women's special sphere.

The independence blueprint adds to these themes a strong emphasis on being self-sufficient and avoiding obligations. Developing an independent self and expressing one's needs and feelings is seen as a precondition to love. In contrast, couples who follow the interdependence blueprint believe that they owe each other mutual support and affection, and that love is a precondition to full self-development.

Sociologists disagree about the relative importance of these two blueprints. Robert Bellah and his associates conclude that independence is becoming the dominant image of love in America. People are increasingly avoiding commitments, they argue and support their interpretation by quoting from Swidler's interviews. For example, a counselor commented: "I guess, if there is anyone who needs to owe anybody anything, it is honesty in letting each other know how they feel about each other, and that if feelings change, to be open and receptive, to accept those changes, knowing that people in a relationship are not cement."[49]

In contrast, my study of 133 adults in 1980 indicates that Interdependence, not Independence, is the dominant blueprint of love. The respondents, who came from diverse social backgrounds, were asked about the "qualities that are most important for a good marriage or love relationship." . . . Contrary to the argument of Bellah et al., the second most frequently mentioned quality was "support and caring." "Good, open communication" was most frequently mentioned, while "tolerance, flexibility and understanding" was third, "honesty" was fourth, and "commitment" was fifth. Individuals who emphasized "support and caring" usually talked about the obligation to be nurturant and attentive, and many of them connected support and caring with self-development. For example, when a 30-year-old minister in San Diego was asked what he most valued in his wife, he replied:

> I trust her to react in a reaffirming way to me when I share with her. . . . I know that she will respond to me in a positive way. She will share the pain or frustration or triumph of the day with me, and I feel like what I have to say about me is very important, because it's me in a sense.

Although there is disagreement about the importance of mutual support and commitment in contemporary relationships, researchers agree on the growing importance of self-fulfillment, flexible roles, and intimate, open communication.

With the decline of the companionship blueprint, the trend from role to self accelerated, producing new, more androgynous images of love.

It is possible that another shift back to traditional roles has begun, partly as a result of the continued economic difficulties of the 70s and 80s. The slight drop in the divorce rate and the reversal of feminist gains in affirmative action and abortion rights may be signs of such a shift. But the evidence that would document this change is not available.

EVIDENCE FROM POPULAR MAGAZINES

The changes in family blueprints that I have just described are clearly reflected in magazine articles that give advice on how to have a happy marriage. I analyzed a sample of articles from 1900 to 1979 and measured the proportion of articles in each decade that endorsed the traditional family duty and companionship blueprints versus the modern themes of self-fulfillment, flexible roles, and intimacy. The results confirm the long-range trend from role to self during the 20th century, and also show that the 20s and 60s were unusually modern while the 50s were unusually traditional. Studies by other researchers show this same pattern of change.

I examined 128 articles on marriage from high circulation magazines like the *Ladies' Home Journal, McCall's,* and the *Reader's Digest.* The articles are addressed primarily to women, and advise them on how to produce a happy, loving marriage and how to overcome feelings of disappointment and loneliness. For each five-year period, I randomly selected eight articles listed in the *Readers' Guide to Periodicals* under the topic "Marriage." The content of each article was coded according to the dominant message that the article seemed to communicate to readers.[50]

The categories used to analyze the articles focused on self-fulfillment, flexible roles, and intimacy and open communication. One category that measured self-fulfillment was "self-sacrifice versus self-fulfillment." An example of endorsing self-sacrifice is a 1909 editorial in *Harper's Bazaar* that advised: "Marriage means self-discipline. Marriage is *not* for the individual, but for the race. . . . Marriage is the slow growth of two persons into one—one person with one pursuit, one mind, one heart, one interest . . . one ideal."[51] In contrast, a *Ladies' Home Journal* article in 1978, illustrating the self-fulfillment theme, warned that it was a myth to believe that marriage should "meet all the emotional needs of both spouses," that it "is an all-encompassing blend of two personalities fused into one. A marriage like this leaves no breathing space for two individuals to retain their own personalities."[52]

A category for measuring flexible roles was "rigid versus flexible female gender role." The traditional side of this category is illustrated by a 1940s article which comments that, compared to men, "women have much less time for action, being absorbed, consciously or unconsciously, by their preoccupation with love and maternity."[53] Intimate communication was measured by the category "avoid conflict, and keep up a front versus communicate openly and confront problems." Illustrating the modern view of communication, an article in the *Reader's Digest* in 1974 asserted that "if spouses are thoughtful toward each other on *all* occasions, they probably have a sick marriage."[54]

Table 1.1 shows the number of articles in each decade that support traditional versus modern themes in these three categories. The percent of modern themes—combining the three categories—gradually rises, as shown at the bottom of the table. There are also discontinuities; for instance, there are more articles endorsing flexible gender roles in the 1920s than in the next three decades. Thus a 1925 article in the *Ladies' Home Journal* proclaimed: "The woman of today acknowledges no master." Women now regard marriage as "a social partnership, an adventure, an experiment even, but it must always be on a fifty-fifty basis."[55] And in every decade, there is considerable variation in what the magazines

are saying, and a substantial number of both traditional and modern themes.

The trend from role to self and the discontinuities in this trend are more clearly displayed in the graph in Figure 1.9. The graph shows the percent of themes in each decade that support self-fulfillment, flexible roles, and intimate communication, combining eight categories that include the three already discussed. For example, "flexible roles" is measured by the previously discussed category about the female role, as well as categories about the male role and the acceptability of divorce. . . .

The graph shows a trend to modern themes over the 20th century. In the first two decades of the century, about 30 percent of the themes are modern, compared to about 70 percent in the 1970s. There is also a clear up-and-down pattern of change, with modern themes predominating in the 20s and again in the 60s and 70s.

The causes of the trend from role to self, as I have discussed, probably include economic prosperity, increasing leisure and education, and the tendency of women as well as men to work for individual wages. The discontinuities can partly be explained by the same factors; in particular, economic hard times apparently reversed the trend in the 30s. Other researchers have emphasized demographic shifts in explaining discontinuities in American family life, and unpopular wars may also be important.[56]

The intriguing association between the women's movement and images of marriage suggests other explanations of the discontinuities—explanations that point to the great importance of gender roles in understanding the American family. A strong women's movement accompanied or preceded the extreme emphasis on personal freedom and self-fulfillment in the 20s and again in the late 60s. The women's movement, as measured by the amount of coverage of women in the *New York Times* and popular magazines, was strongest between 1905 and 1920. It reached its low point between 1950 and the early 60s, and then rose again in the late sixties. . . . The rise

TABLE 1.1

TRENDS IN MAGAZINE ARTICLES ON MARRIAGE, 1900–1979: NUMBER OF ARTICLES SUPPORTING TRADITIONAL VERSUS MODERN THEMES

Traditional [T]		Modern [M]	1900–1909		1910–1919		1920–1929		1930–1939		1940–1949		1950–1959		1960–1969		1970–1979	
			T	M	T	M	T	M	T	M	T	M	T	M	T	M	T	M
1 self-sacrifice compromise	vs.	self-fulfillment individuality	7	1	4	3	5	1	7	2	10	0	11	0	7	7	5	2
2 rigid female role	vs.	flexible female role	10	7	14	4	8	10	11	7	8	9	13	5	8	10	6	13
3 avoid conflict, keep up a front	vs.	communicate openly, confront problems	1	2	2	0	3	2	5	3	4	0	4	6	4	8	3	10
		Percent of modern themes	36%		26%		45%		34%		29%		28%		57%		64%	

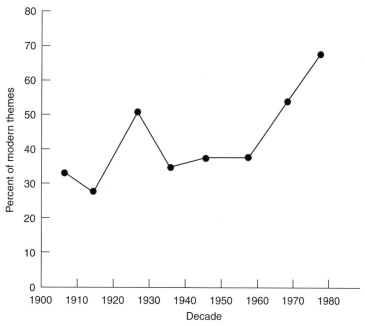

FIGURE 1.9

Modern themes in magazine articles on marriage, 1900–1979: Percent of themes supporting self-fulfillment, flexible roles, and intimacy.

and fall of the women's movement thus parallels the rise and fall of modern images of marriage, as shown in Figure 1.9, except that the high point of the movement around 1910 preceded the change in marital images by about a decade.

This relationship between the women's movement and the trend from role to self is not surprising, and has been noted by social historians. The women's movement usually has urged women to avoid self-sacrifice and traditional gender roles, and participating in the movement probably made women more powerful and independent of their families as they acquired new skills and friends, and new ideas about women's proper place.

The conflict between traditional family roles and women's rights may also produce a self-generating cycle of change. When there is a strong commitment to a traditional family blueprint (i.e., the family duty or companionship blue-

print), individual freedom and self-development are suppressed, especially for women. But freedom and self-development are highly valued in America, leading to a conflict that eventually undermines the blueprint and produces a period of personal liberation like the 1920s. Greater freedom to develop oneself, especially for women, then threatens people's needs for attachments, creating a readiness to accept a new family blueprint. This cyclic tendency, if it exists, will be weakened by the diffusion of the interdependence blueprint, which combines stable attachments and self-development.

Whatever the causes of the changing images of marriage, two patterns of change emerge clearly from my analysis of magazine articles. There has been a gradual trend toward self-fulfillment, flexible roles, and intimate communication, as well as some major discontinuities.

■ Review Questions

1. In what ways do the changing themes of magazine articles reflect a shift "from role to self"?
2. What does the author mean by "androgynous love"?

ENDNOTES

1. Fixing the date of these periods is only approximate, and is based on the sources quoted in this and the previous reading.
2. The Civil War occurred in the middle of this period, but, surprisingly, most historians do not attribute great social consequences to it. Eleanor Flexner's history of women is an exception.
3. O'Neil, 1978, pp. 143–44.
4. Chafe, 1972, p. 49.
5. Fass, 1977.
6. Rothman, 1978.
7. Fass, 1977; Newcomb, 1937.
8. Quoted in Rothman, 1978, p. 43.
9. For a poignant description of how respectable but poor married women had to hide the fact that they were working see Rothman, 1978, Chapter 2. Single life was not unattractive, given the close bonds among women, especially for the privileged few with a college education. The women born between 1865 and 1874 "married later and less frequently than any group before or since," and by the turn of the century "nearly one in five married women was childless" (Ryan, 1979, p. 142).
10. Ryan, 1979, p. 140.
11. Many of its supporters and opponents believed that women's winning the vote would change their role in the family and drastically alter electoral politics. The large amounts of money spent by the liquor industry and urban political machines to fight women's suffrage are an indication of the importance they attributed to it. On the high hopes of many suffragists about the changes that would occur after women got the vote, see Flexner, 1974; and O'Neil, 1978. O'Neil documents the conservative and occasionally racist rhetoric of the suffrage movement.
12. The eight-hour day became common during World War I and the 40-hour week was mandated by New Deal legislation in the thirties (Harris & Levy, 1975, pp. 1, 511). On the declining masculinity of work, see Hantover, 1980, pp. 285–302, and also Filene, 1974.
13. For a supporting argument, see Zaretsky, 1976, and for supporting evidence see Pleck, 1985; and Veroff et al., 1981.
14. On the economic changes, see U.S. Bureau of the Census, 1976, pp. 164–165. On the relation of security and self-development, see Maslow's theory of the hierarchy of needs, 1970.
15. The quotation is from Lynd & Lynd, 1937, p. 80. For a description of this period, also see Chafe, 1972, and Rothman, 1978.
16. Educated people, according to many studies, are more likely to believe that they control their lives and to question authority and traditional rules. See Kohn, 1969.
17. U.S. Bureau of the Census, 1976, pp. 379 and 380. In 1924 B.A.s or first professional degrees were awarded to 55,000 men and 28,000 women, an increase since 1900 of about 200 percent for men and 500 percent for women.
18. I am indebted to Thomas Kemper for this observation.
19. Quoted in Lasch, 1977, p. 31.
20. These quotes are taken from Rothman, 1978, p. 180.
21. Quoted in Lynd & Lynd, 1937, p. 116.
22. See the thought-provoking analysis of magazines from 1921 to 1940 by Johns-Heine and Gerth, 1949.
23. Lynd & Lynd, 1937, p. 118.
24. Newcomb, 1937. In contrast, the Lynds report that high school students in Muncie became more accepting of premarital sex and women's working between 1924 and 1935. This may be an instance of a lag in changes among working-class and provincial people compared to college students.
25. Chafe, 1972, Chapter 4. The proportion of college teachers who were women began to fall in the 30s and continued to decline until the late 50s.
26. Chafe, 1972, p. 105.
27. Quoted in Chafe, 1972, p. 105.

28. Elder, 1974, analyzes the effects of the depression. Virtually all researchers find that middle-class people tend to be more modern. They value companionship between husband and wife more and having children less, and place more emphasis on self-fulfillment, tolerance of diversity, and flexible gender roles. This pattern confirms the hypothesis that economic security, prosperity, and education promote the shift from role to self. The classic study of class and child-rearing values is Melvin Kohn's *Class and Conformity,* 1969. The preference of middle-class people for self-actualization and esteem, and working-class people for belonging and security, is shown in an interesting British study using Abraham Maslow's theory of the hierarchy of needs by Gratton, 1980. Duncan et al., 1973, document the greater importance of job security for working-class people. Also see Gurin et al., 1960; Mason et al., 1976; Gecas, 1979; and Rubin, 1976.

29. U.S. Bureau of the Census, 1976, p. 133.

30. Cherlin, 1981.

31. Chafe, 1972, p. 208.

32. Ibid., p. 178.

33. For a similar interpretation, see Rothman, 1978, p. 218.

34. For an example, see Hicks and Platt's widely quoted and basically sound review of the literature on marital adjustment, published in 1970. Even Komarovsky (1962), usually very sensitive to issues of gender, took for granted the superiority of companionship marriage. She criticized the blue-collar pattern of restricted communication and separate social activities for husbands and wives as a form of "social disorganization," failing to see that the husband's buddies and the wife's close ties with relatives and friends might provide a valuable counterbalance to the tendency of women to be overdependent on their husbands in companionship marriages. Evidence on the role of relatives and friends in limiting wives' dependency on husbands comes from a study of British working-class families by Michael Young and Peter Willmott. They found that wives became more dependent after they moved away from their old community into a suburb.

35. Evidence of the discontent of college-educated wives with their marriage is presented in Campbell et al., 1976. Also Pahl & Pahl, 1971.

36. See Cherlin, 1981, for data on changes in women working and an analysis of how the fifties interrupted many long-term demographic and family trends. For quantitative data on the postwar boom, see U.S. Bureau of the Census, 1976, and Lebergott 1976. Generation and politics may explain the unusual familism of the 1950s. Perhaps the generation that raised their families in the 50s had too many frightening memories of depression and war to feel secure, despite their new prosperity. And perhaps American politics of cold war and McCarthyism diminished people's sense of self-direction and the importance of their personal lives by enhancing the significance of government actions and patriotic values.

37. The phrase "from role to self " was suggested to me by Almond's essay (1977) on the transitions from character to role to self since the 19th century. Also see Turner's influential paper (1976).

38. For more detailed information on these trends see Cherlin, 1981, and U.S. Bureau of the Census, 1982. The survey on premarital sex is reported in Zelnik and Kantner, 1980.

39. Several studies document substantial shifts of public opinion toward personal liberation and away from the standards of the companionship family between the middle of the sixties and the middle of the seventies. See, for example, Yankelovich, 1974. Cherlin, 1981, also suggests that the acceptance of divorce accelerated in the late 60s and early 70s.

40. For a history of the women's movement, see Carden, 1974; and Hole and Levine, 1971. Freeman, 1975, gives an excellent account of its legislative victories. For an analysis of media coverage of the movement, see Cancian and Ross, 1981.

41. Degler, 1980, p. 471.

42. See Friedan, 1963, on the conservative message of Freudian and other therapists in the 1950s.

43. See, for example, Osmond & Martin, 1975.

44. Luker, 1984.

45. Clecak, 1983, reviews this criticism. Christopher Lasch's book, *The Culture of Narcissism,* 1978, is the critical book that had the greatest impact. On the need for commitment, see Yankelovich, 1981.

46. Kidd, 1974 and 1975. Zube's study (1972) of changing concepts of morality in the *Ladies' Home Journal* from 1948 to 1969 comes up

with an interpretation similar to Kidd's. Her quantitative analysis shows a clear shift from values oriented to the future and active "doing," to values oriented to "being" in the present.

47. Bellah et al., 1985, pp. 93 and 100; and Swidler, 1982, pp. 7–8. Similar findings are reported by Quinn, 1982, who did intensive interviews with eleven couples in North Carolina.

48. Harris, 1979.

49. Bellah et al., 1985, p. 101.

50. Here is more detail in the methodology. The high circulation magazines that were included were taken from a list in Kidd, 1975. In the early decades, I also selected articles listed in the *Readers' Guide* from *Harper's* and *Atlantic*. Because of the ease of obtaining articles from *Reader's Digest,* I randomly selected four articles from *Reader's Digest* and four from other magazines, after *Reader's Digest* began publication in the early 1920s. The coding system was originally developed to study changes in magazines between 1950 and 1970; therefore the categories are progressively less applicable as we move toward the beginning of the century, and the earlier articles receive fewer codes in any of the categories. The categories about gender roles are an exception; every article was coded as traditional or modern on these categories. A few articles contained very contradictory messages and were "double-scored," or counted as both traditional and modern on some categories; however, double-scoring was avoided whenever possible. The category system was refined until I reached a criterion of two coders agreeing on 85 percent of the coding for a particular article. This method of measuring changes in popular images of marriage has several problems. The intended audience of the magazines seems to come from a higher social class in the earlier decades, and the content of the articles partly reflects the policies of editors and advertisers and the attitudes of the writers. Nonetheless, the magazines seem to provide a fairly valid measure, since my findings are consistent with the other sources of data described in this chapter.

51. *Harper's Bazaar,* September 1909.

52. Vahanian & Olds, 1978.

53. Maurois, 1940.

54. Lederer & Jackson, 1974.

55. Miller, 1925.

56. Easterlin, 1980, emphasizes the changing size of birth cohorts. He sees very little change in family blueprints and gender roles since World War II. What has changed, in his view, is young people's income relative to the standard of living they grew up with. When their income was relatively high, they lived according to their family ideals, and wives stayed home and had many children as happened in the 50s. When the baby boom generation (or cohort) reached the labor market in the late 70s, wages were relatively low because the cohort was so large that wages were depressed. As a result, they were unable to live according to their ideals and had fewer children. When their children reach the labor market, their income will be relatively high because their cohort is so small, and the cycle will repeat. The relative merits of his theory and mine will be clarified by changes in the family during the recession that began in the 70s. Easterlin predicts a decline in family attachments as relative income declines. I predict a rise because hard times lower people's aspirations for freedom. See Cherlin, 1981, for an excellent analysis and critique of Easterlin. Although I agree with Easterlin that the changes in gender roles are often exaggerated, he exaggerates the stability. For evidence of major changes in women's goals since the late 60s, see Parelius, 1975; Roper & Labeff, 1977; Duncan et al., 1973; Thornton et al., 1983. Cherlin argues that the pattern of family change is not cyclical; rather, there have been gradual changes since 1900 interrupted by the peculiar 50s. Another explanation sociologists have developed is the marriage squeeze argument advanced by Oppenheimer, 1973, and others. They argue that, because women marry men about three years older than themselves, it will be difficult for women to find attractive husbands in historical periods following a rise in fertility, since there will be more younger women on the marriage market than older men. This situation occurred in the 70s, following the baby boom. According to Heer and Grossbard-Schechtman's interpretation (1981), the unfavorable marriage market for women in the 70s helps explain why a growing proportion of women did not marry, why they turned to employment instead and became involved in a women's movement to improve their situation at work.

CHAPTER 2

The History of the Family

Whether feminized or androgynous, love was part of late-nineteenth- and twentieth-century marriage. It is certainly central to marriage today. But it has not always been so. What we recognize as love seems to have played a smaller role in marriage in the past. It was not that people in the past were unfeeling but rather that they had more important things to worry about. A farm husband needed a wife who would be healthy and sturdy, bear many children, and tend the vegetable garden. A farm wife needed a man who would grow and harvest the crop. When men began to earn wages, a woman needed a husband who was a steady provider of income rather than a no-good who couldn't keep a job or who would drink up his pay. Whom to marry was too important a decision to leave to the whims of romantic love, which could fade away, revealing an unreliable or dishonest spouse.

Stephanie Coontz, in the book from which the first reading in this chapter is adapted, *Marriage, A History: From Obedience to Intimacy, or How Love Conquered Marriage,* tells the story of the rise of love as the central force of marriage. Prior to the 1700s, love was seen as separate from marriage. But great changes such as the introduction of wage labor and the migration of young laborers from rural areas to the city undermined parental control over their children. Young adults had more freedom to choose a spouse, and they began to value love. All this happened gradually, over the course of a century or two, and it did not occur among all classes at the same time. But Coontz argues that it eventually produced a profound change in the meaning of marriage that led to the kinds of marriages and relationships we see today.

History is not only about bygone eras; it is also about changes in the recent past and in our lifetimes. Here is an example of a historic change in which you, the reader, most likely will play a role: the emergence of a new life stage between being an adolescent and being fully adult. It is a stage that scholars are calling "early adulthood." It barely existed a half century ago, when people tended to marry young (half of all young women in the 1950s married by age 20), have children quickly, and move into the workforce—in other words, leap from childhood to adolescence to adulthood. Such a quick transition to adulthood is much rarer today. Young adults stay in school longer, cohabit more, and delay childbearing much longer than their parents or grandparents did. Sociologists who study the "life course" of individuals today have noticed this change, labeled it, and thought about its implications for young adults and for the larger society around them. The second reading in this chapter provides an overview of this newly emerging stage of life.

READING 2-1

What's Love Got to Do with It?

A Brief History of Marriage

Stephanie Coontz

It's remarkable to realize that no one under the age of 30 is old enough to actually remember the fairy-tale wedding of Lady Diana Spencer to Prince Charles back in 1981. Yet almost everyone knows about the disillusion and drama that set in a few years later, when it became clear that they weren't going to live "happily ever after." As soon as Diana had the two sons the monarchy needed to serve as "an heir and a spare," Charles returned to his longtime lover, and Diana, bitterly angry, went on to take a series of lovers of her own. As Diana famously complained to a television interviewer, she hadn't known at the time of her wedding that there'd be three persons involved in her marriage. Many individuals still identify so much with the disappointed princess that they've reacted with fury to the announcement that Prince Charles will finally marry the woman with whom he's had a 35-year relationship.

But having only three people involved in a marriage would have seemed downright lonely to most people of the past, and for thousands of years it would have seemed strange for anyone to have entered a marriage with such high expectations for personal happiness as Diana and the millions of her admirers had.

George Bernard Shaw once described marriage as an institution that brings two people together under the influence of the most violent, delusive, and transient of passions, and requires them to

swear they'll remain in that abnormal, exhausting condition until death do them part. His comment pokes fun at the unrealistic expectations attached to the cultural ideal that marriage should be based on true love. But for thousands of years, people would not have gotten the joke, because almost no one believed that people should marry for love. When individuals did advocate such a bizarre belief, it was no laughing matter, but a serious threat to social order.

In ancient India, falling in love before marriage was considered a disruptive, antisocial act. In some Chinese dialects, a term for *love* didn't traditionally apply to feelings between husband and wife: It was used to describe an illicit, socially disapproved relationship. Both the ancient Greeks and medieval Europeans thought lovesickness was a type of insanity, and that it was almost indecent to love a spouse too ardently. The Greek philosopher Plato did hold love in high regard, because he felt that it led men to behave honorably; however, he was referring not to the love of women, "such as the meaner men feel," but to the love of a man for another man, which was the Greek ideal for the purest form of love.

Once the Greeks became Christians, they got far less tolerant of same-sex relationships. But for the first thousand years of Christianity, the church didn't like heterosexual love much better than it liked homosexual love. "It's better to marry than to burn," said Paul, but it's better still to remain single and celibate. Right up until the 16th century, the Christian church taught that married love was only one step above unmarried fornication: The Virgin Mary was the most admired woman; the widow the next. The wife occupied the lowest rung of respectable womanhood.

The hierarchy of good things was different for the aristocracy, but for them, too, the pleasures of marriage were way down on the totem pole. The courtly love poems and songs that have so influenced our own sense of what romance is all about were originally based on

Stephanie Coontz, "What's Love Got to Do with It?" from *Psychotherapy Networker*, May/June 2005, Vol. 29, No. 3, pp. 56–61, 74. Based on her book *Marriage, A History: From Obedience to Intimacy, or How Love Conquered Marriage*, Viking Press. Used by permission of the author.

the notion that adultery was the purest form of love. In 12th-century France, the author of the first treatise on courtly love wrote that marriage is no excuse for not loving. By this he meant that marriage was no excuse for not loving someone *outside* the marriage!

In most cultures of the past, it was inconceivable that young people would choose their spouse on the basis of an unpredictable feeling like love. Marriage wasn't about the happiness of two individuals—it was a political and economic arrangement between two families. For the propertied classes, marriage was a way of consolidating wealth, merging resources, forging political alliances, and even concluding peace treaties.

Marriage was also an economic and political transaction in the lower classes. Farms or businesses could rarely be run by a single person, so prospective partners' skills, resources, tools, and useful in-laws were more important than their attractiveness. For a farmer or artisan, getting married was like picking your most crucial employee, and it was a foolish man indeed who would choose her for her looks, or fire her because he didn't love her anymore.

Certainly, people fell in love in the ancient and medieval world—sometimes even with their own spouse. But marriage was far too vital an economic and political institution to be entered into solely on the basis of something as irrational as love, and too important to be left to the whims of two young people. For thousands of years, the theme song for most courtships and weddings could have been "what's love got to do with it?"

Married love began to get a better reputation with the Protestant Reformation in the 16th century. Protestants argued that the clergy should be allowed, even encouraged, to marry, and that Roman Catholics were wrong to call marriage a necessary evil or a second-best existence to celibacy. Rather, said Luther, marriage was "a glorious estate."

But Protestants were just as suspicious of ardent love between husband and wife as were Roman Catholics, and they were even more hostile toward young people's right to freely choose their own mate. Protestants insisted that a marriage wasn't valid unless the parents agreed to it, even if the couple had gone through a ceremony and later had children together. Luther argued that parents didn't have the right to force a child into a loveless match, but they were totally justified in forbidding a match, no matter how much the couple loved each other, or in annulling a match for which they hadn't given permission. Both Catholic and Protestant theologians criticized women who used endearing nicknames for their husbands, because such familiarity undermined the lines of authority that ought to govern marriage.

It wasn't until the 18th century that a decisive change began to occur in popular attitudes toward love and marriage, spurred by two seismic social revolutions. First, the spread of wage labor made young people less dependent on their parents to get a start in life. A man didn't have to delay marriage until he inherited land or took over a business from his father. A woman could earn her own dowry. This made it harder for parents to control their children's courting.

Second, the freedoms afforded by the market economy had their parallel in new philosophical ideas. During the 18th-century Enlightenment and the age of revolution, influential thinkers across Europe began to champion individual rights and insist that the pursuit of happiness was a legitimate goal. They advocated marrying for love, rather than for wealth or status.

By the end of the 1700s, personal choice of partners had replaced arranged marriage as a social ideal, and individuals were encouraged to make that choice on the basis of love. For the first time in 5,000 years, marriage came to be seen as a private relationship between two individuals, rather than one link in a larger system of political and economic alliances. The measure of a successful marriage was no longer how big a financial settlement was involved, how many useful in-laws were acquired, or how many children were produced, but how well a family met the emotional needs of its individual members.

But these new ideas, conservatives immediately complained, posed a crisis of social order. If marriage was suddenly to be about love and lifelong intimacy, they worried, what would hold a marriage together if love and intimacy disappeared? And how could household order be maintained if marriages were based on love, rather than power?

Traditionalists had good cause to fret. The 1780s and 1790s saw a crisis over these questions, especially in regions influenced by the radical ideas of the American and French revolutions. In America, New Jersey gave women the vote, and several states enacted measures that made it easier for young people to choose their own partners. Most states began to liberalize divorce laws.

The French revolutionaries went further. They redefined marriage as a freely chosen civil contract, made divorce more accessible than it would be again until 1975, and decriminalized homosexual acts, on the grounds that such penalties violated the principle that the state should respect people's private choices. They mandated that families couldn't favor boys over girls in inheritance. Traditionalists thought the world was coming to an end.

At the end of the 18th century, however, the most radical innovations were rolled back. In France, Napoleon repealed the no-fault divorce laws and struck down equal inheritance for women. In America, New Jersey revoked the right of women to vote, and most states adopted restrictions on women's political activity. At the same time, women lost access to many occupations that had formerly been open to them.

But the ideas fostered by these revolutions had made it impossible to fall back on the old saying that women had to obey their husbands as subjects had to obey the king. So people cast about for a new understanding of the relationship between men and women and the nature of marriage—one

that didn't unleash the "chaos" of equality, but didn't insist too much on women's subordination or raise uncomfortable parallels between the right to rebel against political tyrants and women's right to rebel against domestic ones.

The result was a compromise between egalitarian and patriarchal views of marriage. There was a new outrage against forcing women into loveless marriages, reflected in the art and literature of the day. But women, in or out of marriage, weren't extended the same rights as men. Instead, women were said to possess such a unique moral worth and such a delicate constitution that they shouldn't be exposed to the risks that men had to take by participating in business or politics. The exclusion of women from politics, in this new theory, wasn't an assertion of male privilege, but a mark of deference to women's talents and needs.

And those needs began to be defined in totally new ways. In the Middle Ages, popular culture had painted women as the lusty sex, more prone to passion and sexual excess than men. Suddenly this was turned on its head. It became accepted wisdom in the 19th century that the "normal" woman lacked any sexual drives at all—another reason to protect her from too much freedom.

By the early 19th century, idealization of love, marriage, home, hearth, and female purity was the bedrock of popular culture. Poems were written about the "angel in the house" and the sanctity of home, completely overturning an older popular culture that focused on community rather than family celebrations.

When Queen Victoria walked down the aisle wearing white instead of the multicolored costumes of the past, a new "tradition" was instantly invented, and people began to lose the memory of a time when female purity, loving marriage, and domesticity weren't the most cherished subjects of popular culture. One author summed up the new view by saying that if you had just four letters with which to express all the affection and morality and meaning in life, you would simply spell out H-O-M-E.

In the late 18th century, conservatives had warned that unions based on love and the desire for personal happiness were inherently unstable. If love was the most important reason to marry, how could society condemn people who stayed single rather than enter a loveless marriage? If love disappeared from a marriage, why shouldn't the couple be allowed to go their separate ways? If men and women were true soulmates, why should they not be equal partners in society?

In the 19th century, the doctrine that men and women had innately different natures and occupied separate spheres of life seemed to sidestep these problems by allowing people to romanticize love and marriage without unleashing the radical demands that had rocked society in the 1790s. The doctrine of separate spheres held back the inherent individualism of the "pursuit of happiness" by making men and women dependent upon each other, insisting that each party was incomplete without marriage. It justified women's confinement to the home without having to rely on patriarchal assertions about men's right to rule. Men were protecting women, it was said, not dominating them, by reserving political and economic roles for themselves, and women in return would rescue men from material corruption because of their own pure, sexless natures. For a while, the doctrine of female purity seemed to resolve the problem of how to justify women's exclusion from political, economic, and sexual rights without returning to the naked patriarchal controls of the past.

But there were two serious problems with the compromise between the radical implications of love and the traditional constraints of marriage. First of all, the idealized home was out of reach for most of the population, and in fact, middle-class women's domesticity and seclusion depended on the denial of domesticity to the working-class women, men, and children who took over the chores that had formerly taken up the bulk of middle-class wives' time. In the southern United States, slaveholders had no respect for the "sanctity" of marriage, motherhood, or protected childhood when it came to their slaves, and even after emancipation, most African Americans had neither the time nor the resources for wives to be full-time homemakers and children to stay home to be nurtured by their mothers.

In the North, women and children who couldn't survive on their husbands' or fathers' wages worked as domestic servants in other people's homes and provided cheap factory labor. Without their work, middle-class homemakers would have had scant time to minister to the emotional needs of their husbands and children. In mid-19th-century cities, providing enough water to maintain what advice writers called "a fairly clean" home required a servant to lug the equivalent of 100 bottles of water from the public pipe every day.

Even for those who could afford to practice the new ideals of domesticity and gender segregation, there was a problem. The doctrine of difference said that men and women were complementary figures who could be completed only by marriage, but it also drove a wedge between the sexes by emphasizing their differences. Women began to see men as a threat to their pure nature and their more refined friendships. In letters and diaries, women often referred to men as "the grosser sex." For their part, men found it easier to worship an angel in the abstract than to constantly curb their manners and restrain their own enjoyments to put up with the conventions of ladylike behavior on a daily basis.

If the doctrine of difference inhibited emotional intimacy between men and women, the cult of female purity made physical intimacy even more problematic, creating a huge distinction in men's minds between good sex and "good" women. Many men couldn't think about a woman they respected in sexual terms; they often went to prostitutes for sexual relief, and frequently passed venereal diseases on to their wives. For many women, marital sex was a source of anxiety, guilt, or disgust, yet Victorian women suffered from an epidemic of ailments that were almost certainly associated with sexual frustration. They flocked to hydrotherapy centers, where strong volleys of water sometimes relieved their symptoms. Physicians regularly massaged women's pelvic areas to alleviate "hysteria." In fact, the mechanical vibrator was invented at the end of the 19th century to relieve physicians of this time-consuming chore!

No wonder there was a revolt against Victorian prudery and the doctrine of separate spheres. The sexual revolution of the early 20th century wasn't a revolt against marriage—it was an attempt to make marriage more satisfying and to make married love more central to people's identity. And it succeeded dramatically. In the early 20th century, the age of marriage fell, the proportion of men and women who remained single all their lives fell, and the same-sex bonds and intense extended-family ties that had once coexisted with marital ties were devalued, or even labeled deviant. This was when marriage became the happy ending for every story, and when expectations of emotional and sexual satisfaction in marriage led people to elevate marriage above all other personal and family ties. Marriage became a much more important goal, especially for women, and more people reported themselves happy in marriage, than in the past. But the more that people expected to find love and sexual satisfaction in marriage, the more discontented they became when a marriage proved unsatisfying. Divorce rates tripled during the early 1900s. By the end of the 1920s, hundreds of books and articles worried about *The Bankruptcy of Marriage; The Revolt of Women;* and *The Marriage Crisis* and asked, "Is Marriage on the Skids?"

The crisis was put on the back burner during the 1930s and 1940s by the Great Depression and World War II, and in the 1950s, it was almost completely forgotten, as the love-based, male-breadwinner family swept aside all other family forms and values. The reaction against the hardship and turmoil of the '30s and '40s combined with postwar prosperity and unprecedented government subsidies for male-breadwinner families during the 1950s to create what many people see as the Golden Age of Marriage.

By the 1960s, marriage had become nearly universal in North America and Western Europe, with 95 percent of all persons marrying. And as people married at a younger age, life spans lengthened, and divorce rates fell or held steady, individuals were spending much more of their lives in marriage than ever before or since. By 1959, almost half of all American women were married by age 19, and 70 percent were married by age 24. There were also more full-time housewives in society than ever before or since.

Never before had so many people shared the experience of courting their own mates, getting married when they wanted to, and setting up their own households. And never before had married couples been so independent of community groups and extended family ties. The postwar period was characterized by the overwhelming dominance of the nuclear family, male-breadwinner model of marriage. Any departure from this model—whether late marriage, nonmarriage, divorce, single motherhood, or even delayed childbearing—was considered deviant.

A 1957 survey in the United States reported that four out of five people believed that anyone who preferred to remain single was "sick," "neurotic," or "immoral." Even larger majorities agreed that, once married, the husband should be the breadwinner and the wife should stay home. As late as 1961, one survey of young women aged 16 to 21 found that almost all expected to be married by age 22, most wanted to have four children, and they expected to quit work permanently when their first child was born.

But under the surface of that placidity, disillusion and discontent were mounting, for both sexes. Hugh Hefner founded *Playboy* magazine in 1953 as a voice of revolt against male family responsibilities. He urged men to "enjoy the pleasures the female has to offer without becoming emotionally involved"—or, worse yet, financially responsible. *Playboy*'s first issue, in April 1953, featured the article "Miss Gold-Digger of

1953," assailing women who expected husbands to support them.

Housewives had their own discontents. In poll after poll, women who married in the 1950s said that they didn't want their daughters to have the same life that they'd had. Instead, they wanted their daughters to marry later in life and get more education. The limits that these wives and mothers had experienced in their marriages had led them to encourage behaviors in their children that, in combination with the new economic and political trends of the 1960s and 1970s, overturned prior gender roles and marriage patterns. As African Americans, young people, and women challenged the restrictions they'd faced in social life and the economy brought more women into the workforce on new terms, all the old contradictions of the love-based, male-breadwinner marriage reemerged, and this time they exploded.

It took more than 150 years to establish the love-based, male-breadwinner marriage as the dominant model in North America and Western Europe. It took less than 25 years to dismantle it. In barely two decades, marriage lost its role as "the master event," which governed young people's sexual initiation, their assumption of adult roles and work patterns, and their transition into parenthood. People began marrying later. Divorce rates soared. Premarital sex became the norm. Acceptance of gay and lesbian relations increased. The division of labor between husband as breadwinner and wife as homemaker, which sociologists in the 1950s had believed was vital for industrial society, fell apart. And many of the mores that once governed why people marry, what predicts marital satisfaction, who divorces, and how cohabitation affects future marital behavior began to change in fundamental and unexpected ways.

Today researchers chase a moving target as they study the new dynamics and relationships of married life. And all of us struggle to understand and come to terms with these changes in our own families. It doesn't help when the mass media and political pundits assure us that if we just tried harder, we could recapture a Golden Age of "traditional" marriage. Such illusions merely burden us with unrealistic nostalgia for what love and marriage "used to be," feeding our guilt and our fears about family change, instead of showing us the grounds for hope: the fact that many people are now discovering how to sustain commitments and make deeper connections both inside and outside marriage. Our challenge today is to reject romanticized views of the past, which make us feel guilty for not living in a sit-com marriage, and to find ways to help all peoples—whatever kind of family they live in, whether they're currently married or not—build healthier relationships and meet their obligations to dependents.

■ Review Questions

1. Why is it "inconceivable," according to Coontz, that young people in most cultures in the past would have chosen a spouse based on love?
2. How might the rise of marriage based on love have affected the amount of divorce in a society?

READING 2-2

Growing Up Is Harder to Do

Frank F. Furstenberg Jr.

Sheela Kennedy

Vonnie C. McLoyd

Rubén G. Rumbaut

Richard A. Settersten Jr.

In the years after World War II, Americans typically assumed the full responsibilities of adulthood by their late teens or early 20s. Most young men had completed school and were working full-time, and most young women were married and raising children. People who grew up in this era of growing affluence—many of today's grandparents—were economically self-sufficient and able to care for others by the time they had weathered adolescence. Today, adulthood no longer begins when adolescence ends. Ask someone in their early 20s whether they consider themselves to be an adult, and you might get a laugh, a quizzical look, a shrug of the shoulders, or a response like that of a 24-year-old Californian: "Maybe next year. When I'm 25."

Social scientists are beginning to recognize a new phase of life: early adulthood. Some features of this stage resemble coming of age during the late 19th and early 20th centuries, when youth lingered in a state of semi-autonomy, waiting until they were sufficiently well-off to marry, have children, and establish an independent household. However, there are important differences in how young people today define and achieve adulthood from those of both the recent and the more distant past.

This new stage is not merely an extension of adolescence, as has been maintained in the mass media. Young adults are physically mature and often possess impressive intellectual, social and psychological skills. Nor are young people today reluctant to accept adult responsibilities. Instead, they are busy building up their educational credentials and practical skills in an ever more demanding labor market. Most are working or studying or both, and are developing romantic relationships. Yet, many have not become fully adult—traditionally defined as finishing school, landing a job with benefits, marrying and parenting—because they are not ready, or perhaps not permitted, to do so. For a growing number, this will not happen until their late 20s or even early 30s. In response, American society will have to revise upward the "normal" age of full adulthood, and develop ways to assist young people through the ever-lengthening transition.

Among the most privileged young adults—those who receive ample support from their parents—this is a time of unparalleled freedom from family responsibilities and an opportunity for self-exploration and development. For the less advantaged, early adulthood is a time of struggle to gain the skills and credentials required for a job that can support the family they wish to start (or perhaps have already started), and a struggle to feel in control of their lives. A 30-year-old single mother from Iowa laughed when asked whether she considered herself an adult: "I don't know if I'm an adult yet. I still don't feel quite grown up. Being an adult kind of sounds like having things, everything is kind of in a routine and on track, and I don't feel like I'm quite on track."

CHANGING NOTIONS OF ADULTHOOD

Traditionally, the transition to adulthood involves establishing emotional and economic independence from parents or, as historian John Modell described it, "coming into one's own." The life

Frank F. Furstenberg Jr., Sheela Kennedy, Vonnie C. McLoyd, Rubén G. Rumbaut, and Richard A. Settersten Jr., "Growing Up is Harder to Do," *Contexts,* Vol. 3, No. 3, pp. 33–41. © 2004 The American Sociological Association. Used by permission. All rights reserved.

events that make up the transition to adulthood are accompanied by a sense of commitment, purpose and identity. Although we lack systematic evidence on how adulthood was defined in the past, it appears that marriage and parenthood represented important benchmarks. Nineteenth-century American popular fiction, journalism, sermons and self-help guides rarely referred to finishing school or getting a job, and only occasionally to leaving home or starting one's own household as the critical turning point. On the other hand, they often referred to marriage, suggesting that marriage was considered, at least by middle-class writers, as the critical touchstone of reaching adulthood.

By the 1950s and 1960s, most Americans viewed family roles and adult responsibilities as nearly synonymous. In that era, most women married before they were 21 and had at least one child before they were 23. For men, having the means to marry and support a family was the defining characteristic of adulthood, while for women, merely getting married and becoming a mother conferred adult status. As Alice Rossi explained in 1968: "On the level of cultural values, men have no freedom of choice where work is concerned: they must work to secure their status as adult men. The equivalent for women has been maternity. There is considerable pressure upon the growing girl and young woman to consider maternity necessary for a woman's fulfillment as an individual and to secure her status as an adult."

Research conducted during the late 1950s and early 1960s demonstrated widespread antipathy in America toward people who remained unmarried and toward couples who were childless by choice. However, these views began to shift in the late 1960s, rendering the transition to adulthood more ambiguous. Psychologists Joseph Veroff, Elizabeth Douvan, and Richard Kulka found that more than half of Americans interviewed in 1957 viewed someone who did not want to get married as selfish, immature, peculiar or morally flawed. By 1976, fewer than

one-third of a similar sample held such views. A 1962 study found that 85 percent of mothers believed that married couples should have children. Nearly 20 years later, just 40 percent of those women still agreed, and in 1993 only 1 in 5 of their daughters agreed. Arland Thornton and Linda Young-Demarco, who have studied attitudes toward family roles during the latter half of the 20th century, conclude that "Americans increasingly value freedom and equality in their personal and family lives while at the same time maintaining their commitment to the ideals of marriage, family, and children." While still personally committed to family, Americans increasingly tolerate alternative life choices.

To understand how Americans today define adulthood, we developed a set of questions for the 2002 General Social Survey (GSS), an opinion poll administered to a nationally representative sample of Americans every two years by the National Opinion Research Center. The survey asked nearly 1,400 Americans aged 18 and older how important each of the following traditional benchmarks was to being an adult: leaving home, finishing school, getting a full-time job, becoming financially independent from one's parents, being able to support a family, marrying and becoming a parent.

The definition of adulthood that emerges today does not necessarily include marriage and parenthood. As shown in Figure 2.1, the most important milestones are completing school, establishing an independent household and being employed full-time—concrete steps associated with the ability to support a family. Ninety-five percent of Americans surveyed consider education, employment, financial independence and the ability to support a family to be key steps on the path to adulthood. Nonetheless, almost half of GSS respondents do not believe that it is necessary to actually marry or to have children to be considered an adult. As a young mother from San Diego explained, having a child did not make her an adult; instead she began to feel like an adult when she realized that "all of us make

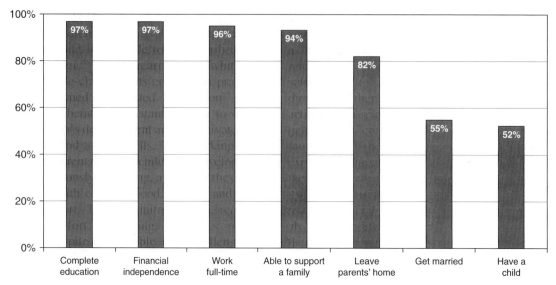

FIGURE 2.1

Percent of Americans who say that an event is at least somewhat important to being considered an adult. (*Source:* General Social Survey 2002. Reprinted by permission.)

mistakes, but you can fix them and if you keep yourself on track . . . everything will come out fine." Compared with their parents and grand-parents, for whom marriage and parenthood were virtually a pre-requisite for becoming an adult, young people today more often view these as life choices, not requirements.

THE LENGTHENING ROAD TO ADULTHOOD

Not only are the defining characteristics of adulthood changing, so is the time it takes to achieve them. To map the changing transitions to adulthood, we also examined several national surveys that contain information on young adults both in this country and abroad. Using U.S. Census data collected as far back as 1900, we compared the lives of young adults over time. We also conducted about 500 in-depth interviews with young adults living in different parts of the United States, including many in recent immigrant groups.

Our findings, as well as the work of other scholars, confirm that it takes much longer to make the transition to adulthood today than de-cades ago, and arguably longer than it has at any time in America's history. Figure 2.2, based on the 1960 and 2000 U.S. censuses, illustrates the large decline in the percentage of young adults who, by age 20 or 30, have completed all of the traditionally defined major adult transitions (leaving home, finishing school, becoming finan-cially independent, getting married and having a child). We define financial independence for both men and women as being in the labor force; however, because women in 1960 rarely com-bined work and motherhood, married full-time mothers are also counted as financially inde-pendent in both years. In 2000, just 46 percent of women and 31 percent of men aged 30 had completed all five transitions, compared with 77 percent of women and 65 percent of men at the same age in 1960.

Women—who have traditionally formed families at ages younger than men—show the

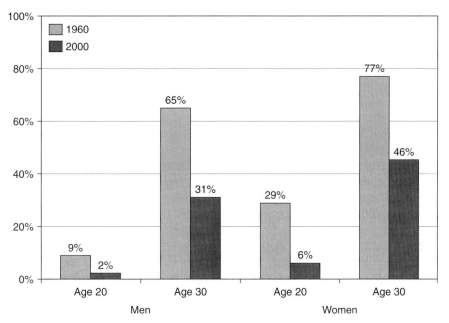

FIGURE 2.2
Percent completing transition to adulthood in 1960 and 2000 using traditional benchmarks
(leaving home, finishing school, getting married, having a child, and being financially
independent).(*Source:* Integrated Public Use Microdata Series extracts [PUMS] of the 1960
and 2000 U.S. Censuses.)

most dramatic changes at early ages. Although
almost 30 percent of 20-year-old women in 1960
had completed these transitions, just 6 percent
had done so in 2000. Among 25-year-olds (not
shown), the decrease is even more dramatic:
70 percent of 25-year-old women in 1960 had
attained traditional adult status, in 2000 just
25 percent had done so. Yet, in 2000, even as
they delayed traditional adulthood, 25-year-old
women greatly increased their participation in
the labor force to levels approaching those of
25-year-old men. The corresponding declines for
men in the attainment of traditional adult status
are less striking but nonetheless significant. For
both men and women, these changes can largely
be explained by the increasing proportion who
go to college and graduate school, and also by
the postponement of marriage and childbearing.

If we use the more contemporary definition
of adulthood suggested in Figure 2.1—one that

excludes marriage and parenthood—then the
contrasts are not as dramatic. In 2000, 70 percent
of men aged 30 had left home, were financially
independent, and had completed their schooling,
just 12 points lower than was true of 30-year-old
men in 1960. Nearly 75 percent of 30-year-old
women in 2000 met this standard, compared to
nearly 85 percent of women in 1960. Nonetheless, even these changes are historically substantial, and we are not even taking into account
how many of these independent, working, highly
educated young people still feel that they are not
yet capable of supporting a family.

The reasons for this lengthening path to
adulthood, John Modell has shown, range from
shifting social policies to changing economic
forces. The swift transition to adulthood typical
after World War II was substantially assisted
by the government. The GI Bill helped veterans
return to school and subsidized the expansion of

education. Similarly, government subsidies for affordable housing encouraged starting families earlier. At the same time, because Social Security was extended to cover more of the elderly, young people were no longer compelled to support their parents. The disappearance or reduction of such subsidies during the past few decades may help to explain the prolongation of adult transitions for some Americans. The growing cost of college and housing forces many youth into a state of semi-autonomy, accepting some support from their parents while they establish themselves economically. When a job ends or they need additional schooling or a relationship dissolves, they increasingly turn to their family for assistance. Thus, the sequencing of adult transitions has become increasingly complicated and more reversible.

However, the primary reason for a prolonged early adulthood is that it now takes much longer to secure a full-time job that pays enough to support a family. Economists Timothy Smeeding and Katherin Ross Phillips found in the mid-1990s that just 70 percent of American men aged 24 to 28 earned enough to support themselves, while fewer than half earned enough to support a family of three. Attaining a decent standard of living today usually requires a college education, if not a professional degree. To enter or remain in the middle class, it is almost imperative to make an educational commitment that spans at least the early 20s. Not only are more Americans attending college than ever before, it takes longer to complete a degree than in years past. Census data reveal that from 1960 to 2000, the percentage of Americans aged 20, 25, and 30 who were enrolled in school more than doubled. Unlike during the 1960s, these educational and work investments are now required of women as well as men. It is little wonder then that many young people linger in early adulthood, delaying marriage and parenthood until their late 20s and early 30s.

Those who do not linger are likely those who cannot afford to and, perhaps as a result,

views on how long it takes to achieve adulthood differ markedly by social class. Less-educated and less-affluent respondents—those who did not attend college and those at the bottom one-third of the income ladder—have an earlier expected timetable for leaving home, completing school, obtaining full-time employment, marriage and parenthood. Around 40 percent of the less well-off in the GSS sample said that young adults should marry before they turn 25, and one-third said they should have children by this age. Far fewer of the better-off respondents pointed to the early 20s, and about one-third of them said that these events could be delayed until the 30s. These social class differences probably stem from the reality that young people with more limited means do not have the luxury of investing in school or experimenting with complex career paths.

NEW DEMANDS ON FAMILIES, SCHOOLS, AND GOVERNMENT

The growing demands on young Americans to invest in the future have come at a time of curtailed government support, placing heavy demands on families. Growing inequality shapes very different futures for young Americans with more and less privileged parents.

Early adulthood is when people figure out what they want to do and how best to realize their goals. If they are lucky enough to have a family that can help out, they may proceed directly through college, travel or work for a few years, or perhaps participate in community service, and then enter graduate or professional school. However, relatively few Americans have this good fortune. Youth from less well-off families must shuttle back and forth between work and school or combine both while they gradually gain their credentials. In the meantime, they feel unprepared for marriage or parenting. If they do marry or parent during these years, they often find themselves trying to juggle too many responsibilities and unable to adequately invest in their future. Like the mother from Iowa, they do not feel "on track" or in control of their lives.

More than at any time in recent history, parents are being called on to provide financial assistance (either college tuition, living expenses or other assistance) to their young adult children. Robert Schoeni and Karen Ross conservatively estimate that nearly one-quarter of the entire cost of raising children is incurred after they reach 17. Nearly two-thirds of young adults in their early 20s receive economic support from parents, while about 40 percent still receive some assistance in their late 20s.

A century ago, it was the other way around: young adults typically helped their parents when they first went to work, if (as was common) they still lived with their parents. Now, many young adults continue to receive support from their parents even after they begin working. The exceptions seem to be in immigrant families; there, young people more often help support their parents. A 27-year-old Chinese American from New York explained why he continued to live with his parents despite wanting to move out, saying that his parents "want me [to stay] and they need me. Financially, they need me to take care of them, pay the bills, stuff like that, which is fine."

As young people and their families struggle with the new reality that it takes longer to attain adulthood, Americans must recognize weaknesses in the primary institutions that facilitate this transition—schools and the military. For the fortunate few who achieve bachelor's degrees and perhaps go on to professional or graduate training, residential colleges and universities seem well designed. They offer everything from housing to health care while training young adults. Likewise, the military provides a similar milieu for those from less-privileged families. However, only about one in four young adults attends primarily residential colleges or joins the military after high school. The other three-quarters look to their families for room and board while they attend school and enter the job

market. Many of these youth enter community colleges or local universities that provide much less in the way of services and support.

The least privileged come from families that cannot offer much assistance. This vulnerable population—consisting of 10 to 15 percent of young adults—may come out of the foster care system, graduate from special education programs, or exit jails and prisons. These youth typically lack job skills and need help to secure a foothold in society. Efforts to increase educational opportunities, establish school-to-career paths, and help students who cannot afford postsecondary education must be given higher priority, even in a time of budget constraints. The United States, once a world leader in providing higher education to its citizens, now lags behind several other nations in the proportion of the population that completes college.

Expanding military and alternative national service programs also can help provide a bridge from secondary school to higher education or the labor force by providing financial credit to those who serve their country. Such programs also offer health insurance to young adults, who are often cut off from insurance by arbitrary age limits. Finally, programs for the vulnerable populations of youth coming out of foster care, special education, and mental health services must not assume that young people are fully able to become economically independent at age 18 or even 21. The timetable of the 1950s is no longer applicable. It is high time for policy makers and legislators to address the realities of the longer and more demanding transition to adulthood.

RECOMMENDED RESOURCES

Furstenberg, Frank F., Jr., Thomas D. Cook, Robert Sampson, and Gail Slap, eds. *Early Adulthood in Cross-National Perspective.* London: Sage Publications, 2002. The contributors describe the emergence of this life stage across countries and the wide variation between them in the patterns of adult transitions.

Larson, Reed W., Bradford B. Brown, and Jeylan T. Mortimer, eds. *Adolescents' Preparation for the Future: Perils and Promises.* Ann Arbor, MI: The Society for Research on Adolescence, 2002. The articles in this interdisciplinary book consider how well adolescents in different societies are being prepared for adulthood in a rapidly changing and increasingly global world.

Modell, John. *Into One's Own: From Youth to Adulthood in the United States 1920–1975.* Berkeley, CA: University of California Press, 1989. Modell documents dramatic 20th-century changes in the transition to adulthood and places these shifts within the context of larger economic, political, and technological changes.

Portes, Alejandro, and Rubén G. Rumbaut. *Legacies: The Story of the Immigrant Second Generation.* Berkeley, CA: University of California Press, 2001. This book includes findings from the Children of Immigrants Longitudinal Study on the adaptation of second-generation immigrants during adolescence.

Schoeni, Robert, and Karen Ross. "Material Assistance Received from Families during the Transition to Adulthood." In *On the Frontier of Adulthood: Theory, Research, and Public Policy,* eds. Richard Settersten Jr., Frank Furstenberg Jr., and Rubén Rumbaut. Chicago: University of Chicago Press, 2004. This study estimates the amount of financial assistance given to young adults by their families at different points during early adulthood.

Settersten, Richard A., Jr., Frank F. Furstenberg Jr., and Rubén G. Rumbaut, eds. *On the Frontier of Adulthood: Theory, Research, and Public Policy.* Chicago: University of Chicago Press, 2004. This book describes prolonged and complex patterns of school, work, and family transitions for young adults in America and Western Europe.

Smeeding, Timothy, and Katherin Ross Phillips. "Cross-National Differences in Employment and Economic Sufficiency." *Annals of the American Academy of Political and Social Science* 580 (2002): 103–133. This article examines the economic independence of young adults in seven industrialized countries.

Thornton, Arland, and Linda Young-DeMarco. "Four Decades of Trends in Attitudes toward Family Issues in the United States: The 1960s through the 1990s." *Journal of Marriage and the Family* 63 (2001): 1009–37. The authors review survey data showing changes in Americans' attitudes toward the family.

■ Review Questions

1. What does it mean to be "fully adult" in contemporary American society?
2. Why does it typically take longer to become an adult today than it did in the mid-twentieth century?

Part Two

Gender, Class, and Race-Ethnicity

CHAPTER 3

Gender and Families

Over the past half century, scholarship on gender has grown in substance and stature so much that gender studies is now one of the core areas of inquiry in sociology. The advances have occurred in two stages. In the first stage, roughly the period from 1965 to 1985, sociologists relied heavily on the concept of gender roles. Some demonstrated ways in which parents, the media, and peer groups influenced children's ideas of the proper role for a girl or boy. Other sociologists studied ways in which society reinforced the roles of breadwinner and homemaker. The second stage began in the mid-1980s, when a new wave of gender scholars became dissatisfied with the concept of gender roles. They argued that the simple dichotomy between men's roles and women's roles shouldn't be taken for granted. Instead, argued the revisionists, scholars should examine the tenuous, changing, socially constructed nature of the very idea of a "male role" and a "female role." They also maintained that gender is a master identity, far too broad to be considered just one of life's roles, like the role of professor or student. They argued instead for an approach that focuses on the continual construction and maintenance of gender differences throughout adulthood.

These second-stage scholars drew upon symbolic interaction theory[1] and its offshoot, ethnomethodology.[2] In 1987, Candace West and Don H. Zimmerman put forward the interactionist approach in "Doing Gender," perhaps the most influential article on the sociology of gender in the past 25 years. "We argue," West and Zimmerman wrote, "that gender is not a set of traits, nor a role, but the product of social doings of some sort." These social doings occur through "situated conduct"—interactions between men and women in particular settings (such as a kitchen or a job interview). Gender is an achieved property that is created through countless social interactions that reinforce gender differences. The first selection in this chapter is an excerpt from "Doing Gender."

---

[1]H. Blumer, "Society as Symbolic Interaction," in *Human Behavior and Social Processes,* ed. A. M. Rose (Boston: Houghton Mifflin, 1962).

[2]H. Garfinkel, *Studies in Ethnomethodology* (Englewood Cliffs, NJ: Prentice Hall, 1967).

As more and more married women have remained in the workplace even when they have small children, the question of whether men can and will increase the amount of care they provide to their children has become an important one. Studies show that fathers have increased the number of hours they spend on child care and housework over the past few decades, but in most families mothers retain responsibility for the children and still do more of the work of caring. Nevertheless, in a small but visible number of families, fathers are staying home full-time to care for their children while their wives work for pay outside the home. How do these men go about the task of being the primary caregiver? Do they do it differently from mothers? Can they do it as well as mothers can? Or, as Andrea Doucet put it in the title of her book about Canadian fathers who were the primary caregivers to their children, *Do Men Mother?* In preparation for writing this book, Doucet talked with fathers and their wives and watched them go about their days. She concluded that, yes, men can mother, but they don't do it quite the way mothers do. That is, the ways that men go about the task of child care draw upon some of the more stereotypical, socially approved masculine characteristics (what Doucet, following R. W. Connell,[3] calls "hegemonic masculinity"). Yet these fathers-who-mother seem to be meeting the needs of their children well. The second selection in this chapter is an excerpt from *Do Men Mother?*

[3]Connell, R. W., *Masculinities* (Cambridge, UK: Polity Press, 1995).

READING 3-1

Doing Gender

Candace West

Don H. Zimmerman

In the beginning, there was sex and there was gender. Those of us who taught courses in the area in the late 1960s and early 1970s were careful to distinguish one from the other. Sex, we told students, was what was ascribed by biology: anatomy, hormones, and physiology. Gender, we said, was an achieved status: that which is constructed through psychological, cultural, and social means. To introduce the difference between the two, we drew on singular case studies of hermaphrodites (Money 1968, 1974; Money and Ehrhardt 1972) and anthropological investigations of "strange and exotic tribes" (Mead 1963, 1968).

Inevitably (and understandably), in the ensuing weeks of each term, our students became confused. Sex hardly seemed a "given" in the context of research that illustrated the sometimes ambiguous and often conflicting criteria for its ascription. And gender seemed much less an "achievement" in the context of the anthropological, psychological, and social imperatives we studied—the division of labor, the formation of gender identities, and the social subordination of women by men. Moreover, the received doctrine of gender socialization theories conveyed the strong message that while gender may be "achieved," by about age five it was certainly fixed, unvarying, and static—much like sex.

Since about 1975, the confusion has intensified and spread far beyond our individual classrooms. For one thing, we learned that the relationship

Candace West and Don H. Zimmerman, "Doing Gender," *Gender and Society* 1, No. 2. (June 1987): pp. 125–140. Copyright © 1987 Sociologists for Women in Society. Reprinted by permission of Sage Publications, Inc.

between biological and cultural processes was far more complex—and reflexive—than we previously had supposed (Rossi 1984, especially pp. 10–14). For another, we discovered that certain structural arrangements, for example, between work and family, actually produce or enable some capacities, such as to mother, that we formerly associated with biology (Chodorow 1978 versus Firestone 1970). In the midst of all this, the notion of gender as a recurring achievement somehow fell by the wayside.

Our purpose in this article is to propose an ethnomethodologically informed, and therefore distinctively sociological, understanding of gender as a routine, methodical, and recurring accomplishment. We contend that the "doing" of gender is undertaken by women and men whose competence as members of society is hostage to its production. Doing gender involves a complex of socially guided perceptual, interactional, and micropolitical activities that cast particular pursuits as expressions of masculine and feminine "natures."

When we view gender as an accomplishment, an achieved property of situated conduct, our attention shifts from matters internal to the individual and focuses on interactional and, ultimately, institutional arenas. In one sense, of course, it is individuals who "do" gender. But it is a situated doing, carried out in the virtual or real presence of others who are presumed to be oriented to its production. Rather than as a property of individuals, we conceive of gender as an emergent feature of social situations: both as an outcome of and a rationale for various social arrangements and as a means of legitimating one of the most fundamental divisions of society.

To advance our argument, we undertake a critical examination of what sociologists have meant by *gender,* including its treatment as a role enactment in the conventional sense and as a "display" in Goffman's (1976) terminology. Both *gender role* and *gender display* focus on behavioral aspects of being a woman or a man (as opposed, for example, to biological differences between the two). However, we contend that the notion of gender as a role obscures the work that is involved in producing gender in everyday activities, while the notion of gender as a display relegates it to the periphery of interaction. We argue instead that participants in interaction organize their various and manifold activities to reflect or express gender, and they are disposed to perceive the behavior of others in a similar light.

To elaborate our proposal, we suggest at the outset that important but often overlooked distinctions be observed among *sex, sex category,* and *gender. Sex* is a determination made through the application of socially agreed upon biological criteria for classifying persons as females or males.[1] The criteria for classification can be genitalia at birth or chromosomal typing before birth, and they do not necessarily agree with one another. Placement in a *sex category* is achieved through application of the sex criteria, but in everyday life, categorization is established and sustained by the socially required identificatory displays that proclaim one's membership in one or the other category. In this sense, one's sex category presumes one's sex and stands as proxy for it in many situations, but sex and sex category can vary independently; that is, it is possible to claim membership in a sex category even when the sex criteria are lacking. *Gender,* in contrast, is the activity of managing situated conduct in light of normative conceptions of attitudes and activities appropriate for one's sex category. Gender activities emerge from and bolster claims to membership in a sex category.

We contend that recognition of the analytical independence of sex, sex category, and gender is essential for understanding the relationships among these elements and the interactional work involved in "being" a gendered person in society. While our primary aim is theoretical, there will be occasion to discuss fruitful directions for empirical research following from the formulation of gender that we propose.

We begin with an assessment of the received meaning of gender, particularly in relation to the roots of this notion in presumed biological differences between women and men.

PERSPECTIVES ON SEX AND GENDER

In Western societies, the accepted cultural perspective on gender views women and men as naturally and unequivocally defined categories of being (Garfinkel 1967, pp. 116–18) with distinctive psychological and behavioral propensities that can be predicted from their reproductive functions. Competent adult members of these societies see differences between the two as fundamental and enduring—differences seemingly supported by the division of labor into women's and men's work and an often elaborate differentiation of feminine and masculine attitudes and behaviors that are prominent features of social organization. Things are the way they are by virtue of the fact that men are men and women are women—a division perceived to be natural and rooted in biology, producing in turn profound psychological, behavioral, and social consequences. The structural arrangements of a society are presumed to be responsive to these differences.

Analyses of sex and gender in the social sciences, though less likely to accept uncritically the naive biological determinism of the view just presented, often retain a conception of sex-linked behaviors and traits as essential properties of individuals (for good reviews, see Hochschild 1973; Tresemer 1975; Thorne 1980; Henley 1985). The "sex differences approach" (Thorne 1980) is more commonly attributed to psychologists than to sociologists, but the survey researcher who determines the "gender" of respondents on the basis of the sound of their voices over the telephone is also making trait-oriented assumptions. Reducing gender to a fixed set of psychological traits or to a unitary "variable" precludes serious consideration of the ways it is used to structure distinct domains of social experience (Stacey and Thorne 1985, pp. 307–8).

Taking a different tack, role theory has attended to the social construction of gender categories, called "sex roles" or, more recently, "gender roles" and has analyzed how these are learned and enacted. Beginning with Linton (1936) and continuing through the works of Parsons (Parsons 1951; Parsons and Bales 1955) and Komarovsky (1946, 1950), role theory has emphasized the social and dynamic aspect of role construction and enactment (Thorne 1980; Connell 1983). But at the level of face-to-face interaction, the application of role theory to gender poses problems of its own (for good reviews and critiques, see Connell 1983, 1985; Kessler, Ashendon, Connell, and Dowsett 1985; Lopata and Thorne 1978; Thorne 1980; Stacey and Thorne 1985). Roles are *situated identities*— assumed and relinquished as the situation demands—rather than *master identities* (Hughes 1945), such as sex category, that cut across situations. Unlike most roles, such as "nurse," "doctor," and "patient" or "professor" and "student," gender has no specific site or organizational context.

Moreover, many roles are already gender marked, so that special qualifiers—such as "female doctor" or "male nurse"—must be added to exceptions to the rule. Thorne (1980) observes that conceptualizing gender as a role makes it difficult to assess its influence on other roles and reduces its explanatory usefulness in discussions of power and inequality. Drawing on Rubin (1975), Thorne calls for a reconceptualization of women and men as distinct social groups, constituted in "concrete, historically changing—and generally unequal—social relationships" (Thorne 1980, p. 11).

We argue that gender is not a set of traits, nor a variable, nor a role, but the product of social doings of some sort. What then is the social doing of gender? It is more than the continuous creation of the meaning of gender through human actions (Gerson and Peiss 1985). We claim that gender itself is constituted through interaction.[2] To develop the implications of our claim, we turn to Goffman's (1976) account of "gender display." Our object here is to explore

how gender might be exhibited or portrayed through interaction, and thus be seen as "natural," while it is being produced as a socially organized achievement.

GENDER DISPLAY

Goffman contends that when human beings interact with others in their environment, they assume that each possesses an "essential nature"—a nature that can be discerned through the "natural signs given off or expressed by them" (1976, p. 75). Femininity and masculinity are regarded as "prototypes of essential expression—something that can be conveyed fleetingly in any social situation and yet something that strikes at the most basic characterization of the individual" (1976, p. 75). The means through which we provide such expressions are "perfunctory, conventionalized acts" (1976, p. 69), which convey to others our regard for them, indicate our alignment in an encounter, and tentatively establish the terms of contact for that social situation. But they are also regarded as expressive behavior, testimony to our "essential natures."

Goffman (1976, pp. 69–70) sees *displays* as highly conventionalized behaviors structured as two-part exchanges of the statement-reply type, in which the presence or absence of symmetry can establish deference or dominance. These rituals are viewed as distinct from but articulated with more consequential activities, such as performing tasks or engaging in discourse. Hence, we have what he terms the "scheduling" of displays at junctures in activities, such as the beginning or end, to avoid interfering with the activities themselves. Goffman (1976, p. 69) formulates *gender display* as follows:

> If gender be defined as the culturally established correlates of sex (whether in consequence of biology or learning), then gender display refers to conventionalized portrayals of these correlates.

These gendered expressions might reveal clues to the underlying, fundamental dimensions of the female and male, but they are, in Goffman's view, optional performances. Masculine courtesies may or may not be offered and, if offered, may or may not be declined (1976, p. 71). Moreover, human beings "themselves employ the term 'expression,' and conduct themselves to fit their own notions of expressivity" (1976, p. 75). Gender depictions are less a consequence of our "essential sexual natures" than interactional portrayals of what we would like to convey about sexual natures, using conventionalized gestures. Our *human* nature gives us the ability to learn to produce and recognize masculine and feminine gender displays—"a capacity [we] have by virtue of being persons, not males and females" (1976, p. 76).

Upon first inspection, it would appear that Goffman's formulation offers an engaging sociological corrective to existing formulations of gender. In his view, gender is a socially scripted dramatization of the culture's *idealization* of feminine and masculine natures, played for an audience that is well schooled in the presentational idiom. To continue the metaphor, there are scheduled performances presented in special locations, and like plays, they constitute introductions to or time out from more serious activities.

There are fundamental equivocations in this perspective. By segregating gender display from the serious business of interaction, Goffman obscures the effects of gender on a wide range of human activities. Gender is not merely something that happens in the nooks and crannies of interaction, fitted in here and there and not interfering with the serious business of life. While it is plausible to contend that gender displays—construed as conventionalized expressions—are optional, it does not seem plausible to say that we have the option of being seen by others as female or male.

It is necessary to move beyond the notion of gender display to consider what is involved in doing gender as an ongoing activity embedded in everyday interaction. Toward this end, we return to the distinctions among sex, sex category, and gender introduced earlier.

SEX, SEX CATEGORY, AND GENDER

Garfinkel's (1967, pp. 118–40) case study of Agnes, a transsexual raised as a boy who adopted a female identity at age 17 and underwent a sex reassignment operation several years later, demonstrates how gender is created through interaction and at the same time structures interaction. Agnes, whom Garfinkel characterized as a "practical methodologist," developed a number of procedures for passing as a "normal, natural female" both prior to and after her surgery. She had the practical task of managing the fact that she possessed male genitalia and that she lacked the social resources a girl's biography would presumably provide in everyday interaction. In short, she needed to display herself as a woman, simultaneously learning what it was to be a woman. Of necessity, this full-time pursuit took place at a time when most people's gender would be well-accredited and routinized. Agnes had to consciously contrive what the vast majority of women do without thinking. She was not "faking" what "real" women do naturally. She was obliged to analyze and figure out how to act within socially structured circumstances and conceptions of femininity that women born with appropriate biological credentials come to take for granted early on. As in the case of others who must "pass," such as transvestites, Kabuki actors, or Dustin Hoffman's "Tootsie," Agnes's case makes visible what culture has made invisible—the accomplishment of gender.

Garfinkel's (1967) discussion of Agnes does not explicitly separate three analytically distinct, although empirically overlapping, concepts—sex, sex category, and gender.

Sex

Agnes did not possess the socially agreed upon biological criteria for classification as a member of the female *sex*. Still, Agnes regarded herself as a female, albeit a female with a penis, which a woman ought not to possess. The penis, she insisted, was a "mistake" in need of remedy (Garfinkel 1967, pp. 126–27, 131–32). Like other competent members of our culture, Agnes honored the notion that there *are* "essential" biological criteria that unequivocally distinguish females from males. However, if we move away from the commonsense viewpoint, we discover that the reliability of these criteria is not beyond question (Money and Brennan 1968; Money and Ehrhardt 1972; Money and Ogunro 1974; Money and Tucker 1975). Moreover, other cultures have acknowledged the existence of "cross-genders" (Blackwood 1984; Williams 1986) and the possibility of more than two sexes (Hill 1935; Martin and Voorheis 1975, pp. 84–107; but see also Cucchiari 1981, pp. 32–35).

More central to our argument is Kessler and McKenna's (1978, pp. 1–6) point that genitalia are conventionally hidden from public inspection in everyday life; yet we continue through our social rounds to "observe" a world of two naturally, normally sexed persons. It is the *presumption* that essential criteria exist and would or should be there if looked for that provides the basis for sex categorization. Drawing on Garfinkel, Kessler and McKenna argue that "female" and "male" are cultural events—products of what they term the "gender attribution process"—rather than some collection of traits, behaviors, or even physical attributes. Illustratively they cite the child who, viewing a picture of someone clad in a suit and a tie, contends, "It's a man, because he has a peepee" (Kessler and McKenna 1978, p. 154). Translation: "He must have a pee-pee [an essential characteristic] because I see the *insignia* of a suit and tie." Neither initial sex assignment (pronouncement at birth as a female or male) nor the actual existence of essential criteria for that assignment (possession of a clitoris and vagina or penis and testicles) has much—if anything—to do with the identification of sex category in everyday life. There, Kessler and McKenna note, we operate with a moral certainty of a world of two sexes. We do not think, "Most persons with penises are men, but some may not be" or "Most persons who dress as men have penises." Rather, we take it for granted that sex and sex category are congruent—that knowing the latter, we can deduce the rest.

Sex Categorization

Agnes's claim to the categorical status of female, which she sustained by appropriate identificatory displays and other characteristics, could be *discredited* before her transsexual operation if her possession of a penis became known and after by her surgically constructed genitalia (see Raymond 1979, pp. 37, 138). In this regard, Agnes had to be continually alert to actual or potential threats to the security of her sex category. Her problem was not so much living up to some prototype of essential femininity but preserving her categorization as female. This task was made easy for her by a very powerful resource, namely, the process of commonsense categorization in everyday life.

The categorization of members of society into indigenous categories such as "girl" or "boy," or "woman" or "man," operates in a distinctively social way. The act of categorization does not involve a positive test, in the sense of a well-defined set of criteria that must be explicitly satisfied prior to making an identification. Rather, the application of membership categories relies on an "if-can" test in everyday interaction (Sacks 1972, pp. 332–35). This test stipulates that if people *can be seen* as members of relevant categories, *then categorize them that way*. That is, use the category that seems appropriate, except in the presence of discrepant information or obvious features that would rule out its use. This procedure is quite in keeping with the attitude of everyday life, which has us take appearances at face value unless we have special reason to doubt (Schutz 1943; Garfinkel 1967, pp. 272–77; Bernstein 1986).[3] It should be added that it is precisely when we have special reason to doubt that the issue of applying rigorous criteria arises, but it is rare, outside legal or bureaucratic contexts, to encounter insistence on positive tests (Garfinkel 1967, pp. 262–83; Wilson 1970).

Agnes's initial resource was the predisposition of those she encountered to take her appearance (her figure, clothing, hair style, and so on), as the undoubted appearance of a normal female. Her further resource was our cultural perspective on the properties of "natural, normally sexed persons." Garfinkel (1967, pp. 122–28) notes that in everyday life, we live in a world of two—and only two—sexes. This arrangement has a moral status, in that we include ourselves and others in it as "essentially, originally, in the first place, always have been, always will be, once and for all, in the final analysis, either 'male' or 'female'" (Garfinkel 1967, p. 122).

Consider the following case:

> This issue reminds me of a visit I made to a computer store a couple of years ago. The person who answered my questions was truly a *salesperson.* I could not categorize him/her as a woman or a man. What did I look for? (1) Facial hair: She/he was smooth skinned, but some men have little or no facial hair. (This varies by race, Native Americans and Blacks often have none.) (2) Breasts: She/he was wearing a loose shirt that hung from his/her shoulders. And, as many women who suffered through a 1950s' adolescence know to their shame, women are often flat-chested. (3) Shoulders: His/hers were small and round for a man, broad for a woman. (4) Hands: Long and slender fingers, knuckles a bit large for a woman, small for a man. (5) Voice: Middle range, unexpressive for a woman, not at all the exaggerated tones some gay males affect. (6) His/her treatment of me: Gave off no signs that would let me know if I were of the same or different sex as this person. There were not even any signs that he/she knew his/her sex would be difficult to categorize and I wondered about that even as I did my best to hide these questions so I would not embarrass him/her while we talked of computer paper. I left still not knowing the sex of my salesperson, and was disturbed by that unanswered question (child of my culture that I am). (Diane Margolis, personal communication)

What can this case tell us about situations such as Agnes's (cf. Morris 1974; Richards 1983) or the process of sex categorization in general? First, we infer from this description that the computer salesclerk's identificatory display was ambiguous, since she or he was not dressed or adorned in an unequivocally female or male fashion. It is when such a display *fails* to provide grounds for categorization that factors such as facial hair or tone of voice are assessed to determine membership in a sex category. Second, beyond the fact that this incident could be recalled after "a couple of years," the customer was not only "disturbed" by the ambiguity of the salesclerk's category but also assumed that to acknowledge this ambiguity would be embarrassing to the salesclerk. Not only do we want to know the sex category of those around us (to see it at a glance, perhaps), but we presume that others are displaying it for us, in as decisive a fashion as they can.

Gender

Agnes attempted to be "120 percent female" (Garfinkel 1967, p. 129), that is, unquestionably in all ways and at all times feminine. She thought she could protect herself from disclosure before and after surgical intervention by comporting herself in a feminine manner, but she also could have given herself away by overdoing her performance. Sex categorization and the accomplishment of gender are not the same. Agnes's categorization could be secure or suspect, but did not depend on whether or not she lived up to some ideal conception of femininity. Women can be seen as unfeminine, but that does not make them "unfemale." Agnes faced an ongoing task of *being* a woman—something beyond style of dress (an identificatory display) or allowing men to light her cigarette (a gender display). Her problem was to produce configurations of behavior that would be seen by others as normative gender behavior.

Agnes's strategy of "secret apprenticeship," through which she learned expected feminine decorum by carefully attending to her fiancé's criticisms of other women, was one means of masking incompetencies and simultaneously acquiring the needed skills (Garfinkel 1967, pp. 146–47). It was through her fiancé that Agnes learned that sunbathing on the lawn in front of her apartment was "offensive" (because it put her on display to other men). She also learned from his critiques of other women that she should not insist on having things her way and that she should not offer her opinions or claim equality with men (Garfinkel 1967, pp. 147–48). (Like other women in our society, Agnes learned something about power in the course of her "education.")

Popular culture abounds with books and magazines that compile idealized depictions of relations between women and men. Those focused on the etiquette of dating or prevailing standards of feminine comportment are meant to be of practical help in these matters. However, the use of any such source *as a manual of procedure* requires the assumption that doing gender merely involves making use of discrete, well-defined bundles of behavior that can simply be plugged into interactional situations to produce recognizable enactments of masculinity and femininity. The man "does" being masculine by, for example, taking the woman's arm to guide her across a street, and she "does" being feminine by consenting to be guided and not initiating such behavior with a man.

Agnes could perhaps have used such sources as manuals, but, we contend, doing gender is not so easily regimented (Mithers 1982; Morris 1974). Such sources may list and describe the sorts of behaviors that mark or display gender, but they are necessarily incomplete (Garfinkel 1967, pp. 66–75; Wieder 1974, pp. 183–214; Zimmerman and Wieder 1970, pp. 285–98). And to be successful, marking or displaying gender must be finely fitted to situations and modified or transformed as the occasion demands. Doing gender consists of managing such occasions so that, whatever the particulars, the outcome is seen and seeable in context as gender-appropriate

or, as the case may be, gender-*in*appropriate, that is, *accountable*.

GENDER AND ACCOUNTABILITY

As Heritage (1984, pp. 136–37) notes, members of society regularly engage in "descriptive accountings of states of affairs to one another," and such accounts are both serious and consequential. These descriptions name, characterize, formulate, explain, excuse, excoriate, or merely take notice of some circumstance or activity and thus place it within some social framework (locating it relative to other activities, like and unlike).

Such descriptions are themselves accountable, and societal members orient to the fact that their activities are subject to comment. Actions are often designed with an eye to their accountability, that is, how they might look and how they might be characterized. The notion of accountability also encompasses those actions undertaken so that they are specifically unremarkable and thus not worthy of more than a passing remark, because they are seen to be in accord with culturally approved standards.

Heritage (1984, p. 179) observes that the process of rendering something accountable is interactional in character:

> [This] permits actors to design their actions in relation to their circumstances so as to permit others, by methodically taking account of circumstances, to recognize the action for what it is.

The key word here is *circumstances*. One circumstance that attends virtually all actions is the sex category of the actor. As Garfinkel (1967, p. 118) comments:

> [T]he work and socially structured occasions of sexual passing were obstinately unyielding to [Agnes's] attempts to routinize the grounds of daily activities. This obstinacy points to the *omnirelevance* of sexual status to affairs of daily life as an invariant but unnoticed background in the texture of relevances that compose the changing actual scenes of everyday life. (italics added)

If sex category is omnirelevant (or even approaches being so), then a person engaged in virtually any activity may be held accountable for performance of that activity as a *woman* or a *man,* and their incumbency in one or the other sex category can be used to legitimate or discredit their other activities (Berger, Cohen, and Zelditch 1972; Berger, Conner, and Fisek 1974; Berger, Fisek, Norman, and Zelditch 1977; Humphreys and Berger 1981). Accordingly, virtually any activity can be assessed as to its womanly or manly nature. And note, to "do" gender is not always to live up to normative conceptions of femininity or masculinity; it is to engage in behavior *at the risk of gender assessment.* While it is individuals who do gender, the enterprise is fundamentally interactional and institutional in character, for accountability is a feature of social relationships and its idiom is drawn from the institutional arena in which those relationships are enacted. If this be the case, can we ever *not* do gender? Insofar as a society is partitioned by "essential" differences between women and men and placement in a sex category is both relevant and enforced, doing gender is unavoidable.

RESOURCES FOR DOING GENDER

Doing gender means creating differences between girls and boys and women and men, differences that are not natural, essential, or biological. Once the differences have been constructed, they are used to reinforce the "essentialness" of gender. In a delightful account of the "arrangement between the sexes," Goffman (1977) observes the creation of a variety of institutionalized frameworks through which our "natural, normal sexedness" can be enacted. The physical features of social setting provide one obvious resource for the expression of our "essential" differences. For example, the sex segregation of North American public bathrooms distinguishes "ladies" from "gentlemen" in matters held to be fundamentally biological, even though both "are somewhat similar in the question of waste products and their elimination" (Goffman 1977, p. 315). These settings are furnished with dimorphic equipment (such as urinals for men or elaborate grooming facilities for women), even though both sexes may achieve the same ends through the same means (and apparently do so in the privacy of their own homes). To be stressed here is the fact that:

> The functioning of sex-differentiated organs is involved, but there is nothing in this functioning that biologically recommends segregation; that arrangement is a totally cultural matter . . . toilet segregation is presented as a natural consequence of the difference between the sex classes when in fact it is a means of honoring, if not producing, this difference. (Goffman 1977, p. 316)

Standardized social occasions also provide stages for evocations of the "essential female and male natures." Goffman cites organized sports as one such institutionalized framework for the expression of manliness. There, those qualities that ought "properly" to be associated with masculinity, such as endurance, strength, and competitive spirit, are celebrated by all parties concerned—participants, who may be seen to demonstrate such traits, and spectators, who applaud their demonstrations from the safety of the sidelines (1977, p. 322).

Assortative mating practices among heterosexual couples afford still further means to create and maintain differences between women and men. For example, even though size, strength, and age tend to be normally distributed among females and males (with considerable overlap between them), selective pairing ensures couples in which boys and men are visibly bigger, stronger, and older (if not "wiser") than the girls and women with whom they are paired. So, should situations emerge in which greater size, strength, or experience is called for, boys and men will be ever ready to display it and girls and women, to appreciate its display (Goffman 1977, p. 321; West and Iritani 1985).

Gender may be routinely fashioned in a variety of situations that seem conventionally expressive to begin with, such as those that present "helpless" women next to heavy objects or flat tires. But, as Goffman notes, heavy, messy, and precarious concerns can be constructed from *any* social situation, "even though by standards set in other settings, this may involve something that is light, clean, and safe" (Goffman 1977, p. 324). Given these resources, it is clear that *any* interactional situation sets the stage for depictions of "essential" sexual natures. In sum, these situations "do not so much allow for the expression of natural differences as for the production of that difference itself" (Goffman 1977, p. 324).

Many situations are not clearly sex categorized to begin with, nor is what transpires within them obviously gender relevant. Yet any social encounter can be pressed into service in the interests of doing gender. Thus, Fishman's (1978) research on casual conversations found an asymmetrical "division of labor" in talk between heterosexual intimates. Women had to ask more questions, fill more silences, and use more attention-getting beginnings in order to be heard. Her conclusions are particularly pertinent here:

> Since interactional work is related to what constitutes being a woman, with what a woman *is,* the idea that it *is* work is obscured. The work is not seen as what women do, but as part of what they are. (Fishman 1978, p. 405)

We would argue that it is precisely such labor that helps to constitute the essential nature of women *as* women in interactional contexts (West and Zimmerman 1983, pp. 109–11; but see also Kollock, Blumstein, and Schwartz 1985).

Individuals have many social identities that may be donned or shed, muted or made more salient, depending on the situation. One may be a friend, spouse, professional, citizen, and many other things to many different people—or, to the same person at different times. But we are always women or men—unless we shift into another sex category. What this means is that

our identificatory displays will provide an ever-available resource for doing gender under an infinitely diverse set of circumstances.

Some occasions are organized to routinely display and celebrate behaviors that are conventionally linked to one or the other sex category. On such occasions, everyone knows his or her place in the interactional scheme of things. If an individual identified as a member of one sex category engages in behavior usually associated with the other category, this routinization is challenged. Hughes (1945, p. 356) provides an illustration of such a dilemma:

> [A] young woman . . . became part of that virile profession, engineering. The designer of an airplane is expected to go up on the maiden flight of the first plane built according to the design. He [sic] then gives a dinner to the engineers and workmen who worked on the new plane. The dinner is naturally a stag party. The young woman in question designed a plane. Her co-workers urged her not to take the risk—for which, presumably, men only are fit—of the maiden voyage. They were, in effect, asking her to be a lady instead of an engineer. She chose to be an engineer. She then gave the party and paid for it like a man. After food and the first round of toasts, she left like a lady.

On this occasion, parties reached an accommodation that allowed a woman to engage in presumptively masculine behaviors. However, we note that in the end, this compromise permitted demonstration of her "essential" femininity, through accountably "ladylike" behavior.

Hughes (1945, p. 357) suggests that such contradictions may be countered by managing interactions on a very narrow basis, for example, "keeping the relationship formal and specific." But the heart of the matter is that even—perhaps, especially—if the relationship is a formal one, gender is still something one is accountable for. Thus a woman physician (notice the special qualifier in her case) may be accorded respect for her skill and even addressed by an appropriate title. Nonetheless, she is subject to evaluation in terms of normative conceptions of appropriate attitudes and activities for her sex category and under pressure to prove that she is an "essentially" feminine being, despite appearances to the contrary (West 1984, pp. 97–101). Her sex category is used to discredit her participation in important clinical activities (Lorber 1984, pp. 52–54), while her involvement in medicine is used to discredit her commitment to her responsibilities as a wife and mother (Bourne and Wikler 1978, pp. 435–37). Simultaneously, her exclusion from the physician colleague community is maintained and her accountability *as a woman* is ensured.

In this context, "role conflict" can be viewed as a dynamic aspect of our current "arrangement between the sexes" (Goffman 1977), an arrangement that provides for occasions on which persons of a particular sex category can "see" quite clearly that they are out of place and that if they were not there, their current troubles would not exist. What is at stake is, from the standpoint of interaction, the management of our "essential" natures, and from the standpoint of the individual, the continuing accomplishment of gender. If, as we have argued, sex category is omnirelevant, then any occasion, conflicted or not, offers the resources for doing gender.

We have sought to show that sex category and gender are managed properties of conduct that are contrived with respect to the fact that others will judge and respond to us in particular ways. We have claimed that a person's gender is not simply an aspect of what one is, but, more fundamentally, it is something that one *does,* and does recurrently, in interaction with others. . . .

■ Review Questions

1. What do the authors mean when they say that gender is not a property of individuals but rather a feature of social situations?
2. Can you give an example of a setting you have experienced in which gender differences were assumed to be natural but were really socially created?

ENDNOTES

1. This definition understates many complexities involved in the relationship between biology and culture (Jaggar 1983, pp. 106–13). However, our point is that the determination of an individual's sex classification is a *social* process through and through.
2. This is not to say that gender is a singular "thing" omnipresent in the same form historically or in every situation. Because normative conceptions of appropriate attitudes and activities for sex categories can vary across cultures and historical moments, the management of situated conduct in light of those expectations can take many different forms.
3. Bernstein (1986) reports an unusual case of espionage in which a man passing as a woman convinced a lover that he/she had given birth to "their" child, who, the lover, thought, "looked like" him.

Fathers and Emotional Responsibility

Andrea Doucet

INTRODUCTION

It was the end of summer in 2002 and Denise's ten-month maternity leave was coming to an end. She found herself sleepless in Ottawa, filled with worry. She wasn't concerned about leaving her son, Nathan, but rather about the fact that her son's daytime caregiver would be Martin, her husband. Denise was especially anxious about the bond being formed between Martin and Nathan, a deep bond that would intensify as the two spent days together while she was at work. Night after night, she wrestled with several recurring qualms: Would Nathan become closer to his father than to her? Who would he go to for comfort? Perhaps the most vexing question for her was, Who would Nathan call out for in the middle of the night? As she explained to me in the joint couple interview I conducted with them in October of that year, "I felt threatened when we first decided that Martin would stay home. . . . If he had wanted Daddy in the night instead of me, I would probably have fallen apart. . . . *I wanted to be the mommy.* I wanted to be the one he calls in the middle of the night."

While Denise lay awake worrying about whose name Nathan would call in the dark of night, fathers in other households throughout the city were waking to their children's cries while their wives lay undisturbed beside them. In Richard and Aileen's home, seven-year-old Sarah would walk around to the far side of the bed where

her father lay sleeping. Greg, a joint-custody father of a five-year-old girl, explained to me, "I've always said I have mother's ears. My ex would have never heard that baby cry in a hundred years." Archie, who used to be the one who slept soundly through the nighttime cries, found that after a few months of being at home he was getting up with their infant son, Jordan: "A really interesting thing happened when I started staying home. Up until that point, I would . . . do the night feeding and then go to bed. If the baby woke up after that point, Jean would hear it and would get up with Jordan. After two months of me staying home, she no longer heard when he woke up. It was *me* getting up. It was really bizarre and I still can't account for it."

There is something about responding to a child's tearful cries in the middle of the night that cuts to the heart of parental protection and care. The parent who wakens and lovingly responds to the child's cries—or the parent whose embrace is sought by the sleepy child—is a metaphoric encapsulation of *nurturing.* As beautifully rendered in a traditional lullaby, "Hush, my darling, don't fear, my darling, the lion sleeps tonight," the parent who brings "hush" and calm to the "darling" child embodies emotional bonds and connection.

Denise's profound worry and Archie's noting of a "bizarre" and unaccountable shift in his behaviour exemplify what Sara Ruddick, in *Maternal Thinking,* has termed "preservation" or "protective care": "it simply means to see vulnerability and to respond to it with care, rather than . . . indifference, or flight" (1995, 19). This state of mind and the sets of practices associated with it are also well captured in several decades of feminist scholarship on "care" and the "ethic of care"[1] as including qualities of attentiveness, competence, and responsiveness (Fisher & Tronto, 1990; Gilligan, 1982; Graham, 1983; Noddings, 2003; Tronto, 1989, 1993, 1995). As evinced by the political theorist Joan Tronto in her description of caring, emotional responsibility involves skills that include "*knowledge* about

Andrea Doucet, "Fathers and Emotional Responsibility," in *Do Men Mother?* pp. 109–136, University of Toronto Press © 2006). Reprinted with the permission of the publisher.

others' needs" which the caregiver acquires through "an *attentiveness* to the needs of others" (Tronto, 1989, 176–8; my emphasis). In wanting to denote both the tasks of caring and the responsibility for caring, I have used the term *emotional responsibility* to capture the essence and work of protective care and the responsibility for its enactment (that is, the "response-ability")[2] (Doucet, 2000, 2001, 2004).

FATHERS AND EMOTIONAL RESPONSIBILITY

While there has been some debate on the character, quality, and enactment of care with distinctions drawn between levels and kinds of caregiving (Tronto, 1993), between care as *love* ("caring about") or *labour* ("caring for") (Graham, 1983; Ungerson, 1990; Tronto, 1993), and whether care is a feminine or feminist practice (Larrabee, 1993; Tronto, 1993; Noddings, 2003), the issue of the *gendered* quality of care is less a matter of debate. International research has demonstrated that most of the work and responsibility for protective care and emotional responsibility for children rests with women. Nevertheless, it has also been shown that men can and do take on the work of care. In this vein, Sara Ruddick's assertion that "men can mother" is supported by a large body of research attesting to men's successful efforts with the maternal tasks of "preservation" and "protective care." That is, many studies on fathering have argued that fathers have the desire and the capacity to be protective, nurturing, affectionate, and responsive with their children (Coltrane, 1996; Dienhart, 1998; Doucet, 2004; Dowd, 2000; Lamb, 1981, 1987; Lupton & Barclay, 1997; Parke, 1996; Pleck, 1985; Pruett, 2000; Snarey, 1993).

Given that my research is on self-defined primary-caregiving fathers, it is not surprising that these findings about fathers' capable nurturing are strongly confirmed in my research. Cameron, a stay-at-home father of two preschool children as well as a foster parent of a mentally challenged teenager, tells me, *"I often find myself even ahead of them. I know what they want before they even express it."* When asked to describe his fathering, Jerome, a stay-at-home father for ten years of two school-age children in rural Nova Scotia, chooses only the following words: *"Kind and gentle. Lots of hugs, Protective."* A final example is with Manuel, the comment of his wife, Julie, that he is so tremendously in tune with the children:

> There was a little thing on the radio the other day. Some engineer has decided there are five different kinds of cries from a baby—you know, tired, hungry, uncomfortable. . . . And he has found that most babies fall into the categories of those five cries. He's developed a monitor that will tell you what that cry is. We were listening to this on the CBC, and I said to [our daughter] Lyn, "You know what? Your dad was like that. Just wonderful. Well, I have never seen anybody who just knew [for instance] that that baby needed a sweater taken off. That this little squirm meant that." I tell them things like this and they go, "Oh he is so wonderful!"

All these statements by and about fathers hint at connection, hugging and holding the child, and knowing intuitively what the child wants. But do fathers' stories about caregiving add anything *new* to our understanding of nurturing and emotional responsibility?

In addition to confirming that fathers are indeed nurturing, my research confirms that fathers shed a light on *other* kinds of protective care. While preservation and protective care are usually related to closely holding and looking after children, fathers also specialize in the following kinds of nurturing: fun and playfulness; a physical and outdoors approach; promoting children's considered risk taking; and encouraging children's independence. These findings emerge from fathers' descriptions of their typical daily and weekly routines with their children, their reflections on differences between mothers' and fathers' care, as well as from the fourteen couple interviews, where mothers' views on the differences and similarities between the parents' care were directly discussed. Findings on recurrent patterns of fatherly nurturing are discussed below.

Fun and Playful: "A Bouncing, Rollicking Time"

Many cross-cultural longitudinal studies have demonstrated that fathers use play to connect with their children (Coltrane, 1996; Lamb, 1987; Parke, 1996; Pruett, 2000; Yogman, Cooley, & Kindlon, 1988). This finding is also evident in the fathers' narratives in this study and is repeated across social class and ethnicity and for both heterosexual and gay fathers.

The women in my study also concur with this view. In the couple interviews, where couples place little pieces of paper on their co-constructed Household Portrait, the response is overwhelmingly consistent along distinct gendered lines when they come across the piece of paper that denotes play. Craig, a stay-at-home father of twins says, "My immaturity has come into this in a big way. I can get on the floor and find myself watching their TV programs with them." Kathy places the "play" task slip in Gary's column, indicating this as his domain: "They like playing with their dad. To say I play with them would be a gross exaggeration. I do games and that sort of thing, but Gary's a lot of fun. He's all of about ten years old."

Several fathers use the example of cooking to contrast their approach with their female partners'. Kyle says, "I teach the kids more about cooking than Carol does. Probably because I take the approach that cooking should be fun, and Carol takes the approach that cooking should be perfect." William, who has run fathering groups, offers a similar view: "It is less the practices and more the style. Feeding a kid is feeding your kid. With fathers, there is more fun associated with cooking, more adventure, flexibility, and getting the kids involved in doing it themselves."

Bernard, a forty-two-year-old father who shares custody of a son with two lesbian mothers, notes that the style of parenting that four-year-old Jake receives is different between the moms' house and Dad's house. He evokes an approach to fathering similar to that of most heterosexual fathers:

> When Jake and I are at my house, it's a different pace. They do more domestic stuff at the moms' house. I say, to heck with all that. We are out there doing things, spending time together. Moms' place is domesticated. There are books, photos, a computer, a playroom. He sees that his moms work and that they spend time with female friends—some guys but mainly female friends. He doesn't see them do much outside of that. At my place he sees photos of himself and my family. He sees books. Sports trophies. My golf clubs, my bowling ball. He comes to my bowling group. He sees all this guy stuff. When I go out into the community, he sees a lot of males. It's a *testosterone world here, an estrogen world there.*

This does not mean that mothers don't use fun and play as a way of responding to their children but rather that fathers and mothers highlight this as a dominant *paternal* pattern in relating to infants and young children. Carl, for example, mentions that though they both take turns putting their two preschool daughters to bed, there is a slight difference, with his style being more a "big, bouncing, rollicking time," whereas hers is "very much a cuddle kind of time."

Physical Activities and the Outdoors: "I Get Them Out as Much as Possible"

The majority of fathers in my study talk about making it a point to get their children outdoors as much as possible, to do lots of physical activities with them, and to be very involved with their children's sports (Brandth & Kvande, 1998; Doucet, 2004; Plantin, Sven-Axel, & Kearney, 2003). Three examples illuminate this theme in the fathers' narratives. Robert, a former sign maker who lives in rural Quebec and is home with two boys, talks about his typical daily routine: "I like to spend time outside with them. Spring, summer, winter, fall, if the weather is nice, we're gallivanting outside all over the countryside. I get them out as much as possible . . . to get them away from the routine in the house. It re-energizes me."

Peter, a part-time graphic designer and stay-at-home father of two boys for the past six years, speaks about preferring being outside with his sons to going to community playgroups: "If we have a choice between going to playgroups or going to the river to throw rocks, we will always go down to the river. We like to go to the parks that are wilder so we can be out in nature."

James, a gay divorced father who took a four-month paternity leave with his son, sums up his time at home this way: "We got out every day. We'd be out of the house by ten. He had an afternoon nap, so we would get back at about one-thirty. . . . I saw it as an eighteen-month adventure. People used to comment on how adventurous we were. I would put him on the back of the bike and we would bike to museums, to the island, everywhere."[3]

Mitchell, a former naval officer and a stay-at-home father of three children under the age of six (including twins), reflects that it may be personality and not gender that leads him to be out with the kids. Nevertheless, he adds, concurring with most of the other men's narratives, that he prefers to be outside with them: "I think it has more to do with personality than whether you're male or female. I think if I enjoyed something like painting or more arts and crafts type thing, I'd probably spend more time doing that with the children. But I prefer being outside running around and going to the park."

Can the valuing of physical and outdoor activities be part of nurturing and emotional responsibility? I would argue that, indeed, they represent ways of responding to the physical and developmental needs of children. Fathers reason that being outdoors and engaging in physical exertion is good for children; they get fresh air and exercise, sleep better, and have the opportunity to explore parks and nature trails. Indeed, fathers' encouragement of activity and exercise with young children and recreational sports for school-age children can be seen as having positive physical and mental developmental outcomes (Beauvais, 2001; Kremarik, 2000).[4]

Measured, Practical Reactions: "My First Response Is to Fix the Problem"

Many fathers also remark that their response to emotionally charged situations is to fall back into what is often viewed as masculine ways of being. When Peter's youngest son was severely ill in the hospital, he found himself acting with what would be considered stereotypical masculine responses focused on *doing* rather than on *being:* "My typical male characteristics are lack of emotion or the deferring of emotion, which I found out when we had a very sick child. My first reaction would be action rather than an emotional response."

In a joint interview, Alistair, a writer, and his wife, Claire, a researcher and doctoral student, reflect on how they respond to the children. Her approach is to "make her feel better" and to "get her to tell me," whereas his response is more "measured" and more oriented to trying "to fix the problem." Alistair says, "I think if [our daughter] Georgia is upset, my first response is to try to identify and fix the problem. Whereas your initial response [turns to Claire] is, How can I make you feel better?"

In response to Alistair, Claire notes that at certain times, his more measured and patient response is what is required, particularly as the children grow older and may not always be willing to open up quickly to their parents. She says, "With Georgia, I can see that she's sad. I'll get her to tell me. It won't come pouring out of her. If she's ready to talk, he's there to listen. And he gives an even, measured response. So they will draw on that too." Claire's noting that "they will draw on that too" reminds us that *connection,* strategically disguised here as *distance* or strategic *indifference,* can nevertheless act as a form of protective care in certain contexts.

Promoting Risk Taking: "I Am Quite Willing to Let These Kids Fail"

Fathers' narratives are also replete with evidence that they encourage risk taking. Whether it is on the play structure in the park, exploring, or learning through physically falling or intellectually failing, most fathers claim to be more likely to facilitate their child's trying things out on his or her own. A couple of examples illustrate fathers' comfort with judicious risk taking.

Bernard, mentioned earlier as a gay father who shares custody of his son with two lesbian mothers, talks about his approach to his son's outdoor play, which contrasts to the child's two mothers. His relaxed attitude resonates with many fathers in the study: 'I do consider his safety. I help him to make a decision. If he was climbing a tree, the mothers would be sitting back and watching him and then yelling that that was far enough. . . . They would be more careful. I would be close by him helping him to make the decision about how far he can go; I would guide him through that decision.'

A different kind of risk taking comes from Kyle, an Italian-Canadian father of two daughters who is married to Carol, a German Canadian. They live in a rural area and both work part-time, Kyle as a local city counsellor and Carol as a librarian. In speaking about their daughter Emma, a gifted child who is home-schooled and who often has difficulties adjusting to social situations, Kyle refers to his wife's approach as "setting up structures, lectures, long heart-to-heart talks late at night," while his is best characterized as "more sink or swim. Push her into a situation and then talk to her later about it. I am quite willing to let these kids fail."

Encouraging Children's Independence: "You Guys Can Make Your Own Lunches"

The issue of risk taking and letting children learn in an independent manner is a more narrow articulation of the wider issue of promoting their independence. This fourth aspect of fathers' emotional *connection* with children is, ironically, their role in facilitating processes of *autonomy* in children. That is, most fathers in this study indicate that they play a strong role in promoting the children's physical, emotional, and intellectual independence. Recurring examples in fathers'

accounts include strongly encouraging the kids to be involved in housework, to make their own lunches, engage in independent play, tie their own laces (shoes or skates), and carry their own backpacks to school. As Alistair says, "I might be less likely to go out of my way to help the kids if it's something they can do themselves."

Jacob, a sole custodial father of three young children, also captures this particularly well in noting that "I have always had them help out with chores" and that all three children (eleven, nine, and seven) make their own lunches: "This year I said, 'you guys can make your own lunches.' I lay the ground rules: 'You need a sandwich, or sometimes soup, then fruit and vegetables and a snack.' They can do it with a little guidance—even Pippa [the youngest]."

Versions of this story were repeated by the majority of men interviewed. Initially, this telling of events puzzled me. Is the promotion of children's independence the opposite of protective care, or a fundamental part of it? As I worked laboriously through the reams of interview transcripts, my first interpretation was that this was an example of the father letting go of the child, in contrast to dominant understandings of nurturing and protective care that suggest that the parent is connected to (or holds on to) the child. Gradually, however, I came to view this behaviour as an integral part of nurturing. That is, the protective care of children with its qualities of attentiveness, responsiveness, and competence, involves both holding on and letting go—and it is the careful letting-go that fathers demonstrate particularly well.

UNDERSTANDING FATHERS' NARRATIVES OF EMOTIONAL RESPONSIBILITY

In examining fathers' caregiving, my research reveals several dominant paternal patterns. What are the sources of such differences? Why do they appear so prominently in fathers' narratives? Drawing from both fathers' and mothers' narratives, I have developed six points to assist us in making sense of gendered differences in approaches to, and the enactment of, the emotional responsibility for children. First, both mothers and fathers remark on the residue of gendered upbringing as key factors accounting for differences in caring. Second, there are the strong beliefs by fathers—as well as many mothers—that mothering and fathering are inherently different—as identities and as *embodied* experiences. Third, many fathers speak further about embodiment issues, specifically the social taboos around men and physical touching, with both boys and girls in the preteen and teen years. Fourth, fathers note the leading role played by mothers in determining the balance of emotional responsibility within households. Fifth, fathers' narratives are marked by hegemonic masculinity, evidenced mainly in their devaluation and concurrent distancing from the feminine. Finally, I consider what we learn more broadly about nurturing and parenting by looking at differences in fathering narratives on emotional responsibility. Is it possible that fathers develop a concept of nurturing that incorporates both traditionally feminine and masculine qualities and, indeed, exists *between* maternal *equality* and paternal *difference*?

Growing Up Male: "I Grew Up as a Guy"

It should not be surprising that most fathers exhibit more traditionally masculine qualities in their caregiving, given that most boys grow up in cultures that encourage sport,[5] physical and emotional independence, and risk taking (see Connell 1995; Mac an Ghaill, 1994; Seidler, 1997).[6] Alistair says he learned on the playing fields (and arenas) of boyhood that the rules of the sports take precedence over attention to somebody getting hurt: "We were out playing ball hockey and Vanessa got hurt. It's the kind of accident that happens in ball hockey. Someone gets hurt, and you kind of stand around like a bunch of male apes and you kick them gently and say, 'Well, can you play or not?' We're not a great nurturing bunch. Because you're learning certain things when you're playing ball hockey.

There was my daughter and she was hurt in the face, and, you know, I was concerned. But also *this is ball hockey,* and you learn certain things when you do that."

Devon, a technician and a sole-custody father of a seven-year-old son, notes that danger is just part of "what little boys do": "I grew up as a guy. We did dangerous things. That's what little boys do. A father thing is, should I let him go up the tree? Yeah, but then a little scepticism is there."

In contrast to Devon, as well as to her own husband, Peter, Linda takes a more cautious parenting approach, rooted partly in "having grown up as a girl": "I don't know if boys take more physical risks than girls. I suspect that they do. Having grown up as a girl, I saw boys on the highest bars at the park, or riding their bikes on one wheel. I think that has some bearing on it."

Most sociologists view statements like ones given above as evidence of socialization. Yet it is more than this. As Patricia Yancey Martin has written, gendering processes are deeply ingrained so that they "become almost automatic": "Gendered practices are learned and enacted in childhood and in every major site of social behavior over the life course, including in school, intimate relationships, families, workplaces, houses of worship, and social movements. In time, like riding a bicycle, gendering practices become almost automatic" (Martin, 2003, 352).

Within such automatic gendering processes, there remains the question of how active fathering affects their daughters. That is, will fathers' daughters who "are learning certain things when . . . playing ball hockey" or "riding a bike on one wheel" also grow up to exhibit these traditional masculine qualities? The long-term impact of fathers actively caring for their daughters will, however, only be revealed if and when the daughters become parents.

Embodied Differences between Mothers and Fathers: "A Longer and Tighter Hug"

A second factor that underlies gendered differences in fathers' narratives is their profound belief in distinct differences between mothering and fathering as identities and as embodied experiences. Even where fathers are left literally holding the baby as their ex-wives or ex-partners leave home, or where they express little feelings towards their ex-wives or partners, the majority of fathers still noted that mothers are more protective, nurturing, and emotionally connected. While admitting that his ex-wife is not nurturing, Jack, a sole-custody father living in New Brunswick, nevertheless says, "I still think in general that the most common situation is that women feel that attachment to the children . . . because she's the mother, right?"

Fathers express great confusion over the origins of this special bond. Is it based in biology (hormones, birthing, and breastfeeding), or is it a result of culture and socialization? Some fathers did implicate the latter. For example, Lorne, a papermill foreman and sole-custody father of three in a northern Ontario town, says, "It's the way we programmed ourselves," especially the fact that "boys are not allowed to get emotional in public." A few fathers reiterate these sentiments, but most suggest an embodied basis for the differences between mothers and fathers. Alistair, who stayed home for over a year with his first infant daughter, is aware of the physical connections associated with pregnancy, birth, and breastfeeding, and also of women's overall emotional involvement, especially with young children: "I think you are *so physically* involved as a mother, from the beginning. Nine months of pregnancy—such a commitment—and then into the breastfeeding. And then normally mothers are much more involved with taking care of very small babies. There is a tremendous bond right there. Even when I was taking care of Georgia at home, I didn't have the same physical bond as Claire did with this baby. I think women are more sensitive and more inclined to be emotionally involved."

Gary, a carpenter and stay-at-home father of three boys, succinctly captures many of the fathers' views on this matter when he speaks about how his wife, Kathy, relates to the kids: "Well, like I said, men do nurture. We do give them a hug, tell them it's okay, sit them on our knee. But I just find with the mother they do it more or longer. They give a tighter hug."

Embodiment: "I Am Very Nervous about That Kind of Thing"

It may be that a mother's hug is longer and tighter because there are different social perceptions of fathers' and mothers' acceptable physicality with children. Although the early years—with infants and pre-school children—provide fathers with ample opportunity to hug and hold their children, many fathers of preteen and teenage boys and girls noted that they were more closely scrutinized by society in general. Brandan, a self-employed sole-custodial father of four, draws links between hegemonic masculinity and homophobia (Connell, 1987, 1995; Kaufman, 1999; Kimmel, 1994) when he says, "I hug and kiss them, but it's not the same. And frankly I'm not as comfortable hugging the big guys as the little guys, like, the older guys go, 'Hey, man . . .' I mean, we're not homophobic, but it's something you're raised with."

Similarly, most of the single fathers of preteen and teenage girls say that, in some way, public displays of close physical affection can easily be misinterpreted. Henry, a sole-custodial father of two, currently unemployed, says he is always aware that his actions may be misinterpreted:

As a single dad, all I have to do is breathe at the wrong time, or say the wrong thing in front of the wrong person. I am very conscious of that. For example, one of my daughter's favourite rants is "You can't touch me! You can't hit me!" because she has been taught at school about violence and stuff like that. I don't use that against her any more at twelve years old. A couple of years ago, she would get a smack if she needed one. But I am very conscious of the fact that if she screamed that out in public it's like "whoh!" They could be taken away on a moment's notice. Just on suspicion. So I am very nervous about that kind of thing.

Even several fathers living with female partners relay a subtle sense of unease in embodied father-daughter relations. Alexander, a university professor who took parental leave to be with two of his three daughters and is now a joint-custody father, reflects on how things changed when his daughter reached puberty: "When puberty arrives, the entire dynamic changes. You don't think much of the physical thing that goes on with your kids until then. Embracing and hugging. I am trying to think about the parallel with a mother and son. Obviously the same thing happens to a degree, yet far less starkly."

Fathers Rely on Mothers: "You Can Never Replace the Mother"

References to gender differences in parenting also appear throughout fathers' narratives partly because fathers *rely* on mothers to take on the overall primary care of children (see also Daly, 2002; Stueve & Pleck, 2003). That is, the role and influence of mothers on the processes of fathers *becoming* and *enacting* their caregiving is highly significant within these narratives. In two-parent households, or even in joint-custody households where parents live apart, the father *expects* that the mother will take on the emotional responsibility for the children. Sasha, an African Canadian, a dance instructor, and a joint-custody father, says, "I think it is a spiritual thing. They were with their mom before they came to earth. That is what men do not have, that extra, extra-special thing with the children."

Luke, a stay-at-home father of two girls for twelve years who now works night shifts in a home for mentally challenged adults, says, "You have to recognize that [even] as a stay-at-home father you can never replace the mother. Don't even think about it."

Narratives of Hegemonic Masculinity and Difference: "We're Still Men, Aren't We?"

Fathers also explicitly and deliberately draw attention to differences in mothering and fathering because they want to distance their fathering

from mothering and indeed from any feminine associations attached to it. Archie says that fathers in general respond to children "in a less feminine way. If a kid falls and hurts himself, women would probably rush over more than men. I say, 'Come on, toughen up.' I think there are more differences there. I am not sure how to characterize it."

Indeed, many fathers express confusion about this issue because they simply do not want to equate what they do with the work that women do. As Maurice says when I ask him about housework, "I like to cook. But I wouldn't want to call this women's work."

Theoretical assumptions that can initially assist us in making sense of these processes are those that highlight the way men distance themselves from and devalue the feminine (Bird, 1996; Chodorow, 1978; Connell, 1987, 1995, 2000; Johnson, 1988; Thorne, 1993) as well as theoretical work related to the concept of hegemonic masculinity (Coltrane, 1994; Connell, 1987, 1995, 2000; Kimmel, 1994; Messner, 1997). Although there have been varied discussions of the meaning and relevance of the concept of hegemonic masculinity, one of the authors who coined it, Connell, has recently boiled it down as "the opposite of femininity" (Connell, 2000, 31). The fathers' narratives touched on in this chapter are filled with inchoate contradictions that illuminate how fathers distance themselves from the feminine. Yet, as explained below, some also admit that being a primary-caregiving father allows them the opportunity to find, as one father, Roy, put it, the "feminine in me."

Between Equality and Difference, between Masculine and Feminine

What seems to occur for fathers entering into female-dominated terrain is that by crossing into an area where they have not been traditionally equal to women, they move both between equality and difference and between the stereotypically feminine and masculine. In seeking to find ways of becoming equal or symmetrical to women in their caregiving efforts, men also have hegemonic masculinity at their backs, reminding them that they are men operating in traditional female worlds. Most men, even sole-custody fathers, thus cling to the view that in spite of their most ardent efforts, they can never be mothers or replace the *mothering* done by women. Rather than *duplicate* the maternal terrain travelled, fathers *alter* it to incorporate differences, which could be viewed as more traditionally masculine traits such as independence, autonomy, and sporting interests.

It is notable that most of the gay fathers in this study recognize the need to consider both masculine and feminine in mothering and fathering and to emphasize the importance of traditionally feminine qualities in fathering, particularly in the raising of sons. A good example of these qualities is found in Bernard's narrative. While drawing borders between the moms' house and his own and between "an estrogen world there" and "a testosterone world here," he also points out that he is aware of the need to demonstrate some traditionally feminine qualities in his parenting and to allow Jake to develop his own feminine qualities:

> I do some things that are typical of fathering. I throw a ball and play catch, mini golf, take him on the roller coaster, watch movies, play sports. But I also do non-typical things. I let him cry; I am physically demonstrative. I want to break that generational cycle. I let him play with dolls, watch women superheroes like the Power Puff Girls. He plays with girls and boys. I want him to experience things that he is interested in. . . . If boys were allowed to be whatever they are, I think that would mean they would become fathers who are extremely close to their children. More expression. Less inhibiting. . . . There is male and female in all of us, but the female is pressured out of boys more. The inhibiting of the feminine. Like the censoring of boys' emotions.

CONCLUSIONS

In this chapter I have explored, in Sara Ruddick's terms, the first maternal demand of preservation or protective care, which is at its core an ability to know and attentively respond to the needs of one's children. My own naming of this maternal, or parental, responsibility is that of *emotional responsibility*. The question "Do men mother?" can be answered, at least partially, by asking, Do fathers take on the preservation and protective care of children? Do they resemble mothers in their approach to emotional responsibility?

At first glance, the answer is an affirmative one. My research on primary caregiving fathers joins a large body of scholarship produced over the past two decades that argues that fathers can be just as nurturing and responsive with their children as mothers are. It is well documented that fathers who are actively involved with their children can develop skills that enable them to partake in this task of preservation.

On second glance, the answer to the question, Do men assume emotional responsibility and partake in the task of preservation? is also negative, in the sense that fathers widen our current understandings of protective care, preservation, and ultimately that of emotional responsibility. My research also uncovers some unique dimensions that fathers bring to our understandings of protective care. In examining fathers' caregiving, my work highlights their emphasis on fun and playfulness, especially with infants and young children, physical activities, an outdoors approach, an emphasis on the practical sides of nurturing, and the promotion of independence and risk taking with older children. This occurs for the majority of father across social class, income levels, occupations, ethnicity, and sexuality. While all these dimensions of caring are not normally part of what we consider nurturing behaviour, my argument is that all these elements are important aspects of the emotional responsibility for children. For example, physical and outdoor activities can lead to positive physical and mental developmental outcomes (Beauvais, 2001), which represent, in turn, unique ways of responding to children's needs. Similarly, while the promotion of independence and of risk taking are rarely included in discussions of nurturing, encouraging autonomy in children can be seen as a form of long-term protection and ultimately of connection.

The roots of these strong patterns in fathers' narratives of nurturing can be traced to several key elements in men's lives. This chapter went back to their boyhood, to the embodied experiences of fathers as they move on female-dominated terrains of parenting, to the reliance on mothers, and to the role of hegemonic masculinity. The latter was evident in men's apparent need to emphasize gender differences through the distancing of themselves from the feminine connotations tied up with the work and identities of caring for children.

This chapter has also detailed where and how embodiment figures into the ways that both fathers and mothers accord greater significance to women's emotional connection to children whether symbolically or in practice. In particular, fathers and mothers draw on embodied aspects of early parenting by reference to the physical, emotional, and symbolic experiences of pregnancy, birth, breastfeeding, and post-childbirth recovery. Men and women refer to all the "messy empirical realities of actual flesh and blood bodies" (Monaghan, 2002, 335) and the differing gendered locations of women and men in relation to the passage of children into the world. What remains striking is the belief in the mysterious and symbolic power of *mothering* as something that the majority of men and women inexplicably uphold. Many are perplexed by the strength of this belief, and indeed most are at a complete loss to explain it, but it nevertheless emerges as a dominant theme from fathers' and mothers' narratives. Fathers also draw attention to the way bodies can matter in the physical touching between fathers and preteen/teen daughters, as well as in noting the tensions of men kissing and touching boys in a society where homophobia thrives. . . .

To conclude this chapter, the comments of two fathers are apt descriptions of perceived gender difference in emotional responsibility. Ed, a stay-at-home father of two living in rural Ontario, comments, "We certainly do look at things differently—housework and activities for the children. I tend to be more concerned about *doing things* with the children rather than making sure the house is perfect. Instead of playgroups, we'll go to the park and walk through the forest."

Archie remarks that in the everyday practical care of children "the broad strokes" remain somewhat different: "Some of the stuff by definition is the same. When you have smaller children, the getting through the day is by definition the same—the feeding, the changing have to be the same. Once you start getting into the non-physical, non-life-sustaining, you do get different practices between women and men. Men are going to be outside more, and more physical. But not always. I think in broad strokes, you will find that women tend to be more emotional and supportive." . . .

■ Review Questions

1. Why is it more socially acceptable today for a man to be the main caregiver to his children than it was a half century ago?
2. Is there more than one way to "mother"? Can caregiving fathers be said to mother?

ENDNOTES

1. Perhaps the most well known instigator of this debate is Carol Gilligan (1982) and her book *In a Different Voice*. It is astounding that nearly a quarter century after its first printing, it is still amply cited in scholarship on care or other aspects of female-dominated practice. Two decades of scrutiny, critique, and appreciation of this work is rooted in Gilligan's claim that there is a moral orientation, 'a different voice,' which is often associated with women. This "care voice" or "the ethic of care" is characterized by a commitment to maintaining and fostering the relationships in which one is woven (Gilligan, 1982, 19) and an ethic that emphasizes "attachment, particularity, emotion and intersubjectivity" (Cole & Coultrap-McQuin, 1992, 4–5). In contrast, the "justice voice" or the "ethic of justice"—associated mainly with the work on moral development by Gilligan's colleague and mentor, Lawrence Kohlberg, as well as with the work of the liberal political theorist John Rawls—emphasizes individual rights, equality, autonomy, fairness, rationality, a highly individuated conception of persons, and a concept of duty that is limited to reciprocal non-interference (Gilligan, 1982). In responding to the perception that *different implied women,* Gilligan's work initially caused a "storm of controversy" (Jaggar, 1990, 249) around the problematic equation of women with care and the associated dangers of essentializing women's caregiving. Gilligan, in response, consistently maintained that though the care voice is heard most often in women, it can also be heard in men (Gilligan, 1993).

2. I am grateful to Carol Gilligan for pointing this out to me.

3. All but one of the gay fathers felt that they parented in a mainly masculine way, drawing on similar patterns of behaviour to heterosexual fathers—emphasizing sports and play, outdoor activity, risk taking, and the promotion of independence.

4. The pattern is also in evidence for the nine gay fathers in the study. Three fathers indicate that they are not really sports oriented, whereas the other six are. Of the three who claim not to be interested in sports, the one with an infant says that he nevertheless plays with children at playgroup more than the mothers do.

5. Sport itself also needs to be socially and historically located (Burstyn, 1999). According to Michael Messner, "[M]odern sport is a 'gendered institution' in that it is a social institution constructed by men, largely as a response to a crisis of gender relations in the late nineteenth and early twentieth centuries. The dominant structures and values of sport came to reflect the fears and needs of a threatened masculinity. Sport was constructed as a homosocial world, with a male-dominant division of labour that excluded women. Indeed, sport came to symbolize the masculine structure of power over women" (Messner, 1992, 16).

6. Recent literature on boys in school highlights how these processes begin in boyhood, when exhibiting signs of emotion marks boys as wimps (Pollock, 1987) and as "polluting the male ideal" by "conveying qualities of softness, emotion and embodiment that are dangerously feminine" (Prendergast & Forrest, 1998, 167).

CHAPTER 4

Social Class and Families

The globalization of the world economy has hit blue-collar workers especially hard. Corporations have moved production overseas in order to take advantage of the lower wages paid to workers in the developing world. Computers and other technologies have allowed employers to replace some workers with machines, such as the robots on automobile assembly lines. Consequently, adults without college educations have found it harder to obtain jobs with adequate wages.

These reduced prospects have hurt families in two ways. First, young men who are unemployed, or who are employed but earn low wages, are often reluctant to marry because they don't think that they earn enough to help support a family. Second, the marriages that do exist face more strain because of inadequate incomes. Most generations of Americans have expected to do better economically than their parents' generation. Now, a significant number of working-class families find that those expectations are not being met.

One such family, the Mertens of Des Moines, Iowa, was profiled in the *New Yorker* magazine in 1995 by Susan Sheehan. Her article is the first selection in this chapter. It is a story worth studying for what it says about working-class families

in the United States today. Kenny Merten earned $7 an hour at his first job after marrying Bonita in 1972; his pay rose to $8.95 before he lost that job. Two decades later, working for a highway barricade company, he makes $7.30 an hour. During the two decades, the cost of consumer goods more than tripled because of inflation. Consequently, Kenny would have to be earning over $24 an hour to match the buying power he had in 1972. Instead, his buying power has declined by 70 percent. "There ain't no middle class no more," said Kenny, who had hoped to join it, "there's only rich and poor."

But social class differences encompass more than income, education, and occupation. These differences may be at once more subtle and more profound. Starting with the work of Melvin Kohn and his colleagues,[1] sociologists have noted that middle-class parents tend to raise their children in ways somewhat different from working-class parents. In general, middle-class parents act in ways that encourage autonomy and independence, whereas working-class parents

---

[1]M. L. Kohn, *Class and Conformity: A Study in Values* (Homewood, IL: Dorsey Press, 1969).

more often encourage conformity and obedi-ence to authority. Not all parents fit this pattern, of course; there is substantial variation within social classes. Moreover, as the twentieth cen-tury progressed, parents in all social classes moved toward emphasizing independence.[2]

In the second selection in this chapter, Annette Lareau reports on a study of class differences in how parents act toward their children. Her findings are consistent with the earlier research, but she provides more detail about how the daily lives of children differ across classes. She points to factors such as whether parents heav-ily structure their children's daily lives, how frequently parents engage them in conversation, and to what extent parents involve them with relatives versus school friends. Lareau claims that middle-class parents tend to follow a par-ticular style she calls "concerted cultivation," whereas working-class and lower-class parents have a style she calls "the accomplishment of natural growth." These styles can influence how children (and parents) interact with teach-ers, doctors, and other professionals. Although Lareau studied black families and white fami-lies, she found that class seemed to matter more than race. In fact, she frames the article around the differences between the upbringing of two 10-year-old black boys, one middle-class and the other poor.

---

[2]D. F. Alwin, "From Obedience to Autonomy: Changes in Traits Desired in Children, 1924–1978," *Public Opinion Quarterly* 52 (1988), pp. 33–52.

Ain't No Middle Class

Susan Sheehan

At 10 o'clock on a Tuesday night in September, Bonita Merten gets home from her job as a nursing-home aide on the evening shift at the Luther Park Health Center, in Des Moines, Iowa. Home is a two-story, three-bedroom house in the predominantly working-class East Side section of the city. The house, drab on the outside, was built in 1905 for factory and railroad workers. It has aluminum siding painted an off-shade of green, with white and dark-brown trim. Usually, Bonita's sons—Christopher, who is 16 and David, who is 20 and still in high school (a slow learner, he was found to be suffering from autism when he was eight)—are awake when she comes home, but tonight they are asleep. Bonita's husband, Kenny, who has picked her up at the nursing home—"Driving makes Mama nervous," Kenny often says—loses no time in going to bed himself. Bonita is wearing her nursing-home uniform, which consists of a short-sleeved navy-blue polyester top with "Luther Park" inscribed in white, matching navy slacks, and white shoes. She takes off her work shoes, which she describes as "any kind I can pick up for 10 or 12 dollars," puts on a pair of black boots and a pair of gloves, and goes out to the garage to get a pitchfork.

In the spring, Bonita planted a garden. She and David, who loves plants and flowers, have been picking strawberries, raspberries, tomatoes, and zucchini since June. Bonita's mother, who lives in Washington, Iowa, a small town about a hundred miles from Des Moines, has always had a large garden—this summer, she gave the Mertens dozens of tomatoes from her 32 tomato plants—but her row of potato plants, which had been bountiful in the past, didn't yield a single potato. This is the first year that Bonita has put potato plants in her own garden. A frost has been predicted, and she is afraid her potatoes (if there are any) will die, so instead of plunking herself down in front of the television set, as she customarily does after work, she goes out to tend her small potato strip alongside the house.

The night is cool and moonless. The only light in the back yard, which is a block from the round-the-clock thrum of Interstate 235, is provided by a tall mercury-arc lamp next to the garage. Traffic is steady on the freeway, but Bonita is used to the noise of the cars and trucks and doesn't hear a thing as she digs contentedly in the yellowy darkness. Bonita takes pleasure in the little things in life, and she excavates for potatoes with cheerful curiosity—"like I was digging for gold." Her pitchfork stabs and dents a large potato. Then, as she turns over the loosened dirt, she finds a second baking-size potato, says "Uh-huh!" to herself, and comes up with three smaller ones before calling it quits for the night.

"Twenty-two years ago, when Kenny and me got married, I agreed to marry him for richer or poorer," Bonita, who is 49, says. "I don't have no regrets, but I didn't have no idea for how much poorer. Nineteen-ninety-five has been a hard year in a pretty hard life. We had our water shut off in July *and* in August, and we ain't never had it turned off even once before, so I look on those five potatoes as a sign of hope. Maybe our luck will change."

When Bonita told Kenny she was going out to dig up her potatoes, he remembers thinking, Let her have fun. If she got the ambition, great. I'm kinda out of hope and I'm tired.

Kenny Merten is almost always tired when he gets home, after 5 P.M., from his job at Bonnie's Barricades—a small company, started 10 years ago by a woman named Bonnie Ruggless, that puts up barriers, sandbags, and signs to protect construction crews at road sites. Some days, he drives a truck a hundred and fifty miles to rural counties across the state to set up roadblocks. Other days, he does a lot of heavy lifting. "The heaviest sandbags weigh between 35 and 40 pounds dry," he says. "Wet, they weigh 50 or 60 pounds, depending on how soaked they are. Sand holds a lot of water." Hauling the sandbags is not easy for Kenny, who contracted polio when he was 18 months old and wore a brace on his left leg until he was almost 20. He is now 51, walks with a pronounced limp, and twists his left ankle easily. "Bonnie's got a big heart and hires people who are down on their luck," he says.

Kenny went to work at Bonnie's Barricades two years ago, and after two raises he earns seven dollars and thirty cents an hour. "It's a small living—too small for me, on account of all the debts I got," he says. "I'd like to quit working when I'm 65, but Bonnie doesn't offer a retirement plan, so there's no way I can quit then, with 28 years left to pay on the house mortgage, plus a car loan and etceteras. So I'm looking around for something easier—maybe driving a forklift in a warehouse. Something with better raises and fringe benefits."

On a summer afternoon after work, Kenny sits down in a rose-colored La-Z-Boy recliner in the Merten's living room/dining room, turns on the TV—a 19-inch Sylvania color set he bought secondhand nine years ago for a hundred dollars—and watches local and national news until six-thirty, occasionally dozing off. After the newscasts, he gets out of his work uniform—navy-blue pants and a short-sleeved orange shirt with the word "Ken" over one shirt pocket and "Bonnie's Barricades" over the other—and takes a bath. The house has one bathroom, with a tub but no shower. Last Christmas, Bonita's mother and her three younger brothers gave the Mertens a shower for their basement, but it has yet to be hooked up—by Kenny, who, with the help of a friend, can do the work for much less than a licensed plumber.

Kenny's philosophy is: Never do today what can be put off until tomorrow—unless he really wants to do it. Not that he is physically lazy. If the Mertens' lawn needs mowing, he'll mow it, and the lawn of their elderly next-door neighbor, Eunice, as well. Sometimes he gets up at 4:30 A.M.—an hour earlier than necessary—if Larry, his half uncle, needs a ride to work. Larry, who lives in a rented apartment two miles from the Mertens and drives an old clunker that breaks down regularly, has been married and divorced several times and has paid a lot of money for child support over the years. He is a security guard at a tire company and makes five dollars an hour. "If he doesn't get to work, he'll lose his job," Kenny says. In addition, Kenny helps his half brother Bob, who is also divorced and paying child support, with lifts to work and with loans.

Around 7:30 P.M., Kenny, who has changed into a clean T-shirt and a pair of old jeans, fixes dinner for himself and his two sons. Dinner is often macaroni and cheese, or spaghetti with store-bought sauce or stewed tomatoes from Bonita's mother's garden. He doesn't prepare salad or a separate vegetable ("Sauce or stewed tomatoes *is* the vegetable," he says); dessert, which tends to be an Iowa brand of ice cream, Anderson Erickson, is a rare luxury. Kenny takes the boys out for Subway sandwiches whenever he gets "a hankering" for one. Once a week—most likely on Friday, when he gets paid—he takes them out for dinner, usually to McDonald's. "It's easier than cooking," Kenny says.

Because Bonita works the evening shift, Kenny spends more time with his sons than most fathers do; because she doesn't drive, he spends more time behind the wheel. Christopher, a short, trim, cute boy with hazel eyes and brown hair, is one badge away from becoming an Eagle Scout, and Kenny drives him to many Scouting activities. This summer, Kenny drove Eunice, who is 85, to the hospital to visit her 90-year-old husband, Tony, who had become seriously ill in August. After Tony's death, on September 12th,

Kenny arranged for the funeral—choosing the casket and the flowers, buying a new shirt for Tony, and chauffeuring the boys to the private viewing at the funeral home. "Everyone was real appreciative," he says.

At around eight-thirty on evenings free from special transportation duties, Kenny unwinds by watching more television, playing solitaire, dozing again, and drinking his third Pepsi of the day. (He is a self-described "Pepsiholic.") Around nine-fifty, he drives two miles to the Luther Park nursing home for Bonita.

Bonita Merten leaves the house before 1 P.M., carrying a 16-ounce bottle of Pepsi (she, too, is a Pepsiholic), and catches the bus to work. She is dressed in her navy-blue uniform and white shoes. Since the uniforms cost 33 dollars, Bonita considers herself lucky to have been given a used one by a nurse's aide who quit, and she bought another, secondhand, for 10 dollars. Luther Park recently announced a mandatory change to forest-green uniforms, and Bonita does not look forward to having to shell out for new attire.

Bonita clocks in before one-forty-five, puts her Pepsi in the break-room refrigerator, and, with the other evening aides, makes rounds with the day aides. She and another aide are assigned to a wing with 20 long-term residents. "The residents have just been laid down on top of their beds before we get there," Bonita says. "First, I change water pitchers and give the residents ice—got to remember which ones don't want ice, just want plain water. We pass out snacks—shakes fortified with protein and vitamins, in strawberry, vanilla, or chocolate. They need the shakes, because they ordinarily don't want to eat their meals. While I'm doing that, the other aide has to pass out the gowns, washrags, and towels, and the Chux—great big absorbent pads—and Dri-Prides. They're adult snap pants with liners that fit inside them. We don't call them diapers because they're not actually diapers, and because residents got their pride to be considered."

At three-thirty, Bonita takes a 10-minute break and drinks some Pepsi. "We start getting the residents up and giving showers before our break and continue after," Bonita says. "Each resident gets two showers a week, and it works out so's I have to shower three patients a day."

One aide eats from four-thirty to five, the other from five to five-thirty. Until August 1st, Bonita bought a two-dollar meal ticket if she liked what was being offered in the employees' dining room. When the meal didn't appeal to her—she wouldn't spend the two dollars for, say, a turkey sandwich and a bowl of cream-of-mushroom soup ("I don't like it at all")—she either bought a bag of Cheetos from a vending machine or skipped eating altogether. On August 1st, the nursing home reduced meal tickets to a dollar. "Even a turkey sandwich is worth that much," she says.

The residents eat at five-thirty, in their dining room. "We pass trays and help feed people who can't feed themselves," Bonita says. "Sometimes we feed them like a baby or encourage them to do as much as they can." At six-thirty, Bonita charts their meals—"what percent they ate, how much they drank. They don't eat a whole lot, because they don't get a lot of exercise, either. We clear out the dining room and walk them or wheel them to their rooms. We lay them down, and we've got to wash them and position them. I always lay them on their side, because I like lying on my side. I put a pillow behind their back and a blanket between their legs. We take the false teeth out of those with false teeth, and put the dentures into a denture cup for those that will let us. A lot of them have mouthwash, and we're supposed to rinse their mouth. We're supposed to brush their teeth if they have them. After everyone is down, we chart. We check off that we positioned them and if we changed their liners. I'm supposed to get a 10-minute evening break, but I hardly ever take it. Charting, I'm off my feet, and there's just too much to do. Often we're short—I'll be alone on a hall for a few hours. The last thing we do is make rounds with the shift coming in. I clock out by nine-forty-five. Ninety-nine percent of the time, Kenny picks me up. When I had different hours and he'd be bowling, his half brother Bob picked me up, or I took a cab for five dollars. The bus is one dollar, but it stops running by seven o'clock."

Bonita has worked all three shifts at Luther Park. The evening shift currently pays 50 cents an hour more than the day shift and 50 cents less than the night shift, but days and nights involve more lifting. (In moving her patients, Bonita has injured her back more times than she can remember, and she now wears a wide black belt with straps which goes around her sacroiliac; she also uses a mechanical device to help carry heavy residents between their wheelchairs and their beds.) Bonita's 1994 earnings from Luther Park were only 869 dollars higher than her 1993 earnings, reflecting an hourly increase in wages from six dollars and fifty cents to six-sixty-five and some overtime hours and holidays, for which she is paid time and a half. This July 1st, she received the grandest raise that she has ever had in her life—75 cents an hour—but she believes there is a hold-down on overtime, so she doesn't expect to earn substantially more in 1995. Luther Park gives her a ham for Easter, a turkey for Thanksgiving, 10 dollars for her birthday, and 20 dollars for Christmas.

Bonita rarely complains about working at the nursing home. "I don't mind emptying bedpans or cleaning up the residents' messes," she says. She regards her job, with its time clocks, uniforms, tedious chores, low wages, penny-ante raises, and Dickensian holiday rewards, as "a means to a life."

Bonita and Kenny Merten and their two sons live in a statistical land above the lowly welfare poor but far beneath the exalted rich. In 1994, they earned $31,216 between them. Kenny made $17,239 working for Bonnie's Barricades; Bonita made $13,977 at Luther Park. With an additional $1,212 income from other sources, including some money that Kenny withdrew from the retirement plan of a previous employer, the Mertens' gross income was $32,428. Last year, as in most other years of their marriage, the Mertens spent more than they earned.

The Mertens' story is distinctive, but it is also representative of what has happened to the working poor of their generation. In 1974, Kenny Merten was making roughly the same hourly wage that he is today, and was able to buy a new Chevrolet Nova for less than 4,000 dollars; a similar vehicle today would cost 15,000 dollars—a sum that even Kenny, who is far more prone than Bonita to take on debt, might hesitate to finance. And though Kenny has brought on some of his own troubles by not always practicing thrift and by not always following principles of sound money management, his situation also reflects changing times.

In the 1960s, jobs for high-school graduates were plentiful. Young men could easily get work from one day to the next which paid a living wage, and that's what Kenny did at the time. By the mid-80s, many of these jobs were gone. In Des Moines, the Rock Island Motor Transit Company (part of the Chicago, Rock Island & Pacific Railroad) went belly up. Borden moved out of the city, and so did a division of the Ford Motor Company. Utility companies also began downsizing, and many factory jobs were replaced by service-industry jobs, which paid less. Although there is a chronic shortage of nurse's aides at Luther Park, those who stay are not rewarded. After 15 years of almost continuous employment, Bonita is paid 7 dollars and 40 cents an hour—55 cents an hour more than new aides coming onto the job.

Working for one employer, as men like Kenny's father-in-law used to do, is a novelty now. Des Moines has become one of the largest insurance cities in the United States, but the Mertens don't qualify for white-collar positions. Civil-service jobs, formerly held by high-school graduates, have become harder to obtain because of competition from college graduates, who face diminishing job opportunities themselves. Bonita's 37-year-old brother, Eugene, studied mechanical engineering at the University of Iowa, but after graduation he wasn't offered a position in his field. He went to work for a box company and later took the United States Postal Service exam. He passed. When Bonita and Kenny took the exam, they scored too low to be hired by the Post Office.

Although 31 percent of America's four-person families earned less in 1994 than the Mertens did, Kenny and Bonita do not feel like members of the middle class, as they did years ago. "There ain't no middle class no more," Kenny says. "There's only rich and poor."

This is where the $32,428 that the Mertens grossed last year went. They paid $2,481 in federal income taxes. Their Iowa income-tax bill was $1,142, and $2,388 was withheld from their paychecks for Social Security and Medicare. These items reduced their disposable income to $26,417. In 1994, Bonita had $9.64 withheld from her biweekly paycheck for medical insurance, and $14.21 for dental insurance—a $620.10 annual cost. The insurance brought their disposable income down to $25,797.

The highest expenditures in the Mertens' budget were for food and household supplies, for which they spent approximately $110 a week at various stores and farmers' markets, for a yearly total of $5,720. They tried to economize by buying hamburger and chicken and by limiting their treats. (All four Mertens like potato chips.) Kenny spent about eight dollars per working day on breakfast (two doughnuts and a Pepsi), lunch (a double cheeseburger or a chicken sandwich), and sodas on the road—an additional $2,000 annually. His weekly dinner out at McDonald's with his sons cost between 11 and 12 dollars—600 dollars a year more. Bonita's meals or snacks at work added up to about 300 dollars. Kenny sometimes went out to breakfast on Saturday—alone or with the boys—and the meals he and his sons ate at McDonald's or Subway and the dinners that all four Mertens ate at restaurants like Bonanza and Denny's probably came to another 600 dollars annually. David and Christopher's school lunches cost a dollar-fifty a day; they received allowances of 10 dollars a week each, and that provided them with an

extra 2 dollars and 50 cents to spend. The money the boys paid for food outside the house came to 500 dollars a year. The family spent a total of about $9,720 last year on dining in and out; on paper products and cleaning supplies; and on caring for their cats (they have two). This left them with $16,077.

The Mertens' next-highest expenditure in 1994 was $3,980 in property taxes and payments they made on a fixed-rate, 30-year, 32,000-dollar mortgage, on which they paid an interest rate of 8.75 percent. This left them with $12,097.

In April of 1994, Kenny's 1979 Oldsmobile, with 279,000 miles on it, was no longer worth repairing, so he bought a 1988 Grand Am from Bonita's brother Eugene for 3,000 dollars, on which he made four payments of 200 dollars a month. The Grand Am was damaged in an accident in September, whereupon he traded up to an 11,000-dollar 1991 Chevy Blazer, and his car-loan payments increased to $285 a month. Bonita has reproached Kenny for what she regards as a nonessential purchase. "A man's got his ego," he replies. "The Blazer is also safer—it has four-wheel drive." The insurance on Kenny's cars cost a total of $798, and he spent 500 dollars on replacement parts. Kenny figures that he spends about 20 dollars a week on gas, or about $1,040 for the year. After car expenses of $2,338 and after payments on the car loans of $1,655, the Mertens had $8,104 left to spend. A 10-day driving vacation in August of last year, highlighted by stops at the Indianapolis Motor Speedway, Mammoth Cave, in Kentucky, and the Hard Rock Cafe in Nashville, cost 1,500 dollars and left them with $6,604.

The Mertens' phone bill was approximately 25 dollars a month: the only long-distance calls Bonita made were to her mother and to her youngest brother, Todd, a 33-year-old aerospace engineer living in Seattle. She kept the calls short. "Most of our calls are incoming, and most of them are for Christopher," Bonita says. The Mertens' water-and-sewage bill was about 50 dollars a month; their gas-and-electric bill was about 150 dollars a month. "I have a hard time paying them bills now that the gas and electric companies have consolidated," Kenny says. "Before, if the gas was 75 dollars and the electric was 75 dollars, I could afford to pay one when I got paid. My take-home pay is too low to pay the two together." After paying approximately 2,700 dollars for utilities, including late charges, the Mertens had a disposable income of $3,904.

Much of that went toward making payments to a finance company on two of Kenny's loans. To help pay for the family's 1994 vacation, Kenny borrowed 1,100 dollars, incurring payments of about 75 dollars a month for two years and three months, at an interest rate of roughly 25 percent. Kenny was more reluctant to discuss the second loan, saying only that it consisted of previous loans he'd "consolidated" at a rate of about 25 percent, and that it cost him 175 dollars a month in payments. Also in 1994 he borrowed "a small sum" for "Christmas and odds and ends" from the credit union at Bonnie's Barricades; 25 dollars a week was deducted from his paycheck for that loan. Payments on the three loans—about 4,300 dollars last year—left the Merten family with a budget deficit even before their numerous other expenses were taken into account.

Except in a few small instances (according to their 1994 Iowa income-tax return, Bonita and Kenny paid H & R Block 102 dollars to prepare, their 1993 return, and they gave 125 dollars to charity), it isn't possible to determine precisely what the rest of the Mertens' expenditures were in 1994. Several years ago, Kenny bounced a lot of checks, and he has not had a checking account since. Kenny exceeded the limits on both of their MasterCards a few years ago, and the cards were cancelled. Bonita has a J. C. Penney charge card but says, "I seldom dust if off." Now and then, Bonita went to a downtown outlet store, and if a dress caught her fancy she might put it on layaway. On special occasions, she bought inexpensive outfits for herself and for Kenny. Before last year's summer holiday, she spent seven dollars on a top and a pair of shorts, and

during the trip Kenny bought a 75-dollar denim jacket for himself and about 50 dollars' worth of T-shirts for the whole family at the Hard Rock Cafe. One consequence of Kenny's having had polio as a child is that his left foot is a size 5½ and his right foot a size 7. If he wants a comfortable pair of shoes, he has to buy two pairs or order a pair consisting of a 5½ and a 7. Often he compromises, buying sneakers in size 6½. David wears T-shirts and jeans as long as they are black, the color worn by Garth Brooks, his favorite country singer. Christopher is partial to name brands, and Bonita couldn't say no to a pair of 89-dollar Nikes he coveted last year. The Mertens spent about 700 dollars last year on clothing, and tried to economize on dry cleaning. "I dry-clean our winter coats and one or two dresses, but I avoid buying anything with a 'Dry-clean only' label," Bonita says.

The Mertens' entertainment expenses usually come to a thousand dollars a year, but that amount was exceeded in 1994 when Kenny bought a mountain bike for every member of the family. The bikes (Bonita has yet to ride hers out of the driveway) cost 259 dollars apiece, and Kenny made the final payments on them earlier this year. This July, David rode Kenny's bike to a hardware store, and it was stolen while he was inside. Kenny yelled at David; Bonita told Kenny he was being too hard on him, and Kenny calmed down.

Bonita and Kenny don't buy books or magazines, and they don't subscribe to newspapers. (They routinely borrowed Eunice and Tony's Des Moines *Register* until Tony's death, when Eunice cancelled it.) They rarely go to the movies—"Too expensive," Kenny says—but regularly rent movies and video games, usually at Blockbuster. For amusement, they often go to malls, just to browse, but when they get a serious urge to buy they go to antique stores. Kenny believes in "collectibles." His most treasured possession is an assortment of Currier & Ives dishes and glasses.

The Mertens have never paid to send a fax, or to send a package via Federal Express, and they aren't on-line: they have no computer. They even avoid spending money on postage: Kenny pays his bills in person. Bonita used to send out a lot of Christmas cards, but, she says, "I didn't get a whole lot back, so I quit that, too." They spend little on gifts, except to members of Bonita's family.

Kenny knows how much Bonita loves red roses. Twenty-two years ago, he gave her one red rose after they had been married one month, two after they had been married two months, and continued until he reached 12 red roses on their first anniversary. He also gave her a dozen red roses when she had a miscarriage, in 1973, "to make her feel better." To celebrate the birth of David and of Christopher, he gave her a dozen red roses and one yellow one for each boy. And Kenny gives Bonita a glass rose every Christmas.

On a Sunday evening this summer, the four Mertens went to Dahl's, their supermarket of choice in Des Moines. They bought four rolls of toilet paper (69 cents); a toothbrush (99 cents); a box of Rice Krispies (on sale for $1.99); eight 16-ounce bottles of Pepsi ($1.67); a gallon of 2-percent milk ($2.07); a large package of the least expensive dishwasher detergent ($2.19), the Mertens having acquired their first dishwasher in 1993, for 125 dollars; two jars of Prego spaghetti sauce ($3); a box of Shake 'n Bake ($1.99); two rolls of film ($10.38), one for Kenny, who owns a Canon T50 he bought for 125 dollars at a pawnshop, and one for Christopher to take to Boy Scout camp in Colorado; a battery ($2.99) for Christopher's flashlight, also for camp; a pound of carrots (65 cents); a green pepper (79 cents); some Ziploc bags ($1.89); a Stain Stick ($1.89); a box of 2000 Flushes ($2.89); a package of shredded mozzarella ($1.39) to add to some pizza the Mertens already had in the freezer; and 12 cans of cat food ($3). Bonita bought one treat for herself—a box of toaster pastries with raspberry filling ($2.05). Christopher asked for a Reese's peanut-butter cup (25 cents), a bottle of Crystal Light (75 cents), and a package of Pounce cat treats ($1.05). All three purchases were O.K.'d.

David, who is enchanted by electrical fixtures, was content to spend his time in the store browsing in the light-bulb section. He was born with a cataract in his left eye, and the Mertens were instructed to put drops in that eye and a patch over his "good" right eye for a few years, so that the left eye wouldn't become lazy. Sometimes when they put the drops in, they told David to look up at a light. Today, David's main obsession, which apparently dates back to the eyedrops, is light. "We'd go someplace with David, and if there was a light with a bulb out he'd say, 'Light out,'" Bonita recalls. "We'd tell him, 'Don't worry about that,' and pretty soon he was saying, 'Light out, don't worry about that.'"

At 20, David looks 15. A lanky young man with coppercolored hair, hearing aids in both ears, and eye-glasses with thick lenses, he attends Ruby Van Meter, a special public high school for the city's mentally challenged. He reads at a fifth-grade level, and he doesn't read much. For years, the Mertens have been applying—without success—for Supplemental Security Income for David. In June of this year, when his application for S.S.I. was once again turned down, the Mertens hired a lawyer to appeal the decision. David has held a series of jobs set aside for slow learners (working, for instance, as a busboy in the Iowa state-house cafeteria and in the laundry room of the local Marriott hotel), but he says that his "mood was off" when he was interviewed for several possible jobs this summer, and he drifted quietly through his school vacation. He will not be permitted to remain in school past the age of 21. If David could receive monthly S.S.I. checks and Medicaid, the Mertens would worry less about what will happen to him after they are gone. They have never regarded David as a burden, and although he has always been in special-education classes, they have treated him as much as possible the way they treat Christopher. Say "special ed" to Bonita, and she will say, "Both my boys are very special."

The Dahl's bill came to $44.75. When Kenny failed to take money out of his pocket at the cash register, Bonita, looking upset, pulled out her checkbook. She had expected Kenny to pay for the groceries, and she had hoped that the bill would be 40 dollars or less. But Kenny was short of money. "Aargh," Bonita said, softly.

Bonita didn't want to write checks for groceries, because she has other ideas about where her biweekly paychecks—about 400 dollars take-home—should go. Most of her first check of the month goes toward the mortgage— $331.68 when she pays it before the 17th of the month, $344.26 when she doesn't. Bonita likes to put aside the second check for the two most important events in her year—the family's summer vacation and Christmas. In theory, Kenny is supposed to pay most of the other family expenses and to stick to a budget—a theory to which he sometimes has difficulty subscribing. "I don't like to work off a budget," he says. "I think it restricts you. My way is to see who we have to pay this week and go from there. I rob Peter to pay Paul and try to pay Peter back." In practice, Kenny rarely pays Peter back. With his take-home pay averaging about 235 dollars a week, he can't.

When a consumer counsellor, who does not know the Mertens, was questioned about the family's current financial predicament—specifically, their 1994 income and expenditures—she made numerous recommendations. Among her suggestions for major savings was that the Mertens cut their food bills dramatically, to 5,400 dollars a year. She proposed stretching the Mertens' food dollars by drastically curtailing their eating out and by buying in bulk from the supermarket. She said that Kenny should get rid of his high-interest loans, and use the money he was spending on usurious interest to convert his mortgage from 30 years to 15. The way Kenny and Bonita were going, the counsellor pointed out, they would not finish paying off their current mortgage until they were 79 and 77 years old, respectively. The Mertens' principal asset is 8,000 dollars in equity they have in their house. If the Mertens wanted to retire at 65, they would need more than what they could expect to receive from Social Security.

The counsellor had many minor suggestions for economizing at the grocery store. The Mertens should buy powdered milk and mix it with one-percent milk instead of buying two-percent milk. They should cut down even further on buying meat; beans and lentils, the counsellor observed, are a nutritious and less costly form of protein. She recommended buying raisins rather than potato chips, which she characterized as "high-caloric, high-fat, and high-cost."

The counsellor had one word for the amount— between 1,500 and 2,500 dollars—that the Mertens spent on vacations: "outlandish." Their vacations, she said, should cost a maximum of 500 dollars a year. She recommended renting a cabin with another family at a nearby state park or a lake. She urged the Mertens to visit local museums and free festivals, and go on picnics, including "no-ant picnics"—on a blanket in their living room.

Kenny and Bonita were resistant to most of the suggestions that were passed on to them from the counsellor, who is funded mainly by creditors to dispense advice to those with bill-paying problems. According to Kenny, buying a dozen doughnuts at the supermarket and then taking breakfast to work would be "boring." Bonita says she tried powdered milk in the mid-80s, when Kenny was unemployed, and the kids wouldn't drink it. She does buy raisins, but the boys don't really like them. Bonita and Kenny both laugh at the prospect of a no-ant picnic. "Sitting on the living-room carpet don't seem like a picnic to me," Bonita says.

Bonita surmises that the counsellor hasn't experienced much of blue-collar life and therefore underestimates the necessity for vacations and other forms of having fun. "We couldn't afford vacations in the 80s, and if we don't take them now the kids will be grown," she says. Kenny reacted angrily to the idea of the boys' eating dried beans and other processed foods. "I lived on powdered milk, dried beans, surplus yellow cheese, and that kind of stuff for two years when I was a kid," he says. "I want better for my boys."

Kenny acknowledges that he tried to confine his responses to the consumer counsellor's minor suggestions, because he realizes that her major recommendations are sound. He also realizes that he isn't in a position to act on them. He dreams of being free of debt. He has tried a number of times to get a 15-year mortgage, and has been turned down each time. "We both work hard, we're not on welfare, and we just can't seem to do anything that will make a real difference in our lives," he says. "So I save 10 dollars a bowling season by not getting a locker at the alley to store my ball and shoes, and have to carry them back and forth. So I save 25 dollars by changing my own oil instead of going to Jiffy Lube. So what? Going out to dinner is as necessary to me as paying water bills."

Kenneth Deane Merten was born poor and illegitimate to Ruby Merten in her mother's home, outside Des Moines, on October 5, 1944; his maternal relatives declined to reveal his father's name, and he never met his father. Ruby Merten went on to marry a soldier and had another son, Robert. She divorced Bob's father, and later married Don Summers, a frequently unemployed laborer, with whom she had three more children. "Mr. Summers was so mean he made me stand up all night in the bed when I was eight years old," Kenny recalls. He has never hit his own sons, because "I know what it done to my life and I don't want it to get passed down." The family often moved in haste when the rent was due. Kenny attended eight or ten schools, some of them twice, before he completed sixth grade.

Kenny's mother died of cancer at 27, when he was 14. The three younger children stayed with Don Summers and a woman he married a month later. Kenny and Bob went to live with their maternal grandparents, and their lives became more stable. Even so, Kenny's school grades were low. "I had a hard time with math

and science," he says. "Coulda been because of all the early moving around. I ain't stupid." He spent his high-school years at Des Moines Technical High School and graduated in 1964, when he was almost 20.

Two days later, he found a job as a shipping clerk for *Look* magazine. He kept the job until 1969, and left only when it became apparent that the magazine was cutting back its operations. He drove a cab from 1969 to 1972, drank too much, and did what he calls "some rowdy rambling." He had put much of that behind him when he got a job as a factory worker at EMCO Industries, a manufacturer of muffler parts and machinery bolts, in the fall of 1972, shortly before he met Bonita.

Bonita Anne Crooks was born on October 7, 1946, in Harper, Iowa. Her father, Cloyce Crooks, was employed all his working life by the Natural Gas Pipeline Company; his wife, Pauline, stayed home to take care of Bonita and her three younger brothers. Bonita was required to do chores, for which she was paid, and to deposit those earnings in a bank. She took tap-dancing lessons, wore braces on her teeth, and often went with her family on vacation to places like California and Texas. "Kenny's growing up was a lot worse than mine," she says. In 1965, Bonita graduated from a Catholic high school and became a nurse's aide, while living at home and continuing to bank her money. In 1971, she moved to Des Moines, and the following year she got a job as a key-punch operator for a large insurance company. Keypunching, however, proved too difficult for her (she couldn't combine accuracy with high speed), and she soon transferred within the company to a lower-paying position—that of a file clerk.

Bonita met Kenny in October 1972 on a blind date that had been arranged by a friend of hers. "I had been jilted by a younger man, and I knew Kenny was meant for me on our first date, when he told me he was born on October 5, 1944—exactly two years and two days earlier than me," Bonita says. She and Kenny fell in love quickly and were married in a traditional ceremony at a Catholic church in Harper on June 30, 1973. The newlyweds set off for Colorado on their honeymoon, but Kenny's car, a secondhand 1966 Pontiac Bonneville convertible, broke down, and the couple ended up in the Black Hills of South Dakota. When they were courting, Kenny had asked Bonita what sort of engagement ring she wanted. She had declined a "chunky" diamond, and said that matching wedding bands would suffice. "I suspected Kenny had debts," Bonita says. "I just didn't know how many he had until we got home."

The couple moved into a modest two-bedroom house. Bonita kept her file-clerk job after David's birth, in April 1975, but when she became pregnant with Christopher, who was born in November 1979, her doctor ordered her to bed. From the window of her bedroom, Bonita could see the Luther Park nursing home being built "kinda like next to my back yard." She didn't return to the insurance company, because her pay couldn't cover the cost of day-time care for two children. Kenny was working days at EMCO, so in June 1980 Bonita took a job on the 3-to-11 P.M. shift at Luther Park. She earned more there than she had as a file clerk. On some nights, Kenny drove a cab. He needed two jobs, because he regularly spent more than he and Bonita earned, just as he had overspent his own pay when he was single. Every year or two, he bought a new car. "I shouldn't have bought those new cars, but life with Don Summers made me feel completely insecure," he says. "Driving new cars gave me a sense of self-worth."

Kenny lost his job at EMCO at the end of 1983. He says that he had asked his supervisor for permission to take some discarded aluminum parts, and that permission was granted. But as he was driving off EMCO's premises with the parts in the bed of his pickup he was accused of stealing them. His supervisor then denied having given Kenny permission to take the parts. A demoralized Kenny didn't seek a new job for a year. He had already stopped driving the cab—after being robbed twice—and had started mowing lawns part time in the spring and summer, and doing cleanup work and shovelling snow in the fall and winter. Kenny's business failed—"There were too many unemployed guys like me out there." Many of his prized belongings were repossessed, among them a Curtis-Mathes stereo console. For two weeks in the summer of 1984, the Mertens were without gas or electricity or telephone service. They went on food stamps. Bonita felt guilty about going to work in air-conditioned surroundings while her husband and children were at home in the heat. Kenny felt humiliated when Bonita's parents visited their dark, sweltering house over the Fourth of July weekend. While Kenny has done better financially than most of his side of the family, it pains him that he hasn't done as well as Bonita's brothers, and that they regard him as a spendthrift and an inadequate provider. "When they get down on Kenny, I feel like I'm caught between a rock and a crevice," Bonita says.

Kenny's starting salary at EMCO had been seven dollars an hour. By the time he was terminated, it was eight-ninety-five an hour. In 1985, he found several jobs he liked, but none paid more than seven dollars an hour. One such job was with Bob Allen Sportswear, and he kept it until 1987, when he was let go during the off-season. He occasionally filed unemployment claims, and the family qualified for food stamps and received some groceries from food banks. During the rocky period between 1984 and 1988, Kenny tried to continue making payments on bills that he owed, in order to avoid having to declare bankruptcy, but his debts grew to the point where they exceeded his assets by "I think 12 or 13 thousand dollars"; his creditors—mostly finance companies—got fed up with him, and then he had no choice. The Mertens were able to keep their house and their '79 Olds. Going on food stamps didn't embarrass them—the boys had to eat, and they went off food stamps whenever Kenny had a new job—but the bankruptcy filing was published in the newspaper and made Bonita feel ashamed.

In 1989, after seeing an ad on television, Kenny enrolled in electronics courses at a local vocational school and borrowed 7,200 dollars to pay for his studies. His deficiency in math came back to haunt him, and he eventually dropped out. While at school, he had heard of an opening as a janitor at Ryko Manufacturing, an Iowa manufacturer of car washes. He eventually moved up to a factory job, working full time at Ryko in the early 90s for three years. Those years were happy ones. He got regular raises, and during the April-to-December busy season he earned a lot of overtime. In the summer of 1991, the Mertens flew to Seattle to visit Bonita's brother Todd. They had just enough money to cover one plane fare, and asked Bonita's brother Eugene to lend them the money for the three other tickets. Bonita took three months off that year; by then, she had worked full time at Luther Park for 11 straight years and needed a break. Kenny was proud to be the family's main provider, and wanted Bonita to stay home and take it easy.

In February 1993 Ryko fired Kenny Merten. His supervisors said that the work he did on the assembly line was neither fast enough nor of a sufficiently high quality. He was earning 11 dollars and 80 cents an hour—almost 30,000 dollars a year including overtime—when he was terminated. "In today's job market, first-rate companies like Ryko can afford to be selective," he says. "They want to hire young men."

Around the same time, Luther Park announced that it intended to expand. The nursing home offered the Mertens 39,000 dollars for the house they had lived in for 18 years. Kenny and Bonita accepted the offer, and were allowed to stay on, free of charge, for six months while they went house hunting. After they sold their house, it became apparent that they had been using it to supplement their income. The house they had bought for 14,800 dollars had appreciated handsomely in value, but they had kept remortgaging, and now they owed 29,000 dollars on it. As a

result, they netted only 10,000 dollars from the sale. The purchase price of the Mertens' new home was 40,000 dollars. They spent 2,000 dollars from the sale of the old house on improvements to their new home, and this reduced the amount of the down payment they were able to afford to 8,000 dollars.

Kenny attempted to return to work at several of the companies where he had previously been employed, but they weren't hiring. It took him five months to find his current job with Bonnie's Barricades—far more arduous work, at lower wages than he had been paid at EMCO more than 20 years earlier. "I know I'll never be able to earn 11.80 an hour again," he says. "The most I can hope for is a seven-dollar-an-hour job that doesn't involve swinging sandbags. Maybe if I come home less tired at the end of the day, I can handle an evening job."

This year did not get off to a good start for Kenny. In January, he hocked two rings that Bonita had given him for a hundred dollars, in order to pay a utility bill. Then, three months later, true to form, Kenny spotted two rings at a local pawnshop that he wanted Bonita to have—a 199-dollar opal ring and a 399-dollar diamond-cluster ring. He asked the pawnshop owner to take the two rings out of the showcase and agreed to make periodic 20 dollar payments on them until they were paid off.

Kenny was not worried about how he would pay for the rings, or how he would pay for the family's annual summer vacation. In September of last year, a few days after the Mertens returned from that summer's driving trip, his Grand Am was rear-ended. After the collision, in which Kenny hurt his back, he hired a lawyer on a contingency basis. The young man who had caused the accident had adequate insurance, and Kenny expected to be reimbursed for medical bills and lost wages. (He hadn't been permitted to lift heavy objects for several weeks.) He also expected the insurance company to pay a sizable sum—10 or 15 thousand dollars—for pain and suffering. Kenny's lawyer told him that he could expect the insurance company to settle with him by March. When the insurance money failed to arrive that month, Kenny's lawyer told him to expect an offer in April, then in May, and then in June. In early July, the lawyer said that he could get Kenny 6,500 dollars by the end of the month—just in time to save the Mertens' summer vacation. The insurance payment and the annual vacation had been the focus of Bonita's attention for seven months. "If you don't go on vacation, a year has gone by with nothing to show for it," she says.

Bonita wanted the family to travel to Seattle to visit Todd because he had a new home and she was eager to see it. The Mertens made meticulous plans for a driving trip to the state of Washington. They decided they would get up at 4 A.M. on Saturday, August 5th, and drive to Rapid City, South Dakota. They would visit Mt. Rushmore, and Kenny, who has an eye for landscapes, would take photographs of the Devils Tower, in Wyoming, at sunrise and sunset. They would arrive at Todd's home on Wednesday, August 9th, spend a few days there, and return to Des Moines, by way of the Mall of America, in Bloomington, Minnesota, on August 19th. Both Bonita and Kenny had arranged with their employers to take one week off with pay and one without.

Six days before their departure, however, their lawyer called with crushing news; the insurance payment would not be arriving until September. The following evening, Bonita injured her shoulder lifting a patient at the nursing home, but she was still determined to have her vacation. Although Kenny was behind on almost all his bills—he had just borrowed 75 dollars from David to pay a water bill—he went to a bank and to his credit union on August 2nd to borrow 2,500 dollars to cover the cost of the vacation, figuring he would pay off this newest loan from the insurance money in September. On the evening of August 2nd, Bonita reinjured her shoulder while helping another aide transfer a resident from her wheelchair to her bed.

Both the bank and the credit union turned Kenny down. Not only did he have too much outstanding debt of his own but he had also cosigned a loan on his half brother Bob's car. Without being able to borrow, the Mertens could not go on vacation. To make matters worse, Luther Park had sent Bonita to a doctor, and he informed her that she would require physical therapy three times a week for the next two weeks. The vacation would have to be cancelled. "When Kenny told me he'd been turned down for the loan, his jaw dropped about two inches," Bonita recalls. "Kenny was so shocked and disappointed for me that I couldn't be disappointed for myself."

The Mertens have had their share of disappointments, but they don't stay down long. On the morning they had set aside to pack for their trip, Bonita baked banana bread. That evening, after she finished work, Kenny took the whole family out to dinner. From there they drove to Blockbuster and bought two videos—"Sister Act 2" (David had loved the original) and a Beatles movie. They also rented two movies, and a video game that Christopher wanted. The boys spent the following week at their grandmother's. During the second vacation week, Bonita took David to the Iowa State Fair, in town. "Me and David really had fun together," she says.

Both Mertens spent a little money during the two weeks that they didn't go out West. Bonita made a payment to Fingerhut on a shelf that she had bought for David's room and on a game that she had bought him, and she finished paying Home Interiors for some mirrors, sconces, and a gold shelf that she had bought for her bedroom. "When I buy this stuff, I can see Kenny getting a little perturbed, but he doesn't say anything," she says. Later in August, the front brakes on Kenny's Blazer failed, and replacement parts cost about a hundred dollars. The labor would have cost him twice that much, but Eunice, the next-door neighbor, gave him some furniture that she no longer needed, and he bartered the furniture with a friend who is an auto mechanic.

Kenny and Bonita agreed that driving with faulty brakes through the mountains on their way West would have been dangerous, so it was a blessing in disguise that they had been forced to remain at home.

On Friday, September 22nd, Kenny, feeling unusually fatigued, decided to take the day off from work. After lunch, he drove Bonita to their lawyer's office. The insurance company had agreed to pay Kenny 7,200 dollars. The lawyer would get a third—2,400 dollars—and Kenny owed 1,200 dollars in medical bills, so he would net 3,600 dollars. He had wanted more—to pay off more of his debts and bills—but this was three days after Bonita's lucky potato strike, and she was feeling optimistic. She persuaded Kenny to put the agony of waiting behind them and to accept the offer.

The next day, Kenny drove Bonita, David, and Christopher to the pawnshop. The proprietor, Doug Schlegel, was expecting them. At the cash register, Doug handed Kenny a small manila envelope with the opal ring inside. "Hey, Kiddo!" Kenny called out to Bonita as he removed the ring from the envelope. "Come here!"

Bonita tried to kiss Kenny, but he quickly moved away. "I love you," she said. After Bonita finished working the opal ring down the third finger of her left hand, checking to see whether it fitted properly, Doug told her, "You don't want to let it sit in the sun or put it in hot water."

"I know," Bonita said. "Opals are soft and touchy. They're my birthstone. I have one I bought for myself, but this is lots prettier."

Once the Mertens were back in the Blazer, Bonita asked Kenny, "Is the opal my birthday present?" Her 49th birthday was coming up in two weeks.

"It's a prebirthday present," Kenny replied. He didn't mention his plan to give her the more expensive ring—the one with the diamond cluster—for Christmas, provided he could make the payments in time.

"Thank you, Kenny. I love you," Bonita said.

"Sure," Kenny said. "You love to pick on me and drive me crazy."

Bonita touched Kenny's hand. "Leave me alone, I'm driving," he told her.

When Kenny stopped at a red light, Bonita said, "You're not driving now." But the light suddenly turned green.

Throughout the fall, Kenny Merten refused to fret over the very real possibility that he would have to file for bankruptcy again if he didn't get his financial house in order. He was thinking only as far ahead as Christmas—imagining himself putting the box that held the diamond-cluster ring for Bonita under the tree in their living room and marking it "Open this one last." Kenny predicts that when his brothers-in-law see the ring they will surely disapprove, but he doesn't care. "The rings shouldn't be in the budget, but they are," he says.

Kenny's mother's short life left him with a determination to marry once and to make that marriage succeed—something that few of his relatives have done. Bonita has often said that one reason she loves Kenny is that he surprises her every once in a while.

"Diamonds are a girl's best friend, next to her husband," Kenny says. "And Bonita's worth that ring, every bit of it. After all, she puts up with me."

■ Review Questions ■

1. To what extent were changes in the American economy responsible for the money troubles the Mertens have?
2. What do you think of the consumer counselor's advice to the Mertens?

Invisible Inequality

Social Class and Childrearing in Black Families and White Families

Annette Lareau

In recent decades, sociological knowledge about inequality in family life has increased dramatically. Yet, debate persists, especially about the transmission of class advantages to children. Kingston (2000) and others question whether disparate aspects of family life cohere in meaningful patterns. Pointing to a "thin evidentiary base" for claims of social class differences in the interior of family life, Kingston also asserts that "class distinguishes neither distinctive parenting styles nor distinctive involvement of kids" in specific behaviors (p. 134). . . .

[In this reading] I draw on findings from a small, intensive data set collected using ethnographic methods. I map the connections between parents' resources and their children's daily lives. My first goal, then, is to challenge Kingston's (2000) argument that social class does not distinguish parents' behavior or children's daily lives. I seek to show empirically that social class does indeed create distinctive parenting styles. I demonstrate that parents differ by class in the ways they define their own roles in their children's lives as well as in how they perceive the nature of childhood. The middle-class parents, both white *and* black, tend to conform to a cultural logic of childrearing I call "concerted cultivation." They enroll their children in numerous age-specific organized activities that dominate family life and create enormous labor, particularly for mothers. The parents view these activities as transmitting important life skills to children. Middle-class parents also stress language use and the development of reasoning and employ talking as their preferred form of discipline. This "cultivation" approach results in a wider range of experiences for children but also creates a frenetic pace for parents, a cult of individualism within the family, and an emphasis on children's performance.[1]

The childrearing strategies of white and black working-class and poor parents emphasize the "accomplishment of natural growth."[2] These parents believe that as long as they provide love, food, and safety, their children will grow and thrive. They do not focus on developing their children's special talents. Compared to the middle-class children, working-class and poor children participate in few organized activities and have more free time and deeper, richer ties within their extended families. Working-class and poor parents issue many more directives to their children and, in some households, place more emphasis on physical discipline than do the middle-class parents. These findings extend Kohn and Schooler's (1983) observation of class differences in parents' values, showing that differences also exist in the *behavior* of parents *and* children.

Quantitative studies of children's activities offer valuable empirical evidence but only limited ideas about how to conceptualize the mechanisms through which social advantage is transmitted. Thus, my second goal is to offer "conceptual umbrellas" useful for making comparisons across race and class and for assessing the role of social structural location in shaping daily life.[3]

Last, I trace the connections between the class position of family members—including children—and the uneven outcomes of their experiences outside the home as they interact with professionals in dominant institutions. The pattern of concerted cultivation encourages an *emerging sense of entitlement* in children. All parents and children are not equally assertive;

Annette Lareau, "Invisible Inequality: Social Class and Childrearing in Black Families and White Families," *American Sociological Review*, 2002, Vol. 67 (October). Reprinted with permission from the American Sociological Association and the author.

but the pattern of questioning and intervening among the white and black middle-class parents contrasts sharply with the definitions of how to be helpful and effective observed among the white and black working-class and poor adults. The pattern of the accomplishment of natural growth encourages an *emerging sense of constraint.* Adults as well as children in these social classes tend to be deferential and outwardly accepting in their interactions with professionals such as doctors and educators. At the same time, however, compared to their middle-class counterparts, white and black working-class and poor family members are more distrustful of professionals. These are differences with potential long-term consequences. In an historical moment when the dominant society privileges active, informed, assertive clients of health and educational services, the strategies employed by children and parents are not equally effective across classes. In sum, differences in family life lie not only in the advantages parents obtain for their children, but also in the skills they transmit to children for negotiating their own life paths.

METHODOLOGY

Study Participants

This study is based on interviews and observations of children, aged 8 to 10, and their families. The data were collected over time in three research phases. Phase one involved observations in two third-grade classrooms in a public school in the Midwestern community of "Lawrenceville."[4] After conducting observations for two months, I grouped the families into social class (and race) categories based on information provided by educators. I then chose every third name, and sent a letter to the child's home asking the mother and father to participate in separate interviews. Over 90 percent of parents agreed, for a total of 32 children (16 white and 16 African American). A black graduate student and I interviewed all mothers and most fathers (or guardians) of the children. Each interview

lasted 90 to 120 minutes, and all took place in 1989–1990.

Phase two took place at two sites in a northeastern metropolitan area. One school, "Lower Richmond," although located in a predominantly white, working-class urban neighborhood, drew about half of its students from a nearby all-black housing project. I observed one third-grade class at Lower Richmond about twice a week for almost six months. The second site, "Swan," was located in a suburban neighborhood about 45 minutes from the city center. It was 90 percent white; most of the remaining 10 percent were middle-class black children.[5] There, I observed twice a week for two months at the end of the third grade; a research assistant then observed weekly for four more months in the fourth grade.[6] At each site, teachers and parents described their school in positive terms.[7] The observations took place between September 1992 and January 1994. In the fall of 1993, I drew an interview sample from Lower Richmond and Swan, following the same method of selection used for Lawrenceville. A team of research assistants and I interviewed the parents and guardians of 39 children. Again, the response rate was over 90 percent but because the classrooms did not generate enough black middle-class children and white poor children to fill the analytical categories, interviews were also conducted with 17 families with children aged 8 to 10. (Most of these interviews took place during the summers of 1996 and 1997.)[8] Thus, the total number of children who participated in the study was 88 (32 from the Midwest and 56 from the Northeast).

Family Observations

Phase three, the most intensive research phase of the study, involved home observations of 12 children and their families in the Northeast who had been previously interviewed (see Table 4.1).[9] Some themes, such as language use and families' social connections, surfaced mainly during this phase. Although I entered the field interested in examining the influence of social class on

TABLE 4.1

**FREQUENCY DISTRIBUTION OF CHILDREN IN THE STUDY
BY SOCIAL CLASS AND RACE**

Social class	White	Black	Total
Middle class[a]	18 (Garrett Tallinger) (Melanie Handlon)	18 (Alexander Williams) (Stacey Marshall)	36
Working class[b]	14 (Billy Yanelli) (Wendy Driver)	12 (Tyrec Taylor) (Jessica Irwin)[c]	26
Poor[d]	12 (Karl Greeley) (Katie Brindle)	14 (Harold McAllister) (Tara Carroll)	26
Total sample	44	44	88

Note: The names in each cell of the table indicate the children selected to take place in the family-observation phase of the study.
[a]Middle-class children are those who live in households in which at least one parent is employed in a position that either entails substantial managerial authority or draws upon highly complex, educationally certified skills (i.e., college-level).
[b]Working-class children are those who live in households in which neither parent is employed in a middle-class position and at least one parent is employed in a position with little or no managerial authority and that does not draw on highly complex, educationally certified skills. This category includes lower-level white-collar workers.
[c]An interracial girl who has a black father and a white mother.
[d]Poor children are those who live in households in which parents receive public assistance and do not participate in the labor force on a regular, continuous basis.

children's daily lives, I incorporated new themes as they "bubbled up" from the field observations. The evidence presented here comes mainly from the family observations, but I also use interview findings from the full sample of 88 children where appropriate.[10]

Nine of the 12 families came from the Northeastern classroom sample. The home observations took place, one family at a time, from December 1993 to August 1994. Three 10-year-olds (a black middle-class boy and girl and a white poor boy) who were not part of the classroom sample were observed in their homes during the summer of 1995.[11]

The research assistants and I took turns visiting the participating families daily, for a total of about 20 visits to each home, often in the space of one month.[12] The observations went beyond the home: Fieldworkers followed children and parents as they participated in school activities, church services and events, organized play, visits to relatives, and medical appointments. Observations typically lasted three hours, but sometimes much longer (e.g., when we observed an out-of-town funeral, a special extended family event, or a long shopping trip). Most cases also involved one overnight visit. We often carried tape recorders and used the audiotapes for reference in writing field notes. Writing field notes usually required 8 to 12 hours for each two- or three-hour home visit. Participating families each were paid $350, usually at the end of the visits.

We worked in teams of three. One fieldworker visited three to four times per week; another visited one to two times per week; and I visited once or twice per week, except for the two families for which I was lead fieldworker. The research teams' composition varied with the race of the family. Two white graduate students and I (a middle-aged white woman) visited the white families; for the black families, the teams included one white graduate student, one black graduate student, and me. All black families with male children were visited by teams that included a black male fieldworker. A white male fieldworker observed the poor family with the white boy; the remaining white fieldworkers were female. Team members met regularly to discuss the families and to review the emerging analytic themes.

Our presence altered family dynamics, especially at first. Over time, however, we saw signs of adjustment (e.g., yelling and cursing increased on the third day and again on the tenth). The children, especially, seemed to enjoy participating in the project. They reported it made them feel "special." They were visibly happy to see the fieldworkers arrive and reluctant to let them leave. The working-class and poor black boys were more comfortable with the black male fieldworkers than with the white female ones, especially at first.[13] Overall, however, family members reported in exit interviews that they had not changed their behavior significantly, or they mentioned very specific alterations (e.g., "the house got cleaner").

A Note on Class

I undertook field observations to develop an intensive, realistic portrait of family life. Although I deliberately focused on only 12 families, I wanted to compare children across gender and race. Adopting the fine-grained differentiations characteristic of current neo-Marxist and neo-Weberian empirical studies was not tenable.[14] Further limitations were imposed by the school populations at the sites I selected. Very few students were children of employers or of self-employed workers. I decided to focus exclusively on those whose parents were employees. Authority in the workplace and "credential barriers" are the criteria most commonly used to

differentiate within this heterogeneous group. I assigned the families to a working-class or middle-class category based on detailed information that each of the employed adults provided about the work they did, the nature of the organization that employed them, and their educational credentials. I also included a category traditionally excluded from class groupings: families not involved in the labor market. In the first school I studied, many children were from households supported by public assistance. Omitting them would have restricted the scope of the study arbitrarily.[15]

The three class categories conceal important internal variations. The Williams family (black) and the Tallinger family (white) have very high incomes, both in excess of $175,000; the median income among the middle-class parents was much lower.[16] Income differences among the middle-class families were not associated with differences in childrearing methods. Moreover, no other data in the study showed compelling intraclass divisions. I consider the use of one term—middle class—to be reasonable.

CONCERTED CULTIVATION AND NATURAL GROWTH

The interviews and observations suggested that crucial aspects of family life *cohered*. Within the concerted cultivation and accomplishment of natural growth approaches, three key dimensions may be distinguished: the organization of daily life, the use of language, and social connections. ("Interventions in institutions" and "consequences" are addressed later in this reading.) These dimensions do not capture all important parts of family life, but they do incorporate core aspects of childrearing (Table 4.2). Moreover, our field observations revealed that behaviors and activities related to these dimensions dominated the rhythms of family life. Conceptually, the organization of daily life and the use of language are crucial dimensions. Both must be present for the family to be described as engaging in

TABLE 4.2

SUMMARY OF DIFFERENCES IN CHILDREARING APPROACHES

Dimension observed	Childrearing approach	
	Concerted cultivation	Accomplishment of natural growth
Key elements of each approach	Parent actively fosters and assesses child's talents, opinions, and skills	Parent cares for child and allows child to grow
Organization of daily life	Multiple child leisure activities are orchestrated by adults	Child "hangs out" particularly with kin
Language use	Reasoning/directives Child contestation of adult statements Extended negotiations between parents and child	Directives Rare for child to question or challenge adults General acceptance by child of directives
Social connections	Weak extended family ties Child often in homogeneous age groupings	Strong extended family ties Child often in heterogeneous age groupings
Interventions in institutions	Criticisms and interventions on behalf of child Training of child to intervene on his or her own behalf	Dependence on institutions Sense of powerlessness and frustration Conflict between childrearing practices at home and at school
Consequences	Emerging sense of entitlement on the part of the child	Emerging sense of constraint on the part of the child

one childrearing approach rather than the other. Social connections are significant but less conceptually essential.

All three aspects of childrearing were intricately woven into the families' daily routines, but rarely remarked upon. As part of everyday practice, they were invisible to parents and children. Analytically, however, they are useful means for comparing and contrasting ways in which social class differences shape the character of family life. I now examine two families in terms of these three key dimensions. I "control" for race and gender and contrast the lives of two black boys—one from an (upper) middle-class family and one from a family on public assistance. I could have focused on almost any of the other 12 children, but this pair seemed optimal, given the limited number of studies reporting on black middle-class families, as well as the

aspect of my argument that suggests that race is less important than class in shaping childrearing patterns.

Developing Alexander Williams

Alexander Williams and his parents live in a predominantly black middle-class neighborhood. Their six-bedroom house is worth about $150,000.[17] Alexander is an only child. Both parents grew up in small towns in the South, and both are from large families. His father, a tall, handsome man, is a very successful trial lawyer who earns about $125,000 annually in a small firm specializing in medical malpractice cases. Two weeks each month, he works very long hours (from about 5:30 A.M. until midnight) preparing for trials. The other two weeks, his workday ends around 6:00 P.M. He rarely travels out of town. Alexander's mother, Christina, is a positive, bubbly woman with freckles and long, black, wavy hair.[18] A high-level manager in a major corporation, she has a corner office, a personal secretary, and responsibilities for other offices across the nation. She tries to limit her travel, but at least once a month she takes an overnight trip.

Alexander is a charming, inquisitive boy with a winsome smile. Ms. Williams is pleased that Alexander seems interested in so many things:

> Alexander is a joy. He's a gift to me. He's very energetic, very curious, loving, caring person, that, um . . . is outgoing and who, uh, really loves to be with people. And who loves to explore, and loves to read and . . . just do a lot of fun things.

The private school Alexander attends[19] has an on-site after-school program. There, he participates in several activities and receives guitar lessons and photography instruction.

Organization of Daily Life   Alexander is busy with activities during the week and on weekends (Table 4.3). His mother describes their Saturday morning routine. The day starts early with a private piano lesson for Alexander downtown, a 20-minute drive from the house:

> It's an 8:15 class. But for me, it was a trade-off. I am very adamant about Saturday morning TV. I don't know what it contributes. So . . . it was . . . um . . . either stay at home and fight on a Saturday morning [laughs] or go do something constructive. . . . Now Saturday mornings are pretty booked up. You know, the piano lesson, and then straight to choir for a couple of hours. So, he has a very full schedule.

Ms. Williams's vehement opposition to television is based on her view of what Alexander needs to grow and thrive. She objects to TV's passivity and feels it is her obligation to help her son cultivate his talents.

Sometimes Alexander complains that "my mother signs me up for everything!" Generally, however, he likes his activities. He says they make him feel "special," and without them life would be "boring." His sense of time

is thoroughly entwined with his activities: He feels disoriented when his schedule is not full. This unease is clear in the following field-note excerpt. The family is driving home from a Back-to-School night. The next morning, Ms. Williams will leave for a work-related day trip and will not return until late at night. Alexander is grumpy because he has nothing planned for the next day. He wants to have a friend over, but his mother rebuffs him. Whining, he wonders what he will do. His mother, speaking tersely, says:

> You have piano and guitar. You'll have some free time. [Pause] I think you'll survive for one night. [Alexander does not respond but seems mad. It is quiet for the rest of the trip home.]

Alexander's parents believe his activities provide a wide range of benefits important for his development. In discussing Alexander's piano lessons, Mr. Williams notes that as a Suzuki student,[20] Alexander is already able to read music. Speculating about more diffuse benefits of Alexander's involvement with piano, he says:

> I don't see how any kid's adolescence and adulthood could not but be enhanced by an awareness of who Beethoven was. And is that Bach or Mozart? I don't know the difference between the two! I don't know Baroque from Classical—but he does. How can that not be a benefit in later life? I'm convinced that this rich experience will make him a better person, a better citizen, a better husband, a better father—certainly a better student.

Ms. Williams sees music as building her son's "confidence" and his "poise." In interviews and casual conversation, she stresses "exposure." She believes it is her responsibility to broaden Alexander's worldview. Childhood activities provide a learning ground for important life skills:

> Sports provide great opportunities to learn how to be competitive. Learn how to accept defeat, you know. Learn how to accept winning, you know, in a gracious way. Also it gives him the opportunity to learn leadership skills and how to be a team player. . . . Sports really provides a lot of really great opportunities.

TABLE 4.3

PARTICIPATION IN ACTIVITIES OUTSIDE OF SCHOOL: BOYS

Boy's name/race/class	Activities organized by adults	Informal activities
Middle Class		
Garrett Tallinger (white)	Soccer team Traveling soccer team Baseball team Basketball team (summer) Swim team Piano Saxophone (through school)	Plays with siblings in yard Watches television Plays computer games Overnights with friends
Alexander Williams (black)	Soccer team Baseball team Community choir Church choir Sunday school Piano (Suzuki) School plays Guitar (through school)	Restricted television Plays outside occasionally with two other boys Visits friends from school
Working Class		
Billy Yanelli (white)	Baseball team	Watches television Visits relatives Rides bike Plays outside in the street Hangs out with neighborhood kids
Tyrec Taylor (black)	Football team Vacation Bible School Sunday school (off/on)	Watches television Plays outside in the street Rides bikes with neighborhood boys Visit relatives Goes to swimming pool
Poor		
Karl Greeley (white)	Goes to swimming pool Walks dogs with neighbor	Watches television Plays Nintendo Plays with siblings
Harold McAllister (black)	Bible study in neighbor's house (occasionally) Bible camp (1 week)	Visits relatives Plays ball with neighborhood kids Watches television Watches videos

Alexander's schedule is constantly shifting; some activities wind down and others start up. Because the schedules of sports practices and games are issued no sooner than the start of the new season, advance planning is rarely possible. Given the sheer number of Alexander's activities, events inevitably overlap. Some activities, though short-lived, are extremely time consuming. Alexander's school play, for example, requires rehearsals three nights the week before the opening. In addition, in choosing activities, the Williamses have an added concern— the group's racial balance. Ms. Williams prefers that Alexander not be the only black child at events. Typically, one or two other black boys are involved, but the groups are predominantly white and the activities take place in predominantly white residential neighborhoods. Alexander is, however, part of his church's youth choir and Sunday School, activities in which all participants are black.

Many activities involve competition. Alex must audition for his solo performance in the school play, for example. Similarly, parents and children alike understand that participation on "A," "B," or "All-Star" sports teams signals different skill levels. Like other middle-class children in the study, Alexander seems to enjoy public performance. According to a field note, after his solo at a musical production in front of over 200 people, he appeared "contained, pleased, aware of the attention he's receiving."

Alexander's commitments do not consume *all* his free time. Still, his life is defined by a series of deadlines and schedules interwoven with a series of activities that are organized and controlled by adults rather than children. Neither he nor his parents see this as troublesome.

Language Use   Like other middle-class families, the Williamses often engage in conversation that promotes reasoning and negotiation. An excerpt from a field note (describing an exchange between Alexander and his mother during a car ride home after summer camp) shows the kind of pointed questions middle-class parents ask children. Ms. Williams is not just eliciting information. She is also giving Alexander the opportunity to develop and practice verbal skills, including how to summarize, clarify, and amplify information:

> As she drives, [Ms. Williams] asks Alex, "So, how was your day?"
>
> Alex: "Okay. I had hot dogs today, but they were burned! They were all black!"
>
> Mom: "Oh, great. You shouldn't have eaten any."
>
> Alex: "They weren't *all* black, only half were. The rest were regular."
>
> Mom: "Oh, okay. What was that game you were playing this morning? . . ."

> Alex: "It was [called] 'Watcha doin?'"
>
> Mom: "How do you play?"

Alexander explains the game elaborately—fieldworker doesn't quite follow. Mom asks Alex questions throughout his explanation, saying, "Oh, I see," when he answers. She asks him about another game she saw them play; he again explains. . . . She continues to prompt and encourage him with small giggles in the back of her throat as he elaborates.

Expressions of interest in children's activities often lead to negotiations over small, home-based matters. During the same car ride, Ms. Williams tries to adjust the dinner menu to suit Alexander:

> Alexander says, "I don't want hot dogs tonight."
>
> Mom: "Oh? Because you had them for lunch."
>
> Alexander nods.
>
> Mom: "Well, I can fix something else and save the hot dogs for tomorrow night."
>
> Alex: "But I don't want any pork chops either."
>
> Mom: "Well, Alexander, we need to eat something. Why didn't you have hamburgers today?"
>
> Alex: "They don't have them any more at the snack bar."
>
> Mom asks Alexander if he's ok, if he wants a snack. Alexander says he's ok. Mom asks if he's sure he doesn't want a bag of chips?

Not all middle-class parents are as attentive to their children's needs as this mother, and none are *always* interested in negotiating. But a general pattern of reasoning and accommodating is common.

Social Connections   Mr. and Ms. Williams consider themselves very close to their extended families. Because the Williamses' aging parents live in the South, visiting requires a plane trip. Ms. Williams takes Alexander with her to see his grandparents twice a year. She speaks on the phone with her parents at least once a week and also calls her siblings several times a week. Mr. Williams talks with his mother regularly by phone (he has less contact with his stepfather). With pride, he also mentions his niece, whose Ivy League education he is helping to finance.

Interactions with cousins are not normally a part of Alexander's leisure time. (As I explain below, other middle-class children did not see cousins routinely either, even when they lived nearby.) Nor does he often play with neighborhood children. The huge homes on the Williamses' street are occupied mainly by couples without children. Most of Alexander's playmates come from his classroom or his organized activities. Because most of his school events, church life, and assorted activities are organized by the age (and sometimes gender) of the participants, Alexander interacts almost exclusively with children his own age, usually boys. Adult-organized activities thus define the context of his social life.

Mr. and Ms. Williams are aware that they allocate a sizable portion of time to Alexander's activities. What they stress, however, is the time they *hold back*. They mention activities the family has chosen *not* to take on (such as traveling soccer).

Summary Overall, Alexander's parents engaged in concerted cultivation. They fostered their son's growth through involvement in music, church, athletics, and academics. They talked with him at length, seeking his opinions and encouraging his ideas. Their approach involved considerable direct expenses (e.g., the cost of lessons and equipment) and large indirect expenses (e.g., the cost of taking time off from work, driving to practices, and forgoing adult leisure activities). Although Mr. and Ms. Williams acknowledged the importance of extended family, Alexander spent relatively little time with relatives. His social interactions occurred almost exclusively with children his own age and with adults. Alexander's many activities significantly shaped the organization of daily life in the family. Both

parents' leisure time was tailored to their son's commitments. Mr. and Ms. Williams felt that the strategies they cultivated with Alexander would result in his having the best possible chance at a happy and productive life. They couldn't imagine themselves *not* investing large amounts of time and energy in their son's life. But, as I explain in the next section, which focuses on a black boy from a poor family, other parents held a different view.

Supporting the Natural Growth of Harold McAllister

Harold McAllister, a large, stocky boy with a big smile, is from a poor black family. He lives with his mother and his 8-year-old sister, Alexis, in a large apartment. Two cousins often stay overnight. Harold's 16-year-old sister and 18-year-old brother usually live with their grandmother, but sometimes they stay at the McAllisters' home. Ms. McAllister, a high school graduate, relies on public assistance (AFDC). Hank, Harold and Alexis's father, is a mechanic. He and Ms. McAllister have never married. He visits regularly, sometimes weekly, stopping by after work to watch television or nap. Harold (but not Alexis) sometimes travels across town by bus to spend the weekend with Hank.

The McAllisters' apartment is in a public housing project near a busy street. The complex consists of rows of two- and three-story brick units. The buildings, blocky and brown, have small yards enclosed by concrete and wood fences. Large floodlights are mounted on the corners of the buildings, and wide concrete sidewalks cut through the spaces between units. The ground is bare in many places; paper wrappers and glass litter the area.

Inside the apartment, life is humorous and lively, with family members and kin sharing in the daily routines. Ms. McAllister discussed, disdainfully, mothers who are on drugs or who abuse alcohol and do not "look after" their children. Indeed, the previous year Ms. McAllister called Child Protective Services to report her twin sister, a cocaine addict, because she was neglecting her children. Ms. McAllister is actively involved in her twin's daughters' lives. Her two nephews also frequently stay with her. Overall, she sees herself as a capable mother who takes care of her children and her extended family.

Organization of Daily Life   Much of Harold's life and the lives of his family members revolve around home. Project residents often sit outside in lawn chairs or on front stoops, drinking beer, talking, and watching children play. During summer, windows are frequently left open, allowing breezes to waft through the units and providing vantage points from which residents can survey the neighborhood. A large deciduous tree in front of the McAllisters' apartment unit provides welcome shade in the summer's heat.

Harold loves sports. He is particularly fond of basketball, but he also enjoys football, and he follows televised professional sports closely. Most afternoons, he is either inside watching television or outside playing ball. He tosses a football with cousins and boys from the neighboring units and organizes pick-up basketball games. Sometimes he and his friends use a rusty, bare hoop hanging from a telephone pole in the housing project; other times, they string up an old, blue plastic crate as a makeshift hoop. One obstacle to playing sports, however, is a shortage of equipment. Balls are costly to replace, especially given the rate at which they disappear—theft of children's play equipment, including balls and bicycles, is an ongoing problem. During a field observation, Harold asks his mother if she knows where the ball is. She replies with some vehemence, "They stole the blue and yellow ball, and they stole the green ball, and they stole the other ball."

Hunting for balls is a routine part of Harold's leisure time. One June day, with the temperature and humidity in the high 80's, Harold and his cousin Tyrice (and a fieldworker) wander around the housing project for about an hour, trying to find a basketball:

> We head to the other side of the complex. On the way . . . we passed four guys sitting on the step. Their ages were 9 to 13 years. They had a radio blaring. Two were working intently on fixing a flat bike tire. The other two were dribbling a basketball.
>
> Harold: "Yo! What's up, ya'll."
>
> Group: "What's up, Har." "What's up? "Yo."
>
> They continued to work on the tire and dribble the ball. As we walked down the hill, Harold asked, "Yo, could I use your ball?"
>
> The guy responded, looking up from the tire, "Naw, man. Ya'll might lose it."

Harold, Tyrice, and the fieldworker walk to another part of the complex, heading for a makeshift basketball court where they hope to find a game in progress:

> No such luck. Harold enters an apartment directly in front of the makeshift court. The door was open . . . Harold came back. "No ball. I guess I gotta go back."

The pace of life for Harold and his friends ebbs and flows with the children's interests and family obligations. The day of the basketball search, for example, after spending time listening to music and looking at baseball cards, the children join a water fight Tyrice instigates. It is a lively game, filled with laughter and with efforts to get the adults next door wet (against their wishes). When the game winds down, the kids ask their mother for money, receive it, and then walk to a store to buy chips and soda. They chat with another young boy and then amble back to the apartment, eating as they walk. Another afternoon, almost two weeks later, the children—Harold, two of his cousins, and two children from the neighborhood—and the fieldworker play basketball on a makeshift court in the street (using the fieldworker's ball). As Harold bounces the ball, neighborhood children of all ages wander through the space.

Thus, Harold's life is more free-flowing and more child-directed than is Alexander Williams's. The pace of any given day is not so much planned as emergent, reflecting child-based interests and activities. Parents intervene in specific areas, such as personal grooming, meals, and occasional chores, but they do not continuously direct and monitor their children's leisure activities. Moreover, the leisure activities Harold and other working-class and poor children pursue require them to develop a repertoire of skills for dealing with much older and much younger children as well as with neighbors and relatives.

Language Use Life in the working-class and poor families in the study flows smoothly without extended verbal discussions. The amount of talking varies, but overall, it is considerably less than occurs in the middle-class homes.[21] Ms. McAllister jokes with the children and discusses what is on television. But she does not appear to cultivate conversation by asking the children questions or by drawing them out. Often she is brief and direct in her remarks. For instance, she coordinates the use of the apartment's only bathroom by using one-word directives. She sends the children (there are almost always at least four children home at once) to wash up by pointing to a child, saying one word, "bathroom," and handing him or her a washcloth. Wordlessly, the designated child gets up and goes to the bathroom to take a shower.

Similarly, although Ms. McAllister will listen to the children's complaints about school, she does not draw them out on these issues or seek to determine details, as Ms. Williams would. For instance, at the start of the new school year, when I ask Harold about his teacher, he tells me she is "mean" and that "she lies." Ms. McAllister, washing dishes, listens to her son, but she does not encourage Harold to support his opinion about his new teacher with more examples, nor does she mention any concerns of her own. Instead, she asks about last year's teacher, "What was the name of that man teacher?" Harold says, "Mr. Lindsey?"

She says, "No, the other one." He says, "Mr. Terrene." Ms. McAllister smiles and says, "Yeah. I liked him." Unlike Alexander's mother, she seems content with a brief exchange of information.

Social Connections Children, especially boys, frequently play outside. The number of potential playmates in Harold's world is vastly higher than the number in Alexander's neighborhood. When a fieldworker stops to count heads, she finds 40 children of elementary school age residing in the nearby rows of apartments. With so many children nearby, Harold could choose to play only with others his own age. In fact, though, he often hangs out with older and younger children and with his cousins (who are close to his age).

The McAllister family, like other poor and working-class families, is involved in a web of extended kin. As noted earlier, Harold's older siblings and his two male cousins often spend the night at the McAllister home. Celebrations such as birthdays involve relatives almost exclusively. Party guests are not, as in middle-class families, friends from school or from extra-curricular activities. Birthdays are celebrated enthusiastically, with cake and special food to mark the occasion; presents, however, are not offered. Similarly, Christmas at Harold's house featured a tree and special food but no presents. At these and other family events, the older children voluntarily look after the younger ones: Harold plays with his 16-month-old niece, and his cousins carry around the younger babies.

The importance of family ties—and the contingent nature of life in the McAllisters' world—is clear in the response Alexis offers when asked what she would do if she were given a million dollars:

> Oh, boy! I'd buy my brother, my sister, my uncle, my aunt, my nieces and my nephews, and my grandpop, and my grandmom, and my mom, and my dad, and my friends, not my friends, but mostly my best friend—I'd buy them all clothes . . . and sneakers. And I'd buy some food, and I'd get my brothers and my sisters gifts for their birthdays.

Summary In a setting where everyone, including the children, was acutely aware of the lack of money, the McAllister family made do. Ms. McAllister rightfully saw herself as a very capable mother. She was a strong, positive influence in the lives of the children she looked after. Still, the contrast with Ms. Williams is striking. Ms. McAllister did not seem to think that Harold's opinions needed to be cultivated and developed. She, like most parents in the working-class and poor families, drew strong and clear boundaries between adults and children. Adults gave directions to children. Children were given freedom to play informally unless they were needed for chores. Extended family networks were deemed important and trustworthy.

The Intersection of Race and Class in Family Life

I expected race to powerfully shape children's daily schedules, but this was not evident (also see Conley 1999; Pattillo-McCoy 1999). This is not to say that race is unimportant. Black parents were particularly concerned with monitoring their children's lives outside the home for signs of racial problems.[22] Black middle-class fathers, especially, were likely to stress the importance of their sons understanding "what it means to be a black man in this society" (J. Hochschild 1995). Mr. Williams, in summarizing how he and his wife orient Alexander, said:

> [We try to] teach him that race unfortunately is the most important aspect of our national life. I mean people look at other people and they see a color first. But that isn't going to define who he is. He will do his best. He will succeed, despite racism. And I think he lives his life that way.

Alexander's parents were acutely aware of the potential significance of race in his life. Both were adamant, however, that race should not be used as "an excuse" for not striving to succeed. Mr. Williams put it this way:

> I discuss how race impacts on my life as an attorney, and I discuss how race will impact on his life.

The one teaching that he takes away from this is that he is never to use discrimination as an excuse for not doing his best.

Thus far, few incidents of overt racism had occurred in Alexander's life, as his mother noted:

> Those situations have been far and few between. . . . I mean, I can count them on my fingers.

Still, Ms. Williams recounted with obvious pain an incident at a birthday party Alexander had attended as a preschooler. The grandparents of the birthday child repeatedly asked, "Who is that boy?" and exclaimed, "He's so dark!" Such experiences fueled the Williamses resolve always to be "cautious":

> We've never been, uh, parents who drop off their kid anywhere. We've always gone with him. And even now, I go in and—to school in the morning—and check [in]. . . . The school environment, we've watched very closely.

Alexander's parents were not equally optimistic about the chances for racial equality in this country. Ms. Williams felt strongly that, especially while Alexander was young, his father should not voice his pessimism. Mr. Williams complained that this meant he had to "watch" what he said to Alexander about race relations. Still, both parents agreed about the need to be vigilant regarding potential racial problems in Alexander's life. Other black parents reported experiencing racial prejudice and expressed a similar commitment to vigilance.

Issues surrounding the prospect of growing up black and male in this society were threaded through Alexander's life in ways that had no equivalent among his middle-class, white male peers. Still, in fourth grade there were no signs of racial experiences having "taken hold" the way that they might as Alexander ages. In terms of the number and kind of activities he participated in, his life was very similar to that of Garrett Tallinger, his white counterpart (see Table 4.3). That both sets of parents were fully committed to a strategy of concentrated cultivation was apparent in the number of adult-organized activities the boys were enrolled in, the hectic pace of family life, and the stress on reasoning in parent-child negotiations. Likewise, the research assistants and I saw no striking differences in the ways in which white parents and black parents in the working-class and poor homes socialized their children.

Others (Fordham and Ogbu 1986) have found that in middle school and high school, adolescent peer groups often draw sharp racial boundaries, a pattern not evident among this study's third- and fourth-grade participants (but sometimes present among their older siblings). Following Tatum (1997:52), I attribute this to the children's relatively young ages (also see "Race in America," *The New York Times,* June 25, 2000, p. 1). In sum, in the broader society, key aspects of daily life were shaped by racial segregation and discrimination. But in terms of enrollment in organized activities, language use, and social connections, the largest differences between the families we observed were across social class, not racial groups. . . .

IMPACT OF CHILDREARING STRATEGIES ON INTERACTIONS WITH INSTITUTIONS

Social scientists sometimes emphasize the importance of reshaping parenting practices to improve children's chances of success. Explicitly and implicitly, the literature exhorts parents to comply with the views of professionals (Bronfenbrenner 1966; Epstein 2001; Heimer and Staffen 1998). Such calls for compliance do not, however, reconcile professionals' judgments regarding the intrinsic value of current childrearing standards with the evidence of the historical record, which shows regular shifts in such standards over time (Aries 1962; Wrigley 1989; Zelizer 1985). Nor are the stratified, and limited, possibilities for success in the broader society examined.

I now follow the families out of their homes and into encounters with representatives of dominant institutions—institutions that are directed by middle-class professionals. Again, I focus on Alexander Williams and Harold McAllister. (Institutional experiences are summarized in Table 4.2.) Across all social classes, parents and children interacted with teachers and school officials, healthcare professionals, and assorted government officials. Although they often addressed similar problems (e.g., learning disabilities, asthma, traffic violations), they typically did not achieve similar resolutions. The pattern of concerted cultivation fostered an *emerging sense of entitlement* in the life of Alexander Williams and other middle-class children. By contrast, the commitment to nurturing children's natural growth fostered an *emerging sense of constraint* in the life of Harold McAllister and other working-class or poor children. (These consequences of child-rearing practices are summarized in Table 4.2.)

Both parents and children drew on the resources associated with these two childrearing approaches during their interactions with officials. Middle-class parents and children often customized these interactions; working-class and poor parents were more likely to have a "generic" relationship. When faced with problems, middle-class parents also appeared better equipped to exert influence over other adults compared with working-class and poor parents. Nor did middle-class parents or children display the intimidation or confusion we witnessed among many working-class and poor families when they faced a problem in their children's school experience.

Emerging Signs of Entitlement

Alexander Williams's mother, like many middle-class mothers, explicitly teaches her son to be an informed, assertive client in interactions with professionals. For example, as she drives Alexander to a routine doctor's appointment, she coaches him in the art of communicating effectively in healthcare settings:

> Alexander asks if he needs to get any shots today at the doctor's. Ms. Williams says he'll need to ask the doctor. . . . As we enter Park Lane, Mom

says quietly to Alex: "Alexander, you should be thinking of questions you might want to ask the doctor. You can ask him anything you want. Don't be shy. You can ask anything."

Alex thinks for a minute, then: "I have some bumps under my arms from my deodorant."

Mom: "Really? You mean from your new deodorant?"

Alex: "Yes."

Mom: "Well, you should ask the doctor."

Alexander learns that he has the right to speak up (e.g., "don't be shy") and that he should prepare for an encounter with a person in a position of authority by gathering his thoughts in advance.

These class resources are subsequently *activated* in the encounter with the doctor (a jovial white man in his late thirties or early forties). The examination begins this way:

Doctor: "Okay, as usual, I'd like to go through the routine questions with you. And if you have any questions for me, just fire away." Doctor examines Alex's chart: "Height-wise, as usual, Alexander's in the ninety-fifth percentile."

Although the physician is talking to Ms. Williams, Alexander interrupts him:

Alex: "I'm in the what?"

Doctor: "It means that you're taller than more than ninety-five out of a hundred young men when they're, uh, ten years old."

Alex: "I'm not ten."

Doctor: "Well, they graphed you at ten . . . they usually take the closest year to get that graph."

Alex: "Alright."

Alexander's "Alright" reveals that he feels entitled to weigh in with his own judgment.

A few minutes later, the exam is interrupted when the doctor is asked to provide an emergency consultation by telephone. Alexander listens to the doctor's conversation and then uses what he has overheard as the basis for a clear directive:

Doctor: "The stitches are on the eyelids themselves, the laceration? . . . Um . . . I don't suture eyelids . . . um . . . Absolutely not! . . . Don't even touch them. That was very bad judgment on the camp's part. . . . [Hangs up.] I'm sorry about the interruption."

Alex: "Stay away from my eyelids!"

Alexander's comment, which draws laughter from the adults, reflects this fourth-grader's tremendous ease interacting with a physician.

Later, Ms. Williams and the doctor discuss Alexander's diet. Ms. Williams freely admits that they do not always follow nutritional guidelines. Her honesty is a form of capital because it gives the doctor accurate information on which to base a diagnosis. Feeling no need for deception positions mother and son to receive better care:

Doctor: "Let's start with appetite. Do you get three meals a day?"

Alex: "Yeah."

Doctor: "And here's the important question: Do you get your fruits and vegetables too?"

Alex: "Yeah."

Mom, high-pitched: "Ooooo. . . ."

Doctor: "I see I have a second opinion." [laughter]

Alex, voice rising: "You give me bananas and all in my lunch every day. And I had cabbage for dinner last night."

Doctor: "Do you get at least one or two fruits, one or two vegetables every day?"

Alex: "Yeah."

Doctor: "Marginally?"

Mom: "Ninety-eight percent of the time he eats pretty well."

Doctor: "OK, I can live with that. . . ."

Class resources are again activated when Alexander's mother reveals she "gave up" on a medication. The doctor pleasantly but clearly instructs her to continue the medication. Again, though, he receives accurate information rather than facing silent resistance or defiance, as occurred in encounters between healthcare professionals and other (primarily working-class and poor) families. The doctor acknowledges Ms. Williams's relative power: He "argues for" continuation rather than directing her to execute a medically necessary action:

Mom: "His allergies have just been, just acted up again. One time this summer and I had to bring him in."

Doctor: "I see a note here from Dr. Svennson that she put him on Vancinace and Benadryl. Did it seem to help him?"

Mom: "Just, not really. So, I used it for about a week and I just gave up." Doctor, sitting forward in his chair: "OK, I'm actually going to argue for not giving up. If he needs it, Vancinace is a very effective drug. But it takes at least a week to start. . . ."

Mom: "Oh. OK. . . ."

Doctor: "I'd rather have him use that than heavy oral medications. You have to give it a few weeks. . . ."

A similar pattern of give-and-take and questioning characterizes Alexander's interaction with the doctor, as the following excerpt illustrates:

Doctor: "The only thing that you really need besides my checking you, um, is to have, um, your eyes checked downstairs."

Alex: "Yes! I love that, I love that!"

Doctor laughs: "Well, now the most important question. Do you have any questions you want to ask me before I do your physical?"

Alex: "Um . . . only one. I've been getting some bumps on my arms, right around here [indicates underarm]."

Doctor: "Underneath?"

Alex: "Yeah."

Doctor: "OK. . . . Do they hurt or itch?"

Alex: "No, they're just there."

Doctor: "OK, I'll take a look at those bumps for you. Um, what about you—um . . ."

Alex: "They're barely any left."

Doctor: "OK, well, I'll take a peek. . . . Any questions or worries on your part?" [Looking at the mother]

Mom: "No. . . . He seems to be coming along very nicely."[23]

Alexander's mother's last comment reflects her view of him as a project, one that is progressing "very nicely." Throughout the visit, she signals her ease and her perception of the exam as an exchange between peers (with Alexander a legitimate participant), rather than a communication from a person in authority to his subordinates. Other middle-class parents seemed similarly comfortable. During Garrett Tallinger's exam, for example, his mother took off her sandals and tucked her legs up under her as she sat in the examination room. She also joked casually with the doctor.

Middle-class parents and children were also very assertive in situations at the public elementary school most of the middle-class children in the study attended. There were numerous conflicts during the year over matters small and large. For example, parents complained to one another and to the teachers about the amount of homework the children were assigned. A black middle-class mother whose daughters had not tested into the school's gifted program negotiated with officials to have the girls' (higher) results from a private testing company accepted instead. The parents of a fourth-grade boy drew the school superintendent into a battle over religious lyrics in a song scheduled to be sung as part of the holiday program. The superintendent consulted the district lawyer and ultimately "counseled" the principal to be more sensitive, and the song was dropped.

Children, too, asserted themselves at school. Examples include requesting that the classroom's blinds be lowered so the sun wasn't in their eyes, badgering the teacher for permission to retake a math test for a higher grade, and demanding to know why no cupcake had been saved when an absence prevented attendance at a classroom party. In these encounters, children were not simply complying with adults' requests or asking for a repeat of an earlier experience. They were displaying an emerging sense of entitlement by urging adults to permit a customized accommodation of institutional processes to suit their preferences.

Of course, some children (and parents) were more forceful than others in their dealings with teachers, and some were more successful than others. Melanie Handlon's mother, for example, took a very "hands-on" approach to her daughter's learning problems, coaching Melanie through her homework day after day. Instead of improved grades, however, the only result was a deteriorating home environment marked by tension and tears.

Emerging Signs of Constraint

The interactions the research assistants and I observed between professionals and working-class and poor parents frequently seemed cautious and constrained. This unease is evident, for example, during a physical Harold McAllister has before going to Bible camp. Harold's mother, normally boisterous and talkative at home, is quiet. Unlike Ms. Williams, she seems wary of supplying the doctor with accurate information:

Doctor: "Does he eat something each day—either fish, meat, or egg?"

Mom, response is low and muffled: "Yes."

Doctor, attempting to make eye contact but mom stares intently at paper: "A yellow vegetable?"

Mom, still no eye contact, looking at the floor: "Yeah."

Doctor: "A green vegetable?" Mom, looking at the doctor: "Not all the time." [Fieldworker has not seen any of the children eat a green or yellow vegetable since visits began.]

Doctor: "No. Fruit or juice?"

Mom, low voice, little or no eye contact, looks at the doctor's scribbles on the paper he is filling out: "Ummh humn."

Doctor: "Does he drink milk every day?"

Mom, abruptly, in considerably louder voice: "Yeah."

Doctor: "Cereal, bread, rice, potato, anything like that?"

Mom, shakes her head: "Yes, definitely." [Looks at doctor.]

Ms. McAllister's knowledge of developmental events in Harold's life is uneven. She is not sure when he learned to walk and cannot recall the name of his previous doctor. And when the doctor asks, "When was the last time he had a tetanus shot?" she counters, gruffly, "What's a tetanus shot?"

Unlike Ms. Williams, who urged Alexander to share information with the doctor, Ms. McAllister squelches eight-year-old Alexis's overtures:

Doctor: "Any birth mark?"

Mom looks at doctor, shakes her head no.

Alexis, raising her left arm, says excitedly: "I have a birth mark under my arm!"

Mom, raising her voice and looking stern: "Will you cool out a minute?" Mom, again answering the doctor's question: "No."

Despite Ms. McAllister's tension and the marked change in her everyday demeanor, Harold's whole exam is not uncomfortable. There are moments of laughter. Moreover, Harold's mother is not consistently shy or passive. Before the visit begins, the doctor comes into the waiting room and calls Harold's and Alexis's names. In response, the McAllisters (and the fieldworker) stand. Ms. McAllister then beckons for her nephew Tyrice (who is about Harold's age) to come along *before* she clears this with the doctor. Later, she sends Tyrice down the hall to observe Harold being weighed; she relies on her nephew's report rather than asking for this information from the healthcare professionals.

Still, neither Harold nor his mother seemed as comfortable as Alexander had been. Alexander was used to extensive conversation at home; with the doctor, he was at ease initiating questions. Harold, who was used to responding to directives at home, primarily answered questions from the doctor, rather than posing his own. Alexander, encouraged by his mother, was assertive and confident with the doctor. Harold was reserved. Absorbing his mother's apparent need to conceal the truth about the range of foods he ate, he appeared cautious, displaying an emerging sense of constraint.

We observed a similar pattern in school interactions. Overall, the working-class and poor adults had much more distance or separation from the school than their middle-class counterparts. Ms. McAllister, for example, could be quite assertive in some settings (e.g., at the start of family observations, she visited the local drug dealer, warning him not to "mess with" the black male fieldworker).[24] But throughout the fourth-grade parent-teacher conference, she kept her winter jacket zipped up, sat hunched over in her chair, and spoke in barely audible tones. She was stunned when the teacher said that Harold did not do homework. Sounding dumbfounded, she said, "He does it at home." The teacher denied it and continued talking. Ms. McAllister made no further comments and did not probe for more information, except about a letter the teacher said he had mailed home and that she had not received. The conference ended, having yielded Ms. McAllister few insights into Harold's educational experience.[25]

Other working-class and poor parents also appeared baffled, intimidated, and subdued in parent-teacher conferences. Ms. Driver, who was extremely worried about her fourth-grader's inability to read, kept these concerns to herself. She explained to us, "I don't want to jump into anything and find it is the wrong thing." When working-class and poor parents did try to intervene in their children's educational experiences,

they often felt ineffectual. Billy Yanelli's mother appeared relaxed and chatty in many of her interactions with other adults. With "the school," however, she was very apprehensive. She distrusted school personnel. She felt bullied and powerless. Hoping to resolve a problem involving her son, she tried to prepare her ideas in advance. Still, as she recounted during an interview, she failed to make school officials see Billy as vulnerable:

> Ms. Yanelli: "I found a note in his school bag one morning and it said, 'I'm going to kill you . . . you're a dead mother-f-er. . . .' So, I started shaking. I was all ready to go over there. [I was] prepared for the counselor. . . . They said the reason they [the other kids] do what they do is because Billy makes them do it. So they had an answer for everything."
>
> Interviewer: "How did you feel about that answer?"
>
> Ms. Yanelli: "I hate the school. I hate it."

Working-class and poor children seemed aware of their parents' frustration and witnessed their powerlessness. Billy Yanelli, for example, asserted in an interview that his mother "hate[d]" school officials.

At times, these parents encouraged their children to resist school officials' authority. The Yanellis told Billy to "beat up" a boy who was bothering him. Wendy Driver's mother advised her to punch a male classmate who pestered her and pulled her ponytail. Ms. Driver's boyfriend added, "Hit him when the teacher isn't looking."

In classroom observations, working-class and poor children could be quite lively and energetic, but we did not observe them try to customize their environments. They tended to react to adults' offers or, at times, to plead with educators to repeat previous experiences, such as reading a particular story, watching a movie, or going to the computer room. Compared to middle-class classroom interactions, the boundaries between adults and children seemed firmer and clearer. Although the children often resisted and tested school rules, they did not seem to be seeking to get educators to accommodate their own *individual* preferences.

Overall, then, the behavior of working-class and poor parents cannot be explained as a manifestation of their temperaments or of overall passivity; parents were quite energetic in intervening in their children's lives in other spheres. Rather, working-class and poor parents generally appeared to depend on the school (Lareau 2000), even as they were dubious of the trustworthiness of the professionals. This suspicion of professionals in dominant institutions is, at least in some instances, a reasonable response.[26] The unequal level of trust, as well as differences in the amount and quality of information divulged, can yield unequal *profits* during an historical moment when professionals applaud assertiveness and reject passivity as an inappropriate parenting strategy (Epstein 2001). Middle-class children and parents often (but not always) accrued advantages or profits from their efforts. Alexander Williams succeeded in having the doctor take his medical concerns seriously. Ms. Marshall's children ended up in the gifted program, even though they did not technically qualify. Middle-class children expect institutions to be responsive to *them* and to accommodate their individual needs. By contrast, when Wendy Driver is told to hit the boy who is pestering her (when the teacher isn't looking) or Billy Yanelli is told to physically defend himself, despite school rules, they are not learning how to make bureaucratic institutions work to their advantage. Instead, they are being given lessons in frustration and powerlessness.

WHY DOES SOCIAL CLASS MATTER?

Parents' economic resources helped create the observed class differences in childrearing practices. Enrollment fees that middle-class parents dismissed as "negligible" were formidable expenses for less affluent families. Parents also paid for clothing, equipment, hotel stays, fast food meals, summer camps, and fundraisers. In 1994, the Tallingers estimated the cost of Garrett's activities at $4,000 annually, and that

figure was not unusually high.[27] Moreover, families needed reliable private transportation and flexible work schedules to get children to and from events. These resources were disproportionately concentrated in middle-class families.

Differences in educational resources also are important. Middle-class parents' superior levels of education gave them larger vocabularies that facilitated concerted cultivation, particularly in institutional interventions. Poor and working-class parents were not familiar with key terms professionals used, such as " tetanus shot." Furthermore, middle-class parents' educational backgrounds gave them confidence when criticizing educational professionals and intervening in school matters. Working-class and poor parents viewed educators as their social superiors.

Kohn and Schooler (1983) showed that parents' occupations, especially the complexity of their work, influence their childrearing beliefs. We found that parents' work mattered, but also saw signs that the experience of adulthood itself influenced conceptions of childhood. Middle-class parents often were preoccupied with the pleasures and challenges of their work lives.[28] They tended to view childhood as a dual opportunity: a chance for play, and for developing talents and skills of value later in life. Mr. Tallinger noted that playing soccer taught Garrett to be "hard nosed" and " competitive," valuable workplace skills. Ms. Williams mentioned the value of Alexander learning to work with others by playing on a sports team. Middle-class parents, aware of the "declining fortunes" of the middle class, worried about their own economic futures and those of their children (Newman 1993). This uncertainty increased their commitment to helping their children develop broad skills to enhance their future possibilities.

Working-class and poor parents' conceptions of adulthood and childhood also appeared to be closely connected to their lived experiences. For the working class, it was the deadening quality of work and the press of economic shortages that defined their experience of adulthood and influenced their vision of childhood. It was dependence on public assistance and severe economic shortages that most shaped poor parents' views. Families in both classes had many worries about basic issues: food shortages, limited access to healthcare, physical safety, unreliable transportation, insufficient clothing. Thinking back over their childhoods, these parents remembered hardship but also recalled times without the anxieties they now faced. Many appeared to want their own youngsters to concentrate on being happy and relaxed, keeping the burdens of life at bay until they were older.

Thus, childrearing strategies are influenced by more than parents' education. It is the interweaving of life experiences and resources, including parents' economic resources, occupational conditions, and educational backgrounds, that appears to be most important in leading middle-class parents to engage in concerted cultivation and working-class and poor parents to engage in the accomplishment of natural growth. Still, the structural location of families did not fully determine their childrearing practices. The agency of actors and the indeterminacy of social life are inevitable.

In addition to economic and social resources, are there other significant factors? If the poor and working-class families' resources were transformed overnight so that they equaled those of the middle-class families, would their cultural logic of childrearing shift as well? Or are there cultural attitudes and beliefs that are substantially independent of economic and social resources that are influencing parents' practices here? The size and scope of this study preclude a definitive answer. Some poor and working-class parents embraced principles of concerted cultivation: They wished (but could not afford) to enroll their children in organized activities (e.g., piano lessons, voice lessons), they believed listening to children was important, and they were committed to being involved in their children's schooling. Still, even when parents across all of the classes seemed committed to

similar principles, their motivations differed. For example, many working-class and poor parents who wanted more activities for their children were seeking a safe haven for them. Their goal was to provide protection from harm rather than to cultivate the child's talents per se.

Some parents explicitly criticized children's schedules that involved many activities. During the parent interviews, we described the real-life activities of two children (using data from the 12 families we were observing). One schedule resembled Alexander Williams's: restricted television, required reading, and many organized activities, including piano lessons (for analytical purposes, we said that, unlike Alexander, this child disliked his piano lessons but was not allowed to quit). Summing up the attitude of the working-class and poor parents who rejected this kind of schedule,[29] one white, poor mother complained:

> I think he wants more. I think he doesn't enjoy doing what he's doing half of the time (light laughter). I think his parents are too strict. And he's not a child.

Even parents who believed this more regimented approach would pay off "job-wise" when the child was an adult still expressed serious reservations: "I think he is a sad kid," or, "He must be dead-dog tired."

Thus, working-class and poor parents varied in their beliefs. Some longed for a schedule of organized activities for their children and others did not; some believed in reasoning with children and playing an active role in schooling and others did not. Fully untangling the effects of material and cultural resources on parents and children's choices is a challenge for future research.[30]

DISCUSSION

The evidence shows that class position influences critical aspects of family life: time use, language use, and kin ties. Not all aspects of family life are affected by social class, and there is variability within class. Still, parents do transmit advantages to their children in patterns that are sufficiently consistent and identifiable to be described as a "cultural logic" of childrearing. The white and black middle-class parents engaged in practices I have termed "concerted cultivation"—they made a deliberate and sustained effort to stimulate children's development and to cultivate their cognitive and social skills. The working-class and poor parents viewed children's development as spontaneously unfolding, as long as they were provided with comfort, food, shelter, and other basic support. This commitment, too, required ongoing effort; sustaining children's natural growth despite formidable life challenges is properly viewed as an accomplishment.

In daily life, the patterns associated with each of these approaches were interwoven and mutually reinforcing. Nine-year-old middle-class children already had developed a clear sense of their own talents and skills, and they differentiated themselves from siblings and friends. They were also learning to think of themselves as special and worthy of having adults devote time and energy to promoting them and their leisure activities. In the process, the boundaries between adults and children sometimes blurred; adults' leisure preferences became subordinate to their children's. The strong emphasis on reasoning in middle-class families had similar, diffuse effects. Children used their formidable reasoning skills to persuade adults to acquiesce to their wishes. The idea that children's desires should be taken seriously was routinely realized in the middle-class families we interviewed and observed. In many subtle ways, children were taught that they were entitled. Finally, the commitment to cultivating children resulted in family schedules so crowded with activities there was little time left for visiting relatives. Quantitative studies of time use have shed light on important issues, but they do not capture the interactive nature of routine, everyday activities and the varying ways they affect the texture of family life.[31]

In working-class and poor families, parents established limits; within those limits, children were free to fashion their own pastimes. Children's wishes did not guide adults' actions as frequently or as decisively as they did in middle-class homes. Children were viewed as subordinate to adults. Parents tended to issue directives rather than to negotiate. Frequent interactions with relatives rather than acquaintances or strangers created a thicker divide between families and the outside world. Implicitly and explicitly, parents taught their children to keep their distance from people in positions of authority, to be distrustful of institutions, and, at times, to resist officials' authority. Children seemed to absorb the adults' feelings of powerlessness in their institutional relationships. As with the middle class, there were important variations among working-class and poor families, and some critical aspects of family life, such as the use of humor, were immune to social class.

The role of race in children's daily lives was less powerful than I had expected. The middle-class black children's parents were alert to the potential effects of institutional discrimination on their children. Middle-class black parents also took steps to help their children develop a positive racial identity. Still, in terms of how children spend their time, the way parents use language and discipline in the home, the nature of the families' social connections, and the strategies used for intervening in institutions, white and black middle-class parents engaged in very similar, often identical, practices with their children. A similar pattern was observed in white and black working-class homes as well as in white and black poor families. Thus my data indicate that on the childrearing dynamics studied here, compared with social class, race was less important in children's daily lives.[32] As they enter the racially segregated worlds of dating, marriage, and housing markets, and as they encounter more racism in their interpersonal contact with whites (Waters 1999), the relative importance of race in the children's daily lives is likely to increase.

Differences in family dynamics and the logic of childrearing across social classes have long-term consequences. As family members moved out of the home and interacted with representatives of formal institutions, middle-class parents and children were able to negotiate more valuable outcomes than their working-class and poor counterparts. In interactions with agents of dominant institutions, working-class and poor children were learning lessons in constraint while middle-class children were developing a sense of entitlement.

It is a mistake to see either concerted cultivation or the accomplishment of natural growth as an intrinsically desirable approach. As has been amply documented, conceptions of childhood have changed dramatically over time (Wrigley 1989). Drawbacks to middle-class childrearing, including the exhaustion associated with intensive mothering and frenetic family schedules and a sapping of children's naivete that leaves them feeling too sophisticated for simple games and toys (Hays 1996), remain insufficiently highlighted.

Another drawback is that middle-class children are less likely to learn how to fill "empty time" with their own creative play, leading to a dependence on their parents to solve experiences of boredom. Sociologists need to more clearly differentiate between standards that are intrinsically desirable and standards that facilitate success in dominant institutions. A more critical, and historically sensitive, vision is needed (Donzelot 1979). Here Bourdieu's work (1976, 1984, 1986, 1989) is valuable.

Finally, there are methodological issues to consider. Quantitative research has delineated population-wide patterns; ethnographies offer rich descriptive detail but typically focus on a single, small group. Neither approach can provide holistic, but empirically grounded, assessments of daily life. Multi-sited, multi-person research using ethnographic methods also poses formidable methodological challenges (Lareau 2002). Still, families have proven themselves open to being studied in an intimate fashion. Creating penetrating portraits of daily life that will enrich our theoretical models is an important challenge for the future.

■ Review Questions

1. If you grew up in a middle-class family, answer this question: Did your parents practice concerted cultivation? If you grew up in a working-class or poor family, answer this one: Did your parents practice the accomplishment of natural growth?
2. Why might concerted cultivation lead children to have a greater sense of entitlement when dealing with teachers, doctors, or other professionals?

ENDNOTES

1. In a study of mothers' beliefs about childrearing, Hays (1996) found variations in how working-class and middle-class mothers sorted information, but she concluded that a pattern of "intensive mothering" was present across social classes. My study of behavior found class differences but, as I discuss below, in some instances working-class and poor parents expressed a desire to enroll their children in organized activities.

2. Some significant differences between the study's working-class and poor families (e.g., only the poor children experienced food shortages) are not highlighted here because, on the dimensions discussed in this paper, the biggest differences were between middle-class and nonmiddle-class families. See Lareau (2003) for a more elaborate discussion as well as Lamont (2000) for distinctions working-class families draw between themselves and the poor; see McLanahan and Sandefur (1994) regarding family structure and children's lives.

3. Case studies of nonrandom samples, such as this one, have the limitation that findings cannot be generalized beyond the cases reported. These examples serve to illustrate conceptual points (Burawoy et al. 1991) rather than to describe representative patterns of behavior. A further limitation of this study is that the data were collected and analyzed over an extended period of time (see the "Methodology" section).

4. All names of people and places are pseudonyms. The Lawrenceville school was in a white suburban neighborhood in a university community a few hours from a metropolitan area. The student population was about half white and half black; the (disproportionately poor) black children were bused from other neighborhoods.

5. Over three-quarters of the students at Lower Richmond qualified for free lunch; by contrast, Swan did not have a free lunch program.

6. At both sites, we attended school events and observed many parent-teacher conferences. Also, I interviewed the classroom teachers and adults involved in the children's organized activities. These interview data are not presented here.

7. Both schools had computer labs, art programs, and music programs, but Swan had many more resources and much higher average achievement scores. Graffiti and physical confrontations between students were common only at Lower Richmond. At these two sites and in Lawrenceville, white faculty predominated.

8. I located the black middle-class parents through social networks; the white poor families were located through flyers left at welfare offices and social service programs, and posted on telephone poles. Ten white poor families (only) were paid $25 per interview.

9. Of 19 families asked to participate in the intensive study, 7 declined (a response rate of 63 percent). I tried to balance the observational phase sample by gender, race, and class, and to "mix and match" the children on other characteristics, such as their behavior with peers, their relationships with extended family, and their parents' level of involvement in their education. The aim was to lessen the chance that observed differences in behavior would reflect unknown variables (e.g., church attendance or parents' participation at school). Last, I deliberately included two families (Irwins, Greeleys) who had some "middle-class" traits but who lived in a working-class and poor area, respectively. Including these unusual families seemed conceptually important for disentangling the influences of social class and environment (neighborhood).

10. I analyzed the data for the study as a whole in two ways. I coded themes from the interviews and used Folio Views software to help establish patterns. I also relied on reading the field notes, thinking about similarities and differences across families, searching for disconfirming evidence, and re-reading the field notes.

11. Recruitment to complete the sample was difficult as children needed to be a specific age, race, and class, and to be part of families who were willing to be observed. The white poor boy was recommended by a social service program manager; the black middle-class children were located through extended social networks of mine.

12. We did 12 to 14 observations of the Handlon and Carroll families before settling on the 20-visit pattern. In Alexander Williams's case, the visits occurred over a year. To observe unusual events (e.g., a family reunion), we sometimes went back after formal observations had ended.

13. Families developed preferences, favoring one fieldworker in a team over another. But these preferences were not stable across families, and the field notes did not differ dramatically between fieldworkers. Notes were much more similar than they were different.

14. Wright (1997) uses 12 categories in his neo-Marxist approach. Goldthorpe, a neo-Weberian, operationalizes his class schema at levels of aggregation ranging from 3 to 11 categories (Erikson and Goldthorpe 1993:38–39).

15. Here "poor" refers to the source of income (i.e., government assistance versus labor market) rather than the amount of income. Although lower class is more accurate than poor, it is widely perceived as pejorative. I might have used "underclass," but the literature has defined this term in racialized ways.

16. Dollar figures are from 1994–1995, unless otherwise noted. Income was not used to define class membership, but these data are available from the author.

17. Mr. and Ms. Williams disagreed about the value of their home; the figure here averages what each

reported in 1995. Housing prices in their region were lower—and continue to be lower today—than in many other parts of the country. Their property is now worth an estimated $175,000 to $200,000.

18. Alexander's mother goes by Christina Nile at work, but Mrs. Williams at church. Some other mothers' last names also differ from their children's. Here I assign all mothers the same last names as their children.

19. I contacted the Williams family through social networks after I was unable to recruit the black middle-class families who had participated in the classroom observation and interview phase. As a result, I do not have data from classroom observations or parent-teacher conferences for Alexander.

20. The Suzuki method is labor intensive. Students are required to listen to music about one hour per day. Also, both child and parent(s) are expected to practice daily and to attend every lesson together.

21. Hart and Risley (1995) reported a similar difference in speech patterns. In their sample, by about age three, children of professionals had larger vocabularies and spoke more utterances per hour than the *parents* of similarly aged children on welfare.

22. This section focuses primarily on the concerns of black parents. Whites, of course, also benefited from race relations, notably in the scattering of poor white families in working-class neighborhoods rather than being concentrated in dense settings with other poor families (Massey and Denton 1993).

23. Not all professionals accommodated children's participation. Regardless of these adults' overt attitudes, though, we routinely observed that middle-class mothers monitor and intervene in their children's interactions with professionals.

24. Ms. McAllister told me about this visit; we did not observe it. It is striking that she perceived only the black male fieldworker as being at risk.

25. Middle-class parents sometimes appeared slightly anxious during parent-teacher conferences, but overall, they spoke more and asked educators more questions than did working-class and poor parents.

26. The higher levels of institutional reports of child neglect, child abuse, and other family difficulties among poor families may reflect this group's greater vulnerability to institutional intervention (e.g., see L. Gordon 1989).

27. In 2002, a single sport could cost as much as $5,000 annually. Yearly league fees for ice hockey run to $2,700; equipment costs are high as well (Halbfinger 2002).

28. Middle-class adults do not live problem-free lives, but compared with the working class and poor, they have more varied occupational experiences and greater access to jobs with higher economic returns.

29. Many middle-class parents remarked that forcing a child to take piano lessons was wrong. Nevertheless, they continued to stress the importance of "exposure."

30. Similarly, whether concerted cultivation and the accomplishment of natural growth are new historical developments rather than modifications of earlier forms of childrearing cannot be determined from the study's findings. The "institutionalization of children's leisure" seems to be increasing (Corsaro 1997). Hays (1996) argues that families increasingly are "invaded" by the "logic of impersonal, competitive, contractual, commodified, efficient, profit-maximizing, self-interested relations" (p. 11). In addition to evidence of a new increase in children's organized activities (Sandberg and Hofferth 2001), none of the middle-class parents in the study reported having childhood schedules comparable to their children's. Change over time in parents' intervention in education and in the amount of reasoning in middle-class families also are difficult to determine accurately. Kohn and Schooler's (1983) study suggests little change with regard to reasoning, but other commentators insist there has been a rise in the amount of negotiating between parents and children (Chidekel 2002; Kropp 2001). Such debates can not be resolved without additional careful historical research.

31. The time-use differences we observed were part of the taken-for-granted aspects of daily life; they were generally unnoticed by family members. For example, the working-class Yanellis considered themselves "really busy" if they had one baseball game on Saturday and an extended family gathering on Sunday. The Tallingers and other middle-class families would have considered this a slow weekend.

32. These findings are compatible with others showing children as aware of race at relatively early ages (Van Ausdale and Feagin 1996). At the two sites, girls often played in racially segregated groups during recess; boys tended to play in racially integrated groups.

CHAPTER 5

Race, Ethnicity, and Families

When one thinks about globalization, the following images come to mind: instant communication around the world through the Internet; factories overseas producing clothing, electronics, and automobiles to be sold to Americans; and executives of multinational corporations jetting across oceans. But there is another side to globalization: the movement of people across countries and continents. Migration is increasing worldwide as individuals, aware of opportunities elsewhere, migrate to the wealthier countries. Migration streams are often racially or ethnically specific: Latin Americans to the United States, South and Southeast Asians to the Middle East, Turks and North Africans to Western Europe. In the past, most migrants were men seeking jobs as laborers. For the past few decades, however, the number of migrants who are women has increased. In particular, the increasing demand in wealthier countries for domestic services (nannies, cleaners, gardeners), and for entertainment and sometimes sex work as well, has produced a large stream of women who migrate from Latin America to the United States and from Southeast Asia to wealthier Asian countries and the United States.

As a result, the occupation of domestic servant, once thought to be a thing of the past, is now making a comeback due to the increased demand from harried two-earner families in the United States and other wealthy countries. Fifty years ago, it was common for African American women to work as domestics in the United States (in fact, until 1970 that was the largest occupational group for African American women). But as opportunities for African American women began to improve in the 1960s, they abandoned domestic work for higher-paying, and less degrading, work. Into the void have stepped Latin American and Asian immigrant women who will work for low wages.

What researchers have discovered is that a substantial number of the immigrant domestic workers leave their children in their home countries. In other words, while these immigrants are caring for American children, someone else is caring for their children. The result is a phenomenon that Pierrette Hondagneu-Sotelo and Ernestine Avila, in the first selection in this chapter, call "transnational motherhood." In the Los Angeles area, which they studied, this phenomenon mainly involves Latina immigrants from Mexico,

Guatemala, and El Salvador. In this selection, the authors explore how these transnational mothers conceive of motherhood.

The family lives of ethnic groups of long standing in the United States also have been much discussed. In 1903, the great African American sociologist W. E. B. DuBois wrote in his book *The Souls of Black Folk* that "the problem of the twentieth century is the problem of the color line—the relation of the darker to the lighter races of men in Asia and Africa, in America, and the islands of the sea." Nearly a century later, the "problem" of color still looms large in discussions of American society, including family life. DuBois was referring to the difference between African Americans and Americans of European descent. Although that black/white distinction is still a central part of American life, there are other "colors" now. The largest of the newer groups is composed of people who speak Spanish and mostly trace their ancestry through Latin America. In the American political discourse, they are increasingly lumped together as "Hispanics," even though there are sharp differences among the major Hispanic groups. Another rapidly growing group is composed of people who are even more diverse than Hispanics: immigrants from

the huge expanse of the globe running from South Asia (e.g., India, Pakistan) to Southeast Asia (e.g., Indonesia, Thailand), and on to East Asia (e.g, China, Japan). They do not share a language or common physical features, and yet in the United States they are lumped together in the category "Asian."

With so many immigrants arriving (the current rate of immigration is higher than at any time since the early decades of the twentieth century), the question arises of whether they will marry outside their group. Earlier in American history, intermarriage among major ethnic and racial groups was outlawed in most states. Even as late as 1967, 15 states had laws forbidding marriage between whites and nonwhites. But both the law and American public opinion have changed. In the second selection in this chapter, Zhenchao Qian analyzes trends in intermarriage among blacks, Hispanics, Asians, American Indians, and non-Hispanic whites. He reports that intermarriage is on the rise, although rates for blacks are substantially lower than for other nonwhite groups. In fact, intermarriage is so common among young Asians, Hispanics, and American Indians that one wonders whether these groups will still have their distinctive ethnicities a generation or two from now.

READING 5-1

"I'm Here, but I'm There"

The Meanings of Latina Transnational Motherhood

Pierrette Hondagneu-Sotelo

Ernestine Avila

While mothering is generally understood as practice that involves the preservation, nurturance, and training of children for adult life (Ruddick 1989), there are many contemporary variants distinguished by race, class, and culture (Collins 1994; Dill 1988, 1994; Glenn 1994). Latina immigrant women who work and reside in the United States while their children remain in their countries of origin constitute one variation in the organizational arrangements, meanings, and priorities of motherhood. We call this arrangement "transnational motherhood," and we explore how the meanings of motherhood are rearranged to accommodate these spatial and temporal separations. In the United States, there is a long legacy of Caribbean women and African American women from the South, leaving their children "back home" to seek work in the North. Since the early 1980's, thousands of Central American women, and increasing numbers of Mexican women, have migrated to the United States in search of jobs, many of them leaving their children behind with grandmothers, with other female kin, with the children's fathers, and sometimes with paid caregivers. In some cases, the separations of time and distance are substantial; 10 years may elapse before women are reunited with their children. In this article we confine our analysis to Latina

Pierrette Hondagneu-Sotelo and Ernestine Avila, "'I'm Here, but I'm There': The Meanings of Latina Transnational Motherhood," *Gender and Society*, Vol. 11, No. 5 (October 1997), pp. 548–549 and 553–570. Copyright © 1997 Sociologists for Women in Society. Reprinted by permission of Sage Publications, Inc.

transnational mothers currently employed in Los Angeles in paid domestic work, one of the most gendered and racialized occupations.[1] We examine how their meanings of motherhood shift in relation to the structures of late-20th-century global capitalism.

Motherhood is not biologically predetermined in any fixed way but is historically and socially constructed. Many factors set the stage for transnational motherhood. These factors include labor demand for Latina immigrant women in the United States, particularly in paid domestic work; civil war, national economic crises, and particular development strategies, along with tenuous and scarce job opportunities for women and men in Mexico and Central America; and the subsequent increasing numbers of female-headed households (although many transnational mothers are married). More interesting to us than the macro determinants of transnational motherhood, however, is the forging of new arrangements and meanings of motherhood.

Central American and Mexican women who leave their young children "back home" and come to the United States in search of employment are in the process of actively, if not voluntarily, building alternative constructions of motherhood. Transnational motherhood contradicts both dominant U.S., White, middle-class models of motherhood, and most Latina ideological notions of motherhood. On the cusp of the millennium, transnational mothers and their families are blazing new terrain, spanning national borders, and improvising strategies for mothering. It is a brave odyssey, but one with deep costs. . . .

DESCRIPTION OF RESEARCH

Materials for this article draw from a larger study of paid domestic work in Los Angeles County and from interviews conducted in adjacent Riverside County. The materials include in-depth interviews, a survey, and ethnographic fieldwork. We had not initially anticipated studying women who live and work apart from their children but serendipitously stumbled on this theme in the course of our research.

For this reading, we draw primarily on tape-recorded and fully transcribed interviews with 26 women who work as house cleaners and as live-out or live-in nanny-housekeepers. Of these 26 women, 8 lived apart from their children to accommodate their migration and work arrangements, but other respondents also spoke poignantly about their views and experiences with mothering, and we draw on these materials as well. We also draw, to a lesser extent, on in-depth, fully transcribed interviews with domestic agency personnel. All of the interview respondents were located through informal snowball sampling. The domestic workers interviewed are all from Mexico, El Salvador, and Guatemala, but they are diverse in terms of demographic characteristics (such as education, civil status, and children), immigration (length of time in the United States, access to legal papers), and other job-related characteristics (English language skills, driver's license, cardiopulmonary resuscitation [CPR] training).

While the interviews provide close-up information about women's experiences and views of mothering, a survey administered to 153 paid domestic workers in Los Angeles provides some indicator of how widespread these transnational arrangements are among paid domestic workers. Because no one knows the total universe of paid domestic workers—many of whom lack legal papers and work in the informal sector where census data are not reliable—we drew a non-random sample in three types of sites located in or near affluent areas spanning from the west side of Los Angeles to the Hollywood area. We solicited respondents at evening ESL (English as a second language) classes, at public parks where nannies and housekeepers congregate with the children they care for in the midmorning hours, and we went to bus kiosks on Mondays and Tuesdays during the early morning hours (7:00 A.M. to 9:00 A.M.) when many domestic workers, including live-in workers, are traveling

to their places of employment. While we refrained from conducting the survey in places where only certain types of domestic workers might be found (the employment agencies, or organizations of domestic workers), going to the bus stops, public parks, and ESL classes means that we undersampled domestic workers with access to private cars, driver's licenses, and good English skills. In short, we undersampled women who are earning at the higher end of the occupation.

The study also draws on ethnographic field research conducted in public parks, buses, private homes, a domestic workers' association, and the waiting room of a domestic employment agency. A tape-recorded group discussion with about 15 women—including several who had their children in their countries of origin—in the employment agency waiting room also informs the study. Nearly all of the in-depth interviews, structured survey interviews, and fieldwork were conducted in Spanish. The climate of fear produced by California voters' passage of anti-immigrant legislation in November 1994 perhaps dissuaded some potential respondents from participating in the study, but more important in shaping the interviews is the deeply felt pain expressed by the respondents. The interview transcripts include tearful segments in which the women recounted the daily indignities of their jobs and the raw pain provoked by the forced separation from their young children.

TRANSNATIONAL MOTHERHOOD AND PAID DOMESTIC WORK

Just how widespread are transnational motherhood arrangements in paid domestic work? Of the 153 domestic workers surveyed, 75 percent had children. Contrary to the images of Latina immigrant women as breeders with large families—a dominant image used in the campaign to pass California's Proposition 187—about half (47 percent) of these women have

TABLE 5.1			

DOMESTIC WORKERS: WAGES, HOURS WORKED AND CHILDREN'S COUNTRY OF RESIDENCE

	Live-ins (*n* = 30)	Live-outs (*n* = 64)	House cleaners (*n* = 59)
Mean hourly wage	$3.79	$5.90	$9.40
Mean hours worked per week	64	35	23
Domestic workers with children	(*n* = 16)	(*n* = 53)	(*n* = 45)
All children in the United States (%)	18	58	76
At least one child "back home"	82	42	24

only one or two children. More significant for our purposes is this finding: Forty percent of the women with children have at least one of their children "back home" in their country of origin.

Transnational motherhood arrangements are not exclusive to paid domestic work, but there are particular features about the way domestic work is organized that encourage temporal and spatial separations of a mother-employee and her children. Historically and in the contemporary period, paid domestic workers have had to limit or forfeit primary care of their families and homes to earn income by providing primary care to the families and homes of employers, who are privileged by race and class (Glenn 1986; Rollins 1985; Romero 1992). Paid domestic work is organized in various ways, and there is a clear relationship between the type of job arrangement women have and the likelihood of experiencing transnational family arrangements with their children. To understand the variations, it is necessary to explain how the employment is organized. Although there are variations within categories, we find it useful to employ a tripartite taxonomy of paid domestic work arrangements. This includes live-in and live-out nanny-housekeeper jobs, and weekly housecleaning jobs.

Weekly house cleaners clean different houses on different days according to what Romero (1992) calls modernized "job work" arrangements. These contractual-like employee-employer relations often resemble those between customer and vendor, and they allow employees a degree of autonomy and scheduling flexibility. Weekly employees are generally paid a flat fee, and they work shorter hours and earn considerably higher hourly rates than do live-in or live-out domestic workers. By contrast, live-in domestic workers work and live in isolation from their own families and communities, sometimes in arrangements with feudal remnants (Glenn 1986). There are often no hourly parameters to their jobs, and as our survey results show, most live-in workers in Los Angeles earn below minimum wage. Live-out domestic workers also usually work as combination nanny-housekeepers, generally working for one household, but contrary to live-ins, they enter daily and return to their own home in the evening. Because of this, live-out workers better resemble industrial wage workers (Glenn 1986).

Live-in jobs are the least compatible with conventional mothering responsibilities. Only about half (16 out of 30) of live-ins surveyed have children, while 83 percent (53 out of 64) of live-outs and 77 percent (45 out of 59) of house cleaners do. As Table 5.1 shows, 82 percent of live-ins with children have at least one of their children in their country of origin. It is very difficult to work a live-in job when your children are in the United States. Employers who hire live-in workers do so because they generally want employees for jobs that may require round-the-clock service. As one owner of a domestic employment agency put it,

> They (employers) want a live-in to have somebody at their beck and call. They want the hours that are most difficult for them covered, which is like six thirty in the morning 'till eight when the kids go to school, and four to seven when the kids are home, and it's homework, bath, and dinner.

According to our survey, live-ins work an average of 64 hours per week. The best live-in worker, from an employer's perspective, is one without daily family obligations of her own. The workweek may consist of six very long workdays. These may span from dawn to midnight and may include overnight responsibilities with sleepless or sick children, making it virtually impossible for live-in workers to sustain daily contact with their own families. Although some employers do allow for their employees' children to live in as well (Romero 1996), this is rare. When it does occur, it is often fraught with special problems, and we discuss these in a subsequent section of this article. In fact, minimal family and mothering obligations are an informal job placement criterion for live-in workers. Many of the agencies specializing in the placement of live-in nanny-housekeepers will not even refer a woman who has children in Los Angeles to interviews for live-in jobs. As one agency owner explained, "As a policy here, we will not knowingly place a nanny in a live-in job if she has young kids here." A job seeker in an employment agency waiting room acknowledged that she understood this job criterion more broadly, "You can't have a family, you can't have anyone (if you want a live-in job)."

The subminimum pay and the long hours for live-in workers also make it very difficult for these workers to have their children in the United States. Some live-in workers who have children in the same city as their place of employment hire their own nanny-housekeeper—often a much younger, female relative—to provide daily care for their children, as did Patricia, one of the interview respondents whom we discuss later in this article. Most live-ins, however, cannot afford this alternative; 93 percent of the live-ins surveyed earn below minimum wage (then $4.25 per hour). Many live-in workers cannot afford to bring their children to Los Angeles, but once their children are in the same city, most women try to leave live-in work to live with their children.

At the other end of the spectrum are the house cleaners that we surveyed, who earn substantially higher wages than live-ins (averaging $9.46 per hour as opposed to $3.79) and who work fewer hours per week than live-ins (23 as opposed to 64). We suspect that many house cleaners in Los Angeles make even higher earnings and work more hours per week, because we know that the survey undersampled women who drive their own cars to work and who speak English. The survey suggests that house cleaners appear to be the least likely to experience transnational spatial and temporal separations from their children.

Financial resources and job terms enhance house cleaners' abilities to bring their children to the United States. Weekly housecleaning is not a bottom-of-the-barrel job but rather an achievement. Breaking into housecleaning work is difficult because an employee needs to locate and secure several different employers. For this reason, relatively well-established women with more years of experience in the United States, who speak some English, who have a car, and who have job references predominate in weekly housecleaning. Women who are better established in the United States are also more likely to have their children here. The terms of weekly housecleaning employment—particularly the relatively fewer hours worked per week, scheduling flexibility, and relatively higher wages—allow them to live with, and care for, their children. So, it is not surprising that 76 percent of house cleaners who are mothers have their children in the United States.

Compared with live-ins and weekly cleaners, live-out nanny-housekeepers are at an intermediate level with respect to the likelihood of transnational motherhood. Forty-two percent of the live-out nanny-housekeepers who are mothers reported having at least one of their children in their country of origin. Live-out domestic workers, according to the survey, earn $5.90 per hour and work an average workweek of 35 hours. Their lower earnings, more regimented schedules, and longer workweeks than house cleaners, but higher earnings, shorter hours, and more scheduling flexibility than live-ins explain their intermediate incidence of transnational motherhood.

The Meanings of Transnational Motherhood

How do women transform the meaning of motherhood to fit immigration and employment? Being a transnational mother means more than being the mother to children raised in another country. It means forsaking deeply felt beliefs that biological mothers should raise their own children, and replacing that belief with new definitions of motherhood. The ideal of biological mothers raising their own children is widely held but is also widely broken at both ends of the class spectrum. Wealthy elites have always relied on others—nannies, governesses, and boarding schools—to raise their children (Wrigley 1995), while poor, urban families often rely on kin and "other mothers" (Collins 1991).

In Latin America, in large, peasant families, the eldest daughters are often in care of the daily care of the younger children, and in situations of extreme poverty, children as young as 5 or 6 may be loaned or hired out to well-to-do families as "child-servants," sometimes called *criadas* (Gill 1994).[2] A middle-aged Mexican woman that we interviewed, now a weekly house cleaner, homeowner, and mother of five children, recalled her own experience as a child-servant in Mexico: "I started working in a house when I was 8 . . . they hardly let me eat any food. . . . It was terrible, but I had to work to help my mother with the rent." This recollection of her childhood experiences reminds us how our contemporary notions of motherhood

are historically and socially circumscribed, and also correspond to the meanings we assign to childhood (Zelizer 1994).

This example also underlines how the expectation on the child to help financially support her mother required daily spatial and temporal separations of mother and child. There are, in fact, many transgressions of the mother-child symbiosis in practice—large families where older daughters care for younger siblings, child-servants who at an early age leave their mothers, children raised by paid nannies and other caregivers, and mothers who leave young children to seek employment—but these are fluid enough to sustain ideological adherence to the prescription that children should be raised exclusively by biological mothers. Long-term physical and temporal separation disrupts this notion. Transnational mothering radically rearranges mother-child interactions and requires a concomitant radical reshaping of the meanings and definitions of appropriate mothering.

Transnational mothers distinguish their version of motherhood from estrangement, child abandonment, or disowning. A youthful Salvadoran woman at the domestic employment waiting room reported that she had not seen her two eldest boys, now ages 14 and 15 and under the care of her own mother in El Salvador, since they were toddlers. Yet, she made it clear that this was different from putting a child up for adoption, a practice that she viewed negatively, as a form of child abandonment. Although she had been physically separated from her boys for more than a decade, she maintained her mothering ties and financial obligations to them by regularly sending home money. The exchange of letters, photos, and phone calls also helped to sustain the connection. Her physical absence did not signify emotional absence from her children. Another woman who remains intimately involved in the lives of her two daughters, now ages 17 and 21 in El Salvador, succinctly summed up this stance when she said, "I'm here, but I'm there." Over the phone, and through letters, she regularly reminds her daughters to take their vitamins, to never go to bed or to school on an empty stomach, and to use protection from pregnancy and sexually transmitted diseases if they engage in sexual relations with their boyfriends.

Transnational mothers fully understand and explain the conditions that prompt their situations. In particular, many Central American women recognize that the gendered employment demand in Los Angeles has produced transnational motherhood arrangements. These new mothering arrangements, they acknowledge, take shape despite strong beliefs that biological mothers should care for their own children. Emelia, a 49-year-old woman who left her five children in Guatemala nine years ago to join her husband in Los Angeles, explained this changing relationship between family arrangements, migration, and job demand:

> One supposes that the mother must care for the children. A mother cannot so easily throw her children aside. So, in all families, the decision is that the man comes (to the U.S.) first. But now, since the man cannot find work here so easily, the woman comes first. Recently, women have been coming and the men staying.

A steady demand for live-in housekeepers means that Central American women may arrive in Los Angeles on a Friday and begin working Monday at a live-in job that provides at least some minimal accommodations. Meanwhile, her male counterpart may spend weeks or months before securing even casual day laborer jobs. While Emelia, formerly a homemaker who previously earned income in Guatemala by baking cakes and pastries in her home, expressed pain and sadness at not being with her children as they grew, she was also proud of her accomplishments. "My children," she stated, "recognize what I have been able to do for them."

Most transnational mothers, like many other immigrant workers, come to the United States with the intention to stay for a finite period of time, until they can pay off bills or raise the money for an investment in a house, their children's education, or a small business. Some of these women return to their countries of origin, but many stay. As time passes, and as their stays grow longer, some of the women eventually bring some or all of their children. Other women who stay at their U.S. jobs are adamant that they do not wish for their children to traverse the multiple hazards of adolescence in U.S. cities or to repeat the job experiences they themselves have had in the United States. One Salvadoran woman in the waiting room at the domestic employment agency—whose children had been raised on earnings predicated on her separation from them—put it this way:

> I've been here 19 years, I've got my legal papers and everything. But I'd have to be crazy to bring my children here. All of them have studied for a career, so why would I bring them here? To bus tables and earn minimum wage? So they won't have enough money for bus fare or food?

Who Is Taking Care of the Nanny's Children?

Transnational Central American and Mexican mothers may rely on various people to care for their children's daily, round-the-clock needs, but they prefer a close relative. The "other mothers" on which Latinas rely include their own mothers, *comadres* (co-godmothers) and other female kin, the children's fathers, and paid caregivers. Reliance on grandmothers and comadres for shared mothering is well established in Latina culture, and it is a practice that signifies a more collectivist, shared approach to mothering in contrast to a more individualistic, Anglo-American approach (Griswold del Castillo 1984; Segura and Pierce 1993). Perhaps this cultural legacy facilitates the emergence of transnational motherhood.

Transnational mothers express a strong preference for their own biological mother to serve as the primary caregiver. Here, the violation of the cultural preference for the biological mother is rehabilitated by reliance on the biological grandmother or by reliance on the ceremonially bound comadres. Clemencia, for example, left her three young children behind in Mexico, each with their respective *madrina,* or godmother.

Emelia left her five children, then ranging in ages from 6 to 16, under the care of her mother and sister in Guatemala. As she spoke of the hardships faced by transnational mothers, she counted herself among the fortunate ones who did not need to leave the children alone with paid caregivers:

> One's mother is the only one who can really and truly care for your children. No one else can. . . . Women who aren't able to leave their children with their mother or with someone very special, they'll wire money to Guatemala and the people (caregivers) don't feed the children well. They don't buy the children clothes the mother would want. They take the money and the children suffer a lot.

Both Central American and Mexican women stated preferences for grandmothers as the ideal caregivers in situations that mandated the absence of the children's biological mother. These preferences seem to grow out of strategic availability, but these preferences assume cultural mandates. Velia, a Mexicana who hailed from the border town of Mexicali, improvised an employment strategy whereby she annually sent her three elementary school-age children to her mother in Mexicali for the summer vacation months. This allowed Velia, a single mother, to intensify her housecleaning jobs and save money on day care. But she also insisted that "if my children were with the woman next door (who babysits), I'd worry if they were eating well, or about men (coming to harass the girls). Having them with my mother allows me to work in peace." Another woman specified more narrowly, insisting that only maternal grandmothers could provide adequate caregiving. In a conversation in a park, a Salvadoran woman offered that a biological mother's mother was the one best suited to truly love and care for a child in the biological mother's absence. According to her,

not even the paternal grandmother could be trusted to provide proper nurturance and care. Another Salvadoran woman, Maria, left her two daughters, then 14 and 17, at their paternal grandmother's home, but before departing for the United States, she trained her daughters to become self-sufficient in cooking, marketing, and budgeting money. Although she believes the paternal grandmother loves the girls, she did not trust the paternal grandmother enough to cook or administer the money that she would send her daughters.

Another variation in the preference for a biological relative as a caregiver is captured by the arrangement of Patricia, a 30-year-old Mexicana who came to the United States as a child and was working as a live-in, caring for an infant in one of southern California's affluent coastal residential areas. Her arrangement was different, as her daughters were all born, raised, and residing in the United States, but she lived apart from them during weekdays because of her live-in job. Her three daughters, ages 1½, 6, and 11, stayed at their apartment near downtown Los Angeles under the care of their father and a paid nanny-housekeeper, Patricia's teenage cousin. Her paid caregiver was not an especially close relative, but she rationalized this arrangement by emphasizing that her husband, the girls' father, and therefore a biological relative, was with them during the week.

> Whenever I've worked like this, I've always had a person in charge of them also working as a live-in. She sleeps here the five days, but when my husband arrives he takes responsibility for them. . . . When my husband arrives (from work) she (cousin/paid caregiver) goes to English class and he takes charge of the girls.

And another woman who did not have children of her own but who had worked as a nanny for her aunt stated that "as Hispanas, we don't believe in bringing someone else in to care for our children." Again, the biological ties help sanction the shared child care arrangement.

New family fissures emerge for the transnational mother as she negotiates various aspects of the arrangement with her children, and with the "other mother" who provides daily care and supervision for the children. Any impulse to romanticize transnational motherhood is tempered by the sadness with which the women related their experiences and by the problems they sometimes encounter with their children and caregivers. A primary worry among transnational mothers is that their children are being neglected or abused in their absence. While there is a long legacy of child servants being mistreated and physically beaten in Latin America, transnational mothers also worry that their own paid caregivers will harm or neglect their children. They worry that their children may not receive proper nourishment, schooling and educational support, and moral guidance. They may remain unsure as to whether their children are receiving the full financial support they send home. In some cases, their concerns are intensified by the eldest child or a nearby relative who is able to monitor and report the caregiver's transgression to the transnational mother.

Transnational mothers engage in emotion work and financial compensation to maintain a smoothly functioning relationship with the children's daily caregiver. Their efforts are not always successful, and when problems arise, they may return to visit if they can afford to do so. After not seeing her four children for seven years, Carolina abruptly quit her nanny job and returned to Guatemala in the spring of 1996 because she was concerned about one adolescent daughter's rebelliousness and about her mother-in-law's failing health. Carolina's husband remained in Los Angeles, and she was expected to return. Emelia, whose children were cared for by her mother and sister, with the assistance of paid caregivers, regularly responded to her sister's reminders to send gifts, clothing, and small amounts of money to the paid caregivers. "If they are taking care of my children," she explained, "then I have to show my gratitude."

Some of these actions are instrumental. Transnational mothers know that they may increase the likelihood of their children receiving adequate care if they appropriately remunerate the caregivers and treat them with the consideration their work requires. In fact, they often express astonishment that their own Anglo employers fail to recognize this in relation to the nanny-housekeeper work that they perform. Some of the expressions of gratitude and gifts that they send to their children's caregivers appear to be genuinely disinterested and enhanced by the transnational mothers' empathy arising out of their own similiar job circumstances. A Honduran woman, a former biology teacher, who had left her four sons with a paid caregiver, maintained that the treatment of nannies and housekeepers was much better in Honduras than in the United States, in part, because of different approaches to mothering:

> We're very different back there. . . . We treat them (domestic workers) with a lot of affection and respect, and when they are taking care of our kids, even more so. The *Americana,* she is very egotistical. When the nanny loves her children, she gets jealous. Not us. We are appreciative when someone loves our children, and bathes, dresses, and feeds them as though they were their own.

These comments are clearly informed by the respondent's prior class status, as well as her simultaneous position as the employer of a paid nanny-housekeeper in Honduras and as a temporarily unemployed nanny-housekeeper in the United States. (She had been fired from her nanny-housekeeper job for not showing up on Memorial Day, which she erroneously believed was a work holiday.) Still, her comments underline the importance of showing appreciation and gratitude to the caregiver, in part, for the sake of the children's well-being.

Transnational mothers also worry about whether their children will get into trouble during adolescence or if they will transfer their allegiance and affection to the "other mother."

In general, transnational mothers, like African American mothers who leave their children in the South to work up North (Stack and Burton 1994), believe that the person who cares for the children has the right to discipline. But when adolescent youths are paired with elderly grandmothers, or ineffective disciplinary figures, the mothers may need to intervene. Preadolescent and adolescent children who show signs of rebelliousness may be brought north because they are deemed unmanageable by their grandmothers or paid caregivers. Alternatively, teens who are in California may be sent back in hope that it will straighten them out, a practice that has resulted in the migration of Los Angeles–based delinquent youth gangs to Mexican and Central American towns. Another danger is that the child who has grown up without the transnational mother's presence may no longer respond to her authority. One woman at the domestic employment agency, who had recently brought her adolescent son to join her in California, reported that she had seen him at a bus stop, headed for the beach. When she demanded to know where he was going, he said something to the effect of "and who are you to tell me what to do?" After a verbal confrontation at the bus kiosk, she handed him $10. Perhaps the mother hoped that money will be a way to show caring and to advance a claim to parental authority.

Motherhood and Breadwinning

Milk, shoes, and schooling—these are the currency of transnational motherhood. Providing for children's sustenance, protecting their current well-being, and preparing them for the future are widely shared concerns of motherhood. Central American and Mexican women involved in transnational mothering attempt to ensure the present and future well-being of their children through U.S. wage earning, and as we have seen, this requires long-term physical separation from their children.

For these women, the meanings of motherhood do not appear to be in a liminal stage. That

is, they do not appear to be making a linear progression from a way of motherhood that involves daily, face-to-face caregiving toward one that is defined primarily through breadwinning. Rather than replacing caregiving with breadwinning definitions of motherhood, they appear to be expanding their definitions of motherhood to encompass breadwinning that may require long-term physical separations. For these women, a core belief is that they can best fulfill traditional caregiving responsibilities through income earning in the United States while their children remain "back home."

Transnational mothers continue to state that caregiving is a defining feature of their mothering experiences. They wish to provide their children with better nutrition, clothing, and schooling, and most of them are able to purchase these items with dollars earned in the United States. They recognize, however, that their transnational relationships incur painful costs. Transnational mothers worry about some of the negative effects on their children, but they also experience the absence of domestic family life as a deeply personal loss. Transnational mothers who primarily identified as homemakers before coming to the United States identified the loss of daily contact with family as a sacrifice ventured to financially support the children. As Emelia, who had previously earned some income by baking pastries and doing catering from her home in Guatemala, reflected,

> The money (earned in the U.S.) is worth five times more in Guatemala. My oldest daughter was then 16, and my youngest was 6 (when I left). Ay, it's terrible, but that's what happens to most women (transnational mothers) who are here. You sacrifice your family life (for labor migration).

Similarly, Carolina used the word *sacrifice* when discussing her family arrangement, claiming that her children "tell me that they appreciate us (parents), and the sacrifice that their papa and mama make for them. That is what they say."

The daily indignities of paid domestic work—low pay, subtle humiliations, not enough food to eat, invisibility (Glenn 1986; Rollins 1985; Romero 1992)—mean that transnational mothers are not only stretching their U.S.-earned dollars further by sending the money back home but also, by leaving the children behind, they are providing special protection from the discrimination the children might receive in the United States. Gladys, who had four of her five children in El Salvador, acknowledged that her U.S. dollars went further in El Salvador. Although she missed seeing those four children grow up, she felt that in some ways, she had spared them the indignities to which she had exposed her youngest daughter, whom she brought to the United States at age 4 in 1988. Although her live-in employer had allowed the 4-year-old to join the family residence, Gladys tearfully recalled how that employer had initially quarantined her daughter, insisting on seeing vaccination papers before allowing the girl to play with the employer's children. "I had to battle, really struggle," she recalled, "just to get enough food for her (to eat)." For Gladys, being together with her youngest daughter in the employer's home had entailed new emotional costs.

Patricia, the mother who was apart from her children only during the weekdays when she lived in with her employer, put forth an elastic definition of motherhood, one that included both meeting financial obligations and spending time with the children. Although her job involves different scheduling than most employed mothers, she shares views similar to those held by many working mothers:

> It's something you have to do, because you can't just stay seated at home because the bills accumulate and you have to find a way. . . . I applied at many different places for work, like hospitals, as a receptionist—due to the experience I've had with computers working in shipping and receiving, things like that, but they never called me. . . . One person can't pay all the bills.

Patricia emphasized that she believes motherhood also involves making an effort to spend time with the children. According to this criterion, she explained, most employers were deficient, while she was compliant. During the middle of the week, she explained, "I invent something, some excuse for her (the employer) to let me come home, even if I have to bring the (employer's) baby here with me . . . just to spend time with my kids."

Transnational mothers echoed these sentiments. Maria Elena, for example, whose 13-year-old son resided with his father in Mexico after she lost a custody battle, insisted that motherhood did not consist of only breadwinning: "You can't give love through money." According to Maria Elena, motherhood required an emotional presence and communication with a child. Like other transnational mothers, she explained how she maintained this connection despite the long-term geographic distance: "I came here, but we're not apart. We talk (by telephone). . . . I know (through telephone conversations) when my son is fine. I can tell when he is sad by the way he speaks." Like employed mothers everywhere, she insisted on a definition of motherhood that emphasized quality rather than quantity of time spent with the child: "I don't think that a good mother is one who is with her children at all times. . . . It's the quality of time spent with the child." She spoke these words tearfully, reflecting the trauma of losing a custody battle with her ex-husband. Gladys also stated that being a mother involves both bread-winning and providing direction and guidance. "It's not just feeding them, or buying clothes for them. It's also educating them, preparing them to make good choices so they'll have a better future."

Transnational mothers seek to mesh caregiving and guidance with breadwinning. While breadwinning may require their long-term and long-distance separations from their children, they attempt to sustain family connections by showing emotional ties through letters, phone calls, and money sent home. If at all financially and logistically possible, they try to travel home to visit their children. They maintain their mothering responsibilities not only by earning money for their children's livelihood but also by communicating and advising across national borders, and across the boundaries that separate their children's place of residence from their own places of employment and residence.

Bonding with the Employers' Kids and Critiques of "Americana" Mothers

Some nanny-housekeepers develop very strong ties of affection with the children they care for during long workweeks. It is not unusual for nanny-housekeepers to be alone with these children during the workweek, with no one else with whom to talk or interact. The nannies, however, develop close emotional ties selectively, with some children, but not with others. For nanny-housekeepers who are transnational mothers, the loving daily caregiving that they cannot express for their own children is sometimes transferred to their employers' children. Carolina, a Guatemalan woman with four children between the ages of 10 and 14 back home, maintained that she tried to treat the employers' children with the same affection that she had for her own children "because if you do not feel affection for children, you are not able to care for them well." When interviewed, however, she was caring for 2-year-old triplets—for whom she expressed very little affection—but she recalled very longingly her fond feelings for a child at her last job, a child who vividly reminded her of her daughter, who was about the same age:

> When I saw that the young girl was lacking in affection, I began to get close to her and I saw that she appreciated that I would touch her, give her a kiss on the cheek. . . .
>
> And then I felt consoled too, because I had someone to give love to. But, I would imagine that she was my daughter, ah? And then I would give pure love to her, and that brought her closer to me.

Another nanny-housekeeper recalled a little girl for whom she had developed strong bonds of affection, laughingly imitating how the preschooler, who could not pronounce the "f" sound, would say "you hurt my peelings, but I don't want to pight."

Other nanny-housekeepers reflected that painful experiences with abrupt job terminations had taught them not to transfer mother love to the children of their employers. Some of these women reported that they now remained very measured and guarded in their emotional closeness with the employers' children, so that they could protect themselves for the moment when that relationship might be abruptly severed.

> I love these children, but now I stop myself from becoming too close. Before, when my own children weren't here (in the United States), I gave all my love to the children I cared for (then toddler twins). That was my recompensation (for not being with my children). When the job ended, I hurt so much. I can't let that happen again.

> I love them, but not like they were my own children because they are not! They are not my kids! Because if I get to love them, and then I go, then I'm going to suffer like I did the last time. I don't want that.

Not all nanny-housekeepers bond tightly with the employers' children, but most of them are critical of what they perceive as the employers' neglectful parenting and mothering. Typically, they blame biological mothers (their employers) for substandard parenting. Carolina recalled advising the mother of the above-mentioned little girl, who reminded her of her own child, that the girl needed to receive more affection from her mother, whom she perceived as self-absorbed with physical fitness regimes. Carolina had also advised other employers on disciplining their children. Patricia also spoke adamantly on this topic, and she recalled with satisfaction that when she had advised her current employer to spend more than 15 minutes a day with the baby, the employer had been reduced to tears. By comparison to her employer's mothering, Patricia cited her own perseverance in going out of her way to visit her children during the week:

> If you really love your kids, you look for the time, you make time to spend with your kids. . . . I work all week and for some reason I make excuses for her (employer) to let me come (home) . . . . just to spend time with my kids.

Her rhetoric of comparative mothering is also inspired by the critique that many nanny-housekeepers have of female employers who may be out of the labor force but who employ nannies and hence do not spend time with their children.

> I love my kids, they don't. It's just like, excuse the word, shitting kids . . . . What they prefer is to go to the salon, get their nails done, you know, go shopping, things like that. Even if they're home all day, they don't want to spend time with the kids because they're paying somebody to do that for them.

Curiously, she spoke as though her female employer is a wealthy woman of leisure, but in fact, both her current and past female employers are wealthy business executives who work long hours. Perhaps at this distance on the class spectrum, all class and racially privileged mothers look alike. "I work my butt off to get what I have," she observed, "and they don't have to work that much."

In some ways, transnational mothers who work as nanny-housekeepers cling to a more sentimentalized view of the employers' children than of their own. This strategy allows them to critique their employers, especially homemakers of privilege who are occupied with neither employment nor daily caregiving for their children. The Latina nannies appear to endorse motherhood as a full-time vocation in contexts of sufficient financial resources, but in contexts of financial hardship such as their own, they advocate more elastic definitions of motherhood, including forms that may include long spatial and temporal separations of mother and children.

As observers of late-20th-century U.S. families (Skolnick 1991; Stacey 1996) have noted, we live in an era wherein no one normative family arrangement predominates. Just as no one type of mothering unequivocally prevails in the White middle class, no singular mothering arrangement prevails among Latina immigrant women. In fact, the exigencies of contemporary immigration seem to multiply the variety of mothering arrangements. Through our research with Latina immigrant women who work as nannies, housekeepers, and house cleaners, we have encountered a broad range of mothering arrangements. Some Latinas migrate to the United States without their children to establish employment, and after some stability has been achieved, they may send for their children or they may work for a while to save money, and then return to their countries of origin. Other Latinas migrate and may postpone having children until they are financially established. Still others arrive with their children and may search for employment that allows them to live together with their children, and other Latinas may have sufficient financial support—from their husbands or kin—to stay home full-time with their children.

In the absence of a universal or at least widely shared mothering arrangement, there is tremendous uncertainty about what constitutes "good mothering," and transnational mothers must work hard to defend their choices. Some Latina nannies who have their children with them in the United States condemn transnational mothers as "bad women." One interview respondent, who was able to take her young daughter to work with her, claimed that she could never leave her daughter. For this woman, transnational mothers were not only bad mothers but also nannies who could not be trusted to adequately care for other people's children. As she said of an acquaintance, "This woman left her children (in Honduras) . . . she was taking care (of other people's children), and I said, 'Lord, who are they (the employers) leaving their children with if she did that with her own children!'"

Given the uncertainty of what is "good mothering," and to defend their integrity as mothers when others may criticize them, transnational mothers construct new scales for gauging the quality of mothering. By favorably comparing themselves with the negative models of mothering that they see in others—especially those that they are able to closely scrutinize in their employers' homes—transnational mothers create new definitions of good-mothering standards. At the same time, selectively developing motherlike ties with other people's children allows them to enjoy affectionate, face-to-face interactions that they cannot experience on a daily basis with their own children.

DISCUSSION: TRANSNATIONAL MOTHERHOOD

In California, with few exceptions, paid domestic work has become a Latina immigrant women's job. One observer has referred to these Latinas as "the new employable mothers" (Chang 1994), but taking on these wage labor duties often requires Latina workers to expand the frontiers of motherhood by leaving their own children for several years. While today there is a greater openness to accepting a plurality of mothering arrangements—single mothers, employed mothers, stay-at-home mothers, lesbian mothers, surrogate mothers, to name a few—even feminist discussions generally assume that mothers, by definition, will reside with their children.

Transnational mothering situations disrupt the notion of family in one place and break distinctively with what some commentators have referred to as the "epoxy glue" view of motherhood (Blum and Deussen 1996; Scheper-Hughes 1992). Latina transnational mothers are improvising new mothering arrangements that are borne out of women's financial struggles, played out in a new global arena, to provide the best future for themselves and their children. Like many other women of color and employed mothers, transnational mothers rely on an expanded and sometimes fluid number of family members and paid caregivers. Their caring circuits, however, span stretches of geography and time that are much wider than typical joint custody or "other mother" arrangements that are more closely bound, both spatially and temporally.

The transnational perspective in immigration studies is useful in conceptualizing how relationships across borders are important. Yet, an examination of transnational motherhood suggests that transnationalism is a contradictory process of the late 20th century. It is an achievement, but one accompanied by numerous costs and attained in a context of extremely scarce options. The alienation and anxiety of mothering organized by long temporal and spatial distances should give pause to the celebratory impulses of transnational perspectives of immigration. Although not addressed directly in this article, the experiences of these mothers resonate with current major political issues. For example, transnational mothering resembles precisely what immigration restrictionists have advocated through California's Proposition 187 (Hondagneu-Sotelo 1995).[3] While proponents of Proposition 187 have never questioned California's reliance on low-waged Latino immigrant workers, this restrictionist policy calls for fully dehumanized immigrant workers, not workers with families and family needs (such as education and health services for children). In this respect, transnational mothering's externalization of the cost of labor reproduction to Mexico and Central America is a dream come true for the proponents of Proposition 187.

Contemporary transnational motherhood continues a long historical legacy of people of color being incorporated into the United States through coercive systems of labor that do not recognize family rights. As Bonnie Thornton Dill (1988), Evelyn Nakano Glenn (1986), and others have pointed out, slavery and contract labor systems were organized to maximize economic productivity and offered few supports to sustain family life. The job characteristics of paid domestic work, especially live-in work, virtually impose transnational motherhood for many Mexican and Central American women who have children of their own.

The ties of transnational motherhood suggest simultaneously the relative permeability of borders, as witnessed by the maintenance of family ties and the new meanings of motherhood, and the impermeability of nation-state borders. Ironically, just at the moment when free trade proponents and pundits celebrate globalization and transnationalism, and when "borderlands" and "border crossings" have become the metaphors of preference for describing a mind-boggling range of conditions, nation-state borders prove to be very real obstacles for many Mexican and Central American women who work in the United States and who, given the appropriate circumstances, wish to be with their children. While demanding the right for women workers to live with their children may provoke critiques of sentimentality, essentialism, and the glorification of motherhood, demanding the right for women workers to choose their own motherhood arrangements would be the beginning of truly just family and work policies, policies that address not only inequalities of gender but also inequalities of race, class, and citizenship status.

■ Review Questions

1. Who is caring for the children of transnational mothers while they are caring for American children?
2. How do transnational mothers reconcile being nannies in the United States with their desires to be good mothers to their own children?

ENDNOTES

1. No one knows the precise figures on the prevalence of transnational motherhood, just as no one knows the myriad consequences for both mothers and their children. However, one indicator that hints at both the complex outcomes and the frequencies of these arrangements is that teachers and social workers in Los Angeles are becoming increasingly concerned about some of the deleterious effects of these mother-child separations and reunions. Many Central American women who made their way to Los Angeles in the early 1980s, fleeing civil wars and economic upheaval, pioneered transnational mothering, and some of them are now financially able to bring the children whom they left behind. These children, now in their early teen years, are confronting the triple trauma of simultaneously entering adolescence—with its own psychological upheavals; a new society—often in an inner-city environment that requires learning to navigate a new language, place, and culture; and they are also entering families that do not look like the ones they knew before their mothers' departure, families with new siblings born in the United States, and new stepfathers or mothers' boyfriends.

2. According to interviews conducted with domestic workers in La Paz, Bolivia, in the late 1980s, 41 percent got their first job between the ages of 11 and 15, and one-third got their first job between the ages of 6 and 10. Some parents received half of the child-servant's salary (Gill 1994, 64). Similar arrangements prevailed in preindustrial, rural areas of the United States and Europe.

3. In November 1994, California voters passed Proposition 187, which legislates the denial of public school education, health care, and other public benefits to undocumented immigrants and their children. Although currently held up in the courts, the facility with which Proposition 187 passed in the California ballots rejuvenated anti-immigrant politics at a national level. It opened the doors to new legislative measures in 1997 to deny public assistance to illegal immigrants.

READING 5-2

Breaking the Last Taboo
Interracial Marriage in America

Zhenchao Qian

Guess Who's Coming to Dinner, a movie about a white couple's reaction when their daughter falls in love with a black man, caused a public stir in 1967. That the African-American character was a successful doctor did little to lower the anxieties of white audiences. Now, almost four decades later, the public hardly reacts at all to interracial relationships. Both Hollywood movies and TV shows, including *Die Another Day, Made in America, ER, The West Wing,* and *Friends,* regularly portray interracial romance.

What has changed? In the same year that Sidney Poitier startled Spencer Tracy and Katherine Hepburn, the Supreme Court ruled, in *Loving v. Virginia,* that laws forbidding people of different races to marry were unconstitutional. The civil rights movement helped remove other blatant legal barriers to the integration of racial minorities and fostered the growth of minority middle classes. As racial minorities advanced, public opinion against interracial marriage declined, and rates of interracial marriage grew rapidly.

Between 1970 and 2000, black-white marriages grew more than fivefold from 65 to 363 thousand, and marriages between whites and members of other races grew almost fivefold from 233 thousand to 1.1 million. Proportionately, interracial marriages remain rare, but their rates increased from less than 1 percent of all marriages in 1970 to nearly 3 percent in 2000. This trend shows that the "social distance" between racial

groups has narrowed significantly, although not nearly as much as the social distance between religious groups. Interfaith marriages have become common in recent generations. That marriages across racial boundaries remain much rarer than cross-religion marriages reflects the greater prominence of race in America. While the interracial marriage taboo seems to be gradually breaking down, at least for certain groups, intermarriage in the United States will not soon match the level of intermarriage that European immigrant groups have achieved over the past century.

PUBLIC ATTITUDES

Americans have become generally more accepting of other races in recent decades, probably as a result of receiving more education and meeting more people of other races. Americans increasingly work and go to school with people from many groups. As racial gaps in income narrow, more members of racial minorities can afford to live in neighborhoods that had previously been white. Neighbors have opportunities to reduce stereotypes and establish friendships. Tolerance also grows as generations pass; elderly people with racist attitudes die and are replaced by younger, more tolerant people. The general softening of racial antagonisms has also improved attitudes toward interracial marriage.

In 1958, a national survey asked Americans for the first time about their opinions of interracial marriage. Only 4 percent of whites approved of intermarriage with blacks. Almost 40 years later, in 1997, 67 percent of whites approved of such intermarriages. Blacks have been much more accepting; by 1997, 83 percent approved of intermarriage. Whites' support for interracial marriage—which may to some extent only reflect respondents' sense of what they should tell interviewers—lags far behind their support of interracial schools (96 percent), housing (86 percent), and jobs (97 percent). Many white Americans apparently remain uneasy about interracial inti-

Zhenchao Qian, "Breaking the Last Taboo: Interracial Marriage in America," *Contexts,* Vol. 4, No. 4, pp. 33–37. © 2005 The American Sociological Association. Used by permission. All rights reserved.

macy generally, and most disapprove of interracial relationships in their own families. Still, such relationships are on the increase.

INTERRACIAL DATING

According to a recent survey reported by George Yancey, more than one-half of African-, Hispanic-, and Asian-American adults have dated someone from a different racial group, and even more of those who have lived in integrated neighborhoods or attended integrated schools have done so. Most dates, of course, are casual and do not lead to serious commitments, and this is especially true for interracial dating. Analyzing data from the National Longitudinal Study of Adolescent Health, Kara Joyner and Grace Kao find that 71 percent of white adolescents with white boyfriends or girlfriends have introduced them to their families, but only 57 percent of those with nonwhite friends have done so. Similarly, 63 percent of black adolescents with black boyfriends or girlfriends have introduced them to their families, but only 52 percent of those with nonblack friends have done so. Data from another national survey show similar patterns for young adults aged 18–29 (61 percent versus 51 percent introducing for whites, and 70 percent versus 47 percent for blacks).

While resistance to interracial relationships in principle has generally declined, opposition remains high among the families of those so involved. Interracial couples express concern about potential crises when their families become aware of such relationships. Their parents, especially white parents, worry about what those outside the family might think and fear that their reputations in the community will suffer. Maria Root notes that parents actively discourage interracial romance, often pointing to other peoples' prejudice—not their own—and expressing concern for their child's well-being: "Marriage is hard enough; why make it more difficult?"

The dating and the parental reservations reveal a generation gap: Young men and women today are more open to interracial relationships than their parents are. This gap may be due simply to youthful experimentation; youngsters tend to push boundaries. As people age, they gradually learn to conform. Kara Joyner and Grace Kao find that interracial dating is most common among teenagers but becomes infrequent for people approaching 30. They attribute this shift to the increasing importance of family and friends—and their possible disapproval—as we age. When people are ready to be "serious," they tend to fall in love with people who are just like themselves.

INTERRACIAL COHABITATION AND MARRIAGE

Who pairs up with whom depends partly on the size of the different racial groups in the United States. The larger the group, the more likely members are to find marriageable partners of their own race. The U.S. Census Bureau classifies race into four major categories: whites, African Americans, Asian Americans, and American Indians. Hispanics can belong to any of the four racial groups. Whites form the largest group, about 70 percent of the population, and just 4 percent of married whites aged 20–34 in 2000 had nonwhite spouses. The interracial marriage rates are much higher for American-born racial minorities: 9 percent for African Americans, about 39 percent for Hispanics, 56 percent for American Indians, and 59 percent for Asian Americans (who account for less than 4 percent of the total population). Mathematically, one marriage between an Asian American and a white raises the intermarriage rate for Asian Americans much more than for whites, because whites are so much more numerous. Because of their numbers as well, although just 4 percent of whites are involved in interracial marriages, 92 percent of all interracial marriages include a white partner. About half of the remaining 8 percent are black-Hispanic couples. Racial minorities have more opportunities to meet whites

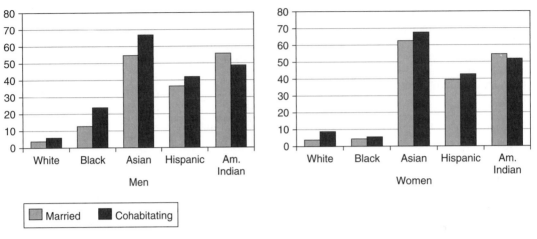

Interracial marriage remains rare among white and black Americans.

FIGURE 5.1

Percentage of Americans in couples married to (dark bars) or cohabiting with (light bars) someone of a different race. (*Source:* 2000 Census.)

in schools, workplaces, and neighborhoods than to meet members of other minority groups.

Some interracial couples contemplating marriage avoid family complications by just living together. In 2000, 4 percent of married white women had nonwhite husbands, but 9 percent of white women who were cohabiting had nonwhite partners (see Figure 5.1). Similarly, 13 percent of married black men had nonblack spouses, but 24 percent of cohabiting black men lived with nonblack partners. Hispanics and Asian Americans showed the same tendency; only American Indians showed the opposite pattern. Black-white combinations are particularly notable. Black-white pairings accounted for 26 percent of all cohabiting couples but only 14 percent of all interracial marriages. They are more likely to cohabit than other minority-white couples, but they are also less likely to marry. The long history of the ban on interracial marriage in the United States, especially black-white marriage, apparently still affects black-white relationships today.

Given differences in population size, comparing rates of intermarriage across groups can be difficult. Nevertheless, statistical models used by social scientists can account for group size, determine whether members of any group are marrying out more or less often than one would expect given their numbers, and then discover what else affects intermarriage. Results show that the lighter the skin color, the higher the rate of intermarriage with white Americans. Hispanics who label themselves as racially "white" are most likely to marry non-Hispanic whites. Asian Americans and American Indians are next in their levels of marriage with whites. Hispanics who do not consider themselves racially white have low rates of intermarriage with whites. African Americans are least likely of all racial minorities to marry whites. Darker skin in America is associated with discrimination, lower educational attainment, lower income, and segregation. Even among African Americans, those of lighter tone tend to experience less discrimination.

RACE AND EDUCATION

Most married couples have similar levels of education, which typically indicates that they are also somewhat similar in social position, background, and values. Most interracial couples also have relatively equal educational attainments. However, when interracial couples do differ in their education, a hierarchy of color is apparent. The darker the skin color of racial minorities, the more likely they are to have married whites "below" them, that is, with less education than themselves. Six of ten African Americans who marry whites with different levels of education marry whites less educated than themselves. Hispanics also tend to marry whites less educated than themselves, but Asian Americans marry whites at about the same educational level.

Highly educated minority members often attend integrated colleges, and their workplaces and neighborhoods are integrated. Although they often develop a strong sense of their group identity in such environments, they also find substantial opportunities for interracial contact, friendship, romance, and marriage. College-educated men and women are more likely to marry interracially than those with less education. The fact that Asian Americans attend college at unusually high rates helps explain their high level of intermarriage with whites. The major exceptions to the interracial influence of higher education are African Americans.

Although middle-class African Americans increasingly live in integrated neighborhoods, they are still much more segregated than other minorities. Well-educated African Americans are less likely to live next to whites than are well educated Hispanics and Asian Americans. One reason is that middle-class black Americans are so numerous that they can form their own middle-class black neighborhoods, while middle-class Hispanic and Asian-American communities are smaller and often fractured by differences in national origin and language. In addition, studies show clearly that whites resist having black neighbors much more than they resist having Hispanic or Asian American neighbors.

Residential and school segregation on top of a long and relentless history of racial discrimination and inequality reduce African Americans'

opportunities for interracial contact and marriage. The geographic distance between blacks and whites is in many ways rooted in the historical separation between the two groups. In contrast, the distance of Hispanics and Asian Americans from whites has more to do with their current economic circumstances; as those improve, they come nearer to whites geographically, socially, and matrimonially.

A MAN AND A WOMAN

Black-white couples show a definite pattern: 74 percent involve a black husband and a white wife. Asian American–white couples lean the other way; 58 percent involve an Asian-American wife. Sex balances are roughly even for couples that include a white and a Hispanic (53 percent involve a Hispanic husband) or a white and an American Indian (49 percent involve Indian husbands).

I mentioned before that most black-white couples have similar educations; nonetheless, white women who marry black men "marry up" more often than those who marry white men. This is especially striking because the pool of highly educated white men greatly outnumbers the pool of highly educated black men. More than half of black husbands of white women have at least some college education, but only two-fifths of black husbands of black women do. In that sense, white wives get more than their "share" of well-educated black husbands. This further reduces the chances that black women, especially highly educated black women, will marry, because they often face shortages of marriageable men. African-American women often resent this. Interviewed by Maria Root, one black man in such a relationship reported being accused of "selling out" and "dissing his black sisters."

Half a century ago, Robert Merton proposed a "status exchange" theory to explain the high proportion of marriages between black men and white women. He suggested that men with high economic or professional status who carry the stigma of being black in a racial caste society "trade" their social position for whiteness by marriage. On the other hand, some social scientists argue that racialized sexual images also encourage marriages between white women and black men. Throughout Europe and the West, people have long seen fair skin tone as a desirable feminine characteristic, and African Americans share those perceptions. For example, Mark Hill found that black interviewers participating in a national survey of African Americans rated black women interviewees with lighter skin as more attractive than those with darker skin. But they did not consider male interviewees with light skin any more attractive than darker-skinned men.

Asian Americans show a different pattern; in most of their marriages with whites, the husband is white. Although Asian-American men are typically more educated than white men, in the mixed couples, white husbands usually have more education than their Asian-American wives. As with white wives of black men, the wives have "married up" educationally. Some speculate that Asian-American women tend to marry white men because they perceive Asian-American men to be rigidly traditional on sex roles and white men as more nurturing and expressive. The emphasis in Asian cultures on the male line of descent may pressure Asian-American men to carry on the lineage by marrying "one of their own." But what attracts white men to Asian-American women? Some scholars suggest that it is the widespread image of Asian women as submissive and hyper-feminine (the "Madame Butterfly" icon).

THE FUTURE OF INTERRACIAL MARRIAGE

Rates of interracial marriage in the future will respond to some conflicting forces: the weakening of barriers between groups; increasing numbers of Hispanics and Asians in the nation; and pos-

sible rising ethnic consciousness. The continued progress of racial minorities in residential integration and economic achievement promotes contact between members of different races as equals. The color line, however, probably will not disappear. Marriage between African Americans and whites is likely to remain rare. Stubborn economic differences may be part of the reason for the persistence of this barrier, but cultural experiences also play a role. In recent years, the middle-class African-American population has grown, yet the persistence of residential segregation reduces the opportunities for contact between blacks and whites. African Americans also maintain a strong racial identity compared to that of other minorities. In the 1990 census, for example, less than 25 percent of children born to a black-white couple were identified by their parents as white—a much lower percentage than for other biracial children. In the 2000 census, blacks identified themselves or their children as multi-racial much less often than did other racial minorities. The stronger racial identities of African Americans, forged by persistent inequality, discrimination, and residential isolation, along with continued white resistance, will hold down the increase in marriages across the black-white divide.

Increases in the relatively high marriage rates of Hispanics and Asian Americans with whites may slow as new immigrants keep arriving from their homelands. Immigration expands the marriage pools for the native-born, who are more able to find spouses in their own racial or ethnic groups. These pools are expanded further by the way the wider society categorizes Hispanics and Asian Americans. They distinguish among themselves by national origin (Cuban versus Mexican or Thai versus Chinese), but whites tend to lump them into two large groups. Common experiences of being identified as the same, along with anti-Latino and anti-Asian prejudice and discrimination, help create a sense of pan-ethnic identity. This in turn inhibits marriage with whites, fosters solidarity within the larger group, and increases marriage rates between varieties of Hispanics and Asian Americans. Interethnic marriage is frequent among American-born Asians despite small group sizes and limited opportunities for contact. For example, in 1990, 18 percent of Chinese-Americans and 15 percent of Japanese-Americans aged 20–34 married spouses of other Asian ethnic groups (compared to 39 percent and 47 percent who married whites).

Many people view the increasing number of interracial marriages as a sign that racial taboos are crumbling and that the distances between racial groups in American society are shrinking. However, marriages across racial boundaries remain rarer than those that cross religious, educational, or age lines. The puzzle is whether interracial marriages will develop as marriages between people of different nationalities did among European immigrants and their descendants in the early 20th century. Diverse in many ways when they entered the country, these 20th-century European Americans, such as Italians, Poles, and Greeks, reached the economic level of earlier immigrants within a couple generations. Their success blurred ethnic boundaries and increased the rate of interethnic marriage. Many of their descendants now define themselves simply as white despite their diverse national origins. For most white Americans, ethnic identities have become largely symbolic.

Similar trends for interracial marriages are unlikely in the near future. The experiences of European Americans show the importance of equal economic achievement in dissolving barriers, so what happens economically to recent immigrants and African Americans will be important.

Even then, the low levels of interracial marriage for middle-class African Americans suggest that this particular color line will persist as a barrier to marriage. And the continuing influx of Asian and Latino immigrants may reinforce those groups' barriers to intermarriage.

RECOMMENDED RESOURCES

Zhenchao Qian. "Breaking the Racial Barriers: Variations in Interracial Marriage between 1980 and 1990." *Demography* 34 (1997): 478–500. An overview of changes in interracial marriage by sex and educational attainment for native-born whites, African Americans, Hispanics, and Asian Americans.

Zhenchao Qian and Daniel T. Lichter. "Measuring Marital Assimilation: Intermarriage among Natives and Immigrants." *Social Science Research* 30 (2001): 289–312. A comparison of interracial marriages between natives and immigrants, showing how immigration may slow down the increases in interracial marriage.

Maria P. P. Root. *Love's Revolution: Interracial Marriage* (Temple University Press, 2001). Presents in-depth interviews with interracial couples.

Howard Schuman, Charlotte Steeh, Lawrence Bobo, and Maria Krysan. *Racial Attitudes in America: Trends and Interpretation* (Harvard University Press, 1997). Using national poll data since 1942, the authors paint a changing picture of racial attitudes for whites and blacks.

George Yancey. "Who Dates Interracially: An Examination of the Characteristics of Those Who Have Dated Interracially." *Journal of Comparative Family Studies* 33 (2002): 179–90. A report on the dating practices of different racial groups.

■ Review Questions

1. Why are rates of intermarriage lower for blacks than for nonblack racial-ethnic groups such as Hispanics and Asians?
2. Why may continued immigration slow the growth of intermarriage for Hispanics and Asians?

Part Three

Sexuality, Partnership, and Marriage

CHAPTER 6

Sexualities

Sociology is here to tell you that sexual behavior, our most private activity, and romantic love, our most personal emotion, are heavily influenced by society. That might be obvious in a society where unmarried women's chastity is closely protected and parents choose their children's spouses. It might even be obvious were we to look back at the United States in the 1950s, when many young men and a majority of young women had first sexual intercourse with the person they chose to marry. But the claim is that although social influences are weaker now, sex and love are still structured in large part by society.

But is sexuality *totally* constructed by society? Consider the differing ways women and men experience sexuality. Don't biological differences between women and men play a role? Indeed, best-selling books in the 1990s, such as *Men Are from Mars, Women Are from Venus,*[1] argued that gender differences in sexuality are largely driven by biology. In contrast, most sociologists continue to insist that biological influences are minimal. In the first reading in this chapter, sociologists Pepper Schwartz and Virginia Rutter search

for a middle ground. Although partial to the position that social influences are greater than biological influences, Schwartz and Rutter maintain that *both* mechanisms must be included in a complete explanation of gender differences in sexual behavior and desire. In making their case, they present clear summaries of the opposing theoretical positions in this debate: sociobiology, which emphasizes evolutionary influences on human behavior, and social constructionism, which emphasizes social control.

Until the latter part of the twentieth century, most long-term sexually intimate relationships took the form of marriage. Beginning in the 1970s, cohabitation—living with a partner without marrying—became an increasingly acceptable form of intimate relationship. More recently, we have seen an apparent increase in intimate relationships among couples who are neither married nor living together. No good data on these couples exists in the United States, but government surveys in Canada and the United Kingdom show them to be increasingly common. In the second selection, a Norwegian sociologist writes about these so-called living apart together, or LAT, relationships, which challenge common notions of family life.

---

[1] John Gray, *Men Are from Mars, Women Are from Venus* (New York: HarperCollins, 1992).

READING 6-1

Sexual Desire and Gender

Pepper Schwartz

Virginia Rutter

SOCIOBIOLOGY AND EVOLUTIONARY PSYCHOLOGY

The past few decades of research on sexuality have produced a new school of human behavior—sociobiology and a related discipline, evolutionary psychology—that explains most gender differences as strategies of sexual reproduction. According to evolutionary psychologist David Buss (1995), "Evolutionary psychologists predict that the sexes will differ in precisely those domains in which women and men have faced different sorts of adaptive problems" (p. 164). By "those domains," Buss refers to reproduction, which is the only human function that depends on a biological difference between men and women.

The key assumption of sociobiological/evolutionary theory is that humans have an innate, genetically triggered impulse to pass on their genetic material through successful reproduction: This impulse is called reproductive fitness. The human species, like other species that sociobiologists study, achieves immortality by having children who live to the age of reproductive maturity and produce children themselves. Sociobiologists and evolutionary psychologists seek to demonstrate that almost all male and female behavior, and especially sexuality, is influenced by this one simple but powerful proposition.

Sociobiologists start at the species level. Species are divided into *r* and *K* reproductive categories. Those with *r* strategies obtain immortality

by mass production of eggs and sperm. The *r* species is best illustrated by fish. The female manufactures thousands of eggs, the male squirts millions of sperm over them, and that is the extent of parenting. According to this theory, the male and female fish need not pair up to nurture their offspring. Although thousands of fertilized fish eggs are consumed by predators, only a small proportion of the massive quantity of fertilized eggs must survive for the species to continue. In the *r* species, parents need not stay together for the sake of the kids.

In contrast, humans are a *K*-strategy species, which has a greater investment in each fertilized egg. Human females and most female mammals have very few eggs, especially compared to fish. Moreover, offspring take a long time to mature in the mother's womb and are quite helpless after they are born, with no independent survival ability. Human babies need years of supervision before they are independent. Thus, if a woman wants to pass on her genes (or at least the half her child will inherit from her), she must take good care of her dependent child. The baby is a scarce resource. Even if a woman is pregnant from sexual maturation until menopause, the number of children she can produce is quite limited. This limitation was particularly true thousands of years ago. Before medical advances of the nineteenth and twentieth centuries, women were highly unlikely to live to the age of menopause. Complications from childbirth commonly caused women to die in their 20s or 30s. Where the food supply was scarce, women were less likely to be successful at conceiving, further reducing the possibility of generating offspring.

Sociobiologists and evolutionary psychologists say that men inseminate, women incubate. The human female's reproductive constraints (usually one child at a time, only so many children over a life cycle, and a helpless infant for a long period of time) shape most of women's sexual and emotional approaches to men and mating. According to their theory, women have good reason to be more selective than men about potential mates. They want to find a man who will stick around and continue to provide resources and protection to this child at least until the child has a good chance of survival. Furthermore, because a woman needs to create an incentive for a man to remain with her, females have developed more sophisticated sexual and emotional skills specifically geared toward creating male loyalty and commitment to their mutual offspring.

Sociobiologists and evolutionary psychologists say that differences in reproductive capacity and strategy also shape sexual desire. Buss asserts that reproductive strategies form most of the categories of desire: Older men generally pick younger women because they are more fertile; younger women seek older men who have more status, power, and resources (a cultural practice known as hypergamy) because such men can provide for their children. Furthermore, health and reproductive capacity make youth generally sexier, and even certain shapes of women's bodies (such as an "ideal" hip-to-waist ratio epitomized by an hourglass figure, which correlates with ability to readily reproduce) are widely preferred (Buss 1994)—despite varying standards of beauty across cultures. Likewise, men who have demonstrated their fertility by producing children are more sought after than men who have not (Buss 1994).

According to evolutionary psychologists, men's tastes for recreational sex, unambivalent lust, and a variety of partners are consistent with maximizing their production of children. Men's sexual interest is also more easily aroused because sex involves fewer costs to them than to women, and the ability for rapid ejaculation has a reproductive payoff. On the other hand, women's taste for relationship-based intimacy and greater investment in each sexual act is congruent with women's reproductive strategies.

In a field that tends to emphasize males' "natural" influence over reproductive strategies, evolutionary anthropologist Helen Fisher (1992) offers a feminist twist. Her study of hundreds of societies shows that divorce, or its informal equivalent, occurs most typically in the third or fourth year of a marriage and then peaks about every four years after that. Fisher hypothesizes that some of the breakups have to do with a woman's attempt to obtain the best genes and best survival chances for her offspring. In both agrarian and hunter-gatherer societies, Fisher explains, women breast-feed their child for three or four years—a practice that is economical and sometimes helps to prevent further pregnancy. At the end of this period, the woman is ready and able to have another child. She reenters the mating marketplace and assesses her options to see if she can improve on her previous mate. If she can get a better guy, she will leave the previous partner and team up with a new one. In Fisher's vision, unlike the traditional sociobiological view (see Table 6.1), different male and female reproductive strategies do not necessarily imply female sexual passivity and preference for lifelong monogamy.

Sociobiologists and evolutionary psychologists tell a fascinating story of how male and female reproductive differences might shape sexuality. To accept sociobiological arguments, one must accept the premise that most animal and human behavior is driven by the instinct to reproduce and improve the gene pool. Furthermore, a flaw of sociobiology as a theory is that it does not provide a unique account of sexual behavior with the potential to be tested empirically. Furthermore, other social science explanations for the same phenomena are supported by more immediate, close-range evidence.

Consider hypergamy, the practice of women marrying men slightly older and "higher" on the social status ladder than they are. Sociobiologists would say women marry "up" to ensure the most fit provider for their offspring. But hypergamy makes little sense biologically. Younger men have more years of resources to provide, and they have somewhat more sexual resources. Empirically, however, hypergamy is fact. It is also a fact that men, overall and in nearly every subculture, have

TABLE 6.1

COMPARISON OF TRADITIONAL AND FEMINIST SOCIOBIOLOGICAL EXPLANATIONS OF GENDER DIFFERENCES IN SEXUALITY

Perspective	Gender difference	Explanation
Traditional	Men seek to maximize number of progeny by changing partners as often as possible. Women seek to maximize well-being of progeny by holding on to their partners as long as possible.	Men have biological capacity to inseminate many women in a short period of time; women's biological job is to incubate and nurture young.
Feminist	Men seek to maximize progeny; women seek to maximize well-being of progeny by exchanging partners when improved options are available.	Men and women both seek to maximize number of partners and quality of partners by exchanging when improved options are available.

access to more rewards and status than women do. Furthermore, reams of imagery—in movies, advertising, novels—promote the appeal of older, more resourceful men. Why not, when older, more resourceful men are generating the images? Social practice, in this case, overrides what sociobiologists consider the biological imperative.

THE SOCIAL ORIGINS OF DESIRE

Your own experience should indicate that biology and genetics alone do not shape human sexuality. From the moment you entered the world, cues from the environment were telling you which desires and behaviors were "normal" and which were not. The result is that people who grow up in different circumstances tend to have different sexualities. Who has not had their sexual behavior influenced by their parents' or guardians' explicit or implicit rules? You may break the rules or follow them, but you can't forget them. On a societal level, in Sweden, for example, premarital sex is accepted, and people are expected to be sexually knowledgeable and experienced. Swedes are likely to associate sex with pleasure in this "sex positive" society. In Ireland, however, Catholics are supposed to heed the Church's strict prohibitions against sex outside of marriage, birth control, and the

expression of lust. In Ireland the experience of sexuality is different from the experience of sexuality in Sweden because the rules are different. Certainly, biology in Sweden is no different from biology in Ireland, nor is the physical capacity to experience pleasure different. But in Ireland, nonmarital sex is clandestine and shameful. Perhaps the taboo adds excitement to the experience. In Sweden, nonmarital sex is acceptable. In the absence of social constraint, it may even feel a bit mundane. These culturally specific sexual rules and experiences arise from different norms, the well-known, unwritten rules of society.

Another sign that social influences play a bigger role in shaping sexuality than does biology is the changing notions historically of male and female differences in desire. Throughout history, varied explanations of male and female desire have been popular. At times, woman was portrayed as the stormy temptress and man the reluctant participant, as in the Bible story of Adam and Eve. At other times, women were seen as pure in thought and deed while men were voracious sexual beasts, as the Victorians would have it.

These shifting ideas about gender are the social "clothing" for sexuality. The concept of gender typically relies on a dichotomy of male versus female sexual categories, just as the tradition of women wearing dresses and men wearing pants has in the past made the shape of men and women appear quite different. Consider high heels, an on-again-off-again Western fashion. Shoes have no innate sexual function, but high heels have often been understood to be "sexy" for women, even though (or perhaps because) they render women less physically agile. (Of course, women cope. As Ginger Rogers, the 1940s movie star and dancing partner to Fred Astaire, is said to have quipped, "I did everything Fred did, only backwards and in high heels.") Social norms of femininity have at times rendered high heels fashionable. So feminine are high heels understood to be that a man in high heels, in some sort of visual comedy gag, guarantees a laugh from the audience. Alternatively, high heels are a required emblem of femininity for cross-dressing men.

Such distinctions are an important tool of society; they provide guidance to human beings about how to be a "culturally correct" male or female. Theoretically, society could "clothe" its members with explicit norms of sexuality that de-emphasize difference and emphasize similarity or even multiplicity. Picture unisex hairstyles and men and women both free to wear skirts or pants, norms that prevail from time to time in some subcultures. What is remarkable about dichotomies is that even when distinctions, like male and female norms of fashion, are reduced, new ways to assert an ostensibly essential difference between men and women arise. Societies' rules, like clothes, are changeable. But societies' entrenched taste for constructing differences between men and women persists.

The Social Construction of Sexuality

Social constructionists believe that cues from the environment shape human beings from the moment they enter the world. The sexual customs, values, and expectations of a culture, passed on to the young through teaching and by example, exert a powerful influence over individuals. When Fletcher Christian sailed into Tahiti in Charles Nordhoff's 1932 account, *Mutiny on the Bounty,* he and the rest of his nineteenth-century English crew were surprised at how sexually available, playful, guilt free, and amorous the Tahitian women were. Free from the Judeo-Christian precepts and straitlaced customs that inhibited English society, the women and girls of Tahiti regarded their sexuality joyfully and without shame. The English men were delighted and, small wonder, refused to leave the island. Such women did not exist in their own society. The women back in England had been socialized within their Victorian culture to be modest, scared of sex, protective of their reputation, and threatened by physical pleasure. As a result, they were unavailable before marriage and did not feel free to indulge in a whole lot of fun after it. The source of the difference was not physiological differences between Tahitian and English women; it was sexual socialization or the upbringing that they received within their differing families and cultures.

If we look back at the Victorian, nineteenth-century England that Nordhoff refers to, we can identify social structures that influenced the norms of women's and men's sexuality. A burgeoning, new, urban middle class created separate spheres in the division of family labor. Instead of sharing home and farm or small business, the tasks of adults in families became specialized: Men went out to earn money, women stayed home to raise children and take care of the home. Although this division of labor was not the norm in all classes and ethnicities in England at the time, the image of middle-class femininity and masculinity became pervasive. The new division of labor increased women's economic dependence on men, which further curbed women's sexual license but not men's. When gender organizes one aspect of life—such as men's and women's positions in the economy—it also organizes other aspects of life, including sex.

In a heterogeneous and individualistic culture like North America, sexual socialization is complex. A society creates an "ideal" sexuality, but different families and subcultures have their own values. For example, even though contemporary society at large may now accept premarital sexuality, a given family may lay down the law: Sex before marriage is against the family's religion and an offense against God's teaching. A teenager who grows up in such a household may suppress feelings of sexual arousal or channel them into outlets that are more acceptable to the family. Or the teenager may react against her or his background, reject parental and community opinion, and search for what she or he perceives to be a more "authentic" self. Variables like birth order or observations of a sibling's social and sexual expression can also influence a person's development.

As important as family and social background are, so are individual differences in response to that background. In the abstract, people raised to celebrate their sexuality must surely have a different approach to enjoying their bodies than those who are taught that their bodies will betray them and are a venal part of human nature. Yet whether or not a person is raised to be at ease with physicality does not always help predict adult sexual behavior. Sexual sybarites and libertines may have grown up in sexually repressive environments, as did pop culture icon and Catholic-raised Madonna. Sometimes individuals whose families promoted sex education and free personal expression are content with minimal sexual expression.

Even with the nearly infinite variety of sexuality that individual experience produces, social circumstances shape sexual patterns. For example, research shows that people who have had more premarital sexual intercourse are likely to have more extramarital intercourse, or sex with someone other than their spouse (Blumstein and Schwartz 1983). Perhaps early experience creates a desire for sexual variety and makes it harder for a person to be monogamous. On the other hand, higher levels of sexual desire may generate both the premarital and extramarital propensities. Or perhaps nonmonogamous, sexually active individuals are "rule breakers" in

other areas also, and resist not only the traditional rules of sex but also other social norms they encounter. Sexual history is useful for predicting sexual future, but it does not provide a complete explanation.

To make explanations more useful, sociologists refer to societal-level explanations as the macro view and to individual-level explanations as the micro view. At the macrolevel, the questions pertain to the patterns among different groups. For example, we may note in our culture that some women wear skirts and all men do not. Why do women and men, generally speaking, differ in this way? Social conflict theory, which examines the way that groups gain and maintain power over resources and other groups, is often used to address macrolevel questions. One might ask: Whose interest does this custom serve and how did it evolve? What does it constrain or encourage? If the custom changes, what social forces have promoted the change? What social forces resist change? Who has power over customs at any given time, and why?

Symbolic interactionism supplements this macrolevel view by looking at the microlevel: How does a particular custom gain its meaning through social interaction? For example, what is really happening when a man opens a door for a woman? Symbolic interactionism proposes that social rules are learned and reinforced through everyday interaction in both small acts, such as a man's paying for a woman's dinner, and larger enactments of male and female roles, such as weddings, manners and advice books, movies, and television. Through such everyday social interaction, norms are confirmed or resisted. When an adult tells a little girl "good girls don't do this," or when boys make fun of her for wanting to be on the football team, or when she observes people scorning or stoning women who venture forth in inappropriate garb (as in countries where women are required to wear a veil), or when she sees women joining a military school getting hazed and harassed, she is learning her society's rules of behavior.

When it comes to sexuality, all these social and behavioral theories hold that biological impulses are subservient to the influence of social systems. Consider high heels again. As anyone who has done so knows, wearing high heels has physical consequences, such as flexed calves while wearing them and aching feet at the end of an evening. But nothing in the physiology of women makes wearing high-heeled shoes necessary, and the propensity to wear high heels is not programmed into women's DNA. A sociobiologist might note that any additional ways a society can invent for women to be sexy accelerate reproductive success. A symbolic interactionist would counter that most rules of sexuality go way beyond what's needed for reproductive success. Footwear has never been shown to be correlated with fertility. Instead, society orchestrates male and female sexuality so that its values are served. A social conflict theorist would go a step further and note that the enactment of gendered fashion norms, individual by individual, serves the political agenda of groups in power (in this case men) at the macrolevel.

An astounding example of gender-based social control of sexuality was the practice of binding the feet of upper-class women in China starting around the tenth century. Each foot was bound so tightly that the last two toes shriveled and fell off. What was left was so deformed that the woman could barely walk and had to be carried. The function was to allow upper-class men to control the mobility of their women. Bound feet, which were thus associated with status and wealth, became erotically charged. Unbound feet were seen as repugnant. By the eighteenth and nineteenth centuries, even poor women participated in this practice. This practice was so associated with sexual acceptability and marriageability that it was difficult to disrupt, even when nineteenth-century missionaries from the West labeled the practice barbaric and unsafe. Only later, in the twentieth century, did foot binding become illegal (Greenhalgh 1977).

Social Control of Sexuality

So powerful are norms as they are transmitted through both social structures and everyday life that it is impossible to imagine the absence of norms that control sexuality. In fact, most images of "liberated" sexuality involve breaking a social norm—say, having sex in public rather than in private. The social norm is always the reference point. Because people are influenced from birth by the social and physical contexts of sexuality, their desires are shaped by those norms. There is no such thing as a truly free sexuality. For the past two centuries in North America, people have sought "true love" through personal choice in dating and mating (D'Emilio and Freedman 1988). Although this form of sexual liberation has generated a small increase in the number of mixed pairs—interracial, interethnic, interfaith pairs—the rule of homogamy, or marrying within one's class, religion, and ethnicity, still constitutes one of the robust social facts of romantic life. Freedom to choose the person one loves turns out not to be as free as one might suppose.

Despite the norm of true love currently accepted in our culture, personal choice and indiscriminate sexuality have often been construed across cultures and across history as socially disruptive. Disruptions to the social order include liaisons between poor and rich; between people of different races, ethnicities, or faiths; and between members of the same sex. Traditional norms of marriage and sexuality have maintained social order by keeping people in familiar and "appropriate" categories. Offenders have been punished by ostracism, curtailed civil rights, or in some societies, death. Conformists are rewarded with social approval and material advantages. Although it hardly seems possible today, mixed-race marriage was against the law in the United States until 1967. Committed same-sex couples continue to be denied legal marriage, income tax breaks, and health insurance benefits; heterosexual couples take these social benefits for granted.

Some social theorists observe that societies control sexuality through construction of a dichotomized or gendered (male-female) sexuality (Foucault 1978). Society's rules about pleasure seeking and procreating are enforced by norms about appropriate male and female behavior. For example, saying that masculinity is enhanced by sexual experimentation while femininity is demeaned by it gives men sexual privilege (and pleasure) and denies it to women. Furthermore, according to Foucault, sexual desire is fueled by the experience of privilege and taboo regarding sexual pleasure. That is, the very rules that control sexual desire shape it and even enhance it. The social world could just as plausibly concentrate on how much alike are the ways that men and women experience sex and emphasize how broadly dispersed sexual conduct is across genders. However, social control turns pleasure into a scarce resource and endows leaders who regulate the pleasure of others with power. . . .

To summarize, social constructionists believe that a society influences sexual behavior through its norms. Some norms are explicit, such as laws against adult sexual activity with minors. Others are implicit, such as norms of fidelity and parental responsibility. In a stable, homogeneous society, it is relatively easy to understand such rules. But in a changing, complex society like the United States, the rules may be in flux or indistinct. Perhaps this ambiguity is what makes some issues of sexuality so controversial today.

AN INTEGRATIVE PERSPECTIVE ON GENDER AND SEXUALITY

Social constructionist explanations of contemporary sexual patterns are typically pitted against the biology of desire and the evolutionary understanding of biological adaptations. Some social constructionists believe there is no inflexible biological reality; everything we regard as either female or male sexuality is culturally imposed. In contrast, essentialists—those who take a biological, sociobiological, or evolutionary point of view—believe people's sexual desires and orientations are innate and hardwired and that social impact is minimal. Gender differences follow from reproductive differences. Men inseminate, women incubate. People are born with sexual drives, attractions, and natures that simply play themselves out at the appropriate developmental age. Even if social constraints conspire to make men and women more similar to each other (as in the 1990s, when the sensitive and nurturing new man is encouraged to get in touch with his so-called feminine, emotional side), people's essential nature is the same: Man is the hunter, warrior, and trailblazer, and woman is the gatherer, nurturer, and reproducer. To an essentialist, social differences, such as the different earning power of men and women, are the consequence of biological difference. In short, essentialists think the innate differences between women and men are the cause of gendered sexuality; social constructionists think the differences between men and women are the result of gendering sexuality through social processes.

Using either the social constructionist or essentialist approach to the exclusion of the other constrains understanding of sexuality. We believe the evidence shows that gender differences are more plausibly an outcome of social processes than the other way around. But a social constructionist view is most powerful when it takes the essentialist view into account. In Table 6.2, we describe this view of gender differences in sexual desire as integrative. Although people tend to think of sex as primarily a biological function—tab B goes into slot A—biology is only one part of the context of desire. Such sociological factors as family relationships and social structure also influence sex. A complex mix of anatomy, hormones, and the brain provides the basic outline for the range of acts and desires possible, but biology is neither where sexuality begins nor where it ends. Social and biological contexts link to define human sexual possibilities.

TABLE 6.2

EXPLANATIONS OF MALE AND FEMALE DIFFERENCES IN SEXUAL DESIRE

Explanations	Causes of desire	Consequences
Essentialist: Desire is biological and evolutionary	Genetically preprogrammed reproductive functions specific to males and females	Male independence in reproduction and female-centered child-rearing practices and passivity are the cause, rather than the result, of gendered social institutions
Social constructionist: Desire is sociological and contextual	Social institutions and social interaction signal and sanction "male" and "female," gendered norms of behavior	Support for or opposition to sex/gender-segregated reproductive and social practices depends on social definitions of men, women, and sexuality
Integrative: Desire is contextual and physical	Bodies, environments, relationships, families, governments shape sexualities	Policies address some biological differences (such as pregnancy and work); emphasize the impact of social forces, interaction, societal programs

The integrative approach follows from a great deal that sexuality researchers have observed. Consider the following example: A research project, conducted over three decades ago, advertised for participants stating that its focus was how physical excitement influences a man's preference for one woman over another (Valins 1966). The researchers connected college men to a monitor that allowed them to hear their heartbeats as they looked at photographs of women models. The men were told that they would be able to hear their heartbeat when it surged in response to each photograph. A greater surge would suggest greater physical attraction. The participants were then shown a photograph of a dark-haired woman, then a blonde, then a red-head. Afterward, each man was asked to choose the picture that he would prefer to take home. In each case, the man chose the photograph of the woman who, as he believed from listening to his own speeding heartbeat, had most aroused him. Or at least the man thought he was choosing the woman who had aroused him most. In reality, the men had been listening to a faked heartbeat that was speeded up at random. The men thus actually chose the women who they believed had aroused them most. In this case, the men's

invented attraction was more powerful than their gut response. Their mind (a powerful sexual organ) told them their body was responding to a specific picture. The participants' physiological experience of arousal was eclipsed by the social context. When social circumstances influence sexual tastes, are those tastes real or sincere? Absolutely. The social world is as much a fact in people's lives as the biological world.

Now let us look at a case where the body's cues were misinterpreted by the mind. An attractive woman researcher stood at the end of a very stable bridge (Dutton and Aron 1974). She approached men after they had walked across the bridge, engaged them in conversation, and then gave the men her telephone number—in case they had further comments, she said. Then the researcher did the same thing with another group of participants, but at the end of an unstable, swinging bridge. People tend to feel a little nervous, excited, or even exhilarated when they make their way across such a bridge. The pulse rises. Adrenaline pumps. Indeed, the anxiety response of walking across the bridge is much like the arousal response caused by meeting a desirable new person. The question was, would that anxiety response confuse men into thinking that they were attracted to the woman at the end of the bridge, more so than the physiologically calm guys who met her on the stable bridge? Yes, a statistically significant, larger number of men from the swinging bridge called the woman. In this case, participants had interpreted an anxiety response as an attraction response, one compelling enough to warrant inviting a stranger on a date. The physical situation transformed the meaning of a casual meeting from anxiety to attraction, again showing the link between biological and social influences. . . .

What do these examples from research illustrate? Sexual desire—in fact, all sexuality—is influenced by the cultural, personal, and situational. But these examples also tell us that people can't escape the biological context of sex and sexuality—nor can they rely on it. Such an integrative approach—the intimate relationship between social context and biological experience—is central to understanding sexuality.

What are the implications of using an integrative approach to sexuality? First, an integrationist will raise questions about biology when social context is emphasized as cause, and will raise questions about social context when biological causes are emphasized. The point is, everything sexual and physical occurs and achieves meaning in a social context.

■ Review Questions

1. Why might women and men have different reproductive strategies?
2. Give an example of the ways in which social institutions seem to influence gender differences in sexuality.

READING 6-2

Living Apart Together
A New Family Form

Irene Levin

Susan and Simon are a couple, and have been so for more than 10 years. The difference between Susan and Simon and many other couples is that they do not share their everyday lives together. They have both been married before and have children from these previous relationships. Susan lives with her children in a neighboring town and

Irene Levin, "Living Apart Together: A New Family Form," *Current Sociology,* March 2004, Vol. 52(2), pp. 223–240. Copyright © 2004. Reproduced with permission of Sage Publications, Inc.

meets Simon every weekend and during holidays. Simon lives alone in the same town as his children, who live with their mother. Simon wants to be close to his children so that he can meet them as often as possible. By living in this current arrangement, Simon can have *both* a couple relationship with Susan *and* a parenting relationship with his children. Susan also likes the current situation because she does not have to choose *between* a partner and her children or make her children move away from their friends in order for her to keep her relationship with Simon.

Susan and Simon are living in a living apart together or LAT relationship—a historically new family form. LAT relationships are a result of changes in our living arrangements. These changes have occurred, little by little, during the past 30 years as a result of changing norms. Previously, it was expected that one would be married in order to live together. Only in marriage was a couple considered to be a "real" couple. Now, however, one can choose to live with one's partner without being married—what we call cohabitation (Trost, 1979; Heimdal and Houseknecht, 2003; Kamp Dush et al., 2003). Today the ritual of marriage is less important and feelings are what matters. Married and cohabiting couples have, however, a lot in common. They live in the same household and in everyday life there is not a lot of difference in their routines. They share "bed and table." The difference is the marriage ritual—cohabiting couples do not have the status of being married. In many aspects of everyday life this does not matter. Their children may not concern themselves about whether or not their parents are married and their routines are often the same in either case. There may be a difference between married and cohabiting couples with regard to differing consequences of relationship breakdown. Generally speaking, economic consequences differ when one of the couple dies, or when the married couple divorces (Hopper, 2001) or the cohabiting couple separates. The exception may be when the cohabiting couple has entered into a special contract.

The question to be considered here is whether two people may be considered to be a couple *without* having a common home. In recent times the answer has become "yes" and a new family form has appeared. To be a couple is no longer dependent upon sharing a common household. It is no longer important for one to be married or to be living in the same household—one can still be a couple, and it is that to which the new term, LAT relationship, refers. Can a LAT relationship be interpreted as a family form? As Levin and Trost (1992) show family can be defined in a range of different terms. The title of this special issue, "Beyond the Conventional Family," suggests that the traditional concept of family and definitions of family norms are increasingly challenged by a range of personal living arrangements. It is argued here that the occurrence of LAT relationships is closely connected to the

occurrence of cohabitation and the changes in norms.

CHANGING NORMS

In the 20th century two major changes occurred in the western world that have affected family situations. One was the emergence of cohabitation (Trost, 1979) and the other was increase in divorce rates (Moxnes, 1990, 2001; Aharons and Rodgers, 1987; Wallerstein and Kelly, 1980). Both of these phenomena occurred before but not to the extent to which they were practiced during this period. Previously, most marriages were dissolved because of the death of one of the spouses. This is shown among other things in the rather high remarriage rate in earlier times. For instance, in England and France during the years 1600–1700, between 25 and 30 percent of all marriages were remarriages (Sogner and Dupâquir, 1981). Nearly all of these remarriages occurred after the death of one of the spouses. As we get closer to the 19th century, the remarriage rate decreased to around 15 percent in Norway (see Sundt, 1975). In the beginning of the 1900s, a new divorce law came into effect (1915) in Norway and remarriages continued to decrease. During the 1900s life expectancy for men and women increased by 25 years. This change in life expectancy must have had many consequences, not the least of which affected marital relations. Previously, when marriages were shorter, death occurred before couples had time to divorce. In our day, divorce has replaced death as one of the main reasons for the dissolution of marriage (Levin, 2001). Today, most marriages dissolve because one of the spouses wants to divorce (Furstenberg and Kiernan, 2001). More often than not, this occurs while children are still living at home.

At the end of the 1960s and the beginning of the 1970s, marriage rates, in most of the western world, started to decrease. In some countries the changes occurred very rapidly, as in Sweden and Denmark, followed by Norway and Finland. In England, this development was somewhat slower than in the Nordic countries, but not as slow as in, for example, Belgium (Trost, 1995). At the same time, the practice of cohabitation began to increase (see Trost, 1979). In the traditional marital system before 1970, four elements were closely connected in time. The prevailing sequence was: the marriage ceremony, moving in together, having sexual intercourse together, having the first child about a year later (Trost, 1993, 1998; Levin and Trost, 2003). The traditional marital system normatively prescribed these four elements, in the given sequence, as the sanctioned practice. With some exceptions, the marriage ceremony and moving in together occurred at the same time, meaning the same day. This seems to have been true for all western societies.

Having sexual intercourse together was only sanctioned after the marriage ceremony. Premarital sex was prohibited for all, but in some countries more than in others, this prohibition was particularly underscored for women. The norm against premarital sex, however, was primarily an ideal norm which did not necessarily translate into a behavioral norm. Norway is a good example of this differentiation: the ideal norm prescribed chastity before marriage but in practice almost all couples had sex before they married. One indicator of this claim is that by the year 1960 one-quarter of all brides in Norway were pregnant at the time of the wedding. The fourth element prescribes that children be born nine to 12 months after the marital ceremony. Preferably and normatively, children should not be born to unwed mothers.

These four elements have lost their normative power and today they are no longer connected to one other. This development is related to the great increase in the rates of cohabitation. It can be argued that cohabitation has become a social institution (Trost, 1979). When cohabitation becomes a social institution of the sort we find in, for example, the Scandinavian countries, there is no normative or expected connection between the four elements that traditionally constituted the marital system. In Sweden, more than half of

all children, and about two-thirds of all first-born children, have unwed mothers. In Norway, the numbers are slightly fewer, but the changes in norms are more or less the same.

Without changes in the normative structure connected to these four elements, LAT relationships would not be as visible or as numerous. The couple would then have probably been defined (by themselves as well as by their own social networks) as "going steady," "engaged to be married" or simply as "lovers." These terms are less definite than a LAT relationship indicates. Prior to normative transformations the couple would not openly stay together overnight. With the changes, they now can do so without any sanctions. Without a general acceptance of cohabitation and its institutionalization which puts it on an equal footing with marriage, LAT relationships would have remained hidden or "invisible" (Levin and Trost, 1999) and they would be much less common than they now are.

The relatively high divorce and separation rates in many western countries might help to make LAT relationships more common and more visible also, especially where cohabitation has become a recognized social institution. Historically, LAT relationships have occurred before but certainly not as commonly as they now do and in the past such relationships were quite hidden from the eyes of others. The higher the divorce and separation rates are, the higher the likelihood not only of remarriages and recohabitations, but also of LAT relationships. Recohabitations always involve a change of home. Either one moves into the other's home or both members of the couple move from separate homes to a common home. In most cases of remarriage the same holds true. But there are instances where married couples remain in separate homes. Some couples who have lived together in a marriage or in a cohabiting relationship cease to live together in a common home without dissolving their relationship; they just form a LAT relationship out of a living together relationship.

Within the context of high rates of divorce today (Moxnes, 1990), many people postdivorce want to start new relationships but they are not ready to risk another divorce. The high rate of divorce and the acceptance of cohabitation as a social institution (Trost, 1995) can account to some extent for the higher incidence of LAT relationships. When Simone de Beauvoir (1908–86) and Jean Paul Sartre (1905–80) established themselves in what we are now calling a LAT relationship, they were seen as being "a little different" from other couples. They were intellectuals and lived, so-called, "Bohemian lives." There are many people today who live in tune with the lifestyle of de Beauvoir and Sartre. They are living in LAT relationships, which have become a new family form in western societies. This is not because the LAT relationship is entirely new, but rather because of the greater visibility and higher frequency of people living in LAT relationships. The greatly elevated numbers make us look upon these couples as representing something new. While journalists both in Norway and in Sweden are now interested in the phenomenon of LAT relationships, there remains little research on the phenomenon.

DEFINING LAT RELATIONSHIPS

The definition of a LAT relationship used here is a couple that does not share a home. Each of the two partners lives in his or her own home in which other people might also live. They define themselves as a couple and they perceive that their close surrounding personal network does so as well. The definition requires three conditions: the couple has to agree that they are a couple; others have to see them as such; and they must live in separate homes. This term refers to homosexual as well as heterosexual couples.

Some consider it unnecessary to give LAT relations a special name. If we go back in time, before cohabitation was common and considered "normal," we had terms such as "going steady"

which designated a premarital form. "Going steady" was usually limited to a certain period of time in which the couple either decided to continue and become a "real" couple and get engaged to be married, or decided to break up the relationship. The "going steady" stage is a part of the LAT relationship and arguably for some the LAT relationship is only a temporary situation which ends up being more like "going steady" ending in relationship dissolution; but for many the LAT relationship is something much more than "going steady," and it lasts over a longer period.

The term "LAT" was first used in the Netherlands, where a Dutch journalist, Michel Berkiel, wrote an article in the *Haagse Post,* in 1978, about a phenomenon he had observed, and in which he lived himself with the person he loved. During one of the morning meetings of the newspaper, while he was writing the article, he asked his colleagues to help him choose a title. Someone suggested that he name the article after a recent movie shown in the Netherlands at that time, titled *Eva and Frank: Living Apart Together.* "Living apart together" seemed too long to him and so he chose to use the acronym LAT or *lat.* Already a word in the Dutch language meaning "stick," this also made its usage easier to accept. The Netherlands is the only country, as far as I know, where the term LAT or *lat* is integrated in everyday speech. In the Scandinavian countries the term *særbo,* in Norwegian, and *särbo,* in Swedish, have now become relatively well-known terms; however, this is more true in Sweden than in Norway.

In France, a different term has been used in a study by Caradec (1996) who uses *cohabitation intermittente* and *cohabitation alternée.* The first term refers to the same phenomenon that is referred to by the phrase LAT relationship—a couple living in separate homes, and looked upon as a couple, by others, and by themselves. The latter term, *cohabitation alternée,* refers to cohabitation where the couple alternates between their two dwellings. Caradec's study claims that nearly 6 percent of the adult population in Paris were living in LAT relationships.

In Germany, Schneider (1996) refers to "partners with different households" or *Partnerschaften mit getrennten Haushalten* in German. Included in his study are only those LAT relationships that have lasted for at least one year. The study is rather special as it contains a majority of "young adults who are in education, mainly studying, or who are in their early period of gainful employment" (Schneider, 1996: 96; my translation). In this study more than 10,000 people, aged 18–61, were interviewed in 1994. He found that 9 percent of the respondents were living in LAT relationships. In the USA, the discussion about LAT relationships is just beginning. There, but also in other places, the term "commuting marriage/cohabitation" is used interchangeably with "dual-households" or "dual-residence living" (see Winfield, 1985). What marks the distinction between commuting marriage/cohabitation and LAT relationships is closely connected to the issue of one's home or domicile. If the two live in *one home* and one (or both of them) has a second apartment where he or she stays when *away from home,* due to their work or studies, these relationships are defined as commuting marital/cohabitational relationships. In order to be a LAT relationship, each partner must have his or her own home, which means that the partners live apart in *two separate residences.*

QUANTITATIVE STUDY

This research on LAT relationships draws upon data collected by both quantitative and qualitative methods. Most of the quantitative data come from Sweden, where we collected data on three different occasions. The first was in August 1993 when SKOP (a Scandinavian opinion research organization) included some of our questions in one of its monthly surveys, with a probability sample of 1021 inhabitants of Sweden, aged 18–74 years. The same questions were asked in a probability sample of 2121 people, aged 18–74 years, in January/February 1998, again by SKOP.[1] Here the relevant question was (in translation): "Do you live in a marriage-like relationship with someone while maintaining separate homes?" This question followed a previous one about being married or cohabiting. There were also questions concerning how frequently they were together and how far away from one another they lived.

The 1993 Swedish opinion research survey found that 6 percent of those respondents who were neither married nor cohabitating affirmed that they were living in a LAT relationship. The survey suggests that Sweden had about 60,000 couples, or 120,000 persons, living in LAT relationships. The data collected in 1998 found that the relative number of persons living in LAT relationships had increased to 12 percent of those respondents who were neither married nor cohabiting. This suggests that at least 130,000 couples or 260,000 people were living in LAT relationships at that time. Some of these couples are same-sex couples but the majority are heterosexual couples.

In the year 2001, a third data collection was undertaken which showed a slight increase in LAT relationships from the survey results in 1998. Fourteen percent of the respondents that were neither married nor cohabiting said that they were living in a LAT relationship in 2001. This suggests that the numbers had risen to about 300,000 people or about 150,000 couples.[2]

At that time we knew very little about how many LAT relationships there were in Norway. However, in 2002, the Norwegian Bureau of Statistics collected data in order to find out how many LAT relationships there were in Norway. Approximately 1000 people, aged 18–74, were interviewed. Eight percent of those who said that they were neither married nor cohabiting saw themselves as living in LAT relationships. The interview study suggests that about 60,000–70,000 people or 30,000–35,000 couples were living in a LAT relationship in Norway, in 2002.

QUALITATIVE STUDY

In our research we have also interviewed 100 people living in LAT relationships. The interviews were in-depth and structured, but not standardized. The interviews were between one and three hours in length. In order to visualize interviewees' conception of family, a three-step method was used (Levin, 1993). First they were asked: "Who is in your family—could you make a list?" Second, "Could you place your family on this sheet of paper according to closeness and distance to you?" Third, they were interviewed about their relationships to their family members and especially their living arrangements.

In some cases we were able to identify people in a LAT relationship but were unable to interview these couples. These people were given a short semi-standardized questionnaire which they answered and sent back to us.

The sample is a convenience sample, and we found our informants in a variety of ways. Sometimes at lectures or presentations, when we had mentioned LAT relationships, people in the audience approached us. We were interviewed in Norwegian and Swedish magazines and newspaper articles in which we solicited people living in LAT relationships to take part in the research. When people asked us about our research and we mentioned the LAT study, some volunteered to be interviewed and others told us about parents, children or friends in LAT relationships. The age range of our informants in the qualitative study is from 20 to 80 years.

The interviewees may be divided into two subgroups:

1. Those who would like to live together but for one reason or another have decided not to do so.
2. Those who would not live together even if they could, and who want to remain a couple *living apart together.*

I start by describing some patterns we found in the first subgroup.

WE WOULD HAVE LIVED TOGETHER IF IT WERE NOT FOR ONE OR MORE REASONS . . .

Responsibility and Care

One reason why some people choose to live in LAT relationships has to do with their feelings of responsibility for other people. This feeling of responsibility is so strong that they do not want a new relationship to another person to impinge upon their deeply felt duties. In particular, it is the responsibility and care for children still living at home and for older parents that are given as reasons for *not living together* with new partners. If another person moves into his or her apartment or if he or she moves away to another apartment, major changes will occur. When it comes to relationships with older parents, people often did not want to leave them alone as this can be a way of forcing them to move into a home for the aged. These are people who do not believe that their children or their parents have appropriated their own decision-making. Rather, they understand their relationship to the new partner as unrelated to the relationship and responsibility they have for their children or for their parents. Here LAT relationships imply that one simply does not have to move *everyone* into the same living arrangement.

People in this situation look upon the new couple relationship as an *addition to* the relationships they already have and not as being *instead of* those other relationships. The new couple relationship is not allowed to threaten or replace already existing relationships. It is simply easier to give each relationship "its due" by not creating a stepfamily household. By keeping the home as it is, it is easier to keep relationships, with children or aged parents, as they are. Even for a parent who is not the custodian of his or her children, to move to another home can be seen as *cheating* one's own children, to leave the child's parental home for the sake of another adult. The following example illustrates such a situation.

Fred and Freda were first an unmarried LAT and they later got married but kept their LAT relationship until all of the children had moved out of their homes. Fred was 56 years old and Freda was 51 at the time of the interview. They met 10 years before when Fred's three children were living at home with him in his custody. At that time, his children were 14, 16, and 20 years old. Freda had two children. They were 10 and 14 years old, and in her custody. Her ex-husband took care of their children every second weekend and during some holidays. Fred and Freda were decided that they would not move in together until their own children had grown up and left home. Both lived in the same city, 15 minutes apart by public transportation. They met and fell in love and felt that they were a couple very quickly, but it took about a year until they were in a LAT relationship, according to their view at the time of the interview. At the beginning of the relationship, they stayed overnight at each other's home during weekends. They did not tell their children about their true relationship at first, but introduced each other to their children as old and good friends. Neither of them wanted to push the other or to be pushed into relationships with one another's children. After some time, the children on both sides accepted their parent's new relationship.

Two years before the interview took place, Freda and Fred were married. They continued to live in a LAT relationship at the time of the interview. We later learned that they now do live together, after having spent 10 years of their lives in a LAT relationship, both as unmarried and married LATs.

When it comes to caring for elderly parents, LAT relationships can be a solution for those who want to continue to care for their elderly parents and still keep a relationship with a new partner. Often, people in this situation have lived in close contact and proximity to their parents for many years. They might have liked or disliked this arrangement, but they accepted it as a particular feature of their own lives. When the elderly mother or father dies, or becomes severely ill, there are no choices for these people. They dutifully accept the long-term care of their aged or disabled parent.

Taking care of elderly or disabled parents is a strongly felt duty, and a very high priority in the value system and self-understanding of many of those we interviewed that were in this particular situation. If they fail to provide a high level of personal care, they know that they themselves will suffer severely, with feelings of guilt, for not behaving in accordance with their own standards of responsibility and morality. For others in this situation, it is a way of "repaying" the older generation for what it has done for the child in earlier stages of life. Perhaps some respondents had received important help and support with their own children from their parents. All in all, it seems to be preferable for them to remain in their existing surroundings and to continue to care for the elderly parent. It may seem easier, all things considered, to have a LAT relationship, with their partner living in another home. In this way, one can avoid choosing between the aged (and sometimes disabled) parent and the new partner. They can have both.

A strong feeling of responsibility and the duty to care for children and aged parents existed in these people long before they met their new partners. In these examples, the respondents perceive that they are *significant others* for their children and for their parents. If they do not act in accordance with their feelings of responsibility, they know that feelings of guilt will result. The LAT relationship allows them to care for children or aged parents *and* maintain a relationship with a new partner. For these people, the situation is not "either/or" but "both/and." By caring for those others who are so closely related to them they are caring for themselves, too.

They Work or Study in Different Places

In many ways, reconciling the demands created by work or study with a relationship with someone in a different geographic location is tackled by relying upon a similar way of thinking. People in this situation do not want to choose *either* their partner *or* their job. They want both and they decide to keep both. A consequence of this decision requires them to live in separate homes. This might be looked upon as a more temporary condition, in light of their own perceptions, because one's job, at some future date, may be changed. Their couple relationship and their jobs are important to them and they want to maintain both. If either moved to their partner's domicile, career opportunities would diminish. This might not be solely a question of money. Even if the other person could support him or her, the arrangement would not be acceptable. Being economically independent is a value of high importance for these people. This characteristic is sometimes referred to as the tendency towards individualization. A century ago, and even half a century ago, people were seldom able to think in the same terms as these people now do. Individualization is more pronounced today. There is more acceptance for the idea that couples need to find ways to better accommodate one another's needs for self-realization. Formerly, the matter was framed as a way of showing one's love: "If you love me enough, you will relocate." The job and the partner are seen as being in competition, and one has to choose between them. In particular there would have been social expectations pressurizing the woman to relocate. Ordinarily, she was the one who was expected to give up her job and her friends. Today, there is acceptance of the idea that she can keep her job and her friends, as well as her relationship with children, parents, and other relatives, and at the same time have a relationship with a man and maintain separate dwellings.

This situation also includes students who study in different places. We were somewhat surprised when we received answers from students defining themselves as LAT partners. We, in our old-fashioned way, saw them more as "going steady." This is a way of seeing their relationship as less serious and uses the traditional marital system as the guiding model (Trost, 1979). However, these students told us that if it were not for their studies, they would have been living together as a cohabiting couple. Since their studies are preventing them, they define themselves as LAT partners.

Cohabitation, as a socially accepted phenomenon, has changed the definition of the situation for these students, relative to what would have been the case earlier, when cohabitation was generally frowned upon by large groups of people. Our material consists solely of people who define themselves as living in a LAT relationship. This means that we have no access to any data from people who define themselves as "going steady." It would have been interesting to compare those defining themselves in a LAT relationship with those who do not do so, but who do see themselves as "going steady." For students, the LAT relationship is a temporary one. They expect to live together after graduation and find jobs near their common home.

Given the technological realities of our contemporary lives, the world seems to be getting smaller and smaller. Telephones, faxes, emails, airplanes, all function to make it easier and easier to keep in contact with people living far away. Some of our informants report that they live on different continents. One of the respondents in our study told us that she lives in Norway and he in Malaysia. For some periods in their relationship, she has lived with him in Malaysia, and he with her in Oslo. They define their two homes as theirs in common, but pay the expenses for them separately.

These couples look upon their lives as a process that changes all the time. Their decisions are only made *for the time being*. When their working situation changes, they may also change their living arrangements. At the same time, they are aware that moving to their partner's home might very well mean losing a lot of the friendships and the close quality of their own social network. Moving away will probably lessen one's contacts with children and grandchildren.

The next subgroup we consider is very different from the first one. Whereas people in the first subgroup do not really want to be in a LAT relationship, for the people in this subgroup the LAT relationship is the *preferred* living arrangement.

THOSE WHO WOULD NOT WISH TO LIVE TOGETHER EVEN IF THEY COULD DO SO, AND STILL WANT TO REMAIN AS A COUPLE

They Don't Want to Repeat the Same Mistake Twice

People in this situation often choose this way of living in order to avoid creating the same conditions that led to the break-up of a former marriage or cohabitation. For many years, they had all experienced living together with another person in a couple relationship—a living situation that ended in divorce or separation. In order to try being in a new couple relationship they feel it is important for them to structure the situation so that another break-up will not occur. They believe that living together, in itself, will change the way each of them relates to the other and that those changes could threaten the relationship's survival. Choosing to live apart is a strategy used in order to avoid another painful separation.

The following example illustrates this approach. A woman had been married for 23 years and had three children from that marriage. When her husband asked her for a divorce, because he had started a relationship with his secretary, her whole world fell apart. But somehow, she managed to pull herself together. She bought an apartment and found meaning in her life as a mother, as a grandmother, and as a professional woman. Time passed, and she began to like her new situation. She enjoyed the freedom of only being responsible for herself, but did not use this freedom to meet new men. She simply did what she wanted to do whenever she wanted to do so, and she enjoyed the realization that no one expected her to "boil the potatoes" each and every

day. She liked being able to join her colleagues for a glass of beer, after work, without inconveniencing anybody else. Eventually, she met a man with whom she fell in love. He was living half an hour's car drive away, and he wanted them to live together like ordinary couples do, in the same home. However, she was worried about making the same mistake twice. Her divorce had been too much of a shock for her, and she would do anything to avoid repeating that experience. She refused his offer to live together, but her refusal was not a sign of her lack of affection and love. On the contrary, she says that she loves him very much, but she does not want to tell him *just how much* she loves him. She says that she would rather live alone during the week and meet him on weekends and spend holidays together. She does not dare to live with him "full-time." The risk is connected to her understanding of her marriage and of its break-up and divorce.

She believes that the break-up of her marriage resulted from the fact that she became less interesting as a woman. She is afraid that she will do the same things that eventually made her boring to her husband. She believes that she knows herself very well, and she is certain that she would begin to perform all the traditional housewife activities. She would prepare food for him when he came home from work, and she would become the person responsible for all their home comforts. This is the behavior she would expect from herself and they are related to her own self-esteem and to her identity as a woman. Since she loves him very much, she does not want to risk the good relationship they share, just to live under the same roof, with all of the everyday duties which he (or she) might define as humdrum and boring. She simply does not want to experience another break-up. She has decided to live in a LAT relationship in order to maintain a good couple relationship and to learn the lesson of her past experiences. Her answer to the question "Do you think that you might move in together one day?" is that they probably will do so when she retires, "if he still wants me."

Retired Couples

For retired people, the situation is somewhat different even though the result is the same. These people too do not want to live together even though they are a couple and love one another. Since one or both are not working any more, there is the possibility of moving in together; but deciding to move in together would create difficult practical decisions and necessitate some sacrifices. For instance, who would make the move? Whose furniture would be redundant? Since both might have lived in a one-person home for many years, a lot of the *things* they own are connected to memories of important happenings from their previous lives. The things are *cherished* as symbols of shared experiences. They are reminders of people, and are not just *dead things* as some people may seem to believe—and as such, they are important to them for their own well-being.

Another reason for not wanting to trade two homes for one is their relationship to children and grandchildren. It may be easier to maintain those relationships if they keep their own homes, rather than living together with a partner in one home. One woman told us that she lives 30 km away from her partner and that she sees him every weekend and every Wednesday, and that they go on holiday together. Moving in together is not discussed as a serious possibility because she gets what she wants from their relationship *as it is.* Why would (or should) she change it? When he is ill, she goes over to his home in order to help him. However, he does not do the same when she is ill. When that happens, she gets help from neighbors and from her daughter-in-law. She likes the situation as it is and it has suited her for 18 years. Early on in their relationship they talked of moving in together but it is not a question they discuss any more. They are quite satisfied with their relationship.

She has been hurt by her partner's criticism of her relationship with her disabled son who lives away. When he comes home her partner feels that she favors him. This criticism was unacceptable for the woman and she gave her partner an ultimatum. Now things have cooled down again and the relationship is back to normal. She is very happy with matters as they stand. One of the things that she most enjoys is their Sunday dinners. She drives them to a neighboring town and he pays for their meal in a nice restaurant. He is also very generous when it comes to giving her gifts and that is something she greatly appreciates.

From Marriage or Cohabitation to a LAT Relationship

Most of the LAT relationship patterns we found consist of people who begin their LAT relationship without first deciding whether or not their relationship was headed for cohabitation or marriage. For some of our respondents the situation has been the other way around. They started as a married or cohabiting couple and the LAT relationship was a solution to difficulties they experienced in those relationships. They lived together for several years but found that they got on each other's nerves in the course of everyday life together. At the same time, they love each other and feel bound to one another. For that reason, they do not want a divorce or a final end to their relationship. It is not what they want, nor is it what their children want. As a solution, one of the partners moves to a nearby apartment and in so doing an alternative way of living, an arrangement that might better fit their lifestyles, for the time being, is undertaken.

An example of this situation is Paul and Paula who met about 20 years ago. They soon became a couple and moved in together. A few years later, they had their first child, and a few years after that their second one. For several years their relationship had been deteriorating and it had become boring. They were finding one another irritating. They still loved one another, but a year before our interview, they decided to separate. They sold their house and bought two apartments just a few minutes' walk from one another. Their children stay with their mother, but they both spend a lot of time with their father, who also spends a lot of time in his ex-cohabitant's apartment, which is larger than his own. This is their way of saving their couple relationship, which in both their opinions would have ended in a break-up without the LAT relationship.

They are clearly still *significant others* to one another and they both want to maintain their relationship but everyday life together simply became too trying. By having two separate homes they hope to be able to maintain the emotions necessary for them to be a loving couple, for each other, and to be good parents to their children. Here the LAT relationship is an alternative to ending their couple relationship. For some people, this alternative might be a peaceful way to a slow divorce without any abrupt changes for themselves or their children.

EXPLAINING LATS

This article has presented a range of situations where the LAT relationship has been established by couples in ways which differ from marriage or cohabitation. Couples often choose a LAT relationship as their living arrangement in order to avoid choosing between (the felt responsibility to care for) an elderly parent, or their own children, and the new partner, which sharing a home would present. An alternative arrangement is partly made possible by LAT relationships because the pressure upon couples "to settle down together" in a common dwelling has decreased. More and more people are accepting the "both/and" solution that LAT relationships provide. As Lewis and Meredith (1989) remark, some adult children live together with a parent, not only because of their sense of duty to care for the parent, but also because they enjoy spending time together with the parent.

A question frequently asked is whether or not LAT relationships occur in all classes within society. Is it a decision that only the financially well-off can make? Our findings show that one can find LAT relationships among all sorts of people. This does not imply that being financially well-off does not make the living arrangements easier to manage. Certainly long-distance LAT relationships require the couple to spend more money on telephone calls and travel, and one home is cheaper to maintain than two. There is no argument with these matters of fact. In most cases, however, in our research, where LAT relationships are found to exist, the couple already each have their own home and are used to paying for their own home expenses.

Why is it that the number of LAT relationships has been increasing? Why have we not noticed or registered LAT relationships before? There may be more than one answer to these questions. One factor is the mortality rate. The lower the mortality rate, the greater the likelihood for a person not only to live longer, but also to experience divorce, the death of a spouse and separation from a non-marital cohabitant, and thus, the greater the likelihood, *ceteris paribus,* for the person to enter into a LAT relationship, or some other new relationship, for that matter. When mortality rates were higher, a greater number of marriages were dissolved by the death of one of the spouses. The need for divorce lessens, therefore, when mortality rates are high.

The closer society got to the 20th century, the greater the decline in remarriages, the greater the rise in the divorce rates, and the greater the fall in mortality rates. The remarriage rate near the middle of the 19th century was about 20 percent, in Norway, but by 1885, it had decreased to about 15 percent (see Sundt, 1975). The remarriage rate continued to decrease during the 20th century, and the lowest rate was reached just before the outbreak of the Second World War, when the remarriage rate was approximately 8 percent (Levin, 1994). During the same period of time, divorce increased and new laws regulating divorce in Norway in 1915 and in Sweden in 1916 came into effect. These laws accepted fault and no-fault grounds for divorce and subsequently the divorce rate continued to increase.

A second factor that has contributed to the increase in LAT relationships has to do with changes in the labor market. A higher degree of specialization is required, these days, and that means a demand for higher levels of education for most job applicants. Fewer people can simply decide to relocate and assume that they will be able to find a good job. This is true for both men and women. Working women are less able to follow their husbands and find a job when they relocate. The relatively short history of the full-time housewife is almost over, in many countries, and in some others, this role has already become a thing of the past. In order to really understand the new structure of relationships between women and men, including LAT relationships, one has to look into the many processes promoting gender equality and equity in contemporary society.

A third factor has to do with the frequency of travel and with the availability and use of IT communication. People on holiday, or travelling because of their job, meet people living in other places. Some of these meetings result in couples falling in love. Many of these relationships will last, and if one or both cannot or does not want to relocate, they might form a long-distance LAT relationship. Travel for leisure or for work will probably increase, even though advances in IT communication continue apace. Couples are being generated on the Internet. Some of those *virtual* relationships may develop into long-distance LAT relationships. We will probably see an important increase in LAT relationships in the near future, and the growth will include married and unmarried couples choosing to live in a LAT relationship.

Traditionally, informal social norms prescribed that a couple should live in the same home. Sharing a domicile was the taken-for-granted pattern for couples. In cases where the two could not live together, living arrangements were considered to be merely temporary. With the high divorce rate, the increasing numbers of women who are gainfully employed, and the considerable victories that have been won, by women, in the battle for equity, society and its norms have changed. The move towards greater gender equality and equity has had consequences for intimacy and for couple relationships (see Giddens, 1994). Few men, but many women, see advantages in LAT relationships. Therefore the woman is usually the active one in suggesting to move apart.

To summarize, only a few decades ago, marriage was the sole socially approved institution for couples planning to live together. Cohabitation was frowned upon and seen as a deviant phenomenon. There has been a remarkable change in the acceptance of cohabitation. These days, it is more often seen as being a viable option, and it has become an accepted social institution, in its own right, alongside marriage. Without this acceptance of cohabitation, LAT relationships would not have emerged. One might say that cohabitation, as a socially accepted institution, was a prerequisite for the establishment of LAT relationships. The recognition of LAT relationships as a new social phenomenon, in several western societies, and the documented rise in its frequency, as well as the general increasing awareness of the term "LAT relationship," are factors at work today that may some day establish the LAT relationship as a generally recognized and accepted social institution in many more countries.

There are many reasons for predicting that LAT relationships will be more common in the near future. The labor market will probably not return to the relatively simple structure it had only a few decades ago. Specialization will probably continue to increase, affecting even more job-holders. Holiday and work-related travel probably will not decrease, even if IT communication becomes even more important. In fact, IT communication might be used more frequently as a way for people to meet new partners. Same-gender couples may increasingly "come out of the closet" and cohabit or form LAT relationships. Divorce and separation rates will probably not decrease, and new partnerships will be formed in increasing numbers. The LAT relationship may become a more common way for dealing with a difficult marriage or non-marital cohabitation. The mortality rate will probably continue to decrease in most countries, and that means that people will live longer, and probably be healthier, and thus more prone to find new partners.

NOTES

The research reported on in this article was carried out with Professor Jan Trost, Uppsala University, Sweden.

1. This second survey was financed by SKOP and by the Magnus Bergwall Foundation.
2. If the percentages in England were the same as in Sweden, there would be, approximately, 750,000 couples living in LAT relationships.

■ Review Questions

1. Are LAT relationships "families"?
2. Why might couples choose not to live together?

CHAPTER 7

Cohabitation and Marriage

A majority of marriages now begin with a period of cohabitation—the couple first lives together without marrying. Prior to about 1970, cohabitation was frowned upon and was very rare except among the poor. Today, it is widely accepted. This new relationship stage has greatly changed the ways couples think about marriage. A half century ago, women and men married soon after high school or college and expected to cope with tight budgets for a while until they achieved financial stability. But today, many young couples are postponing marriage until after they have achieved financial stability. Marriage was the start of young adulthood in the mid-twentieth century; today it is often the end of it. The interviews with cohabiting couples that Pamela J. Smock, Wendy D. Manning, and Meredith Porter describe in the first reading in this chapter illustrate this change.

While presenting excerpts from these interviews, the authors also write about the process of sociological research. They contrast "quantitative" and "qualitative" studies. The former are the statistical studies of survey or government data that dominate much of social scientific research. Reading 1-1, "The Family in Trouble: Since When? For Whom?" is an example of a quantitative study. Qualitative studies consist of analyses of what people say or do in real life or what they have written in diaries or letters. Many qualitative studies involve detailed, first-person observations of a small sample of individuals or families over a long time period, a method that is called "ethnography" by anthropologists. The Smock et al. reading does not have the intensive, long-term observations of an ethnography, but it is qualitative because the authors rely on the words that people said to them in discussion groups (i.e., person *x* said to us . . .) rather than on statistical summaries (i.e., 75 percent of the sample said "yes"). Although sociologists sometimes define themselves as either quantitative or qualitative researchers, the two methods can be used to complement each other. Smock et al. have done statistical research in the past. They chose to conduct a qualitative study because it could help them understand the meanings of the patterns they were seeing in their statistical data. By alternating between quantitative and qualitative studies, the authors hope to combine a broad statistical portrait of cohabitors with an in-depth understanding of what they are thinking.

Kathryn Edin and Maria Kefalas conducted an ethnographic study to answer the question of why women in low-income families have been postponing marriage but not postponing having children—with the result that the percentage of children born outside of marriage has risen dramatically among low-income women. This phenomenon has been puzzling social scientists and policy makers. In order to understand it better, Edin and Kefalas studied women and men in eight low-income neighborhoods in the Philadelphia area for over two years. The authors wanted to learn more about the nature of intimate relationships in low-income communities and about low-income women's attitudes and values about childbearing and marriage. They published their findings in a 2005 book, *Promises I Can Keep: Why Poor Women Put Motherhood before Marriage.* The second reading in this chapter is an article they wrote for the magazine *Contexts* summarizing what they found.

READING 7-1

"Everything's There Except Money"
How Money Shapes Decisions to Marry among Cohabitors

Pamela J. Smock

Wendy D. Manning

Meredith Porter

The last few decades have ushered in significant changes in family patterns (Casper & Bianchi, 2002; Thornton, Fricke, Axinn, & Alwin, 2001; Thornton & Young-Demarco, 2001). After a brief period characterized by early marriage and low levels of divorce after World War II, recent decades have been marked by lower levels of childbearing, higher divorce rates, increases in the average age at marriage, rising nonmarital childbearing, and rising levels of cohabitation. Although most Americans still marry at some point and the vast majority express strong desires to marry, unmarried cohabitation has dramatically transformed the marriage process. Today, the majority of marriages and remarriages begin as cohabiting relationships. Most young men and women have cohabited or will cohabit, cohabitation has increased in all age groups, and cohabitation is increasingly a context for childbearing and childrearing (Bumpass & Lu, 2000; Casper & Bianchi; Manning, 2002).

Given that cohabitation is now the modal path to marriage, an important issue is whether and under what circumstances cohabitation leads to marriage. A long line of research in the social sciences has drawn on data from surveys to examine the economic determinants of marriage. More recently, studies have emerged examining similar

Pamela J. Smock, Wendy D. Manning, and Meredith Porter, "'Everything's There Except Money': How Money Shapes Decisions to Marry among Cohabitors," *Journal of Marriage and Family* 67 (August 2005): 680–696. Reprinted by permission.

issues for cohabiting unions (e.g., Clarkberg, 1999; Oppenheimer, 2003; Sassler & McNally, 2003). . . .

CURRENT INVESTIGATION

Our study builds on prior work by exploring how cohabiting men and women link economic circumstances and the marriage decision-making process. One motivation for this work is that it is difficult with quantitative research alone to understand why education, income, or employment measures are positively and significantly correlated with marriage. Our general aim is to triangulate existing quantitative studies with new qualitative data to explore what positive economic circumstances mean to cohabiting men and women and how those meanings shape marriage decisions. As Lin (1998) argues, analyses based on quantitative data can often provide us with the *what*—that two or more variables are related and that there may be a credible causal story—but they cannot necessarily provide us with the *how* and the *why*.

We thus draw on data from 115 in-depth interviews with men and women who are now, or were recently, cohabiting to explore whether and how financial issues are involved in cohabitors' thoughts and feelings about marriage. Our approach is informed by the social psychological paradigm of symbolic interactionism, which posits that individual behavior is based not only on what is, but also on individuals' interpretations of what is. This perspective assumes that individuals categorize and construct their social world, subjectively define situations, and use these interpretations to adapt their behavior (Mead, 1934; Stryker, 1972). Most broadly, the symbolic interactionist paradigm holds that identifying subjective meanings and interpretations is essential for understanding individual behavior.

Our study adds to extant knowledge in two additional ways. First, we focus on working- and lower middle-class individuals. The few qualitative studies on our general topic tend to focus on the disadvantaged, particularly low-income mothers. We purposefully set out to study young men and women who have not made it solidly into the middle class, but, for the most part, are not officially poor or involved in the welfare system. A quantitative study spanning the years from 1960 to 2000 underscores the importance of this endeavor. Ellwood and Jencks (2001) show that the increase in single parenthood over the past 40 years has been concentrated in the middle and lower thirds of the educational distribution, and not just the lower third.

Second, we interview both parents and nonparents and restrict our focus to cohabiting (or recently cohabiting) young adults rather than including those in an array of relationship statuses. Our exclusive focus on cohabitors is important because the modal path to marriage is through cohabitation. Including those who are childless is useful because it reflects the actual composition of cohabiting couples today; approximately 60% of cohabiting unions do not include children (Fields & Casper, 2001).

METHOD

Our analysis is based on semistructured in-depth interviews with 115 young adults who were currently cohabiting or had recently cohabited. For the latter group, the median time since the end of the cohabitation in either dissolution or marriage (see below) was one and a half years, with the majority having ended the cohabitation within the last 3 years. Our interview strategy drew on the idea of the relationship as "career" by asking how and why cohabiting relationships began, perceptions of the future of the relationship at the beginning of the cohabitation, numerous aspects of the relationship itself, views on prerequisites for marriage, perceptions of how being married would differ from cohabiting, perceptions of how cohabitation differs from dating, and how and why the cohabiting relationship ended (if relevant).

At the time of interview, 47% of our sample were cohabiting, 26% were married (after having cohabited with their spouse or someone else), 26% were currently single after having recently cohabited, and one respondent was divorced after having cohabited and then married. The respondents were interviewed in 2002, largely between April and October, and were 18–36 years old, with a median age of 26, at the time of interview. Additionally, our sample is diverse such that we have at least 15 interviews with each gender and race/ethnic group (White, Black, Latino, or Latina).

The respondents all live in the vicinity of Toledo, Ohio, which has a sociodemographic distribution quite similar to that of the entire nation. For example, 2000 Census data indicate that the populations of the Metropolitan Statistical Area of Toledo and the nation are similar in terms of race (13% in Toledo and 12% in the United States are Black), education (80% in Toledo and 84% in the United States are high school graduates), median income ($50,046 in Toledo and $50,287 in the United States), and marital status (74% in Toledo and 76% in the United States are married couple families).

We recruited our sample by means of personal contacts, as well as encounters with potential respondents in various parts of the community (e.g., local coin laundry, grocery stores, restaurants, the neighborhood, parties). This was a time-consuming effort in that the key requirement was to interview a racially and ethnically diverse sample of men and women who were currently cohabiting or recently cohabiting. In addition, to meet the demographic specifications of the sample, some respondents were referred by community organizations or agencies or were recruited in areas in which the pool of prospective participants had a greater probability of being a specific race or ethnicity. Note, though, that respondents were not necessarily clients of the agencies but often employees of them; thus, we remained cognizant of seeking interviews largely with working- and lower middle-class men and women. Some interviews were conducted immediately following an introduction but most were

TABLE 7.1

DISTRIBUTION OF SAMPLE (%) ACCORDING TO RACE, GENDER, EDUCATION, INCOME, AND EMPLOYMENT STATUS

%	White male 19.1	White female 25.2	Black male 13.9	Black female 14.8	Latino 13.0	Latina 13.9	Total 100.0
Educational attainment							
Less than high school	4.5	3.4	18.8	0	33.3	25	12.2
High school or GED	22.7	10.3	31.3	41.2	40.0	18.8	25.2
Technical or some college	50.0	48.3	43.8	41.2	20.0	56.3	44.3
College graduate	22.7	37.9	6.3	17.6	6.7	0.0	18.3
Personal income							
Less than $20,000	22.2	50	56.3	64.7	69.2	92.9	57.3
$20,000–$40,000	50.0	50.0	31.3	35.3	30.8	7.1	35.4
More than $40,000	27.8	0.0	12.5	0.0	0.0	0.0	7.3
Employment status							
Employed	95.5	93.1	81.3	88.2	53.3	62.5	81.7
Not employed	4.5	6.9	18.7	11.8	46.6	37.5	18.2
N	22	29	16	17	15	16	115

scheduled for a later time. Additionally, the sample was partially a snowball sample, with approximately 30% of the respondents referred from the pool of participating respondents.

The interviews were semistructured and lasted, on average, 2 hours, with the mean length of a transcribed interview being 39 pages. Although semistructured interviews provide some organization, they also allow the interviewer to probe with follow-up questions and pursue additional lines of inquiry. Generally, in-depth interviews are an excellent method for exploring perceptions, behavioral patterns, and their cognitive justifications, ultimately helping to illuminate the causal processes that quantitative social science seeks to uncover (Weiss, 1994). We used one interviewer for all interviews: She is a member of the community who is experienced in interviewing racially and economically diverse populations in the area, and our reading of the transcripts suggests that she achieved outstanding rapport with the vast majority of respondents.

Table 7.1 shows the distribution of our sample according to education, personal income, and employment status. Our sample can be characterized as largely working class and lower middle

class (i.e., high school graduates and those with some college or technical school training). The educational breakdown of our sample is as follows: less than high school (12.2%), high school (25%), some college (44.3%), college graduate or more (18.3%). The majority of our respondents are currently employed (82%), although a few are enrolled in school full time, and some are both employed and enrolled in school part time. Yearly individual incomes range from about $10,000 per year to $55,000 per year, with the majority (57%) earning less than $20,000 per year and only 7% earning more than $40,000. Couple incomes range from approximately $15,000 to $60,000, with most reporting combined incomes in the $20,000 to $40,000 range (not in table). Income varies significantly by race/ethnicity and gender. White men and women are the most highly educated; White men are most likely to earn at least $40,000 per year; and over half of all Latinos and Blacks earn less than $20,000 per year. Also noteworthy is that Latinos and Latinas are least likely to be currently employed. Finally, a range of parenthood statuses is represented in our data: 45% are childless, 23% have a biological child with their partner, 6% have a biological child from a prior relationship, 10% have a stepchild(ren), with the remainder having some combination of stepchildren and biological children from a prior relationship (not in table).

Our coding proceeded whereby categories were derived as they emerged from the data. We used a computer program called Atlas/ti to aid in our data management and analyses. The program assists with coding and analysis of qualitative data (Weitzman, 1999), and provides tools to manage, store, extract, compare, explore, and reassemble meaningful pieces of data flexibly and systematically. The development of our coding scheme was an intensive, iterative analytic task. Essentially, coding applies a meaning or interpretation to a segment of data—in our case, textual data from the interviews. It consists of creating categories and marking segments of the data with these codes. A single paragraph or sentence may have one code or several and these may be overlapping with other text segments.

The authors each read a subset of transcripts, coding them independently. We then examined *intercoder reliability* by using a merge function in the program to juxtapose codes, review similarity of code lists, compare the number of codes derived, and assess consistency between coders in segments of text coded (i.e., where segments begin and end). Although we had few interpretive disagreements, we used the merge function as a tool to explore and discuss the meaning of minor discrepancies in our interpretations and, eventually, to generate a coding scheme capturing our consensus on the issues.

Our analyses involved first searching for instances in the interviews in which the issue of money was raised by the respondent either in response to a question about "what would need to be in place for marriage" or at other points in the interview when respondents raised the issue themselves. We then analyzed the context in which finances were raised—that is, whether and how respondents themselves made the connection between economic factors and marriage. We organize our results around several emergent

themes regarding aspects of finances, providing representative quotations to illustrate these themes. Note that the interviewer did not probe to specifically seek *economic* prerequisites for marriage. Thus, the findings we report here may be conservative estimates of the salience of economics in marital decision making among cohabitors.

RESULTS

We asked cohabitors about their views on marriage prerequisites, or what kinds of things needed to be "in place" to decide to marry; we also take account of instances in which these issues were raised or elaborated by the respondent at other points in the interview. To obtain a broad view of this issue, Table 7.2 categorizes individuals into four groups: mentioned only economic issues, mentioned only relationship/individual qualities, mentioned both types of issues, and gave no response. Economic aspects include money, jobs, assets (e.g., houses, savings), or education. Relationship/individual factors include concerns such as needing more time in the relationship, quality of the relationship, age/maturity, and substance abuse or violence.

As shown in Table 7.2, most respondents perceive both relationship and economic factors as important for marriage. Approximately 23% named only economic criteria or only relationship criteria; nearly 50% named both. Thus, overall, 72% of the sample identified at least one economic factor as a prerequisite for the relationship to result in marriage. Table 7.2 also suggests that the prominence of economic concerns may vary by race, with Blacks more likely to cite economic factors than Latinos or Whites (82% vs. 67% and 71% among Whites and Latinos, respectively).

In the remainder of the paper we explore the specific aspects of economics that cohabitors believe important for marriage. Five central themes emerged from the data: (a) having enough money, (b) the ability to pay for a "real" wedding,

TABLE 7.2

DISTRIBUTION OF SAMPLE (%) BY PERCEIVED PREREQUISITES FOR MARRIAGE

Total sample	*N* 115	Only economic 22.6	Only relationship 23.5	Relationship and economic 49.6	No mention of either 4.3
Gender					
Male	53	20.8	24.5	47.2	7.5
Female	62	24.2	22.6	51.6	1.6
Race/ethnicity					
White	51	25.5	29.4	41.2	3.9
Black	33	18.2	18.2	63.6	0.0
Latinos/Latinas	31	22.6	19.4	48.4	9.7

(c) achieving a set of financial goals before marriage, (d) the male partner's capacity to be an economic provider, and (e) lack of money as a source of stress and relationship conflict.

Money as Capstone in the Cohabitation-Marriage Sequence: "Everything's There Except Money"

About one third of those citing any economic factor mentioned money needed to be in place for them to marry (or have married) their cohabiting partner. Leroy, who is 29 years old and recently unemployed, says, "I don't really know 'cause the love is there uh . . . trust is there. Everything's there except money." Similarly, 25-year-old Ofilia says, "Money, it's just money. Nothing else." And Joseph, 31 years old, says, "Basically everything was in place, just basically it gets back to the money." Patricio, a 20-year-old unemployed young man who dropped out of high school, puts it perhaps most straightforwardly: "If I ever got rich I would marry Melissa." Calvin, who is 24 and also unemployed, says, "I want to be financially okay when I, when I've decided to take that step."

Other respondents are somewhat more specific. The idea of marriage appears to be associated with having attained a certain "comfortable" financial status. Holly, a 36-year-old store supervisor whose cohabiting relationship dissolved without marriage, describes how getting married should signify that one is no longer struggling economically:

I: Ok. How then, like what would have had to been in place for you to have gotten married?

R: Money.

I: Ok. Tell me a little bit about what that means.

R: Money means um . . . stability. I don't want to struggle, if I'm in a partnership, then there's no more struggling, and income-wise we were still both struggling.

The implication is that one does not marry if one is struggling financially; marriage both connotes and requires a certain level of economic stability. Holly's comment about financial stability was echoed in some other cohabitors' concerns. Donald, a roofer, tries to describe what he means: "We feel when we get financially, you know what I'm saying, stable, then we will be ready."

Andy, a 26-year-old computer technician whose relationship recently ended, also talks about wanting to be financially comfortable, but expresses it in negative terms, mainly focusing on debt: "I'm still at a financially unstable point because of like school loans. And I don't want to impose that upon anybody else. Like that's one of my major things before I get married, I want to be paid up. . . ."

Thus, empathizing with what he thinks a future partner might feel, Andy will not marry unless he is basically debt free. This concern was echoed by several others as they thought about what needed to be in place to marry: Getting "bills paid down," "caught up on some bills," and dealing with student loans, all inhibited the sense of being ready to marry.

Heidi, an assistant manager at a shoe store, lives with her boyfriend and her boyfriend's parents. She implies that marriage, but not cohabitation, requires economic and residential independence, which boils down to having enough money:

> Right now, we wouldn't be able to afford, you know, to be out on our own. . . . To have to pay rent . . . to pay bills . . . I mean, I realize that you're going to have rent and I realize that you're going to have you know, utilities and groceries and furnishings and stuff like that. I don't think he realizes that half the time, and he's like, "Hmmm, so let's go!" I think that we need to have more income coming in so we can be able to do that.

Money and the Symbolic Meaning of the Wedding Ceremony: A Real Wedding

For some cohabitors, the issue of enough money is tied directly to the ability to afford a wedding. Overall, one fifth of those mentioning any economic issue as important for marriage mentioned weddings, or more precisely, the cost of weddings, as an impediment to getting married. This is especially noteworthy because the interviewer never raised the issue of weddings, and it emerged without prompting.

Respondents often cite saving to have a real wedding as a prerequisite to marriage. Abram, a 27 year old, said he knew right away that he wanted to marry his girlfriend, but "we never saved up enough money to have the wedding we wanted." (He also mentioned the cost of a honeymoon as part of what he considers a proper wedding.) Another respondent, Vicente, currently cohabiting with his fiancée, posited that the purpose of cohabitation is actually to pay for a wedding: "I mean cohabitation, I think it's alright I mean. You see someone you love and if you want to have a big wedding, you can't afford it, you go live with them until you can afford it."

Other respondents said they simply could not afford a wedding, even if they had plans to marry. Petra, who works as an administrative assistant, reported that her boyfriend tells her he "wants to marry me and that he wants a big wedding and, you know, he wants the whole nine yards, but right now we can't really afford it." And, for Ofilia, having a wedding competes monetarily with raising children; she and her boyfriend do not have enough money to do both:

> . . . he gave me a ring, he asked me to marry him a long time ago. We talked about getting married, it's just we don't have anyone to pay for the wedding and I don't want to go downtown. So, it's on us . . . and when we came down to the decision of do we want kids or do we want the marriage and for now we wanted the kids. . . .

Typically, respondents who talked about weddings aim to have sufficient financial resources for a relatively large wedding. But for others the impediment is just being able to afford an engagement ring or a modest wedding. Geraldine, a 28-year-old law clerk, reported that her partner was "trying to sell his trumpet" to pay for her ring. Indeed, even very modest weddings may pose a serious obstacle to marriage for working- and middle-class young adults. Ben, a 30-year-old railroad conductor, said he did not know how he would come up with $5,000 for a wedding, exclaiming "Weddings are expensive!"

Several men and women made a distinction between a "church" wedding and a "downtown" (or "courthouse" or "justice of the peace") wedding; this distinction was quite salient to them. When asked whether she and her partner had considered marriage, Terri, a beautician, says:

> I did, I did a lot. He just said he wasn't ready or we don't have the money, you know wait until we get our finances straight. Well, you never can get your finances straight, it don't matter how long and I don't want a big wedding, I already told him that, I want to go downtown and that's it, it's not going to cost that much but for some odd reason he just,

I don't think he ever wants to get married to be truthful.

Here, note that Terri believes that her partner's persistent desire to wait until their finances are "straight"—despite her willingness to compromise on a downtown weddings—amounts to a strategy to avoid marriage.

Heidi, too, decides that although she yearns for a church wedding, a downtown wedding would be acceptable:

I've always wanted a church wedding. You know . . . I want to walk down the aisle with my Dad, and you know, I want to dance with my Grandpa (laughs). . . . But if it came down to the point where Eric was just like, I really don't want to have a church wedding, let's just go downtown, I, I love him so much, I want to be with him so much, that I probably would do it.

Among other cohabitors, especially some women, the resistance to "going downtown" was formidable. Annie, a 22-year-old home health care aid, explains that she's just waiting for her boyfriend to change his mind because "until he does, we just won't get married. I'm not going downtown. . . . I say, you don't want a big wedding, we're not going to get married." Gloria, a 25-year-old woman who works for a telephone company says, "We're gonna do it right. So, we wouldn't rush a wedding like—let's just go get married 'justice of peace.'. . . We want to have a big wedding. We want to have, you know, both of our families enjoy it." Here, one can see that perceptions of prerequisites for marriage also involve relations to others such as family members. Asked whether he is considering marriage, Leroy answered:

R: Well, it crossed my mind. Um . . . I always said I just couldn't afford it. If I could afford it I probably would be married by now. . . . You can't get married for free.

I: Ok. But you could go down to the justice of the peace, you could have a simple church wedding, you could, I mean. . . .

R: But that's the poor people way.

Despite the fact that Leroy is nearly poor—having recently lost a job paying him about $15,000 per year—it is vital to him to have a real wedding rather than a "poor people" wedding. Leroy goes on to explain his reactions to his cousin's recent wedding. Although it was in a church, it was small, simple, and inexpensive. There were no bridesmaids, groomsmen, or flower girls, leading Leroy to say that "it just didn't seem like a wedding" and it was more like a "get together." Kerry, a homemaker, appears to agree. She reports that her sister-in-law told her, "Oh, don't go downtown, you should have a wedding!"—implying that marriage by a justice of the peace is not considered a "real wedding." Other cohabitors also spoke of "just" going downtown, with the implication that this is a minimal, lesser sort of wedding.

James, a 36-year-old carpenter, describes how he and his girlfriend are trying to save up for a house, so he suggested that they go downtown to marry and then have a real wedding in a couple of years when they could afford it:

And her thing was "No, I don't want to do that. I want to go back home, I want to have this big ceremony with my mother by my side." My thing was "We just can't afford it, your mother doesn't have any money. It's not like she's going to pay for anything. I'm going to pay for this and we can't afford it. You know. So, no we can't do it." Then her thing was "Well, no I'm not going down to the court house and getting married." You know, and that was about the extent of our conversation.

Wesley, a 22 year old who works as a supervisor at a manufacturing plant, was quite specific about the need for a little "financial time" because of his girlfriend's desire for a "big 30, 40 thousand thing and I'm not quite ready for that . . . we need to get some more of my student loans paid off and stuff like that before I can even do that."

It is noteworthy that in all cases the young couples appear to have sole responsibility to pay for the wedding; parents or other relatives are not mentioned as potential resources. These young adults, unlike their more privileged, upper middle class counterparts, are unable to rely on family members to absorb the cost, or even some of the cost, of a wedding. This is not surprising, given their modest backgrounds, including that over 60% did not grow up with their two biological married parents (not in table).

Money as Part of the Respectability Package: "After X, Y, and Z, We'll Get Married"

A theme that emerged in the interviews is the importance of accomplishing a *set* of financially related goals before marriage. Respondents who mention any one economic factor as a prerequisite for marriage tend to mention more than one. These responses were generally stated as "when we have x, y, and z, we'll get married."

LaTonya, a 24-year-old customer service supervisor, says of her partner: "So he thinks that he needs to graduate and be making more money and, you know, buy me a house and a really big ring and all that kind of thing before we get married." Russell, 19 years old and unemployed, says, "For us to get married we'd have to have a lot. Like we'd have to both have good jobs, money, and a place to stay. And all of that." Fred, a 22-year-old UPS worker, states: "If I had the money, I would, I'd get married, but all that wedding and stuff and I want to get my own place before—I want to settle down before I get married." For Fred, financial resources for a wedding and a home are required before marriage. Malcolm, a 25-year-old waiter, wants a car and a good career prior to marriage: "I don't have a car. . . . I want a nice dependable car, I want a good job as far as career-wise. . . . I want to either be back at school or take a path to going back to school or being in school and being successful and on my way to graduating." Ellen, a graduate student and part-time Medicaid eligibility worker, says, "I think, have enough money set aside, and maybe even living in our own apartment or a house maybe?"

Candace, 25 years old and currently on worker's compensation, provides a more elaborate response. She talks about how she and her partner are interested in marrying, but there are some things they want first:

> Um, we have certain things that we want to do before we get married. We both want very good jobs, and we both want a house, we both want reliable transportation. I'm about to start taking cake decorating classes, and so I can have me some good income, and he—he's trying his best you know? He's been looking out for jobs everywhere, and we—we're trying. We just want to have—we gotta have everything we need before we say "Let's get married."

Although Candace and her partner have discussed these issues at some length and generally agree on their goals, lack of money still intervenes. Candace has passed the General Educational Development (GED) tests and she is not quite sure how many years of schooling her partner has. Their relatively low levels of schooling and unemployed status suggest that they may have enormous difficulty achieving their goals of well-paying jobs in order to marry.

As suggested by several of the above quotations, home ownership is often part of the desired package. Approximately 22% of those mentioning at least one economic factor say that owning their own home is an important prerequisite for marriage.

The case of Peter, 28 years old and in sales, who did end up marrying his partner, is illustrative. Reflecting on the timing of the marriage, he says, "Probably the biggest thing of all . . . was a . . . just a financial stability before we would jump into something like that. I didn't want to get married and go living in an apartment or townhouse. I wanted to save on up to, you know, buy a home, start a family." These results are consistent with a quantitative analysis showing that housing opportunities influence young adults' living arrangements. Hughes (2003) finds that people are more likely to be married when potential earnings are high and housing costs are low.

Sandra, 19 years old, voices a similar concern. She and her partner live half of the time at her parents' house and half at his parents' house. She explained that they are not yet ready for marriage because they lack the resources to set up an independent household, which to her is necessary for marriage:

> I feel like we don't have the resources, I mean he lives here, and my mom always says you know, "if you want to get married, you can live here and it wouldn't matter," 'cause, but I, I wouldn't feel right. I feel like if you get married, you need to go out on your own, and start your own life, and I'm not ready for that right now. And neither is he.

Another factor sometimes mentioned in the set of economic prerequisites for marriage is finishing school. This is consistent with both quantitative (e.g., Manning & Smock, 1995; Thornton, Axinn, & Teachman, 1995) and qualitative research (Sassler, 2004), suggesting that school enrollment inhibits marriage among cohabitors.

Finishing school is not necessarily viewed as an end in itself but as part of a package, tied to attaining economic stability. As Geraldine, a teacher who ended up marrying her partner, says, "I wanted to be graduated from college. . . . I wanted to have a job." Gloria, who also married her partner, has a similar view about the timing of her marriage: "See, I had the degree and I was ready to move to this next step which would be my mate . . . because I've done the schooling and I've secured the job with the security, financial security."

Money and Gendered Expectations: "The Guy Takes Care of the Woman and His Kids"

Another theme that emerged in our interviews is a perception on the part of some cohabitors that men's economic situations are relatively more important than women's for marriage. This came across in two ways. First, it was more common for women than for men to be concerned about their *partner's* jobs. About three times as many women than men reported that they wanted a change in some aspect of their partner's employment (e.g., get a job or get a better paying job) in

order to marry. Additionally, whereas women might mention wanting to finish their degrees and get their career on track before marriage, both men and women made far more references to men's jobs and men's income stability. This is of particular interest, given that cohabitors express more gender-egalitarian views than those who do not cohabit (e.g., Clarkberg, Stolzenberg, & Waite, 1995).

Second, a significant minority of our respondents directly expressed the expectation that men should be able to "provide for" or "support" a family. Such views were expressed by one third of those mentioning at least one economic factor ($n = 26$) and about equally by women and men.

For example, Henry, a 33-year-old information systems manager, reflects: "Had I been . . . in a financial position where I was able to take care of myself and a family, then it might have moved things along quicker." Jamal, 27 years old, says, "What would make me ready? Knowing that I could provide. . . ." Victor, a 27-year-old male, states that "the male's financially responsible for like, you know, the household, paying the bills."

The following interchange with Hector, a 20-year-old student, clearly reveals gendered expectations. Here he is describing why he and his former cohabiting partner did not marry:

> R: . . . if I do get married I need myself to be able to support [her] as well as me and everybody else that gets brought into this family. That's what I, that's what you know, I ideally what I was brought up to be. The guy takes care of the woman and his kids. . . .
>
> I: Is that machismo?
>
> R: Not machismo. That's just how I was brought up. I mean I . . . I could be wrong. I'm probably wrong to most people now because women are taking care of themselves, which is fine.
>
> I: You're more of a traditionalist.
>
> R: Yeah.

I: So you wanted to be able to support her financially?

R: Right.

Sometimes the belief that men are more responsible for the finances in a marriage comes out in subtler ways. Lester, an 18-year-old house painter, says that in order to marry his partner, "I would have to be able to take care of myself before I'd be able to take care of a family." This implies his expectation that it would be his responsibility to take care of a family. Perhaps less realistically, Donald, who is 30 years old and currently cohabiting, muses that he would marry his partner "if I was to hit the lottery and could take her somewhere and we wouldn't have to worry about no problems for the rest of our life."

Women also sometimes express views that men have more responsibility for providing in marriage than women. Kerry, a 25-year-old married homemaker, reflects on what had to be in place for her to marry her partner: "I don't know if he was really thinking about what marriage meant. You know, he was gonna have to take care of us, and have a family now, and be a provider. He was just being kind of immature still. . . ." Kerry also says that they were "trying to get him into a career that, you know, was gonna make enough money for us. . . . And then worry about getting married. . . ." Gloria puts it this way:

> I'm just saying that I feel like, ok, I do want my man to make more money than me, I believe he needs to be the breadwinner and I also feel like, as a wife . . . those are my responsibilities to keep the house clean and all this. . . .

(Gloria went on to say that the minute she would start helping her husband to earn money, then household chores ought to be split.) Candace explains her hesitancy to marry her partner because she needs to know whether "he can take care of us"—Candace has four children—if anything happens to her to prevent her from working.

A case in which we did hear a woman talking about needing to be able to support a family herself was Geraldine's. When describing how she wanted to finish school and start a job before marriage she explained, "If anything happened, or if he died or something, or we did end up getting divorced somewhere down the line, I wouldn't be destitute." Thus, her concern with economic independence, seemingly a prerequisite for marriage, was more a precaution in case of her partner's death or a divorce.

Money and Relationship Quality: "Whenever We'd Get in Fights, It'd Be About Money"

Although not typically referenced in the quantitative literature on the economic determinants of marriage or cohabitation, there is a body of research linking forms of economic distress to marital quality and stability (e.g., Clark-Nicolas & Gray-Little, 1991; Conger et al., 1990; Fox & Chancey, 1998; Johnson & Booth, 1990). Studies suggest that perceived economic hardship has negative effects on relationship quality and is positively related to thoughts of divorce, that employment uncertainty and low income are associated with psychological distress among husbands and wives, and that husbands' job insecurity has a significant positive effect on wives' reports of marital conflict and thoughts of divorce. One study of farm families, for example, suggests that economic hardship is related to thoughts of divorce, with depression accounting for about half of this effect (Johnson & Booth). Another finds that perceived economic adequacy—as measured by adequacy of income for food, clothing, medical care, leisure, and monetary surplus left at month's end—is a significant predictor of marital satisfaction (Clark-Nicolas & Gray-Little).

Our interviews with cohabitors are consistent with these findings, suggesting that financial constraints are sometimes perceived as a source of relationship conflict affecting relationship quality and the sense of a stable future. Over one quarter of the total sample ($n = 31$) told us that money was a problem area when asked about conflict in their relationships. Larry, for example, reports that he had no hopes for the future with his partner at the beginning of their relationship because they argued about "how we're going to pay for these bills. . . ." Aileen, a 32-year-old computer technician, says about her partner:

> [He] doesn't work enough, sometimes. He like, you know, he won't go to work for four days, so his paycheck will be half of what it should be. And then he'll want to pay his bills, before he gives, gives me the money that I, I need. And that pisses me off.

Vicente, when asked about the stability of his relationship, says that "just finances, pretty much, is about the only instability in the relationship." And when asked about the main source of conflict in her relationship, Rose, a married, 27-year-old medical worker, had this to say:

> R: Money.
>
> I: Money. Okay. Does that mean like choices in what each other spends it on?
>
> R: Oh no. Just 'cause we don't have enough . . . to pay all the bills at one time.

The severity of the problem varies of course with economic resources. Thus, although some cohabitors may feel money is a source of tension, they are able to resolve ensuing conflicts. As described by Ellen, a graduate student: "Sometimes when it's dwindling down before we're gonna get paid, and it's like not really a conflict, it's just like, 'What are we gonna do?' And then, like the last fight we had, we fought about money a little bit, we kind of just didn't talk for 10 minutes, then we just started talking about it . . . and we worked it out."

Notably, in the event that financial circumstances improve and stabilize, relationship quality can be positively affected. Ben, now married to his partner, reports that "I think things stabilized quite a bit too with when I started working for the railroad. It stabilized us a lot more. We were making better money . . . it wasn't an up and down, it was a constant." In his prior job, "it was a lot of stress. It was a lot of 'Okay, am I gonna be able to make my bills this month?'" Recalling this earlier time, Ben says:

> It's hard when you don't have money and you can't get what you want to get and you . . . might not be able to get all the groceries that you want to get, you might not be able to put gas in your car to go somewhere. . . . So, I think it's helped us a lot being able to do what we want, when we want, and get the things that we need.

CONCLUSION

Drawing on in-depth interviews with 115 young adults, we find that cohabitors believe that economic circumstances matter for marriage in several different ways. First, having "enough" money is a common consideration, alongside the view that marriage signifies that one is no longer struggling economically. Second, we find that lack of money is associated with relationship conflict, suggesting a significant indirect pathway by which financial difficulties inhibit marriage. Third, although our sample is largely nonpoor, having sufficient money or savings to afford a real wedding is also a concern. Going downtown to the courthouse is not deemed a real wedding, and some cohabitors say they will delay marriage until they can afford a church wedding and reception. Noteworthy is that these young couples, generally from modest backgrounds, anticipate paying for their weddings themselves, without help from parents. Fourth, it is often not attaining a single financial goal, but several as a package, that is perceived as necessary for marriage. Cohabitors' thoughts on this issue often took the form of "after x, y, and z, we'll get married." Most commonly, this economic package includes home ownership, getting out of debt, and financial stability (not living from paycheck to paycheck).

Finally, we find that some cohabitors, both men and women, tend to think that the decision to marry hinges on the male partner's ability to fulfill the breadwinner role—despite the prevailing view that cohabitors are less invested in traditional normative practices than those who do not cohabit. Our study illustrates that some cohabitors are making a direct and conscious connection between willingness to marry and the male partner's ability to provide. This finding is consistent with quantitative studies that have found that men's economic situations may matter more for marriage than women's (e.g., Oppenheimer, 2003; Smock & Manning, 1997; Xie et al., 2003). Landale and Forste (1991, p. 603) speculate that cohabitation is an adaptive family strategy that allows for union formation in the face of economic uncertainty because it makes few unambiguous demands on the man as breadwinner.

Interestingly, the notion of marriage as preferably occurring after economic stability has been achieved contrasts sharply with the experiences of the working-class married couples studied some three decades ago by Rubin (1976). Rubin describes how financial difficulties pervaded the early years of marriage in her sample. Our results suggest that, today, those years of economic struggle often occur during cohabitation rather than marriage.

Why have perceptions about economic readiness to marry altered since Rubin's study? This question is intricately tied to the issue of the retreat from marriage in general over the past 30 years, a topic that numerous social scientists have pondered; a recent issue of this journal (November, 2004) is, in fact, devoted to the topic. As emphasized by Cherlin (2004), although marriage remains quite desirable, as all surveys show, its practical importance has decreased. At the same time, Cherlin argues that marriage has become the most prestigious family form and indicator of achievement, with even the wedding symbolic of such achievement (see, also, Furstenberg, 1995). We agree with this assessment and underscore that the increasing acceptability and prevalence of living together unmarried, as well as having children outside of marriage, have raised the bar as far as marriage is concerned. As long as a living arrangement is available that has become normative and offers many of the same benefits as marriage (i.e., companionship, financial economies of scale, sexual access, and even

procreation), there is no reason why marriage should occur unless expectations, economic and otherwise, are met.

Our research has several limitations. First, our interviews were geared to attaining a wide array of information so that the focus on the prerequisites for marriage comprised only a relatively small part of the interview. Had this issue been our main focus, we would have had more and richer data, allowing us to further explore issues such as those raised by Terri (who suspects her partner of using financial concerns as a tactic to avoid marriage). Second, our findings are based on a nonrepresentative sample of cohabitors who were living in the Toledo, Ohio, area. Given this, and the qualitative nature of our study, the results cannot be generalized to a larger population. A third limitation is that we rely on data from respondents at one point in time. We plan follow-up interviews with respondents who were cohabiting at the time of the interview to gain a better understanding of the dynamics of cohabiting relationships.

Nonetheless, our findings make several contributions to extant knowledge. First, our data suggest that the associations between money and marriage . . . are more than correlations. Cohabitors consciously draw on perceptions of their economic position in thinking about whether and when to marry. In this way, our data triangulate already existing quantitative data, making a stronger case for a causal relationship between marriage and economic opportunity as well as eliciting particular aspects of economics salient to young adults that are generally unmeasured in the data used by [previous] studies. . . . Our study also identifies relationship *processes* such as stresses and conflict over money that likely partially account for the quantitative association between good economic circumstances and marriage.

Second, qualitative work to date on the economic barriers to marriage has focused on disadvantaged, unmarried parents, primarily mothers (e.g., Edin, 2000; Gibson et al., 2003). By widening the socioeconomic spectrum to include the working and lower middle classes, our study enlarges the discourse on marriage and its retreat. Our work underscores the ubiquity of financial problems confronting those in our society who are not privileged economically, who may be just a step or two away from poverty, and the linkage between financial struggles and the retreat from marriage (Ellwood & Jencks, 2001; Lichter, Graefe, & Brown, 2003; Oppenheimer, 2003; Smock, 2004).

Third, our study has two implications for how social scientists study marriage. First, our findings can inform the development of new measures . . . to investigate why economic circumstances influence marriage decisions. We would suggest, as one example, that gauging perceptions of financial difficulties (e.g., perceived economic adequacy) could enhance our understanding of relationship quality, stability, and the transition to marriage (see Clark-Nicolas & Gray-Little, 1991).

Finally, family demographers Bumpass and Sweet (2001) have argued that, to be motivated to marry, cohabitors must feel that marriage will change their lives. This reasoning is consistent with the arguments of some scholars that marriage itself causes changes that lead to higher incomes and other positive outcomes (Waite, 1995, 2000). Our findings suggest a slightly different take on these matters, at least in terms of economic factors. We find that cohabitors feel that marriage ought to occur once something has *already* changed. In the end, our results suggest that a feeling of readiness to marry hinges not on the hope of a comfortable financial future but on the sense that it has already been attained.

■ Review Questions

1. Why do many cohabitors reject the idea of a "downtown" (i.e., civil marriage at a courthouse) marriage even though it is much less expensive?
2. What do the authors mean when they write, "We find that cohabitors feel that marriage ought to occur once something has *already* changed"?

READING 7-2

Unmarried with Children

Kathryn Edin

Maria Kefalas

Jen Burke, a white tenth-grade dropout who is 17 years old, lives with her stepmother, her sister, and her 16-month-old son in a cramped but tidy row home in Philadelphia's beleaguered Kensington neighborhood. She is broke, on welfare, and struggling to complete her GED. Wouldn't she and her son have been better off if she had finished high school, found a job, and married her son's father first?

In 1950, when Jen's grandmother came of age, only 1 in 20 American children was born to an unmarried mother. Today, that rate is 1 in 3—and they are usually born to those least likely to be able to support a child on their own. In our book, *Promises I Can Keep: Why Poor Women Put Motherhood before Marriage,* we discuss the lives of 162 white, African American, and Puerto Rican low-income single mothers living in eight destitute neighborhoods across Philadelphia and

Kathryn Edin and Maria Kefalas, "Unmarried with Children," *Contexts,* Vol. 4, No. 2, pp. 16–22. © 2005 The American Sociological Association. Used by permission. All rights reserved.

its poorest industrial suburb, Camden. We spent five years chatting over kitchen tables and on front stoops, giving mothers like Jen the opportunity to speak to the question so many affluent Americans ask about them: Why do they have children while still young and unmarried when they will face such an uphill struggle to support them?

ROMANCE AT LIGHTNING SPEED

Jen started having sex with her 20-year-old boyfriend Rick just before her 15th birthday. A month and a half later, she was pregnant. "I didn't want to get pregnant," she claims. "*He* wanted me to get pregnant." "As soon as he met me, he wanted to have a kid with me," she explains. Though Jen's college-bound suburban peers would be appalled by such a declaration, on the streets of Jen's neighborhood, it is something of a badge of honor. "All those other girls he was with, he didn't want to have a baby with any of them," Jen boasts. "I asked him, 'Why did you choose me to have a kid when you could have a kid with any one of them?' He was like, 'I want to have a kid with *you*.'" Looking back, Jen says she now believes that the reason "he wanted me to have a kid that early is so that I didn't leave him."

In inner-city neighborhoods like Kensington, where child-bearing within marriage has become rare, romantic relationships like Jen and Rick's proceed at lightning speed. A young man's avowal, "I want to have a baby by you," is often part of the courtship ritual from the beginning. This is more than idle talk, as their first child is typically conceived within a year from the time a couple begins "kicking it." Yet while poor couples' pillow talk often revolves around dreams of shared children, the news of a pregnancy— the first indelible sign of the huge changes to come—puts these still-new relationships into overdrive. Suddenly, the would-be mother begins to scrutinize her mate as never before, wondering whether he can "get himself together"— find a job, settle down, and become a family man—in time. Jen began pestering Rick to get a real job instead of picking up day-labor jobs at nearby construction sites. She also wanted him to stop hanging out with his ne'er-do-well friends, who had been getting him into serious trouble for more than a decade. Most of all, she wanted Rick to shed what she calls his "kiddie mentality"— his habit of spending money on alcohol and drugs rather than recognizing his growing financial obligations at home.

Rick did not try to deny paternity, as many would-be fathers do. Nor did he abandon or mistreat Jen, at least intentionally. But Rick, who had been in and out of juvenile detention since he was 8 years old for everything from stealing cars to selling drugs, proved unable to stay away from his unsavory friends. At the beginning of her seventh month of pregnancy, an escapade that began as a drunken lark landed Rick in jail on a car-jacking charge. Jen moved back home with her stepmother, applied for welfare, and spent the last two-and-a-half months of her pregnancy without Rick.

Rick sent penitent letters from jail. "I thought he changed by the letters he wrote me. I thought he changed a lot," she says. "He used to tell me that he loved me when he was in jail. . . . It was always gonna be me and him and the baby when he got out." Thus, when Rick's alleged victim failed to appear to testify and he was released just days before Colin's birth, the couple's reunion was a happy one. Often, the magic moment of childbirth calms the troubled waters of such relationships. New parents typically make amends and resolve to stay together for the sake of their child. When surveyed just after a child's birth, eight in ten unmarried parents say they are still together, and most plan to stay together and raise the child.

Promoting marriage among the poor has become the new war on poverty, Bush style. And it is true that the correlation between marital status and child poverty is strong. But poor single mothers already believe in marriage. Jen insists that she will walk down the aisle one day, though she admits it might not be with Rick. And demographers still project that more than seven in ten women who had a child outside of marriage will eventually wed someone. First, though, Jen wants to get a good job, finish school, and get her son out of Kensington.

Most poor, unmarried mothers and fathers readily admit that bearing children while poor and unmarried is not the ideal way to do things. Jen believes the best time to become a mother is "after you're out of school and you got a job, at least, when you're like 21. . . . When you're ready to have kids, you should have everything ready, have your house, have a job, so when that baby comes, the baby can have its own room." Yet given their already limited economic prospects, the poor have little motivation to time their births as precisely as their middle-class counterparts do. The dreams of young people like Jen and Rick center on children at a time of life when their more affluent peers plan for college and careers. Poor girls coming of age in the inner city value children highly, anticipate them eagerly, and believe strongly that they are up to the job of mothering—even in difficult circumstances. Jen, for example, tells us, "People outside the neighborhood, they're like, 'You're 15! You're pregnant?' I'm like, it's not none of their business. I'm gonna be able to take care of my kid. They have nothing to worry about." Jen says she has concluded that "some people . . . are better at having kids at a younger age. . . . I think it's better for some people to have kids younger."

WHEN I BECAME A MOM

When we asked mothers like Jen what their lives would be like if they had not had children, we expected them to express regret over forgone opportunities for school and careers. Instead, most believe their children "saved" them. They describe their lives as spinning out of control before becoming pregnant—struggles with parents and peers, "wild," risky behavior, depression, and school failure. Jen speaks to this poignantly. "I was just real bad. I hung with a real bad crowd.

I was doing pills. I was really depressed. . . . I was drinking. That was before I was pregnant." "I think," she reflects, "if I never had a baby or anything, . . . I would still be doing the things I was doing. I would probably still be doing drugs. I'd probably still be drinking." Jen admits that when she first became pregnant, she was angry that she "couldn't be out no more. Couldn't be out with my friends. Couldn't do nothing." Now, though, she says, "I'm glad I have a son . . . because I would still be doing all that stuff."

Children offer poor youth like Jen a compelling sense of purpose. Jen paints a before-and-after picture of her life that was common among the mothers we interviewed. "Before, I didn't have nobody to take care of. I didn't have nothing left to go home for. . . . Now I have my son to take care of. I have him to go home for. . . . I don't have to go buy weed or drugs with my money. I could buy my son stuff with my money! . . . I have something to look up to now." Children also are a crucial source of relational intimacy, a self-made community of care. After a nasty fight with Rick, Jen recalls, "I was crying. My son came in the room. He was hugging me. He's 16 months and he was hugging me with his little arms. He was really cute and happy, so I got happy. That's one of the good things. When you're sad, the baby's always gonna be there for you no matter what." Lately she has been thinking a lot about what her life was like back then, before the baby. "I thought about the stuff before I became a mom, what my life was like back then. I used to see pictures of me, and I would hide in every picture. This baby did so much for me. My son did a lot for me. He helped me a lot. I'm thankful that I had my baby."

Around the time of the birth, most unmarried parents claim they plan to get married eventually. Rick did not propose marriage when Jen's first child was born, but when she conceived a second time, at 17, Rick informed his dad, "It's time for me to get married. It's time for me to straighten up. This is the one I wanna be with. I had a baby with her, I'm gonna have another baby with her."

Yet despite their intentions, few of these couples actually marry. Indeed, most break up well before their child enters preschool.

I'D LIKE TO GET MARRIED, BUT . . .

The sharp decline in marriage in impoverished urban areas has led some to charge that the poor have abandoned the marriage norm. Yet we found few who had given up on the idea of marriage. But like their elite counterparts, disadvantaged women set a high financial bar for marriage. For the poor, marriage has become an elusive goal—one they feel ought to be reserved for those who can support a "white picket fence" lifestyle: a mortgage on a modest row home, a car and some furniture, some savings in the bank, and enough money left over to pay for a "decent" wedding. Jen's views on marriage provide a perfect case in point. "If I was gonna get married, I would want to be married like my Aunt Nancy and my Uncle Pat. They live in the mountains. She has a job. My Uncle Pat is a state trooper; he has lots of money. They live in the [Poconos]. It's real nice out there. Her kids go to Catholic school. . . . That's the kind of life I would want to have. If I get married, I would have a life like [theirs]." She adds, "And I would wanna have a big wedding, a real nice wedding."

Unlike the women of their mothers' and grandmothers' generations, young women like Jen are not merely content to rely on a man's earnings. Instead, they insist on being economically "set" in their own right before taking marriage vows. This is partly because they want a partnership of equals, and they believe money buys say-so in a relationship. Jen explains, "I'm not gonna just get into marrying him and not have my own house! Not have a job! I still wanna do a lot of things before I get married. He [already] tells me I can't do nothing. I can't go out. What's gonna happen when I marry him? He's gonna say he owns me!"

Economic independence is also insurance against a marriage gone bad. Jen explains, "I want to have everything ready, in case something goes wrong. . . . If we got a divorce, that would be my house. I bought that house, he can't kick me out or he can't take my kids from me." "That's what I want in case that ever happens. I know a lot of people that happened to. I don't want it to happen to me." These statements reveal that despite her desire to marry, Rick's role in the family's future is provisional at best. "We get along, but we fight a lot. If he's there, he's there, but if he's not, that's why I want a job . . . a job with computers . . . so I could afford my kids, could afford the house. . . . I don't want to be living off him. I want my kids to be living off me."

Why is Jen, who describes Rick as "the love of my life," so insistent on planning an exit strategy before she is willing to take the vows she firmly believes ought to last "forever"? If love is so sure, why does mistrust seem so palpable and strong? In relationships among poor couples like Jen and Rick, mistrust is often spawned by chronic violence and infidelity, drug and alcohol abuse, criminal activity, and the threat of imprisonment. In these tarnished corners of urban America, the stigma of a failed marriage is far worse than an out-of-wedlock birth. New mothers like Jen feel they must test the relationship over three, four, even five years' time. This is the only way, they believe, to insure that their marriages will last.

Trust has been an enormous issue in Jen's relationship with Rick. "My son was born December 23rd, and [Rick] started cheating on me again . . . in March. He started cheating on me with some girl—Amanda. . . . Then it was another girl, another girl, another girl after. I didn't wanna believe it. My friends would come up to me and be like, 'Oh yeah, your boyfriend's cheating on you with this person.' I wouldn't believe it. . . . I would see him with them. He used to have hickies. He used to make up some excuse that he was drunk—that was always his excuse for everything." Things finally came to a head when Rick got another girl pregnant. "For a while, I forgave him for everything. Now, I don't forgive him for nothing." Now we begin to understand the source of Jen's hesitancy. "He wants me to marry him, [but] I'm not really sure. . . . If I can't trust him, I can't marry him, 'cause we would get a divorce. If you're gonna get married, you're supposed to be faithful!" she insists. To Jen and her peers, the worst thing that could happen is "to get married just to get divorced."

Given the economic challenges and often perilously low quality of the romantic relationships among unmarried parents, poor women may be right to be cautious about marriage. Five years after we first spoke with her, we met with Jen again. We learned that Jen's second pregnancy ended in a miscarriage. We also learned that Rick was out of the picture—apparently for good. "You know that bar [down the street]? It happened in that bar. . . . They were in the bar, and this guy was like badmouthing [Rick's friend] Mikey, talking stuff to him or whatever. So Rick had to go get involved in it and start with this guy. . . . Then he goes outside and fights the guy [and] the guy dies of head trauma. They were all on drugs, they were all drinking, and things just got out of control, and that's what happened. He got fourteen to thirty years."

THESE ARE CARDS I DEALT MYSELF

Jen stuck with Rick for the first two and a half years of his prison sentence, but when another girl's name replaced her own on the visitors' list, Jen decided she was finished with him once and for all. Readers might be asking what Jen ever saw in a man like Rick. But Jen and Rick operate in a partner market where the better-off men go to the better-off women. The only way for someone like Jen to forge a satisfying relationship with a man is to find a diamond in the rough or improve her own economic position so that she can realistically compete for more upwardly mobile partners, which is what Jen is trying to do now. "There's this kid, Donny, he works at my job. He works on C shift. He's a supervisor! He's funny, three years older, and he's not a geek or

anything, but he's not a real preppy good boy either. But he's not [a player like Rick] and them. He has a job, you know, so that's good. He doesn't do drugs or anything. And he asked my dad if he could take me out!"

These days, there is a new air of determination, even pride, about Jen. The aimless high school dropout pulls ten-hour shifts entering data at a warehouse distribution center Monday through Thursday. She has held the job for three years, and her aptitude and hard work have earned her a series of raises. Her current salary is higher than anyone in her household commands—$10.25 per hour, and she now gets two weeks of paid vacation, four personal days, 60 hours of sick time, and medical benefits. She has saved up the necessary $400 in tuition for a high school completion program that offers evening and weekend classes. Now all that stands between her and a diploma is a passing grade in mathematics, her least favorite subject. "My plan is to start college in January. [This month] I take my math test . . . so I can get my diploma," she confides.

Jen clearly sees how her life has improved since Rick's dramatic exit from the scene. "That's when I really started [to get better] because I didn't have to worry about what *he* was doing, didn't have to worry about him cheating on me, all this stuff. [It was] then I realized that I had to do what I had to do to take care of my son. . . . When he was there, I think that my whole life revolved around him, you know, so I always messed up somehow because I was so busy worrying about what *he* was doing. Like I would leave the [GED] programs I was in just to go home and see what he was doing. My mind was never concentrating." Now, she says, "a lot of people in my family look up to me now, because all my sisters dropped out from school, you know, nobody went back to school. I went back to school, you know? . . . I went back to school, and I plan to go to college, and a lot of people look up to me for that, you know? So that makes me happy . . . because five years ago nobody looked up to me. I was just like everybody else."

Yet the journey has not been easy. "Being a young mom, being 15, it's hard, hard, hard, you know." She says, "I have no life. . . . I work from 6:30 in the morning until 5:00 at night. I leave here at 5:30 in the morning. I don't get home until about 6:00 at night." Yet she measures her worth as a mother by the fact that she has managed to provide for her son largely on her own. "I don't depend on nobody. I might live with my dad and them, but I don't depend on them, you know." She continues, "There [used to] be days when I'd be so stressed out, like, 'I can't do this!' And I would just cry and cry and cry. . . . Then I look at Colin, and he'll be sleeping, and I'll just look at him and think I don't have no [reason to feel sorry for myself]. The cards I have I've dealt myself so I have to deal with it now. I'm older. I can't change anything. He's my responsibility—he's nobody else's but mine—so I have to deal with that."

Becoming a mother transformed Jen's point of view on just about everything. She says, "I thought hanging on the corner drinking, getting high—I thought that was a good life, and I thought I could live that way for eternity, like sitting out with my friends. But it's not as fun once you have your own kid. . . . I think it changes [you]. I think, 'Would I want Colin to do that? Would I want my son to be like that . . . ?' It was fun to me but it's not fun anymore. Half the people I hung with are either . . . Some have died from drug overdoses, some are in jail, and some people are just out there living the same life that they always lived, and they don't look really good. They look really bad." In the end, Jen believes, Colin's birth has brought far more good into her life than bad. "I know I could have waited [to have a child], but in a way I think Colin's the best thing that could have happened to me. . . . So I think I had my son for a purpose because I think Colin changed my life. He *saved* my life, really. My whole life revolves around Colin!"

PROMISES I CAN KEEP

There are unique themes in Jen's story—most fathers are only one or two, not five years older than the mothers of their children, and few fathers have as many glaring problems as Rick—but we heard most of these themes repeatedly in the stories of the 161 other poor, single mothers we came to know. Notably, poor women do not reject marriage; they revere it. Indeed, it is the conviction that marriage is forever that makes them think that divorce is worse than having a baby outside of marriage. Their children, far from being liabilities, provide crucial social-psychological resources—a strong sense of purpose and a profound source of intimacy. Jen and the other mothers we came to know are coming of age in an America that is profoundly unequal—where the gap between rich and poor continues to grow. This economic reality has convinced them that they have little to lose and, perhaps, something to gain by a seemingly "ill-timed" birth.

The lesson one draws from stories like Jen's is quite simple: Until poor young women have more access to jobs that lead to financial independence—until there is reason to hope for the rewarding life pathways that their privileged peers pursue—the poor will continue to have children far sooner than most Americans think they should, while still deferring marriage. Marital standards have risen for all Americans, and the poor want the same things that everyone now wants out of marriage. The poor want to marry too, but they insist on marrying well. This, in their view, is the only way to avoid an almost certain divorce. Like Jen, they are simply not willing to make promises they are not sure they can keep.

RECOMMENDED RESOURCES

Kathryn Edin and Maria Kefalas. *Promises I Can Keep: Why Poor Women Put Motherhood before Marriage* (University of California Press, 2005). An account of how low-income women make sense of their choices about marriage and motherhood.

Christina Gibson, Kathryn Edin, and Sara McLanahan. "High Hopes but Even Higher Expectations: The Retreat from Marriage among Low-Income Couples," *Journal of Marriage and Family* 67 (December 2005), pp. 1301–1312. The authors examine the rising expectations for marriage among unmarried parents.

Sharon Hays. *Flat Broke with Children: Women in the Age of Welfare Reform* (Oxford University Press, 2003). How welfare reform has affected the lives of poor moms.

Annette Lareau. *Unequal Childhoods: Class, Race, and Family Life* (University of California Press, 2003). A fascinating discussion of different child-rearing strategies among low-income, working-class, and middle-class parents.

Timothy J. Nelson, Susan Clampet-Lundquist, and Kathryn Edin. "Fragile Fatherhood: How Low-Income, Non-Custodial Fathers in Philadelphia Talk about Their Families." In *The Handbook of Father Involvement: Multidisciplinary Perspectives,* ed. Catherine Tamis-LeMonda and Natasha Cabrera (Lawrence Erlbaum Associates, 2002). What poor, single men think about fatherhood.

■ Review Questions

1. Have low-income women rejected marriage?
2. Are their standards for marriage too high?

CHAPTER 8

Work and Families

The movement of mothers into the paid workforce is one of the most significant changes in family life over the past half century. Because most mothers are employed outside the home, they cannot do as much housework and childrearing as they used to. Men are doing more work in the home but not enough to fully compensate. Many parents are now paying childcare providers or cleaning services to perform tasks mothers used to do for free. It is now clear how valuable was the unpaid labor mothers did in the home and how expensive it is to replace.

The families most in need of replacing household labor are the growing numbers of two-earner couples and single parents. Neither has the luxury of having a partner caring for their homes and children full-time. The time squeeze is greatest among couples in which both partners have demanding professional or technical jobs and are also raising children. They sometimes complain of overwork. But as Kathleen Gerson and Jerry A. Jacobs show in the first selection in this chapter, the problem for other Americans is underwork. Many people without college educations have had difficulty finding the full-time work they desire. So, while the members of some

American families are concerned about having too much work, others are concerned about having not enough.

With more and more mothers working outside the home, a major question for sociologists is why an unequal division of labor between mothers and fathers still exists inside the home. A number of sociologists, seeking to unravel this puzzle, have turned to the persistence of beliefs about culturally appropriate behavior for women and men. People have "gender ideologies," to use Arlie Hochschild's term, that stubbornly affect what they do around the house. It is important to the self-image of many men that their wives be seen as the main workers around the house because, they think, men aren't supposed to do much work around the house. Hochschild studied some working-class husbands who did a great deal of domestic work but insisted that they were just helping out their wives.

For women, the inner conflict can be greater. Those who were raised after the feminist revolution of the 1960s typically believe that women should be able to work outside the home and that their husbands should share the housework and child care. But they also may want to prove to their husbands that they are fulfilling the role of a good wife; and this desire may lead them to display how much housework they still do. Or they may want to do more of the housework to support the ego of a husband who is not earning much money and therefore is not fulfilling the culturally prescribed male role. Faced with these tensions, as well as with the grim economic situation of many divorced women, wives may accept an unequal division of labor despite their preferences for greater sharing.

In "Joey's Problem: Nancy and Evan Holt," a chapter from her book *The Second Shift: Working Parents and the Revolution at Home,* Hochschild tells the story of a married couple who do not share the housework and child care equally even though the wife works full-time outside the home. Nancy struggles to reconcile the reality of the division of labor in her marriage with her ideals. Hochschild provides an insightful account of the tensions in their marriage and how they were resolved.

READING 8-1

The Work-Home Crunch

Kathleen Gerson

Jerry A. Jacobs

More than a decade has passed since the release of *The Overworked American,* a prominent 1991 book about the decline in Americans' leisure time, and the work pace in the United States only seems to have increased. From sleep-deprived parents to professionals who believe they must put in long hours to succeed at the office, the demands of work are colliding with family responsibilities and placing a tremendous time squeeze on many Americans.

Yet beyond the apparent growth in the time that many Americans spend on the job lies a more complex story. While many Americans are working more than ever, many others are working less. What is more, finding a balance between work and other obligations seems increasingly elusive to many workers—whether or not they are actually putting in more time at work than workers in earlier generations. The increase in harried workers and hurried families is a problem that demands solutions. But before we can resolve this increasingly difficult time squeeze we must first understand its root causes.

AVERAGE WORKING TIME AND BEYOND

"There aren't enough hours in the day" is an increasingly resonant refrain. To most observers, including many experts, the main culprit appears to be overwork—our jobs just take up too much of our time. Yet it is not clear that the average American is spending more time on the job. Although it may come as a surprise to

those who feel overstressed, the average work week—that is, hours spent working for pay by the average employee—has hardly changed over the past 30 years. Census Bureau interviews show, for example, that the average male worked 43.5 hours a week in 1970 and 43.1 hours a week in 2000, while the average female worked 37.1 hours in 1970 and 37.0 hours in 2000.

Why, then, do more and more Americans feel so pressed for time? The answer is that averages can be misleading. Looking only at the average experience of American workers misses key parts of the story. From the perspective of individual workers, it turns out some Americans are working more than ever, while others are finding it harder to get as much work as they need or would like. To complicate matters further, American families are now more diverse than they were in the middle of the 20th century, when male-breadwinner households predominated. Many more Americans now live in dual-earner or single-parent families where all the adults work.

These two trends—the growing split of the labor force and the transformation of family life—lie at the heart of the new time dilemmas facing an increasing number of Americans. But they have not affected all workers and all families in the same way. Instead, these changes have divided Americans into those who feel squeezed between their work and the rest of their life, and those who have more time away from work than they need or would like. No one trend fits both groups.

So, who are the time-squeezed, and how do they differ from those with fewer time pressures but who may also have less work than they may want or need? To distinguish and describe the two sets of Americans, we need to look at the experiences of both individual workers and whole families. A focus on workers shows that they are increasingly divided between those who put in very long work weeks and who are concentrated in the better-paying jobs, and those who put in comparatively short work weeks, who are more likely to have fewer educational credentials and

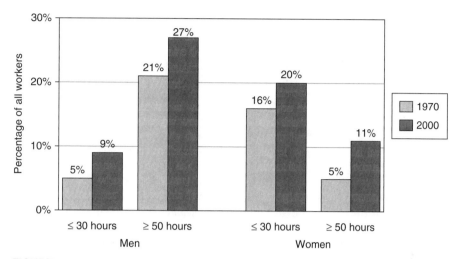

FIGURE 8.1

The percentage of men and women who put in 30 or fewer hours and who put in 50 or more hours a week in 1970 and 2000. (*Source:* March Current Population Surveys; nonfarm wage and salary workers.)

are more likely to be concentrated in the lower-paying jobs.

But the experiences of individuals does not tell the whole story. When we shift our focus to the family, it becomes clear that time squeezes are linked to the total working hours of family members in households. For this reason, two-job families and single parents face heightened challenges. Moreover, women continue to assume the lion's share of home and childcare responsibilities and are thus especially likely to be squeezed for time. Changes in jobs and changes in families are putting overworked Americans and underemployed Americans on distinct paths, are separating the two-earner and single-parent households from the more traditional households, and are creating different futures for parents (especially mothers) than for workers without children at home.

A GROWING DIVIDE IN INDIVIDUAL WORKING TIME

In 1970, almost half of all employed men and women reported working 40 hours a week. By 2000, just 2 in 5 worked these "average" hours.

Instead, workers are now far more likely to put in either very long or fairly short work weeks. The share of working men putting in 50 hours or more rose from 21 percent in 1970 to almost 27 percent in 2000, while the share of working women putting in these long work weeks rose from 5 to 11 percent.

At the other end of the spectrum, more workers are also putting in shorter weeks. In 1970, for example, 5 percent of men were employed for 30 or fewer hours a week, while 9 percent worked these shortened weeks in 2000. The share of employed women spending 30 or fewer hours on the job also climbed from 16 percent to 20 percent (see Figure 8.1). In total, 13 million Americans in 2000 worked either shorter or longer work weeks than they would have if the 1970s pattern had continued.

These changes in working time are not evenly distributed across occupations. Instead, they are strongly related to the kinds of jobs people hold. Managers and professionals, as one might expect, tend to put in the longest work weeks. More than 1 in 3 men in this category now work 50 hours or more per week, compared to only 1 in 5 for men in other occupations. For women, 1 in 6 professionals and managers work these long weeks, compared to fewer than 1 in 14 for women in all other occupations. And because jobs are closely linked to education, the gap in working time between the college educated and those with fewer educational credentials has also grown since 1970.

Thus, time at work is growing most among those Americans who are most likely to read articles and buy books about overwork in America. They may not be typical, but they are indeed working more than their peers in earlier generations. If leisure time once signaled an elite lifestyle, that no longer appears to be the case. Working relatively few hours is now more likely to be concentrated among those with less education and less elite jobs.

Workers do not necessarily prefer these new schedules. On the contrary, when workers are asked about their ideal amount of time at work, a very different picture emerges. For example, in a 1997 survey of workers conducted by the Families and Work Institute, 60 percent of both men and women responded that they would like to work less while 19 percent of men and women said that they would like to work more. Most workers—both women and men—aspire to work between 30 and 40 hours per week. Men generally express a desire to work about 38 hours a week while women would like to work about 32 hours. The small difference in the ideal working time of men and women is less significant than the shared preferences among them. However, whether their jobs require very long or comparatively short work weeks, this shared ideal does stand in sharp contrast to their job realities. As some workers are pressured to put in more time at work and others less, finding the right balance between work and the rest of life has become increasingly elusive.

OVERWORKED INDIVIDUALS OR OVERWORKED FAMILIES?

Fundamental shifts in family life exacerbate this growing division between the over- and under-

worked. While most analyses of working time focus on individual workers, time squeezes are typically experienced by families, not isolated individuals. A 60-hour work week for a father means something different depending on whether the mother stays at home or also works a 60-hour week. Even a 40-hour work week can seem too long if both members of a married couple are juggling job demands with family responsibilities. And when a family depends on a single parent, the conflicts between home and work can be even greater. Even if the length of the work week had not changed at all, the rise of families that depend on either two incomes or one parent would suffice to explain why Americans feel so pressed for time.

To understand how families experience time squeezes, we need to look at the combined working time of all family members. For example, how do married couples with two earners compare with those anchored by a sole, typically male, breadwinner? For all married couples, the work week has indeed increased from an average of about 53 hours in 1970 to 63 hours in 2000. Given that the average work week for individuals did not change, it may seem strange that the couples' family total grew so markedly. The explanation for this apparent paradox is both straightforward and crucial: married women are now far more likely to work. In 1970, half of all married-couple families had only male breadwinners. By 2000, this group had shrunk to one-quarter (see Figure 8.2). In 1970, one-third of all married-couple families had two wage-earners, but three-fifths did in 2000. In fact, two-earner families are more common today than male-breadwinner families were 30 years ago.

Each type of family is also working a little more each week, but this change is relatively modest and certainly not large enough to account for the larger shift in total household working time. Two-earner families put in close to 82 working hours in 2000 compared with 78 hours in 1970. Male-breadwinner couples worked 44 hours on average in 1970 and 45 hours in 2000.

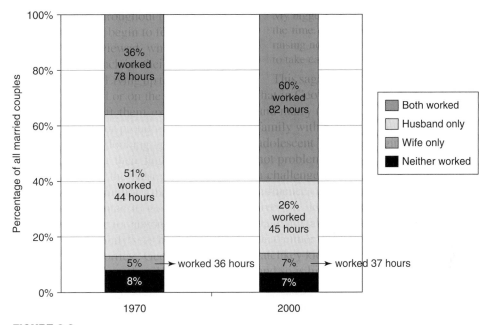

FIGURE 8.2
Total hours of work per week for married couples, 1970 and 2000. (*Source:* March Current Population Surveys; nonfarm married couples aged 18–64.)

The vast majority of the change in working time over the past 30 years can thus be traced to changes in the kinds of families we live in rather than to changes in how much we work. Two-earner couples work about as much today as they did 30 years ago, but there are many more of them because more wives are working.

Single parents, who are overwhelmingly mothers, are another group who are truly caught in a time squeeze. They need to work as much as possible to support their family, and they are less likely to be able to count on a partner's help in meeting their children's daily needs. Although these households are not displayed in Figure 8.2, Census Bureau data show that women headed one-fifth of all families in 2000, twice the share of female-headed households in 1970. Even though their average work week remained unchanged at 39 hours, the lack of child care and other support services leaves them facing time squeezes at least as sharp. Single fathers remain a much smaller group, but their ranks have also

grown rapidly. Single dads work almost as much as single moms—37 hours per week in 2000. Even though this represents a drop of two hours since 1970, single fathers face time dilemmas as great as those facing single mothers. Being a single parent has always posed daunting challenges, and now there are more mothers and fathers than ever in this situation.

At the heart of these shifts is American families' growing reliance on a woman's earnings—whether or not they depend on a man's earnings as well. Women's strengthened commitment to paid employment has provided more economic resources to families and given couples more options for sharing the tasks of breadwinning and caretaking. Yet this revolution in women's work has not been complemented by an equal growth in the amount of time men spend away from the job or in the availability of organized child care. This limited change at the workplace and in men's lives has intensified the time pressures facing women.

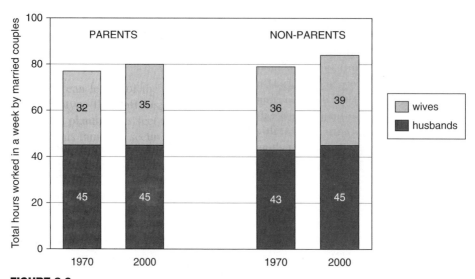

FIGURE 8.3

Average hours of work per week of couples (parents and non-parents). (*Source:* March Current Population Surveys; nonfarm married couples aged 18–64.)

DUAL-EARNER PARENTS AND WORKING TIME

The expansion of working time is especially important for families with children, where work and family demands are most likely to conflict. Indeed, there is a persisting concern that in their desire for paid work, families with two earners are shortchanging their children in time and attention. A closer looks reveals that even though parents face increased time pressure, they cope with these dilemmas by cutting back on their combined joint working time when they have children at home. For example, U.S. Census data show that parents in two-income families worked 3.3 fewer hours per week than spouses in two-income families without children, a slightly wider difference than the 2.6 hours separating them in 1970. Working hours also decline as the number of children increase. Couples with one child under 18 jointly averaged 81 hours per week in 2000, while couples with three or more children averaged 78 hours. Rather than forsaking their children, employed parents are taking steps to adjust their work schedules to make more time for the rest of life.

However, it is mothers, not fathers, who are cutting back. Fathers actually work more hours when they have children at home, and their working hours increase with the number of children. Thus, the drop in joint working time among couples with children reflects less working time among mothers. Figure 8.3 shows that in 2000, mothers worked almost 4 fewer hours per week than married women without children. This gap is not substantially different than in 1970.

This pattern of mothers reducing their hours while fathers increase them creates a larger gender gap in work participation among couples with children compared to the gender gap for childless couples. However, these differences are much smaller than the once predominant pattern in which many women stopped working for pay altogether when they bore children. While the transition to raising children continues to have different consequences for women and men, the size of this difference is diminishing.

It is also important to remember that the rise in working time among couples is not concentrated among those with children at home. Though Americans continue to worry about the consequences for children when both parents go to work, the move toward more work involvement does not reflect neglect on the part of either mothers or fathers. On the contrary, employed mothers continue to spend less time at the workplace than their childless peers, while employed fathers today do not spend substantially more time at work than men who are not fathers.

SOLVING THE TIME PRESSURE PUZZLE

Even though changes in the average working time of American workers are modest, many American families have good reason to feel overworked and time-deprived. The last several decades have witnessed the emergence of a group of workers who face very long work weeks and live in families that depend on either two incomes or one parent. And while parents are putting in less time at work than their peers without children at home, they shoulder domestic responsibilities that leave them facing clashes between work demands and family needs.

The future of family well-being and gender equality will depend on developing policies to help workers resolve the time pressures created by the widespread and deeply rooted social changes discussed above. The first step toward developing effective policy responses requires accepting the social transformations that sent women into the workplace and left Americans wishing for a balance between work and family that is difficult to achieve. Unfortunately, these changes in the lives of women and men continue to evoke ambivalence.

For example, mothers continue to face strong pressures to devote intensive time and attention to child rearing. Indeed, generally they want to, despite the rising economic and social pressure to hold a paid job as well. Even though most contemporary mothers are counted on to help support their families financially, the United States has yet to develop the childcare services and flexible jobs that can help workers meet their families' needs. Whether or not mothers work outside the home, they face conflicting expectations that are difficult to meet. These social contradictions can be seen in the political push to require poor, single mothers to work at a paid job while middle-class mothers continue to be chastised for spending too much time on their jobs and away from home.

To a lesser but still important extent, fathers also face intensifying and competing pressures. Despite American families' increasing reliance on women's earnings, men face significant barriers to family involvement. Resistance from employers and co-workers continues to greet individual fathers who would like to spend less time at work to care for their children. For all the concern and attention focused on employed mothers, social policies that would help bring men more fully into the work of parenting get limited notice or support. New time squeezes can thus be better understood by comparing the large changes in women's lives with the relative lack of changes in the situation for men. The family time bind is an unbalanced one.

Even as family time has become squeezed, workers are also contending with changes in the options and expectations they face at work. Competitive workplaces appear to be creating rising pressures for some workers, especially professionals and managers, to devote an excessive amount of time to their jobs, while not offering enough work to others. In contrast to these bifurcating options, American workers increasingly express a desire to balance the important work of earning a living and caring for a new generation.

Finding solutions to these new time dilemmas will depend on developing large scale policies that recognize and address the new needs of 21st century workers and their families. As we suggest in our book, *The Time Divide,* these policies need to address the basic organization of American work and community institutions. This includes revising regulations on hours of work and providing benefit protections to more workers, moving toward the norm of a shorter work week, creating more family-supportive workplaces that offer both job flexibility and protections for employed parents, and developing a wider array of high-quality, affordable childcare options.

Extending protections, such as proportional benefits and overtime pay, to workers in a wider range of jobs and occupations would reduce the built-in incentives employers have to extract as much work as possible from professionals and managers while offering less work to other employees. If professionals and managers were given overtime pay for overtime work, which wage workers are now guaranteed under the Fair Labor Standards Act, the pressures on these employees to put in endless workdays might lessen. . . . Similarly, if part-time workers were offered fringe benefits proportional to the hours they work (such as partial pensions), there would be fewer reasons for employers to create jobs with work weeks so short that they do not provide the economic security all families need.

Reducing the average work week to 35 hours would also reduce the pressures on workers and help them find a better work-family balance. While this goal may seem utopian, it is important to remember that the 40-hour standard also seemed unimaginably idealistic before it was adopted in the early 20th century. Other countries, most notably France, have adopted this standard without sacrificing economic well-being. A shorter work week still would allow for variation in work styles and commitments, but it would also create a new cultural standard that better reflects the needs and aspirations of most contemporary workers. It would also help single parents meet their dual obligations and allow couples to fashion greater equality in their work and caretaking responsibilities.

Time at work is clearly important, but it is not the whole story. The organization of the workplace and the structure of jobs also matters, especially for those whose jobs and occupations require intensive time at work. Among those putting in very long work weeks, we find that having job flexibility and autonomy helps ease the perceived strains and conflicts. The work environment, especially in the form of support from supervisors and co-workers, also makes a difference. In addition, we find that workers with access to such family-friendly options as flexible work schedules are likely to use them, while workers without such benefits would like to have them.

Flexibility and autonomy are only useful if workers feel able to use them. Women and men both express concern that making use of "family-friendly" policies, such as extended parental leaves or nonstandard working hours, may endanger their future work prospects. Social policies need to protect the rights of workers to be involved parents without incurring excessive penalties at the workplace. Most Americans spend a portion of their work lives simultaneously immersed in work for pay and in parenting. Providing greater flexibility at the workplace will help workers develop both short-and longer-term strategies for integrating work and family life. However, even basic changes in the organization of work will not suffice to meet the needs of 21st-century families. We also need to join the ranks of virtually all other industrialized nations by creating widely available, high-quality and affordable child care. In a world where mothers and fathers are at the workplace to stay, we need an expanded network of support to care for the next generation of workers.

These changes will not be easy to achieve. But in one form or another, they have been effectively adopted in other societies throughout the modern world. While no one policy is a cure-all, taken together they offer a comprehensive approach for creating genuine resolutions to the time pressures that confront growing numbers of American workers and their families. Ultimately, these new time dilemmas cannot be resolved by chastising workers (and, most often, mothers) for working too much. Rather, the time has come to create more flexible, family-supportive, and gender-equal workplaces and communities that complement the 21st-century forms of work and family life.

RECOMMENDED RESOURCES

Bond, James T. *Highlights of the National Study of the Changing Workforce.* New York: Families and Work Institute, 2003. Bond reports findings from a major national survey of contemporary American workers, workplace conditions, and work-family conflict.

Gornick, Janet, and Marcia Meyers. *Families that Work: Policies for Reconciling Parenthood and Employment.* New York: Russell Sage Foundation, 2003. This important study compares family-supportive policies in Europe and the United States.

Hays, Sharon. *The Cultural Contradictions of Motherhood.* New Haven, CT: Yale University Press, 1997. Hays examines how American mothers continue to face pressure to practice intensive parenting even as they increase their commitment to paid work.

Heymann, Jody. *The Widening Gap: Why America's Working Families Are in Jeopardy and What Can Be Done about It.* New York: Basic Books, 2000. Drawing from a wide range of data, this study makes a compelling case for more flexible work structures.

Hochschild, Arlie. *The Time Bind: When Home Becomes Work and Work Becomes Home.* New York: Metropolitan Books, 1997. This is a rich study of how employees in one company try to reconcile the tensions between spending time at work and caring for their families.

Jacobs, Jerry A., and Kathleen Gerson. *The Time Divide: Work, Family, and Gender Inequality.* Cambridge, MA: Harvard University Press, 2004. An overview of trends in working time, our book shows why and how time pressures have emerged in America over the past three decades, how they are linked to gender inequality and family change, and what we can do to alleviate them.

Robinson, John P., and Geoffrey Godbey. *Time for Life. The Surprising Ways Americans Use Their Time.* University Park: Pennsylvania State University Press, 1999. Drawing on time diaries, Robinson and Godbey conclude that Americans' leisure time has increased.

Schor, Juliet. *The Overworked American: The Unexpected Decline of Leisure.* New York: Basic Books, 1991. This early and original analysis of how Americans are overworked sparked a national discussion on and concern for the problem.

■ Review Questions

1. How does a person's education affect how many hours per week she or he is likely to work outside the home?
2. How have changes in the kinds of families Americans live in affected what the authors call the "work-home crunch"?

Joey's Problem: Nancy and Evan Holt

Arlie Hochschild

Nancy Holt arrives home from work, her son, Joey, in one hand and a bag of groceries in the other. As she puts down the groceries and opens the front door, she sees a spill of mail on the hall floor, Joey's half-eaten piece of cinnamon toast on the hall table, and the phone machine's winking red light: a still-life reminder of the morning's frantic rush to distribute the family to the world outside. Nancy, for seven years a social worker, is a short, lithe blond woman of 30 who talks and moves rapidly. She scoops the mail onto the hall table and heads for the kitchen, unbuttoning her coat as she goes. Joey sticks close behind her, intently explaining to her how dump trucks dump things. Joey is a fat-cheeked, lively four-year-old who chuckles easily at things that please him.

Having parked their red station wagon, Evan, her husband, comes in and hangs up his coat. He has picked her up at work and they've arrived home together. Apparently unready to face the kitchen commotion but not quite entitled to relax with the newspaper in the living room, he slowly studies the mail. Also 30, Evan, a warehouse furniture salesman, has thinning pale blond hair, a stocky build, and a tendency to lean on one foot. In his manner there is something both affable and hesitant.

From the beginning, Nancy describes herself as an "ardent feminist," an egalitarian (she wants a similar balance of spheres and equal power). Nancy began her marriage hoping that she and

Evan would base their identities in both their parenthood and their careers, but clearly tilted toward parenthood. Evan felt it was fine for Nancy to have a career, if she could handle the family too.

As I observe in their home on this evening, I notice a small ripple on the surface of family waters. From the commotion of the kitchen, Nancy calls, "Eva-an, will you *please* set the table?" The word *please* is thick with irritation. Scurrying between refrigerator, sink, and oven, with Joey at her feet, Nancy wants Evan to help; she has asked him, but reluctantly. She seems to resent having to ask. (Later she tells me, "I *hate* to ask; why should I ask? It's begging.") Evan looks up from the mail and flashes an irritated glance toward the kitchen, stung, perhaps, to be asked in a way so barren of appreciation and respect. He begins setting out knives and forks, asks if she will need spoons, then answers the doorbell. A neighbor's child. No, Joey can't play right now. The moment of irritation has passed.

Later as I interview Nancy and Evan separately, they describe their family life as unusually happy—except for Joey's "problem." Joey has great difficulty getting to sleep. They start trying to put him to bed at 8:00. Evan tries but Joey rebuffs him; Nancy has better luck. By 8:30 they have him *on* the bed but not *in* it; he crawls and bounds playfully. After 9:00 he still calls out for water or toys, and sneaks out of bed to switch on the light. This continues past 9:30, then 10:00 and 10:30. At about 11:00 Joey complains that his bed is "scary," that he can only go to sleep in his parents' bedroom. Worn down, Nancy accepts this proposition. And it is part of their current arrangement that putting Joey to bed is "Nancy's job." Nancy and Evan can't get into bed until midnight or later, when Evan is tired and Nancy exhausted. She used to enjoy their love-making, Nancy tells me, but now sex seems like "more work." The Holts consider their fatigue and impoverished sex life as results of Joey's problem.

The official history of Joey's problem—the interpretation Nancy and Evan give me—begins with Joey's fierce attachment to Nancy, and Nancy's strong attachment to him. On an afternoon walk through Golden Gate Park, Nancy devotes herself to Joey's every move. Now Joey sees a squirrel; Nancy tells me she must remember to bring nuts next time. Now Joey is going up the slide; she notices that his pants are too short—she must take them down tonight. The two enjoy each other. (Off the official record, neighbors and Joey's baby-sitter say that Nancy is a wonderful mother, but privately they add how much she is "also like a single mother.")

For his part, Evan sees little of Joey. He has his evening routine, working with his tools in the basement, and Joey always seems happy to be with Nancy. In fact, Joey shows little interest in Evan, and Evan hesitates to see that as a problem. "Little kids need their moms more than they need their dads," he explains philosophically; "All boys go through an oedipal phase."

Perfectly normal things happen. After a long day, mother, father, and son sit down to dinner. Evan and Nancy get the first chance all day to talk to each other, but both turn anxiously to Joey, expecting his mood to deteriorate. Nancy asks him if he wants celery with peanut butter on it. Joey says yes. "Are you sure that's how you want it?" "Yes." Then the fidgeting begins. "I don't like the strings on my celery." "Celery is made up of strings." "The celery is too big." Nancy grimly slices the celery. A certain tension mounts. Every time one parent begins a conversation with the other, Joey interrupts. "I don't have anything to drink." Nancy gets him juice. And finally, "Feed me." By the end of the meal, no one has obstructed Joey's victory. He has his mother's reluctant attention and his father is reaching for a beer. But talking about it later, they say, "This is normal when you have kids."

Sometimes when Evan knocks on the baby-sitter's door to pick up Joey, the boy looks past his father, searching for a face behind him: "Where's Mommy?" Sometimes he outright refuses to go home with his father. Eventually Joey even swats at his father, once quite hard, on the face for "no reason at all." This makes it hard to keep imagining Joey's relation to Evan as "perfectly normal." Evan and Nancy begin to talk seriously about a "swatting problem."

Evan decides to seek ways to compensate for his emotional distance from Joey. He brings Joey a surprise every week or so—a Tonka truck, a Tootsie Roll. He turns weekends into father-and-son times. One Saturday, Evan proposes the zoo, and hesitantly, Joey agrees. Father and son have their coats on and are nearing the front door. Suddenly Nancy decides she wants to join them, and as she walks down the steps with Joey in her arms, she explains to Evan, "I want to help things out."

Evan gets few signs of love from Joey and feels helpless to do much about it. "I just don't feel good about me and Joey," he tells me one evening; "that's all I can say." Evan loves Joey. He feels proud of him, this bright, good-looking, happy child. But Evan also seems to feel that being a father is vaguely hurtful and hard to talk about.

The official history of Joey's problem was that Joey felt the "normal" oedipal attachment of a male child to his mother. Joey was having the emotional problems of growing up that any parent can expect. But Evan and Nancy add the point that Joey's problems are exacerbated by Evan's difficulties being an active father, which stem, they feel, from the way Evan's own father, an emotionally remote self-made businessman, had treated him. Evan tells me, "When Joey gets older, we're going to play baseball together and go fishing."

As I recorded this official version of Joey's problem through interviews and observation, I began to feel doubts about it. For one thing, clues to another interpretation appeared in the simple pattern of footsteps on a typical evening. There was the steady pacing of Nancy, preparing dinner in the kitchen, moving in zigzags from counter to refrigerator to counter to stove. There were the lighter, faster steps of Joey, running in large figure eights through the house, dashing from his

Tonka truck to his motorcycle man, reclaiming his sense of belonging in this house, among his things. After dinner, Nancy and Evan mingled footsteps in the kitchen, as they cleaned up. Then Nancy's steps began again: click, click, click, down to the basement for laundry, then thuck, thuck, thuck up the carpeted stairs to the first floor. Then to the bathroom where she runs Joey's bath, then into Joey's room, then back to the bath with Joey. Evan moved less—from the living room chair to Nancy in the kitchen, then back to the living room. He moved to the dining room to eat dinner and to the kitchen to help clean up. After dinner he went down to his hobby shop in the basement to sort out his tools; later he came up for a beer, then went back down. The footsteps suggest what is going on: Nancy was at work on her second shift.

BEHIND THE FOOTSTEPS

Between 8:05 A.M., and 6:05 P.M., both Nancy and Evan are away from home, working a "first shift" at full-time jobs. The rest of the time they deal with the varied tasks of the second shift: shopping, cooking, paying bills; taking care of the car, the garden, and yard; keeping harmony with Evan's mother who drops over quite a bit, "concerned" about Joey, with neighbors, their voluble baby-sitter, and each other. And Nancy's talk reflects a series of second-shift thoughts: "We're out of barbecue sauce . . . Joey needs a Halloween costume . . . The car needs a wash . . ." and so on. She reflects a certain "second-shift sensibility," a continual attunement to the task of striking and restriking the right emotional balance between child, spouse, home, and outside job.

When I first met the Holts, Nancy was absorbing far more of the second shift than Evan. She said she was doing 80 percent of the housework and 90 percent of the childcare. Evan said she did 60 percent of the housework, 70 percent of the childcare. Joey said, "I vacuum the rug, and fold the dinner napkins," finally concluding, "Mom and I do it all." A neighbor agreed with

Joey. Clearly, between Nancy and Evan, there was a "leisure gap": Evan had more than Nancy. I asked both of them, in separate interviews, to explain to me how they had dealt with housework and childcare since their marriage began.

One evening in the fifth year of their marriage, Nancy told me, when Joey was two months old and almost four years before I met the Holts, she first seriously raised the issue with Evan. "I told him: 'Look, Evan, it's not working. I do the housework, I take the major care of Joey, *and* I work a full-time job. I get pissed. This is *your* house too. Joey is *your* child too. It's not all *my* job to care for them.' When I cooled down I put to him, 'Look, how about this: I'll cook Mondays, Wednesdays, and Fridays. You cook Tuesdays, Thursdays, and Saturdays. And we'll share or go out Sundays.' "

According to Nancy, Evan said he didn't like "rigid schedules." He said he didn't necessarily agree with her standards of housekeeping, and didn't like that standard "imposed" on him, especially if she was "sluffing off" tasks on him, which from time to time he felt she was. But he went along with the idea in principle. Nancy said the first week of the new plan went as follows. On Monday, she cooked. For Tuesday, Evan planned a meal that required shopping for a few ingredients, but on his way home he forgot to shop for them. He came home, saw nothing he could use in the refrigerator or in the cupboard, and suggested to Nancy that they go out for Chinese food. On Wednesday, Nancy cooked. On Thursday morning, Nancy reminded Evan, "Tonight it's your turn." That night Evan fixed hamburgers and French fries and Nancy was quick to praise him. On Friday, Nancy cooked. On Saturday, Evan forgot again.

As this pattern continued, Nancy's reminders became sharper. The sharper they became, the more actively Evan forgot—perhaps anticipating even sharper reprimands if he resisted more directly. This cycle of passive refusal followed by disappointment and anger gradually tightened, and before long the struggle had spread to the task of doing the laundry. Nancy said it was only fair that Evan share the laundry. He agreed in principle, but anxious that Evan would not share, Nancy wanted a clear, explicit agreement. "You ought to wash and fold every other load," she had told him. Evan experienced this "plan" as a yoke around his neck. On many weekdays, at this point, a huge pile of laundry sat like a disheveled guest on the living-room couch.

In her frustration, Nancy began to make subtle emotional jabs at Evan. "I don't know *what's* for dinner," she would say with a sigh. Or "I can't cook now; I've got to deal with this pile of laundry." She tensed at the slightest criticism about household disorder; if Evan wouldn't do the housework, he had absolutely *no* right to criticize how she did it. She would burst out angrily at Evan. She recalled telling him: "After work *my* feet are just as tired as *your* feet. I'm just as wound up as you are. I come home. I cook dinner. I wash and I clean. Here we are, planning a second child, and I can't cope with the one we have."

About two years after I first began visiting the Holts, I began to see their problem in a certain light: as a conflict between their two gender ideologies. Nancy wanted to be the sort of woman who was needed and appreciated both at home and at work—like Lacey, she told me, on the television show "Cagney and Lacey." She wanted Evan to appreciate her for being a caring social worker, a committed wife, and a wonderful mother. But she cared just as much that she be able to appreciate *Evan* for what *he* contributed at home, not just for how he supported the family. She would feel proud to explain to women friends that she was married to one of these rare "new men."

A gender ideology is often rooted in early experience, and fueled by motives formed early on and such motives can often be traced to some cautionary tale in early life. So it was for Nancy. Nancy described her mother:

> My mom was wonderful, a real aristocrat, but she was also terribly depressed being a housewife. My dad treated her like a doormat. She didn't have any self-confidence. And growing up, I can remember

her being really depressed. I grew up bound and determined not to be like her and not to marry a man like my father. As long as Evan doesn't do the housework, I feel it means he's going to be like my father—coming home, putting his feet up, and hollering at my mom to serve him. That's my biggest fear. I've had bad dreams about that.

Nancy thought that women friends her age, also in traditional marriages, had come to similarly bad ends. She described a high school friend: "Martha barely made it through City College. She had no interest in learning anything. She spent nine years trailing around behind her husband [a salesman]. It's a miserable marriage. She hand washes all his shirts. The high point of her life was when she was 18 and the two of us were running around Miami Beach in a Mustang convertible. She's gained seventy pounds and she hates her life." To Nancy, Martha was a younger version of her mother, depressed, lacking in self-esteem, a cautionary tale whose moral was "if you want to be happy, develop a career and get your husband to share at home." Asking Evan to help again and again felt like "hard work" but it was essential to establishing her role as a career woman.

For his own reasons, Evan imagined things very differently. He loved Nancy and if Nancy loved being a social worker, he was happy and proud to support her in it. He knew that because she took her caseload so seriously, it was draining work. But at the same time, he did not see why, just because she chose this demanding career, *he* had to change *his own* life. Why should her personal decision to work outside the home require him to do more inside it? Nancy earned about two-thirds as much as Evan, and her salary was a big help, but as Nancy confided, "If push came to shove, we could do without it." Nancy was a social worker because she loved it. Doing daily chores at home was thankless work, and certainly not something Evan needed her to appreciate about him. Equality in the second shift meant a loss in his standard of living, and despite all the high-flown talk, he felt he hadn't *really* bargained for it. He was happy to help Nancy at home if she needed help; that was fine. That was only decent. But it was too sticky a matter "committing" himself to sharing.

Two other beliefs probably fueled his resistance as well. The first was his suspicion that if he shared the second shift with Nancy, she would "dominate him." Nancy would ask him to do this, ask him to do that. It felt to Evan as if Nancy had won so many small victories that he had to draw the line somewhere. Nancy had a declarative personality; and as Nancy said, "Evan's mother sat me down and told me once that I was too forceful, that Evan needed to take more authority." Both Nancy and Evan agreed that Evan's sense of career and self was in fact shakier than Nancy's. He had been unemployed. She never had. He had had some bouts of drinking in the past. Drinking was foreign to her. Evan thought that sharing housework would upset a certain balance of power that felt culturally "right." He held the purse strings and made the major decisions about large purchases (like their house) because he "knew more about finances" and because he'd chipped in more inheritance than she when they married. His job difficulties had lowered his self-respect, and now as a couple they had achieved some ineffable "balance"—tilted in his favor, she thought—which, if corrected to equalize the burden of chores, would result in his giving in "too much." A certain driving anxiety behind Nancy's strategy of actively renegotiating roles had made Evan see agreement as "giving in." When he wasn't feeling good about work, he dreaded the idea of being under his wife's thumb at home.

Underneath these feelings, Evan perhaps also feared that Nancy was avoiding taking care of *him*. His own mother, a mild-mannered alcoholic, had by imperceptible steps phased herself out of a mother's role, leaving him very much on his own. Perhaps a personal motive to prevent that happening in his marriage—a guess on my part, and unarticulated on his—underlay his strategy of passive resistance. And he wasn't

altogether wrong to fear this. Meanwhile, he felt he was "offering" Nancy the chance to stay home, or cut back her hours, and that she was refusing his "gift," while Nancy felt that, given her feelings about work, this offer was hardly a gift.

In the sixth year of her marriage, when Nancy again intensified her pressure on Evan to commit himself to equal sharing, Evan recalled saying, "Nancy, why don't you cut back to half-time; that way you can fit everything in." At first Nancy was baffled: "We've been married all this time, and you *still* don't get it. Work is important to me. I worked *hard* to get my MSW. Why *should* I give it up?" Nancy also explained to Evan and later to me, "I think my degree and my job has been my way of reassuring myself that I won't end up like my mother." Yet she'd received little emotional support in getting her degree from either her parents or in-laws. (Her mother had avoided asking about her thesis, and her in-laws, though invited, did not attend her graduation, later claiming they'd never been invited.)

In addition, Nancy was more excited about seeing her elderly clients in tenderloin hotels than Evan was about selling couches to furniture salesmen with greased-back hair. Why shouldn't Evan make as many compromises with his career ambitions and his leisure as she'd made with hers? She couldn't see it Evan's way, and Evan couldn't see it hers.

In years of alternating struggle and compromise, Nancy had seen only fleeting mirages of cooperation, visions that appeared when she got sick or withdrew, and disappeared when she got better or came forward.

After seven years of loving marriage, Nancy and Evan had finally come to a terrible impasse. Their emotional standard of living had drastically declined: they began to snap at each other, to criticize, to carp. Each felt taken advantage of: Evan, because his offering of a good arrangement was deemed unacceptable, and Nancy, because Evan wouldn't do what she deeply felt was "fair."

This struggle made its way into their sexual life—first through Nancy directly, and then through Joey. Nancy had always disdained any form of feminine wiliness or manipulation. Her family saw her as "a flaming feminist" and that was how she saw herself. As such, she felt above the underhanded ways traditional women used to get around men. She mused, "When I was a teenager, I vowed I would *never* use sex to get my way with a man. It is not self-respecting; it's demeaning. But when Evan refused to carry his load at home, I did, I used sex. I said, 'Look, Evan, I would not be this exhausted and asexual every night if I didn't have so much to face every morning.'" She felt reduced to an old "strategy," and her modern ideas made her ashamed of it. At the same time, she'd run out of other, modern ways.

The idea of a separation arose, and they became frightened. Nancy looked at the deteriorating marriages and fresh divorces of couples with young children around them. One unhappy husband they knew had become so uninvolved in family life (they didn't know whether his unhappiness made him uninvolved, or whether his lack of involvement had caused his wife to be unhappy) that his wife left him. In another case, Nancy felt the wife had "nagged" her husband so much that he abandoned her for another woman. In both cases, the couple was less happy after the divorce than before, and both wives took the children and struggled desperately to survive financially. Nancy took stock. She asked herself, "Why wreck a marriage over a dirty frying pan?" Is it really worth it?

UPSTAIRS-DOWNSTAIRS: A FAMILY MYTH AS "SOLUTION"

Not long after this crisis in the Holts' marriage, there was a dramatic lessening of tension over the issue of the second shift. It was as if the issue was closed. Evan had won. Nancy would do the second shift. Evan expressed vague guilt but beyond that he had nothing to say. Nancy had wearied of continually raising the topic, wearied of the lack of resolution. Now in the exhaustion of defeat, she wanted the struggle to be over too.

Evan was "so good" in *other* ways, why debilitate their marriage by continual quarreling. Besides, she told me, "Women always adjust more, don't they?"

One day, when I asked Nancy to tell me who did which tasks from a long list of household chores, she interrupted me with a broad wave of her hand and said, "I do the upstairs; Evan does the downstairs." What does that mean? I asked. Matter-of-factly, she explained that the upstairs included the living room, the dining room, the kitchen, two bedrooms, and two baths. The downstairs meant the garage, a place for storage and hobbies—Evan's hobbies. She explained this as a "sharing" arrangement, without humor or irony—just as Evan did later. Both said they had agreed it was the best solution to their dispute. Evan would take care of the car, the garage, and Max, the family dog. As Nancy explained, "the dog is all Evan's problem. I don't have to deal with the dog." Nancy took care of the rest.

For purposes of accommodating the second shift, then, the Holts' garage was elevated to the full moral and practical equivalent of the rest of the house. For Nancy and Evan, "upstairs and downstairs," "inside and outside," was vaguely described like "half and half," a fair division of labor based on a natural division of their house.

The Holts presented their upstairs-downstairs agreement as a perfectly equitable solution to a problem they "once had." This belief is what we might call a "family myth," even a modest delusional system. Why did they believe it? I think they believed it because they needed to believe it, because it solved a terrible problem. It allowed Nancy to continue thinking of herself as the sort of woman whose husband didn't abuse her—a self-conception that mattered a great deal to her. And it avoided the hard truth that, in his stolid, passive way, Evan had refused to share. It avoided the truth, too, that in their showdown, Nancy was more afraid of divorce than Evan was. This outer cover to their family life, this family myth, was jointly devised. It was an attempt to agree that there was no conflict over the second shift, no tension between their versions of manhood and womanhood, and that the powerful crisis that had arisen was temporary and minor.

The wish to avoid such a conflict is natural enough. But their avoidance was tacitly supported by the surrounding culture, especially the image of the woman with the flying hair. After all, this admirable woman also proudly does the "upstairs" each day without a husband's help and without conflict.

After Nancy and Evan reached their upstairs-downstairs agreement, their confrontations ended. They were nearly forgotten. Yet, as she described their daily life months after the agreement, Nancy's resentment still seemed alive and well. For example, she said:

> Evan and I eventually divided the labor so that I do the upstairs and Evan does the downstairs and the dog. So the dog is my husband's problem. But when I was getting the dog outside and getting Joey ready for childcare, and cleaning up the mess of feeding the cat, and getting the lunches together, and having my son wipe his nose on my outfit so I would have to change—then I was pissed! I felt that I was doing *everything*. All Evan was doing was getting up, having coffee, reading the paper, and saying, "Well, I have to go now," and often forgetting the lunch I'd bothered to make.

She also mentioned that she had fallen into the habit of putting Joey to bed in a certain way: he asked to be swung around by the arms, dropped on the bed, nuzzled and hugged, whispered to in his ear. Joey waited for her attention. He didn't go to sleep without it. But, increasingly, when Nancy tried it at eight or nine, the ritual didn't put Joey to sleep. On the contrary, it woke him up. It was then that Joey began to say he could only go to sleep in his parents' bed, that he began to sleep in their bed and to encroach on their sexual life.

Near the end of my visits, it struck me that Nancy was putting Joey to bed in an "exciting" way, later and later at night, in order to tell Evan something important: "You win; I'll go on doing all the work at home, but I'm angry about it and I'll make you pay." Evan had won the battle but

lost the war. According to the family myth, all was well: the struggle had been resolved by the upstairs-downstairs agreement. But suppressed in one area of their marriage, this struggle lived on in another—as Joey's problem, and as theirs.

NANCY'S "PROGRAM" TO SUSTAIN THE MYTH

There was a moment, I believe, when Nancy seemed to *decide* to give up on this one. She decided to try not to resent Evan. Whether or not other women face a moment just like this, at the very least they face the need to deal with all the feelings that naturally arise from a clash between a treasured ideal and an incompatible reality. In the age of a stalled revolution, it is a problem a great many women face.

Emotionally, Nancy's compromise from time to time slipped; she would forget and grow resentful again. Her new resolve needed maintenance. Only half aware that she was doing so, Nancy went to extraordinary lengths to maintain it. She could tell me now, a year or so after her "decision," in a matter-of-fact and noncritical way: "Evan likes to come home to a hot meal. He doesn't like to clear the table. He doesn't like to do the dishes. He likes to go watch TV. He likes to play with his son when he feels like it and not feel like he should be with him more." She seemed resigned.

Everything was "fine." But it had taken an extraordinary amount of complex "emotion work"—the work of *trying* to feel the "right" feeling, the feeling she wanted to feel—to make and keep everything "fine." Across the nation at this particular time in history, this emotion work is often all that stands between the stalled revolution on the one hand, and broken marriages on the other.

It would have been easier for Nancy Holt to do what some other women did: indignantly cling to her goal of sharing the second shift. Or she could have cynically renounced all forms of feminism as misguided, could have cleared away any ideological supports to her indignation, so as to smooth her troubled bond with Evan. Or, like her mother, she could have sunk into quiet depression, disguised perhaps by overbusyness, drinking, overeating. She did none of these things. Instead, she did something more complicated. She became *benignly* accommodating.

How did Nancy manage to accommodate graciously? How did she really live with it? In the most general terms, she had to bring herself to *believe* the myth that the upstairs-downstairs division of housework was fair, and that it had resolved her struggle with Evan. She had to decide to accept an arrangement which in her heart of hearts she had felt was unfair. At the same time, she did not relinquish her deep beliefs about fairness.

Instead, she did something more complicated. Intuitively, Nancy seemed to *avoid* all the mental associations that reminded her of this sore point: the connections between Evan's care of the dog and her care of their child and house, between her share of family work and equality in their marriage; and between equality and love. In short, Nancy refused to consciously recognize the entire chain of associations that made her feel that something was wrong. The maintenance program she designed to avoid thinking about these things and to avoid the connections between them, was, in one way, a matter of denial. But in another way, it was a matter of intuitive genius.

First, it involved dissociating the inequity in the second shift from the inequity in their marriage, and in marriages in general. Nancy continued to care about sharing the work at home, about having an "equal marriage" and about other people having them too. For reasons that went back to her depressed "doormat" mother, and to her consequent determination to forge an independent identity as an educated, middle-class woman for whom career opportunities had opened up in the early 1980s, Nancy cared about these things. Egalitarianism as an ideology made sense of her biography, her circumstances, and the way she had forged the two. How could she *not* care? But to ensure that her concern for equality did not

make her resentful in her marriage to a man remarkably resistant to change, she "rezoned" this anger-inducing territory. She made that territory much smaller: only if Evan did not take care of the dog would she be indignant. Now she wouldn't need to be upset about the double day *in general.* She could still be a feminist, still believe in 50–50 with housework, and still believe that working toward equality was an expression of respect and respect the basis of love. But this chain of associations was now anchored more safely to a more minor matter: how lovingly Evan groomed, fed, and walked the dog.

For Evan, also, the dog came to symbolize the entire second shift: it became a fetish. Other men, I found, had second-shift fetishes too. When I asked one man what he did to share the work of the home, he answered, "I make all the pies we eat." He didn't have to share much responsibility for the home; "pies" did it for him. Another man grilled fish. Another baked bread. In their pies, their fish, and their bread, such men converted a single act into a substitute for a multitude of chores in the second shift, a token. Evan took care of the dog.

Another way in which Nancy encapsulated her anger was to think about her work in a different way. Feeling unable to cope at home, she had with some difficulty finally arranged a half-time schedule with her boss at work. This eased her load, but it did not resolve the more elusive moral problem: within their marriage, her work and her time "mattered less" than Evan's. What Evan did with his time corresponded to what he wanted her to depend on him for, to appreciate him for; what she did with her time did not. To deal with this, she devised the idea of dividing all of her own work in the new schedule into "shifts." As she explained: "I've been resentful, yes. I was feeling mistreated, and I became a bitch to live with. Now that I've gone part-time, I figure that when I'm at the office from eight to one, and when I come home and take care of Joey and make dinner at five—all that time from eight to six is my shift. So I don't mind making dinner every night *since it's on my shift*. Before, I had to make dinner on time I considered to be *after* my shift and I resented always having to do it."

Another plank in Nancy's maintenance program was to suppress any comparison between her hours of leisure and Evan's. In this effort she had Evan's cooperation, for they both clung hard to the notion that they enjoyed an equal marriage. What they did was to deny any connection between this equal marriage and equal access to leisure. They agreed it couldn't be meaningfully claimed that Evan had more leisure than Nancy or that his fatigue mattered more, or that he enjoyed more discretion over his time, or that he lived his life more as he preferred. Such comparisons could suggest that they were both treating Evan as if he were *worth more* than Nancy, and for Nancy, from that point on, it would be a quick fall down a slippery slope to the idea that Evan did not love and honor her as much as she honored and loved him.

For Nancy, the leisure gap between Evan and herself had never seemed to her a simple, practical matter of her greater fatigue. Had it been just that, she would have felt tired but not indignant. Had it been only that, working part-time for a while would have been a wonderful solution, as many other women have said, "the best of both worlds." What troubled Nancy was the matter of her worth. As she told me one day: "It's not that I mind taking care of Joey. I love doing that. I don't even mind cooking or doing laundry. It's that I feel sometimes that Evan thinks his work, his time, is worth more than mine. He'll wait for me to get the phone. It's like his time is more sacred."

As Nancy explained: "Evan and I look for different signs of love. Evan feels loved when we make love. Sexual expression is very important to him. I feel loved when he makes dinner for me or cleans up. He knows I like that, and he does it sometimes." For Nancy, feeling loved was connected to feeling her husband was being considerate of her needs, and honoring her ideal of sharing and equity. To Evan, "fairness" and respect seemed impersonal moral concepts, abstractions rudely imposed on love. He thought he expressed his respect for Nancy by listening carefully to her opinions on the elderly, on welfare, on all sorts of topics, and by consulting her on major purchases. But who did the dishes had to do with a person's role in the family, not with fairness and certainly not with love. In my interviews, a surprising number of women spoke of their fathers helping their mothers "out of love" or consideration. As one woman said, "My dad helped around a lot. He really loved my mom." But in describing their fathers, not one man I interviewed made this link between help at home and love.

SUPPRESSING THE POLITICS OF COMPARISON

In the past, Nancy had compared her responsibilities at home, her identity, and her life to Evan's, and had compared Evan to other men they knew. Now, to avoid resentment, she seemed to compare herself more to *other working mothers*— how organized, energetic, and successful she was compared to them. By this standard, she was doing great: Joey was blooming, her marriage was fine, her job was all she could expect.

Nancy also compared herself to single women who had moved further ahead in their careers, but they fit another mental category. There were two kinds of women, she thought—married and single. "A single woman could move ahead in her career but a married woman has to do a wife's work and mother's work as well." She did not make this distinction for men.

When Nancy decided to stop comparing Evan to men who helped more around the house, she had to suppress an important issue that she had often discussed with Evan: How *unusually* helpful was Evan? How unusually lucky was she? Did he do more or less than men in general? Than middle-class, educated men? What was the "going rate"?

Before she made her decision, Nancy had claimed that Bill Beaumont, who lived two doors down the street, did half the housework without being reminded. Evan gave her Bill Beaumont, but said Bill was an exception. Compared to *most men,* Evan said, he did more. This was true if "most men" meant Evan's old friends. Nancy felt "upwardly mobile" compared to the wives of those men, and she believed that they looked upon Evan as a model for their own husbands, just as she used to look up to women whose husbands did more than Evan. She also noted how much the dangerous "unionizer" she had appeared to a male friend of theirs:

> One of our friends is a traditional Irish cop whose wife doesn't work. But the way they wrote that marriage, even when she had the kid and worked full time, she did everything. He couldn't understand our arrangement where my husband would help out and cook part time and do the dishes once in a while and help out with the laundry [an arrangement that didn't last]. We were *banned* from his house for a while because he told Evan, "Every time your wife comes over and talks to my wife, I get in trouble." I was considered a flaming liberal.

When the wife of Joe Collins, a neighbor on the other side, complained that Joe didn't take equal responsibility, Joe in turn would look down the invisible chain of sharing, half-sharing, and nonsharing males to someone low on his wife's list of helpful husbands and say, "At least I do a hell of a lot more than *he* does." In reply, Joe's wife would name a husband she knew who took fully half the responsibility of caring for the child and the home. Joe would answer that this man was either imaginary or independently wealthy, and then cite the example of another male friend who, though a great humorist and fisherman, did far less at home.

I began to imagine the same evening argument extending down the street of this middle-class Irish neighborhood, across the city to other cities, states, regions . . . wives pointing to husbands who did more, husbands pointing to men who did less. Comparisons like these—between Evan and other men, between Nancy and other women—reflect a semiconscious sense of *the going rates for a desirable attitude or behavior*

in an available member of the same and opposite sex. If most of the men in their middle-class circle of friends had been given to drinking heavily, beating their wives, and having affairs, Nancy would have considered herself "lucky" to have Evan, because he didn't do those things. But most of the men they knew weren't like that either, so Nancy didn't consider Evan "above the going rate" in this way. Most of those men only halfheartedly encouraged their wives to advance at work, so Nancy felt lucky to have Evan's enthusiastic encouragement.

This idea of a "going rate" indicated the market value, so to speak, of a man's behavior or attitudes. If a man was really "rare," his wife intuitively felt grateful, or at least both of them felt she ought to. How far the whole culture, and their particular corner of it, had gotten through the feminist agenda—criminalizing wife battery, disapproving of a woman's need for her husband's "permission" to work, and so on—became the cultural foundation of the judgment about how rare and desirable a man was.

The "going rate" was a tool in the marital struggle, useful in this case mainly on the male side. If Evan could convince Nancy that he did as much as or more than "most men," she couldn't as seriously expect him to do more. Like most other men who didn't share, Evan felt the male "norm" was evidence on his side: men "out there" did less. Nancy was lucky he did as much as he did.

Nancy thought men "out there" did more at home but were embarrassed to say so. Given her view of "men out there," Nancy felt less lucky than seemed right to Evan, given his picture of things. Besides that, Nancy felt that sheer rarity was not the only or best measure. She felt that Evan's share of the work at home should be assessed, not by comparing it to the real inequalities in other people's lives, but by comparing it to the ideal of sharing.

Comparisons between Evan and the going rate of male helpfulness was one basis on which to appraise Evan's offerings to their marriage and the credit and gratitude due him for those offerings. The more rare, the more credit. Their ideals of manhood and womanhood formed another basis. The closer to the ideal, the more credit. And the harder it was to live up to the ideal, the more pride-swallowing it took, or the more effort shown, the more credit. Since Evan and Nancy didn't see this going rate the same way, since they differed in their ideals, and since Evan hadn't actually shown much effort in changing, Nancy had not been as grateful to Evan as he felt she should have been. Not only had she not been grateful, she'd resented him.

But now, under the new "maintenance program" to support the necessary myth of equality in her marriage, Nancy set aside the tangles in the give and take of credit. She thought now in a more "segregated" way. She compared women to women, and men to men, and based her sense of gratitude on that way of thinking. Since the going rate was unfavorable to women, Nancy felt she should feel more grateful for what Evan gave her (because it was so rare in the world) than Evan should feel for what she gave him (which was more common). Nancy did not have to feel grateful because Evan had compromised his own views on manhood; actually he had made few concessions. But she did feel she owed him gratitude for supporting her work so wholeheartedly; that was unusual.

For his part, Evan didn't talk much about feeling grateful to Nancy. He actually felt she wasn't doing enough around the house. But he said this in a curious way that avoided an Evan-Nancy comparison. He erased the distinction between Nancy and himself: his "I" disappeared into "we," leaving no "me" to compare to "you." For example, when I asked him if he felt that he did enough around the house, he laughed, surprised to be asked point-blank, and replied mildly: "No, I don't think so. No. I would have to admit that we probably could do more." Then using "we" in an apparently different way, he went on: "But I also have to say that I think we could do more in terms of the household chores than we really do. See, we let a lot more slide than we should."

Nancy made no more comparisons to Bill Beaumont, no more unfavorable comparisons to the "going rate." Without these frames of reference, the deal with Evan seemed "fair." This did not mean that Nancy ceased to care about equality between the sexes. On the contrary, she cut out magazine articles about how males rose faster in social welfare than females, and she complained about the condescending way male psychiatrists treat female social workers. She pushed her feminism "out" into the world of work, a safe distance away from the upstairs-downstairs arrangement at home.

Nancy now blamed her fatigue on "everything she had to do." When she occasionally spoke of conflict, it was conflict between her job and Joey, or between Joey and housework. Evan slid out of the equation. As Nancy spoke of him now, he had no part in the conflict.

Since Nancy and Evan no longer conceived of themselves as comparable, Nancy let it pass when Evan spoke of housework in a "male" way, as something he "would do" or "would not do," or something he did when he got around to it. Like most women, when Nancy spoke of housework, she spoke simply of what had to be done. The difference in the way she and Evan talked seemed to emphasize that their viewpoints were "naturally" different and again helped push the problem out of mind.

Many couples traded off tasks as the need arose; whoever came home first started dinner. In the past, Evan had used flexibility in the second shift to camouflage his retreat from it; he hadn't liked "rigid schedules." He had once explained to me: "We don't really keep count of who does what. Whoever gets home first is likely to start dinner. Whoever has the time deals with Joey or cleans up." He had disparaged a female neighbor who kept strict track of tasks as "uptight" and "compulsive." A couple, he had felt, ought to be "open to the flow." Dinner, he had said, could be anytime. The very notion of a leisure gap disappeared into Evan's celebration of happy, spontaneous anarchy. But now that the struggle was over, Evan didn't talk of dinner at "anytime." Dinner was at six.

Nancy's program to keep up her gracious resignation included another tactic: she would focus on the *advantages* of losing the struggle. She wasn't *stuck* with the upstairs. Now, as she talked she seemed to preside over it as her dominion. She would do the housework, but the house would feel like "hers." The new living room couch, the kitchen cabinet, she referred to as "mine." She took up "supermom-speak" and began referring to *my* kitchen, *my* living room curtains, and, even in Evan's presence, to *my* son. She talked of machines that helped *her,* and of the work-family conflict itself as *hers.* Why shouldn't she? She felt she'd earned that right. The living room reflected Nancy's preference for beige. The upbringing of Joey reflected Nancy's ideas about fostering creativity by giving a child controlled choice. What remained of the house was Evan's domain. As she remarked: "I never touch the garage, not ever. Evan sweeps it and straightens it and arranges it and plays with tools and figures out where the equipment goes—in fact, that's one of his hobbies. In the evening, after Joey has settled down, he goes down there and putzes around; he has a TV down there, and he figures out his fishing equipment and he just plays around. The washer and dryer are down there, but that's the only part of the garage that's my domain."

Nancy could see herself as the "winner"—the one who got her way, the one whose kitchen, living room, house, and child these really were. She could see her arrangement with Evan as *more* than fair—from a certain point of view.

As a couple, Nancy and Evan together explained their division of the second shift in ways that disguised their struggle. Now they rationalized that it was a result of their two *personalities.* For Evan, especially, there was no problem of a leisure gap; there was only the continual, fascinating interaction of two personalities. "I'm lazy," he explained. "I like to do what I want to do in my own time. Nancy isn't as lazy as I am. She's compulsive and very well organized." The

comparisons of his work to hers, his fatigue to hers, his leisure time to hers—comparisons that used to point to a problem—were melted into freestanding personal characteristics, his laziness, her compulsiveness.

Nancy now agreed with Evan's assessment of her, and described herself as "an energetic person" who was amazingly "well organized." When I asked her whether she felt any conflict between work and family life, she demurred: "I work real well overnight. I pulled overnights all through undergraduate and graduate school, so I'm not too terribly uncomfortable playing with my family all evening, then putting them to bed, making coffee, and staying up all night [to write up reports on her welfare cases] and then working the next day—though I only do that when I'm down to the wire. I go into overdrive. I don't feel any conflict between the job and the child that way at all."

Evan was well organized and energetic on his job. But as Nancy talked of Evan's life at home, he neither had these virtues nor lacked them; they were irrelevant. This double standard of virtue reinforced the idea that men and women cannot be compared, being "naturally" so different.

Evan's orientation to domestic tasks, as they both described it now, had been engraved in childhood, and how could one change a whole childhood? As Nancy often reminded me, "I was brought up to do the housework. Evan wasn't." Many other men, who had also done little housework when they were boys, did not talk so fatalistically about "upbringing," because they were doing a lot of it now. But the idea of a fate sealed so very early was oddly *useful* in Nancy's program of benign resignation. She needed it, because if the die had been cast in the dawn of life, it was inevitable that she should work the extra month a year.

This, then, was the set of mental tricks that helped Nancy resign herself to what had at one time seemed like a "bad deal." This was how she reconciled believing one thing and living with another.

HOW MANY HOLTS?

In one key way the Holts were typical of the vast majority of two-job couples: their family life had become the shock absorber for a stalled revolution whose origin lay far outside it—in economic and cultural trends that bear very differently on men and women. Nancy was reading books, newspaper articles, and watching TV programs on the changing role of women. Evan wasn't. Nancy felt benefited by these changes; Evan didn't. In her ideals and in reality, Nancy was more different from her mother than Evan was from his father, for the culture and economy were in general pressing change faster upon women like her than upon men like Evan. Nancy had gone to college; her mother hadn't. Nancy had a professional job; her mother never had. Nancy had the idea that she should be equal with her husband; her mother hadn't been much exposed to that idea in her day. Nancy felt she should share the job of earning money, and that Evan should share the work at home; her mother hadn't imagined that was possible. Evan went to college, his father (and the other boys in his family; though not the girls) had gone too. Work was important to Evan's identity as a man as it had been for his father before him. Indeed, Evan felt the same way about family roles as his father had felt in his day. The new job opportunities and the feminist movement of the 1960s and '70s had transformed Nancy but left Evan pretty much the same. And the friction created by this difference between them moved to the issue of second shift as metal to a magnet. By the end, Evan did less housework and childcare than most men married to working women—but not much less. Evan and Nancy were also typical of nearly 40 percent of the marriages I studied in their clash of gender ideologies and their corresponding difference in notion about what constituted a "sacrifice" and what did not. By far the most common form of mismatch was like that between Nancy, an egalitarian, and Evan, a transitional.

But for most couples, the tensions between strategies did not move so quickly and powerfully to issues of housework and childcare. Nancy pushed harder than most women to get her husband to share the work at home, and she also lost more overwhelmingly than the few other women who fought that hard. Evan pursued his strategy of passive resistance with more quiet tenacity than most men, and he allowed himself to become far more marginal to his son's life than most other fathers. The myth of the Holts' "equal" arrangement seemed slightly more odd than other family myths that encapsulated equally powerful conflicts.

Beyond their upstairs-downstairs myth, the Holts tell us a great deal about the subtle ways a couple can encapsulate the tension caused by a struggle over the second shift without resolving the problem or divorcing. Like Nancy Holt, many women struggle to avoid, suppress, obscure, or mystify a frightening conflict over the second shift. They do not struggle like this because they started off wanting to, or because such struggle is inevitable or because women inevitably lose, but because they are forced to choose between equality and marriage. And they choose marriage. When asked about "ideal" relations between men and women in general, about what they want for their daughters, about what "ideally" they'd like in their own marriage, most working mothers "wished" their men would share the work at home.

But many "wish" it instead of "want" it. Other goals—like keeping peace at home—come first. Nancy Holt did some extraordinary behind-the-scenes emotion work to prevent her ideals from clashing with her marriage. In the end, she had confined and miniaturized her ideas of equality successfully enough to do two things she badly wanted to do: feel like a feminist, and live at peace with a man who was not. Her program had "worked." Evan won on the reality of the situation, because Nancy did the second shift. Nancy won on the cover story; they would talk about it as if they shared.

Nancy wore the upstairs-downstairs myth as an ideological cloak to protect her from the contradictions in her marriage and from the cultural and economic forces that press upon it. Nancy and Evan Holt were caught on opposite sides of the gender revolution occurring all around them. Through the 1960s, 1970s, and 1980s masses of women entered the public world of work—but went only so far up the occupational ladder. They tried for "equal" marriages, but got only so far in achieving it. They married men who liked them to work at the office but who wouldn't share the extra month a year at home. When confusion about the identity of the working woman created a cultural vacuum in the 1970s and 1980s, the image of the supermom quietly glided in. She made the "stall" seem normal and happy. But beneath the happy image of the woman with the flying hair are modern marriages like the Holts', reflecting intricate webs of tension, and the huge, hidden emotional cost to women, men, and children of having to "manage" inequality. Yet on the surface, all we might see would be Nancy Holt bounding confidently out the door at 8:30 A.M., briefcase in one hand, Joey in the other. All we might hear would be Nancy's and Evan's talk about their marriage as happy, normal, even "equal"—because equality was so important to Nancy.

■ Review Questions

1. Contrast Nancy's and Evan's gender ideologies.
2. What "family myth" did the Holts create to resolve their disagreement over housework and child care?

Part Four

Links across
the Generations

CHAPTER 9

Children and Parents

The study of "parenting" used to be in reality the study of "mothering." A half century ago, childrearing was seen as mothers' work. Although mothers still do the majority of childrearing, fathers have increased their share; and more and more social scientists have studied what fathers do. In this chapter, I present two selections that explore fathering at opposite ends of our culture. In the first selection, W. Bradford Wilcox discusses the role fathers play in Conservative Protestant families. This kind of Protestantism is sometimes called "evangelical," a term the author uses in this piece. It encompasses religious groups who emphasize a born-again experience of individual faith in Jesus Christ and a view of the Bible as the literal word of God and the primary source of moral guidance. The Southern Baptist Convention, the Assemblies of God, and the Pentecostal Assemblies of the World are examples of Conservative Protestant churches. Its followers consider the husband to be the head of the household. They generally reject egalitarian gender philosophies and tolerance of nonmarital family forms. They approve of corporal punishment of children in moderation.

The stereotypical Conservative Protestant father is a harsh, distant parent who rules by strict discipline and punishment. But Wilcox argues

that this stereotype is inaccurate. To be sure, Conservative Protestant fathers are more prone to spank their children. Yet in other ways, the author argues, these men look a lot like the loving, involved "new" father much admired by social liberals. Wilcox labels this mixture of the old and new fathering styles as "neotraditional."

At the other end of the continuum of fathering are gay men who wish to become fathers but who cannot do so within the framework of heterosexual partnerships and who, unlike lesbians, cannot give birth. Rather, they must seek out opportunities to construct biological and social fatherhood in ways that are innovative and nontraditional. Their experiences illuminate, usually by contrast, the taken-for-granted assumptions about how one ordinarily becomes and remains a parent. In the second selection, Judith Stacey reports on this new world of gay parenthood in the large gay population in Los Angeles. Gay men can become fathers in a number of ways, but all of them require determination and hard work. Not all gay men want to be fathers enough to undertake such a project, but Stacey, in this excerpt from a longer article, shows us the remarkable stories of several who do. Their experiences raise questions about the nature and boundaries of parenthood.

READING 9-1

Religion and the Domestication of Men

W. Bradford Wilcox

A wife should "submit herself graciously" to her husband's leadership, and a husband should "provide for, protect, and lead his family." So proclaimed the Southern Baptist Convention—the nation's largest evangelical Protestant denomination—in 1998. Statements like this, and religious support for gender traditionalism and antifeminist public policies more generally, indicate how conservative religious institutions have helped to stall the gender revolution of the last half century. The crucial role that Phyllis Schlafly's Eagle Forum played in defeating the ERA in the 1970s is but one example.

Beneath the politics, we know less about how religious institutions influence individual men. Journalists, academics, and feminists have been skeptical—to say the least—about the influence of religion on American family men. Journalists Steve and Cokie Roberts responded to the 1998 Southern Baptist statement, for instance, by writing that such thinking "can clearly lead to abuse, both physical and emotional." Similarly, sociologists Julia McQuillan and Myra Marx Ferree have argued that evangelical Protestantism is an influential force "pushing men toward authoritarian and stereotypical forms of masculinity and attempting to renew patriarchal relations."

Academics, journalists, and feminists raise an important question: Are religious institutions, especially conservative ones such as evangelical Protestantism or Mormonism, a force for patriarchy?

W. Bradford Wilcox, "Religion and the Domestication of Men," *Contexts*, Vol. 5, No. 4, pp. 42–46. © 2006 The American Sociological Association. Used by permission. All rights reserved.

Critics have yet to examine how religious institutions, particularly conservative ones, have also become deeply concerned about the family revolution of the last half century. Increases in divorce, nonmarital childbearing, and premarital sex in the society at large and in their own ranks have disturbed many conservative churches, organizations, and leaders. Partly as a consequence of this revolution, and partly because feminism has raised women's expectations of men in the society at large and within conservative churches, conservative religious institutions have turned their focus on men with the aim of encouraging them to devote more time, attention, and emotional energy to their families. They hope to strengthen families that seem increasingly vulnerable to fragmentation.

Does religion domesticate men in ways that make them more engaged and attentive husbands and fathers? To answer this question, I focus not only on white, middle-class families, but also on the urban poor, who have borne the brunt of our nation's retreat from marriage.

In my research, I have relied on quantitative data—primarily the National Survey of Families and Households and the Fragile Families and Child Wellbeing Study—and on qualitative interviews with over 150 clergy, churchgoing, and secular men and women living in cities across the country to determine how religion is associated with men's approach to family life.

A FORCE FOR PATRIARCHY?

So how do religious institutions affect men who are married with children? In my book, *Soft Patriarchs and New Men: How Christianity Shapes Fathers and Husbands,* I find some evidence that religion is a force for patriarchy.

When it comes to work and family life, evangelical Protestantism (theologically conservative churches such as the Southern Baptist Church, Assemblies of God, the Presbyterian Church of America, and nondenominational evangelical churches) fosters gender inequality. Evangelical

Protestant family men are more likely to endorse traditional gender attitudes than other men. For instance, I found that 58 percent of churchgoing, evangelical men who are married with children believe it is "much better for everyone if the man earns the main living and the woman takes care of the home and family," compared to only 44 percent of churchgoing, mainline Protestant men and 37 percent of unaffiliated men. (Mainline Protestantism encompasses churches such as the Episcopal Church, Presbyterian Church (USA), the Lutheran Church (ELCA), and the United Methodist Church.)

These attitudes, reinforced by church-based activities and social networks, matter. Evangelical Protestant husbands do an hour less housework per week than other American husbands; not surprisingly, the division of household labor is less equal in evangelical homes than in other American homes. Sociologists Jennifer Glass and Jerry Jacobs have shown that women raised in evangelical Protestant families are more likely to focus on motherhood than work: they marry earlier, bear children earlier, and work less than other women in the United States. So it is true that evangelical Protestantism—but not mainline Protestantism, Reform Judaism, and Roman Catholicism—appears to steer men (and women) toward gender inequality.

Evangelical Protestantism also steers fathers in a patriarchal direction when it comes to discipline. Drawing in part on their belief in original sin and on biblical passages that seem to promote a strict approach to discipline—"He who spares the rod hates his son, but he who loves him is careful to discipline him" (*Proverbs* 13:24)— evangelical Protestant leaders, such as Focus on the Family [former] President James Dobson, stress the divine authority of parents and the need for parents to take a firm hand with their children. As Dobson writes, "If a little child is taught to disrespect the authority of his parents, systematically from the tender years of childhood—to mock their leadership, to 'sass' them and disobey their instructions, to exercise extreme self-will

from the earliest moments of awareness—then it is most unlikely that this same child will turn his face up to God, about 20 years later, and say humbly, 'Here I am Lord; send me!'"

Many evangelical fathers take these views to heart. They are more likely to value obedience in their children. They are also more likely to spank their children when they do not get that obedience. Specifically, evangelical fathers are significantly more likely to use corporal punishment on their children than Catholic, Jewish, and unaffiliated fathers. In important respects, evangelical Protestantism appears to be a force for patriarchal authority and gender relations.

TURNING THE HEARTS OF MEN TOWARD THEIR FAMILIES

But this is not the whole story about religion and men in the United States. Because they are worried about the social and religious consequences of divorce and nonmarital childbearing, and because they view the vocations of marriage and parenthood in a transcendent light, churches and family ministries have devoted countless radio broadcasts, books, and sermons to the task of encouraging Americans to make their marriages and children a top priority.

Conservative religious groups, such as Promise Keepers and the Southern Baptist Convention, have been particularly attentive to the family failures of men. Recognizing that men are often the weak link in families—because they fail to focus emotionally and practically on their wives and children, and because they are often absent, physically or financially—evangelical Protestant churches and ministries have generally taken the lead in the religious world in calling on men to put their families first. Drawing also on a therapeutic emphasis that entered evangelical Protestantism in the 1970s, evangelical elites urge men to be emotionally and practically engaged with their wives and children.

For instance, one popular book among evangelicals, *If Only He Knew: What No Woman Can*

Resist, by therapist Gary Smalley, chides husbands for their insensitivity toward their wives. He lists 122 ways in which husbands are insufficiently attuned emotionally to their wives—from "not inviting her out on special romantic dates from time to time" to "being easily distracted when she is trying to talk"—and exhorts men to comfort, to listen, to praise, and to communicate with their wives. Likewise, popular Christian pastor Charles Swindoll urges men to model God's love to their children in the following way: "Your boy must be very aware that *you love him.* . . . When is the last time you took him in your arms and held him close so no one else could hear, and whispered to him how happy you are to have him as your son?"

Mainline Protestant, Catholic, and Reform Jewish congregations also encourage men to invest in their families, although they do it more in the context of encouraging both men and women to honor the Golden Rule by treating their spouses and especially their children with care and consideration. As sociologist Penny Edgell reports in her book *Religion and Family in a Changing Society,* moderate-to-liberal congregations in these traditions criticize lives centered around careers or materialism and stress the importance of putting family life first.

This emphasis on family seems to be bearing fruit. I found that men who are religious—especially evangelical fathers and husbands—are more involved and affectionate with their children and wives than are unaffiliated family men. As fathers, religious men spend more time in one-on-one activities like reading to their children, hug and praise their kids more often, and keep tabs on the children more than unaffiliated fathers do. For instance, churchgoing fathers spend 2.9 hours per week with their children in youth activities such as soccer, Boy Scouts, and religious youth groups, and churchgoing evangelical fathers spend 3.2 hours per week on these activities, compared to 1.6 hours for unaffiliated fathers.

As husbands, religious men are more affectionate and understanding with their wives, and they spend more time socializing with them, com-pared to husbands who are not regular churchgoers. I also found—contrary to the expectations of critics—that churchgoing, evangelical married men have the lowest rates of reported domestic violence of any major religious or secular group in the United States. (On the other hand, evangelical married men who do not attend church regularly have the highest rates of domestic violence.) Not surprisingly, wives of religious men report higher levels of marital happiness than wives of men who are not religious.

Religious family men—especially more conservative ones—combine elements of the new and the old in their approach to family life. They are more likely to have unequal marriages and to take a strict approach to discipline; but they are also more emotionally and practically engaged than the average secular or nominally religious family man. In a word, their approach to family life can be described as neotraditional. . . .

RELIGION IN MEN'S LIVES

The United States has witnessed two distinct but related revolutions in the last half century: a gender revolution marked by increased equality in the opportunities, rewards, and responsibilities that men and women face, and a family revolution marked by the weakening of marriage as the central institution for organizing sex, childbearing, childrearing, and adult life more generally. The gender revolution has not completely triumphed, in part because men have not taken up an equal share of housework and childcare. My research and that of others suggests another reason: religious institutions—particularly more conservative ones like the Southern Baptist Convention— often lend ideological and practical support to traditional gender attitudes and family behaviors; thus, feminist, academic, and journalistic critics are rightly concerned about how some religious institutions reinforce gender inequality.

But critics miss how religious institutions— especially more conservative ones—also encourage men to put their families first. Most of the institutions that men encounter in their daily lives—work, popular culture, and sports, for instance—do not push men to invest in family life. But religious institutions—especially traditional ones worried about the well-being of the family in the modern world—do encourage men to focus on their families. They provide men with messages, rituals, and activities that help them to see their roles as husbands and fathers as meaningful and important, and to improve their performance of these roles.

Churchgoing family men in the United States are more involved and affectionate fathers and husbands, compared to their peers who are secular or just nominally religious. Their wives report greater marital happiness, and are therefore less likely to divorce them. At least in urban America, these men also appear more likely to engage in "decent" behavior—for example, holding regular jobs and avoiding drug and alcohol abuse—than their less religious peers.

This neotraditional approach to family life, combining a progressive insistence on men's active engagement in family life with a traditional insistence on some degree of gender complementarity in family life, has not received much scholarly attention. But if we seek to understand family pluralism and family change in the United States in all of its complexity, we must keep these neotraditional men and their families in our sociological imagination.

RECOMMENDED RESOURCES

John P. Bartkowski. *Remaking the Godly Marriage: Gender Negotiation in Evangelical Families* (Rutgers University Press, 2001). Evangelical Protestant couples draw selectively on both essentialist and feminist gender ideals in negotiating married life.

Penny Edgell. *Religion and Family in a Changing Society* (Princeton University Press, 2005). Men, more than women, attend church to socialize their children, and are thus more likely than women to be attracted to churches that cater to traditional families.

Sally Gallagher. *Evangelical Identity and Gendered Family Life* (Rutgers University Press, 2003). The conventional critique of evangelical Protestant gender politics does not capture the ambiguities and heterogeneity of gender beliefs and behaviors in this subculture.

Jennifer Glass and Jerry Jacobs. "Childhood Religious Conservatism and Adult Attainment among Black and White Women." *Social Forces* 84 (2005): 555–579. Evangelical Protestantism puts many women on a trajectory toward early motherhood and marriage and away from full-time employment.

W. Bradford Wilcox. *Soft Patriarchs, New Men: How Christianity Shapes Fathers and Husbands* (University of Chicago Press, 2004). The impact of religion on mainline and evangelical Protestant family men.

■ Review Questions ■

1. In what ways are the evangelical fathers traditional in their approach to family life?
2. In what ways do they differ from the traditional pattern of fatherhood?

READING 9-2

Gay Parenthood and the Decline of Paternity as We Knew It

Judith Stacey

Because let's face it, if men weren't always hungry for it, nothing would ever happen. There would be no sex, and our species would perish. (Sean Elder, 2004)

Unlucky in love and ready for a family, [Christie] Malcomson tried for 4½ years to get pregnant, eventually giving birth to the twins when she was 38. Four years later, again without a mate, she had Sarah. "I've always known that I was meant to be a mother," Malcomson, 44, said. "I tell people, 'I didn't choose to be a single parent. I choose to be a parent.'" (Lornet Turnbull, 2004)

His partner at the time was also interested in adopting. In fact, the shared desire to have a family had been one of the things that brought the two together in the first place. . . . So it was a blow when his partner began to back off. By February 1996, the partner had changed his mind about the adoption altogether. It sundered their relationship and was the direct cause of their breakup. (David Strah and Susanna Margolis, 2003:116)

The increasing visibility of gay and lesbian parenthood arouses widespread expectations, hopes, and fears that public acceptance of homosexuality will cause its incidence to increase. A recent book opens with the conventional wisdom on this trend; "Like it or not—and granted that most Americans still do not—millions of children are already being raised by gay and lesbian parents, and their numbers are increasing at an ever-accelerating pace" (Bernstein, 2005:xvi). Similarly, opponents and advocates of same-sex marriage alike seem to presume that legalization will expand the numbers

of children with gay parents and that, conversely, bans on gay marriage would work to reduce lesbian and gay parenthood (see, for example, Gallagher, 2003). This article, however, draws upon ethnographic research on gay male intimacy and kinship in Los Angeles to advance the counter-intuitive claim that inverse outcomes are more likely. Growing public visibility of gay parenthood, I suggest, both signals and fosters dramatic transformations in the meaning of contemporary parenthood generally, and of paternity particularly. Paradoxically, however, these developments are likely to reduce the incidence of gay paternity at the same time that they will enhance its quality and legitimacy. The very success gay men have begun to achieve in openly pursuing parenthood against the odds exposes conditions governing contemporary family life that represent the decline of paternity as we knew it. This does not augur the demise of male parenthood, however, but its creative, if controversial, reconfiguration.

Most analyses of postmodern transformations of intimacy feature the emergent quality of adult unions, often placing gays and lesbians on the frontier (Bech, 1997; Beck and Beck-Gernsheim, 1995; Giddens, 1992; Kipnis, 2003; Seidman, 1991; Stacey, 1996, 1998; Weeks et al., 2001). Giddens (1992), for example, portrays gays and lesbians as vanguard explorers of "confluent love," his ideal-typical conception of "the pure relationship" entered and sustained for the sake of reciprocal emotional and erotic satisfaction, rather than the dictates of social obligation and economic necessity. The contemporary pursuit of parenthood, although far less examined, evinces a similar shift from obligation to desire, as Ulrich Beck and Elisabeth Beck-Gernsheim (1995) have noted. In fact, although adult quests for parental intimacy are decidedly asymmetrical rather than "confluent," arguably they represent desire for "the pure relationship" in extremis. Here too, gay men and lesbians serve as post-modern family pioneers. Gay male parenthood, in particular, occupies terrain even more avant-garde than do gay cultures of adult eros and intimacy.

Parenthood in advanced industrial societies today proceeds, or demurs, within the terms of the postmodern family condition—a permanent condition of family diversity and dissent (see Stacey, 1998). Historical forces swept the modern industrial family order of "first love, then marriage, and last the baby carriage" into the dustbin of history. The effects of globalizing capital and media, reproductive technologies, and transnational social movements for gender and sexual rights are irreversible. Gone is the industrial male family wage that underwrote the male breadwinner—female homemaker gender regime. Widespread access to contraception, abortion, and reproductive technologies have irrevocably unhinged the links between heterosexuality, marriage, and procreation. Grass roots feminism, gay liberation, and backlash campaigns for "family values" have turned the conduct of personal life into a terrain of fractious political struggle. We must feed our appetites for intimacy today from a disorderly smorgasbord of familial patterns and practices.

Parenthood, like intimacy more generally, has become, above all, contingent. Paths to parenthood no longer appear natural, obligatory, or uniform, but are necessarily reflexive, uncertain, self-fashioning, plural, and politically embattled. So too are parenting structures, unmoored from marriage, coupling or even biological reproduction. Now that children represent an enormous economic and social responsibility rather than a source of family labor or social security, an emotional rather than economic calculus governs the pursuit of parenthood. "The men and women who decide to have children today," as Beck and Beck-Gernsheim point out, "certainly do not do so because they expect any material advantages. Other motives closely linked with the emotional needs of the parents play a significant role; our children mainly have 'a psychological utility'" (1995:105). Amidst the threatening upheavals, insecurities and alienation of global capitalism, children present adults with renewed opportunities for hope, meaning, and connection. Contemporary adults who desire parenthood, in other words, primarily seek the intimate bonds children seem to promise. More reliably than a confluent lover or contemporary spouse, parenthood beckons to many hungering for lasting love, intimacy, and kinship—for that elusive "haven in a heartless world."

Gay men who openly seek parenthood confront these features of postmodern parenthood in magnified form. Prospective gay male parents necessarily operate from cultural premises antithetical to what Townsend (2002) terms "the package deal"—marriage, work and fatherhood—of now eroding, modern masculinity. By choosing to become primary parents to children, gay men challenge conventional definitions of masculinity and particularly paternity and even dominant gender and sexual norms of gay culture itself. Thus, gay sex columnist and comic Dan Savage self-parodies the cultural stakes involved when he and his partner were deciding to adopt a child: "Terry and I would be giving up certain things that, for better or worse, define what it means to be gay. Good things, things we enjoyed and that had value and meaning for us. Like promiscuity" (1999:26).

Moreover, gay men pursue their parental quest despite enormous challenges, without access to customary biological, cultural, institutional or legal means. Raised as males, most gay men do not receive direct cultural socialization in the feminine labors of "love and ritual"—kin work, emotion work, domestic labor, childcare, nurturing. Yet, unlike heterosexual men, they cannot rely on women to perform these services for them. Because women are not the primary objects of their affections, gay men express masculine erotic desires unconstrained by women's wishes or by reproductive consequences. On the contrary, gay men have to struggle for access to "the means of reproduction," without benefit of default scripts for achieving or practicing gay parenthood. Here they confront a range of challenging and difficult options—foster care, diverse forms of domestic and international adoption, hired or volunteered forms of surrogacy whether "traditional" or gestational, sperm provision in order to co-parent with women, or even resorting to an instrumental approach to heterosexual procreation.

Compared with maternity, the social character of paternity has always been more visible than its biological status. Indeed, prior to DNA testing, most modern societies mandated a marital presumption of paternity. Gay male paternity intensifies this emphasis on social rather than biological definitions of parenthood. Available routes to genetic gay male parenthood are either formidably expensive or socially and emotionally very difficult to negotiate. Consequently most prospective gay male parents pursue purely social paths to parenthood through adoption and foster care.[1] Moreover, profound racial and sexual asymmetry marks the demographic conditions of the adoption marketplace. Prospective parents are disproportionately white, while available children are disproportionately from darker, racially or nationally subordinate groups. Since most public and private adoption agencies as well as birth mothers rank married heterosexual couples as the most desirable adoptive parents, gay men engage in elevated rates of trans-racial parenthood for which their higher rates of cross-racial intimacy and partnering may incline them.[2] The multi-racial character of such families visually signals the predominantly social character of gay parenthood. For all of these reasons, gay men provide frontier terrain for exploring contemporary transformations in the meanings and motives for paternity.

FINDING POP LUCK IN THE CITY OF ANGELS

Gay male narratives of parental desire and decision-making from my ethnographic study of gay male intimacy and kinship in Los Angeles help to illuminate the changing character and calculus of contemporary paths to parenthood and childlessness. While San Francisco and New York have generated the lion's share of research on gay culture, Los Angeles, as geographer Moira Kenny points out, "is the greatest hidden chapter in American gay and lesbian history" (2001:7). In addition, despite its anti-family image, LA represents a multi-ethnic Mecca for gay parenthood. According to data reported in Census 2000, both the greatest number of same-sex couple households and of such couples who are raising children in the nation reside in Los Angeles County.[3] It seems likely therefore that the numbers here exceed those of any similar sized region in the world. The county openly places children under its custody into foster care or adoption in gay single and dual-parent households, and numerous local, private adoption agencies, lawyers, and services specialize in facilitating domestic and international adoptions for a gay clientele. Domestic partnership legislation in California authorizes second-parent adoption, and family court judges have awarded pre-birth, dual-parent custody rights to prospective co-parenting, same-sex couples.

Gay fatherhood is exceptionally institutionalized and visible in Los Angeles. Organized groups of "Gay Fathers" formed in the city as early as the mid-1970s. "Gay Fathers Coalition International" held its national conference in LA in 1985, united with lesbian parent groups, and generated Gay and Lesbian Parents Coalition International, the forerunner of Family Pride, Incorporated, currently among the leading national grass roots gay family organizations (Miller, 2001:226–29). The City of Angels is also the surrogacy capital of the gay globe. "Growing Generations," founded there in 1996, is the world's first gay and lesbian-owned professional surrogacy agency explicitly serving an international clientele of prospective gay parents.[4] Moreover, several of its first clients were among nine gay male families who in 1998 organized the PopLuckClub (PLC), a pioneering local support group for gay fathers and their children (see www.popluckclub.org). The thriving PLC sponsors monthly gatherings, organizes special events, and provides information, referrals, support and community to a membership that in July

2002 included 205 family units, 65 of which were headed by single parents (PLC, 2002).

Between January 1999 and July 2003, I conducted field research on gay male family formations and aspirations in Los Angeles, including lengthy multi-session, life history interviews with 50 self-identified gay men and with members of their designated kin, community and affinity groups, like the PLC.[5] I interviewed individuals, couples, and collective household members both separately and jointly, generally in their homes. I also accompanied informants to numerous family, community, and public events, including a baby christening, a memorial service, playgroups, birthday and holiday parties, a beach party, religious services, public forums, pride and AIDS marches, film screenings, restaurant dates, commitment ceremonies, a house-warming, political benefits and meetings and so on.

All but three of my primary informants were born between 1955 and 1976. They came of age and came out after the Stonewall era of gay liberation and after the AIDS crisis was widely recognized. Popular discourses about safe sex, the gayby boom, gay marriage, domestic partnerships and "families we choose" informed their sense of familial prospects. They represent the first cohort of gay men young enough to contemplate parenthood outside heterosexuality and mature enough to be in a position to choose or reject it. The men and their families encompass diverse racial, ethnic, national, geographic, religious, and social class backgrounds and practice varied relational and residential options. My research sample includes single men, open and monogamous couples, and a committed trio; it encompasses men who reside or parent alone or with friends, lovers, former lovers, biological and adopted kin, and children of every conceivable origin.[6]

Indeed, I intentionally oversampled for gay fathers. Nationally 22 percent of male same-sex-couple households recorded in Census 2000 included children under the age of 18 (Simmons and O'Connell, 2003:10). However, fathers comprise approximately 50 percent of my sample overall and more than 60 percent of the men who were currently in same-sex couples. Depending on which paternal definition one employs, between 24 and 29 of my 50 primary interviewees were fathers of 35 children, and 4 men who were not yet parents declared their firm intention to become so.[7] Only 16 men (32 percent), in contrast, depicted themselves as childless more or less by choice.

Also by design, I sampled to include the full gamut of contemporary gay paths to paternity. Although most children who currently live with gay fathers in the U.S. are progeny of their fathers' former heterosexual relationships, this was true of only six of the 34 children parented by men in my study. Instead, the vast majority were products of varieties of planned gay parenthood. Fifteen were adopted (or in the process of becoming so) through county and private agencies or via independent, open adoption agreements with birth mothers; four were foster care children; five children were conceived through surrogacy contracts, both gestational and "traditional"; and four were conceived via sperm provided to lesbians with whom three men had agreed to co-parent. In addition, five men had formerly served as foster parents to numerous teenagers, and several expected to continue to accept foster placements. Two men, however, were biological but not social parents, one by intention the other unwittingly.[8]

The fathers and children in my sample are racially and socially diverse, and their families, like gay parent-families nationally, are much more likely to be multi-racial and multi-cultural than are other families in the U.S., or perhaps anywhere else. Two-thirds of the gay-father families in my study are multi-racial. The majority (15) of the 24 gay men currently parenting dependent children are white, but most (21) of their 34 children are not.[9] Even more striking, only 2 of the 15 adopted children are white, both of these obtained through open, independent adoption arrangements with birth mothers; 7 adoptees are black or mixed race, and 6 Latino. In contrast, 9 of their 12 adoptive parents are white, and one each is black, Latino and Asian American. It is difficult to assess how racially representative this is of gay men, gay parents and their families in the city, the state, or in the nation. Although the dominant cultural stereotype of gay men and gay fathers is white and middle class, Census 2000 data report rather surprisingly that racial minorities comprised a higher proportion of same-sex couple-parent households in California than was true for heterosexual married couples.[10] The vast majority of the children in these families, however, are progeny of their gay parents' former heterosexual relationships.[11] Contemporary gay paths to paternity have become far more diverse and complex.

THE PASSION-FOR-PARENTHOOD CONTINUUM

Gay men I interviewed in Los Angeles expressed a range of attitudes toward parenthood—from religious vocation to unabashed aversion—that register the contingent and emotionally driven character of contemporary paternity. On one end of the passion-for-parenthood continuum clustered individuals I label "predestined parents." Compelled by a potent, irrepressible longing, these men report having always known that they wished to parent and being ready to move heaven and earth to do so. Few, if any, predestined parents consciously seek single parenthood, but like Christie Malcomson, the single mother quoted in the second epigraph at the beginning of this article, they will brave this daunting trail rather than forgo parenthood entirely. In fact, their desire to parent often trumps the desire for a partner, and a predestined parent will eventually forsake a mate who forces him to choose between the two. On the far opposite end of the spectrum lie the absolute "parental refuseniks" for whom parenthood holds less than no appeal. A few gay men even regard freedom from the pressure to parent to be one of the compensatory rewards of their stigmatized sexual identity. Displaying inverse priorities to a predestined parent, a pure refusenik's antipathy to parenthood is so

potent that he will forfeit dyadic intimacy rather than accede to the parental yearnings of an unequivocally motivated mate. Arrayed between these two poles lies a wide palette of inclinations held by less determined souls. Persuasive life partners or circumstances can recruit or divert these potential "situational parents" into or away from the world of Pampers and playgrounds that the two other groups fervently embrace or eschew.

Predestined Progenitors

Eighteen men who achieved paternity and four who plan to do so portrayed their passion for parenthood in terms sufficiently ardent to classify as predestined parents. A shared yearning for parenthood united three fortunate pairs in my research sample; five men sought parenthood without an intimate partner; five others induced situational partners to support their quest; while primordial parental desires led two men to form married heterosexual families that they later left. Two sample narratives indicate characteristic challenges and triumphs of diverse paths to predestined parenthood.

1. Predestined Pairing Eddie Leary and Charles Tillery, an affluent, white, Catholic couple, are parents to a preschool girl and infant twin sons born through gestational surrogacy. The children are genetic half-siblings, all conceived by the same egg donor and the same gestational surrogate, but the first with Charles's sperm, and the twins with Eddie's. At the time I interviewed them, the couple had been together for 16 years. Eddie told me that they had discussed their shared desire to parent on their very first date. In fact, by then Eddie had already entered a heterosexual marriage primarily for that purpose, but he came out to his wife and left the marriage before achieving it. Directly echoing Christie Malcomson, Eddie claimed that he always knew that he "was meant to be a parent." He recalls that in childhood whenever adults had posed the cliched question to him, "What do you want to be when you grow up?" his ready answer was "a daddy."

Charles and Eddie met and spent their first 10 years together in Chicago building successful careers in corporate law and gliding through the glamorous DINC (double income, no children) fast lane of life. By their mid-30s, however, they were bored and asking themselves the existential question, "is this all there is?" They had already buried more friends than their parents had by their 60s, which, Eddie believes, "gives you a sense of gravitas." In addition, he reports, "my biological clock was definitely ticking." In the mid-1990s, they migrated to LA, lured by the kind of gay family life-style and the ample job opportunities it seemed to offer. They spent the next five years riding an emotional roller coaster attempting to achieve parenthood.

First Eddie and Charles considered adoption, but became discouraged when they learned that then-Governor Pete Wilson's administration was preventing joint adoptions by same-sex couples. Blessed with ample financial and social resources, they decided to shift their eggs, so to speak, into the surrogacy basket. One of Charles's many cousins put the couple in touch with her college roommate, Sally, a married mother of two in her mid-30s living in Idaho. Sally loved both bearing and rearing children and had been fantasizing about bestowing the gift of parenthood on a childless couple. Although her imaginary couple had not been two gay men, she and Eddie bonded instantly, and she agreed to serve as the men's gestational surrogate.

To secure an egg donor and manage the complex medical and legal processes involved during the period just before "Growing Generations" opened, Eddie and Charles were among the first gay clients of a surrogate parenthood agency that primarily assists infertile heterosexual couples. Shopping for DNA in the agency's catalog of egg donors, they selected Marya, a Dutch graduate student who had twice before subsidized her education by serving as an anonymous donor for married couples. Marya had begun to long for maternity herself, however, and was loathe to subject her body and soul yet again to the gruel-

ing and hormonally disruptive process. Yet when she learned that the new candidates for her genes were gay men eager to meet her, she found herself flattered and taken with the prospect of openly aiding such a quest. She too felt an immediate affinity with Eddie and agreed to enter a collaborative egg donor relationship with him and Charles. In her experiences serving as egg donor for infertile married couples, Marya explained, "the mother there can get a little jealous and a little threatened, because she's already feeling insecure about being infertile, and having another woman having that process and threatening the mother's role, I think is a big concern." With a gay couple, in contrast, "you get to be—there's no exclusion, and there's no threatened feelings."

Because Eddie is a few years older than Charles, he was first to provide sperm, and all four parties were thrilled when Sally became pregnant on the second IVF attempt. Elation turned to despair, however, when the pregnancy miscarried in the 13th week. Eddie describes himself as devastated, saying that he "grieved and mourned the loss of my child, just as if I'd been the one carrying it." In fact, Sally recovered from the trauma and was willing to try again before Eddie, who simply "couldn't bear the risk of losing another of my children." Instead, Charles provided the sperm for what became the couple's firstborn child, Heather. Two years later, eager for a second child, they persuaded both reluctant women to subject their bodies to one more attempt at a successful pregnancy, this time with Eddie's sperm. A pair of healthy twins arrived one year later,[12] with all four procreative collaborators, as well as Sally's husband, present at the hospital to welcome the boys into what has become a remarkable, surrogacy-extended family.

Occasionally Marya visits her genetic progeny, but Eddie and Sally have developed an extraordinary, deep, familial bond. They engage in daily, lengthy, intimate, long-distance conversations. "Mama, Sally," as Heather calls her, makes regular use of the Leary-Tillery guest room, accompanied sometimes by her husband and children. Often she times her visits to substitute as co-parent with Eddie during Charles's frequent business trips. The two families have taken joint vacations, skiing or camping together in the Rockies, and once Marya came along. Sally's ten-year-old daughter and eight-year-old son refer to Heather as their surrogate sister.

Eddie and Charles jointly share legal custody of all three children, awarded dual-parent status via pre-birth decrees. From the start, they agreed that Eddie, a gourmet cook who designed the family's state-of-the-culinary-art kitchen, would stay home as a full-time parent, and Charles would be the family's breadwinner. A hired non-residential nanny assists Eddie while Charles is out earning the tofu, sometimes minding the twins when Eddie and Heather join the weekly play-group of PLC at-home-dads and tots. Charles, for his part, blessed with Herculean energy and scant need for sleep, plunges into his full-scale, second shift of baby feedings, diapers, baths, and bed-time storytelling the moment he returns from the office. Although Eddie admits to some nagging concerns that he "may have committed career suicide by joining the mom's club in the neighborhood," he also believes he's met his calling: "I feel like this is who I was meant to be."

2. Parent Seeking Partner When I interviewed Tonatiuh Hidalgo, a 34-year-old, single father and Mexican immigrant in 2001, he was in the final stages of adopting his four-year-old black foster son, Ramon. Tonatiuh was a sexual migrant to Los Angeles who ran away from home when he was only 15 in order to conceal his unacceptable sexual desires from his large, commercially prominent, urban Mexican family. He paid a coyote at the border and survived a harrowing illegal immigration experience that culminated in a footrace across the California desert with an INS patrol in hot pursuit. Then, by working at a Taco Bell, Tona put himself through high school. Through his keen intelligence, linguistic facility, and prodigious work ethic and drive, he built a stable career managing a designer furniture show-room and secured U.S. citizenship as well.

Four years after his sudden disappearance, Tonatiuh returned home to come out to his family, cope with their painful reactions to his homosexuality, and begin to restore his ruptured kinship bonds. During one of the annual visits he has made since then he fell in love with Juan, a Mexican language teacher. Tona claims that he informed his new lover of his desire to parent right at the outset, and Juan seemed enthusiastic, "so, I thought we were the perfect match," Tona brought his boyfriend back to Los Angeles, and they lived together for five years. However, when Tona began to pursue his lifelong goal of parenthood, things fell apart. To initiate the adoption process, Tona enrolled the couple in the county's mandatory foster care class. However, Juan kept skipping class and neglecting the homework, and so he failed to qualify for foster parent status. This jeopardized Tona's eligibility for adoptive parenthood as well. The county presented him with a "Sophie's choice." They would not place a child in his home unless Juan moved out.

Despite Tona's primal passion for parenthood, "at the time," he self-critically explained, "I made the choice of staying with him, a choice that I regret. I chose him over continuing with my adoption." This decision ultimately exacted a fatal toll on the relationship. In Tona's eyes, Juan was preventing him from fulfilling his lifelong dream of having children. His resentment grew, but it took another couple of years before his passion for parenthood surpassed his diminishing passion for his partner. That is when Tona moved out and renewed the adoption application as a single parent.

Ramon is the first of three children that Tona has "definitely decided" to adopt, whether or not he finds another partner. He plans to adopt two more, preferably a daughter and another son, in that order. Removed at birth from crack-addicted parents, Ramon had lived in three foster homes in his first three years of life, before the county placed him with Tonatiuh in its fost-adopt program. Ramon suffered from food allergies, anxiety, and hyperactivity when he arrived, and the social worker warned Tona to anticipate learning disabilities as well. Instead, after nine months under Tonatiuh's steady, patient, firm and loving care, Ramon was learning rapidly and appeared to be thriving. And so was Tonatiuh. He feels so lucky to have Ramon whom he no longer perceives as racially different from himself: "To me he's like my natural son. I love him a lot, and he loves me too much. Maybe I never felt so much unconditional love." In fact, looking back, he attributes the long, painful years he spent struggling to accept his own homosexuality to his discomfort with gay male sexual culture and its emphasis on youth and beauty. "I think it made me fear that I was going to grow old alone," he reflects. "Now I don't have to worry that I'm gay and I'll be alone."

For in addition to the intimacy Tonatiuh savors with Ramon, his son proved a vehicle for building much closer bonds with most of his natal family. Several of Tona's eleven siblings have also migrated to Los Angeles, among these a married brother, his wife, and children who provide indispensable back-up support to the single-father family. Ramon adores his cousins with whom he and his father spend almost every weekend and holiday. Ramon has acquired a devoted abuela as well. Tonatiuh's mother now travels regularly from Mexico to visit her dispersed brood and, after years of disapproval and disappointment, she has grown to admire and appreciate her gay son above all her progeny. Tona reported with pride that during a recent phone call she had stunned and thrilled him when she said, "you know what? I wish that all your brothers were like you. I mean that they liked guys." Astonished, Tona asked her, "why do you say that?" She replied, "I don't know. I just feel that you're really good to me, you're really kind. And you're such a good father." Then she apologized for how badly she had reacted when Tona told the family that he was gay, and she told him that now she's really proud of him. "Now I don't have to accept it," Tona quoted her,

"because there's nothing to accept. You're natural, you're normal. You're my son, I don't have to accept you." And she went on and on. It was so nice, it just came out of her. And now she talks about gay things, and she takes a cooking class from a gay guy and tells me how badly her gay cooking teacher was treated by his family when they found out, and how unfair it is, and all.

Although Tona has begun to create the family he has always wanted, he still dreams of sharing parenthood with a mate more compatible than Juan: "I would really love to meet someone, to fall in love." The man of his dreams is

> someone family-oriented. Now that's really important, family-oriented, because I am very close to my family. I always do family things, like my nephews' birthday parties, going to the movies with them, family dinners, etc. But these are things that many gay men don't like to do. If they go to a straight family party, they get bored.

Consequently, Tona is pessimistic about finding a love match. Being a parent, moreover, severely constrains his romantic pursuits. He doesn't want to subject Ramon, who has had so much loss and instability in his life, to the risk of becoming attached to another new parental figure who might leave. In addition, he doesn't want Ramon "to think that gay men only have casual relationships, that there's no commitment. But," he observes with disappointment, "I haven't seen a lot of commitment among gay men." He takes enormous comfort, however, in knowing that even if he never finds another boyfriend, "I will never really be alone. And I guess that's one of the joys that a family brings."

While Eddie, Charles, and Tonatiuh all experienced irrepressible parental yearnings, they pursued very different routes to realizing this common "destiny." Gestational surrogacy, perhaps the newest, the most "high tech," and certainly the most expensive path to gay parenthood, is available primarily to affluent *couples,* the overwhelming majority of whom are white and seeking genetic progeny.[13] Adoption, on the other hand, is one of the oldest forms of "alternative" parenthood.

It involves bureaucratic and social rather than medical technologies, and the fost-adopt program which Tonatiuh employed represents the least expensive and generally the most accessible route to gay paternity. Thus, like Tonatiuh, most single gay prospective parents pursue this avenue which most states now make available to single adults as well as couples, an index of expediency more than tolerance.[14] Most states and counties allow gay men to shop for parenthood in their overstocked warehouse of "hard to place" children, the majority of whom, like Ramon, have been removed from families judged negligent, abusive, or incompetent. Most of the state's stockpiled children, also like Ramon, are children of color and disproportionately boys with "special needs."

In short, the demographics of contrasting routes to gay parenthood starkly expose racial-class disparities in the market value of children in the U.S. Affluent, mainly white couples like Charles and Eddie can literally purchase the means to eugenically reproduce white infants in their own idealized image, selecting desired traits in egg donors like Marya with whom to mate their own DNA. In contrast, for gay men who are less privileged and/or uncoupled, public agencies provide a grab-bag of displaced children who are generally older, darker, and less healthy.[15]

Somewhere in between these two poles lie forms of independent, open adoption and individually negotiated co-parenting arrangements with women, particularly lesbians who desire sperm donors willing to serve as male co-parents as well. Independent adoption agencies enable middle-class gay men, again primarily but not exclusively white and coupled, to adopt healthy infants of a variety of hues. Bernardo Fernandez, a middle-class black man I interviewed, successfully employed this route to parenthood with intimate consequences almost inverse to Tona's. Bernardo initiated the process of independent adoption while he was single, but then enjoyed the good fortune of falling in love with a man who also had always wanted to parent. Two other predestined parents in my study are now

co-parenting children conceived through donor insemination with lesbian friends.[16] In one case, a single predestined dad provided the sperm to a close friend, but in the second case a situational dad whose partner is a predestined parent agreed to be the biological father for a lesbian couple who are his long-term friends.

The final category of predestined parents in my study consists of four men with irrepressible parental yearnings who, at the time, were not yet parents but declared themselves committed to becoming so and were actively weighing their options. Three of these men are white and one black; two are coupled and two single, social statuses that inflected their calculations about the incentives, opportunities and risks of different strategies. Damian, for example, a 34-year-old, single white observant Catholic, was still struggling to make his peace with what he viewed as his homosexual nature and the barrier it posed to his potent conventional familial longings and values. Unhappily single and discouraged by the prospects of finding the sort of committed relationship he desired, Damian was not willing to forfeit his parental desires as well. He had been tempted by, but rejected the option of entering a heterosexual marriage of convenience. "I have a very close female friend," Damian reported, "who would marry me in a heartbeat if I wanted to marry and have a kid. I've actually thought about it, but then if I had a kid with Colleen, I'd have to share. And what if we broke up, or things fell apart? Then what?" To achieve a more secure form of primary parental status, Damian had decided to pursue some form of adoption. Michael, a black single man, arrived at a similar conclusion but through a somewhat different calculus. He confessed with some embarrassment that his desire to parent was so compelling that he had contemplated engaging in closeted heterosexual courtship through which he might impregnate an unsuspecting prospective co-parent. Michael found the ethics of that strategy troubling, "but the problems of doing that seem less than the problem of not have a kid at all." He rejected this prospect in favor of adoption, however, because like Damian, he was not interested in a parenting relationship that might not allow him to live with his children full-time. Gay predestined dads articulate cravings, anxieties and strategies for achieving intimacy that the contemporary quest for parenthood has come to represent.

PATHS TOWARD OR AWAY FROM PARENTHOOD

Gay male parental narratives presented in the previous sections open a window onto the vagaries of contemporary transformations of parenthood generally, and paternity specifically. Because I oversampled for fathers, predestined parents are disproportionately represented in my study. Their narratives reveal complex connections between partnership and parenthood. Most, if not all, fervently motivated parents strongly wish to combine the two forms of intimacy. Some make parenthood a pivotal courtship criterion, and the luckiest of these, like Eddie and Charles, successfully mate compatible predestined partners. However, if push comes to shove, parenthood trumps partnership for predestined parents and can even thwart it, as we have seen. Thus, although Tonatiuh deeply desired and attempted to combine partnership and parenthood, he was ultimately unwilling to sacrifice the latter on the altar of dyadic intimacy. Conversely, parenthood can prove a pathway to partnership for a fortunate few who, like Bernardo, find that their parental status enhances their appeal to other predestined gay parents.

Occasionally, moreover, passionate pursuit of gay paternity becomes an unexpected conduit to more complex kinship forms. Gestational surrogacy bequeathed Eddie and Charles a rich set of reproductive technologically extended kin. Bernardo developed such a close, familial bond with the social worker at the independent adoption agency who matched him with his son's birth mother that he actually chose to move across country to facilitate a second adoption and to raise

his children in her community and with her active involvement. And three men in my study who participated in insemination and co-parenting arrangements with lesbians within a three- and a four-parent family respectively thereby acquired augmented sets of kin ties as well.[17]

However much gay male culture may connote sexual and commercial self-indulgence to mainstream commentators, I encountered very few parental refuseniks in my research. Rather, the vast majority of the gay men I studied neither avidly yearn for parenthood nor categorically spurn it. Most agreed that they would be likely to succumb, with varying levels of resistance or grace, to the entreaties or demands of a determined partner, as Glenn Miya did when issued an ultimatum by his partner Steve Llanusa.[18] In the absence of such pressure, however, most gay men appear willing to forgo parenthood without serious reflection or regrets. A study of the desire to parent among 94 gay men in New York (Beers, 1996:50) reported that 19 of the men affirmed their desire to parent, 11 did not wish parenthood, while the vast majority (58) acknowledged their ambivalence.[19] There are good reasons to believe that such ambivalence represents the dominant parental outlook not just of gay men, but of contemporary men more generally.

Although women and men occupy all points along the spectrum of parental desire, they do not do so equally. As with most social characteristics, gender differentiates the means and distribution of such sentiments. For example, a Dutch study that compared planned lesbian and heterosexual parent families (Bos, 2004) found that the mean strength of desire to have children was weakest for heterosexual fathers. Lesbian biological mothers scored highest on desire for parenthood measures followed by lesbian social mothers and then heterosexual mothers.[20] Moreover, many social indices suggest that women handily dominate the predestined end of the parental yearnings arc, while men would win a refusenik derby hands down. Increasing numbers of single women today who are disappointed in love nonetheless, like Christie Malcomson, "choose to be a parent" (see Hertz and Ferguson, 1997). In contrast, the ranks of men who emulate Tonatiuh, Damian, Bernardo, or Michael by pursuing parenthood solo are thin indeed.[21] To be sure, men's biological procreative disadvantage represents a significant barrier to gender equity here, but it is one that gay men appear more motivated than their heterosexual counterparts to hurdle.[22] Likewise, evidence suggests that straight men are disproportionately less likely than gay men like Eddie to regard full-time, at-home parenting as their calling. In fact, an analysis of at-home parenting data in the 2000 Census (Gates cited in Bellafante, 2004) found that gay male couple parenting families were even slightly more likely than married heterosexual or lesbian couple parents to include a full-time at-home parent.[23] Finally, data on the comparative weakness of paternal ties to children post-divorce is disturbingly strong (see Furstenberg and Cherlin, 1991; Stephens, 1996).

Indeed, there are many reasons to believe that a predestined urge to parent is even less common among straight men than among gays. For one thing, by definition, if not by disposition, gay men are already gender dissidents. Engaging in nurturing, care-taking, and domestic activities is simultaneously more necessary for gay men and less likely to be threatening to their masculine identity. Secondly, gay men are more likely to be single than heterosexual men or women of any sexual orientation (see Bell and Weinberg, 1978; Laumann et al., 2000).[24] A greater proportion of them, therefore, have cause, like Tonatiuh, Damian, and Michael, to adopt a compensatory parental strategy in their search for intimacy. On the carrot side of the ledger, moreover, despite decades of feminist efforts to redress gender imbalances, contemporary conditions of work and parenthood offer gay men access to a broader array of parenting activities, rewards, and support networks than most heterosexual fathers enjoy. Gay men can assume, share, and negotiate primary parenthood with far less pressure to navigate around gender scripts or

in deference to women's biological or cultural parental advantages. Gay fatherhood, that is to say, represents terrain more akin to motherhood than to dominant forms of heterosexual paternity. Indeed, the ideological divisions over appropriate parenting standards that erupted sporadically on the PLC listserve seemed so familiar that I dubbed them the "Mr Mommy Wars."[25] In addition, gay support groups, events, and services organized by and for gay parents, children and families, like the PLC, COLAGE, and family week in Provincetown provide gay men with levels of community support for primary parenting that very few heterosexual fathers enjoy.

The unmooring of heterosexual masculinity and paternity exposes the predominantly situational character of contemporary fatherhood and fatherlessness. No longer a requisite route to masculine adult social status, paternity has become increasingly situational, contingent primarily on the fate of romantic attachments. To attain parenthood today requires the unequivocal yearning of at least one adult or an accidental pregnancy. Consequently postmodern maternity is increasingly situational as well, a fact reflected in declining fertility rates and satirized in popular culture. A widely circulated ironic 1980s feminist greeting card, for example, featured a Warhol-style female character who lamented, "Oh dear, I forgot to have children!" Nonetheless, the majority of even postfeminist women still seem to skew toward the predestined pole of the desire-to-parent continuum. Most men, in contrast, regardless of their sexual inclinations, array along the situational bandwidth. Heterosexual "situations" continue to lead a preponderance of straight men into paternity. Homosexual situations, on the other hand, currently lead most gay men to childlessness.[26]

However obvious, even tautological, this contrast may now appear, it was not always the case. Instead, the overwhelming majority of contemporary gay fathers became parents while they were enmeshed in closeted homosexual situations.[27] Whereas men with homoerotic desires routinely used to enter heterosexual marriages in attempts to suppress or shield their stigmatized yearnings, hard-won gains in social acceptance of homosexuality have diminished the incentives for this strategy. The paradoxical consequences of the shift from closeted to open homosexuality, therefore, are a simultaneous rise in the visibility and quality of gay fatherhood and a decline in its incidence. Beyond the closet, far fewer gay men will become situational parents.

Contemporary openly gay paternity, which by definition is never accidental, requires the determined efforts of at least one gay man whose passion for parenthood is unequivocally predestined. A man, that is, whose parental desire might more accurately be understood as maternal than as paternal. "For most heterosexual men," Jesse Green (1999:48) observes:

> the birth of a child, a son especially, seems to confirm their masculinity, however idiotic the connection may be. Was it possible that, for a gay man, adopting a son would have the opposite effect? A single father would be first a mother, and thus, in a way, *less* of a man.

Rather than a bid to achieve legitimate masculine status, intentional gay parenthood represents a search for enduring love and intimacy in a world of contingency and flux.

Of course, nothing is distinctively gay about this quest. Hegemonic hetero-masculinity also decreasingly depends upon paternity or marriage. Indirectly, therefore, gay male paths to planned parenthood highlight the erosion of traditional incentives for pursuing the status of fatherhood as we knew it. Parenthood, like adult mating practices, has entered the terrain of the pure relationship. The facetious observation about our endangered species in the first epigraph to this article may be halfway accurate. Without "masculine" cravings for sex and "feminine" yearnings for progeny, paternity, but not male parenthood, might wither away.

Acknowledgements

I am grateful for comments from Tim Biblarz, Jeffrey Escoffier, Don Kulick, Harvey Molotch, Joe Saltzer, Arlene Stein, and two anonymous reviewers for *Sexualities* and to generous research assistance from Jenna Appelbaum and Sarah Lowe. A National Endowment for the Humanities Fellowship supported portions of the field research from which this article draws.

■ Review Questions ■

1. Who are the parents of Heather and the twins? Eddie? Charles? Sally? Marya?
2. Why might gay parenthood be more akin to motherhood than to conventional fatherhood?

ENDNOTES

1. Here too, however, gays encounter discrimination. While one national study found that 60 percent of adoption agencies accept applications from homosexual clients, only 39 percent of the agencies in this group had placed at least one child with a gay or lesbian potential parent during the target period, and only 19 percent of these agencies actively recruit prospective gay and lesbian parents (Brodzinsky et al., 2003).

2. California Census 2000 data report that 24 percent of same-sex couples were interracial compared with 15 percent of heterosexual married couples. Compared with children of married couples, children of same-sex couples were twice as likely to be adopted, and children of same-sex parents were disproportionately of Hispanic and non-white race and ethnic origins (Sears and Badgett, 2004:7, 11, 13). Of the children adopted in California between October 1, 2001, and

September 30, 2002, for example, 41 percent were Hispanic, 23 percent black, non-Hispanic, and only 29 percent were white, non-Hispanic (U.S. Dept. of Health and Human Services, 2003). Qualitative studies of gay fathers likewise report high percentages of cross-racial adoption. See Sbordone, 1993; Schacher et al., 2005.

3. The 2000 Census reports 25,173 same-sex couples in Los Angeles County, of which 14,468 are male. With 8015 of its reported same-sex couples raising children, Los Angeles County ranks first in the nation (Sears and Badgett, 2004:5, 11). This vastly understates the incidence of gay parentage, because it does not include single parents, dual-household parents, or gay parents who did not report a same-sex partnership.

4. http://www.growinggenerations.com (see also Strah with Margolis, 2003:133–41).

5. I conducted formal in-depth, multi-session interviews, each session of two to five hours' duration with 50 gay men. In addition I conducted formal interviews with 20 of their designated kin, including siblings, roommates, former lovers, co-parents, surrogates, and informal interviews with many more, as well as with community members. Primary informants were recruited through referrals from individuals with access to diverse networks and populations, through notices I placed in a variety of gay newsletters and list-serves, and through volunteers in audiences who attended invited public lectures on gay family issues I delivered at local workplaces, public events, and community groups. From volunteers, I selected for diversity in race, class, and family patterns.

6. Among the primary interviewees 30 are white, 7 African American or Afro-Caribbean, 7 Latino, 4 Asian American, and 2 of mixed race (one Latino Asian, the other Latino Anglo); legal and undocumented immigrants were represented in each racial category. At the time of their interviews, 15 of the 50 men were more or less single, 30 were coupled, and 3 formed a committed trio. Several of the single men resided in collective households marked by ambiguous and/or changing relationships.

7. Twenty-four men were actively parenting children. In addition, two men were stepfathers to a partner's nonresidential children; one man with

his mother formerly co-foster-parented teenagers; four of the adoptive fathers had also formerly fostered teenagers, and two of these intended to resume this practice in the future; one man served as a known sperm donor for lesbian couple friends; and one man was a genetic father who does not parent his offspring.

8. One, a sperm dad who nicknamed himself a "spad," had facilitated a lesbian friend's desire to conceive a child with a donor willing to be an avuncular presence in her child's life. The other unwittingly impregnated a former girlfriend who chose to keep the child and agreed not to reveal its paternity.

9. Of the gay parents 5 are Latino, 3 are black or Caribbean, and one is Asian American; 13 of their 34 children are white, 9 Latino, 8 black, Caribbean or mixed race, and 4 multi-racial Asian.

10. Nearly 40 percent of same-sex parents in the state identified themselves as black, mixed race, or of another race compared with 28 percent of married-couple parents; 53 percent of parents in same-sex couples were white against 58 percent of married-couple parents. According to these Census data, whites are slightly overrepresented among individuals in same-sex couples in California and Asian Americans are significantly underrepresented, but percentages of Hispanic, black and mixed race individuals are proportional to their numbers in the state (Sears and Badgett, 2004:7, 16).

11. In the 2000 Census, 76 percent of children residing in male same-sex couple households were described as their "natural born" children (Gary Gates, personal communication, May 17, 2005).

12. Multiple births occur frequently with IVF, because physicians implant multiple embryos to increase the odds of successful gestation.

13. In fact the surrogacy agency Charles and Eddie used does not accept single applicants.

14. At the time of writing, Florida is the only state that explicitly bans all adoptions by gay and lesbian adults, although it allows gays and lesbians to serve as foster parents. Several states permit adoptions by single homosexuals, but forbid same-sex couples from adopting. Utah, for example, prohibits adoption or foster care to homes that include adults who are not related by blood or marriage. Ironically, this law provoked at least one gay male couple in Salt Lake City to become

fathers through surrogacy instead. Proposals to restrict or ban gay adoption and/or foster care have been introduced in several state legislatures or proposed as referenda.

15. Although non-Hispanic blacks represent only 12.5 percent of the U.S. population, the percentages of children who entered the national foster care system in September 2001 that were non-Hispanic white and black were relatively equal, 38 percent and 37 percent respectively. Black children, moreover, disproportionately remain in the foster care system—45 percent of the children who had exited foster care during the previous fiscal year were white, non-Hispanic, while only 30 percent were black, non-Hispanic. And although there are more black than white children waiting for adoption (45% of the children waiting to be adopted in September 2001 were non-Hispanic black and 34% were non-Hispanic white), more white than black children are adopted. Of the children adopted the previous fiscal year, 38 percent were white and 35 percent were black (U.S. Department of Health and Human Services, Administration on Children, Youth, and Families, Children's Bureau, March 2003). Race has also been shown to affect the amount of time that children have to wait for adoption completion and legalization (Kapp et al., 2001).

16. National cultural and institutional frameworks influence notable cross-national variations in preferred forms of gay and lesbian parenthood, Co-parenting arrangements between lesbians and gay male sperm donors, for example, appear to be more popular in Sweden than in the U.S. or Ireland (see Ryan-Flood, 2005).

17. Two such families are described in Stacey, 2004.

18. It is important to note, however, that a situational path to parenthood does not predict an individual's emotional or behavioral response to actual parenthood. Like Glenn, many men who enter parenthood somewhat reluctantly can become "born-again" dads once they bond with their actual children. Also like Glenn, some situational fathers even come to desire or to assume a primary, at-home parenting role. Two other men in my sample exhibited this pattern, as do several men whose stories are reported in Strah with Margolis, 2003.

19. Beers built upon a prior study (Sbordone, 1993) that compared 78 gay men who chose to become fathers after they came out with 83 gay men who were not (yet) fathers. That study, which only allowed dichotomous responses to the desire to parent question, reported that 46 percent of the non-fathers said that they did not want to become parents.

20. Somewhat surprisingly, however, the mean strength of desire to have children did not differ significantly between heterosexual women and men in this study who were already parents (Bos, 2004). No gay male parents were included in this study.

21. According to the National Committee for Single Adoptive Parents, men comprise approximately one in seven of the people who contact the organization (cited in Shireman, 1995).

22. Data on adoptive family structure indicate how infrequently single men attempt (and/or succeed at) adoption. During the fiscal year 2001, 67 percent of adoptive families were headed by married couples, 1 percent by unmarried couples, 30 percent by single women, and 2 percent by single men (U.S. Department of Health and Human Services, Administration for Children, Youth, and Families, Children's Bureau, March 2003).

23. Among 9328 same-sex couples with children randomly selected for analysis by Gary Gates, research director at the Williams Project, UCLA, 26 percent of male couples and 22 percent of female couples included an at-home parent, compared with 25 percent of heterosexual married couples with children (Gates in Bellafante, 2004:A1). While gender differences in income may contribute to the lower incidence of full-time parenting among lesbian couples, average earnings of gay men are lower than among heterosexual men (Badgett, 2001).

24. In Bell and Weinberg's classic study (1978) of homosexualities, 29 percent of the male sample compared with 75 percent of the female sample were in stable couple relationships (1978:91, 97). Laumann et al. (2000) estimate that over a third of the men in their sample population who had only male partners in the past year were living with a partner at the time of the interview, compared to two-thirds of the men who had only female partners in the past year (2000:314).

25. Among these were value conflicts over the legitimacy of leaving children with nannies and over exposing children to sexualized imagery in the annual gay pride march.

26. Lesbian situations likely lie somewhere in between. Nationally, 33 percent of declared female same-sex couple households included children under 18, compared with 22 percent of male same-sex couple households and 46 percent of married-couple households. (Simmons and O'Connell, 2003).

27. See Census data reported in note 11.

CHAPTER 10

Older People and Their Families

Many observers of the changing lives of children have concluded that the family is in crisis. The litany is familiar: more divorce, more step-families, more childbearing outside of marriage, more day care, more sex and violence in the media, and so forth. Even commentators who disagree with this position feel compelled to explain why divorce, day care, and so on don't have the negative effects that one might expect. In other words, when you look at the family from the vantage point of its youngest members, the changes that occurred during the last half of the twentieth century seem problematic.

But when you look at families from the vantage point of their oldest members, the picture is quite different. The changes that occurred in the lives of older people in the last half of the twentieth century were generally positive: longer life expectancy, higher incomes, and greater independence. The better health and greater affluence of older people has allowed them to lead independent lives while still retaining frequent contact with their children and grandchildren—a style of life both older people and their children, for the most part, preferred.

Yet when a family crisis arises, older people are often willing and able to help. In fact, gerontologist Vern L. Bengtson argues that the great social changes in American families over the past several decades have increased the importance of multigenerational bonds in family life—a trend he thinks will continue in the early twenty-first century. Longer lives and better health for older people, he notes, mean more shared years of life for grandparents, parents, and children. The increases in divorce and in childbearing outside marriage have lessened the importance of the nuclear family, he maintains, and have made parents more reliant on their own aging parents.

Not everyone agrees with Bengtson—his scenario may be a bit too rosy. But it is an interesting and provocative argument. In the first reading in this chapter, Bengtson presents his case.

One place where multigenerational bonds would be expected to dominate family life is the inner city, where marriage has declined among low-income minority populations. Because of divorce and childbearing outside marriage, there are relatively few nuclear families. Instead, many

223

middle-aged grandmothers are deeply involved in their young grandchildren's lives. But what happens to these grandmothers later in life when they are old and need care and companionship? What happens to self-reliant women when their health begins to fail? And who will care for older men who, in many cases, have lived apart from their children for decades?

Katherine S. Newman sought answers to these questions by returning to some of the same inner-city neighborhoods—and some of the same people—she had observed in her earlier book *No Shame in My Game.* In her more recent book, *A Different Shade of Gray,* excerpted here, she writes about the family lives of inner-city adults in late midlife and old age.

Beyond the Nuclear Family

The Increasing Importance of Multigenerational Bonds

Vern L. Bengtson

During the past decade, sociologists have been engaged in an often heated debate about family change and family influences in contemporary society. This debate in many ways reflects the legacy of Ernest W. Burgess (1886–1965), the pioneer of American family sociology. It can be framed in terms of four general hypotheses, each of which calls attention to significant transitions in the structure and functions of families over the 20th century.

The first and earliest hypothesis concerns the *emergence of the "modern" nuclear family form* following the Industrial Revolution. This transition (suggested by Burgess in 1916 and elaborated by Ogburn, 1932, and Parsons, 1944) proposed that the modal structure of families had changed from extended to nuclear, and its primary functions had changed from social-institutional to emotional-supportive. The second hypothesis concerns the *decline of the modern nuclear family* as a social institution, a decline said to be attributable to the fact that its structure has been truncated (because of high divorce rates) and its functions further reduced (Popenoe, 1993). A third hypothesis can be termed the *increasing heterogeneity of family forms,* relations that extend beyond biological or conjugal relationship boundaries. Growing from the work of feminist scholars (Coontz, 1991; Skolnick, 1991; Stacey, 1990), and research on racial and ethnic minority families

Vern L. Bengtson, "Beyond the Nuclear Family: The Increasing Importance of Multigenerational Bonds," *Journal of Marriage and Family* 63 (February 2001), pp. 1–16. Reprinted by permission.

(Burton, 1995; Collins, 1990; Stack, 1974), this perspective suggests that family structures and relationships should be redefined to include both "assigned" and "created" kinship systems (Cherlin, 1999). I suggest a fourth hypothesis for consideration: the *increasing importance of multigenerational bonds.* I propose that relations across more than two generations are becoming increasingly important to individuals and families in American society; that they are increasingly diverse in structure and functions; and that in the early 21st century, these multigenerational bonds will not only enhance but in some cases replace nuclear family functions, which have been so much the focus of sociologists during the 20th century.

In this reading, I first summarize the "Burgess legacy" in American family sociology and relate it to the four hypotheses summarized above. Then I suggest some foundations for my hypotheses concerning the increasing importance and diversity of multigenerational relationships, starting from a discussion of macrosocial trends (population aging and intergenerational family demography) and moving to micro-social dimensions (solidarity and types of cross-generational relationships). I conclude with some suggestions about future research that will be needed to examine further the role of multigenerational bonds in 21st century society.

THE BURGESS LEGACY: AS FAMILIES HAVE CHANGED, HAVE THEY DECLINED IN IMPORTANCE? . . .

The Emergence of the "Modern" Nuclear Family Form

Burgess' groundbreaking analyses of the American family started from a consideration of macrosocial trends brought about by the Industrial Revolution and continued with his exploration of the microsocial dynamics within families. One of his earliest concerns was the family as an aspect of social organization in the context of social evolution. His first book (Burgess, 1916) would today be regarded as a polemic in support of the traditional extended family and its functions because he argued that this family form was necessary for the socialization of children if social evolution were to continue. Within the next decade, however, he shifted his perspective. From the structural "functions" of families applied to the modernizing societies of the early 20th century, he turned to an emphasis on family members' "interactions."

Burgess' hypothesis was that families had changed. He broke from late-19th-century views of the extended family structure as the bedrock of social organization and progress to say, "The family in historical times has been, and at present is, in transition from an institution to a companionship" (Burgess, 1926, p. 104). He focused on the nuclear family and its changing functions as the consequence of industrialization and modernization, arguments echoed later by Ogburn (1932), Davis (1941), and Parsons (1944). His thesis was that urbanization, increased individualism and secularism, and the emancipation of women had transformed the family from a social institution based on law and custom to one based on companionship and love.

Burgess advanced his position very quietly in a number of scholarly journal publications. These appeared to have escaped notice by the popular press at that time, quite unlike today's debates about the family. He argued that the family had become more specialized in its functions and that structural and objective aspects of family life had been supplanted by more emotional and subjective functions. This he termed the "companionship" basis of marriage, which he suggested had become the underlying basis of the "modern" family form.

But Burgess went further. He proposed that the most appropriate way to conceptualize and study the family was as "a unity of interacting personalities" (Burgess, 1926). By this he meant three things: First, "the family" is essentially a *process,* an interactional system influenced by each of its members; it is not merely a *structure,* or a

household. Second, the behaviors of one family member—a troubled child, a detached father—could not be understood except in *relationship* to other family members, their ongoing patterns of interactions, and personalities developing and changing through such interactions. This conceptualization provided the intellectual basis for the first marriage and family counseling programs in the United States. Third, the central *functions* of families had changed from being primarily structural units of social organization to being relationships supporting individuals' needs. Marriage was transformed from a primarily economic union to one based on sentiment and companionship.

Thus, Burgess represented a bridge between 19th-century conceptions of the family as a unit in social evolution to 20th-century ideas of families as supporting individuals' needs. His work also provided a bridge in sociological theory, from structural-functionalism to symbolic interactionism and phenomenology. But in all this, Burgess' focus was on the nuclear family, a White, middle-class, two-generation family; and the family forms emerging in the 21st century will, as I argue below, look much different than the family that Burgess observed.

The Decline of the Modern Nuclear Family Form

The "decline of the family" in American society is a theme that has become the focus of increasingly heated debates by politicians, pundits, and family sociologists during the last decade. David Popenoe (1993), the most articulate proponent of this position, has argued that there has been a striking decline in the family's structure and functions in American society, particularly since 1960. Moreover, his hypothesis is that recent family decline is "more serious" than any decline in the past, because "what is breaking up is the nuclear family, the fundamental unit stripped of relations and left with two essential functions that cannot be performed better elsewhere: child-rearing and the provision to its members of affection and companionship" (Popenoe, p. 527).

Supporters of the family decline hypothesis have focused on the negative consequences of changing family structure, resulting from divorce and single parenting, on the psychological, social, and economic well-being of children. Furthermore, they suggest that social norms legitimating the pursuit of individual over collective goals and the availability of alternate social groups for the satisfaction of basic human needs have substantially weakened the social institution of the family as an agent of socialization and as a source of nurturance for family members (Popenoe).

There is much to support Popenoe's hypothesis. There has been a significant change in nuclear family structure over the past 50 years, starting with the growing divorce rate in the 1960s, which escalated to over half of first marriages in the 1980s (Amato & Booth, 1997; Bumpass, Sweet, & Martin, 1990). There also has been an increase in single-parent families, accompanied by an increase in poverty for the children living in mother-headed families (McLanahan, 1994). The absence of fathers in many families today has created problems for the economic and emotional well-being of children (Popenoe, 1996).

At the same time, the "family decline" hypothesis is limited, and to some critics flawed, by its preoccupation with the family as a coresident household and the nuclear family as its primary representation. Popenoe defined the family as "a relatively small domestic group of kin (or people in a kinlike relationship) consisting of at least one adult and one dependent person" (Popenoe, 1993, p. 529). Although this might be sufficient as a demographic definition of a "family household," it does not include important aspects of family functions that extend beyond boundaries of coresidence. There is nothing in Popenoe's hypothesis to reflect the function of multigenerational influences on children—the role of grandparents in socializing or supporting grandchildren, particularly after the divorce of middle-generation parents (Johnson & Barer, 1987; Minkler & Rowe, 1993). Nor is there any mention of what Riley and Riley (1993) have called the "latent matrix of kin connections," a web of "continually shifting linkages that provide the potential for activating and intensifying close kin relationships" in times of need by family members (Riley & Riley, p. 169). And there is no consideration of the longer years of shared lives between generations, now extending into many decades, and their consequences for the emotional and economic support for family members across several generations (Bengtson & Allen, 1993; Silverstein & Litwak, 1993).

The Increasing Heterogeneity of Family Forms

A third hypothesis has been generated by feminist scholars (Coontz, 1991; Osmond & Thorne, 1993; Skolnick, 1991; Stacey, 1993, 1996; Thorne & Yalom, 1992) and researchers studying minority families (Burton, 1995; Collins, 1990; Stack, 1974). This hypothesis can be summarized as follows: Families are changing in both forms and meanings, expanding beyond the nuclear family structure to involve a variety of kin and nonkin relationships. Diverse family forms are emerging, or at least being recognized for the first time, including the matriarchal structure of many African American families. Stacey (1996) argued that the traditional nuclear family is increasingly ill-suited for a postindustrial, postmodern society. Women's economic and social emancipation over the past century has become incongruent with the nuclear "male breadwinner" family form and its traditional allocation of power, resources, and labor. We have also seen a normalization of divorce and of stepparenting in recent years. Many American families today are what Ahrons (1994) has described as "binuclear." Following divorce and remarriage of the original marital partners and parents, a stable, child-supportive family context may emerge. Finally, because some four million children in the United States are being raised by lesbian or gay parents (Stacey & Biblarz, 2001), these and other alternative family forms "are here . . . and let's get used to it!" (Stacey, 1996, p. 105).

In responding to Popenoe, Stacey (1996) argued that the family is indeed in decline—if what we mean by "family" is the nuclear form of dad, mom, and their biological or adopted kids. This form of the family rose and fell with modern industrial society. In the last few decades, with the shift to a postindustrial domestic economy within a globalized capitalist system and with the advent of new reproductive technologies, the modern family system has been replaced by what Stacey has called "the postmodern family condition," a pluralistic, fluid, and contested domain in which diverse family patterns, values, and practices contend for legitimacy and resources. Stacey suggested that family diversity and fluidity are now "normal," and the postmodern family condition opens the possibility of egalitarian, democratic forms of intimacy, as well as potentially threatening levels of insecurity.

The Increasing Importance of Multigenerational Bonds

I want to suggest a fourth hypothesis about family transitions during the 20th century that builds on those of Burgess, Popenoe, Stack, and Stacey but reflects the recent demographic development of much greater longevity. It is this: *Relations across more than two generations are becoming increasingly important to individuals and families in American society.* Considering the dramatic increase in life expectancy over the past half century, this is not a particularly radical departure from conventional wisdom. But I suggest a corollary to this hypothesis, which I hope will lead to spirited debate: *For many Americans, multigenerational bonds are becoming more important than nuclear family ties for well-being and support over the course of their lives.*

I will attempt to provide a foundation for this hypothesis in the remainder of this article. First, I argue that changes in intergenerational demography (changing societal and family age structures, creating longer years of "shared lives") have resulted in increased opportunities—and needs—for interaction, support, and mutual influence across more than just two generations. Second, I will note the strength of intergenerational

solidarity over time and the diversity of cross-generational types. Third, because the increase in marital instability and divorce over the last several decades has weakened the ability of nuclear families to provide the socialization, nurturance, and support needed by family members, I argue that kin across several generations will increasingly be called upon to provide these essential family functions in 21st-century society.

THE MACROSOCIOLOGY OF INTERGENERATIONAL RELATIONSHIPS

The demographic structure of American families has changed significantly in recent years. We hear most about two trends: The increase in divorce rates since the 1960s, with one out of two first marriages ending in divorce (Cherlin, 1992); and the increasing number of children living in single-parent households, often accompanied by poverty (McLanahan & Sandefur, 1994; Walker & McGraw, 2000). But there is a third trend that has received much less attention: The increased longevity of family members and the potential resource this represents for the well-being of younger generations in the family.

Multigenerational Family Demography: From Pyramids to Beanpoles

First consider how much the age structure of the U.S. population has changed over the past 100 years. Treas (1995b) provided a valuable overview of these changes and their consequences for families. In 1900, the shape of the American population structure by age was that of a pyramid, with a large base (represented by children under age 5) progressively tapering into a narrow group of those aged 65 and older. This pyramid characterized the shape of the population structure by age in most human societies on record, from the dawn of civilization through the early Industrial Revolution and into the early 20th century (Laslett, 1976; Myers, 1990). But by 1990, the age pyramid for American society had come to look more like an irregular triangle.

By 2030, it will look more like a rectangle, with strikingly similar numbers in each age category starting from children and adolescents through those above the age of 60. The story here is that because of increases in longevity and decreases in fertility, the population age structure of the United States, like most industrialized societies, has changed from a pyramid to a rectangle in just over a century of human historical experience.

Second, consider the implications of these macrosocietal changes in age distribution for the generational structure of families in American society. At the same time, there have been increases in life expectancy over the 20th century, decreases in fertility have occurred, and the population birthrate has decreased from 4.1 in 1900 to 1.9 in 1990 (Cherlin, 1999). This means that the age structure of most American families has changed from a pyramid to what might be described as a "beanpole" (Bengtson, Rosenthal, & Burton, 1990), a family structure in which the shape is long and thin, with more family generations alive but with fewer members in each generation. Whether the "beanpole" structure adequately describes a majority of families today has been debated (Farkas & Hogan, 1995; Treas, 1995a). Nevertheless, the changes in demographic distribution by age since 1900 are remarkable, and the progression "from pyramids to beanpoles" has important implications for family functions and relationships into the 21st century.

The Changing "Kin Supply" Structure across Generations What might be lost in a review of macrosocial demographic trends are the consequences for individual family members and their chances of receiving family support. For example, the "family decline" hypothesis of Popenoe (1993) suggests that U.S. children are at greater risk today because of the breakdown of the nuclear family structure and the too-frequent disappearance of fathers. The decrease in mortality rates over the last century suggests a more optimistic story, however: The increasing availability of extended intergenerational kin (grandparents, great-grandparents, uncles, and aunts) has become a resource for children as they grow up and move into young adulthood.

Peter Uhlenberg (1996) examined the profound effects that mortality changes over the 20th century have had on the "supply" of kin available for support of family members in American society. He noted that for children born in 1900, the chances of being an orphan (both parents dying before the child reached age 18) were 18%. But for children born in 2000, 68% will have four *grand*parents still living by the time they reach 18. Further along the life course, by the time these children are themselves facing the responsibilities of rearing children, the effects of mortality declines on the availability of older kin for support are even more substantial. For those born in 1900, by age 30 only 21% had *any* grandparent still living. For those born in 2000, by age 30, 76% will still have at least one grandparent alive. Today it is more likely that 20-year-olds will have a grandmother still living (91%) than 20-year-olds alive in 1900 had a mother still living (83%; Uhlenberg).

Another perspective on this issue is provided by Wachter (1997) in computer simulations about availability of kin for 21st-century family members. He examined implications of longevity, fertility, and divorce for the future. He noted that although low fertility rates in the late 20th century will lead to a shortage of kin for those reaching retirement around 2030, the effects of divorce, remarriage, and family blending are expanding the numbers and types of stepkin, "endowing the elderly of the future with kin networks that are at once problematic, rich, and varied" (Wachter). The implication is that stepkin are increasing the kin supply across generations, becoming potential sources of nurture and support for family members in need, and that this may compensate, in part, for lower fertility rates (Amato & Booth, 1997).

Longer Years of "Shared Lives" across Generations Other implications of these demographic changes over the 20th century should be noted. First, we now have more years of "cosurvivorship between generations" than ever before in human history (Bengtson, 1996; Goldscheider, 1990). This means that more and more aging parents and grandparents are available to provide for family continuity and stability across time (Silverstein, Giarrusso, & Bengtson, 1998). This also means a remarkable increase in multigenerational kin representing a "latent network" (Riley & Riley, 1993) who can be activated to provide support and well-being for younger family members. The increased longevity of parents, grandparents, great-grandparents, and other older family members in recent decades represents a resource of kin available for help and support that can be, and frequently is, activated in times of need (King, 1994; Silverstein, Parrott, & Bengtson, 1995). These older kin will also be in better health (Hayward & Heron, 1999).

At the same time, there are potentially negative consequences of the "longer years of shared lives" across generations. One involves protracted years of caregiving for dependent elders (Bengtson, Rosenthal, & Burton, 1995). A second involves protracted conflict—what an 84-year-old mother in the Longitudinal Study of Generations termed a "life-long lousy parent-child relationship." Family researchers have not adequately addressed intergenerational conflicts throughout the adult years (Clarke, Preston, Raskin, & Bengtson, 1999). Because of longer years of shared lives, intergenerational relationships—in terms of help given or received, solidarity or conflict or both—will be of increasing importance for family life in the future.

Finally, to the story of multigenerational family demography and its changes over the 21st century must be added a recognition of "alternative family forms," reflected in gay and lesbian couples raising children (Kurdek & Schmidt, 1987), never-married singles and couples raising children (Smock & Manning, 1997), and other nonbiological but socially significant family forms. We know little about the intergenerational relationships of these variations beyond the White, middle-class, two-generation household

in America today. What they represent in "latent kin support networks" or "cosurvivorship across generations" must be a focus of future research.

When Parenting Goes across Several Generations

A function not addressed by Burgess was the importance of grandparents to family members' well-being, an understandable oversight given the historical period when he was writing, when the expected life span of individuals was almost 3 decades shorter than today. Popenoe (1993) also did not discuss the importance of grandparents in the potential support they represent for younger generation members.

Grandparents provide many unacknowledged functions in contemporary families (Szinovacz, 1998). They are important role models in the socialization of grandchildren (Elder, Rudkin, & Conger, 1994; King & Elder, 1997). They provide economic resources to younger generation family members (Bengtson & Harootyan, 1994). They contribute to cross-generational solidarity and family continuity over time (King, 1994; Silverstein et al., 1998). They also represent a bedrock of stability for teenage moms raising infants (Burton & Bengtson, 1985).

Perhaps most dramatic is the case in which grandparents (or great-grandparents) are raising grandchildren (or great-grandchildren). Over four million children under age 18 are living in a grandparent's household. Frequently this is because these childrens' parents are incapacitated (by imprisonment, drug addiction, violence, or psychiatric disorders) or unable to care for their offspring without assistance (Minkler & Rowe, 1993). Research by Harris (2000) indicates that about 20,000 children in Los Angeles County alone are now the responsibility of grandparents or great-grandparents because of recent court decisions concerning the parents' lack of competence. In Harris' study, one grandmother had been assigned by the court as guardian to 13 of her grandchildren, born to two of her daughters, each of whom had been repeatedly imprisoned on crack cocaine charges (Harris & Pedersen, 1997). Similar instances are related by Minkler and Rowe in their study of crack-addicted parents in the San Francisco area.

When Parents Divorce and Remarry, Divorce and Remarry

The rising divorce rate over the last half of the 20th century has generated much concern about the fate of children (McLanahan & Sandefur, 1994). The probability that a marriage would end in divorce doubled between the 1960s and the 1970s, and half of all marriages since the late 1970s ended in divorce (Cherlin, 1992). About 40% of American children growing up in the 1980s and 1990s experienced the breakup of their parents' marriages (Bengtson, Rosenthal, & Burton, 1995; Furstenberg & Cherlin, 1991), and a majority of these also experienced their parents' remarriage and the challenges of a "blended family."

In the context of marital instability, the breakup of nuclear families, and the remarriage of parents, it is clear that grandparents and step-grandparents are becoming increasingly important family connections (Johnson & Barer, 1987). Two-fifths of divorced mothers move during the first year of the divorce (McLanahan, 1983), and most of these move in with their parents while they make the transition to single parenting (Goldscheider & Goldscheider, 1993).

When Help Flows across Generations, It Flows Mostly Downward

An unfortunate stereotype of the older generation today is of "greedy geezers" who are spending their children's inheritance on their own retirement pleasures (Bengtson, 1993). This myth is not in accord with the facts. Intergenerational patterns of help and assistance flow mostly from the older generations to younger generations in the family. For example, McGarry and Schoeni (1995) have shown that almost one-third of U.S. parents gave a gift of $500 or more to at least one of their adult children during the past year;

however, only 9% of adult children report providing $500 to their aging parents. Similar results are reported by Bengtson and Harootyan (1994) and Soldo and Hill (1993).

Silverstein et al. (1995) noted that intergenerational support patterns ebb and flow over time. Multigenerational families represent "latent kin networks" of support (Riley & Riley, 1993) that often are enacted only in times of crisis. This is similar to Hagestad's (1996) notion of elders as the "Family National Guard": Although remaining silent and unobserved for the most part, grandparents (and great-grandparents) muster up and march out when an emergency arises regarding younger generation members' well-being.

THE MICROSOCIOLOGY OF INTERGENERATIONAL RELATIONSHIPS

Although there have been important changes in the demography of intergenerational relationships since the 19th century, population statistics about family and household structure tell only one part of the story. At the behavioral level, these changes have more immediate consequences in the ways family members organize their lives and pursue their goals in the context of increasing years of intergenerational "shared lives." How to conceptualize and measure these intergenerational interactions has become increasingly important since Burgess (1926) put forth his definition of the family as "a unity of interacting personalities."

The Solidarity Model: Dimensions of Intergenerational Relationships

In discussing these social-psychological approaches to intergenerational relations, I should first identify the study from which my colleagues and I have examined them, the Longitudinal Study of Generations (LSOG). This study began as a cross-sectional survey of more than 2,044 three-generational family members, sampled from more than 840,000 members of the primary HMO serving Southern California at that time (see Bengtson,

1975 and 1996, for details of the sampling procedures). It has continued as a longitudinal study with data collected at 3-year intervals, adding the great-grandchild generation in 1991.

A concern in the LSOG since it began 3 decades ago has been the conceptualization and measurement of intergenerational relationships. We use the theoretical construct of *intergenerational solidarity* as a means to characterize the behavioral and emotional dimensions of interaction, cohesion, sentiment, and support between parents and children, grandparents and grandchildren, over the course of long-term relationships. We define six conceptual dimensions of intergenerational solidarity (Bengtson & Mangen, 1988; Bengtson & Schrader, 1982; Roberts, Richards, & Bengtson, 1991).

1. Affectual solidarity: the sentiments and evaluations family members express about their relationship with other members (How close do you feel to your father or mother? How well do you get along with your child or grandchild? How much affection do you feel from them?)
2. Associational solidarity: the type and frequency of contact between intergenerational family members
3. Consensual solidarity: agreement in opinions, values, and orientations between generations
4. Functional solidarity (assistance): the giving and receiving of support across generations, including exchange of both instrumental assets and services as well as emotional support
5. Normative solidarity: expectations regarding filial obligations and parental obligations, as well as norms about the importance of familistic values
6. Structural solidarity: the "opportunity structure" for cross-generational interaction reflecting geographic proximity between family members

The theoretical rationale for these six dimensions and the adequacy (or limitations) of their measurement in survey research have been described at length in a volume by Mangen, Bengtson, and Landry (1988) and in subsequent articles (Roberts & Bengtson, 1990; Roberts et al., 1991; Silverstein et al., 1995). The solidarity paradigm has proven useful in research by other investigators (Amato & Booth, 1997; Lee, Netzer, & Coward, 1994; Marshall, Matthews, & Rosenthal, 1993; Rossi & Rossi, 1990). It can be seen as exemplifying an operational definition of the life course theoretical perspective (Bengtson & Allen, 1993; Elder, Rudkin, & Conger, 1994).

The Strength of Intergenerational Relationships Over Time

Using longitudinal data from the LSOG, we have been able to chart the course of intergenerational solidarity dimensions over time. Our design allows consideration of the development and aging of each of the three and now four generations in our sample, as well as the sociohistorical context of family life as it has changed over the years of the study (Bengtson et al., 2002).

One consistent result concerns the high levels of affectual solidarity (reflecting the emotional bonds between generations) that have been found over six times of measurement, from 1971 to 1997 (Bengtson et al., 2000). Three things should be noted. We find that the average solidarity scores between grandparents and parents, parents and youth, grandparents and grandchildren are high, considerably above the expected midpoint of the scale. Second, these scores are remarkably stable over the 26 years of measurement; there are no statistically significant differences by time of measurement, and the scores are correlated over time between .5 and .8. Third, there is a "generational bias" in these reports: Parents consistently report higher affect than their children do over time, as do grandparents compared with grandchildren. This supports the "intergenerational stake" hypothesis first proposed 30 years ago (Bengston & Kuypers, 1971; Giarrusso, Stallings, & Bengtson, 1995). The older generation has a greater psychosocial investment, or "stake," in their joint relationship than does their younger generation, and this influences their perceptions and evaluations of their common intergenerational relationships.

These results indicate the high level of emotional bonding across generations and the considerable stability of parent-child affectual relationships over long periods of time.

At the same time, it should be noted that not all intergenerational relationships display such high levels of emotional closeness. We find that about one in five relationships are characterized by either significant conflict (Clarke et al., 1999) or detachment. . . .

The Effects of Changing Family Forms on Intergenerational Influence

Situating multigenerational families in sociohistorical context allows us to broaden our inquiry about their importance and functionality. How have intergenerational influences changed over recent historical time? Are families still important in shaping the developmental outcomes of its youth? What have been the effects of changing family structures and roles, the consequences of divorce and maternal employment, on intergenerational influences? We used the 30-year LSOG to explore these issues.

An important feature of the LSOG is that enough time has elapsed since its start in 1971 that the ages at which members of different generations were assessed have begun to overlap. This provides what we call a generation-sequential design. A limitation of existing data sets has been that researchers could not track changes across generations within specific families over decades of time, nor draw conclusions about the relationship between historical change in family structures and intergenerational influence and socialization outcomes. The LSOG is unique because of its accumulation of parallel longitudinal assessments for multiple generations within the same families in different historical periods.

Within a life course framework that focuses on the interplay of macroeconomic and microrelational processes, Bengtson, Biblarz, and Roberts (2002) examined the development and cultivation of youth's achievement orientations: Their educational and occupation career aspirations, their values, and their self-esteem. Achievement orientations are viewed as personal attributes that may be passed down, or "transmitted," from generation to generation in families, promoting continuity over multiple generational lines across many decades of history. We also know that parent-child affectual bonds can mediate this process. It is therefore useful to study these intergenerational transmission processes. In so doing, we can empirically examine the hypotheses concerning family decline or intergenerational family importance and diversity.

Our analysis (Bengtson et al., 2002) contrasted the achievement orientations of Generation X youth (18- to 22-year-olds) today with their baby-boomer parents when they were about the same age in 1971. We know that Generation Xers have grown up in families that were quite different in structure than their parents' families were. How has this affected their achievement orientations: their aspirations, values, and self-esteem?

Figure 10.1 illustrates just how different the family context of these two successive generations has been. Generation Xers were much more likely than their baby-boomer parents to have grown up in a family with less than two siblings, with a father and mother who were college graduates, with a mother who was working full time, and, above all, in a divorced household (40% for Generation Xers, 20% for their baby boomer parents). Given these differences, how do the two generations compare in terms of family solidarity and achievement orientations?

Our analysis suggests that today's Generation Xers are surprisingly similar to what their baby-boomer parents were on these measures at the same age, almost 30 years ago. This suggests that despite changes in family structure and socioeconomic context, intergenerational influences on youths' achievement orientations remain strong. Generation Xers whose parents divorced were slightly less advantaged in terms of achievement orientations than Generation Xers who came from nondivorced families but were nevertheless higher on these outcome measures than were their baby-boomer parents at

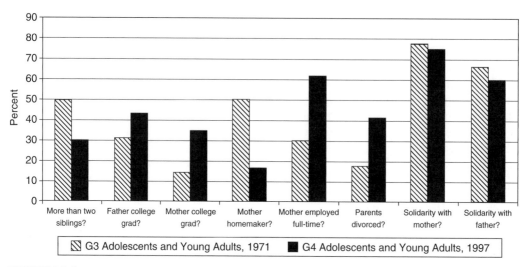

FIGURE 10.1

Historical changes in family structure and parental attributes: "Generation X" compared with their baby-boomer parents at the same age. (*Source:* Vern L. Bengtson, "Beyond the Nuclear Family: The Increasing Importance of Multigenerational Bonds," *Journal of Marriage and Family* 63 (February 2001), pp. 1–16. Reprinted with permission.

the same age, regardless of family structure. We also found that maternal employment has not negatively affected the aspirations, values, and self-esteem of youth across these two generations, despite the dramatic increase in women's labor force participation over the past 3 decades. Finally, we found that Generation Xer women have considerably higher educational and occupational aspirations in 1997 than did their baby-boomer mothers almost 30 years before. In fact, Generation X young women's aspirations were higher than Generation X young men's.

These findings challenge the hypothesis that families are declining in function and influence and that "alternative" family structures spell the downfall of American youth. Multigenerational families continue to perform their functions in the face of recent social change and varied family forms. . . .

MULTIGENERATIONAL FAMILY BONDS: MORE IMPORTANT THAN EVER BEFORE?

My hypothesis is that multigenerational family bonds are important, more so than family

research has acknowledged to date. I have argued that demographic changes over the 20th century ("from pyramids to beanpoles" and "longer years of shared lives") have important implications for families in the 21st century, particularly with regard to the "latent network" of family support across generations. I have suggested that multigenerational relationships are increasingly diverse in structure and functions within American society. I propose that because the increase in marital instability and divorce has weakened so many nuclear families, these multigenerational bonds will not only enhance but in some cases replace some of the nuclear family functions that have been the focus of so much recent debate.

To test this hypothesis concerning the increasing importance of multigenerational bonds will require research such as the following: First, we will need to examine longitudinal data to trace the salience over time of the multigenerational model. My argument (following Riley & Riley, 1993) is that multigenerational relations represent a "latent kin network" that may be inactive and unacknowledged for long periods of time, until a family crisis occurs. Such is the case when grandparents are called to help in the raising of grandchildren; when family elders become incapacitated and adult children and other kin provide caregiving support. Fortunately, by now we have several large ongoing longitudinal studies (such as the National Survey of Families and Households, Health and Retirement Survey, Analysis of Household Economics and Demography, etc.) that can be used to examine the activation of latent kin networks over time.

[Second, w]e will need trend data so as to examine whether multigenerational families are indeed interacting more and fulfilling more functions for members in the 21st century than in the past. We need to explore how trends in longevity, elder health, the beanpole intergenerational structure, and the aging of baby boomers are affecting intergenerational solidarity and support.

Third, we need more data on the ethnic and racial diversity of American family forms. We need to examine multigenerational influences across and within special populations, such as minority families and first- and second-generation immigrants. For example, considerable evidence shows that for many African Americans, extended kin relationships are more salient than they are for White families (Burton, 1995). As has been observed so many times in our recent history, minority patterns can signal changes on the horizon for White majority families.

We also need data reflecting the increasing diversity of American family forms beyond biological and conjugal relationships. We need to examine the multigenerational relationships of gay and lesbian families and of never-married parents.

We need cross-national data to examine how multigenerational relations are changing and the implications of these changes. For example, in the face of rapid industrialization and population aging, we are seeing changes in the meaning and expression of "filial piety" in Asian societies. In Korea and Japan, for example, multigenerational household sharing is becoming less prevalent (Bengtson & Putney, 2000). What does this imply in terms of Confucian norms about caring for one's parents? We need also to examine the

changing mix between state and family provisions for the elderly. Paradoxically, it appears that Eastern societies are becoming more dependent on state provisions for the elderly, whereas Western societies are facing declining governmental resources and placing more responsibilities on families (Bengtson & Putney).

Finally, we need to focus on policy implications of the growing importance of multigenerational bonds. What can be done to strengthen multigenerational family supports? Grandparent visitation rights have been challenged recently in the U.S. Supreme Court; what does this mean in light of other court decisions to place more responsibility on grandparents as court-mandated guardians of grandchildren?

CONCLUSION: BEYOND THE NUCLEAR FAMILY

Are families declining in importance within American society? Eight decades ago, Ernest W. Burgess addressed this question from the standpoint of family transformations across the 19th and 20th centuries. His hypothesis was that families and their functions had changed from a social institution based on law and custom to a set of relationships based on emotional affect and companionship (Burgess, 1926). But this did not mean a loss of social importance. He suggested that the modern family should be considered as "a unity of interacting personalities" (Burgess) and that future research should focus on the interactional dynamics within families. In all this, Burgess' focus, and that of those who followed him (Ogburn, 1932; Parsons, 1944), was on the nuclear family form.

Eight decades later, this question—are families declining in importance?—has resurfaced. Some family experts have hypothesized that families have lost most of their social functions along with their diminished structures because of high divorce rates and the growing absence of fathers in the lives of many children (Popenoe, 1993). A contrasting hypothesis is that families are becoming more diverse in structure and forms (Skolnick, 1991; Stacey, 1996).

In this article, I have suggested another hypothesis, one that goes beyond our previous preoccupation with the nuclear or two-generation family structure. This concerns the increasing importance of multigenerational bonds and the multigenerational extension of family functions. I want to be clear about this hypothesis because it differs from contemporary wisdom about the most pressing problems of American families today and because I hope it will generate much debate. I have proposed that (a) multigenerational relationships (those involving three or more generations) are becoming increasingly important to individuals and families in American society; (b) these multigenerational relationships are increasingly diverse in structure and functions; and (c) for many Americans, multigenerational bonds are becoming more important than nuclear family ties for well-being and support over the course of their lives.

Burgess was right, many decades ago: The American family is in transition. But it is not only in transition "from institution to companionship," as he argued. Over the century, there have been significant changes in the family's structure and functions. Prominent among them has been the extension of family bonds, of affection and affirmation, of help and support, across several generations, whether these be biological ties or the creation of kinlike relationship. But as families have changed, they have not necessarily declined in importance. The increasing prevalence and importance of multigenerational bonds represent a valuable new resource for families in the 21st century.

■ Review Questions

1. What are the reasons why, in Bengtson's opinion, multigenerational ties are becoming more important to many Americans than nuclear family ties?
2. What are the characteristics of the "beanpole family"? What are its strengths and limitations?

READING 10-2

Men and Women
Together and Apart in the Later Years

Katherine S. Newman

"King, you don't understand. I don't want everything. That's not why I'm living . . . to want things. I done lived thirty-five years without things. I got enough for me. I just want to wake up in the bed beside you in the morning. . . . Your job is to be around so this baby can know you its daddy. Do that. For once, somebody do that. Be that. That's how you be a man, anything else I don't want."

—Tonya, speaking to her husband, King,
in August Wilson's play *King Hedley II*[1]

In the backyard of a run-down tenement in the Hill District, August Wilson's fictional Pittsburgh neighborhood, two African-American couples are wrestling with the history of their relationships. Elmore wants to reclaim his relationship with Ruby, now in her sixties, after a long absence. King (Ruby's grown son) wants to please Tonya, his thirty-five-year-old wife who is pregnant with his child, though she loudly proclaims that she does not want to bring a baby into a world—or a marriage—like this. King and Elmore have both been in and out of jail as

© 2003 by Katherine S. Newman. This piece originally appeared in *A Different Shade of Gray: Midlife and Beyond in the Inner City* by Katherine S. Newman. Reprinted by permission of The New Press. www.thenewpress.com.

a consequence of hot-headed murders, outbursts against men who wronged them in the past. Tonya and Ruby are fed up with the excuses, the absences, and the disappointments. They have learned the hard way how to live without men.

Ruby makes it clear that Elmore needs to make up for lost time if he wants to win her affection. She wants new dresses, some jewelry, and twenty dollars for some food, right now. Then she'll think about marrying Elmore. Tonya wants nothing of the kind from King. She knows he will do something crazy in order to "be a real man," something that will land him in jail. She cautions him, pleads with him, begs him not to sacrifice their lives together for the sake of "things." "I don't need things," she tells him. "I saw what they cost. I can live without them and be happy." Most of all, Tonya does not want to hear that King is stealing on her account. Her first husband followed that pathway to the penitentiary. Her teenage daughter, Natasha, hardly knows her father because he has been in jail for half her life. Like King, Ruby's first husband robbed in order to provide for his family, but this brought them nothing but grief. She wants King to abandon that destructive path.

[Natasha's] daddy been in jail for half her life. She wouldn't know him if she saw him. For what? The same stuff you be talking. How he gonna get his. He don't want it all. He just want his little bit. What he got now. He ain't got nothing . . . Natasha don't even know what a daddy is. I don't want that for my children.

It is not the fate of black women, Wilson's plays tell us, to hold their men for long. Whatever happiness they can cobble together is sure to be temporary, cut short by the ambitions of men who have few options for making something of themselves. Hemmed in by racism, by disappearing jobs, by the erosion of the old black middle class and the ascendance of new generations who reject their values, these fictional men are waging a losing battle to find themselves in the world. As King explains to Tonya, he has to claim a place in a world that defines manhood in material ways.

I ain't gonna stop living. The world ain't gonna change and all of a sudden get better because I be somebody's daddy. I can't go and get no job just because I'm gonna be somebody's daddy . . . I'm just trying to do my get. Get you the things you want.

Tonya and King are more eloquent than ordinary people, but this is all that separates Wilson's characters from very real New Yorkers. Surprisingly, though, we see very little in social science about how men and women in poor, minority communities think about their relations with each other in later life.

Virtually all of the research literature focuses instead on "disrupted" patterns of family formation, and with some reason. The sharp increase in single-parent households, always at greater risk for poverty, attracts the attention of anyone concerned with the fate of adults and the children they raise.[2] Yet the consequences of single parenthood do not end when the children are grown. What happens to the men who father children and then "disappear"? Where do they go when they hit their fifties? What are their lives like when they are no longer young enough to live a high life? To what extent, if at all, do they maintain ties to the women they have loved, to the children they helped bring into the world? If these men come looking for their families, asking to be let into their lives, will they be welcomed? Or are they shown the door, cut off from their children and the women they have known because it is less risky to leave the past behind than to open up to future disappointment?

And what of the women, who have soldiered on, raising children by themselves, often on the most meager of incomes? How does the experience of single parenthood affect the way their lives unfold when they hit their sixties? Popular culture provides us with images of what ought to happen to men and women in old age: gray-haired couples living out their lives together, mutually supportive as physical decline inevitably intrudes. Does this happen in the inner city?

The scholarship that has been done would incline most experts to answer, "No." Once lovers break up—early on in the relational "careers" of young adults—they are finished, period. My research suggests this is not always so. Men and women *do* try to reconnect on the other side of the age spectrum. They engage in a complicated dance of longing and bad blood, of water that has passed under the bridge long ago, and fears of what the future might bring if a relationship falls apart again. That leeriness operates on aging adults and the adult children whom they have raised, who also have something at stake in reconnecting to fathers lost to them in their youth. It's a risky business, but one that unfolds often enough to make the question of relationships between men and women part of life in late middle age.

It doesn't happen to everyone, of course. Many poor women and men of color grow old by themselves. Widowhood arrives early. A rocky history of never-married parenthood, or serial divorce, leaves a void that is never filled. Old age may pass in the company of adult children and grandchildren, or with good friends who have stuck together through many years of difficult times. But the bond between husband and wife may not be part of the picture, even when a man has come knocking.

Some men establish new relationships in their later years, especially with younger women. Men are in short supply and can often rely on this scarcity to start over again rather than entangle themselves with former lovers or ex-wives. A goodly number, too, pass into their senior years without any romantic attachments, hanging on the fringes of their sisters' households or daughters' families. . . .

THICK SKINS AND HARD SHELLS

The distinguished sociologist of race, Orlando Patterson,[3] has issued a challenge to romantic—or, at least, benign—portraits of African-American families. Conventional wisdom, he argues, posits either that black families have remained strong even in the face of overwhelming numbers of never-married mothers and high divorce rates or that there is nothing race-specific about these patterns. Scholars rushing to the defense of black single mothers have argued with great conviction that there is nothing pathological or debilitating about these families.[4] Or, if there is something broken about broken families, it is a consequence of poverty and the economic marginalization of black men rather than of poisonous gender relations.

Nonsense, answers Patterson. Slavery hammered the self-respect of black men and undermined the stability of African-American families. Poverty creates pressures of its own, but the black working and middle classes look only marginally better where marriage is concerned. Survey evidence presented in Patterson's work offers a blistering portrait of distrust between men and women in the black community. Women seem to believe men are generally no good: irresponsible, self-absorbed, looking out for number one. Men spit back that women are domineering, calculating, and manipulative. It's a catastrophe, Patterson tells us, and one that has lasting consequences, particularly for the more than 50 percent of black children growing up in single-parent households today.[5]

By many measures, marriage is in rocky condition in the United States, and not just among minority families. The divorce rate doubled in the 1960s and '70s, owing in part to the expansion in women's labor-force participation and the more generous provision of welfare benefits, both of which freed women from financial dependence upon men and from relationships they deemed destructive. A million children experience a parental divorce every year.[6] Yet Patterson suggests that more is at stake in the case of African Americans than these secular, cross-race trends. The preexisting tensions that he argues hold sway over men and women in the black community are so bad that they don't even get to the point of divorce; they don't marry in the first place.

Patterson makes important points based on survey research, but as with all work of this kind there is more to this than meets the statistical eye. First, as I noted earlier, this "never married" designation is a multifaceted category. Many of the people in it are what we might call "behaviorally married," even when they lack the paperwork. Others are closer to the object of Patterson's scorn: the one-night-stand relationship, resulting in a child, which can never progress because it is steeped in bad blood. And like the 50 percent of marriages that dissolve into divorce, some of these never-marrieds begin at one end of this continuum—acting in consort as full partners—only to dissolve into something that looks a lot like divorce, often of the bitter variety. We are poorly positioned to examine these patterns given the current resources of survey research. They cannot accurately capture the nuances. This is unfortunate because much of the Western world is in the midst of a fundamental change in patterns of marriage that we do not yet understand. We won't make much progress if we cannot figure out how to describe the "semi-marriages" that characterize cohabitation with children that is so evident in, for instance, inner-city New York.

These patterns are mainly of interest to those concerned with family formation. They matter a great deal, however, throughout the life course and come home to roost when men and women reach their mature years. Brief encounters, even those that bring children into the world, rarely resurface when former partners reach their elder years. Men don't try to reconnect and women usually have no idea what has become of them. Relationships of greater duration often take a different path. Cohabiting mothers . . . both permit and encourage ongoing contact between dads and kids. These are the cohabitations that are more likely to reemerge in middle age or the elder years, albeit with many of the reservations and worries that August Wilson's fictional women express. But for every [man], who remained in contact with his kids, there is another man who makes the effort only to face a slamming door. They are rebuffed by their former partners, who are bitter about being abandoned or convinced the fathers will be a bad influence in their kids' lives.

Ironically, older women often realize too late that cutting their ex-partners out has hurt their (now adult) children. When they see the pattern recur in the next generation, they often try to make up for lost time. They encourage their cohabiting daughters who suffer a breakup to let their grandkids maintain some kind of relationship with the errant fathers. This is delicate ground, for the adult daughters are often looking to their mothers to take sides, to validate their own damaged feelings by ratifying the daughter's decision to sever her ties with her partner. Yet from the vantage point of their own mature lives, these grandmothers often risk the ire of their daughters and tell them to let the children keep in touch with their fathers. Such grandmothers are trying to repair, at a distance, wounds that opened up in the course of their own adult lives.

Cheryl Naylor's experience illustrates the ways in which relationships that come and go in the space of early adulthood come back to have an impact on a woman's mature years. Elegantly thin, Cheryl is now nearly sixty years old, her features worn by time. A chain-smoking fan of Kool 100s, she is most at ease stretched out on the long, black leather sectional couch that sits in the living room of her two-bedroom apartment. The housing project where she lives is one of the better-known public developments in central Harlem and she has been a resident for nearly twenty years now. The walls are festooned with baby pictures and posters of rap groups she likes.

Cheryl met her first serious boyfriend in the neighborhood where she grew up. She was eighteen when she first noticed him, sitting on the stoop of the apartment building next door.

> He was nice looking all right. He had just came from the South, I think. He was likin' one of my girlfriends, but she didn't like him and me and her used to be together all the time. And he asked her who I was and it just started like that. So I met his mother and his brothers. By being right across the streets I used to always go up to his mother's house.

They started hanging out on the sidewalk outside the apartment building, leaning against the cars on the curb, and graduated to going out to the movies together. Cheryl's mother was wary of Lucas; she didn't think he was right for her daughter, and she took to looking out the window, watching over them, telegraphing her disapproval.

> She just kept saying he wasn't no good. You know how them mothers was back then. He wasn't no good; he wasn't no future for me and stuff like that. I don't know what made her say that because she never really saw that much of him. I guess she heard what the neighbors were saying about him.

Mama's dour gaze did not dissuade Cheryl from pursuing her relationship with Lucas, but it did convince her that she had to keep at least one big secret: she was pregnant. Even as a teenager Cheryl was tall and slender; her figure helped her to conceal the baby. She was nearly eight months along when her mother finally discovered the truth.

> I worked in a hospital at the time and didn't used to get home until about 1:00 A.M. Lucas called me at about 3:00 A.M. one day and [my mother] picked up the other extension. I answered the phone, but she could tell [something was up] because he kept saying, "Did you tell your mother yet? You told her?" I said, "No, I ain't gonna tell her." And she said to me, "Who's that, that black snake!"

Things went from bad to worse thereafter. Cheryl went crying to her brothers, asking them to intervene. Then Lucas's mother came calling to try to reason with Cheryl's mother. She wanted to see a marriage take place, but Cheryl was somewhat reluctant herself and Lucas seemed resistant. The truth of that interchange is buried in the past. Whatever the intentions and desires were, no wedding took place. Instead, Cheryl carried the pregnancy to term for the "whole, miserable nine months." They stayed together as girlfriend and boyfriend from the distance of separate houses for a time, but they never did try to form a family. Eventually their relationship unraveled, mainly because Cheryl was disappointed in the meagerness of Lucas's own contributions toward their daughter's care.

Nonetheless, Lucas "recognized" his daughter, meaning he made it public that he was the father and extended the helping hands of his own mother toward her granddaughter.

> His mother, every week, used to send cases of Carnation milk and baby food and stuff like that. And I told her that I appreciated it, even though I was working. I said, he's not gonna never do anything, and I took him to court and everything. But he always somehow bailed out of it or something for child support. I never got child support from him.

Cheryl appreciated the way Lucas's mother "did the right thing." But she was annoyed that Lucas himself had been let off the hook. Lucas's own contributions were limited to occasional donations of cash over the two or three years that followed Yvonne's birth. Sensing that this was the most she was ever going to see out of him led Cheryl to reject the idea of marrying him in the first place.[7]

Eventually, Lucas took up with Robin (a friend of Cheryl's) and they had four or five children together. Because Cheryl and Robin were friends, they didn't fight over Lucas. In fact, Robin admonished Lucas about the importance of taking care of baby Yvonne. Robin and Lucas managed to make a go of things. They still live together in a big house in Queens where Robin has established a real estate business. They have grandchildren whom Cheryl knows. "They really doing all right. They come over here every now and then. Robin calls me; we talk on the phone and it's just like it was way back there in the sixties and seventies."

Cheryl is more comfortable maintaining her friendship with Robin than any semblance of her former relationship with Lucas. Even so, over the years he has been an occasional figure in his daughter Yvonne's life. "He'll come and see her every now and then. You know, he'd give her money to give me or something like that, but really he never was into her life [in a big way]."

Cheryl's experience with Lucas was the norm as she remembers it. A few of her more fortunate friends married Prince Charming and rode out of Harlem. But this was the exceptional case, not the rule. Most of the time, boys would get together with girls until the babies started coming and would disappear thereafter.

> Some of my friends was all right. They went off and got married. And they lived happily ever after. The other ones was in predicaments like I was. They had babies and the guys stepped off; they never saw them anymore and they had to fend for theirselves. They had to get up and start going to work for theirselves to take care of their children.

This pattern stands in contrast to Cheryl's own childhood and the experience of her own parents. Her mother and father both grew up in intact families and Cheryl was, by her own admission, much closer to her dad than her mom as she grew up. It was not a matter of long-standing custom that men were rotten deserters. In Cheryl's own generation, though, expectations for a happy marriage, or even a long-lasting partnership, receded sharply, to be replaced by low aspirations for intimacy. After Lucas, who was a disappointment, Cheryl has experienced mostly short stints when she felt she mattered to her man. The father of her second child did not work out any better than Lucas.

> He was never here; he was always back and forth, in and out, in and out. Him and his mother had a terrible relationship. He always hated his mother and used to tell me [so]. I said, you not gonna have a good life, you hate your mother.

Cheryl moved in with her own mother and went out to work to support herself and her two children. She would hear periodically about her ex-partner's "career" in jail and the other relationships he started (and finished), but she didn't give him a lot of thought.

The third—and last—of Cheryl's men turned out to be a more durable presence in her life, but for that reason an even more profound disappointment. By this time she was in her mid-thirties. She was working as a waitress in a bar and met

Rodney on the job. It was, perhaps, not the most propitious of circumstances for beginning a new relationship, but Cheryl was looking for someone to love, and Rodney seemed to be in search of a new home, and a stepmother for his own children. She fell into the role, almost without thinking. Rodney would call her up and ask her to come over to his mother's house and she took him up on the invitation. She braved the hostility of Rodney's then-girlfriend, the mother of his children, and gradually established a relationship with him, and perhaps even more so with his children.

Rodney moved in slowly, but eventually he became a fixture in Cheryl's life. More than anything, though, Cheryl grew attached to his children. They were the magnet that drew her into the relationship.

> His kids started coming. That's just how it was. But I love kids and I just fell in love with his kids. His daughter had that thick hair with the wave in it that comes down her back. I'd love them kids; I still love them.

Rodney and Cheryl were together for nearly a decade. The early years were wonderful, despite the tensions with his ex-lover. Cheryl felt she had found a man who not only loved her, but who would help her care for Yvonne and her younger daughter, Janet. She set limits on his authority over them and he adhered to them, while doing the same for his kids.

> The first three years was beautiful. . . . He had good rapport with my kids. I told him, "You're not their father, but they're goin' to have to respect you. Don't hit my kids. You can chastise them but don't put your hands on them." And they loved Rodney to death. They called him Daddy and everything. We went to dinner all the time. Every weekend he would take us up to Sammy's [a well-known restaurant]. One week he would just take me, the next week he would take Yvonne and Janet and some of the kids from our building. We went to amusement parks. You know it was just really good.

As Cheryl looks back, this was just about the happiest part of her life. Her kids had a dad; his kids had a more responsible mom in Cheryl than they did in their own mother; Rodney and Cheryl had each other. But it didn't last. Simultaneously, Yvonne went off the rails and Rodney's daughter Quanda sank into total rebellion. Yvonne started running away from home, indulging in drugs, and storming through the apartment in defiance when Cheryl tried to discipline her. Quanda was worse, as Cheryl discovered by prying into her diary.

Cheryl turned to Rodney, warning him that Quanda could not continue her weekend visits if she was going to dabble in drugs and sex. No change. Quanda continued to indulge, particularly since she met no resistance from her own mother who was, by this time, a crack cocaine user and a heavy drinker. The mother neglected Quanda and her siblings, who would turn to Cheryl, calling to complain that there was no food in the house. Cheryl did what she could from a distance and earned the enduring love of Rodney's sons, and the equally permanent enmity of Quanda. Telling them they should respect their mother, no matter how badly she behaved, Cheryl stood up for what she thought was a better model of child rearing. To be truthful, the model wasn't working very well with her own daughter Yvonne.

Coincident with these traumas, Rodney began to insist that Cheryl stay close to home. Cheryl's cousin had offered her a job working as a teacher's aide in a Muslim school in Queens. The job required that she travel from Harlem to Jamaica Bay, but she enjoyed it since it was a step up from working in the bar where she had met Rodney. Cheryl couldn't understand why Rodney was losing his temper over her whereabouts, because she was always home by six o'clock to cook dinner. He issued an ultimatum: "It's me or the job." She turned him down.

Rodney's insistence was particularly irritating because he was becoming a less dependable figure himself. He would disappear for a day or two without explanation. Rodney ditched the construction job he had held down for most of their years together. Cheryl wasn't sure where the money was coming from, but she began to hear from other women in his life who wanted some. They would call, ask for Rodney, and hang up when Cheryl said he wasn't there. The calls grew a bit bolder: women demanding Rodney pay their rent, or buy Pampers for their children. One showed up on Cheryl's doorstep holding a baby she claimed, loud enough for all the neighbors to hear, was Rodney's child. That was the end for Cheryl. She issued an ultimatum of her own: get out. Cheryl gave Rodney thirty days to pack up and leave. The next week, his belongings disappeared from her house and that was that.

The disappointment she felt was powerful enough to convince Cheryl that there really are no good men in this world. Women should be suspicious of men's intentions, she says, and ready to treat them instrumentally. She does not want any man in her house or her life.

> When that box [of Rodney's belongings] was gone and all his stuff was outta my house, I knew that he was gone. And that was that. He just left. And after that I said I wouldn't even let [repair]men come into my house. I used to just hate men. To this day, I don't want any of them in my life. I'm getting over it now, gradually. The first year, it was hard. I'm not gonna lie to you. . . . Now I don't want nobody to come back in my house and put no shoes under my bed.

Cheryl "got over" Rodney, and now after many years on her own she wants nothing to do with men at all. She has become the kind of woman Orlando Patterson bemoans when he writes about poisonous relations between black men and women. Yet she did not start out from that position. For many years she believed that love was possible and she acted on that assumption through several relationships. Belatedly, and bitterly, she has concluded she was wrong about all that.

Cheryl knows that her youngest daughter Janet has inherited some of this ill will. Much as Cheryl bears these internal scars, she did not wish them on her daughters. Hence she has tried to make amends by encouraging Janet to keep her own ex-partner in touch with the son they share. Janet was resistant, having also learned through her own bad experience that men are not to be trusted and that women have to make do on their own. It fell to Cheryl to try to maintain the links between her grandson and his father.

> Janet told me that she was glad her father wasn't in my life because it made me a stronger woman. And her son's father is the same way. My daughter has been taking care of her own son for sixteen years on her own. You know, she don't ask [that man] for anything. But when [the father] Tom comes around my house, her son sees his father. Like Janet said, there will never be no real relationship there because he don't even know how to converse with this kid because he's never around him. But they sit outside, they play basketball.
>
> Janet said, "Ma, take [my son] upstairs when [he comes around]." And I said, "No, Janet. He don't see his father, so let him stay out there and play." They stayed outside until like two or three o'clock in the morning. I looked out the window and there they was out there playing [basketball]. I said, "Tom, don't you think it's time for that boy to come upstairs?" And he said, "Okay Miss Cheryl, I'm gonna bring him up." And he sent him up. And the boy looked so happy that day because he really loved his father. He knows his father.

Tom is not the perfect father or son-in-law. Yet his son knows him and his lineage. He doesn't have a dad he can rely on for steady advice or support, but he does not suffer the confusion of not having a clue about where he comes from. As Cheryl explains, he has a set of kinship coordinates, a sense of location.

> He knows his father. He know his grandmother. He [knew] his [other] grandmother before she passed away and his aunts and uncles. Whenever they come and get him, or ask Janet [if] he can go, she always let him go.

Getting Janet to this point, moving her beyond bitterness, has not been easy either. Cheryl has had to pull her over that hurdle.

> Years ago, Janet would say, "Ma, if Tom ever died, my son is not going to his funeral." And I sat her down and said, "Janet, you can't do that; it's

not right. He'll never forgive you for doing that. He know now, he's sixteen. He understand. He know that his father never did anything for him. But when [Tom] do come around, he try to be with him. So you can't do that. If he pass away today or tomorrow, that still his son. You can't deny that. Maybe he wasn't nothing, but that's still his son and that's still his father. And that wouldn't be right. I might not be here to see it, but you will regret what you did because he would tell you about it in years to come."

Bringing Janet around to this way of thinking took some courage because Cheryl could easily have been defined as a hypocrite, unwilling to admit the mistakes she made in raising her own two daughters. As it happens, she does recognize the error of her ways and regrets much of the pathway she herself took as a mother. She blames herself for the tension between her two daughters, the jealousy that pitted them against each other and hurled Yvonne into such a state of fury that she lashed out physically at Janet and then turned around and hurt herself. She blames herself for the drug habit Yvonne developed, which landed her on Rikers Island and bequeathed to the next generation a twisted life of acting out, flunking out, and striking out in retaliation for neglect and abuse.

The only real pride Cheryl takes in surveying her family is vested in Janet. The younger daughter has made her own mistakes and fallen off the deep end more than once. But Cheryl worked hard to rescue this one and turn her around. Today she has a regular job as a beautician and earns a decent living. She has raised her son, without his father but with enough of a backbone to keep him out of trouble. Janet has become a new woman and a solace to Cheryl, the mainstay of the family. She is the person Cheryl knows will keep her company in her own old age.

Thousands of African-American women in inner-city neighborhoods have known this kind of disappointment in their lives. They are reaching their late fifties, as has Cheryl, with a rocky history of broken marriages or no marriages at all, with sons and daughters who go on to repeat their experience. They have learned to fend for themselves as the sole workers in the household, to lean on their mothers to help them raise their children, and to return the favor to succeeding generations when they become grandmothers themselves. Emotional satisfaction endures less in the bond that ties men to women than in the vertical link that binds mothers to children. The company they keep is only episodically punctuated by lovers or husbands, brothers and fathers. Mostly, it is a community of women.

From the perspective of the middle class, including its African-American members, this is a poor substitute for a real family, which is supposed to have, at its core, a couple. From an economic perspective, there can be no doubt that families like Cheryl's are disadvantaged in almost every respect. They are poorer, the children who grow up in them often have problems in school or get in trouble with the law. Girls, like Yvonne and Janet, are "at risk" for repeating their mothers' experience. All of this is true. Yet there is another truth that bears observation as well: there is strength in these women and they are, in many respects, better off than the men whom they have cast off or who have let them go. They *do* have family to lean on. There are constants in their lives, alongside the hardship. Cheryl does have Janet and together they have Janet's son.

When Cheryl was thirty, she felt bad about the men in her life. She was reconciled to a cordial, though distant, relation to Lucas, but felt burned and resentful toward Rodney. Now that she is nearly sixty, she has come out on the other side of this stress. Yes, she wishes it might have turned out more like the storybook weddings she dreamed about as a young girl. But no, she is not living out her life as a sob sister. On the other side of middle age, that couple-centered existence doesn't matter as much to her. So many of the women she knows never had it either. They are the norm in her inner-city neighborhood, not the exception. Hence what matters to her most is not the lack of marriage but the presence of her

daughter and her grandson. She knows that Janet will be there for her over the long haul and feels blessed that she has someone to rely on. The people she feels sorry for are the ones who don't have such a daughter, who only have kids like Yvonne out on Rikers Island. Everyone needs to have at least one person they can count on and that much Cheryl has for sure.

FROM THE MEN'S SIDE

Sociologists focus their attention on poor families primarily from the viewpoint of women and children. Men are present in scholarly writings only peripherally, often because they have absented themselves from the families they helped to create. But they don't just disappear. How do *they* think about the trajectories of their relations with the womenfolk? Virtually everything we know about this subject from the man's angle is really about boys, or rather adolescents. Elijah Anderson's provocative essays[8] provide key insights into the competitive psychology of young men, intent mainly on proving their mettle to their fellow males using the currency of female attention. As he tells it, the boys are not interested in what one might call a relationship. They are interested in "getting one over" on the girls, on getting the sexual goods from as many admiring girls as possible for use in bragging rights.

Journalists and social scientists have seized on this kind of instrumental behavior as a prime mover in the story of broken families. The disinterest that men show in "settling down" or being "responsible fathers" leads directly to female-headed households, increased risk of family poverty, the absence of role models for children (especially male children), and a growing suspicion among women that men are just no good.[9] To be fair, women often come to the conclusion that two can play this game and, like Cheryl, decide they are the ones who want out of binding commitments. In the main, though, it is men who are seen (both by women and by themselves) as free agents. But for how long? Is this a pattern of disconnection that lasts throughout the life cycle? What happens when men begin to feel their age?

Some men we interviewed who have now reached sixty-five look back on their wilder days as something of a burden. Living up to an image of virility, performing in bed or on the streets, often to impress other men, left them exhausted, and not particularly satisfied or proud of themselves. They don't claim to be looking for sympathy, nor would they deny that their high-living days weren't fun at times, but they also note (quietly and not for public consumption) that there were times when they just wanted to go home, relax, and forget about posturing for anyone else's sake.

Geoffrey Powers certainly sees his life in this light. Now in his late forties, Geoffrey comes from a South Carolina farm family. He moved to New York to join his older brother, the first of his seven siblings to move north in the 1970s. They had heard there were good jobs in New York and the opportunities for young, black men in the rural South were not very appetizing. Geoffrey did not get much of an education. The GED he acquired after dropping out of high school was not nearly as important as the carpentry he learned in the Job Corps. With these blue-collar skills in his back pocket, Geoffrey made a solid living in the building trades. These days he works as a shipping manager for a firm in Queens, where he hopes to stay until he turns seventy. Geoffrey has come a long way and he knows it. He grew up in a house with no inside toilet and not enough food on the table. Today he can look forward to retiring on his pension in the rent-controlled apartment he now lives in.

In his youth, Geoffrey did his share of "acting foolish," running around on the streets and getting into trouble. Job Corps training came his way because he was regarded as "at risk" and it did the trick in terms of providing him with skills. But Geoffrey had a field day in New York. He partied, drank more than he should have, had lots of girlfriends. He finally found a girl he really treasured and they had a child together, even as he was living at home with his older sister.

My biggest problem was, well, I had no real job at the time. And I didn't know nothing about really raising no kids. I didn't know how to keep money to take care of my kid.

This saga sounds quite familiar by now, except that in Geoffrey's case he finally did settle down and marry (a different woman). He had a second family with his new wife and they now have two adolescent children, a girl and a boy. They are not problem-free kids and Geoffrey often finds it a challenge to separate them from the untoward influences of the poor neighborhood where they live. He lectures his son about drugs and his daughter about boys and is never entirely sure that either sermon has hit its mark. They are latchkey kids because Geoffrey is a working man and so is his wife.

Yet there is a lot of pleasure in such a stolid, settled life, with basic rhythms that change very little from day to day. Among them is the knowledge that he no longer has to walk on the wild side. Indeed, Geoffrey takes satisfaction from raising his second set of teenagers with more care than those he had when he was not much more than a teenager himself.

> I'm proud of my family, proud of my kids. I'm proud of being able to get up and go to work every day. I'm proud of just being still alive! My family, though, that's the best part, the proudest part of my life. I really ain't got too much in my life but my family. Failure is when you sitting in the street being a wino. You ain't got no job, you don't have a place to live. That's a big failure. But me? I mean, I got an apartment, I go to work every day. That's a blessing in disguise.

Most of all, Geoffrey is glad that he lived long enough to outgrow the pathways that he followed when he was a young man without much sense of obligation toward anyone else. Those wild days might have been fun for a while, but they got to be wearing.

> I don't hang on the street like I used to, you know. I don't run around. When I come home from work, I [am] tired. I go to bed. There's a big change in me. I used to be on the street all night long. Can't do

that no more. I'm at the middle age time when you just come from work, go home and take a bath, eat your supper and get to bed. 'Cause I have to work every day now.

These days he can let all of the pressures of that macho stereotype flow off his back. Geoffrey's focus is on planting his feet in one place and making sure his family is secure.

> When you get to be forty . . . that's the time you're supposed to be done, situated, ready to just . . . watch your kids grow up and be helping your kids out. You go to work and sit back and relax and pay the bills. And take care of your family. Life changes for the better. No more hotdogging. No more running around. I think it's time to settle down and just look after family.

On occasion Geoffrey regrets that it took him so long to come around to this settled version of himself. He left a lot of trouble in his wake before he figured out that the old street-gang lifestyle wasn't for him. There is that lost daughter and a lost common-law wife and no amount of excuses can really make up for those errors of judgment. Like the other men we interviewed, Geoffrey has come to a belated recognition of the collateral damage done when he was "young and foolish." By the time it registered in the life of his first child and her mother, it was really too late for Geoffrey to remedy the past. What he could do was to try again and that is exactly what he did.

Middle-aged men in the inner city who have not managed to stabilize as well as Geoffrey also seek some kind of home life in their later years. More often than not, they look to settle down at last with a new and untainted woman or someone they've known as an acquaintance for a long time but were not romantically involved with in the past. Their "new" partners are beyond the childbearing phase, though they may be responsible for someone else's kids off and on. Like an old married couple, they mainly attend to each other. Old men try to find some peace and comfort in the arms of the one kind of woman they may not have had for a long time: a wife.

Clark is a case in point. A brown-skinned, muscular man whose body has seen better days, Clark is now fifty-seven years old. He lives in a one-room studio apartment in a housing development in Harlem that was once a middle-class enclave but is now inhabited mainly by the working poor. The whole apartment is about 300 square feet, with a kitchen in one corner and a computer in another. A nice-looking man, whose 5 foot 9 inch frame is overburdened by muscle that has gone to seed, Clark has had a rocky road since adolescence. Like many other men he knows, Clark comes from stable, working stock. But his own life has not been so stable, and his downward drift crisscrossed the lives of several women.

Clark was born in Brooklyn, one of six children. Both of his parents were from South Carolina and came up to New York as teenagers, in the river of African Americans that flowed out of the Deep South during the Great Migration.[10] They met as teenagers in the Bronx and married in their early twenties. Clark's mother was an educated woman who found a job as an elementary schoolteacher, and his father worked as an auto mechanic. Together they made a good living, but with so many children to provide for the household was always a bit chaotic. Misbehavior brought forth spanking from their father. Mother took a different tack: she would "brow beat" the kids, urging them to buckle down, get an education, work hard. With hindsight, Clark says, he recognizes she was right. In his youth, though, he wanted to have his own way. He saw his mom as old-fashioned, out of touch, with "ideas that were for her time," while he wanted to "pursue what [he] wanted to pursue." Clark humored his mother by heading off to school, and then pleasured himself by cutting classes. Ultimately, he skipped school, playing hooky.

Clark's parents drifted apart emotionally in their later years. They remained under the same roof until the day his dad died, but the tight bond between them loosened and Clark knew it. "When I was younger," he says casting his mind back to childhood, "everything was hunkydory." Clark could just see that his parents did not seem to share very much with each other after a time. "The relationship was strained," he says. "They didn't speak as much and my father spent a lot of time out of the house. . . . They just grew apart."

Clark's interest in the opposite sex kindled at thirteen or fourteen, but wasn't serious until he was sixteen. That was the year he met Sandra. Sandra and Clark lived in the same neighborhood and passed each other on the way to school. But Clark wasn't the only guy in the picture. "All of the guys wanted to be with her," he says smiling broadly. She was "hotsy totsy," he remembers, but she was also widely known as a "good girl," who was respected for her virtues.

> You know how guys are, right? They will stand around and brag [about girls] even when they have no basis in fact to do so. And you never heard [Sandra's] name come up in those kind of conversations. She always carried herself well. She was somebody you could take home to your mother.

And he did. Clark's mother, the schoolteacher, liked Sandra a lot. Clark was in a slight state of shock since he didn't expect to gain approval for any of his relationships. "It was scary," he says with a laugh. "Scary when your mother likes someone . . ."

Her churchgoing family, especially her father, a deacon, ensured Sandra's standing. Accorded much respect in the neighborhood, Sandra's kin took it for granted that she would only go out with a "good boy," and Clark—son of a schoolteacher and a steadily employed father—fit the bill. No fool he, Clark joined the church choir, even though "you know, I can't sing at all." With this fiction, he "got past her father," and they started dating under the watchful, and approving, eyes of both sets of parents. They went to movies, dinner, and long walks on the promenade facing the magnificent harbor alongside Brooklyn Heights. Clark and Sandra were an item for nearly three years, although they saw other people as well (or at least Clark did). But he knew his mother did not approve of anyone other than Sandra.

> My mother was a mental disciplinarian. [I would see girls in between] and you would know immediately, immediately how my mother felt about it. She didn't have to say a word. She could be standing at the refrigerator with her back turned. If I brought somebody into the house that she didn't like, a young lady, especially while I was Sandra's [steady], she didn't say anything. And you know what, the girl could feel [the chill]. My mother might not say a word. You might not even see the expression. It's just like the whole house got cold.

Though not one to keep his mother happy, Clark tended to stick with Sandra. And she returned the affection, giving him the one gift that really signaled how much she loved him: her virginity.

Given this praiseworthy young lady, he might have felt on the top of the world were it not for the troublesome influence of his peers. Boys in Clark's neighborhood were impressed that he "got Sandra," but having one steady girlfriend was not exactly their idea of success. Just in case something happened with "your main girl," you should always have some action on the side. The point, as Elijah Anderson would say, was to compete.

> It's not even cheating, really. It is, but we're talking at the time as a young guy. You're gonna try to, as many young boys do, try to meet as many women as you possibly can. Whether or not anything happens between you and the young lady [as a consequence] is kind of irrelevant. The thing is to meet as many as you can. That was the attitude at the time.

What the boys were interested in was not the occasional churchgoing, good girl so much as the number of conquests they could brag about to one another. Hanging out on the stoop of their Brooklyn flats, Clark and his buddies gathered in groups to take in the perpetual show of women "on parade." They compared notes on a girl's body, her walk, the way her clothes fit. "Typical, ridiculous stuff," he laughs, the stuff of short relationships and temporary commitments. "We didn't want to hear about marriage at that age. Marriage? Please!"

Truth be told, Clark was happy enough to bask in Sandra's attention. But all around him he saw a different model of men and women together. Even his father, loyal spouse that he was, was constantly the subject of sidelong glances and inappropriate attention from other women. "Women used to speak to my father," Clark remembers, "and it was probably a source of tension between him and my mother." As far as Clark knows, his dad never acted on impulse and declined to pursue whatever it was that was "on offer." His attractiveness, Clark thought, might have been a "weapon against my mother, because she could be quite intimidating mentally." Smart, professional, and respected, Clark's mother cut a higher-class figure than her auto mechanic husband, at a time when it was not "done" for wives to be superior in status.[11]

When Clark ventured out into the territory of boy/girl relations, he was operating with contradictory "instructions." He had his parents to look to, a long-married couple, but one where temptations from the outside were visible even to the children. And he had his friends, none of whom were lucky enough to find a girl of Sandra's caliber and who substituted a numbers game for relationships of any great meaning. For them, masculinity was a matter of conquest, and a deliberate eschewing of the kind of "go steady" commitment that Sandra expected.

Competing models finally got the better of Clark, and not just with respect to Sandra. He started to lose face because he was acting too much like the good boy her deacon father admired and too little like the badass his friends put some store in. So Clark started cutting school more often. He dabbled in the drug trade for a bit of fast cash. Clark started going out with other girls in a secretive, evasive fashion. Worst of all, he was hard-hearted in the face of Sandra's extreme disappointment and played the big man, the tough guy. He became the one that was "hard to get" and impossible to keep.

> We just grew apart. Yeah, she didn't like the direction some parts of my life was going in. I wanted

to do what I wanted to do. And you know, at that age, there's a lot of ego involved. So it was like, "You can't get with my program." We eventually just drifted apart.

It didn't take long for Clark to find another lady and this one was different than Sandra. Tricia was easygoing, independent, and didn't hang on Clark. She had long legs and tight shorts—all the requirements. Clark had felt a bit burdened by Sandra's middle-class expectations about high school, church, and loyalty. Tricia was different.

> She didn't try to pressure [me] on a lot of stuff. She had an attitude like . . . she was always secure in herself. You know, you do your thing and I'll do my thing. A lot of women want you to account for every second of your time. Tricia wasn't like that. She was secure enough I guess by herself to let [me] go off without pressing [me] about where I was gonna go. And trust in you and herself enough to know that [I was] gonna come back.

Other girls—Sandra included—were possessive, annoyed by the flirtatious behavior of other young girls with boys who were spoken for. Clark found the flings fun and the jealousy of girlfriends a drag. Tricia never pulled that chain; so as far as Clark was concerned she was the perfect girl, and they became an item.

Indeed, they saw each other fairly steadily for about three years. Out of the blue one day, or so Clark remembers, Tricia went into the bathroom and came out leaking water. She had a full-term baby on the way.

> Up until my daughter was born, the day she was born, neither one of us thought about kids. I didn't even know [Tricia] was pregnant. . . . [Tricia] didn't grow at all. She had no stomach . . . her face was a little fat and her butt got big. The day her water broke, we were going crazy. We took her to the hospital and she had the baby, who was about four or five pounds. . . . She was underweight. But, no, we never planned on anything.

Clark moved in with Tricia and her parents after Sonya was born. Despite their reservations about Clark, Tricia's parents seem to have accepted his role in their grandchild's life. Even though she was not the result of careful planning, Sonya was loved, "a happy addition to the family," he says with satisfaction. Tricia looked after the baby for a time and then went to work in a hospital, leaving her mother on child-care duty. Clark got a job in shipping and receiving and began making his "little money" contributions to the coffers of the extended household. He took Sonya out for walks, and while he admits he wasn't one for the diapers, as he looks back on her infancy he sees himself as a dutiful and attentive father, within limits. Tricia and her mother were the full-time caregivers for Sonya. What he did was play a part that was, from his perspective, far more involved than many other men who had children in his peer group. At twenty-two, he was helping to support his daughter and living with her mother. He was not an absentee dad.

Clark and Tricia talked about getting married off and on, but seem to have felt little urgency about the prospect. More important to Tricia was just the fact that Clark was still there and still hers. They were managing financially, with the pooled resources of the several generations in Tricia's household, and Clark's steady job was part of the equation. But whatever they learned from the accidental birth of Sonya didn't stick because, within a year or so, another baby girl was on the way. Now the pressures on Clark to form an independent household began to grow. To make matters worse, both Clark and Tricia boosted their drug use from an occasional indulgence to a more serious habit. Money started to become a big problem.

> I used drugs casually before we met. But during the time I was with her, that's when I started indulging heavily. Heavily. I got in with a group of guys who were also making money and it looked good, wearing glamorous clothes. Always had a bunch of money in their pockets. But with all of that stuff came a whole lot of other stuff. I was out there [selling]. The lifestyle, everything. I went for it.

Space was very tight in Tricia's parents' house and her parents were distraught about the erratic behavior that Clark began to display. Tricia

was working, drugs notwithstanding, but Clark started disappearing without warning, flashing leather jackets they knew he couldn't afford on his clerk's income. They didn't get mad, they just got worried, and tried repeatedly to talk sense into Clark. He couldn't hear them.

> I was like a son to them. They tried to talk to me as you would to a son, but my mind was in the streets. My own mother was going crazy too. I had a lot of opportunities that I passed by, that I blew through stupidity, not staying in focus and know what my goals were supposed to be.
>
>   My mother says I'm scared of success. She said, "Every time you get close to something, you find a way to blow it."

Her views were pretty far from Clark's mind at the time, though. He was fixed on "the streets" and Tricia was focused on moving out on their own. With two baby girls and the uncomfortable, prying eyes of his "in-laws" watching them, the couple was desperate for a little privacy.

> She really wanted to get out of [her parents' house]. We wanted to get out of there. We wanted to get our own place, naturally. And I felt like I wasn't making enough money. I guess you never make enough money. And whatever little money we made, we spent on drugs, too. So there's never enough money in that situation.

They didn't move out. Clark blew the chance by diving headlong into the drug trade until he attracted the attention of the police.[12] In some respects, he was relieved. Clark was not exactly the king of the mountain. He was trying to make it in a business for which he was temperamentally unsuited. "I am not a killer-type guy, you know. I am not ruthless." Ruthless is what you have to be to become a successful drug dealer. In retrospect, he realizes he was terrified of the trade. "They committed heinous crimes and hurt people." "Thank God there are prisons" for people like that because, as Clark sees it, "I would never want to see those guys on the street or to be near my daughters." He did not have the fortitude to follow in their footsteps.

Busted under Rockefeller's draconian drug laws, he started cycling in and out of jail. After eight years of life with Tricia, he found himself doing some serious time, leaving his "wife" at wit's end. They broke up in 1989, during Clark's third stint in jail. With a lot of time on his hands, and the benefit of hindsight, he knows now that she didn't have much choice but to break it off. She had just had enough of him, and probably of her own drug troubles. Tricia had two kids to take care of and parents to whom she needed to prove she could be trusted. Clark had to go.

> She told me that she would always love me, but that she was not making jail a part of her life. That threw me for a loop 'cause it wasn't like I didn't love her. But she cut me off. I was still in love with her and tried to hold her. But if a woman's fed up, don't you try to hold on. That was one of the lessons she taught me. That took a lot of my self-esteem. 'Cause she had to be brutal with me to get me to understand that it was really over. I used to call the house. . . . She used to hang up on me. You can't keep a person there who doesn't want to be there.

It took many years for him to work his way toward some kind of reconciliation with Tricia. They were never together again as a couple, but they found some kind of peace between them that enabled Clark to reconnect with his daughters in middle age.

> I wasn't there for them as a father. They never had the opportunity to be around me and I didn't have the chance to be around them as much as I would have like to, or as much as they would have liked me to.

To Tricia's everlasting credit, she did not prevent Clark from connecting with his daughters even when he was in jail. She made sure they sent him cards and kept in touch with him no matter where he was and no matter how recalcitrant he became.

> I stayed in touch off and on. Guilt kills, though. When you're wrong and you know it, you sit up in the cell sometimes and think. . . . I won't even bother them. I would stop writing to them.

> I stopped writing to everybody for years. I just wouldn't even call home. The correctional officials would tell me to call home and I wouldn't.

Reverting to his father's "strong, silent" mode of noncommunication, Clark closed himself off from everyone in his family and cut his links to his children before they had much of a chance to develop in the first place. Yet Tricia persisted in trying to keep a line open.

> I'm grateful to Tricia for that. She never tried to keep my daughters from me. She never talked bad about me. And I will always respect her for that because she could have. She never talked bad about me. None of that. My mother, other people told me, "[Tricia] never [badmouthed] you."

Clark's family was brought into the circle and kept close so that the girls would know their kin on his side.

> She let the children know my mother, my sisters. You understand? She knew that the loss of her relationship with me affected her [ability to] integrate the children with all aspects of the family.

When Clark got out of jail, Tricia cultivated his affection, not for herself but for her kids. Eventually he came out of his shell and shed some of the shame he'd built up in prison.

He found some joy in reconnecting to the kids, though he never tried to push the father/daughter relationship very far. Instead, Clark kindled a quiet kind of friendship with his children and through it hoped to make up for some lost time. Perhaps his take is self-serving, but today he believes they understand—in ways they could not have known in their childhood—that he made big mistakes in his life. The crater that opened up where a father was supposed to be developed not because he didn't care about them, but because he cared more about himself.

> They understand that I love them. Yeah, [they think], my father did some stupid things. He's been in prison. He's done it on more than one occasion, but he loves me. And now they're able to understand that. They understand it's not nothing that I

specifically did to them, you know. Daddy didn't leave you because Daddy didn't want to be with you. You understand. Daddy left because he was an asshole. Okay.

Clark expects no sympathy or understanding for this destructive drift. He just feels better knowing that his kids realize it was indeed his self-absorbed mistakes and not any disregard for them that left a big zero where a father should have been standing. That recognition cleared the way for him to reconnect with his daughters as a friend. "I call them up, 'Watcha doin'?' You know, I'm knowing my daughters now. We are rebuilding our relationship now. They are pretty cool about it."

Clark might not have been able to reconstruct his family life years later if it had not been for Ramona, the woman he ultimately married. She gave him new hope and some of the emotional reserves that he needed to put his life back together after his jail term. Clark and Ramona met in Phoenix House, the drug-rehab program where he got a job as a staff counselor. Clark's job involved designing and monitoring treatment programs for as many as ten and twenty people at a time, running encounter groups where all kinds of hostilities and fears are aired, and young drug addicts are "busted down," their egos battered into submission. Only then will they accept their responsibility for treatment, or so the Phoenix House philosophy goes. Clark was seen as a successful graduate of the program, a veteran of more than a year's worth of tough love.

When Clark arrived in the Bronx facility to collect a group of new drug-treatment "clients," he found Ramona standing on the steps, looking quite fetching. "I swear to God," Clark says with a slightly sheepish grin, "this might sound corny, but when I looked at her I knew she was gonna be mine." He didn't say a word to Ramona, but his heart skipped a beat or two and he scurried around looking for her records. Clark managed to get Ramona assigned to Phoenix House where he knew he'd get a chance to get a bit closer. They spent weeks circling each other. Ramona was suspicious of his attention and Clark, well, he was too cool to let on about his intentions. They sparred over her treatment, with Clark taking advantage of the authority his counseling position afforded.

> She was leaning against the wall when she came in, and in Phoenix House you are not supposed to lean against the wall. No. You stand up straight. You're not supposed to have your hand in your pocket or nothing like that. Right? So I'm a counselor, so I give out "haircuts" on the floor. A haircut is when you verbally chastise somebody. So Ramona is leaning on the wall. "Get up off my wall!" I let her have it. She was just coming out of induction [intake] and knows the basics, but she don't know [exactly] where this guy's coming from.

Clark started visiting her "encounters," group counseling sessions designed to get the anger out. He would "let her have it" some more and then walk out. Eventually, for reasons known perhaps only to Ramona, they started having more civilized conversations. They fell for each other to the point where all Clark wanted was to get Ramona out of Phoenix House and into his house. She obliged by dropping out of the program and joining him at home.

They lived together for the next eleven years or so and then finally tied the knot. Their wedding day was one of the high points of his life, Clark says. They have been together now for sixteen years, though their lives have hardly been trouble free. Clark's drug problems always linger in the background and threaten to erupt, despite the fact that he was once a poster boy for Phoenix House, praised for having overcome his habit, his prison record, and his bad attitude. He has been in and out of jail during his years with Ramona, most recently for posing as a janitor and stealing laptop computers and pocketbooks from midtown offices. Ramona sticks by him and is always waiting for him upon his return, but it has not been an easy ride. She faces a lot of criticism from her family for putting up with Clark. They are right, lord knows, that he has serious problems. He doesn't blame them for being worried.

"They want to see her happy," he says, "but with someone who is doing something with his life." Unfortunately, and with cause, "they don't see it coming from me."

> I don't want to be responsible for anybody's happiness in that way because I have a history of letting people down. I build people up to the point where they depend on me for a lot of things. I deliver up to a certain point and then I just . . . [blow it]. I carry a lot of guilt because I have disappointed a lot of people . . . a lot of people, and myself as well. I have seen people cry over me. I don't like to disappoint people. So don't make me responsible for your happiness. I like a woman who have lives other than me . . . who have their own job, own career and their own interests other than me.

The last time we interviewed Clark, he had been on release for a month and swore that this time it would be different. For better or for worse, though, Ramona and Clark remain a couple. It is more than he deserves, as Clark is all too quick to point out.

Entering middle age with a rocky biography and limited prospects for an economically feasible "retirement," Clark is almost entirely dependent upon his wife's fortunes. He has no money, no job, and no serious prospects for one. What he has is Ramona. To a more limited extent, he also has his daughters, thanks to Tricia's desire to keep their father in the picture. Most men with prison records of this kind are not so fortunate; they lose everyone.[13] It is hard to know the degree to which necessity has been the mother of invention in Clark's case.[14]

If we want to know what growing old is going to mean for Clark and Ramona, we can see at this point that it is probably going to be shared. At least if the past sixteen years is any guide, Clark will most likely remain "coupled," while Cheryl will not. Older men, even those with very complicated pasts, are "in demand" in communities where so many men have disappeared from women's lives.

Pulling the lens backward from the details of these individual lives, it seems clear that the story of men and women in the inner city remains complex throughout middle age and the elder years. For some, like Reynaldo's parents, it is a story that looks to a census taker like a marriage that dissolved into divorce, even though the divorce was "in name only," to protect welfare benefits. Those on the inside know that this is a long-"married" couple that can now dandle a couple of grandchildren on their knees. . . .

Clark, too, has found a family in Ramona, and has tentatively reached out to the children he left behind through his many bouts in jail and the end of his relationship with their mother. Though he hates to admit it, his relationship with Ramona is really "her call," since she is the one with steady employment and he is, for all intents and purposes, dependent upon her. That is rarely a recipe for stability and his history does not suggest much stability in his future. Yet he would retort that he and Ramona have been together for sixteen years now and if that is not evidence of staying power, what is?

It is a long run that women like Cheryl have not really known in their lives, sometimes by choice and other times by default. They are without much male company nowadays and have not been active in the romance department for some time. Still, they are hardly alone in any other sense. For years now they have had their children and now their grandchildren for company. It is not always quite what they wanted. At times they would have been just as happy to be alone, or at least free from obligation, especially from their teenage grandchildren, who are often a source of trouble in their lives. Yet each of them has one special child who has managed to hang in there and made their elder years more worthwhile, and certainly not bereft of company.

During the 1970s, minority families—particularly "the black family"—came under heavy attack as deviant, destructive, and the source of our poverty problem. Liberal social scientists rushed to the rescue, pointing to the resilience of single-parent households, the creative use of social networks and private safety nets to shore up a poverty-stricken community, the essential dignity of mothers and the struggling, and morally culpable, absent fathers. From the vantage point of a new century, it seems only fair to note that the resilience and heroic effort is real enough. *A Different Shade of Gray* is filled with stories of women (and sometimes men) who have shouldered burdens that would break most people. They are the only safety net under their children, the main caretakers who look after the elderly, and even the final safe haven for men who may have been an irregular presence for twenty years. Their steadfastness in the face of adversity is to be admired.

At the same time, the costs of problematic family life are enormous and should not be cast aside in a rush to avoid "blaming the victim." The emotional toll that failed relationships take, particularly on women, can be devastating to self-esteem and foster a hard shell as they try to shield themselves from future disappointments. Children are damaged by the loss of their fathers, and even if they reconnect when they are all grown up, they are less trusting and more likely to repeat the family breakdown in their own lives. Finally, the financial costs, to which we return in the conclusion, are enormous. Without two incomes to support a household, it is increasingly difficult to escape the clutches of poverty; if they had had more money in the bank, they would probably have departed along with the millions of others who took to the highways and headed for the suburbs. Lacking income, they were stuck in deteriorating neighborhoods, unable to amass the equity in housing, the savings in bank accounts, or the social security that comes to married people. As inequality has grown in the United States since the mid-1970s, single parents have fallen further and further behind married couples in financial terms. The consequences for their children, in school performance, in health outcomes, and in risks of poverty, are severe and lasting.

August Wilson's fictional character Tonya knew all this without cracking the cover of a sociology textbook. That's why she wanted King to stay with her, whatever the cost to his manhood. "Be there," she said. But by the end of *King Hedley II*, Tonya's worst nightmare comes to pass: King dies, killed accidentally by his own mother. It is a sorrowful and sobering tale without even a semblance of a happy ending. We come away respecting the sacrifices Tonya and Ruby have made to raise their kids, acknowledging the noble aims King and Elmore have for wanting to make something of themselves. We know as well that those many years of separation and disappointment have taken a huge toll on everyone onstage—and in the real world, too.

■ Review Questions ■

1. What led Cheryl to urge her daughter Janet to keep the father of Janet's children in the children's lives?
2. Why are older men in African American communities more isolated from kin than are older women?

ENDNOTES

1. All quotations taken from August Wilson, *King Hedley II: A Play in Two Acts* (1999). Performed May 24, 2000, by Huntington Theatre Company, Boston.
2. See Andrew J. Cherlin, ed., *The Changing American Family and Public Policy* (Washington, D.C.: Urban Institute Press, 1988); Frank F. Furstenberg, Jr., and Andrew J. Cherlin, *Divided Families: What Happens to Children When Parents Part* (Cambridge, MA: Harvard University Press, 1991); Andrew J. Cherlin, *Marriage, Divorce, Remarriage* (revised and enlarged edition) (Cambridge, MA: Harvard University Press, 1992); Irwin Garfinkel, Sara S.

McLanahan, Philip Robins, eds., *Child Support and Child Well-Being* (Washington, D.C.: Urban Institute Press 1994); Sara McLanahan, Irwin Garfinkel, and Dorothy Watson, *Family Structure, Poverty, and the Underclass* (Madison: University of Wisconsin-Madison, Institute for Research on Poverty, 1987); Sara McLanahan and Gary Sandefur, *Growing Up with a Single Parent: What Hurts, What Helps* (Cambridge, MA: Harvard University Press, 1994); Sara McLanahan and Karen Booth, *Mother-Only Families: Problems, Reproduction, and Politics* (Madison: University of Wisconsin-Madison, Institute for Research on Poverty, 1988); Irwin Garfinkel and Sara S. McLanahan, *Single Mothers and Their Children: A New American Dilemma* (Washington, D.C.: Urban Institute Press, 1986).

3. Orlando Patterson, *Rituals of Blood: Consequences of Slavery in Two American Centuries* (New York: Civitas/CounterPoint, 1998), writes: "Afro-Americans are the most unpartnered and isolated group of people in America and quite possibly in the world. Unlike any other group of Americans, most of them will go through most of their adult lives without any deep and sustained attachment to a non-kin companion" (p. 4). Patterson argues that gender relations in the black world are as bitter and dysfunctional as they could be. Patterson cites a study conducted at Temple University in which working- and lower-class blacks were asked if there was distrust and even hatred between black men and black women. Sixty-six percent of men and 74 percent of women answered affirmatively (p. 5). Patterson traces much of the problem to the legacy of slavery. He argues that while other groups in the United States have faced similar economic and social problems, such as "rural and urban poverty, ethnic persecution, and economic discrimination," only blacks exhibit such strained gender relations and the high rate of paternal abandonment (p. 159). What sets Afro-Americans apart is the historical fact of slavery and no explanation of Afro-American families is complete without a discussion of the slave system. The slavery system conducted an "[assault] on the roles of father and husband" and produced a hostile environment for "pregnancy, women, childbirth, infancy, and childrearing" (p. 159).

4. See Robert William Fogel and Stanley Engerman, *Time on the Cross: The Economics of*

American Negro Slavery* (Boston: Little, Brown, 1974); Eugene Genovese, *Roll, Jordan Roll* (New York: Pantheon Books, 1974); Herbert G. Gutman, *The Black Family in Slavery and Freedom, 1750–1925* (New York: Pantheon, 1976); Paul J. Lammermier, "The Urban Black Family in the Nineteenth Century: A Study of Black Family Structure in the Ohio Valley, 1850–1880," *Journal of Marriage and the Family* 35 (August 1973), pp. 440–56; Charles Vert Willie, *Black and White Families: A Study in Complementarity* (New York: General Hall, 1985).

5. This pattern refers to children in any single-parent family. Patterson, *Rituals of Blood,* writes: "Sixty percent of Afro-American children are now being brought up without the emotional or material support of a father" (p. 4).

6. Andrew J. Cherlin, "Generation Ex-: Review of the Unexpected Legacy of Divorce: A 25-Year Study by Judith S. Wallerstein, Julia Lewis and Sandra Blakeslee: Hyperion Press," *The Nation,* December 11, 2000, pp. 62–64. Divorce rates have skyrocketed over the past century. About half of all marriages contracted in 1967 will end in divorce. Of the marriages contracted a hundred years earlier, only about 5 percent ended in divorce. Steven Ruggles, "The Rise of Divorce and Separation in the United States, 1880–1990," *Demography* 34 (2) (November 1997), pp. 455–66. See also Cherlin, *Marriage, Divorce, Remarriage;* Teresa Castro Martin and Larry L. Bumpass, "Recent Trends in Marital Disruption," *Demography* 26 (1) (February 1989), pp. 37–51; David Lester, "Trends in Divorce and Marriage around the World," *Journal of Divorce and Remarriage* 25 (1–2), pp. 169–71.

7. Kathryn Edin, "What Do Low-Income Single Mothers Say about Marriage?" *Social Problems* 47 (1) (February 2000), pp. 112–33, provides a discussion of women's reluctance to marry. She interviews 292 low-income single mothers and finds that several factors contribute to the women's reluctance to marry. The economic position of potential husbands is very important. Most of the women believe that the man should earn considerably more than minimum wage before he becomes marriage material. The women assess a man's economic position by looking at the regularity of his earnings, the effort expended to keep his job, and the sources of his income. Irregular earnings, illegal

sources of income, and little effort in maintaining or looking for work all disqualify potential mates as spouses. Other studies substantiate Edin's findings. See Pamela J. Smock and Wendy D. Manning, "Cohabiting Partners' Economic Circumstances and Marriage," *Demography* 34 (3) (August 1997), pp. 331–41, and Wendy D. Manning and Pamela J. Smock, "Why Marry? Race and the Transition to Marriage among Cohabitors," *Demography* 32 (4) (November 1995), pp. 509–20. Kathryn Edin also finds that women are reluctant to marry for non-monetary reasons. The respondents believe that a woman's social standing is tied to that of her husband. Thus, only a man who can bring a woman "respectability" is viewed as a good match. If the man is not able to maintain a job, then his class standing disqualifies him from consideration. Issues of control also enter into marriage decisions. Many women are unwilling to enter into marriage if they believe they will have to fulfill a subservient role. Finally, many women avoid marriage because of their distrust of men in general and because of their fear of domestic violence.

8. Elijah Anderson, *Streetwise,* suggests that "sexual relations, exploitative and otherwise" are as common among middle-class teenagers as they are among the lower-class adolescent respondents. In contrast to the middle-class youths, however, the young men see "no future to derail" by having a child (p. 113). Thus sex, and the offspring as the result, becomes a source of status for the boys. Anderson finds that the young fathers who maintain strong links to their peer group, often "congregate on street corners, boasting about their sexual exploits and deriding conventional family life" (p. 112). This boasting is important because it provides proof of the man's sexual prowess. Finding willing female partners requires men to have a good game: gaining a girl's confidence and favor enough for her to sleep with him. Seducing many different women garners the boy more respect from his friends while continued rejection by women earns him strong ridicule. See also Anderson, *Code of the Street,* pp. 142–78; and Anderson, "Sex Codes and the Family Life among Poor Inner-City Youths," pp. 59–78.

9. Timothy Nelson, Kathryn Edin, and Susan Clampet-Lundquist, "'Doin' the Best I Can': How Low-Income Non-Custodial Fathers in Philadelphia Talk about Their Families," unpublished manuscript (May 16, 2000), find in their sample of low-income, noncustodial fathers that few of them provide consistent financial support to all of their offspring. Many of the men are highly involved when the children are initially born yet this involvement tends to drop off sharply as the children get older. This is particularly true if the relationship between the man and the child's mother is not amicable. Despite this fact, Nelson et al. find that fatherhood has strong symbolic meaning for the men. Indeed, the authors assert that "low-income non-custodial fathers generally ascribe tremendous importance to their children and firmly believe that their lives would be infinitely less meaningful without [them]" (p. 2). Many of the men in the study describe their lives in "before and after": before having children and after having them. Contrary to what the researchers expected, most of the men said that becoming fathers changed their lives for the better. Many of the men describe fatherhood as their salvation: having children had prompted them to change their ways or at least cut back on dangerous behavior. Many also describe the "irrevocable nature of one's status as a father" (p. 22). Unlike other relationships, this bond could not be broken. The authors suggest that fatherhood holds such a cherished position in these men's lives for several reasons. First, children provide the only opportunity for the men to experience social advancement. Secondly, children provide a means of achieving "immortality" (p. 23). Having children leaves some evidence that you were "on the planet" (p. 24). See also Kathryn Edin, Timothy Nelson, and Rechelle Paranal, "Fatherhood and Incarceration as Potential Turning Points in the Criminal Careers of Unskilled Men," unpublished manuscript (May 5, 2001).

10. The Great Migration began between World War I and World War II and gathered steam as the factories pumped out munitions for the war effort. Altogether, some 5 million African Americans decamped from the rural South and journeyed first to the southern cities and then to the northern cities where booming factories were short of labor. See Nicholas Lemann, *The Promised Land: The Great Black Migration and How It Changed America* (New York: Knopf, 1991).

11. Research has shown that people of similar socioeconomic status usually marry one another. This is commonly measured using education: the spouses

have equivalent levels of education. However, persons with dissimilar amounts of education do get married. During the 1990s, when marriage (or cohabitation) occurred between people of dissimilar educational attainment, it was more likely for the woman to be better educated than the man. Zhenchao Qian, "Changes in Assortative Mating: The Impact of Age and Education, 1970–1990," *Demography* 35 (3) (August 1998), pp. 279–92. Moreover, these dissimilar unions were more likely to take place between people of lower educational attainment. Robert Mare, "Five Decades of Educational Assortative Mating," *American Sociological Review* 56 (February 1991), pp. 15–32. See also Matthijs Kalmijn, "Assortative Mating by Cultural and Economic Occupational Status," *American Journal of Sociology* 100 (2) (September 1994), pp. 422–52; Matthijs Kalmijn, "Status Homogamy in the United States," *American Journal of Sociology* 97 (2) (September 1991), pp. 496–523; and Robert Mare, "Five Decades of Educational Assortative Mating," *American Sociological Review* 56 (February 1991), pp. 15–32.

12. See Bruce Western and Katherine Beckett, "How Unregulated Is the US Labor Market?: The Penal System as a Labor Market Institution," *American Journal of Sociology* 104 (4) (January 1999), pp. 1030–60. The number of people incarcerated in the United States has risen dramatically since 1980. In 1980, 500,000 people were in prison. By 1996 the number of people had risen to more than 1.6 million (pp. 1034–1035). Moreover, an increasing percentage of inmates are black. Afro-Americans accounted for 22 percent of the prison population in 1930. Sixty-two years later blacks comprised more than half of the country's inmates (p. 1035). Prison time has become part of many black men's lives: one out of every three black male youth "was under some form of state supervision" and about 7 percent of black male adults were serving time in 1995 (p. 1035). This situation is not found with whites. While the incarceration rate (incarceration per 100,000) for blacks in 1992–93 was 1,947, the rate was only 306 for whites (p. 1036, Table 2). The United States has a much larger prison population than other industrialized countries. Western and Beckett argue that this is not a product of higher crime

rates in the United States. Instead, they suggest that incarceration rates have risen because of "more aggressive prosecutorial practices, tougher sentencing standards, and intensified criminalization of drug-related activity" (p. 1037). The United States imprisons more drug and property offenders than other industrialized countries. In 1994, for instance, about 30 percent of state prison inmates were convicted of nonviolent drug offenses. In contrast, nonviolent offenders made up only 6 percent of the state prison population in 1979 (p. 1037). See also Bruce Western, Jeffrey R. Kling, and David F. Weiman, "The Labor Market: Consequences of Incarceration," *Crime and Delinquency* 47 (3) (July 2001), pp. 410–27.

13. Edin, Nelson, and Paranal, "Fatherhood and Incarceration as Potential Turning Points in the Criminal Careers of Unskilled Men," conducted a study between 1995 and 2001 of 300 low-income noncustodial fathers living in Philadelphia and Charleston. The researchers find that many men who are incarcerated attempt to reconnect with their families after they are released. However, this process can be quite difficult and in many cases incarceration severely damages relationships that were fragile to begin with. Nearly all of those respondents who had a romantic relationship before going to prison saw their relationship crumble due to incarceration. Their girlfriends either broke it off and/or began a relationship with someone else. After the men were released, their former partners often refused to reestablish the connection. This refusal to let the men back in their lives also caused problems in the relationship between the father and the child. "[Mothers] are generally the conduit through which communication with children flows"; thus the men had a more difficult time remaining in their children's lives (p. 8). The researchers even found some cases in which fathers attempted to reconnect with their girlfriends/wives and children but were unable to because they could not find them. The women had moved away without notifying the father (p. 22). U.S. law can also make it more difficult for fathers to reunite with their children. The 1997 ASFA adds more criteria to a previous law, which enables the state to terminate the parents' rights if the child has been in foster care for fifteen or more months out of the last

twenty-two months. John Hagen and Juleigh Petty Coleman, "Returning Captives of the American War on Drugs: Issues of Community and Family Reentry," *Crime and Delinquency* 47 (3) (July 2001), pp. 352–67. See also C. F. Hairston, "The Forgotten Parent: Understanding the Forces that Influence Incarcerated Fathers' Relationships with their Children," *Child Welfare* 77 (5), pp. 617–39; Sara McLanahan and Bruce Western, "Fathers Behind Bars," *Contemporary Perspectives in Family Research* 2 (1996), pp. 309–24; Robert J. Sampson and John H. Laub, "Crime and Deviance over the Life Course: The Salience of Adult Social Bonds," *American Sociological Review* 55 (1990), pp. 609–27.

14. Economic necessity, and the need for caretaking services, keeps many a middle-class couple together too. Data collected since 1860 show a general rise in divorce rates over the past 150 years. However, the divorce rate has fluctuated with economic expansion and depression. Cherlin, *Marriage, Divorce, Remarriage,* finds that the annual divorce rate increased after every major war. In contrast, it decreased during the Great Depression. There is no reason to believe this is the case because somehow people get along so much better under conditions of economic stress. More likely, men and women who would be even more vulnerable apart stick together out of necessity. Indeed, Cherlin argues this very point: because jobs and housing were scarce, many couples chose to stay together (or at least to postpone their divorce). Cherlin, *Marriage, Divorce, Remarriage,* pp. 21, 23. By the same token, it has been suggested that welfare freed up poor women from a degree of dependence and that divorce rates rose in response to their freedom. That freedom can evaporate, as it has in Clark's case, when there are no good options for economic independence. Indeed, he has to hope that he and Ramona stick with their relationship, because without it he would be in deep, deep trouble.

Part Five

Conflict, Disruption, and Reconstitution

CHAPTER 11

Domestic Violence

The problem of violence against women in families and in other intimate settings is not new. Yet only within the past few decades has much attention been paid to it, thanks mostly to the feminist movement. Government responses were initially modest. The U.S. Congress did not pass the Violence Against Women Act until the summer of 1994, when the murder of Nicole Simpson, O.J. Simpson's wife, focused the public's attention on battered women. Since then, however, there has been much public and scholarly attention to the topic.

Physical abuse by a spouse or romantic partner is sometimes not just an isolated act but, rather, part of a broader attempt by the man to control the woman. In fact, Michael P. Johnson, in the first selection, argues that we should distinguish between two kinds of domestic violence. The first, and most common, kind occurs in couples who have an occasional dispute that leads to some moderately violent act, such as slapping or hitting, by both men and women. Most surveys that ask about abuse, Johnson says, capture responses about this "situational" kind of violence. Less common but more damaging, he argues, is a pattern of severe, repeated violence on the part of men who seek to control their partner's behavior. The helping professionals who run shelters for battered women see the victims of these "intimate terrorists," as Johnson calls them.

How should law enforcement respond to domestic violence? Before the 1980s, when the police were called by a victim of intimate partner violence, who was almost always a woman, they rarely arrested the alleged assailant, almost always a boyfriend or husband. But starting in the 1980s, police departments, under pressure from advocates for battered women, began arresting the violent man more often in domestic violence calls. In an influential experiment in Minnesota, police officers were randomly assigned to arrest the batterer rather than merely offering mediation or telling the man to leave the location. If they were assigned to arrest a batterer, they did so whether or not the victim requested it. Supporters of mandatory arrest laws argued that some victims did not request an arrest or press charges because they were afraid of retaliation by the man or did not want him to go to jail. The mandatory arrest policy took the matter out of the victims' hands.

The results of the experiment suggested that men who were arrested were less likely to commit future violence. In response, many states and localities enacted laws that required the police to arrest an assailant if probable cause existed that he (or, more rarely, she) had been violent. But the mandatory arrest policy has been controversial. Subsequent studies have shown that it is not always better to arrest the perpetrator; rather, it depends on the situation. As a result, some advocates and observers are backing off from supporting mandatory arrests. But what kind of guidance does one then provide to the police and the courts? In the second reading, Amy Leisenring reviews and comments on this issue. In doing so, she returns to the distinctions between different kinds of domestic violence that Johnson makes in the first reading.

READING 11-1

Control and Violence in Intimate Relationships

Michael P. Johnson

One woman we interviewed told us that she was first beaten on her honeymoon and when she cried and protested, her husband replied, "I married you so I own you."[1]

In order to understand the nature of an individual's use of violence in an intimate relationship, you have to understand its role in the general control dynamics of that relationship. Some people use violence as one of many tactics in a general strategy aimed at taking complete control over their partner, as in the case of the newlywed husband quoted above. Others may become violent in order to resist their partner's attempts to control them. For still others, their violent behavior may have little to do with control. In this chapter I will distinguish among four types of intimate partner violence that are defined by the extent to which the perpetrator and his or her partner use violence in order to attempt to control the relationship. The four types constitute a typology of *individual* violence that is rooted in information about the couple and defined by the control context within which the violence is embedded (Table 11.1).

In *intimate terrorism,* the perpetrator uses violence in the service of general control over his or her partner; the partner does not. In *violent resistance,* the partner is violent and controlling—an intimate terrorist—and the resister's violence arises in reaction to that attempt to exert general control.[2] In *mutual violent control,* both members of the couple use violence in attempts to gain general control over their partner. Thus, three of the four types of intimate partner violence are

Michael P. Johnson, *A Typology of Domestic Violence* (Boston: Northeastern University Press, 2008). Chapter 1, pp. 5–24, "Control and Violence in Intimate Relationships." © University Press of New England, Lebanon, NH. Reprinted with permission.

TABLE 11.1

TYPES OF DOMESTIC VIOLENCE

Intimate Terrorism
The individual is violent and controlling.
The partner is not.

Violent Resistance
It is the partner who is violent and controlling.
The individual is violent, but not controlling.

Situational Couple Violence
Although the individual is violent,
neither partner is both violent and controlling.

Mutual Violent Resistance
Both individual and partner are violent and controlling.

organized around attempts to exert or thwart general control. In the fourth type of intimate partner violence, *situational couple violence,* the perpetrator is violent (and his or her partner may be as well); however, neither of them uses violence to attempt to exert general control.

The control that forms the basis of this typology of intimate partner violence and is the defining feature of intimate terrorism, is more than the specific, short-term control that is often the goal of violence in other contexts. The mugger wants to control you only briefly in order to take your valuables and move on, hopefully never to see you again. In contrast, the control sought in intimate terrorism is general and long term. Although each particular act of intimate violence may appear to have any number of short-term, specific goals, it is embedded in a larger pattern of power and control that permeates the relationship. This is the violence employed by the newlywed batterer quoted above, who sees his behavior as the embodiment of his "ownership" of his partner.

The core idea of this book is that this "intimate terrorism"—violence deployed in the service of general control over one's partner—is quite a different phenomenon than violence that is not motivated by an interest in exerting general control over one's partner. I would argue, also, that intimate terrorism is what most of us *mean* by "domestic violence." This is the violence that

FIGURE 11.1
The Power and Control Wheel. (*Source:* Domestic Violence/Intimate Terrorism adapted from Ellen Pence and Michael Paymar, *Education Groups for Men Who Batter: The Duluth Model* [New York: Springer, 1993].)

has received massive media attention, and that has been the focus of thirty years of feminist activism and research in the United States.

INTIMATE TERRORISM AND OTHER TYPES OF PARTNER VIOLENCE

Intimate Terrorism

Our discussion of the four types of partner violence begins with intimate terrorism because it involves the general exercise of coercive control that is the heart of the distinctions posed here. Figure 11.1 is a widely used graphical representation of partner violence deployed in the service of general control. This diagram and the understanding of domestic violence that lies behind it were developed over a period of years from the testimony of battered women in the Duluth, Minnesota, area, testimony that convinced the staff of the Duluth Domestic Abuse Intervention

Project that the most important characteristic of the violence that they encountered was that it was embedded in a general pattern of power and control.[3] A *pattern* of power and control cannot, of course, be identified by looking at violence in isolation or by looking at one incident. It can only be recognized from information about the use of multiple control tactics over time, allowing one to find out whether a perpetrator uses more than one of these tactics to control his or her partner, indicating an attempt to exercise general control.

Let's work our way around the "spokes" of the diagram, clockwise, beginning with economic abuse at one o'clock. It is not unusual for an intimate terrorist to deprive his partner of control over economic resources.[4] He controls all the money. She is allowed no bank account and no credit cards. If she works for wages, she has to turn over her paychecks to him. He keeps all the cash and she has to ask him for money when she needs to buy groceries or clothes for herself or the children. He may require a precise accounting of every penny, demanding to see the grocery bill and making sure she returns every bit of the change. This economic abuse may be justified through the next form of control, male privilege: "I am the man of the house, the head of the household, the king in my castle." Of course, this use of male privilege can cover everything. As the man of the house, his word is law. He doesn't have to explain. She doesn't disagree with him. She is to do his bidding without question. And she doesn't talk back. All of this holds even more rigidly in public, where he is not to be humiliated by smart-talk from "his woman."

How does he use the children to support his control? First of all, they, too, know he is the boss. He makes it clear that he controls not only them, but their mother as well. He may use them to back him up, to make her humiliation more complete by forcing them into the room to assist him as he confronts her, asking them if he isn't right, and making them support his control of her. He may even have convinced them that he *should* be in charge, that he does know

what is best (father knows best), and that she is incompetent or stupid or immoral. In addition, he may use her attachment to the children as a means of control, by threatening to take them away from her or hurt them if she isn't a "good wife and mother." Of course, being a good wife and mother means doing as he says.

Then there's isolation. Keep her away from everyone else. Make *himself* her only source of information, of support, of money, of everything. In a rural setting he might be able to literally isolate her, moving to a house trailer in the woods, with one car that he controls, no phone, keeping her there alone. In an urban setting, or if he needs her to go out to work, he can isolate her, though less literally, by driving away her friends and relatives and intimidating the people at work, so that she has no one to talk to about what's happening to her. When she's completely isolated, and what he tells her about herself is all she ever hears about herself, he can tell her over and over again that she's worthless, humiliate her, demean her, emotionally abuse her. She's ugly, stupid, a slut, a lousy wife, an incompetent mother. She only manages to survive because he takes care of her. She'd be helpless without him. And who else is there to tell her otherwise? Maybe he can convince her that she can't live without him.

Related to this emotional abuse is minimizing or denying his own abuse, and blaming her for what is going on in the relationship. It's her crazy behavior or incompetence or sexual misconduct that requires him to control her the way he does, in her own best interests. How could she see him as abusive? He's never really hurt her. On the contrary, she's the abusive partner. She's so out of touch with reality that maybe she should get some help.

If she resists, intimidate her. Show her what might happen if she doesn't behave. Scream at her. Swear at her. Let her see his rage. Smash things. Or maybe a little cold viciousness will make his point. Kick her cat. Hang her dog. That ought to make her think twice before she decides not to do as he says. Or threaten her. Threaten to hit her, or beat her, or pull her hair out, or burn her. Or tell her he'll kill her, maybe the kids, too.

Put all these means of control together, or even a few of them, and the abuser builds what Catherine Kirkwood calls a "web" of abuse.[5] He entraps and enslaves his partner. If she manages to thwart one means of control, there are others at his disposal. Wherever she turns, there is another way he can control her. Sometimes she is ensnared by multiple strands. She can't seem to escape—she is trapped. But with the addition of violence, there is more than entrapment. There is terror.

For this reason the diagram does not include the violence as just another means of control, another spoke in the wheel. The violence is depicted, rather, as the rim of the wheel, holding all the spokes together. When violence is added to such a pattern of power and control, the abuse becomes much more than the sum of its parts. The ostensibly nonviolent tactics that accompany that violence take on a new, powerful, and frightening meaning, controlling the victim not only through their own specific constraints, but also through their association with the general knowledge that her partner will do anything to maintain control of the relationship, even attack her physically. Most obviously, the threats and intimidation are something more than idle threats if he has beaten her before. But beyond that, his "request" to see the grocery receipts becomes a "warning" if he has put her into the hospital this year. His calling her a stupid slut may feel like the beginning of a vicious physical attack. As battered women often report, "All he had to do was look at me that way, and I'd jump." What is for most of us the safest place in our world, home, is for her a place of constant fear.

Violent Resistance

What is a woman to do when she finds herself terrorized in her own home?[6] At some point, most women in such relationships do fight back physically. For some, this is an instinctive reaction to being attacked, and it happens at the first blow—almost without thought. For others, it doesn't happen until it seems he is going to continue to assault her if she doesn't do something to stop him. For most women in heterosexual relationships, the size difference ensures that violent resistance won't help, and may make things worse, so they turn to other means of coping. For a few, eventually it seems that the only way out is to kill him.

The critical defining pattern of violent resistance is that the resister is violent but *not* controlling and is faced with a partner who is *both* violent and controlling; i.e., he is an intimate terrorist. Violence in the face of intimate terrorism may arise from any of a variety of motives. She may (at least at first) believe that she can defend herself, that her violent resistance will keep him from attacking her further. That may mean that she thinks she can stop him right now, in the midst of an attack, or it may mean that she thinks that if she fights back often enough he will eventually decide to stop attacking her physically. Even if she doesn't think she can stop him, she may feel that he shouldn't be allowed to attack her without getting hurt some himself. This desire to hurt him in return even if it won't stop him can be a form of communication ("What you're doing isn't right and I'm going to fight back as hard as I can"), or it may be a form of retaliation or payback, along the lines of "He's not going to do that without paying some price for it." In a few cases, she may be after serious retaliation, attacking him when he is least expecting it and doing her best to do serious damage, even killing him. But there is another, more frequent motive for such premeditated attacks—escape. Sometimes, after years of abuse and entrapment, a victim of intimate terrorism may feel that the only way she can escape from this horror is to kill her tormenter. Such cases have been the focus of some media attention, as in movies such as *The Burning Bed, Sleeping with the Enemy,* and *Enough.* More importantly, the "battered woman defense" has achieved some credibility in the courts;[7] governors and parole boards have been considering clemency, pardons, or parole in cases in which the motive for the murder of an abusive partner was clearly to escape from a seemingly hopeless situation.[8]

Situational Couple Violence

Probably the most common type of partner violence does not involve any attempt on the part of either partner to gain general control over the relationship. The violence is situationally provoked, as the tensions or emotions of a particular encounter lead someone to react with violence. Intimate relationships inevitably involve conflicts, and in some relationships one or more of those conflicts may escalate to violence. The violence may be minor and singular, with one argument at some point in the relationship escalating to the level that someone pushes or slaps the other, is immediately remorseful, apologizes, and never does it again. Or it could be a chronic problem, with one or both partners frequently resorting to violence, minor or severe. I don't want to minimize the danger of such violence. Situationally provoked violence can be life-threatening.

The motives for such violence vary. A physical reaction might feel like the only way one's extreme anger or frustration can be expressed. It may well be intended to do serious injury as an expression of anger. It may primarily be an attempt to get the attention of a partner who doesn't seem to be listening. Or there could be a control motive involved, albeit not one that is part of a general pattern of coercive control. One partner may simply find that the argument is not going well for him or her, and decide that one way to win this is to get physical.

The critical distinctions among types of violence have to do with general patterns of power and control, not with the ostensible motives for specific incidents of violence. Thus, many of the separate violent incidents of situational couple violence may look exactly like those involved in intimate terrorism or violent resistance. The difference is in the general power and control dynamic of the relationship, not in the nature of

any one assault. If it appears that neither partner is generally trying to control the other—i.e., the relationship does not involve the use of a range of control tactics by one or both of the partners—then we are dealing with situational couple violence. It is simply that one or more disagreements have resulted in violence. The violence may even be frequent, if the situation that provokes the violence is recurring, as when one partner frequently feels that the other is flirting, and the confrontations over that issue regularly lead one or the other of them to lash out. And the violence may be quite severe, including even homicide. What makes it situational couple violence is that it is rooted in the events of a particular situation rather than in a relationshipwide attempt to control.

Mutual Violent Control

Finally, in a very small number of cases, both members of the couple are violent and controlling, each behaving in a manner that would identify him or her as an intimate terrorist if it weren't for the fact that their partner also seems to be engaged in the same sort of violent attempt to control the relationship. We know very little about the dynamics of such relationships other than that they seem to involve the "mutual combat" that researchers have for decades attributed to any relationship in which both partners reported that they had been violent. In most such cases, however, that so-called mutual violence was a product of intimate terrorism with violent resistance, or situational couple violence in which both partners had been violent. With mutual violent control, we have the true mutuality of two people fighting for general control over the relationship. . . .

Not Asking the Right Questions: The Battered Husband Fiasco

In 1977, in one of the first publications to come out of the groundbreaking 1975 National Family Violence Survey, Suzanne Steinmetz ignited a decades-long and not-yet-dead debate about the nature of partner violence. Her article, "The Battered Husband Syndrome," argued that there were as many battered husbands in U.S. families as there were battered wives.[9] Her article was immediately answered with intense criticism, a great scholarly debate ensued, and over the years hundreds of studies have addressed the issue of gender symmetry in partner violence.[10] While we have amassed a great deal of scientific evidence that men are far and away more likely than women to be perpetrators of domestic violence,[11] there also appears to be considerable evidence that women are just as likely as men to attack their partners.[12] The debate on this issue has been so acrimonious that, in the late 1990s, I was unable to persuade the protagonists to take part in a panel discussion of the issue at scholarly meetings, the parties basically refusing to be in the same room with each other. How did we come to have two groups of renowned scholars presenting ostensibly credible evidence for their obviously contradictory positions regarding the simplest possible question about partner violence: "Who does it?"?

The answer is that a terrible mistake characterized research on partner violence from the beginning of its development in the early 1970s. No one was thinking about distinguishing among types of partner violence. Researchers assumed that "violence was violence," that although there might be differences in how often and how severely partners assaulted each other, intimate partner violence was essentially one phenomenon. There were two major groups of social scientists doing this early research, but doing it from quite different perspectives and using different sources of data.[13] The "family violence scholars" were interested in violence between parents and their children and between siblings, as well as violence between spouses. Violence was seen as an outcome of family conflict. They did large-scale surveys, interviewing large numbers of U.S. husbands and wives, and were distressed to find that family conflict led many spouses, siblings, and parents to assault other family members in the privacy of their own homes.[14] The "feminist scholars" were focused more specifically on wife abuse. They studied agency data from the police, courts, emergency rooms, and shelters, and they interviewed women who had come to these agencies for help. Violence was seen as a product of patriarchal family traditions and general male dominance in the society. They were appalled at the number of women who were terrorized in their own homes.[15] The two groups of scholars did, however, have at least one thing in common: they each thought that their own research identified the true nature of partner violence. They have been at an impasse over the gender issue for almost thirty years.

The simple solution to this dilemma (simple once you see it) is that the two groups are studying different kinds of partner violence.[16] How can this be? In general, the studies that demonstrate the predominance of male violence involve agency data (courts, police agencies, hospitals, and shelters), while the studies that show gender symmetry involve the "representative" samples of large-scale survey research. Both of these research strategies are heavily biased, the former through its use of biased sampling frames (agency client lists), the latter through refusals. Although the biases of agency data are generally taken to be obvious,[17] representative sample surveys are mistakenly assumed to be unbiased. In fact, the final samples of so-called random sample surveys are *not* random—due to refusals. I have estimated, for example, that the refusal rate in the National Family Violence Surveys was approximately 40 percent rather than the 18 percent usually reported.[18] Could there be two qualitatively different forms of partner violence, one gender-symmetric and overrepresented in general surveys, the other male-perpetrated and overrepresented in agency samples?

In my early work (1995) on this question, I identified a number of agency-based studies and general surveys that used the same set of questions to assess the nature of partner violence.[19] My conclusion from comparing these findings was that the two sampling strategies identify partner violence that differs not only in gender symmetry, but also in a variety of other important ways. Agency samples identify partner violence that is more frequent, more likely to escalate, more severe, less likely to be mutual, and perpetrated almost entirely by men. This gender-asymmetric pattern resonated for me with feminist analyses of partner violence as one tactic in a general pattern of controlling behaviors used by some men to exercise general control over "their" women.[20] The asymmetry of such control contrasted dramatically, it seemed to me, with the family violence perspective's predominantly symmetric image of partner violence as a matter of conflict. I hypothesized that there were two qualitatively different forms/patterns of partner violence—one part of a general strategy of power and control (intimate terrorism), the other involving violence that is not part of a general pattern of control, probably a product of the escalation of couple conflict into violence (situational couple violence).[21] I argued that each research group was unknowingly studying only one of these two types of violence. Couples involved in situational couple violence are unlikely to become agency clients, because such situationally provoked violence does not, in most cases, call for police intervention, emergency room visits, Protection from Abuse orders, an escape to a shelter, or a divorce. Couples involved in intimate terrorism are unlikely to agree to participate in general surveys—the victims out of fear of reprisal from the batterer, the batterers out of fear of exposing themselves to intervention by the police or other agencies. Although these arguments seemed reasonable enough, my 1995 paper provides no direct evidence of their validity because, at that time, no one had made such distinctions among types of violence.

Here is the evidence. The data come from a unique study designed by Irene Frieze in the 1970s. The women she interviewed came from a variety of sources, including agencies (courts and shelters) and a general sample. Thus, if my theory

was correct, her sample was likely to include both situational couple violence and intimate terrorism (and its response, violent resistance). One source of respondents was a flyer placed in laundromats. The second source was a shelter sample of women who had sought help at one of the Pittsburgh area shelters for battered women. Another group consisted of women who had filed for a Protection from Abuse order (PFA) in the courts. The fourth source was women who lived on the same block as the women in each of the first three groups; i.e., this group had not been selected because of violence and, therefore, probably was quite similar to the typical general survey sample.

From the lengthy interview protocols, I chose one question to determine whether the husband and/or wife had been violent, as reported by the wife: "Has he (Have you) ever actually slapped or pushed you (him) or used other physical force with you (him)?" I also selected eleven questions tapping control tactics that did not involve violence toward one's partner. From them, I constructed a coercive control scale and split it into a high-control group and a low-control group. The information regarding the violence and control of both partners was then used to designate each spouse as either nonviolent or involved in one of the four types of partner violence. Given my initial interest in the gender debate, my first question was whether the Pittsburgh data supported my idea that (a) the violence in general survey samples consists mostly of situational couple violence, while the violence in agency samples is mostly intimate terrorism and violent resistance, and (b) situational couple violence is gender-symmetric, intimate terrorism is mostly male-perpetrated, with violent resistors therefore mostly women.

First, let's nail down the sampling argument. Do general survey samples tap primarily situational couple violence, while agency samples give access primarily to intimate terrorism (and violent resistance)? Looking first at male violence, Table 11.2 shows that in the Pittsburgh

TABLE 11.2

MEN'S VIOLENCE IN DIFFERENT SAMPLES

	Survey sample (n = 37)	Court sample (n = 35)	Shelter sample (n = 50)
Mutual violent control	0%	11%	2%
Intimate terrorism	11%	46%	66%
Violent resistance	3%	6%	4%
Situational couple violence	86%	37%	28%

TABLE 11.3

WOMEN'S VIOLENCE IN DIFFERENT SAMPLES

	Survey sample (n = 29)	Court sample (n = 29)	Shelter sample (n = 38)
Mutual violent control	0%	14%	3%
Intimate terrorism	3%	7%	5%
Violent resistance	10%	41%	61%
Situational couple violence	86%	31%	32%

study's general sample (a type of sample that is typical of family violence research), the violent men are involved mostly in situational couple violence, with only 11 percent of their violence being intimate terrorism. In the agency samples, intimate terrorism is much more typical, representing 46 percent of the men's violence in the court data and 66 percent in the shelter data. Table 11.3 presents the data regarding women's violence, which are the other side of the same picture. Situational couple violence dominates the women's violence in the survey sample, while violent resistance is the largest category in the shelter sample, with the court data being intermediate.

Before we move on, let's think about this for a moment. The results for the general sample are much as predicted: targets of intimate terrorism are evidently not willing to participate in general surveys, and we can reasonably assume that any findings from general surveys apply to situational couple violence, not to intimate terrorism. The data from the courts and the shelter, however, surprised me. I had expected agency data to be heavily dominated by men's intimate terrorism and women's violent resistance, but there are considerably more cases of situational couple violence than I had thought there would be. Where did I go wrong? I had mistakenly assumed that only intimate terrorism would frighten women enough to send them to the courts for a Protection from Abuse order, or to a shelter for support or temporary housing. I hadn't paid close enough attention to my own statements that even situational couple violence can be quite frequent and/or severe. And I

TABLE 11.4

GENDER SYMMETRY OF TYPES OF VIOLENCE

	Husbands	Wives	(n)
Intimate terrorism	89%	11%	(81)
Violent resistance	15%	85%	(61)
Situational couple violence	55%	45%	(167)
Mutual violent control*	50%	50%	(16)

*Mutual violent control is symmetrical by definition in heterosexual relationships.

hadn't taken seriously enough the evidence from general surveys (thus dealing with situational couple violence) that men's situational couple violence is much more likely than women's to produce injuries.[22] Shelters and courts are places that women turn to when they fear for their safety. Although intimate terrorism is certainly the type of violence that is most likely to produce such a reaction, situational couple violence involving a man assaulting a woman can also be severe enough or frequent enough to be quite frightening. Thus, although the relatively large number of cases of situational couple violence in the shelter and court samples was somewhat surprising, in retrospect the pattern makes sense.[23] General samples involve almost entirely cases of situational couple violence, while agency samples involve a mix of intimate terrorism and the most frightening cases of situational couple violence.[24]

The data in Tables 2 and 3 establish that the different sampling strategies do, indeed, tap different kinds of violence. Are the gender differences in violence type such that those biases could have created the gender debate? The answer clearly is "Yes," as you can see from Table 11.4. Eighty-nine percent of the intimate terrorists in the Pittsburgh data were men.[25] Of course, it follows that in this sample of heterosexual couples almost all of the violent resistance comes from women (85 percent). In dramatic contrast to the clear gendering of intimate terrorism and violent

resistance is situational couple violence, which is close to gender-symmetric, at least by the crude criterion of prevalence. . . . Mutual violent control, which is very rare, is gender-symmetric by definition in heterosexual couples, because it is defined by both partners' being violent and controlling.[26]

That explains the gender fiasco, doesn't it? Men and women are equally involved only in situational couple violence.[27] When someone goes on television or publishes a paper to pronounce that the survey evidence proves that women are as violent as men in intimate relationships, they are suggesting that women are as likely as men to be batterers and abusers—intimate terrorists. And the suggestion is not subtle. They tell stories about some of the few women who are, indeed, intimate terrorists,[28] or they are on a talk show in which the panel consists of "girls who beat up their boyfriends" or "men who are afraid of their wives." But we have just shown that *survey* data about violence are only about situational couple violence, not intimate terrorism. Intimate terrorism is in fact perpetrated almost entirely by men.

And situational couple violence isn't anything like intimate terrorism. Here are some data about the violence perpetrated by the men from the Pittsburgh study. The violence in men's intimate terrorism is quite frequent; the modal number of incidents in these marriages is one hundred.[29] The modal number of violent events in men's situational couple violence is one. Intimate terrorism escalated in severity of violence in 72 percent of the cases; situational couple violence escalated in only 29 percent. In terms of injuries, the violence of intimate terrorism was severe in 67 percent of the cases, compared to 29 percent of the cases of situational couple violence. These data do not leave much doubt that intimate terrorism and situational couple violence are not the same phenomenon.[30] We need to make these distinctions.

■ Review Questions

1. How does what Johnson calls "intimate terrorism" differ from what he calls "situational couple violence"?
2. Why do surveys find many more reports of the "situational" form of violence than of the "terrorism" form?

ENDNOTES

1. R. Emerson Dobash and Russell P. Dobash, *Violence against Wives: A Case against Patriarchy* (New York: Free Press, 1979), 94.
2. I have avoided using the term "perpetrator" here because it implies that the violent resister is the primary initiator of the violence in the relationship. That certainly is not the case for violent resistance. A violent resister is, however, a perpetrator in the sense of having committed a violent act, and should that violence come to the attention of the criminal justice system, "perpetrator" is the term that would be applied.
3. Ellen Pence and Michael Paymar, *Education Groups for Men Who Batter: The Duluth Model* (New York: Springer, 1993).
4. I am going to use gendered pronouns here because, as I will show later, the vast majority of intimate terrorists are men terrorizing female partners. That does not mean that women are never intimate terrorists. There are a small number of women who do terrorize their male partners, and there are also women in same-sex relationships who terrorize their partners. I will discuss both of these situations later. Suzanne K. Steinmetz, "The Battered Husband Syndrome," *Victimology* 2, no. 3-sup-4 (1977–78); Claire M. Renzetti, *Violent Betrayal: Partner Abuse in Lesbian Relationships* (Thousand Oaks, Calif.: Sage, 1992).
5. Catherine Kirkwood, *Leaving Abusive Partners: From the Scars of Survival to the Wisdom for Change* (Newbury Park, Calif.: Sage, 1993).

6. Once again, I will use gendered pronouns because most violent resisters are women in heterosexual relationships. There certainly are also violent resisters in same-sex relationships and in the small number of cases in which a woman is able to terrorize her male partner.
7. Lenore E. Walker, "Legal Self-Defense for Battered Women," in *Battering and Family Therapy: A Feminist Perspective,* ed. Marsali Hansen and Michele Harway (Thousand Oaks, Calif.: Sage, 1993); Lenore E. Walker, *Terrifying Love: Why Battered Women Kill and How Society Responds* (New York: Harper & Row, 1989).
8. Linda L. Ammons, "Dealing with the Nastiness: Mixing Feminism and Criminal Law in the Review of Cases of Battered Incarcerated Women—a Tenth-Year Reflection," *Buffalo Criminal Law Review* 4 (2001).
9. Steinmetz, "The Battered Husband Syndrome."
10. Elizabeth Pleck et al., "The Battered Data Syndrome: A Comment on Steinmetz's Article," *Victimology* 2 (1978).
11. Russell P. Dobash et al., "The Myth of Sexual Symmetry in Marital Violence," *Social Problems* 39, no. 1 (1992).
12. John Archer, "Sex Differences in Aggression between Heterosexual Partners: A Meta-Analytic Review," *Psychological Bulletin* 126, no. 5 (2000).
13. I use the word "groups" here loosely. Although some of the scholars within each group have collaborated with each other, these groups are identified primarily by the theoretical frameworks that drive their work and the sources from which they generally gather

their information. Michael P. Johnson, "Patriarchal Terrorism and Common Couple Violence: Two Forms of Violence against Women," *Journal of Marriage and the Family* 57, no. 2 (1995); Demie Kurz, "Social Science Perspectives on Wife Abuse: Current Debates and Future Directions," *Gender & Society* 3, no. 4 (1989): 489–505.

14. Richard J. Gelles, "Violence in the Family: A Review of Research in the Seventies," *Journal of Marriage & the Family* 42, no. 4 (1980); Murray A. Straus, "A General Systems Theory Approach to a Theory of Violence between Family Members," *Social Science Information* 12, no. 3 (1973); Murray A. Straus, Richard J. Gelles, and Suzanne K. Steinmetz, *Behind Closed Doors: Violence in the American Family* (Garden City, N.Y.: Doubleday, 1980).

15. Dobash and Dobash, *Violence against Wives;* Dell Martin, *Battered Wives* (New York: Pocket Books, 1976); Mildred Daley Pagelow, *Woman-Battering: Victims and Their Experiences* (Newbury Park, Calif.: Sage, 1981); Maria Roy, ed., *Battered Women: A Psychosociological Study of Domestic Violence* (New York: Van Nostrand Reinhold, 1977); Lenore E. Walker, *The Battered Woman* (New York: Harper & Row, 1979).

16. Johnson, "Patriarchal Terrorism and Common Couple Violence."

17. Murray A. Straus, "Injury and Frequency of Assault and the 'Representative Sample Fallacy' in Measuring Wife Beating and Child Abuse," in *Physical Violence in American Families.*

18. Johnson, "Patriarchal Terrorism and Common Couple Violence."

19. Much of the gender debate in the literature has centered on the inadequacies of these questions, called the Conflict Tactics Scales or CTS, as a means to assess partner violence. Dobash et al., "The Myth of Sexual Symmetry in Marital Violence"; Straus, "The Conflict Tactics Scales." Whatever the inadequacies of the CTS may be, it is the most widely used instrument for assessing level of partner violence. Comparing studies that all used the CTS eliminated this potential source of bias.

20. Dobash and Dobash, *Violence against Wives;* Pence and Paymar, *The Duluth Model;* Evan Stark and Anne Flitcraft, *Women at Risk: Domestic Violence and Women's Health* (Thousand Oaks, Calif.: Sage, 1996).

21. The terminology I use has changed somewhat over the years, although the definitions have remained the same. My 1995 paper refers to "patriarchal terrorism" and "common couple violence." I soon abandoned the former term because it begs the question of men's and women's relative involvement in this form of controlling violence. It also implies that all such intimate terrorism is somehow rooted in patriarchal structures, traditions, or attitudes. I still believe that intimate terrorism is perpetrated primarily by men in heterosexual relationships and that in such cases the violence is, indeed, rooted in patriarchal traditions. However, it is clear that there are women who are intimate terrorists in both heterosexual and same-sex relationships. Renzetti, *Violent Betrayal.* Furthermore, it is not necessarily the case that all intimate terrorism, even men's, is rooted in patriarchal ideas or structures. With regard to "common couple violence," I abandoned it in favor of "situational couple violence" because the former terminology implies to some readers that I feel that such violence is acceptable. I also prefer the new terminology because it more clearly identifies the roots of this violence in the situated escalation of conflict.

22. Jan E. Stets and Murray A. Straus, "Gender Differences in Reporting Marital Violence and Its Medical and Psychological Consequences," in *Physical Violence in American Families.*

23. It is also possible that there is a measurement error issue involved in this finding. The difference between situational couple violence (SCV) and intimate terrorism (IT) amounts to being on one side or the other of a cutoff between "low" and "high" on the Coercive Control Scale. The choice of cutoff is somewhat arbitrary, and there are likely to be some low-control cases that may actually involve intimate terrorism. This is one of those areas in social science where I am convinced that a reasonably well designed qualitative interview could give us better information than can an "objective" scale. In fact, there is even a quantitative approach, called cluster analysis, that I believe does a better job of identifying the types; when I use that approach, the Pittsburgh data look a little more as expected. Only 29 percent of the male violence in the court sample is identified as situational couple violence (compared to 37 percent with the arbitrary cutoff); 19 percent is identified

as situational couple violence in the shelter sample (compared to 28 percent with the arbitrary cutoff). Michael P. Johnson, "Conflict and Control: Symmetry and Asymmetry in Domestic Violence," in *Couples in Conflict,* ed. Alan Booth, Ann C. Crouter, and Mari Clements (Mahwah, N.J.: Lawrence Erlbaum, 2001), 102.

24. Looking, for example, at the frequency of violence from male partners involved in situational couple violence, we see that the average number of violent incidents is one in the general Pittsburgh sample, fifteen in the court sample, and twelve in the shelter sample. Similarly, situational couple violence involves serious injury to the woman in 19 percent of the cases in the general sample, 64 percent in the court sample, and 50 percent in the shelter sample.

25. If I use the cluster analysis approach, intimate terrorism is 97 percent male perpetrated. Situational couple violence is 56 percent male perpetrated. Johnson, "Conflict and Control," 100.

26. Nevertheless, the debate about gender symmetry continues, and there is very little published empirical work that addresses the issue in terms of the gender symmetry of intimate terrorism versus situational couple violence. There is one study (done in England) that quite closely replicates my findings. Graham-Kevan and Archer (2003) used control measures completely different from those I constructed from the Pittsburgh data and a sample that included 43 women shelter clients, 4 male batterer intervention participants, 104 students (mixed gender), and 97 male prisoners (not selected for domestic violence). They found that 87 percent of the intimate terrorists were men and 90 percent of the violent resisters were women, while situational couple violence was 45 percent male and 55 percent female. Their data also confirm the sampling pattern, with 75 percent of the men's violence in their nonselected sample being situational couple violence, as compared with 10 percent in their shelter sample. Nicola Graham-Kevan and John Archer, "Intimate Terrorism and Common Couple Violence: A Test of Johnson's Predictions in Four British Samples," *Journal of Interpersonal Violence* 18, no. 11 (2003): 1256, 1260.

There are also two recent studies that raise some questions about the gender distribution of intimate terrorism, finding intimate terrorism to be roughly gender symmetric. Nicola Graham-Kevan and John Archer, "Using Johnson's Domestic Violence Typology to Classify Men and Women in a Non-Selected Sample," unpublished (2005); Denis Laroche, "Aspects of the Context and Consequences of Domestic Violence: Situational Couple Violence and Intimate Terrorism in Canada," report, Government of Québec, Institut de la statistique du Québec, 2005. However, both of these studies use general samples. The problem with a general sample is that, as Graham-Kevan and Archer, and I, have shown, such samples include very little intimate terrorism. Because we have no well-defined criterion for the level of control required to identify intimate terrorism, authors generally resort to a cluster analysis approach. In a sample with little or no intimate terrorism, the cluster analysis will still identify a high-control cluster, but it is likely to consist mostly of situational couple violence, perhaps with a few cases of intimate terrorism. Thus, the gender distribution for the so-called intimate terrorism will be more like that of situational couple violence.

27. And mutual violent control, which is very rare.

28. Steinmetz, "The Battered Husband Syndrome."

29. I must admit, I used the mode here in part for dramatic effect, although it is true that 11 percent of the intimate terrorists are reported to have been violent one hundred times, and 32 percent of the men involved in situational common violence had been violent only once. The modal figure of one hundred reported by wives for intimate terrorists is certainly inflated, because it is up in the range where women would not be giving precise estimates, but choosing numbers that approximated their experiences. The means and medians may not provide as dramatic a picture, but the differences are still clear. The means for intimate terrorism and situational couple violence are forty-four and ten, respectively. The medians are nineteen and three, respectively.

30. Remember that the types are defined in terms of control context, not the frequency or severity of the violence. The hypothesized differences in frequency and severity of the violence are derived from theory. It is assumed that attempts by husbands to exert general control over their wives will be met by considerable resistance in the United States, where marriage is seen by most women as a partnership. Thus, the intimate terrorist will in some cases turn to violence repeatedly and may escalate its severity in order to gain control.

Controversies Surrounding Mandatory Arrest Policies and the Police Response to Intimate Partner Violence

Amy Leisenring

INTRODUCTION

Understandings of and responses to violence against women by an intimate partner have changed drastically in the last several decades in the USA. While in the 1960s, intimate partner violence was primarily understood as a personal and private issue and was largely ignored by the police and criminal justice system, it is now viewed as a major social problem and is taken much more seriously. Pressure from feminist groups and battered women's advocates has led to numerous reforms within the criminal justice system. One of the most significant reforms has been the implementation of policies that encourage or mandate the arrest of offenders, often referred to as "mandatory arrest policies." (Many jurisdictions have also adopted "no-drop" prosecution policies that encourage or mandate the prosecution of offenders but a discussion of such policies is beyond the scope of this paper.) Mandatory arrest policies have been the source of much controversy and debate; researchers, activists, victim's advocates, policy-makers, and law enforcement officials disagree about the effectiveness of such policies and the ultimate effects that they have on the lives of the women that they were designed to protect. . . .

Mandatory and pro-arrest (or presumptive) policies are common today in the majority of jurisdictions in the USA. A mandatory arrest law

Amy Leisenring, "Controversies Surrounding Mandatory Arrest Policies and the Police Response to Intimate Partner Violence," *Sociology Compass* 2/2 (2008): 451–466. Reprinted with permission.

requires the police to arrest an offender if there is probable cause to believe that intimate partner violence has occurred (Schneider 2000). Pro-arrest policies or presumptive policies encourage arrest but allow officers a bit more discretion. In the last two decades, numerous districts have adopted aggressive arrest policies: currently, 31 states have passed mandatory arrest laws (American Civil Liberties Union 2007). Such laws and policies remove the decision to press charges from the victim. They also reduce the likelihood that responding officers will use their own judgment to decide whether or not to make an arrest, which in the past, often resulted in inaction by many police officers. Policies that mandate or encourage arrest of abusers are seen as sending a message to police officers to "take domestic assaults seriously; treat them criminally" (Gosselin 2000, 316). However, these policies have been the subject of much controversy and debate.

DEBATES OVER REFORMS

Mandatory arrest polices have been highly controversial, both in and outside of feminist circles. At issue are a number of questions, mainly: (i) Who should have control over what happens when the police respond to an intimate partner violence case: the state, the police, or the victim? (ii) Are mandatory arrest policies in the best interest of all victims? (iii) Do mandatory arrest policies have an impact on the behavior of perpetrators? In this section, I will review the central debates surrounding each of these questions and discuss what the research shows surrounding these issues.

Mandatory Arrest Policies and Issue of Control

A central issue surrounding mandatory arrest policies is the issue of control. Because these policies either mandate or encourage police officers who respond to intimate partner violence calls to arrest the perpetrator, ostensibly the decision-making power about what happens to an offender is removed from both the victim and police and rests with the state. Many argue that this is a good thing and favor mandatory arrest policies because they help the state to send a uniform message to the community that intimate partner violence is a serious crime and is a matter of public concern instead of a private issue between the two people involved (Schneider 2000). Battered women's advocates in favor of mandatory arrest laws argue that such laws hold agents of the state such as police officers responsible for fulfilling the government's responsibility to protect its citizens (Stark 2004). Furthermore, as Stark (1993) states, "making battering the only crime in which police discretion is removed acknowledges a special social interest in redressing the legacy of discriminatory treatment of women by law enforcement" (p. 662).

Others argue that removing or lessening responding police officers decision-making powers through mandatory arrest policies is positive (see Stark 1993 for discussion). Such policies control the behavior of police officers and hold them accountable for taking action. Many feminists and battered women's activists see this as beneficial given the typical police response of minimal or no action when they have responded to intimate partner violence calls in the past. Indeed, as Stark (1993) points out, arrests for assaults rose 70% from 1984 to 1989 due to the implementation of mandatory arrest laws.

Finally, some have also argued that having policies that mandate the arrest of abusers is helpful to victims because it takes the pressure off of victims to make the decision whether or not to arrest their batterer (see Stewart 2001 for discussion). This makes it less likely that batterers will hold victims responsible for their arrest and thus retaliate at a later date. Mandating arrest also helps to ensure that the offender will be arrested for breaking a law regardless of the wishes of the victim. Indeed, a study conducted by Buzawa and Austin (1993) revealed that the actions taken by police officers who respond to intimate partner violence calls were largely influenced by victims'

preferences for what they wanted to have happen to their abusers. The officers were more likely to arrest a perpetrator if this is what the victim desired and less likely to arrest a perpetrator if it went against the victim's wishes. Supporters of mandatory arrest policies argue that these policies will help to ensure that all offenders of intimate partner violence are arrested.

Even though mandatory arrest policies are supposed to remove the discretion of police officers who respond to intimate partner violence calls and diminish the likelihood that police will respond negatively to victims, current research demonstrates that gender bias within the system still exists and that many female victims continue to have negative experiences with the police. For example, Stephens and Sinden (2000) found that the majority of battered women in their study who had more than one encounter with law enforcement officials for intimate partner violence reported that police officers commonly minimized the seriousness of their situation, doubted their story, conveyed attitudes of nonchalance and indifference, and/or were rude and condescending. Similarly, a study by Belknap and Hartman (2000) of victim advocates' reports found that while some advocates reported favorable police behaviors and responses, many believe that there are still a "significant" portion of cases in which police response is unfavorable or even hostile.

Finally, not everyone believes that taking away control from battered women during the police response to intimate partner violence calls is a good thing; some argue that removing victims from major-decision-making roles in their cases is not always in the best interest of the women who experience intimate partner violence (Dasgupta 2003; Ford 1991; Hilton 1993; Mills 2003). Some researchers and battered women's advocates argue that mandatory arrest policies disempower women because they limit women's agency and ability to act in their own best interests, ignore their opinions, and revictimize them through forced submittal to state power (Ferraro and Pope 1993; Ford 1991; McLeod 1983). Many women who call the police do not want their batterer arrested (Ferraro and Pope 1993; Stewart 2001). There are multiple reasons a woman may not want her batterer to be arrested and/or jailed: she may depend on him for income and/or housing for herself and/or her children, she may be afraid he will be even angrier when he gets out of jail and his violence against her will escalate, she may not trust the system, she may prefer he receive counseling and support instead of prosecution and punishment, and/or she may not want to end her relationship with him. As Gelles (1993) argues, some women who do not wish their abuser to be arrested use their call to the police and/or the resulting police visit as a means of controlling their abuser's behavior. Because mandatory arrest policies remove this option from women, some have argued that they also remove power from abused women. And, as Rajah et al. (2006) point out, some see the removal of control from female victims as particularly problematic because "women who are denied decision-making power in mandatory arrest encounters may be dissatisfied with the criminal justice response to intimate partner violence and discouraged from calling the police in future domestic disputes" (p. 899).

What does research show about how victimized women themselves view mandatory arrest policies and the amount of control they have in the police response to violence perpetrated against them? Studies indicate that there is mixed support from battered women for such policies. Smith (2001) surveyed 93 battered women staying at emergency shelters and found that while the majority of the women were supportive of mandatory policies, their support varied by race, marital status, and the extent of their injuries, suggesting that some women desire more control over the outcomes of their cases. For example, while 79% of the white women in her sample were supportive of the adoption of mandatory arrest policies, only 53% of the black women in her study were supportive of such policies, suggesting that "Black women prefer more power and control over the arrest decision than White

women" (p. 102). Single and divorced women were more supportive of mandatory arrest policies than married or separated women. Smith concludes that her findings lend support to the claim that universalistic policies are not likely the best means of addressing the individual needs of victims. Similarly, Bohmer et al. (2002), who conducted focus groups with both victims of intimate partner violence and service providers for intimate partner violence victims, found that while support for mandatory policies was mixed among the providers, clients were even less likely to support such policies. The foremost concern of the clients was "their future financial and personal well-being" and they saw the criminal justice system as "being an impediment to that future rather than a source of help" (p. 84). As one victim in this study stated of her abuser: "Well I need him to pay the bills more than I need him to pay for the violence" (p. 82). Such findings have led to broader questions about whether or not mandatory arrest policies serve the best interests of all battered women.

Mandatory Arrest Policies and Victims' Best Interests

Again, many argue that because mandatory arrest policies have led to police officers taking intimate partner violence more seriously, they are beneficial to battered women. The findings from a study conducted by Jones and Belknap (1999) suggest that the implementation of a pro-arrest policy in one jurisdiction served to improve the likelihood of a "strong" police response to intimate partner violence. Epstein (1999) discusses a study conducted in 1990 in the District of Columbia that found that police officers who responded to intimate partner violence calls were arresting accused batterers in only 5% of all cases; furthermore, they failed to arrest in over 80% of cases where the victim had visible injuries. After the city implemented a mandatory arrest law, the rate of arrest of offenders by responding police officers rose from 5% to 41%. Epstein (1999) argues that mandatory arrest policies appear to benefit those victims who desire the arrest of their abusers. Furthermore, research also demonstrates that under mandatory arrest policies more intimate partner violence victims are reporting the violence that they experience to the police (Cho and Wilke 2005).

A number of critics of mandatory arrest policies have argued that these policies are not in the best interest of all abused women. A major argument stems from the recognition that abused women's experiences are diverse and multifaceted—there is no one universal victimized woman's experience. Some critics see uniform responses to intimate partner violence as problematic because such responses fail to take into account the diversity of women's situations based on structural factors such as race, culture, and class and individual factors such as different women's desires and needs (Crenshaw 1994; Dasgupta 2003; Mills 1996). For example, Epstein (1999) makes the argument that the recent reforms to immigration law in the USA may lead abused immigrant women to reject the criminal justice system as a means of addressing the violence in their lives because of fear that their abuser will be deported.

Similarly, some have argued that using arrest as the main means of addressing intimate partner violence exacerbates problems in minority and/or poor communities where police have often demonstrated inappropriate behavior and women may be mistrustful of the police (Sparks 1997). For example, Crenshaw (1994) argues that some women of color may be reluctant to call the police because they do not want to subject their abuser to a criminal justice system that has historically discriminated against men of color. Research on this topic has been mixed. One study cited by Epstein (1999) found that African American abused women worried that reporting abusers to the police "could further contribute to the social stereotyping of black men as particularly violent" (p. 137). However, a 2000 study by Rennison and Welchans (as cited in Stark 2004) found that some women of color actually report their victimization at higher rates (67% for black

women and 65% for Hispanic women) than other groups, including white women (50%).

Still others who argue that mandatory arrest policies are not always in victimized women's best interests point to the increasing number of studies showing that a growing number of women are arrested under these policies. Evidence suggests that in some jurisdictions after mandatory arrest policies were implemented the number of women arrested for intimate partner violence substantially increased (Hirschel and Buzawa 2002; Miller 2001). For example, female aggregate felony intimate partner violence arrest rates increased more than 500% in California from 1987 to 1997 (DeLeon-Granados et al. 2006). Dual arrests—where women are arrested along with their male partners and ex-partners—appear to be the most common scenario under which women are arrested for intimate partner violence (Finn and Bettis 2006). While a possible explanation for the rise in women's arrest rates for intimate partner violence is that their use of violence has increased (DeLeon-Granados et al. 2006), many scholars and battered women's advocates argue that this is not the case. For example, while acknowledging that some women who are arrested for intimate partner violence do actually assault their partners, Osthoff (2002) argues that many women are wrongly arrested for engaging in acts of self-defense or when their abusers falsely accuse them of violence.

Indeed, a study conducted by Finn and Bettis (2006) that explored police officers' justifications for using dual arrest did find that even though police officers are required by law to fully investigate the context in which an act of intimate partner violence occurs, many are hesitant to do so. Finn and Bettis state that the officers "for the most part, fail to take into consideration factors that would help [them] distinguish an assault that was part of an ongoing pattern of battering from one that was not" (p. 282). This is tied to a criticism of mandatory arrest policies that centers on what Stark (2004) terms the "incident-specific understanding" of battering held by the criminal justice system (p. 1321). Under current practice, when police respond to an intimate partner violence call, they are required to make an arrest based on whether or not an incident of violence has occurred; thus, they often fail to take into consideration the context in which the abuse has occurred and the continuous cycle of control and abuse that is common to many abusive relationships.

Mandatory Arrest Policies and Effect on Offenders' Behavior

Debate also exists surrounding if/how mandatory arrest policies impact the behavior of offenders and whether or not these policies actually prevent intimate partner violence. Once again, research examining the effectiveness of mandatory arrest policies in deterring future violence has produced contradictory results (Belknap 2001; Schmidt and Sherman 1996). In the 1980s Sherman and Berk's (1984) Minneapolis experiment showed that arresting batterers helped to serve as a deterrent to future violence and resulted in the implementation of mandatory arrest policies all around the USA (Schmidt and Sherman 1996). However, in the 1990s, replication studies of the Minneapolis experiment in six other cities reflected both deterrent and backfiring effects of arrest (Schmidt and Sherman 1996). For example, based on the replication studies, researchers concluded that (i) arrest reduces intimate partner violence in some cities but increases it in others; (ii) arrest reduces intimate partner violence among employed people but increases it among unemployed people; and (iii) arrest reduces intimate partner violence in the short term but may increase it in the long run (Sherman 1992). These replication studies paint a very muddy and confusing picture regarding the effectiveness of arrest in deterring intimate partner violence. Sherman (1992) himself has retracted the importance of the results of his original Minneapolis experiment and argues that mandatory arrest laws should be repealed.

Other studies examining the success of mandatory arrest policies also have produced mixed results. Maxwell et al. (2002) found that while in general arrest is associated with a decrease in subsequent intimate partner violence, 40% of victims in their sample experienced repeat victimizations. They conclude that "arresting suspects, although effective on average, is not a panacea for all victims of intimate partner violence" (p. 72). Simpson et al. (2006) argue that research on the impact of mandatory arrest policies on police actions and behavior is somewhat limited and the results are contradictory. They found that in the state of Maryland there was a significant and positive impact of legislation encouraging arrest on the likelihood of police officers to arrest offenders in intimate partner violence cases.

Some research suggests that mandatory arrest policies are not executed uniformly across all populations and that racial and class disparities exist surrounding responding police officers' decisions about who to arrest. For example, Avakame and Fyfe (2001) found that police are more likely to arrest an offender if the victim is a wealthy, white, older, suburban female. They also found that the police are more likely to arrest if the offender is African American, if the offender is under the influence of drugs and alcohol, if the assault occurred in a suburban or rural area (as opposed to an urban area), and if there was injury to the victim. The study of Maxwell et al. (2002) showed that according to official arrest records more men of color were likely to reoffend but if victim interviews were consulted then white men were more likely to reoffend. The authors argue that this discrepancy may be due to a greater willingness of African American women to call the police and a greater likelihood of police officers to arrest African American offenders. In their study, Simpson et al. (2006) found that the implementation of a mandatory arrest policy did not differentially impact the arrest probabilities for African Americans and whites.

Data from the Bureau of Justice Statistics indicate that the rate of nonfatal incidents of intimate partner violence dropped from 5.8 per 1,000 residents in 1993 to 2.6 per 1,000 residents in 2004

(Catalano 2006). These data also show a 26% decline between 1993 and 2004 in the number of females murdered by an intimate partner and a 45% decline in the number of males murdered by an intimate partner (Catalano 2006). Because many battered women end up killing their batterer in self-defense when they believe that the state has failed to protect them (Belknap 2001; Schneider 2000), it is possible that the decrease in the number of males murdered by an intimate partner is a sign that increased intervention by the criminal justice system has provided battered women with the resources they need to safely exit their abusive relationship without having to kill their abuser. However, these trends also may be the function of the increased efforts of the battered women's and shelter movement over the past several decades which have aided women in safely exiting violent relationships. As some critics have pointed out, the exact relationship between criminal justice reforms and the decrease in intimate partner violence is unclear (Dasgupta 2003). Thus, drawing specific conclusions from trends about the success or failure of criminal justice reforms such as mandatory arrest policies is risky at best. A study conducted by the National Institute of Justice determined that "no one policy affects all groups the same way in terms of decreasing violence" (as cited in Dasgupta 2003, 9).

FUTURE DIRECTIONS

How are we to make sense of the conflicting and contradictory findings of the numerous studies that examine mandatory arrest policies and their impact on victims and offenders? Given that the findings of most of these studies are not consistent, how can we determine whether or not mandatory arrest policies are successful in preventing intimate partner violence and whether they are beneficial to the victims of such violence? Returning to Johnson's (2005, 2006) argument that there are different types of intimate partner violence is useful when trying to answer these questions. The existence of different types of

intimate partner violence likely helps to explain the lack of consistent findings surrounding the effects of mandatory arrest policies: the impact of arrest on perpetrators and/or victims may differ depending upon the type of intimate partner violence that exists in a relationship. Johnson and Ferraro (2000) argue, "Partner violence cannot be understood without acknowledging important distinctions among types of violence, motives of perpetrators, the social locations of both partners, and the cultural contexts in which violence occurs" (p. 948). And obviously, if we cannot understand partner violence we cannot develop a response that will successfully reduce and eradicate partner violence.

Clearly, a more aggressive police response to intimate partner violence by the criminal justice system has helped to solidify the message that such violence is not socially acceptable. Evidence suggests that policies that encourage the arrest and prosecution of abusers help some victimized women in some instances. However, the creation of laws and policies that treat all intimate partner violence cases uniformly are problematic if they fail to recognize the various types of domestic violence; place too much emphasis on particular incidents of violence; and fail to understand victim's experiences with violence in the context of their entire relationship (Mahoney 1994; Wittner 1998). Uniform policies appear unable to account for and address the complex nature of intimate partner violence and the diversity of abused women's needs, desires, and experiences. A growing number of studies seem to suggest that mandatory law enforcement policies do not always serve the best interests of all victimized women, nor do they appear to be the sole solution to stopping intimate partner violence and guaranteeing the safety of women who are abused. Research indicates that in some cases (such as those in which victimized women are arrested), mandatory arrest policies may do more harm for abused women than good.

Thus, it seems that if as a society we truly are invested in the idea of stopping intimate partner violence, several things are necessary. First, we need more research that looks at how the needs and desires of the victims of various types of intimate partner violence may differ and how these needs may be best met. Similarly, we need research that examines if/how mandatory arrest policies differently impact the various types of intimate partner violence. For example, research is needed to answer questions such as whether or not arrest is more effective for those who perpetrate situational couple violence than for those men who perpetrate intimate terrorism. Second, there needs to be more training for agents of the criminal justice system such as police officers to help them better understand and recognize the different types of violence and the dynamics and patterns of abuse that exist in violent relationships. As Johnson (2005) points out, the response and intervention strategies that are most successful in eradicating intimate partner violence will likely vary depending on the type of violence. Finally, we must question the value of mandatory policies that dictate the uniform treatment of all intimate partner violence cases and acknowledge that such policies have had many unintended consequences. Instead of uniform policies, we should encourage responses that recognize the complexity of intimate partner violence and victims' experiences. These are challenging tasks, for sure, but they are neccessary in order to ensure the safety of all victims of intimate partner violence.

■ Review Questions ■

1. Why do some advocates think that it is necessary to require the police to arrest a batterer even if the victim does not want him to be arrested?
2. In what situations do you think that mandatory arrests would be justified?

CHAPTER 12

Divorce

The experience of having one's parents divorce is now common in childhood. Perhaps 40 percent of American children under age 18 will witness their parents' divorce. The process is often very difficult. Nearly all children are upset when they first learn of the separation, although a minority who are in highly conflicted families also may feel some relief. For the first year or two, commonly referred to in the literature as the "crisis period," difficulties are likely to persist. What is the longer-term picture?

This chapter presents two perspectives on this topic. The first is by Sara McLanahan, a sociologist. She focuses on the social and economic consequences: the chances of dropping out of high school, having a child outside of marriage, or having trouble finding a job. Her reading of the literature is that most children adequately adjust to divorce and avoid serious long-term problems but that the risk of undesirable outcomes increases. She also addresses questions such as the following: Do some of the apparent effects of divorce actually reflect conditions that were present in the family prior to the divorce? Why exactly does father absence make a difference?

And what policies might be adopted to reduce divorce and its harmful effects?

The second selection is by two psychologists, Joan B. Kelly and Robert E. Emery. They focus on the psychological outcomes of divorce, such as behavior problems, anxiety, and depression. Like McLanahan, they conclude that divorce raises the risk of experiencing problems but that most children do not experience serious problems as a result of their parents' divorce. But why, they then ask, do we commonly hear that most children are harmed by divorce in the long-term? The answer, they argue, is that many adults whose parents divorced can function well in life but still have painful memories of the divorce and its aftermath. When we ask them about their family lives, they can easily call up these memories. Nevertheless, most such people go about their lives without much difficulty. We should not minimize the painful reflections they have, say the authors; but we should not make the mistake of confusing their pain with pathology. They may have painful reflections, but their adult lives are not compromised by antisocial behavior, depression, or the inability to hold a job.

READING 12-1

Life without Father

What Happens to the Children?

Sara McLanahan

Over half of all children born in the United States today will, if current trends continue, live apart from at least one of their biological parents—usually the father—before they reach adulthood. A substantial proportion (about one-fifth) will never live with their fathers. These families are economically vulnerable and they disproportionately represent ethnic minorities. As almost all Americans have either experienced divorce or are close to people who have, the consequences of divorce are of personal as well as social interest.

The conventional wisdom on the issue of father absence has shifted dramatically over the past four decades. During the 1960s, most people viewed divorce and out-of-wedlock childbearing as leading inevitably to delinquency, school failure, and other social problems. During the 1970s, the pendulum swung in the opposite direction. Leading sociologists argued that single motherhood was just another lifestyle reflecting women's growing economic independence and freedom to leave unhappy marriages. Since the mid-1980s, a new consensus holds that although most children of divorced parents do all right, growing up without a father increases the risk of numerous undesirable outcomes. Whether these outcomes are caused by the divorce itself, as opposed to something else about the family, remains controversial.

THE SCOPE OF THE PROBLEM

Children raised apart from a biological parent are disadvantaged in numerous ways. They are more

likely to drop out of high school, less likely to attend college, and less likely to graduate from college than children raised by both biological parents. Girls from father-absent families are more likely to become sexually active at a younger age and to have a child outside of marriage. Boys who grow up without their fathers are more likely to have trouble finding (and keeping) a job in young adulthood. Young adult men and women from one-parent families tend to work at low-paying jobs.

The popular perception of these effects is subjective. High school graduation is one example. Some argue that the effects of father absence are small, noting that most children living apart from their fathers graduate from high school (80 percent, as compared with 90 percent for children in two-parent families). Others argue that the effects are large, noting that dropout rates double (from 10 percent to 20 percent) when fathers are gone. Most of the outcomes described above follow this pattern and therefore are subject to these two conflicting interpretations.

Although father absence is much more common among ethnic minorities and low-income families, the penalties associated with single parenthood appear to be more or less similar for children from all socioeconomic backgrounds. Where differences do exist, the costs tend to be higher for children from white and middle-class backgrounds than for children from more disadvantaged backgrounds. In other words, children from advantaged backgrounds seem to lose more when their fathers leave. Possible explanations are that living without a father is more common in poorer communities, or children from middle-class families have more to lose. In most instances, children of widowed mothers fare better than children of divorced and never-married mothers, perhaps because widows experience less economic insecurity (they are eligible for social security benefits) or because a father's death disrupts a child's family and friendship ties less than a divorce does. Also, a child is less likely to feel rejected by a parent who dies than a parent who is absent by choice.

Some believe that children of never-married mothers fare worse than children raised by divorced mothers. The evidence suggests otherwise. Once differences in parents' economic circumstances are taken into account, these two groups of children do equally well. What about children who grow up in stable cohabiting unions? Unfortunately, social scientists can say little about whether a child born to unmarried parents who stay together is disadvantaged relative to a child born to married parents who stay together. Since cohabitation was relatively rare until recently, and since long-term cohabiting unions are still very rare, we know little about the long-term effects on children of this family arrangement.

Remarriage is another instance where general perceptions are distorted. Children in stepfamilies fare no better than children in single-parent families and in some instances fare worse. Frank Furstenberg and Andrew Cherlin, two leading family sociologists, attribute this finding to the lack of established societal guidelines about how stepfamilies should operate. Parents and children therefore constantly negotiate over their rights and responsibilities. Other researchers claim that biological parenthood benefits children more than step-parenthood for genetic reasons.

DOES FATHER ABSENCE CAUSE POOR OUTCOMES IN CHILDREN?

While most researchers agree that father absence is associated with adverse outcomes among children, they disagree over whether it causes those outcomes. Many think that parental conflict is the source of the problem. We know that conflict is bad for children, and we also know that parents who divorce experience more conflict than parents who stay together. Conflict is not the whole story, however. Many couples that divorce do not experience high levels of conflict.

Other scholars argue that the negative outcomes associated with father absence are due to flaws in the character or genes of one or both of the parents. Alcoholism and depression, for

example, can cause both family instability as well as poor outcomes in children. One way to test this theory is to look at children before and after their parents separate. If the "flawed individual" argument is correct, we would expect the children in these families to be doing poorly even before their parents' divorce. Andrew Cherlin and his colleagues have taken this approach, using a large study that followed children born in England in 1958. They found that some, but not all, of the harm suffered by children whose fathers were absent could be explained by conditions that preceded the divorce.

The economist Jonathan Gruber has taken a different approach. Noting that parents (irrespective of their flaws) are less likely to divorce in states that make divorce more difficult, he compared children in these two types of states. Gruber found that those who grew up in states with easy access to divorce obtained less education and had lower incomes as adults than children who grew up in states that discouraged divorce.

Yet another way to assess whether divorce causes children to do worse is to compare children who have the same parents (or parent) but experience different family structures. Sibling differences can occur if the parents divorce after the first child grows up but before the last child leaves home, or if a single mother remarries, has a second child, and remains married to the second husband. Researchers find that in families like these, both siblings fare worse than children raised by two parents, suggesting that the problem is the parents (or parent) rather than the divorce itself.

In sum, the evidence is mixed with respect to whether divorce causes children to have problems or whether the problems associated with divorce are due to poor parenting or even poor genes.

WHY DOES FATHER ABSENCE MAKE A DIFFERENCE?

Three general factors account for the disadvantages associated with father absence: economic deprivation, poor parenting and lack of social support. Economic insecurity is probably the most important reason why children who live apart from their fathers tend to be less successful. In the United States, where childrearing is primarily a private rather than a public responsibility, parental income is significant. It determines the quality of child care and health care that children receive, and it also determines the quality of their education. School quality is closely related to where parents live, with the best schools typically found in more expensive neighborhoods. According to the U.S. Census Bureau, in 1995, the median income of two-parent families with children under age 18 was just over $50,000, as compared with just under $18,000 for female-headed families. Half of families headed by single mothers live below the poverty line, as compared with 10 percent of two-parent families. Of course, many single-mother families were poor even before the father left the household, but in most instances, the departure of the father reduced their economic prospects even further.

Income cannot account for all of the disadvantages of children without fathers, however. The fact that children in stepfamilies do just as poorly as children in single-mother families tells us that something other than financial deprivation is at work. The most obvious problem is that a father's absence reduces a child's access to parental attention. Interacting with the estranged mother and building a new relationship with the child can be a difficult and painful experience for a nonresident father, and many men respond by disengaging from the children.

A father's absence may also affect the quality of the mother-child relationship. The economic hardship and insecurity of single parenthood can bring on depression and psychological distress, thereby interfering with good mothering. Even among middle-class families, the departure of the father from the household can trigger disruptions in household routines such as meals and bedtimes, and undermine discipline. With their time, energy, and spirit stretched thin, some single mothers become too lenient and others become too rigid or strict. Neither mothering style bodes well for children.

The loss of social support is the third reason why father absence matters. The sustaining web of facilities, programs, people, and care providers that back up parents' efforts is likely to decline when families are forced to move, which is often the case after divorce (and remarriage). The longer a family resides in the same community or neighborhood, the more likely the parent is to know about opportunities for the child. The mother is more likely to know about after-school programs and the names of the best teachers, and to have the connections and influence to access these resources. Even children who do not move may lose touch with people and other valuable resources. For example, many children lose access to their father's family and friends, and they may also be cut off from their mother's family and friends if she is too stressed and weary to maintain old relationships.

WHAT CAN BE DONE?

The United States is not the only country that has experienced increases in divorce and nonmarital childbearing in the past four decades. Indeed, although divorce is more common in the United States, bearing children out of wedlock is more common in the Scandinavian countries. Yet the conditions that single mothers face there are very different. For example, the poverty rate—measured as having income below 50 percent of median income—for single-mother families is 55 percent in the United States, 52 percent in Canada, 24 percent in the Netherlands, 46 percent in the U.K. and 7 percent in Sweden. Although part of this difference is due to differences in who becomes a single mother (single mothers in the United States are younger, less educated and more likely to be nonwhite than single mothers in other countries), most of the difference is due to welfare-state policies. Whereas in the United States, government assistance reduces poverty rates by about 15 percent, in Sweden public support reduces poverty by 90 percent.

Given that poverty rates among single mothers are much lower in other nations than in the United States, the effects of single motherhood might be expected to be much more benign elsewhere. Yet this is not always the case. Although children in single-mother families fare better in Sweden, where their poverty rates are low, they also appear to do well in Canada, where poverty rates are high. And, somewhat surprisingly, they do poorly in the U.K. and the Netherlands, where poverty rates are lower than in the United States. So the cross-national picture is something of a puzzle and suggests (once again) that economic deprivation is not the whole story.

Aside from easing the economic problems of children without fathers, we can try to reduce their risks more directly. First, we can make sure that parents are informed about the potential risks associated with the father's departure and the ways in which they can minimize the risks. While information alone is not likely to have a huge effect on divorce (or nonmarital childbearing), it may encourage some parents to try to rebuild their marriage and it may encourage others to work harder at maintaining a cooperative relationship after divorce.

Second, we can make sure that social policies do not discourage marriage. Although this point may seem obvious to most people, our current tax and transfer system is not neutral. Rather, it contains numerous "marriage penalties" that discourage permanent unions for couples at all income levels. These penalties include categorical restrictions that limit benefits to certain groups of parents (e.g., single mothers) as well as "income tests" and tax schedules that favor one-parent families over two-parent families in some instances.

For instance, take a couple in which both parents have little education and both work for low wages. This couple must choose between living together and getting very little help from the government or living apart and getting a great deal of help, including cash assistance, child care subsidies and health care subsidies. If the mother believes that the father's employment prospects are poor, she may decide that living alone is more beneficial economically than living with her child's father.

Working-class families also face a "marriage penalty." One of the most popular (and fastest growing) programs in the United States is the Earned Income Tax Credit, a program that provides a subsidy to parents with low incomes. A single mother earning $12,000 a year can receive an additional $3,000 from the government. If she lives with a man who earns $15,000, however, the family receives nothing. One way to deal with the disincentives inherent in income-tested programs is to make the individual, rather than the family, the basis for determining taxes and transfers. If we followed this course, people's taxes and transfers would not be affected by their decisions to marry or cohabit. Of course, such an approach would be very expensive because more families would qualify for benefits. But it would probably also increase the incidence of marriage.

A third way to minimize the potential harm associated with a father's departure is to insist that fathers support their children even when they live elsewhere. This means establishing paternity for children born outside wedlock and enforcing child-support obligations for all children with an absent father. Unlike our welfare and tax systems, which discourage marriage, child-support enforcement reduces divorce and nonmarital childbearing. It not only prevents fathers from leaving but also mitigates the negative effects of their going by reducing the economic insecurity of single mothers. In short, child-support enforcement is a win-win policy, which is one reason why it has received broad bipartisan support in Congress. Unfortunately for low-income children, the situation is not quite so rosy. Since welfare benefits are reduced by one dollar for each dollar of child support a mother receives, child-support collections do not improve the economic status of children in welfare households. This policy saves welfare dollars, but it does not benefit children's welfare. It may even harm children by increasing tension and conflict between low-income parents.

What about joint custody and visitation? Real joint custody is hard to sustain, and moderate levels of visitation do not appear to help children much. What does seem to help is a close father-child relationship, which depends on the parents' ability to minimize conflict after divorce. Because of this finding, some states have started to mandate parent workshops and counseling sessions at the time of divorce to inform parents of the benefits (to their children) of maintaining a positive coparenting relationship and to increase their communication skills.

Finally, if we are serious about keeping fathers and their children together, we should be doing much more for "fragile families," defined as unmarried parents who are raising a child together. Not only is this group of families growing much faster than divorcing families, in most instances, the parents in these families have high hopes for a future together at the time their child is born. Yet because of their marginal financial circumstances, these parents face many barriers to achieving a stable family life, including potentially harmful government policies. Helping these families form and maintain a stable union is not a matter of changing the minds of parents who no longer want to be together. Rather, it is a matter of helping them achieve their goals. Policies that strengthen fragile families should appeal both to conservatives who want to promote marriage and to liberals who want to increase the "marriage-ability" of low-income parents.

■ Review Questions   ■

1. How can it be true that most children of divorced parents do all right *and* that divorce raises the risks of undesirable outcomes?
2. What specific aspects of father absence appear detrimental to children after divorce?

READING 12-2

Children's Adjustment Following Divorce

Risk and Resilience Perspectives

Joan B. Kelly

Robert E. Emery

DIVORCE AS RISK FOR CHILDREN

A large body of empirical research confirms that divorce increases the risk for adjustment prob-

Joan B. Kelly and Robert E. Emery, "Children's Adjustment Following Divorce: Risk and Resilience Perspectives," *Family Relations* Vol. 52, No. 4 (2003): 352–362. Reprinted by permission of the publisher.

lems in children and adolescents (for reviews, see Amato, 2000; Emery, 1999; Hetherington, 1999; Kelly, 2000; McLanahan, 1999; Simons et al., 1996). Children of divorce were significantly more likely to have behavioral, internalizing, social, and academic problems when compared with children from continuously married families. The extent of risk is at least twice that of children in continuously married families (Hetherington, 1999; McLanahan; Zill, Morrison, & Coiro, 1993). Although 10% of children in continuously married families also have serious psychological and social problems, as measured on objective tests, estimates are that 20–25% of children from divorced families had similar problems (Hetherington & Kelly, 2002; Zill & Schoenborn, 1990). The largest effects are seen in externalizing symptoms, including conduct disorders, antisocial behaviors, and problems with authority figures and parents. Less robust differences are found with respect to depression, anxiety, and self-esteem. Whereas preadolescent boys were at greater risk for these negative outcomes than girls in several studies (see Amato, 2001; Hetherington, 1999), no gender differences specifically linked to divorce were found in other studies (Sun, 2001; Vandewater & Lansford, 1998). The complex interaction between gender, age at separation, preseparation adjustment, sex of custodial parent, quality of relationships with both parents, and extent of conflict confounds efforts to clarify findings regarding gender.

Children in divorced families have lower academic performance and achievement test scores compared with children in continuously married families. The differences are modest and decrease, but do not disappear, when income and socioeconomic status are controlled (for review, see McLanahan, 1999). Children from divorced families are two to three times more likely to drop out of school than are children of intact families, and the risk of teenage childbearing is doubled. However, it appears that youngsters are already at risk for poorer educational performance and lowered expectations well before separation. For example, the risk for school dropout is associated with poverty or low income prior to separation, and this may be exacerbated by the further decline in economic resources following separation (Pong & Ju, 2000). Further, in looking at parental resources available to children prior to separation, parents provided less financial, social, human, and cultural capital to their children compared with parents who remained married (Sun & Li, 2001), and parent-child relationships were less positive (Sun, 2001). Adolescents from divorced families scored lower on tests of math and reading both prior to and after parental separation compared with adolescents in married families, and their parents were less involved in their adolescents' education (Sun & Li, 2002).

The increased risk of divorced children for behavioral problems is not diminished by remarriage. As with divorce, children in stepfamily homes are twice as likely to have psychological, behavioral, social, and academic problems than are children in nondivorced families (Bray, 1999; Hetherington & Kelly, 2002; Zill, 1998; Zill & Schoenborn, 1990).

Children from divorced families have more difficulties in their intimate relationships as young adults. Compared with young adults in continuously married families, young adults from divorced families marry earlier, report more dissatisfaction with their marriages, and are more likely to divorce (Amato, 1999, 2000; Chase-Lansdale, Cherlin, & Kierman, 1995). Relationships between divorced parents and their adult children also are less affectionate and supportive than those in continuously married families (Amato & Booth, 1996; Zill et al., 1993). When divorced parents denigrated the other parent in front of the children, young adults were more likely to report angry and less close relationships with the denigrating parents (Fabricius & Hall, 2000). Somewhat surprising is the finding that young adults whose parents had low-conflict marriages and then divorced had more problems with intimate relationships, less social support of friends and relatives, and lower psychological well-being compared with children whose high-conflict parents divorced (Booth & Amato, 2001). Parents in low-conflict marriages who divorced differed in certain dimensions, including less integration in the community and more risky behaviors, and this may place their children at greater risk. Further research is needed to understand the aspects of parenting and parent-child relationships in these low-conflict marriages that negatively affect the later relationships of their offspring.

Higher divorce rates for children of divorced families compared with those in still-married families are substantiated in a number of studies (Amato, 1996; McLanahan & Sandefur, 1994; Wolfinger, 2000). The risk of divorce for these young adults is related to socioeconomic factors, as well as life course decisions such as cohabitation, early marriage, and premarital childbearing; attitudes toward marriage and divorce; and interpersonal behaviors, all of which are associated with marital instability (Amato, 1996, 2000). The number and cumulative effect of family structure transitions is linked to the higher probability of divorce; three or more transitions (divorce, remarriage, redivorce) greatly increase the risk of offspring divorce (Wolfinger).

PROTECTIVE FACTORS REDUCING RISK FOR CHILDREN OF DIVORCE

In the last decade, researchers have identified a number of protective factors that may moderate the risks associated with divorce for individual children and that contribute to the variability in outcomes observed in children of divorce. These include specific aspects of the psychological adjustment and parenting of custodial parents, the type of relationships that children have with their nonresident parents, and the extent and type of conflict between parents.

Competent Custodial Parents and Parenting

Living in the custody of a competent, adequately functioning parent is a protective factor associated with positive outcomes in children. Overall, one of the best predictors of children's psychological functioning in the marriage (Cummings & Davies, 1994; Keitner & Miller, 1990) and after divorce (Emery et al., 1999; Hetherington, 1999; Johnston, 1995; Kaiter et al., 1989; Kline et al., 1990) is the psychological adjustment of custodial parents (usually mothers) and the quality of parenting provided by them. A particular cluster of parenting behaviors following divorce is an important protective factor as well. When custodial parents provide warmth, emotional support, adequate monitoring, discipline authoritatively, and maintain age-appropriate expectations, children and adolescents experience positive adjustment compared with children whose divorced custodial parents are inattentive, less supportive, and use coercive discipline (Amato, 2000; Buchanan et al., 1996; Hetherington, 1999; Krishnakumar & Buehler, 2000; Maccoby & Mnookin, 1992).

Nonresident Parents

There is a potential protective benefit from the timely and appropriate parenting of nonresident parents. Frequency of visits between fathers and children generally is not a reliable predictor of children's outcomes, because frequency alone does not reflect the quality of the father-child relationship. In one study, boys and younger children, but not girls or older children, were better adjusted with frequent and regular contact with their fathers (Stewart, Copeland, Chester, Malley, & Barenbaum, 1997). In the context of low conflict, frequent visits between fathers and children is associated with better child adjustment, but where interparental conflict is intense, more frequent visits were linked to poorer adjustment, presumably because of the opportunities for more direct exposure of the children to parental aggression and pressures (Amato & Rezac, 1994; Hetherington & Kelly, 2002; Johnston, 1995).

Frequency of contact also has beneficial effects when certain features of parenting are present in nonresident parents. A meta-analysis of 57 studies found that children who had close relationships with their fathers benefited from frequent contacts when their fathers remained actively involved as parents (Amato & Gilbreth, 1999). When fathers helped with homework and projects, provided authoritative parenting, and had appropriate expectations for their children, the children had more positive adjustment and academic performance than did those with less involved fathers. More paternal involvement in children's schooling was also associated with better grades and fewer repeated grades and suspensions (Nord, Brimhall, & West, 1997). The combination of fathers engaging in activities with their children and providing financial support was associated with increased probability of completing high school and entering college compared with activities alone or activities combined with very low financial support (Menning, 2002). Indeed, when both parents engage in active, authoritative, competent parenting, adolescent boys from divorced families had no greater involvement in delinquent behavior than did those in continuously married families (Simons and Associates, 1996).

New reports about joint custody, compared with sole custody, also suggest a protective effect for some children. A meta-analysis of 33 studies of sole- and joint-physical custody studies reported that children in joint-custody arrangements were better adjusted on multiple objective measures, including general adjustment, emotional and behavioral adjustment, and academic achievement compared with children in sole-custody arrangements (Bausermann, 2002). In fact, children in joint custody were better adjusted regardless of the level of conflict between parents, and they did not differ in adjustment from the children in still-married families. Although the joint-custody parents had less conflict prior to separation and after divorce than did sole-custody parents, these differences did not affect the advantage of joint custody. Lee (2002) also reported positive effects of dual residence on children's behavioral adjustment, although the effects were suppressed by high interparental conflict and children's sadness.

In sharp contrast to the 1980s, some findings suggest that between 35% and 40% of children may now have at least weekly contacts with their fathers, particularly in the first several years after divorce (Brayer & O'Connell, 1998; Hetherington, 1999; Seltzer, 1991, 1998). This may reflect changes in legal statutes and social contexts that now encourage shared legal decision-making, less restrictive views of paternal time with children, and greater opportunities for interested fathers to engage more fully in active parenting. Mothers also are more satisfied with higher levels of paternal involvement than they were 20 years ago (King & Heard, 1999), possibly reflecting changing cultural and work-related trends and

the increased role of the father in raising children (Doherty, 1998; Pleck, 1997).

Diminished Conflict between Parents Following Divorce

Low parental conflict is a protective factor for children following divorce. Although we know little about the thresholds at which conflict becomes a risk factor following divorce in different families, some conflict appears to be normative and acceptable to the parties (King & Heard, 1999). Young adults whose parents had low conflict during their earlier years were less depressed and had fewer psychological symptoms compared with those whose parents had continued high conflict (Amato & Keith, 1991; Zill et al., 1993). When parents have continued higher levels of conflict, protective factors include a good relationship with at least one parent or caregiver; parental warmth (Emery & Forehand, 1994; Neighbors, Forehand, & McVicar, 1993; Vandewater & Lansford, 1998); and the ability of parents to encapsulate their conflict (Hetherington, 1999). Several studies found no differences in the amount of conflict between parents in sole- or joint-custody arrangements (Braver & O'Connell, 1998; Emery et al., 1999; Maccoby & Mnookin, 1992), although results from a meta-analysis found more conflict in sole-custody families prior to and after divorce (Bausermann, 2002).

Most parents diminish their conflict in the first 2–3 years after divorce as they become disengaged and establish their separate (or remarried) lives. Studies indicate that between 8% and 12% of parents continue high conflict 2–3 years after divorce (Hetherington, 1999; King & Heard, 1999; Maccoby & Mnookin, 1992). The relatively small group of chronically contentious and litigating parents are more likely to be emotionally disturbed, character-disordered men and women who are intent on vengeance and/or on controlling their former spouses and their parenting (Johnston & Campbell, 1988; Johnston & Roseby, 1997). Such parents use disproportionate resources and time in family courts, and their children are more likely to be exposed to parental aggression. When one or both parents continue to lash out during transitions between households, mediation experience indicates that children can be protected from this exposure through access arrangements that incorporate transfers at neutral points (e.g., school, day care).

Related to the level of conflict between parents postdivorce is the effect of the coparental relationship. Research shows that between 25% and 30% of parents have a cooperative coparental relationship characterized by joint planning, flexibility, sufficient communication, and coordination of schedules and activities. However, more than half of parents engage in parallel parenting, in which low conflict, low communication, and emotional disengagement are typical features. Although there are distinct advantages of cooperative coparenting for children, children thrive as well in parallel parenting relationships when parents are providing nurturing care and appropriate discipline in each household (Hetherington, 1999; Hetherington & Kelly, 2002; Maccoby & Mnookin, 1992; Whiteside & Becker, 2000).

RESILIENCE OF CHILDREN OF DIVORCE

Despite the increased risk reported for children from divorced families, the current consensus in the social science literature is that the majority of children whose parents divorced are not distinguishable from their peers whose parents remained married in the longer term (Amato, 1994, 2001; Chase-Lansdale et al., 1995; Emery, 1999; Emery & Forehand, 1994; Furstenberg & Kiernan, 2001; Hetherington, 1999; Simons and Associates, 1996; Zill et al., 1993). There is considerable overlap between groups of children and adolescents in married and postdivorce families, with some divorced (and remarried) children functioning quite well in all dimensions, and some children in married families experiencing severe psychological, social, and academic difficulties (Amato, 1994, 2001; Hetherington, 1999). Whereas a slight widening of the differences

between children from married and divorced families is found in studies in the 1990s, the magnitude of the differences remains small (Amato, 2001). Both large-scale studies with nationally representative samples and multimethod longitudinal studies using widely accepted psychological and social measures and statistics indicate that the majority of children of divorce continue to fall within the average range of adjustment (Amato, 2001; Hetherington & Kelly, 2002; Zill et al., 1993).

Not to minimize the stresses and risk to children that separation and divorce create, it is important to emphasize that approximately 75–80% of children and young adults do not suffer from major psychological problems, including depression; have achieved their education and career goals; and retain close ties to their families. They enjoy intimate relationships, have not divorced, and do not appear to be scarred with immutable negative effects from divorce (Amato, 1999, 2000; Laumann-Billings & Emery, 2000; McLanahan, 1999; Chase-Lansdale et al., 1995). In fact, Amato (1999) estimated that approximately 42% of young adults from divorced families in his study had well-being scores above the average of young adults from nondivorced families.

As we indicated here, the differences in children's lives that determine their longer-term outcomes are dependent on many circumstances, among them their adjustment prior to separation, the quality of parenting they received before and after divorce, and the amount of conflict and violence between parents that they experienced during marriage and after divorce. Children from high-conflict and violent marriages may derive the most benefit from their parents' divorces (Amato, Loomis, & Booth, 1995; Booth & Amato, 2001) as a result of no longer enduring the conditions that are associated with significant adjustment problems in children in marriages. Once freed from intense marital conflict, these findings suggest that parenting by custodial parents improves, although research is needed to explain more specifically what aspects of parent-child relationships and family functioning facilitate recovery in these young-sters. Clearly, the links between level of marital conflict and outcomes for children are complex. For children whose parents reported marital conflict in the midrange, divorce is associated with only slightly lower psychological well-being (Booth & Amato, 2001). If this midrange marital conflict represents approximately 50% of the families that divorce, as others have found, then the large number of resilient children seen in the years following divorce is not surprising.

UNDERSTANDING CONTRADICTORY FINDINGS ON ADULT CHILDREN OF DIVORCE

These broadly based findings of long-term resiliency are at odds with the 25-year longitudinal study that has received widespread attention. In *The Unexpected Legacy of Divorce* (Wallerstein, Lewis, Blakeslee, 2000), the authors report that children of divorce, interviewed in young adulthood, do not survive the experience of divorce and that the negative effects are immutable. These young adults are described as anxious, depressed, burdened, failing to reach their potential, and fearful of commitment and failure.

What accounts for these enormously disparate findings? Many of these differences can be traced to methodological issues and may relate as well to the clinical interpretations of participant interviews about their experiences as divorced young adults. An essential methodological concern is that this study (Wallerstein & Kelly, 1980; Wallerstein & Blakeslee, 1989; Wallerstein et al., 2000) was a qualitative study, used a clinical sample, and no comparison group of married families existed from the start. The data were collected in clinical interviews by experienced therapists, and no standardized or objective measures of psychological adjustment, depression, anxiety, self-esteem, or social relationships were used. The goal of the study, initiated in 1969 when information about children of divorce was extremely limited, was to describe in detail the responses of children and parents to the initial separation and divorce, and then to see how they fared over the first 5 years in comparison with their initial reports and behaviors (Wallerstein & Kelly). . . .

Aside from sampling and methodological concerns, another explanation for the marked divergence in longer-term outcomes of divorced offspring may be a confusion of pain and pathology. Like young adults participating in more objective assessments of pain, participants in the Wallerstein study may have reported considerable distress in reflecting upon their parents' divorce. However, painful reflections on a difficult past are not the same as an inability to feel and function competently in the present.

PAINFUL MEMORIES AS LONGER-TERM RESIDUES OF DIVORCE

A third perception of the short- and longer-term effects of divorce may be a useful complement and balance to risk and resilience perspectives. Painful memories and experiences may be a lasting residue of the divorce (and remarriage) process for many youngsters and young adults. However, it is important to distinguish pain or distress about parental divorce from longer-term psychological symptoms or pathology. Clearly, divorce can create lingering feelings of sadness, longing, worry, and regret that coexist with competent psychological and social functioning. Substantial change and relationship loss, when compounded for some by continuing conflict between parents, represents an ongoing unpleasant situation over which the child or adolescent may have no control. Research that includes standardized and objective measures of both psychological adjustment and painful feelings is useful in disentangling differences in long-term outcomes reported in young adults from divorced families. Such research may help to explain some of the apparent conflict between studies using clinical and quantitative methods.

A decade after divorce, well-functioning college students reported continued pain and distress about their parents' divorces (Laumann-Billings & Emery, 2000). Compared with students in still-married families, they reported more painful childhood feelings and experiences, including worry about such things as their parents attending major events and wanting to spend more time with their fathers. They did not blame themselves for parental divorce, and 80% thought that the divorce was right for their parents. Feelings of loss were the most prevalent of the painful feelings, and the majority reported they missed not having their father around. Many questioned whether their fathers loved them. Despite these painful feelings and beliefs, these young adults did not differ on standardized measures of depression or anxiety from a comparison sample of students in still-married families. These findings were replicated in a second sample of low-income young adults who were not college students. Among factors associated with more pain among children from divorced families were living in sole mother or father custody, rather than a shared custody arrangement, and higher levels of post-divorce parental conflict. When children's parents continued their high conflict, these young adults reported greater feelings of loss and paternal blame and were more likely to view their lives through the filter of divorce (Laumann-Billings & Emery). Young adults in both samples also reported lower levels of loss when they had lived in joint physical custody and were less likely to see life through the filter of divorce. As would be expected, there is no question that divorce impacted the lives of many of these young adults and that parental attitudes and behavior affected the degree of painful feelings lingering after divorce. Although tempting, this impact should not be confused with or portrayed as poor psychological adjustment.

Feelings of loss also were reported by half of 820 college students a decade after divorce in another study (Fabricius & Hall, 2000). Subjects indicated that they had wanted to spend more time with their fathers in the years after divorce. They reported that their mothers were opposed to increasing their time with fathers. When asked which of nine living arrangements would have been best for them, 70% chose "equal time" with each parent, and an additional 30% said a "substantial" number of overnights with their fathers, preferences that were similar in a sample of young adults in nondivorced families. The typical amount of contact reported in this and other studies between children and their fathers was every other weekend. One can infer from these findings that for many years, many of these students experienced some degree of painful longing for the absent parent that might have been alleviated with more generous visiting arrangements. An analysis of the amount of contact and closeness to fathers indicated that with each increment of increased contact between these children and their fathers, there was an equal increase in young adults reporting closeness to their fathers and a corresponding decrease in anger toward their fathers. Further, the increased feelings of closeness toward fathers did not diminish their reported closeness to mothers (see Fabricius, 2003). Further, increasing increments of father contact were linked to incremental amounts of support paid by fathers for their children's college (Fabricius, Braver, & Deneau, 2003). In fact, students who perceived their parents as opposed to or interfering with contact with the nonresident parent were more angry and less close to those parents than were students who reported their parents as more supportive of contact with the nonresident parents.

Another source of pain may be the extent to which adult children feel that they had no control over their lives following divorce. As indicated earlier, the majority of children and adolescents are not adequately informed about the divorce and its implications for their lives (Dunn et al., 2001). They also are not consulted for their ideas regarding access arrangements and how they are working for them, both emotionally and practically (Kelly, 2002; McIntosh, 2000; Smart & Neale, 2000). The young adults cited earlier who longed to spend increased time with their fathers either perceived that they had no control over this arrangement or in reality did not have control. In lacking a voice in these divorce arrangements, not only did they miss their fathers over an extended period, but they were left with lingering doubts as to whether their fathers loved them. The substantial presence of involved nonresident parents in children's lives after divorce may be an important indicator to many children that they are valued and loved.

Transitions between two households constitute another arena where many children do not have sufficient input and control, particularly as they move into adolescence, and this may cause lingering angry or painful feelings. Whereas 25% of youngsters had *some* to *many* negative feelings about transitions between households, 73% had *some* to *many* positive feelings about the transitions. There was a significant association between positive feelings about transitions and being given a voice or role in some decision-making about the arrangements (Dunn et al., 2001). Although some research calls attention to the importance of children having a voice in formulating or shaping postdivorce parenting plans, there is the danger of burdening children with decisions that the adults cannot make. Giving children the right to be heard, if not done with sensitivity and care, may give children the responsibility for making an impossible choice between their two parents. There is a distinction between providing children with the possibility of input regarding their access arrangements and the inherent stresses of decision-making—a distinction with which children themselves seem quite familiar and comfortable (Kelly, 2002; McIntosh, 2000; Smart & Neale, 2000).

IMPLICATIONS FOR PRACTICE AND INTERVENTIONS

There are a number of important implications for practice and intervention that derive from this analysis of children's adjustment following divorce. Rather than communicating a global or undifferentiated view of the impact of divorce, research has begun to identify particular factors that increase children's risk following divorce and, equally important, those that are protective and promote resiliency in children and adolescents. Understanding this literature is central to promoting policies and developing and assessing services that have the potential to help mitigate family problems so that adjustment problems among children from divorced families are diminished. There are few better examples than the importance of adopting a systems approach (including family systems and broader social and legal systems) to helping these children. Whatever its specific nature or focus, interventions are more likely to benefit children from divorced families if they seek to contain parental conflict, promote authoritative and close relationships between children and *both* of their parents, enhance economic stability in the postdivorce family, and, when appropriate, involve children in effective interventions that help them have a voice in shaping more individualized and helpful, access arrangements (Kelly, 2002). . . .

■ Review Questions

1. What is the difference between having painful memories and having long-term psychological problems?
2. What "protective factors" reduce the risk that children will have serious problems after their parents get a divorce?

CHAPTER 13

Stepfamilies

At current rates, about one-third of all adults can expect to marry, divorce, and remarry during their lifetimes—a far higher proportion than in previous generations. When neither spouse has children from previous marriages, remarried life can be very similar to life in first marriages. To be sure, the spouses tend to be older, more established in their careers, and more set in their preferences about personal life, but the basic day-to-day interaction isn't all that different. However, when one or both partners has children from a previous marriage, then the remarriage creates a stepfamily. Stepfamilies also are formed when a woman who is raising a child born outside of marriage marries a man other than the father. In both types of stepfamilies, the new stepparent must adjust to the immediate presence of the children of the other spouse. This adjustment can be difficult, not just for the stepparent but for the biological parent and the stepchildren as well. If the stepchildren have contact with their noncustodial biological parent (who is usually their father), they create links with other households as they make visits to him. In this situation, it can be difficult for the remarried couple to forge a strong, viable partnership because of the tugs and pulls of stepchildren, biological children, and former spouses.

Moreover, family law and policy tend to ignore stepparents. In many states, they have few rights and responsibilities and cannot even sign a stepchild's permission form to go on a field trip. Mary Ann Mason argues in the first selection that this situation needs to change. She advocates modifications of law and public policy that would recognize the contribution of stepparents and more clearly define their position. But it's not easy to decide what changes would be best. Sometimes giving more responsibility to stepparents, such as requiring them to contribute to the support of their stepchildren, could make it easier for noncustodial biological parents to shirk their responsibilities. Mason thoughtfully considers these complications, describes the various positions legal observers take, and makes her recommendations.

Mason's article deals with what we might call conventional stepfamilies—those that are formed when an adult who is living with her (or, more rarely, his) biological child marries a partner who is unrelated to the child. But with the rise of cohabitation, other stepfamily-like families are

295

becoming more numerous. For instance, an adult living with her biological child may be cohabiting with, but not married to, a partner who is unrelated to the child. The partners, usually men, may show a great range of commitment to the mother and child: They may be as involved with the children as the best of stepfathers, or, on the other hand, they may have little to do with the children and may be in the household only for a short time before their relationships with the mothers end. How should we think about these cohabiting stepfamily-like households? Moreover, what are the experiences of the children living in them?

In the second selection, Sandi Nelson, Rebecca L. Clark, and Gregory Acs compare the well-being of children in these cohabiting families, which they sometimes call mother-boyfriend families, with (1) children who are living in conventional stepfamilies (mother married to stepparent), which they call blended families; (2) children living with unpartnered single parents; and (3) children living with two biological parents. They tabulate parents' reports on their living arrangements and on how their children are faring from a large national survey. Other studies have shown that children living in conventional stepfamilies have about the same levels of well-being as children living with a single parent—in other words, the presence of the stepparent doesn't, on balance, help or hinder them. In this article, Nelson, Clark, and Acs find evidence that children living in so-called mother-boyfriend families may have the lowest levels of well-being of the four types of families mentioned above.

The Modern American Stepfamily
Problems and Possibilities

Mary Ann Mason

Cinderella had one, so did Snow White and Hansel and Gretel. Our traditional cultural myths are filled with the presence of evil stepmothers. We learn from the stories read to us as children that stepparents, particularly stepmothers, are not to be trusted. They may pretend to love us in front of our biological parent, but the moment our real parent is out of sight they will treat us cruelly and shower their own children with kindnesses. Few modern children's tales paint stepparents so harshly, still the negative image of stepparents lingers in public policy. While the rights and obligations of biological parents, wed or unwed, have been greatly strengthened in recent times, stepparents have been virtually ignored. At best it is fair to say that as a society we have a poorly formed concept of the role of stepparents and a reluctance to clarify that role.

Indeed, the contrast between the legal status of stepparents and the presumptive rights and obligations of natural parents is remarkable. Child support obligations, custody rights, and inheritance rights exist between children and their natural parents by virtue of a biological tie alone, regardless of the quality of social or emotional bonds between parent and child, and regardless of whether the parents are married. In recent years policy changes have extended the rights and obligations of natural parents, particularly in regard to unwed and divorced parents, but have not advanced with regard to stepparents. Stepparents in most states

Mary Ann Mason, "The Modern American Stepfamily: Problems and Possibilities" in Mary Ann Mason, Arlene Skolnik, Stephen D. Sugarman (eds.), *All Our Families,* Oxford University Press, Chapter 5, pp. 96–97, 102–116. © 2003. Used by permission of Oxford University Press.

have no obligation during the marriage to support their stepchildren, nor do they enjoy any right of custody or control. Consistent with this pattern, if the marriage terminates through divorce or death, they usually have no rights to custody or even visitation, however longstanding their relationship with their stepchildren. Conversely, stepparents have no obligation to pay child support following divorce, even if their stepchildren have depended on their income for many years. In turn, stepchildren have no right of inheritance in the event of the stepparent's death (they are, however, eligible for Social Security benefits in most cases).[1]

Policymakers who spend a great deal of time worrying about the economic and psychological effects of divorce on children rarely consider the fact that about 70 percent of mothers are remarried within six years. Moreover, about 28 percent of children are born to unwed mothers, many of whom eventually marry someone who is not the father of their child. In a study including all children, not just children of divorce, it was estimated that one-fourth of the children born in the United States in the early 1980s will live with a stepparent before they reach adulthood.[2] These numbers are likely to increase in the future, at least as long as the number of single-parent families continues to grow. In light of these demographic trends, federal and state policies affecting families and children, as well as policies governing private-sector employee benefits, insurance, and other critical areas of everyday life, may need to be adapted to address the concerns of modern stepfamilies. . . .

STEPFAMILIES IN LAW AND PUBLIC POLICY

Both state and federal law set policies that affect stepfamilies. Overall, these policies do not reflect a coherent policy toward stepparents and stepchildren. Two competing models are roughly evident. One, a "stranger" model, followed by most states, treats the residential stepparent as if he or she were a legal stranger to the children, with no rights and no responsibilities. The other, a "dependency" model, most often followed by federal policymakers, assumes the residential stepfather is, in fact, supporting the stepchildren and provides benefits accordingly. But there is inconsistency in both state and federal policy. Some states lean at times toward a dependency model and require support in some instances, and the federal government sometimes treats the stepparent as if he or she were a stranger to the stepchildren, and ignores them in calculating benefits.

State law governs the traditional family matters of marriage, divorce, adoption, and inheritance, while federal law covers a wide range of programs and policies that touch on the lives of most Americans, including stepfamilies. As the provider of benefits through such programs as Temporary Aid for Needy Families (TANF) and Social Security, the federal government sets eligibility standards that affect the economic well-being of many stepfamilies. In addition, as the employer of the armed forces and civil servants, the federal government establishes employee benefits guidelines for vast numbers of American families. And in its regulatory role, the federal government defines the status of stepfamilies for many purposes ranging from immigration eligibility to tax liability.

Not covered in this chapter or, to my knowledge, yet systematically investigated are the wide range of private employee benefit programs, from medical and life insurance through educational benefits. These programs mostly take their lead from state or federal law. Therefore, it is fair to guess that they suffer from similar inconsistencies.

State Policies

State laws generally give little recognition to the dependency needs of children who reside with their stepparent; they are most likely to treat the stepparent as a stranger to the children, with no rights or obligations. In contrast to the numerous state laws obligating parents to support natural children born out of wedlock or within a previous marriage, only a few states have enacted statutes which specifically impose an affirmative duty on stepparents. The Utah stepparent support statute, for example, provides simply that "A stepparent shall support a stepchild to the same extent that a natural or adoptive parent is required to support a child."[3] This duty of support ends upon the termination of the marriage. Most states are silent on the obligation to support stepchildren.[4]

A few states rely on common law, the legal tradition stemming from our English roots. The common law tradition leans more toward a dependency model. It dictates that a stepparent can acquire the rights and duties of a parent if he or she acts *in loco parentis* (in the place of a parent). Acquisition of this status is not automatic; it is determined by the stepparent's intent. A stepparent need not explicitly state the intention to act as a parent; he or she can "manifest the requisite intent to assume responsibility by actually providing financial support or by taking over the custodial duties."[5] Courts, however, have been reluctant to grant *in loco* parental rights or to attach obligations to unwilling stepparents. In the words of one Wisconsin court, "A good Samaritan should not be saddled with the legal obligations of another and we think the law should not with alacrity conclude that a stepparent assumes parental relationships to a child."[6]

At the extreme, once the status of *in loco parentis* is achieved, the stepparent "stands in the place of the natural parent, and the reciprocal rights, duties, and obligations of parent and child subsist." These rights, duties, and obligations include the duty to provide financial support, the right to custody and control of the child, immunity from suit by the stepchild, and, in some cases, visitation rights after the dissolution of the marriage by death or divorce.

Yet stepparents who qualify as *in loco parentis* are not always required to provide support in all circumstances. A subset of states imposes obligation only if the stepchild is in danger of becoming dependent on public assistance. For example, Hawaii provides that

> A stepparent who acts in loco parentis is bound to provide, maintain, and support the stepparent's stepchild during the residence of the child with the stepparent if the legal parents desert the child or are unable to support the child, thereby reducing the child to destitute and necessitous circumstances.[7]

Just as states do not regularly require stepparents to support their stepchildren, they do not offer stepparents the parental authority of custody and control within the marriage. A residential stepparent generally has fewer rights than a legal guardian or a foster parent. According to one commentator, a stepparent "has no authority to make decisions about the child—no authority to approve emergency medical treatment or even to sign a permission slip for a field trip to the fire station."[8]

Both common law and state statutes almost uniformly terminate the stepparent relationship upon divorce or the death of the custodial parent. This means that the support obligations, if there were any, cease, and that the stepparent has no rights to visitation or custody. State courts have sometimes found individual exceptions to this rule, but they have not created any clear precedents. Currently only a few states authorize stepparents to seek visitation rights, and custody is almost always granted to a biological parent upon divorce. In the event of the death of the stepparent's spouse, the noncustodial, biological parent is usually granted custody even when the stepparent has, in fact, raised the child. In one such Michigan case, *Henrickson v. Gable*,[9] the children, aged nine and ten when their mother died, had lived with their stepfather since infancy and had rarely seen their biological father. In the ensuing custody dispute, the trial court left the children with their stepfather, but an appellate court, relying upon a state law that created a strong preference for biological parents, reversed this decision and turned the children over to their biological father.

Following the stranger model, state inheritance laws, with a few complex exceptions, do not recognize the existence of stepchildren. Under existing state laws, even a dependent stepchild whose stepparent has supported and raised the child for many years is not eligible to inherit from the stepparent if there is no will. California provides the most liberal rule for stepchild recovery when there is no will, but only if the stepchild meets relatively onerous qualifications. Stepchildren may inherit as the children of a deceased stepparent only if "it is established by clear and convincing evidence that the stepparent would have adopted the person but for a legal barrier."[10] Very few stepchildren have been able to pass this test. Similarly a stepchild cannot bring a negligence suit for the accidental death of a stepparent. In most instances, then, only a biological child will inherit or receive legal compensation when a stepparent dies.

Federal Policies

The federal policies that concern us here are of two types: federal benefit programs given to families in need, including TANF and Supplemental Security Income (SSI), and general programs not based on need, including Social Security as well as civil service and military personnel employee benefits. Most of these programs follow the dependency model. They go further than do most states in recognizing or promoting the actual family relationship of residential stepfamilies. Many of them (although not all) assume that residential stepparents support their stepchildren and accordingly make these children eligible for benefits equivalent to those afforded to other children of the family.

Despite the fact that federal law generally recognizes the dependency of residential stepchildren, it remains wanting in many respects. There is a great deal of inconsistency in how the numerous federal programs and policies treat the stepparent-stepchild relationship, and the very definitions of what constitutes a stepchild are often quite different across programs. Most of the programs strive for a dependency-based definition, such as living with or receiving 50 percent of support from a stepparent. However, some invoke the vague definition, "actual family relationship," and some do not attempt any definition at all, thus potentially including non-residential stepchildren among the beneficiaries. In some programs the category of stepchild is entirely absent or specifically excluded from the list of beneficiaries for some programs.

Even where program rules permit benefits for dependent stepchildren as for natural children, the benefits to stepchildren are typically severed by death or divorce.[11] While Social Security does cover dependent stepchildren in the event of death, several programs specifically exclude stepchildren from eligibility for certain death benefits. Under the Federal Employees' Retirement System, stepchildren are explicitly excluded from the definition of children in determining the default beneficiary, without concern for the stepchild's possible dependency. All stepchildren are similarly excluded from eligibility for lump-sum payments under the Foreign Service Retirement and Disability System and the CIA Retirement and Disability program.[12]

Stepchildren are even more vulnerable in the event of divorce. Here the stranger model is turned to. As with state law, any legally recognized relationship is immediately severed upon divorce in nearly all federal programs. The children and their stepparents become as strangers. Social Security does not provide any cushion for stepchildren if the deceased stepparent is divorced from the custodial parent. Under Social Security law, the stepparent-stepchild relationship is terminated immediately upon divorce and the stepchild is no longer eligible for benefits even if the child has in fact been dependent on the insured stepparent for the duration of a very long marriage.[13] If the divorce were finalized the day before the stepparent's death, the child would receive no benefits.

In sum, current federal policy goes part way toward defining the role of the stepparent by

assuming a dependency model in most programs, even when state law does not, and providing benefits to stepchildren based on this assumption of stepparent support. However, as described, existing federal stepparent policy falls short in several critical areas. And state laws and policies fall far short of federal policies in their consideration of stepfamilies, for the most part treating stepparents as strangers with regard to their stepchildren.

NEW POLICY PROPOSALS

Proposals for policy reform regarding stepfamilies are scant in number and, so far, largely unheard by policymakers. Most of the proposals come from legal scholars, a few from social scientists. Stepparents have not been organized to demand reform, nor have child advocates. All the reforms have some disagreements with the existing stranger and dependency models, but few offer a completely new model.

All of the proposals I review base their arguments to a greater or lesser degree on social science data, although not always the same data. The proposers may roughly be divided into three camps. The first, and perhaps smallest camp, I call *negativists.* These are scholars who view stepfamilies from a sociobiological perspective, and find them a troublesome aberration to be actively discouraged. The second, and by far largest group of scholars, I term *voluntarists.* This group acknowledges both the complexity and the often distant nature of stepparent relationships, and largely believes that law and policy should leave stepfamilies alone, as it does now. If stepparents wish to take a greater role in their stepchildren's lives, they should be encouraged to do so, by adoption or some other means. The third camp recognizes the growing presence of stepfamilies as an alternate family form and believes they should be recognized and strengthened in some important ways. This group, I call them *reformists,* believes the law should take the lead in providing more rights or obligations to stepparents. The few policy initiatives from this group range from small specific reforms regarding such issues as inheritance and visitation to my own proposal for a full-scale redefinition of stepparents' rights and obligations.

The negativist viewpoint on stepparenting, most prominently represented by sociologist David Popenoe, relies on a sociobiological theory of reproduction. According to this theory, human beings will give unstintingly to their own biological children, in order to promote their own genes, but will be far less generous to others. The recent rise in divorce and out-of-wedlock births, according to Popenoe, has created a pattern of essentially fatherless households that cannot compete with the two-biological-parent families.

Popenoe believes the pattern of stepparent disengagement revealed by many researchers is largely based on this biological stinginess.

> If the argument . . . is correct, and the family is fundamentally rooted in biology and at least partly activated by the "genetically selfish" activities of human beings, childbearing by non relatives is inherently problematic. It is not that unrelated individuals are unable to do the job of parenting, it is just that they are not as likely to do the job well. Stepfamily problems, in short, may be so intractable that the best strategy for dealing with them is to do everything possible to minimize their occurrence.

Moreover, Popenoe cites researchers on the greatly increased incidence of child abuse by stepfathers over natural fathers, who suggest that "stepchildren are not merely 'disadvantaged' but imperiled."[14] This argument is not so farfetched, he claims, in fact it is the stuff of our folk wisdom. Snow White and Hansel and Gretel had it right; stepparents are not merely uncaring, they may be dangerous.

Popenoe goes beyond the stranger model, which is neutral as to state activity, and suggests an active discouragement of stepparent families. He believes the best way to obstruct stepfamilies is to encourage married biological two-parent families. Premarital and marital counseling, a longer waiting period for divorce, and a redesign of the current welfare system so that marriage and family are empowered rather than denigrated are among his policy recommendations. He is heartened by what he calls the "new familism," a growing recognition of the need for strong social bonds, which he believes can best be found in the biological two-parent family.[15]

The second group of scholars, whom I call voluntarists, generally believe that the stepparent relationship is essentially voluntary and private and the stranger model most clearly reflects this. The legal bond formed by remarriage is between man and wife—stepchildren are incidental; they are legal strangers. Stepparents may choose, or not choose, to become more involved with everyday economic and emotional support of their stepchildren; but the law should not mandate this relationship, it should simply reflect it. These scholars recognize the growth of stepfamilies as a factor of modern life and neither condone nor condemn this configuration. Family law scholar David Chambers probably speaks for most scholars in this large camp when he says,

> In most regards, this state of the law nicely complements the state of stepparent relationships in the United States. Recall the inescapable diversity of such relationships—residential and non-residential, beginning when the children are infants and when they are teenagers, leading to comfortable relationships in some cases and awkward relationships in others, lasting a few years and lasting many. In this context it seems sensible to permit those relationships to rest largely on the voluntary arrangements among stepparents and biologic parents. The current state of the law also amply recognizes our nation's continuing absorption with the biologic relationship, especially as it informs our sensibilities about enduring financial obligations.[16]

Chambers is not enthusiastic about imposing support obligations on stepparents, either during or following the termination of a marriage, but is interested in promoting voluntary adoption. He would, however, approve some middle ground where biological parents are not completely cut off in the adoption process.

Other voluntarists are attracted by the new English model of parenting, as enacted in the Children Act of 1989. Of great attraction to American voluntarists is the fact that under this model a stepparent who has been married at least two years to the biological parent may voluntarily petition for a residence order for his or her spouse's child. With a residence order the stepparent has parental responsibility toward the child until the age of sixteen. But this order does not extinguish the parental responsibility of the noncustodial parent.[17] In accordance with the Children Act of 1989, parents, biological or otherwise, no longer have parental rights, they have only parental responsibilities, and these cannot be extinguished upon the divorce of the biological parents. In England, therefore, it is possible for three adults to claim parental responsibility. Unlike biological parental responsibility, however, stepparent responsibility does not usually extend following divorce. The stepparent is not normally financially responsible following divorce, but he or she may apply for a visitation order.

The third group, whom I call reformists, believe that voluntary acts on the part of stepparents are not always adequate, and that it is necessary to reform the law in some way to more clearly define the rights and responsibilities of stepparents. The American Bar Association Family Law Section has been working for some years on a proposed Model Act to suggest legislative reforms regarding stepparents' obligations to provide child support and rights to discipline, visitation, and custody. A Model Act is not binding anywhere; it is simply a model for all states to consider. Traditionally, however, Model Acts have been very influential in guiding state legislative reform. In its current form, the ABA Model Act would require stepparents to assume a duty of support during the duration of the remarriage only if the child is not adequately supported by the custodial and noncustodial parent. The issue is ultimately left to the discretion of the family court, but the Model Act does not require that the stepparent would need to have a close relationship with a stepchild before a support duty is imposed. The Model Act, however, does not describe what the rule should be if the stepparent and the custodial parent divorce.

The proposed statute is rather more complete in its discussion of stepparent visitation or custody rights following divorce. It takes a two-tiered approach, first asking if the stepparent has standing (a legal basis) to seek visitation and then asking if the visitation would be in the best interests of the child. The standing question is to be resolved with reference to five factors, which essentially examine the role of the stepparent in the child's life (almost an *in loco parentis* question), the financial support offered by the stepparent, and the detriment to the child from denying visitation. The court, if it finds standing, then completes the analysis with the best interests standard of the jurisdiction. The Model Act's section on physical custody also requires a two-tiered test, requiring standing and increasing the burden on the stepparent to present clear and convincing proof that he or she is the better custodial parent.

The ABA Model Act is a worthwhile start, in my opinion, but it is little more than that. At most it moves away from a stranger model and provides a limited concept of mandatory stepparent support during a marriage, acknowledging that stepchildren are at least sometimes dependent. It also gives a stepparent a fighting chance for visitation or custody following a divorce. It fails to clarify stepparents' rights during the marriage, however, and does not deal with the issue of economic support at the period of maximum vulnerability, the termination of the marriage through death and divorce. Moreover, the Model Act, and, indeed, all the existing reform proposals, deal only with traditional legal concepts of parenthood defined by each state and do not consider the vast range of federal programs, or other public and private programs, that define the stepparent-stepchild relationship for purposes of benefits, insurance, or other purposes.

I propose, instead, a new conceptualization of stepparent rights and responsibilities, a de facto parent model, that will cover all aspects of the stepparent-stepchild relationship and will extend to federal and private policy as well. My first concern in proposing a new framework is the welfare of the stepchildren, which is not adequately dealt with in either the stranger or the dependency model. The failure of state and, to a lesser extent, federal policy to address coherently the financial interdependencies of step relationships, described earlier in this chapter, means that children dependent upon a residential stepparent may not receive adequate support or benefits from that parent during the marriage, and they may not be protected economically in the event of divorce or parental death.

The longitudinal studies of families described earlier in this chapter suggest that the most difficult periods for children are those of marital transition, for example, divorce and remarriage. Families with a residential stepfather have a much higher family income than mother-headed single families; indeed, their household incomes look much like nuclear families.[18] However, research demonstrates that stepfamilies are fragile and are more likely to terminate in divorce than biological families. The event of divorce can quite suddenly pull the resources available for the children back to the single-parent level. Currently children are at least financially cushioned by child support following the divorce of their biological parents, but have no protective support following the breakup of their stepfamily. Nor are they protected in the event of the death of the stepparent, which is certainly another period of vulnerability (as discussed earlier, only a small minority continue to receive support from non-custodial parents).

A second reason for proposing a new framework is to strengthen the relationship of the stepparent and stepchildren. While research generally finds that stepparents are less engaged in parenting than natural parents, research studies do not explain the causes; others must do so. In addition to the sociobiologists' claim for stingy, genetically driven behavior, sociologists have posited the explanation of "incomplete institutionalization."[19] This theory is based on the belief that, by and large, people act as they are expected to act by society. In the case of stepfamilies, there are unclear or absent societal norms and standards for how to define the remarried family, especially the role of the stepparent in relation to the stepchild.

Briefly, my new model requires, first of all, dividing stepparents into two subclasses: those who are de facto parents and those who are not. De facto parents would be defined as "those stepparents legally married to a natural parent who primarily reside with their stepchildren, or who provide at least 50 percent of the stepchild's financial support." Stepparents who do not meet the de facto parent requirements would, in all important respects, disappear from policy.

For the purposes of federal and state policy, under this scheme, a de facto parent would be treated virtually the same as a natural parent during the marriage. The same rights, obligations, and presumptions would attach vis-à-vis their stepchildren, including the obligation of support. These rights and duties would continue in some form, based on the length of the marriage, following the custodial parent's death or divorce from the stepparent, or the death of the stepparent. In the event of divorce the stepparent would have standing to seek custody or visitation but the stepparent could also be obligated for child support of a limited duration. Upon the death of a stepparent, a minor stepchild would be treated for purposes of inheritance and benefits as would a natural child.

So far this proposal resembles the common law doctrine of *in loco parentis,* described earlier, where the stepparent is treated for most purposes (except inheritance) as a parent on the condition that he or she voluntarily agrees to support the child. In the de facto model, however, support is mandatory, not voluntary, on the grounds both that it is not fair to stepchildren to be treated by the law in an unequal or arbitrary manner, and that child welfare considerations are best met by uniform support of stepchildren. Furthermore, in the traditional common law *in loco parentis* scenario, the noncustodial parent had died and was not a factor to be reckoned with. Under this scheme, creating a de facto parent category for stepparents would not invalidate the existing rights and obligations of a noncustodial biological parent. Rather, this proposal would empower a stepparent as an additional parent.

Multiple parenting and the rights and obligations of the stepparent and children following divorce or death are controversial and difficult policy matters that require more detailed attention than the brief exposition that can be offered here. Multiple parenting is the barrier upon which many family law reform schemes, especially in custody and adoption, have foundered. It is also one of the reasons that there has been no consistent effort to reformulate the role of stepparents. Working out the details is critical. For instance, mandating stepparent support raises a central issue of fairness. If the stepparent is indeed required to support the child, there is a question about the support obligations of the noncustodial parent. Traditionally, most states have not recognized the stepparent contribution as an offset to child support.[20] While this policy promotes administrative efficiency, and may benefit some children, it may not be fair to the noncustodial parent. An important advance in recognizing the existence of multiple parents in the nonlinear family is to recognize multiple support obligations. The few states that require stepparent obligation have given limited attention to apportionment of child support obligations, offering no clear guidelines. I propose that state statutory requirements for stepparent obligation as de facto parents also include clear guidelines for apportionment of child support between the noncustodial natural parent and the stepparent.

Critics of this proposal may say that if the custodial parent's support is reduced, the child will have fewer resources. For some children, this may be true, but as discussed earlier in this chapter, only about 25 percent of all stepchildren receive child support and the average amount is less than $2000 per year.[21] Therefore, a reduction of this small amount of support to a minority of stepchildren would not have a large overall effect compared with the increased resources of living with a stepparent that most stepchildren enjoy. And, certainly, the additional safety net of protection in the event of the death of the stepparent or divorce from the custodial parent would benefit all stepchildren. In addition, under the de facto scheme, the reduction of the support payment for the noncustodial parent may help to sweeten the multiple parenting relationship.

Let us apply this model to the Jones-Hutchins family introduced earlier. If Ray Jones, the noncustodial parent, were paying $6000 a year support for his two children (on the high end for noncustodial parents according to the National Survey for Children and Families), his payments could be reduced by as much as half, since Sam Hutchins's income is $50,000 per year and he has no other dependents. It should be emphasized, however, that in most stepfamilies there would be no reduction in support, because the noncustodial parent is paying no support. In the Jones-Hutchins family the $3000 relief would certainly be welcome to Ray, who is also now living with and helping to support his new wife's child. The relief would likely make him somewhat friendlier toward Sam, or at least more accepting of his role in his children's lives. It also might make him more likely to continue support past eighteen, since he would not feel as financially pinched over the years. More important, while the children would lose some support, they would have the security that if Sam died they would be legal heirs and default beneficiaries to his life insurance. They could also ask for damages if his death were caused by negligence or work-related events. And if he and their mother divorced, they could continue for a time to be considered dependents on his health and other benefits and to receive support from him.

Another facet of multiple parenting is legal authority. If stepparents are required to accept parental support obligations, equal protection and fairness concerns dictate that they must also be given parental rights. Currently, state laws, as noted earlier, recognize only natural or adoptive parents; a stepparent currently has no legal authority over a stepchild, even to authorize a field trip. If stepparents had full parental rights, in some cases, as when the parents have shared legal custody, the law would be recognizing the parental rights of three parents, rather than two. While this sounds unusual, it is an accurate reflection of how many families now raise their children. Most often, however, it would be only the custodial parent and his or her spouse, the de facto parent, who would have authority to make decisions for the children in their home.

In the Jones-Hutchins family this policy would give Sam more recognition as a parent. Schools, camps, hospitals, and other institutions that require parental consent or involvement would now automatically include him in their consideration of the children's interests. Since Sam is the more day-to-day parent, their biological father, Ray, may not mind at all. If he did mind, the three of them would have to work it out (or in an extreme event, take it to mediation or family court). In fact, since only a minority of noncustodial dads see their children on a regular basis, three-parent decision making would be unusual.

Critics of this scheme may argue that adoption, not the creation of the legal status of de facto parent, is the appropriate vehicle for granting a stepparent full parental rights and responsibilities.[22] If, as discussed earlier, nearly three-quarters of stepchildren are not being supported by their noncustodial parents, policy initiatives could be directed to terminating the nonpaying parents' rights and promoting stepparent adoption. Adoption is not possible, however, unless the parental rights of the absent natural parent have been terminated—a difficult procedure against a reluctant parent. Normally, the rights of a parent who maintains contact with his or her child cannot be terminated even if that parent is not contributing child support. And when parental rights are terminated, visitation rights are terminated as well in most states. It is by no means clear that it is in the best interests of children to terminate contact with a natural parent, even if the parent is not meeting his or her obligation to support.[23] As discussed earlier, a large percentage (another 25 percent or so) of noncustodial parents continue some contact with their children, even when not paying support.[24] And while stepparent adoption should be strongly encouraged when it is possible, this solution will not resolve the problem of defining the role of stepparents who have not adopted.

Extending, in some form, the rights and obligations following the termination of the marriage by divorce or death is equally problematical. Currently, only a few courts have ruled in favor of support payments following divorce, and these have been decided on an individual basis. Only one state, Missouri, statutorily continues stepparent support obligations following divorce.[25] It would clearly be in the best interests of the child to experience continued support, since a significant number of children may sink below the poverty line upon the dissolution of their stepfamily.[26]

Since the de facto model is based on dependency, not blood, a fair basis for support following divorce or the death of the custodial parent might be to require that a stepparent who qualified as a de facto parent for at least one year must contribute child support for half the number of years of dependency until the child reached majority. If a child resided with the stepparent for four years, the stepparent would be liable for support for two years. If the biological noncustodial parent were still paying support payments, the amount could be apportioned. While it may be said that this policy would discourage people from becoming stepparents by marrying, it could also be said to discourage divorce once one has become a stepparent. Stepparents might consider working harder at maintaining a marriage if divorce had some real costs.

Conversely, stepparents should have rights as well as responsibilities following divorce or the death of the custodial parent. Divorced or widowed stepparents should be able to pursue visitation or custody if they have lived with and supported the child for at least one year. Once again, multiple parent claims might sometimes be an issue, but these could be resolved, as they are now, under a primary caretaker, or a best interest standard.

The death of a stepparent is a particular period of vulnerability for stepchildren for which they are unprotected by inheritance law. While Social Security and other federal survivor benefits are based on the premise that a stepchild relies on the support of the residential stepparent and will suffer the same hardship as natural children if the stepparent dies, state inheritance laws, notoriously archaic, decree that only biology, not dependency, counts. State laws should assume that a de facto parent would wish to have all his dependents receive a share of his estate if he died without a will. If the stepchildren are no longer dependent, that assumption would not necessarily prevail. The same assumption should prevail for insurance policies and compensation claims following an accidental death. A dependent stepchild, just as a natural child, should have the right to sue for loss of support.

On the federal front, a clear definition of stepparents as de facto parents would eliminate the inconsistencies regarding stepparents which plague current federal policies and would clarify the role of the residential stepparent. For the duration of the marriage, a stepchild would be treated as a natural child for purposes of support and the receipt of federal benefits. This treatment would persist in the event of the death of the stepparent. The stepchild would receive all the survivor and death benefits that would accrue to a natural child.[27]

In the case of divorce, the issue of federal benefits is more complicated. Stepchildren and natural children should not have identical coverage for federal benefits following divorce, again, but neither is it good policy to summarily cut off children who have been dependent, sometimes for many years, on the de facto parent. A better policy is to extend federal benefits for a period following divorce, based on a formula that matches half the number of years of dependency, as earlier suggested for child support. For instance, if the stepparent resided with the stepchild for four years, the child would be covered by Social Security survivor benefits and other federal benefits, including federal employee benefits, for a period of two years following the divorce. This solution would serve children by at least providing a transitional cushion. It would also be relatively easy to administer. In the case of the death of the biological custodial parent, benefits could be similarly extended, or continued indefinitely if the child remains in the custody of the stepparent.

All other private benefits programs would similarly gain from the application of a clear definition of the rights and obligations of residential stepparents. While these nongovernmental programs, ranging from eligibility for private health and life insurance and annuities to access to employee child care, are not reviewed in this chapter, they almost surely reflect the same inconsistencies or silences evident in federal and state policies.

Ultimately, state law defines most of these stepfamily relationships, and it is difficult, if not impossible to achieve uniform reform on a state-by-state basis. In England it is possible to pass a single piece of national legislation, such as the Children Act of 1989, which completely redefines parental roles. In America, the process of reform is slower and less sure. Probably the first step in promoting a new policy would be for the federal government to insist all states pass stepparent general support obligation laws requiring stepparents acting as de facto parents (by my definition) to support their stepchildren as they do their natural children. This goal could be accomplished by making stepparent general support obligation laws a prerequisite for receiving federal welfare grants. Federal policy already assumes this support in figuring eligibility in many programs, but it has not insisted that states change their laws. Precedent for this strategy has been set by the Family Support Acts of 1988 in which the federal government mandated that states set up strict child support enforcement laws for divorced parents and unwed fathers at TANF levels in order to secure AFDC funding.[28] The second, larger step would be to require limited stepparent support following divorce, as described previously. Once the basic obligations were asserted, an articulation of basic rights would presumably follow.

CONCLUSION

Stepfamilies compose a large and growing sector of American families that is largely ignored by public policy. Social scientists tell us that these families have problems. Stepparent-stepchildren relationships, poorly defined by legal and social norms, are not as strong or nurturing as those in non-divorced families, and stepchildren do not do as well in school and in other outside settings. Still, stepfamily relationships are important in lifting single-parent families out of poverty. When single or divorced mothers marry, the household income increases by more than threefold, rising to roughly the same level as nuclear families. A substantial portion of these families experiences divorce, however, placing the stepchildren at risk of falling back into poverty. It makes good public policy sense then, both to strengthen these stepfamily relationships and to cushion the transition for stepchildren should the relationship end.

■ Review Questions

1. Give an example of how the law follows the "stranger model" of stepparenting.
2. Should stepparents have the same obligation to support the children in their families as biological parents do?

ENDNOTES

1. Mary Ann Mason and David Simon, "The Ambiguous Stepparent: Federal Legislation in Search of a Model," *Family Law Quarterly* 29:446–448, 1995.
2. E. Mavis Heatherington and Kathleen M. Jodl, "Stepfamilies as Settings for Child Development," in Alan Booth and Judy Dunn (eds.), *Stepfamilies: Who Benefits? Who Does Not?* (Hillsdale, N.J.: L. Erlbaum 1994), 55; E. Mavis Heatherington, "An Overview of the Virginia Longitudinal Study of Divorce and Remarriage: A Focus on Early Adolescence," *Journal of Family Psychology* 7:39–56, 1993.
3. Utah Code Ann. 78-45-4.1.
4. Margaret Mahoney, *Stepfamilies and the Law* (Ann Arbor: University of Michigan Press, 1994), 13–47.
5. Miller v. United States, 123 F.2d 715, 717 (8th Cir. 1941).
6. Niesen v. Niesen, 157 N.W.2d 660, 664 (Wis. 1968).
7. Hawaii Revised Stat. Ann., Title 31, Sec. 577-4.
8. David Chambers, "Stepparents, Biologic Parents, and the Law's Perceptions of 'Family' after Divorce," in S. Sugarman and H. H. Kay (eds.), *Divorce Reform at the Crossroads* (New Haven: Yale University Press, 1990), 102–129.
9. Henrickson v. Gable.
10. Cal. Prob. Code, Sec. 6408.
11. Mason and Simon, "The Ambiguous Stepparent: Federal Legislation in Search of a Model," 449.

12. Ibid., pp. 460–466.
13. 42 U.S.C. sec. 416(e), 1994.
14. M. Daly and M. Wilson, *Homicide* (New York: Aldine de Gruyter, 1988), 230.
15. Barbara Whitehead, "A New Familism?" *Family Affairs,* Summer, 1992.
16. Chambers, "Stepparents, Biologic Parents, and the Law's Perceptions of 'Family' after Divorce," 26.
17. Mark A. Fine, "Social Policy Pertaining to Stepfamilies: Should Stepparents and Stepchildren Have the Option of Establishing a Legal Relationship?" in Booth and Dunn (eds.), *Stepfamilies,* 199.
18. Mary Ann Mason and Jane Mauldon, "The New Stepfamily Needs a New Public Policy," *Journal of Social Issues* 52(3):5, Fall 1996.
19. Andrew Cherlin, "Remarriage as an Incomplete Institution," *American Journal of Sociology* 84:634–649, 1978.
20. S. Ramsey and J. Masson, "Stepparent Support of Stepchildren: A Comparative Analysis of Policies and Problems in the American and British Experience," *Syracuse Law Review* 36:649–666, 1985.
21. Mason and Mauldon, "The New Stepfamily," 7.
22. Joan Hollinger (ed.) et al., *Adoption Law and Practice* (New York: Matthew Bender, 1988).
23. Katherine Bartlett, "Re-thinking Parenthood as an Exclusive Status: The Need for Alternatives When the Premise of the Nuclear Family Has Failed," *Virginia Law Review* 70:879–903, 1984.
24. Mason and Mauldon, "The New Stepfamily," 5.
25. Vernon's Ann. Missouri Stats. 453.400, 1994.
26. Mason and Mauldon, "The New Stepfamily," 5.
27. Mason and Simon, "The Ambiguous Stepparent," 471.
28. 100 P.L. 485; 102 Stat. 2343 (1988).

READING 13-2

Beyond the Two-Parent Family

How Teenagers Fare in Cohabiting Couple and Blended Families

Sandi Nelson

Rebecca L. Clark

Gregory Acs

Although the rapid rise in cohabitation has been well documented, little is known about how children fare in cohabiting families compared with children in traditional two-parent, stepparent,

Sandi Nelson, Rebecca L. Clark, and Gregory Acs, "Beyond the Two-Parent Family: How Teenagers Fare in Cohabiting Couple and Blended Families" from *New Federalism: National Survey of America's Families,* Series B, No. B-31, May 2001, by The Urban Institute

and single-parent households (Bumpass and Raley 1995; Manning and Lichter 1996; Smock and Manning 1997).[1] Previous research on the effects of living arrangements on child outcomes has shown that, in general, children living with their married biological parents exhibit the lowest rates of behavioral problems and perform better at school, while children in single-parent families tend to fare worse across these outcomes.

In this brief, we use data from the 1997 National Survey of America's Families (NSAF)[2] to examine whether children living in cohabiting families with their mothers and their mothers' boyfriends (who are not related to the children) are any better or worse off than children living with just a single mother. We also compare outcomes for children living in families in which their mothers have married their boyfriends (forming "blended" families) with outcomes for children living with a single mother as well as with outcomes for children living with married biological parents.[3] Specifically, we focus on behavioral problems among

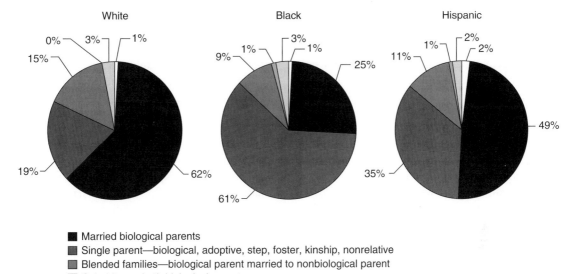

Married biological parents
Single parent—biological, adoptive, step, foster, kinship, nonrelative
Blended families—biological parent married to nonbiological parent
Cohabitors—both biological parents
Cohabitors—one biological parent with boyfriend/girlfriend
Other—married and unmarried adoptive, foster, kinship, and nonrelative couples

FIGURE 13.1

Teenagers' (12- to 17-year-olds) living arrangements, by race: 1997. (*Source:* Urban Institute calculations from the 1997 National Survey of America's Families. *Note:* Only teenagers whose respondent parent(s) were either the most knowledgeable adult or the spouse/partner were included.)

teenagers (12- to 17-year-olds). We begin by documenting the living arrangements of teenagers and then use a multivariate, regression-based model to examine how living arrangements affect teenagers' behavioral outcomes.

LIVING ARRANGEMENTS OF TEENAGERS

Figure 13.1 shows the living arrangements of teenagers by race/ethnic group.[4] Most white teenagers (62 percent) live with married biological parents; in contrast, 49 percent of Hispanic teenagers and only 25 percent of black teenagers live in such families. Whites are also the most likely to live in blended families: 15 percent of them do, compared with 9 and 11 percent of blacks and Hispanics, respectively. For black teenagers, the most common living arrangement is with a single parent; a significant share of Hispanic teenagers live in single-parent families

(35 percent), while about one in five white teenagers live in such families.

The percentage of teenagers living in cohabiting families is relatively low (3 to 4 percent) and does not vary dramatically across race/ethnic groups; however, there are some important differences in the types of cohabiting families. About one-quarter of black teenagers and nearly one-third of Hispanic teenagers in cohabiting families live with both biological parents—that is, they live with both their mother and father, but their parents are not married. In contrast, virtually all white teenagers in cohabiting families live with one biological parent and that parent's boyfriend or girlfriend.

HOW TEENAGERS FARE IN BLENDED AND COHABITING FAMILIES

Next we examine whether differences in living arrangements affect teenagers' behavioral and emotional well-being. We specifically focus on three outcomes: (1) whether the teenager has emotional or behavioral problems;[5] (2) whether the teenager exhibits a low level of school engagement;[6] and (3) whether the teenager has been suspended or expelled from school in the past year.[7, 8] We use a multivariate approach to isolate the impact of living arrangements on these outcomes by controlling for other important differences across teenagers, such as parental education and family income levels.[9]

In general, families with a husband or boyfriend present have higher incomes than families with a single mother. By taking income differences into account, we can detect any advantages (or disadvantages) conferred on teenagers through having a man present beyond the additional income he may provide. However, the additional income itself may provide an important benefit: If a boyfriend's or stepfather's income lifts a teenager out of poverty, the teenager's behavioral outcomes are likely to improve.

For ease of presentation and interpretation, we use our multivariate results to generate predicted probabilities for each outcome for each of four separate living arrangements: living with married biological parents, living in a blended family, living with cohabitors (a single mother and her boyfriend who is not related to the teenager),[10] and living with a single mother.[11] We conduct separate analyses for three race/ethnic groups (whites, blacks, and Hispanics) and present the predicted probabilities for each outcome separately (see Table 13.1).

TEENAGERS IN COHABITING FAMILIES

White and Hispanic teenagers living in cohabiting families fare worse, on average, than those living with single mothers. White teenagers living with cohabitors are significantly more likely to exhibit low school engagement than those living with a single mother (39.3 and 27.9 percent, respectively). Similarly, white teenagers living with cohabitors are more likely to be suspended

or expelled from school than those living with a single mother (23.0 and 11.3 percent, respectively). In addition, white teenagers living with cohabitors are just as likely as those living with a single mother to have emotional and behavioral problems.

Similarly, for Hispanic teenagers, living in a cohabiting family significantly increases the likelihood of exhibiting problem behaviors relative to living with a single mother across all three outcome measures. Hispanic teenagers living with cohabitors have a 37.7 percent chance of experiencing emotional and behavioral problems, while those living with a single mother have only a 10.8 percent chance. The differences for school behavior are just as dramatic: Hispanic teenagers living with a single mother have a 38.3 percent likelihood of having low engagement with school and a 15.2 percent chance of being suspended or expelled; those living with cohabitors have a 66.2 and 42.0 percent likelihood, respectively.

The impact of cohabitation on black teenagers is less dramatic. Black teenagers living in cohabiting families have the same levels of emotional and behavioral problems and school engagement as black teenagers living with single mothers. However, they are more likely to have been suspended or expelled than those living with single mothers (56.4 and 30.6 percent, respectively). Overall, black teenagers with a cohabiting mother are no better off than those with a single mother; on some measures they are actually worse off.

TEENAGERS IN BLENDED FAMILIES

Although cohabitation rates are increasing, far more teenagers live in blended families, and some may argue that outcomes for teenagers would improve if single mothers and cohabitors were to marry, forming blended families. Table 13.1 shows that living in a blended family is neither better nor worse than living in a single-mother family for white teenagers in terms of the behavioral outcomes we consider. Indeed, for teenagers in both blended and single-mother families,

TABLE 13.1

THE RELATIONSHIP BETWEEN LIVING ARRANGEMENTS AND THREE BEHAVIORAL PROBLEM INDICATORS AMONG 12- TO 17-YEAR-OLDS

Living arrangement	Predicted percentage of teenagers with emotional and behavioral problems	Predicted percentage of teenagers with low levels of school engagement	Predicted percentage of teenagers suspended or expelled from school in the past year
White teenagers living with			
Married biological parents	3.6	18.9	7.1
Blended—mother and step- or adoptive father	10.1[a]	23.8[a]	9.5[a]
Cohabitors—mother and boyfriend	10.0[a]	39.3[a,b]	23.0[a,b]
Single mother	9.7[a]	27.9[a]	11.3[a]
Hispanic teenagers living with			
Married biological parents	2.8	17.1	9.7
Blended—mother and step- or adoptive father	8.1[a]	34.9[a]	23.1[a,b]
Cohabitors—mother and boyfriend	37.7[a,b]	66.2[a,b]	42.0[a,b]
Single mother	10.8[a]	38.3[a]	15.2[a]
Black teenagers living with			
Married biological parents	6.1	25.7	10.4
Blended—mother and step- or adoptive father	6.1[b]	36.1[a]	18.9[a,b]
Cohabitors—mother and boyfriend	14.9[a]	37.1	56.4[a,b]
Single mother	11.7[a]	32.5[a]	30.6[a]

Source: Urban Institute calculations from logit estimates of determinants of emotional and behavioral problems, low school engagement, and suspensions and expulsions on data from the 1997 National Survey of America's Families.
Differences are significant at the 90 percent confidence level.
a. Statistically significant difference from teenagers living with married biological parents.
b. Statistically significant difference from teenagers living with a single mother.
Note: Predicted probabilities for teenagers with unmarried biological parents are not shown because of insufficient sample sizes.

the chance of exhibiting behavioral or emotional problems and the chance of being expelled or suspended is about 1 in 10; the chance of having low school engagement is about 1 in 4. Thus, although outcomes for white teenagers in blended families are no better than those for white teenagers in single-mother families when other factors are held constant, blended arrangements do not have the same negative outcomes as those associated with cohabitation.

In these respects, Hispanic teenagers are similar to white teenagers. Hispanic teenagers living in blended families are equally likely to have emo-

tional and behavioral problems and to exhibit low levels of school engagement as are teenagers living with single mothers, and they are more likely to be expelled or suspended from school (23.1 and 15.2 percent, respectively). Overall, living in a blended family rather than with a single mother is not associated with better outcomes for Hispanics.

In contrast, black teenagers living in blended families generally fare better than their counterparts living with single mothers: They are less likely to have emotional and behavioral problems (6.1 and 11.7 percent, respectively) and to have been suspended or expelled (18.9 and 30.6

percent, respectively). Black teenagers in blended and single-mother families have similar levels of low school engagement (36.1 and 32.5 percent, respectively). Overall, a black teenager, unlike a white or Hispanic teenager, is better off in a blended family than in a single-mother family.

TEENAGERS LIVING WITH MARRIED BIOLOGICAL PARENTS

Not surprisingly, teenagers living with married biological parents are far less likely to exhibit behavioral problems than are those living with cohabitors and those living in blended families. Indeed, only 3.6 percent of white teenagers living with married biological parents have emotional and behavioral problems, 18.9 percent have low levels of school engagement, and 7.1 percent have been suspended or expelled. The predicted incidences of these problems for Hispanic teenagers in married biological parent families are similar to those for whites.

Compared with black teenagers who live in cohabiting families, those living with married biological parents are significantly less likely to experience emotional and behavioral problems (14.9 and 6.1 percent, respectively) and to have been suspended or expelled from school (56.4 and 10.4 percent, respectively); they are also less likely to exhibit low school engagement (37.1 and 25.7 percent, respectively), but the difference is not statistically significant. Black teenagers living with married biological parents also run a significantly lower risk of poor outcomes relative to those who live in blended families on two of the three measures, although they are equally likely to experience emotional and behavioral problems. Black teenagers in both blended and married biological parent families have a 6.1 percent chance of exhibiting emotional and behavioral problems.

CONCLUSION

The living arrangements of teenagers vary significantly by race and ethnicity, with white teenagers far more likely to live with married biological parents and black teenagers more likely to live in single-parent families. Further, these differences in living arrangements are associated with differences in teenagers' behavior.

Specifically, our analysis of the relationship between teenagers' living arrangements and their behavioral outcomes shows that living with a single mother and her boyfriend is no better than living with a single mother. In many cases (particularly for whites and Hispanics), it is significantly worse. The most favorable outcomes we observe are for teenagers living with their biological parents who are married to each other. Beyond that arrangement, for white and Hispanic teenagers, living in a blended or single-mother family is relatively interchangeable, and living with cohabitors is associated with the poorest behavioral outcomes. For black teenagers, however, living in a blended family is associated with better outcomes than living with either a single mother or with cohabitors.

Our analysis is subject to certain limitations. First, we find a correlation between cohabitation and poorer behavioral outcomes for teenagers. This may indicate that the teenager's problems stem from the presence of a cohabitor; however, there are several other potential explanations. For example, a single mother with a troubled teenager may be more likely to seek out a partner than a single mother without a troubled teenager. Alternatively, unmeasured characteristics of the mother may affect both child outcomes and her marital/cohabitation status. It may also be the case that differences in outcomes for children living with a mother and her boyfriend compared with a mother and a stepfather are related to the quality of the mother–partner relationship.

Second, there may be different outcomes for teenagers living with cohabitors, depending on whether the cohabitors are both biological parents of the teenager or are a mother with her current boyfriend. Unfortunately, our analysis is constrained by the small number of cases of cohabiting biological parents, particularly when we separate the population by the race/ethnicity of the teenager. Consequently, we only present results for cohabiting families in which the male is the mother's boyfriend, not the biological father of the teenager.

Third, our analysis is limited to only three outcomes: two addressing school problems and one dealing with emotional and behavioral problems.

Finally, this analysis examines the relationship between behavioral problems and living arrangements for 12- to 17-year-olds only. Younger children may benefit from having their biological father present even if he is not married to the child's mother. Future analyses should address the relationship between behavioral problems and living in both types of cohabiting couple families for children of all ages.

The number of children living with cohabiting couples is increasing despite legislators' efforts to encourage the formation and maintenance of married two-parent families through the Personal Responsibility and Work Opportunity Reconciliation Act (PRWORA) of 1996. Our research suggests that cohabiting couple families are not simply an extension of traditional married biological or blended parent families. Instead, children in these types of families represent a unique group that is particularly at risk for behavioral problems, often more so than their counterparts in single-mother families. Policymakers and researchers should be mindful of these differences when formulating and examining policies that may influence family living arrangements.

■ Review Questions

1. Should a family in which a mother is cohabiting with a partner be called a stepfamily, or should that term be reserved for families in which the partners are married?
2. Why might children in cohabiting (step)families have more difficulties than children in married stepfamilies?

ENDNOTES

1. Cohabiting couple families comprise two distinct types of living arrangements: children living with unmarried biological parents and children living with one biological parent and that parent's partner.
2. The 1997 NSAF provides information on a nationally representative sample of the civilian noninstitutionalized population under age 65 and their families. The survey contains information on more than 44,000 households. Information on the children in the NSAF was obtained from the parent or guardian in the household most knowledgeable about the child's education and health care. For 72 percent of the children, this respondent—labeled the most knowledgeable adult (MKA)—was the mother. For more information on NSAF survey methods, see Dean Brick et al. (1999).

3. McLanahan and Sandefur (1994) examine the outcomes for children in stepfamilies. Whether stepchildren are more similar to their counterparts living with married biological parents or to those living with a single parent varies depending on the race/ethnicity and sex of the child and the specific outcome considered. Note that McLanahan and Sandefur define children in stepfamilies as those who live with only one biological parent who is married. For this analysis, we prefer the term "blended families" instead of stepfamilies, because we include biological parents married to stepparents and adoptive parents in our definition of blended families.
4. White and black teenagers who were identified as having Hispanic ethnicity were coded as Hispanics in this analysis.

5. For the emotional and behavioral problems indicator, the MKA was asked whether the child exhibited signs of external distress (not getting along with other kids, acting too young for his or her age, lying, or cheating) and internal distress (sadness, depression, or feelings of worthlessness) in the past month. The MKA was asked to decide whether the focal child exhibited the behavior often, sometimes, or never. The responses were coded on a three-point scale, with 1 for often, 2 for sometimes, and 3 for never. A composite measure of behavioral and emotional problems was derived from the responses. Responses were totaled to create a scale score ranging from 6 to 18. A child whose MKA responses totaled 12 points or fewer on the behavioral problems scale received a value of 1 for high levels of behavioral problems. Children whose score was greater than 12 points received a value of 0. This scale was originally developed from the Child Behavior Checklist for the National Health Interview Survey (NHIS) as an indicator of children's mental health. See NSAF Methodology Report 6: 1997 Benchmarking Measures of Child and Family Well-Being.

6. To assess school engagement, the MKA was asked about the extent to which the child did schoolwork only when forced to, did just enough to get by, always did homework, and cared about doing well in school. The response categories were coded 1 for all of the time, 2 for most of the time, 3 for some of the time, and 4 for none of the time. The responses to these four questions were combined to generate a measure of school engagement. Responses were totaled to create a scale score ranging from 4 to 16. A child whose MKA responses totaled 10 points or fewer on the school engagement scale received a value of 1 for low school engagement. Children whose score was greater than 10 points received a value of 0. Jim Connell and Lisa J. Bridges at the Institute for Research and Reform in Education in California created the school engagement scale in 1996, which includes the four indicators used in the NSAF school engagement index. See NSAF Methodology Report 6: 1997 Benchmarking Measures of Child and Family Well-Being.

7. For suspensions and expulsions, the MKA was asked whether the child had been suspended (both in and out of school) or expelled from school in the past 12 months.

8. Moore et al. (2000) examine the incidence of several emotional and behavioral outcomes for children using both the 1997 and 1999 waves of the NSAF. They report that in 1997, 8.8 percent of teenagers had emotional and behavioral problems and 13.9 percent had been expelled or suspended from school; their findings for 1999 are similar.

9. Our universe includes 12- to 17-year-olds who live with their biological mother in one of five types of living arrangements: married biological parents, unmarried biological parents, blended parents (i.e., with a stepfather or adoptive father), mother cohabiting with a male who is unrelated to the child, and mother only. The universe is further restricted to teenagers whose MKA was either the biological mother or the mother's spouse or partner.

The variables included in the regression model include the child's living arrangement (married biological parents, unmarried biological parents, blended parents, cohabiting mother, or single mother); the child's gender; the MKA's education level (less than a high school education, a high school degree or GED, or more than a high school education); and the child's social family's poverty level (less than 100%, 100%–200%, or more than 200% of the federal poverty level). Full results of the logit regression analysis are available upon request.

Note that the family income includes the income of unmarried partners and relatives of unmarried partners. Because research suggests that unmarried partners do not necessarily share resources with their partner or their partner's children, using this broad definition of family income may overstate the resources available to the child.

10. Because of insufficient sample sizes, the regression results for teenagers living with unmarried biological parents are not presented. Not only is this type of living arrangement rare for teenagers, it also represents a very select population because it is an extremely stable nonmarital arrangement.

11. Predicted probabilities are computed using the appropriate living arrangement variables and the mean characteristics for the sample for all the other (non-living-arrangement) variables. Unadjusted probabilities of teenagers' behavioral outcomes by race/ethnicity compare favorably with adjusted probabilities and are available upon request.

Part Six

Family and Society

CHAPTER 14

The Family, the State, and Social Policy

In 1996, the U.S. Congress passed the most sweeping changes since the Great Depression in the program that provides cash assistance to poor families with children. President Bill Clinton, who had promised in his 1992 campaign to "end welfare as we know it," overcame misgivings about the bill and signed it. With the stroke of his pen, "welfare," as the program is commonly called, was transformed from an open-ended source of income to a program that required work and limited the amount of time that families could spend on the rolls.

What was the effect of "welfare reform," as it was called? The number of people enrolled in the main welfare program, now renamed Temporary Assistance for Needy Families, or TANF, plunged by more than half. Many of the former recipients found work at least some of the time. But how did it affect their daily lives and their children's daily lives? Did it cause great harm, as liberals warned? Did it improve their lives as conservatives hoped? Jason DeParle, who had covered welfare reform as a reporter for the *New York Times,* set out to answer these questions by focusing on the lives of three African-American women in Wisconsin, the state that had gone furthest in requiring welfare

recipients to work. They are Angie Jobe; Jewell Reed, who is the sister of the now-incarcerated father of Angie's children; and Jewell's cousin Opal Caples. This excerpt from DeParle's *American Dream: Three Women, Ten Kids, and a Nation's Drive to End Welfare,* focuses on Angie, whose work as a nursing aide made her a welfare reform "success story." What success means in this context is the theme of this first selection.

When the welfare reform legislation was reauthorized in 2006, there was much debate about whether to include funds to promote marriage. (The final bill did include these funds.) Indeed, marriage had emerged as a public-policy issue in the early 2000s. But while attention first focused on promoting heterosexual marriage among the poor, the legalization of same-sex marriage in Massachusetts in 2004 and throughout Canada in 2005 quickly focused attention on whether same-sex marriage, or even same-sex domestic partnerships, should be allowed. It is a divisive issue with passionate supporters and opponents. Some opponents see it as a moral issue, while some supporters see it as a civil rights issue. In the second selection, William Meezan and Jonathan Rauch analyze same-sex marriage as a family policy issue. Legalizing same-sex marriage, the authors say, could make same-sex parenting (even among nonmarried gay men and lesbians) more widely accepted socially. So it is reasonable to ask what the consequences of growing up with gay or lesbian parents are for children. If the consequences are negative, some policymakers might oppose same-sex marriage even if they have no moral objections; and if there are no negative consequences, more observers might favor it. The authors review the evidence and comment on its implications.

American Dream

Money: Milwaukee, Summer 1999

Jason DeParle

"Who the hell is FICA?" Angie fumed. "They be eatin' my ass *up*." If Opal and Marcus were one source of frustration, her pay stub was another and closer to her heart. Leaving welfare, juggling multiple jobs, Angie had done all a welfare reformer could ask. And she had done it with a kind of willed faith that work would eventually pay. "I want my own house," she said, after some Brown Street kids tossed a rock through her window. "With a fence!"

On the surface, she was making good progress. Had she stayed on welfare,[1] her cash and food stamps would have come to about $14,400 a year. In her first three years off welfare, her annual income (in constant dollars) averaged more than $24,900. On paper, she was up more than $10,000—a gain of nearly 75 percent.

Yet it didn't feel that way. Usually she said she has "a little more money, but it ain't that much." On a bleak day, she said, "No, I'm not better off economically—not yet."

While that may just sound like Angie grousing, it's a pretty fair read of the evidence. Like almost all recipients, Angie never lived on welfare alone; she had boyfriends of varying means and a series of (mostly) covert jobs. Quantifying the help from her boyfriends is hard. But through the tax returns lying in the bottom of her closet and her old welfare records, it's possible to see how Angie's part of the finances really worked. A comparison of her last four years on welfare

Jason DeParle, "American Dream: Money: Milwaukee, Summer 1999" from *American Dream: Three Women, Ten Kids, and a Nation's Drive to End Welfare*, pp. 282–291, 321–322. Copyright © 2004 by Jason DeParle. Used by permission of Viking Penguin, a division of Penguin Group USA, Inc., and of Darhansoff, Verrill, Feldman Literary Agents, NY.

with her first three years off produces a box score that looks like this:[2]

	On welfare	Off welfare
Earnings:	$ 6,500	$ 16,100
Tax Credits:	$ 2,300	$ 5,600
Payroll Taxes:	$ −500	$ −1,200
Cash Welfare:	$ 8,400	$ 0
Food Stamps:	$ 4,800	$ 4,400
Total Income:	$21,500	$ 24,900

As a strategy for promoting work, the law did its job: Angie's annual earnings more than doubled. Adding in tax credits (and subtracting FICA), the amount she brought home from the workplace rose by $12,200 a year. Yet the drop in welfare and food stamps cost her $8,800. On balance, she was up $3,400, a gain of 16 percent.

Or was she, really? The more she worked, the more her work expenses increased. There was bus fare, babysitting, work uniforms, and snacks from the vending machine. In Angie's case, the child-care costs were minimal, since the kids mostly minded themselves. But figure just $30 week for bus rides and the stolen car, a conservative estimate, and you wipe out nearly half the gain. In leaving welfare, Angie also lost her health insurance. The kids remained on Medicaid, which was crucial with Kesha's asthma attacks. But for twenty of her first thirty-six months off the rolls, Angie earned just enough to get disqualified. On welfare, she could call a cab and get driven to a doctor for free. But, with pains shooting down her back from lifting patients, Angie walked around uninsured.

Other than her back, Angie was healthy. Jewell was not. After she left welfare, her earnings rose *sixfold*,[3] to nearly $13,000 a year. But her public aid fell 93 percent—she lost all of her welfare and most of her food stamps after she failed to file the monthly earnings reports required of people who work.[4] While her overall income rose from about $14,700 to $16,600 (a gain of 13 percent), she also lost her health insurance for two years, and Jewell had bleeding ulcers. "I just dealt with that pain," she said. "I just got a lot of Tums, Rolaids, stuff like that." In the end, she was hospitalized and her wages were garnished to pay the bill, a circumstance that struck her as nothing unusual. "Anybody that works is gonna get their check garnished," she said. "Everybody in Milwaukee owes a hospital bill."

In going to work, Angie and Jewell didn't just face new expenses. They also faced new uncertainty. Angie's income soared for a year, when she bought a car and worked two jobs. Then it crashed for three months after the car was stolen. So the experience registered less like a stable advance than a roller coaster ride. In Jewell's case, the ride was particularly steep. Her income leaped to $25,000 when she worked in the Alzheimer's ward, then fell to $8,000 the next year when she lost her job and focused on Ken. On welfare, they had a senile landlady who forgot to collect the rent. Off welfare, Jewell had rent to pay and her nephew Quinten to feed. Angie had Opal and Brierra.

So *did* they come out ahead in economic terms? Probably, a bit. And their earnings may grow with time,[5] which wouldn't happen on welfare. Still, three years after they left the rolls, their material lives didn't *feel* much different. Their economic progress, such as it was, vanished in the noise of living.

To understand the economics of the postwelfare years, you have to juggle two competing ideas. The first is that most poor single mothers fared better than expected. The second is that they continued to lead terribly straitened lives. Earnings surged, welfare fell, and net incomes inched up—but not necessarily enough to keep the lights on. By national standards, Angie was a great success: she earned 50 percent to 75 percent more than the average woman leaving the rolls.[6] Sifting through the piles of economic data, it's hard to know what to emphasize most—the amazing ability of poor mothers to work or the questions about what their work will achieve?

The case for encouragement starts with earnings trends:[7] from 1994 to 2001, the poorest half of single mothers saw their annual earnings *double*. That universe includes most of the women who left welfare as well as many who might have gone on it absent the new law. (Among the poorest quarter of single mothers, the rise in earnings was proportionally even greater: 150 percent.) Mostly that's because the women worked more. But the wages of entry-level workers also rose. While it was common to talk of recipients being shoved into minimum-wage jobs, most earned in the range of $7.50 to $8.25 an hour (in today's terms)—well above the legal minimum.

Poverty rates brought more good news. Most of the conservatives who backed the law would have been happy to replace welfare with work, even if poverty levels didn't change. But poverty rates fell sharply—for some groups to record lows. Poverty rates are arbitrary and odd, and they generally undercount need. Crudely devised four decades ago as a multiple of food costs, the formula hasn't changed other than to grow with inflation. The numbers undercount poverty by ignoring work expenses and the increased costs of housing and health care (which have far outpaced inflation). But they also ignore billions distributed through certain programs like food stamps and tax credits. Their all-or-nothing quality is oblivious to nuance: the year she left welfare, Angie would have been poor with $18,437 and not poor with a dollar more. Nonetheless, the numbers retain an important symbolism, and since the methodology behind them hasn't changed, they can be useful in tracking trends.

Poverty rates didn't just fall; they plunged.[8] And they plunged most among those groups targeted by the bill. America's child poverty rates, the highest in the industrial world, hadn't changed in fifteen years. Suddenly they dropped more than 20 percent. Poverty among blacks, Hispanics, and single mothers fell to all-time lows. Nearly *half* the country's black children were poor when [President Bill] Clinton first pledged to end welfare. By the time he left office the figure had fallen by more than a third, to 30 percent. The last president to preside over an economic expansion,

Ronald Reagan, removed 290,000 Americans from poverty. The Clinton years multiplied that figure 22 times, moving 6.4 million people across the poverty line. More than half lived in families headed by single mothers. "This is the first recovery in three decades where everybody got better at the same time,"[9] Clinton said, just before leaving office. "I just think that's so important."

The bad news is that while incomes rose, they rose from distressingly low levels. Extrapolating from an hourly wage of $7.50, one would expect to see annual earnings of about $15,600. But most women leaving welfare earned much less. A few found only part-time work. Many more went months between jobs. In her first year and a half off the rolls, Jewell quit one nursing home (too much work), got fired at another (chronic tardiness), and ran through four temp jobs. Even Angie, a much more experienced worker, went jobless for two and a half months after her car was stolen and she fell into a funk. Only about a third of those leaving welfare nationwide held jobs in every quarter of the following year.[10]

So what did former recipients really earn? In ballpark terms, if you count everyone leaving welfare (including those without jobs), the average woman earned less than $9,000 in her first year off the rolls. Count workers alone, and the figure grows to about $12,000.[11] Count steady workers (excluding those who go back on welfare), and you can get to $14,500. Their paychecks did grow with time; in Wisconsin, the earnings of the average "leaver" rose 26 percent over three years.[12] Still, their annual earnings over the three-year stretch averaged just $10,400 (even when you exclude those who didn't work at all). With earnings of $12,700, Jewell was well ahead of the pack. With $16,100 Angie was a star.

Nationally, most people leaving welfare did come out ahead, at least on paper. But that wasn't the case in Wisconsin. Maria Cancian and three colleagues at the University of Wisconsin examined the records of eight thousand of the state's former welfare families. Although their earnings and tax credits surged, their public aid dropped even faster, cutting their total income by about $2,600 in the first year, a loss of 20 percent. Even after three years, a minority of those leaving the rolls—40 percent—had incomes higher than when they were on welfare. Wisconsin had unusually high benefits, so families leaving welfare had more to lose, and in cutting the rolls so deeply the state pushed more marginal cases out the door. The before-after comparison might look different in, say, Chicago. Nonetheless, the Cancian study recorded something of note: the most celebrated welfare program in the world on average left poor people even poorer.[13]

A focus on averages can leave things out. Even as poverty levels fell, the ranks of single mothers in "extreme poverty"[14]—living below half the poverty line—rose by nearly 20 percent. Nationally, about one welfare mother in five earned nothing after leaving the rolls. How they survived remains unclear. There was no parallel rise in public destitution, no sidewalk encampments of homeless families, as Daniel Patrick Moynihan had feared. *Spending* among the very poor rose,[15] even as their incomes fell, suggesting they had more resources—boyfriends or relatives to take them in—than the Census Bureau could measure. While reliable data on the very poor are scarce, the best guess is that about 7 percent of single mothers grew poorer in the second half of the 1990s.[16] The worst of them, like Amber Peck in Milwaukee, parceled out their kids, then trudged through the snow to sleep on church floors.

Opponents of the bill sometimes cite such families as evidence of its failure. But a policy that fails the most marginalized few isn't necessarily a failure overall, especially if it brings significant improvement to the lives of most others. What's more surprising is how much hardship persisted among the seeming winners, among workers like Angie and Jewell. By warning, as Senator Moynihan did, of "cholera epidemics," critics set the bar for suffering awfully high. Large numbers of welfare-to-work *successes* report problems in obtaining basic necessities[17]— fewer problems, perhaps, than when they were on welfare, but not dramatically fewer. Depending how the question is asked, a quarter to a half of former recipients report shortages of food. Similar percentages cite an inability to pay rent and utilities. Half said they lacked health insurance at a given moment, meaning that many more experienced a period without insurance sometime in their first few years off the rolls. Sheldon Danziger and four academic colleagues tracked seven hundred Michigan families for four years.[18] Those who moved from welfare to work had nearly twice the annual income of those who stayed on welfare but "similar levels of material hardship." They were less likely to go without food or shelter but much more likely to go without needed medical care.

In my own travels through postwelfare life, I was struck by how many working families complained about facing depleted cupboards[19]—or about just plain going hungry. I spent some time with Michelle Crawford, the Milwaukee woman [Wisconsin Governor] Tommy Thompson featured in his legislative address. ("I want to run for president," she remembered him telling her, "and I want you on my team.") While her pride in landing a job was real, so were her struggles to buy a commodity as basic as milk. To fool the kids, she sweetened a powdered mix and hid it in store-bought jugs. "Then we ran out of sugar," she said. Food wasn't on my mind when I stopped by Pulaski High School to talk to some students with welfare-to-work moms. But it was on the minds of the kids, who commandeered the conversation with macabre jokes about Ramen noodles and generic cereal. When I asked how many had recently gone to bed hungry, four out of five raised their hands. "Go to my house, look in the refrigerator—you'll be lucky if there's a gallon of milk," said a senior named Tiffany Fiegel. Then she burst into tears.

The persistence of so much hardship poses a paradox.[20] If incomes were rising, and poverty falling, why did so many people skip meals and fall behind on the rent? The answer is that the near poor live only slightly better than the poor.

The Economic Policy Institute, a Washington research and advocacy group, examined two databases that measure hardships like shortages of food or medical care. Material deprivation did fall once families crossed the poverty line. But it only fell a bit. Real freedom from grinding need didn't occur until families reached twice the poverty line—until a woman like Angie, with four kids, had an income of nearly $40,000. In Wisconsin, fewer than one former recipient in ten had an income of twice the poverty line the year after leaving the rolls.[21] If past trends hold true, most never will:[22] a decade after leaving AFDC, two-thirds of former welfare families still hadn't gotten that far.

One can quibble about the math, but the basic point is clear: there's a threshold that families have to cross to feel their lives have changed. And most haven't crossed it. Angie went from 103 percent of the poverty line during her last four years on welfare to 114 percent during her first three years as a worker. With an extra mouth to feed in Quinten, Jewell went the other way, from 98 percent of the poverty line on welfare to 93 percent off it.[23] "How well am I doing?" Angie said one day. "I ain't gonna call me poor—but I *am* poor." The Census Bureau couldn't have put it any better.

To say that Angie lived on $25,000 makes her life sound more forgiving than it was.[24] The tax money came just once a year and went mostly to big-ticket items—cars, refrigerators, bedroom sets. Food stamps went to food. [Her boyfriend] Marcus pitched in, but his help was erratic and typically in-kind—a package of pork chops, a new coat—as opposed to something Angie could count on for the bills. (Help from Opal was similarly sporadic.) What Angie really lived on was her take-home pay, about $1,120 a month. The result was come-and-go-economics: what comes, goes.

Nearly 60 percent went to shelter costs: $450 to rent and $200 to utilities.

Seventy-five dollars went to Walgreen's for items, like toothpaste and toilet paper, that food stamps wouldn't buy.

Seventy-five dollars went to Jewel-Osco, for groceries when the food stamps ran out.

Fifty dollars went to the Lorillard Tobacco Company, since Angie's body wouldn't function without a pack of Newports every other day.

What was left was about $270 a month, or $9 a day. With that, Angie had to buy the remaining stuff of her life: bus fare, haircuts, gerbil food, video games, winter coats, check-cashing fees, doctors' bills, Colt 45s, Halloween candy, Christmas presents, Kesha's color-guard uniform, Redd's rap discs, Von's basketball shoes, Darrell's birthday party at Chuck E. Cheese, and the occasional pizza supreme. It was a budget with no room for error. And a life with lots of error. "Cash money in my hands?" Angie said. "It's like the wind blows and it's gone."

The biweekly pay cycle had a rhythm all its own: two weeks of anticipation followed by the realization that the money had been spoken for twice. As a rule, food came before rent, and rent before utilities, which Angie relegated to the lower-order status of optional necessity.[25] "If you ain't got no place to stay, all the gas and the lights in the world wouldn't make no difference," she said. In her first six months on Brown Street, she paid on the light bill once. "Paid on" is how she put it, since the bill was never fully paid. She owed more than $1,400, but with Kesha using a nebulizer the power company was slow to disconnect. The week after the fight with Marcus, Angie picked up a $490 paycheck, hoping to treat herself to an outfit and a plastic plant. Once she paid the rent and bought a bus pass, she had $23 and 12 days to go. Among Angie's coping skills was a healthy dose of denial: she refused to open the bills. "If I ain't got the money, I ain't got the money," she said. "No need to be worrying myself to death."

By the spring, the tax money was gone; Michael was cutting Opal's check; and Marcus lost his job when the corner grocery closed. To cap it off, a bureaucratic screwup cost Angie her food stamps. Angie was too proud to say that anyone in the house went hungry—"We survive! Ain't nobody starving in there!"—but it wasn't unusual at the end of the month to find the refrigerator reduced to a box of fish sticks and a bottle of ketchup. Half the household fights, it seemed, revolved around a shortage of food. Opal was supposed to help stock the fridge, but she sold some of her stamps for spending money and kept a cache of snacks locked in her room. One morning, after she beat Darrell to the last drop of milk for the cereal, the five-year-old flung himself to the floor.

"What you crying for, boy?" she said.

"I ain't got nothing to eat! I'm hungry!" he said.

"You need a good butt-whipping, Darrell!" Opal said.

Darrell wasn't the only one missing a meal. Called in to work on her thirty-third birthday, Angie was broke and didn't eat all day. The loss of her food stamps left her incensed. The program required an eligibility review every three months. Arriving for her most recent appointment, she discovered her caseworker had gone on a leave of absence. In welfare jargon, that had left Angie in a "vacant zone"; she no longer had a designated worker but could see whomever was free. No one was. A few weeks later, Angie got a notice saying she had been cut off for failing to complete the review.

"QUESTIONS: Ask your Worker," it said.

"Worker Name: VACANT."

It took two months of calling to get another appointment. When she did, the bus broke down, she got there late, and no one would see her again. Having worked until midnight the previous night, Angie was out of patience; she responded with an off-color tirade that nearly got her thrown out of the office. A supervisor calmed her down, but she still had to come back the following day, when ten minutes of paper pushing restored her stamps. The foul-ups had cost her $500, but she arrived home trying to pretend she didn't care. "Hell no, because I *work!*" she said. "I done got over all that, waiting on food stamps! I *hate* to be bothered with them. I wish I had a job that paid

$10, $11 an hour—I wouldn't *have* to be bothered with them."

"That still ain't enough," Opal said.

"You could make it," Angie said. "You just have to budget."

But Angie didn't earn $11 an hour. She earned $7.82,[26] and while her income placed her in the postwelfare elite, it still didn't pay the bills. She needed a pool job to make more money, and she needed a car to work the pool. With some of her friends moonlighting as home health aides, Angie put in an application. "I need two jobs to get me what I need!" she said. "One job ain't gonna make it."

A SHOT AT THE AMERICAN DREAM

So how had the new law changed her life? Had ending welfare worked? While I had posed versions of the question before, they never seemed to grab her, and I was starting to understand why. On welfare, Angie was a low-income single mother, raising her children in a dangerous neighborhood in a household roiled by chaos. She couldn't pay the bills. She drank lots of beer. And her kids needed a father. Off welfare, she was a low-income single mother, raising her children in a dangerous neighborhood in a household roiled by chaos. She couldn't pay the bills. She drank lots of beer. And her kids needed a father. "We're surviving!" is all Angie said. "'Cause that's what we have to do."

Were the kids proud that she works? It was a question that often arose when I talked about Angie with middle-class friends, most of whom took it as an article of faith that the answer had to be yes. Angie paused. "I don't think the kids think about that," she said. "They'd like it if I'd just sit around with them all day." She raised her voice to a mimicking squeal: "'Why you always at work?' Shoot! Why you think I gotta work? Ain't none a you got a job!" It was pos-

sible, of course, that the kids felt prouder than she knew and that the power of the example she set would become clearer with time. I asked if she thought her struggles to grind out a low-wage living would encourage the kids to stay in school. "Do I think they're going to finish high school? Hell, no!" Angie said. Watching her own mother struggle hadn't inspired her. "I just hope they understand what I'm doing, trying to make they life a little better. I ain't expecting nobody to be no rocket scientist. Just get up and make a life for yourself. And don't be selling no drugs."

Did she worry that Kesha would follow her path and become a teenage mom? "Sex ain't what's on Kesha's mind now," Angie said. "When she's ready, she'll let me know."

Marcus wasn't so sure. Kesha did spend a lot of time with that eighteen-year-old boy upstairs. . . .

Angie shot him a censuring look.

"No—I know she ain't having sex," he said. After a pause, he whispered, "She might as well move up there."

Angie yawned and talked on. In the hours between midnight and dawn, she found her sacred space, turning the jumble of junk and a flickering TV into her makeshift sanctuary. Finally, the beer cans were empty. The GED workbook was covered with dust. The kitchen clock flashed its usual time: 88:88. In the real world, it was almost 3:00 A.M., and in two hours Angie's alarm clock would drag her cussing from her sleep. She wasn't betting that an $8 or $9 an hour job would prove anyone's salvation, the kids' or her own. Still, by the time the sun rose over Milwaukee, she would be at the nursing home, complaining that she was broke and tired and desperate for a little sleep. Then she would get someone dressed and fed and ready for the day. Angie wasn't one to boast, but that did make her proud. "I work," she said.

■ Review Questions ■

1. Why did Angie's net income go up by only 16 percent when she got a job that paid her $24,900 per year?
2. Has welfare reform been a success in the case of Angie and her family?

ENDNOTES

1. Had she stayed on welfare: If Angie had gone on W-2 in 1999, she would have gotten $673 a month in cash and $417 in food stamps, or $13,080 a year. Expressed in 2003 dollars, the measure I use throughout this chapter unless otherwise noted, that's $14,400.

2. How Angie's finances worked: "On welfare" refers to Angie's last four full years on AFDC, 1992 through 1995. "Off welfare" covers her first three years after leaving, 1997 through 1999. She left midway through 1996, making it a unique year that I placed in neither category. Earnings records are from tax returns and the state wage files kept to track eligibility for unemployment insurance; cash and food stamp figures come from state records. Angie's 1992 and 1993 earnings are estimates based on partial data; all other figures are actual. The numbers have been adjusted for inflation and expressed in constant 2003 dollars.

   One thing to notice is that even when Angie was on AFDC, her welfare check accounted for only 38 percent of her income. Another 29 percent came from earnings (after taxes); 22 percent from food stamps; and 11 percent from tax credits. If that suggests she wasn't as "dependent" on AFDC as she seemed, it also explains why taking it away may do less, for good or ill, than either side assumed. A fuller picture of Angie's finances would have to quantify the contributions of boyfriends and relatives which other research suggests typically add another 15 to 20 percent, further diminishing the role of AFDC. (See Kathryn Edin and Laura Lein, *Making Ends Meet* [New York: Russell Sage Foundation, 1997], 44.) Another thing to keep in mind is that Angie's monthly income was less stable than these multi-year averages

suggest. Both of her peak-income years—$26,000 at the post office in 1994 and $27,400 at the nursing pool in 1997—were followed by years with steep losses. Her income fell nearly a third in 1995, when she got discouraged and quit, and by 20 percent in 1998, after her car got stolen. That is, the anxiety of living on sums like these is even greater than the numbers suggest. For more financial data see www.jasondeparle.com.

3. Jewell's earnings rose *sixfold:* Her box score looked like this:

	On welfare	Off welfare
Earnings	$1,900	$ 12,700
Tax credits	700	4,000
Payroll taxes	(−100)	(−1,000)
AFDC	7,800	0
Food stamps	4,400	900
Total	$14,700	$ 16,600

   Jewell's 1994 earnings and tax credits are estimates; all other numbers are actual. Amounts expressed in 2003 dollars.

4. Monthly earnings reports: The state stopped requiring the reports in August 1997, a month after Jewell lost her stamps.

5. Earnings may grow with time.

6. Angie earned at least 50 percent more: In her first three years off welfare, Angie's earnings averaged more than $16,100 a year. By contrast, a typical woman leaving the Wisconsin rolls earned between about $9,000 and $10,400. Angie's first two jobs, at Clement Manor and Mercy Rehab, paid hourly wages of $8.33 and $7.46 (in 2003 dollars), placing her squarely in the middle of former recipients nationwide; her annual earnings were higher than average only because she worked more steadily.

7. Case for encouragement: From 1994 to 2001, annual earnings among the poorest half of single mothers rose from $4,500 to $8,800; earnings among the poorest quarter rose from $1,500 to $3,900. Total income grew more modestly, rising 32 percent to $17,000 for the poorest half and rising 16 percent to $10,000 among the poorest quarter. Over the same years, hourly wages for women at the 20th percentile rose by 14 percent, to $7.79. (Author's communication with Jared Bernstein of the Economic Policy Institute.)

As for former recipients, Acs and Loprest found them earning about $8.25 an hour; Elise Richer and two colleagues produced an estimate of $8.20; Ron Haskins came up with about $7.50 (all in 2003 dollars). Converting a midpoint estimate of $7.85 back into late-nineties dollars suggests the average leaver earned about 35 percent above the minimum wage. (Acs and Loprest, "ASPE Leavers Study," table 3; Elise Richer, Steve Savner, and Mark Greenberg, "Frequently Asked Questions about Working Welfare Leavers," CLASP, Nov. 2001, 13; Ron Haskins, "Effects of Welfare Reform on Family Income and Poverty," in Blank and Haskins, *The New World of Welfare,* 109.)

8. Poverty rates plunged: Among children, the poverty rate fell from 21.8 percent in 1994 to 16.3 percent in 2001; among blacks, from 30.6 percent to 22.5 percent; among Hispanics, 30.7 percent to 21.4 percent; and among people living in single-mother homes, from 38.7 percent to 28.6 percent. In 2003, the poverty threshold was $12,682 for a mother with one child; $14,824 for a mother of two; $18,725 for a mother of three; and $21,623 for a mother of four.

9. "First recovery in three decades": Clinton interview with five reporters from *The New York Times,* Nov. 30, 2000.

10. A third held jobs: Acs and Loprest, "ASPE Leavers Study," Executive Summary and table 3.3.

11. Average earnings: $9,000 and $12,000, Acs and Loprest, "ASPE Leavers Study," table 3.5. (The $9,000 includes an adjustment to account for nonworkers.) $14,500 comes from the same study, table 3.7. All figures expressed in 2003 dollars.

12. Wisconsin earnings growth, three-year mean: Maria Cancian and others, "Before and After TANF: The Economic Well-Being of Women Leaving Welfare" (Madison: Institute for Research

on Poverty, Special Report, no. 77), May 2000, table 8; figures in 2003 dollars.

13. Poor people even poorer: The Cancian study examined eight thousand families who left the rolls in late 1995, just before Angie and Jewell. Over the next year, they gained $2,900 in earnings and tax credits but lost $5,500 in cash and food stamps. That reduced their total income from $13,600 on aid to $11,000 off it. (Ibid., fig. 2, in 2003 dollars.) The study appeared six months after W-2 won the Innovations Award and received almost no attention.

14. Extreme poverty: Sheila R. Zedlewski and others, "Extreme Poverty Rising, Existing Government Programs Could Do More," Urban Institute, April 1, 2002; they use an alternate definition of poverty that includes food stamps.

15. *Spending* among the very poor: Ron Haskins, "Effects of Welfare Reform," in Blank and Haskins, *The New World of Welfare,* 116–19.

16. About 7 percent grew poorer: Analysis of Census Bureau data by Wendell Primus; Christopher Jencks and Joseph Swingle find the tipping point somewhere between the 5th and 10th percentile in "Without a Net," *The American Prospect,* Jan. 3, 2000.

17. Basic necessities: Shortages of food, rent, Acs and Loprest, "ASPE Leavers Study," tables 6.2–3; half uninsured, Bowen Garrett and John Holahan, "Welfare Leavers, Medicaid Coverage, and Private Health Insurance," The Urban Institute, B-13, March 2000.

18. Michigan families: Sheldon Danziger and others, "Does It Pay to Move from Welfare to Work?" *Journal of Policy Analysis and Management* 21, no. 4 (2002): 671–92.

19. Depleted cupboards: While I regularly encountered food shortages in my travels in Milwaukee, surveys by the United States Department of Agriculture indicated that food hardships declined in the late 1990s among the broader population, for some groups dramatically. One report found: "the prevalence of children's hunger declined by about half, from 1.1 percent of all households with children in 1995 to 0.6 percent in 1999." It's possible, of course, for both "food insecurity" and outright "hunger" (two different measures) to be declining yet still common among former welfare recipients. Mark Nord and Gary Bickel, "Measuring

Children's Food Insecurity in U.S. Households, 1995–99," Economic Research Service, USDA, *Food Assistance and Nutrition Research Report,* Number 24, April 2002, Abstract.

20. Persistence of hardship: Heather Boushey and others, *Hardships in America: The Real Story of Working Families* (Washington, DC: Economic Policy Institute, 2001), esp. table 4.

21. Fewer than one in ten reach twice the poverty line: Maria Cancian and Daniel R. Meyer, "Alternative Measures of Economic Success among TANF Participants," July 2003, table 2 (most but not all of the families they surveyed had left the rolls).

22. Most never will: Among former AFDC families, the share with incomes above 200 percent of the poverty line was 12 percent in the first year, 27 percent after five years, and 33 percent after ten years. Daniel R. Meyer and Maria Cancian, *Journal of Applied Social Sciences* 25, no. 1 (Winter/Fall 2000–2001).

23. Poverty status of Angie and Jewell: These numbers include food stamps and tax credits, which

the official numbers omit. Angie's peak year rose from 121 percent of the poverty line on welfare to 127 percent off it—hardly any difference. Likewise, Jewell's rose from 117 percent on welfare to 121 percent off it. She did, however, experience more income fluctuation after leaving welfare. In her first full year off the rolls, when she mostly went jobless, her income fell to a new low of 54 percent of the poverty line.

24. What Angie really lived on: In her first three years off welfare, Angie's annual earnings after payroll taxes averaged $14,850 (in 2003 dollars), or $1,238 a month. To show how this fit her 1999 expenses on Brown Street, I converted it into 1999 dollars; that leaves her with monthly take-home pay of $1,121.

25. Optional necessity: Angie's phone had long been cut off, but I had one installed in the summer of 1999, to make it easier to reach her.

26. She earned $7.82: That was her nominal wage in the spring of 1999, her third year off the rolls; the equivalent in 2003 dollars is $8.64.

READING 14-2

Gay Marriage, Same-Sex Parenting, and America's Children

William Meezan

Jonathan Rauch

Although Americans are deeply divided over same-sex marriage, on one point most would agree: the issue has moved from the obscure fringes to the roiling center of the family-policy debate in a startlingly brief time. In May of 1970,

William Meezan and Jonathan Rauch, "Gay Marriage, Same-Sex Parenting, and America's Children," *The Future of Children,* Vol. 15, No. 2, Fall 2005, pp. 98–107, 110. *From The Future of Children,* a collaboration of The Woodrow Wilson School of Public and International Affairs at Princeton University and The Brookings Institution.

Jack Baker and Mike McConnell applied for a marriage license in Hennepin County, Minnesota. They were turned down. For a generation, subsequent efforts in other venues met the same fate. In the 1990s, Hawaii's state supreme court seemed, for a time, likely to order same-sex marriage, but a state constitutional amendment preemptively overruled the court. Vermont's civil-union program, adopted in 2000 by order of Vermont's high court, offered state (though not federal) benefits to same-sex couples. That program, however, was seen as a substitute for full-fledged marriage. No state, it seemed, was prepared to grant legal matrimony to same-sex couples.

Last year [2004], that taboo broke. Under order of its state supreme court, Massachusetts began offering marriage licenses to same-sex couples. More than forty states, by contrast, have enacted laws or, in some cases, constitutional amendments declaring they would *not* recognize same-sex marriage—a trend that escalated in 2004 when thirteen states passed constitutional amendments banning same-sex marriage.[1] The issue pits left against right and, perhaps more significant, old against young: Americans over age forty-four oppose same-sex marriage by a decisive majority, but a plurality of Americans under age thirty support it.[2] Today, across generations and geography, the country is divided over the meaning of marriage as it has not been since the days when states were at odds over interracial marriages and no-fault divorces—if then.

For many of its advocates, same-sex marriage is a civil rights issue, plain and simple. For many of its opponents, it is just as simply a moral issue. In reality, it is both, but it is also a family-policy issue—one of the most important, yet least studied, family-policy issues on the American scene today. The most controversial of its family-policy aspects is the question: how might same-sex marriage affect the well-being of American children?

COUNTING THE CHILDREN

To begin thinking about gay marriage and children, it is useful to pose another question: which children? Consider three groups of children. First, there are those who are now being raised, or who would in the future be raised, by same-sex couples even if same-sex marriage were unavailable. No one knows just how many American children are being raised by same-sex couples today. The 2000 census counted about 594,000 households headed by same-sex couples, and it found children living in 27 percent of such households.[3] The census did not, however, count the number of children in each home. So all we can say is that, conservatively, at least 166,000 children are being raised by gay and lesbian couples.[4] Many of these children, whatever their number, would be directly affected by the introduction of same-sex marriage—a point we will return to later in this article.

On the obverse is a second group that is much larger but on which the effects, if any, of same-sex marriage are entirely unclear: children *not* being raised by same-sex couples—which is to say, children being raised by opposite-sex couples, married or unmarried, or by single parents. How might same-sex marriage affect these children? Or, to put it another way, how (if at all) might homosexual marriage affect heterosexual behavior? Some opponents, such as the journalist Maggie Gallagher and Massachusetts Governor Mitt Romney, argue that same-sex marriage will signal governmental indifference to whether families contain both a mother and a father.[5] Such legal and cultural indifference, they fear, would further erode the norm of childrearing by both biological parents; more children would end up in fatherless homes. On the other hand, some advocates, such as Jonathan Rauch, argue that same-sex marriage will signal the government's (and society's) preference for marriage over other family arrangements, reinforcing marriage's status at a time when that status is under strain.[6] Same-sex marriage, in this view, would encourage marriage over nonmarriage and thus would benefit adults and children alike. Still others believe that same-sex marriage will have little or no effect of any sort on heterosexual families, if only because the number of gay and lesbian couples is small. There is, however, no evidence at all that bears directly on this question, at least in the American context, because until last year same-sex marriage had never been tried in the United States.[7]

In principle, a third class of children might be affected by same-sex marriage: additional children, so to speak, who might grow up with same-sex couples as a direct or indirect result of the legalization of same-sex marriage. Although even many opponents of same-sex marriage believe that gay and lesbian people should be allowed to foster and adopt children under certain circumstances, they worry that legalizing same-sex marriage would send an irrevocable cultural signal that same-sex parenting and opposite-sex parenting are interchangeable, when in fact they may not be equally good for children. In any case, the advent of same-sex marriage would probably make same-sex parenting easier legally and more widely accepted socially, particularly for couples adopting children from the child welfare system. It is thus not surprising that questions about same-sex parenting come up time and again in discussions of same-sex marriage. To those questions we turn next.

WHAT ARE SAME-SEX FAMILIES?

To speak of same-sex parenting is, almost by definition, to bundle together an assortment of family arrangements. Most children of opposite-sex parents got there the old-fashioned way, by being the biological children of both parents. Because same-sex couples cannot conceive together, their children arrive by a multiplicity of routes into families that assume a variety of shapes. In many cases (no one knows just how many), children living with gay and lesbian couples are the biological offspring of one member of the couple, whether by an earlier marriage or relationship, by arrangement with a known or anonymous sperm donor (in the case of lesbian couples), or by arrangement with a surrogate birth mother (in the case of male couples). Though, again, numbers are unavailable, male couples seem more likely than female couples to adopt children who are not biologically related to either custodial parent. It is worth noting that these different paths to parenthood lead to disparate destinations. The family dynamics of a female couple raising one partner's biological son from a previous marriage may be quite different from the dynamics of, say, a male couple raising a biologically unrelated son adopted from foster care.

Legal arrangements vary, too. Nonbiological parents in same-sex couples who seek to be legally recognized as parents must adopt, and the rules that govern adoption are as diverse as the state legislatures that pass adoption laws, the state agencies that promulgate adoption regulations, and the state courts that interpret them.

All the states allow married couples to apply jointly—as couples—for adoption (but marriage is no guarantee that the adoption will be approved); and all the states allow unmarried individuals to apply for adoption. Only one state, Utah, denies adoption to unmarried couples (heterosexual and homosexual). And so marriage and adoption, though intertwined, are treated as distinct matters by the law and the courts.

Beyond that point, the rules diverge, especially for same-sex couples. Florida, uniquely, bans homosexual individuals from adopting. Mississippi explicitly bans adoption by same-sex couples. At the other end of the spectrum, as of mid-2004 nine states and the District of Columbia permitted same-sex couples to apply jointly for adoption, meaning that both members of the couple could be simultaneously granted parental status. In almost two dozen other states, courts in either the whole state or in some jurisdictions allow "second-parent" adoptions, under which one gay or lesbian partner can petition to become the second parent of the first partner's biological or previously adopted child. (For instance, a gay man could first adopt as a single parent, and then his partner could apply to become the child's other legal parent.) In the remaining states, same-sex couples are not eligible for either joint or second-parent adoption, which means that any children they might be raising are legally related to only one custodial parent.[8]

To study same-sex parenting, then, is to study not one phenomenon but many. As of this writing, indeed, the many same-sex couples whom researchers have studied share just one common trait: not one of them was legally married.[9] So—with suitable caveats about the diversity of same-sex family relationships and structures—what can we say about same-sex parenting and its impact on children? As it happens, the literature on same-sex parenting and its effects on children is significant and growing. For the present article, we reviewed most of it: more than fifty studies, many literature reviews, and accounts of a number of dissertations and conference papers dating back to the 1970s.

WHY SAME-SEX PARENTING IS HARD TO STUDY

This body of research grew partly out of court cases in which lesbian and gay parents (or co-parents) sought to defend or obtain custody of children.[10] Many researchers approached the subject with a sympathetic or protective attitude toward the children and families they studied. Critics have accused researchers of downplaying differences between children of gay and straight parents, especially if those differences could be interpreted unfavorably—a charge that has been debated in the field.[11] We will not enter that debate here, beyond noting that the best defense against bias is always to judge each study, whatever its author's motivation, critically and on its merits.

More significant, we believe, are the daunting methodological challenges that the researchers faced, especially at first.

Difficulty Finding Representative Samples

Perhaps the most important such challenge is that researchers have no complete listing of gay and lesbian parents from which to draw representative samples (probability samples, as researchers call them). To find study participants, they have often had to rely on word-of-mouth referrals, advertisements, and other recruiting tools that may produce samples not at all like the full population of gay and lesbian parents. All but one of the studies we examined employed samples composed of either totally or predominantly white participants. Almost all the participants were middle- to upper-middle-class, urban, well educated, and "out." Most were lesbians, not gay men. Participants were often clustered in a single place. It may be that most same-sex parents *are* white, relatively affluent lesbians, or it may be merely that these parents are the easiest for researchers to find and recruit, or both may be partly true. No one knows. Absent probability samples, generalizing findings is impossible.

Small Sample Sizes

Gay- and lesbian-headed families can be difficult to locate, and funding for this research has been sparse.[12] Those factors and others have forced researchers to deal with the challenge of small samples. Most studies describing the development of children raised in gay or lesbian homes report findings on fewer than twenty-five children, and most comparative studies compare fewer than thirty children in each of the groups studied. Other things being equal, the smaller the number of subjects in the groups studied, the harder it is to detect differences between those groups.[13]

Comparison Groups

The question is often not just how well same-sex parents and their children fare, but compared with whom? Should a single lesbian mother be compared with a single heterosexual mother? If so, divorced or never married? Should a two-mother family be compared with a two-biological-parent family, a mother-father family headed by one biological parent and one stepparent, or a single-parent family? It all depends on what the researcher wants to know. Identifying appropriate comparison groups has proved vexing, and no consistent or wholly convincing approach has emerged. Many studies mix family forms in both their homosexual and heterosexual groups, blurring the meaning of the comparison being made. Some studies do not use comparison groups at all and simply describe children or adults in same-sex households. Some, in fact, have argued that comparing gay and straight families, no matter how closely matched the groups, is inappropriate inasmuch as it assumes a "heterosexual norm" against which same-sex parents and their children should be judged.[14]

Subject-Group Heterogeneity

As we noted, families headed by same-sex parents are structurally very different from one another. That fact presents researchers with another challenge, because studies are most accurate when each of the groups being examined or compared is made up of similar individuals or families. When the pool of potential subjects is small, as it is for same-sex parents, assuring within-group homogeneity is often difficult. Thus some studies use "mixed" groups of lesbian-headed households, yielding results that are difficult to interpret. For example, partnered lesbians are often included with single lesbians, with all called "single" by the author; children who live both in and outside the home are discussed as a single group; children born into homes that originated both as heterosexual marriages and as lesbian households are included in the same sample; and separated and divorced women are mixed with never-married women and called "single." In at least one of the studies reviewed, children of transsexuals and lesbians, children who are both biological and adopted, and parents who are both biological and adopters are treated as a single group.

Measurement Issues

Another challenge is to gauge how well children are faring. Few studies collect data from the children directly, and even fewer observe the children's behavior—the gold standard for research of this kind, but more expensive and time-consuming than asking parents and children to evaluate themselves. Some studies use nonstandardized measures, while others use either measures with poor reliability and validity or measures whose reliability and validity were either not known or not reported.

Another measurement issue arises from the sometimes dated content of the measures used. In one 1986 study, for example, dressing in pants and wanting to be a doctor or lawyer were considered masculine for girls, and seeking leadership roles was considered a display of dominance.[15] Those classifications look rather quaint today.

Statistical Issues

To some extent, researchers can compensate for heterogeneous samples and nonequivalent comparison groups by using statistical methods that control for differences, particularly in studies with larger samples. Not all studies have done so, especially in the era before today's advanced software made statistical work considerably easier. Some studies thus did not perform appropriate statistical analyses when that was possible. Others did not report the direction of the significant relationships that they found, leaving unclear which group of children fared better. Most failed to control for potentially confounding factors, such as divorce stress or the status of a current relationship with a former partner.

Putting the Research Challenges in Perspective

This is an imposing catalog of challenges and shortcomings, and it needs to be seen in context. The challenges we describe are by no means unique to the research on same-sex parenting, and neither are the flaws that result.[16] Studying small, hard-to-locate populations is inherently difficult, especially if the subject pool is reticent. One of us, Meezan, has been conducting and reviewing field research on foster and adoptive families since the 1970s; he finds that the studies reviewed here are not under par by the standards of their discipline at the time they were conducted.

WHAT THE EVIDENCE SHOWS—AND MEANS

So what do the studies find? Summarizing the research, the American Psychological Association concluded in its July 2004 "Resolution on Sexual Orientation, Parents, and Children,"

> There is no scientific basis for concluding that lesbian mothers or gay fathers are unfit parents on the basis of their sexual orientation. . . . On the contrary, results of research suggest that lesbian and gay parents are as likely as heterosexual parents to provide supportive and healthy environments for their children. . . . Overall, results of research suggest that the development, adjustment, and well-being of children with lesbian and gay parents do not differ markedly from that of children with heterosexual parents.[17]

Our own review of the evidence is consistent with that characterization. Specifically, the research supports four conclusions.

First, lesbian mothers, and gay fathers (about whom less is known), are much like other parents. Where differences are found, they sometimes favor same-sex parents. For instance, although one study finds that heterosexual fathers had greater emotional involvement with their children than did lesbian co-mothers, others find either no difference or that lesbian co-mothers seem to be more involved in the lives of their children than are heterosexual fathers.[18]

Second, there is no evidence that children of lesbian and gay parents are confused about their gender identity, in either childhood or adulthood, or that they are more likely to be homosexual. Evidence on gender behavior (as opposed to identification) is mixed; some studies find no differences, whereas others find that girls raised by lesbians may be more "masculine" in play and aspirations and that boys of lesbian parents are less aggressive.[19] Finally, some interesting differences have been noted in sexual behavior and attitudes (as opposed to orientation). Some studies report that children, particularly daughters, of lesbian parents adopt more accepting and open attitudes toward various sexual identities and are more willing to question their own sexuality. Others report that young women raised in lesbian-headed families are more likely to have homosexual friends and to disclose that they have had or would consider having same-sex sexual relationships.[20] (Just how to view such differences in behavior and attitude is a matter of disagreement. Where conservatives may see lax or immoral sexual standards, liberals may see commendably open-minded attitudes.)

Third, in general, children raised in same-sex environments show no differences in cognitive abilities, behavior, general emotional development, or such specific areas of emotional development as self-esteem, depression, or anxiety. In the few cases where differences in emotional development are found, they tend to favor children raised in lesbian families. For example, one study reports that preschool children of lesbian mothers tend to be less aggressive, bossy, and domineering than children of heterosexual mothers. Another finds more psychiatric difficulties and a greater number of psychiatric referrals among children of heterosexual parents.[21] The only negative suggestion to have been uncovered about the emotional development of children of same-sex parents is a fear on the part of the children—which seems to dissipate during adolescence when sexual orientation is first expressed—that they might be homosexual.[22]

Finally, many gay and lesbian parents worry about their children being teased, and children often expend emotional energy hiding or otherwise controlling information about their parents, mainly to avoid ridicule. The evidence is mixed, however, on whether the children have heightened difficulty with peers, with more studies finding no particular problems.[23]

The significance of this body of evidence is a matter of contention, to say the least. Steven Nock, a prominent scholar reviewing the literature in 2001 as an expert witness in a Canadian court case, found it so flawed methodologically that the "only acceptable conclusion at this point is that the literature on this topic does not constitute a solid body of scientific evidence," and that "all of the articles I reviewed contained at least one fatal flaw of design or execution. . . . Not a single one was conducted according to generally accepted standards of scientific research."[24] Two equally prominent scholars, Judith Stacey and Timothy Biblarz, vigorously disputed the point: "He is simply wrong to say that all of the studies published to date are virtually worthless and unscientific. . . . If the Court were to accept Professor Nock's primary criticisms of these studies, it would have to dismiss virtually the entire discipline of psychology."[25]

We believe that both sides of that argument are right, at least partially. The evidence provides a great deal of information about the particular families and children studied, and the children now number more than a thousand.[26] They are doing about as well as children normally do. What the evidence does not provide, because of the methodological difficulties we outlined, is much knowledge about whether those studied are typical or atypical of the general population of children raised by gay and lesbian couples. We do not know how the *normative* child in a same-sex family compares with other children. To make the same point a little differently, those who say the evidence shows that many same-sex parents do an excellent job of parenting are right. Those who say the evidence falls short of showing that same-sex parenting is equivalent to opposite-sex parenting (or better, or worse) are also right.

Fortunately, the research situation is improving, so we may soon have clearer answers. Over the past several decades researchers have worked to improve their methods, and the population of

gay and lesbian parents has become easier to study. Studies using larger samples are appearing in the literature, the first long-term study following the same group of people over time has been published, and studies using representative, population-based samples have appeared. More studies now use standardized instruments with acceptable reliability and validity. Recent studies are much more likely to match comparison groups closely and are also more likely to use statistical methods to control for differences both within and between the study groups.

We identified four studies—all comparatively recent (dating from 1997)—that we believe represent the state of the art, studies that are as rigorous as such research could today reasonably be expected to be (see table). Their conclusions do not differ from those of the main body of research.

FOUR STRONG STUDIES

How do children of lesbian or gay parents fare and compare? Following are summaries of four methodologically rigorous studies.

Wainwright, Russell, and Patterson (2004)

Methodology: Drawing on a nationally representative sample of more than 12,105 adolescents in the National Study of Adolescent Health, the authors compared forty-four adolescents being raised by female same-sex couples with forty-four raised by heterosexual couples. The comparison groups were matched child for child (not on group averages) on many traits, and the study samples did not differ on numerous demographic characteristics from the national sample of 12,105. Metrics were mostly standardized instruments with good reliability and validity, and many were the most commonly used measures in the field. Multivariate analysis was used to determine the impact of family type, controlling for other demographic and social factors.

Findings: "No differences in adolescents' psychosocial adjustment," including depressive symptoms, anxiety, and self-esteem; no differences in grade-point averages or problems in school. Adolescents with same-sex parents reported feeling more connected to school. The authors found that "it was the qualities of adolescent-parent relationships rather than the structural features of families (for example, same- versus opposite-sex parents) that were significantly associated with adolescent adjustment. . . . Across a diverse array of assessments, we found that the personal, family, and school adjustment of adolescents living with same-sex parents did not differ from that of adolescents living with opposite-sex parents."

Golombok and Others (2003)

Methodology: In southwest England, researchers drew on a geographic population study of almost 14,000 mothers and their children to identify eighteen lesbian-mother families (headed both by lesbian couples and single mothers) and then added twenty-one lesbian mothers identified through personal referrals, a lesbian mothers' support organization, and advertisements. The twenty-one supplementary subjects were "closely comparable" to the eighteen drawn from the population study. The resulting sample of thirty-nine "cannot be deemed truly representative of the population of lesbian-mother families" but "constitutes the closest approximation achieved so far." Those families were compared with seventy-four families headed by heterosexual couples and sixty families headed by single heterosexual mothers. Standardized measures were administered and interview data were coded by personnel blind to the family's type and structure and were checked for reliability.

(continued)

FOUR STRONG STUDIES (*continued*)

Findings: "Children reared by lesbian mothers appear to be functioning well and do not experience negative psychological consequences arising from the nature of their family environment." After the authors controlled for initial differences between groups (age of children, number of siblings) and the number of statistical comparisons made, "the only finding that remained significant. . . was greater smacking of children by fathers than by co-mothers." Also, "boys and girls in lesbian-mother families were not found to differ in gender-typed behavior from their counterparts from heterosexual homes." Children did better psychologically with two parents, regardless of whether the parents were same-sex or opposite-sex couples, than with a single mother.

Chan, Raboy, and Patterson (1998)

Methodology: Using a sample drawn from people who used the same sperm bank (in California), and thus controlling for the effects of biological relatedness, the researchers compared four family structures: lesbian couples (thirty-four), lesbian single mothers (twenty-one), heterosexual couples (sixteen), and single heterosexual mothers (nine). Participation rates were significantly higher for lesbian couples than for others. Though education and income levels were above average for all groups, lesbian parents had completed more education, and lesbian and coupled families had higher incomes; otherwise, group demographics were similar. Information on children's adjustment was collected from parents and teachers, using standardized measures with good reliability and validity.

Findings: "Children's outcomes were unrelated to parental sexual orientation," for both single-parent and coupled families. "On the basis of assessments of children's social competence and behavior problems that we collected, it was impossible to distinguish children born to and brought up by lesbian versus heterosexual parents." Sample size was large enough to detect large or medium effects but not small ones, so family structure had either small or nonexistent effects.

Brewaeys and Others (1997)

Methodology: Using a sample drawn from the fertility clinic at Brussels University Hospital, thirty lesbian-couple families who conceived through donor insemination (DI) were compared with thirty-eight heterosexual families who conceived through DI and thirty heterosexual families who conceived naturally. Response rates were generally good, but better for lesbian co-mothers than for heterosexual fathers. Statistical analysis controlled for demographic differences between comparison groups and for number of comparisons made, and good metrics were used.

Findings: Children's emotional and behavior adjustment "did not differ" between lesbian and opposite-sex families, and "boys and girls born in lesbian mother families showed similar gender-role behaviour compared to boys and girls born in heterosexual families." The quality of parents' relationship with each other did not differ across the two family types, nor did the quality of interaction between children and biological parents. "However, one striking difference was found between lesbian and heterosexual families: social mothers [that is, nonbiological lesbian parents] showed greater interaction with their children than did fathers."

Sources: Jennifer L. Wainwright, Stephen T. Russell, and Charlotte J. Patterson, "Psychosocial Adjustment, School Outcomes, and Romantic Relationships of Adolescents with Same-Sex Parents," *Child Development* 75, no. 6 (December 2004): 1886–98, quotes pp. 1892, 1895; Susan Golombok and others, "Children with Lesbian Parents: A Community Study," *Developmental Psychology* 39, no. 1 (January 2003): 20–33, quotes pp. 30, 31; Raymond Chan, Barbara Raboy, and Charlotte J. Patterson, "Psychosocial Adjustment among Children Conceived via Donor Insemination by Lesbian and Heterosexual Mothers," *Child Development* 69, no. 2 (April 1998): 443–57, quotes p. 453; A. Brewaeys and others, "Donor Insemination: Child Development and Family Functioning in Lesbian Mother Families," *Human Reproduction* 12, no. 6 (1997): 1349–59, quotes pp. 1356, 1357.

It bears emphasizing that the issue of same-sex parenting is directly relevant to same-sex marriage only to the extent that the latter extends the scope of the former. Gay and lesbian couples make up only a small share of the population, not all of those couples have or want children, and many who do have or want children are likely to raise them whether or not same-sex marriage is legal.

The number of additional children who might be raised by same-sex couples as a result of same-sex marriage is probably small. Moreover, an important question, where family arrangements are concerned, is always, "Compared with what?" We doubt that same-sex marriage would shift any significant number of children out of the homes of loving heterosexual parents and into same-sex households; and, to the extent that same-sex marriage helps move children out of foster care and into caring adoptive homes, the prospect should be welcomed. If the past several decades' research establishes anything, it is that the less time children spend in the public child welfare system, the better. Put simply, research shows that the state makes a poor parent for many of the children in its custody, particularly compared with stable, loving, developmentally appropriate environments.

AN OPPORTUNITY TO LEARN

It is important, we think, to recognize that social science cannot settle the debate over same-sex marriage, even in principle. Some people believe the United States should have same-sex marriage as a matter of basic right even if the change proves deleterious for children; others believe the country should reject same-sex marriage as a matter of morality or faith even if the change would benefit kids. Consequential factors are but one piece of a larger puzzle; and, as is almost always the case, social research will for the most part follow rather than lead the national debate.

Both authors of this paper are openly gay and advocates of same-sex marriage, a fact that readers should weigh as they see fit. In any case, our personal judgments about the facts presented here are no better than anyone else's. Two points, however, seem to us to be both incontrovertible and important.

First, whether same-sex marriage would prove socially beneficial, socially harmful, or trivial is an empirical question that cannot be settled by any amount of armchair theorizing. There are plausible arguments on all sides of the issue, and as yet there is no evidence sufficient to settle them.

Second, the costs and benefits of same-sex marriage cannot be weighed if it cannot be tried—and, preferably, compared with other alternatives (such as civil unions). Either a national constitutional ban on same-sex marriage or a national judicial mandate would, for all practical purposes, throw away the chance to collect the information the country needs in order to make a properly informed decision.

As it happens, the United States is well situated, politically and legally, to try same-sex marriage on a limited scale—without, so to speak, betting the whole country. As of this writing, one state (Massachusetts) is marrying same-sex couples, two others (Vermont and Connecticut) offer civil unions, and several more (notably California) offer partner-benefit programs of one sort or another. Most other states have preemptively banned gay marriage, and some have banned civil unions as well. The upshot is that the nation is running exactly the sort of limited, localized experiment that can repay intensive study.

In particular, the clustering in four neighboring states of all three kinds of arrangement—same-sex marriage in Massachusetts, civil unions in Vermont and Connecticut, and neither in New Hampshire—offers a near-ideal natural laboratory. A rigorous study of how children fare when they are raised in these various arrangements and environments would not be easy to design and execute, and it would require a considerable amount of time and money; but the knowledge gained would make the debate over gay marriage better lit and perhaps less heated, to the benefit of all sides of the argument.

■ Review Questions

1. Why has it been so difficult to study the consequences for children of growing up in gay and lesbian families?
2. What do the studies, limited though they may be, find?

ENDNOTES

1. The thirteen were Arkansas, Georgia, Kentucky, Louisiana, Michigan, Mississippi, Missouri, Montana, North Dakota, Oklahoma, Ohio, Oregon, and Utah.
2. *Los Angeles Times* poll, March 27–30, 2004. Among respondents under age thirty, 44 percent supported same-sex marriage and 31 percent supported civil unions; 22 percent favored neither.
3. U.S. Census Bureau, *Married-Couple and Unmarried-Partner Households: 2000* (February 2003). See also Gary J. Gates and Jason Ost, *The Gay and Lesbian Atlas* (Washington: Urban Institute, 2004), p. 45.
4. Because same-sex couples, especially those with children, may be reluctant to identify themselves to census takers, and because small populations are inherently difficult to count, this number is likely to be an undercount. See Gates and Ost, *The Gay and Lesbian Atlas* (see note 3). Other estimates range much higher. See, for example, Frederick W. Bozett, "Gay Fathers: A Review of the Literature," in *Psychological Perspectives on Lesbian and Gay Male Experiences,* edited by Linda Garnets and Douglas Kimmel (Columbia University Press, 1993), pp. 437–57.
5. See, for example, Maggie Gallagher, "What Is Marriage For?" *Weekly Standard,* August 4–11, 2003; and Mitt Romney, testimony before the U.S. Senate Judiciary Committee, June 22, 2004.
6. Jonathan Rauch, *Gay Marriage: Why It Is Good for Gays, Good for Straights, and Good for America* (New York: Times Books, 2004).
7. As of this writing, the Netherlands, Belgium, and several Canadian provinces had adopted same-sex marriage, but only recently. The effects, if any, on the welfare of children and families are both unclear and disputed. See, for example, Stanley Kurtz, "The End of Marriage in Scandinavia," *Weekly Standard,* February 2, 2004; and in rebuttal, M. V. Lee Badgett, *Will Providing Marriage Rights to Same-Sex Couples Undermine Heterosexual Marriage? Evidence from Scandinavia and the Netherlands,* Discussion Paper (Council on Contemporary Families and Institute for Gay and Lesbian Strategic Studies, July 2004). Also in rebuttal, William N. Eskridge, Darren R. Spedale, and Hans Ytterberg, "Nordic Bliss? Scandinavian Registered Partnerships and the Same-Sex Marriage Debate," *Issues in Legal Scholarship,* Article 4, available at www.bepress.com/ils/iss5/art4/.
8. The authors are indebted to the Human Rights Campaign, the Lambda Legal Defense and Education Fund, and the National Adoption Information Clearinghouse for information on state adoption policies. Because adoption policies are often set by courts on a case-by-case basis, adoption rules are in flux and vary within as well as between states. The summary counts presented here are subject to interpretation and may have changed by the time of publication.
9. At this writing, same-sex marriage was too new in Massachusetts to have generated any research results.
10. "A third perspective from which [research] interest in lesbian and gay families with children has arisen is that of the law. . . . Because judicial and legislative bodies in some states have found lesbians and gay men unfit as parents because of their sexual orientation, lesbian mothers and gay fathers have often been denied custody or visitation with their children following divorce." Charlotte Patterson, "Lesbian Mothers, Gay Fathers, and Their Children," in *Lesbian, Gay and Bisexual Identities over the Lifespan: Psychological Perspectives,* edited by Anthony R. D'Augelli and Charlotte Patterson (Oxford University Press, 1995), p. 264.
11. Judith Stacey and Timothy J. Biblarz examine twenty-one studies and find that "researchers frequently downplay findings indicating difference regarding children's gender and sexual preferences and behavior." Judith Stacey and Timothy Biblarz, "(How) Does the Sexual Orientation of Parents Matter?" *American Sociological Review* 66 (April 2001): 159–83. Golombok and others reply that it is Stacey and Biblarz who "have overemphasized the differences that have been reported between children with lesbian and heterosexual parents." Susan Golombok and others, "Children with Lesbian Parents: A Community Study," *Developmental Psychology* 39, no. 1 (January 2003): 21.
12. For example, as best we can discern, none of the studies reviewed for this article was funded by the federal government, the major source of social science research funding in the United States.

13. For example, Tasker and Golombok note that there was only a 51 percent chance of detecting a moderate effect size in their sample, and an even lower possibility (if any at all) of detecting a small effect size. See Fiona Tasker and Susan Golombok, *Growing Up in a Lesbian Family* (New York: Guilford Press, 1997).

14. From the perspective of gay men, Gerald Mallon states, "Usually, explorations of gay parenting focus on the differences between gay and straight parents. [I] approach this topic through a gay-affirming lens, meaning that I do not take heterosexuality as the norm and then compare gay parenting to that model and discuss how it measures up. In most cases heterosexually oriented men become fathers for different reasons and in different ways than do gay men. Comparisons of gay fathers to heterosexual fathers are therefore inappropriate." Gerald Mallon, *Gay Men Choosing Parenthood* (Columbia University Press, 2004), p. xii. From a lesbian perspective, Victoria Clarke states, "In the rush to prove. . . . our similarities to heterosexual families, oppressive norms of femininity, masculinity, and heterosexuality are reinforced. The use of sameness arguments suppresses feminist critiques of the family as a prime site of hetero-patriarchal oppression. . . . By taking mainstream concerns seriously, lesbian and gay psychologists inadvertently invest them with validity and reinforce the anti-lesbian agendas informing popular debates about lesbian parenting." Victoria Clarke, "Sameness and Differences in Lesbian Parenting," *Journal of Community and Applied Social Psychology* 12 (2002): 218.

15. Richard Green and others, "Lesbian Mothers and Their Children: A Comparison with Solo Parent Heterosexual Mothers and Their Children," *Archives of Sexual Behavior* 15, no. 2 (1986): 167–83.

16. For example, similar issues arise in the study of transracial adoption: "Study findings that support greater use of transracial adoption as a placement option . . . are fraught with conceptual and methodological limitations. . . . For instance, many have small sample sizes and no—or inappropriate—comparison groups. While they tend to be cross-sectional, those that are longitudinal are potentially biased from sample attrition." Devon Brooks and Richard P. Barth, "Adult Transracial and Intracial Adoptees: Effects of Race, Gender, Adoptive

Family Structure, and Placement History on Adjustment Outcomes," *American Journal of Orthopsychiatry* 69 (January 1999): 88.

17. Available at www.apa.org/pi/lgbc/.

18. A. Brewaeys and others, "Donor Insemination: Child Development and Family Functioning in Lesbian Mother Families," *Human Reproduction* 12 (1997): 1349–59; David K. Flaks and others, "Lesbians Choosing Motherhood: A Comparative Study of Heterosexual Parents and Their Children," *Developmental Psychology* 31 (1995): 105–14; Golombok and others, "Children with Lesbian Parents" (see note 11), pp. 20–33; Katrien Vanfraussen, Ingrid Ponjaert-Kristoffersen, and Anne Brewaeys, "Family Functioning in Lesbian Families Created by Donor Insemination," *American Journal of Orthopsychiatry* 73, no. 1 (January 2003): 78–90.

19. Green and others, "Lesbian Mothers and Their Children" (see note 15); Beverly Hoeffer, "Children's Acquisition of Sex Role Behavior in Lesbian-Mother Families," *American Journal of Orthopsychiatry* 51, no. 3 (1981): 536–44; Ailsa Steckel, "Psychosocial Development of Children of Lesbian Mothers," in *Gay and Lesbian Parents,* edited by Frederick W. Bozett (New York: Praeger, 1987), pp. 75–85.

20. Lisa Saffron, *"What about the Children?" Sons and Daughters of Lesbian and Gay Parents Talk about Their Lives* (London: Cassell, 1996); Tasker and Golombok, *Growing Up in a Lesbian Family* (see note 13). It is unclear whether the young women are more likely to *engage* in same-sex relations, more likely to *disclose* them, or some combination of the two.

21. Steckel, "Psychosocial Development of Children of Lesbian Mothers" (see note 19); Susan Golombok, Ann Spencer, and Michael Rutter, "Children in Lesbian and Single-Parent Households: Psychosexual and Psychiatric Appraisal," *Journal of Child Psychology and Psychiatry* 24, no. 4 (1983): 551–72.

22. Karen G. Lewis, "Children of Lesbians: Their Point of View," *Social Work* 25 (May 1980): 198–203; Ann O'Connell, "Voices from the Heart: The Developmental Impact of Mother's Lesbianism on Her Adolescent Children," *Smith College Studies in Social Work* 63, no. 3 (June 1993): 281–99; S. J. Pennington, "Children of Lesbian Mothers,"

in *Gay and Lesbian Parents,* edited by Bozett (see note 19), pp. 58–74.

23. Phillip A. Belcastro and others, "A Review of Data Based Studies Addressing the Effects of Homosexual Parenting on Children's Sexual and Social Functioning," *Journal of Divorce and Remarriage* 20, nos. 1–2 (1993): 105–22; Frederick W. Bozett, "Children of Gay Fathers," *Gay and Lesbian Parents,* edited by Bozett (see note 19), pp. 39–57; Margaret Crosbie-Burnett and Lawrence Helmbrecht, "A Descriptive Empirical Study of Gay Male Stepfamilies," *Family Relations* 42 (1993): 256–62; Nanette Gatrell and others, "The National Lesbian Family Study: Interviews with Mothers of Five-Year-Olds," *American Journal of Orthopsychiatry* 70, no. 4 (October 2000): 542–48; Tamar D. Gershon, Jeanne M. Tschann, and John M. Jemerin, "Stigmatization, Self-Esteem, and Coping among the Adolescent Children of Lesbian Mothers," *Journal of Adolescent Health* 24, no. 6 (June 1999): 437–45; Golombok, Spencer, and Rutter, "Children in Lesbian and Single-Parent Households" (see note 21); Golombok and others, "Children with Lesbian Parents" (see note 11); Jan Hare, "Concerns and Issues Faced by Families Headed by a Lesbian Couple," *Families in Society* 75 (1994): 27–35; Ghazala Afzal Javaid, "The Children of Homosexual and Heterosexual Single Mothers," *Child Psychiatry and Human Development* 24 (1993): 235–48; Suzanne M. Johnson and Elizabeth

O'Connor, *The Gay Baby Boom: The Psychology of Gay Parenthood* (New York University Press, 2002); Lewis, "Children of Lesbians" (see note 22); O'Connell, "Voices from the Heart" (see note 22); Pennington, "Children of Lesbian Mothers" (see note 22); Tasker and Golombok, *Growing Up in a Lesbian Family* (see note 13); Norman Wyers, "Homosexuality and the Family: Lesbian and Gay Spouses," *Social Work* 32 (1987): 143–48.

24. Steven L. Nock, affidavit in the superior court of Ontario, Canada, *Halpern et al. v. Canada* and *MCCT v. Canada* (2001), at items 141 (p. 47) and 115 (p. 39).

25. Judith Stacey and Timothy Biblarz, affidavit in the superior court of Ontario, Canada, *Halpern et al. v. Canada* and *MCCT v. Canada* (2001), at items 4 (p. 3) and 14 (p. 7).

26. Anderssen and others' review of the literature up until 2000, which did not cover all of the studies through that date, puts the number of children studied at 615. Norman Anderssen, Christine Amlie, and Erling Andre Ytteroy, "Outcomes for Children with Lesbian or Gay Parents: A Review of Studies from 1978 to 2000," *Scandinavian Journal of Psychology* 43 (2002): 335–51. Since that time, larger-scale studies, some with samples larger than 200, have been undertaken. Stacey and Biblarz, in their affidavit (see note 25) at item 41 (p. 19), cite more than 1,000 children, and 500 observed in "22 of the best studies."

References

CHAPTER 1

Reading 1-2

Almond, Richard. 1977. "Character, Role and Self: Evolution in Personality Styles." Unpublished manuscript. Palo Alto, California.

Bellah, Robert; Richard Madsen; William Sullivan; Ann Swidler; and Steven Tipton. 1985. *Habits of the Heart.* Berkeley: University of California Press.

Campbell, Angus; Philip Converse; and Willard L. Rodgers. 1976. *The Quality of American Life.* New York: Russell Sage.

Cancian, Francesca, and Bonnie Ross. 1981. "Mass Media and the Women's Movement." *Journal of Applied Behavioral Science* 17:9–26.

Carden, Maren L. 1974. *The New Feminist Movement.* New York: Russell Sage Foundation.

Chafe, William H. 1972. *The American Woman.* New York: Oxford University Press.

Cherlin, Andrew. 1981. *Marriage, Divorce, Remarriage.* Cambridge, Massachusetts: Harvard University Press.

Clecak, Peter. 1983. *America's Quest for the Ideal Self.* New York: Oxford University Press.

Degler, Carl N. 1980. *At Odds: Women and the Family in America from the Revolution to the Present.* New York: Oxford University Press.

Duncan, Otis Dudley; Howard Schuman; and Beverly Duncan. 1973. *Social Change in a Metropolitan Community.* New York: Russell Sage.

Easterlin, Richard A. 1980. *Birth and Fortune.* New York: Basic Books.

Elder, Glen. 1974. *Children of the Great Depression.* Chicago: University of Chicago Press.

Fass, Paula S. 1977. *The Damned and the Beautiful.* New York: Oxford University Press.

Filene, Peter. 1974. *Him/Her/Self: Sex Roles in Modern America.* New York: Harcourt Brace Jovanovich.

Flexner, Eleanor. 1974. *Century of Struggle.* New York: Atheneum.

Freeman, Jo. 1975. *The Politics of Women's Liberation.* New York: David McKay.

Friedan, Betty. 1963. *The Feminine Mystique.* New York: Norton.

Gecas, V. 1979. "The Influence of Social Class on Socialization." In W. Burr et al. (eds.), *Contemporary Theories about the Family,* Vol. I. New York: Free Press.

Gratton, Lynda C. 1980. "Analysis of Maslow's Need Hierarchy with Three Social Class Groups." *Social Indicators Research* 7:463–76.

Gurin, Gerald; J. Veroff; and S. Feld. 1960. *Americans View Their Mental Health.* New York: Basic Books.

Hantover, Jeffrey P. 1980. "The Boy Scouts and the Validation of Masculinity." In Elizabeth Pleck and Joseph Pleck, *The American Man*. Englewood Cliffs, New Jersey: Prentice Hall.

Harris, Louis, and Associates. 1979. *The Playboy Report on American Men*. Playboy Inc.

Harris, William H., and Judith Levy (eds.). 1975. *The New Columbia Encyclopedia*. New York: Columbia University Press.

Heer, David M., and Amyra Grossbard-Shechtman. 1981. "The Impact of the Female Marriage Squeeze and the Contraceptive Revolution on Sex Roles and the Women's Liberation Movement in the U.S. 1960–1975." *Journal of Marriage and the Family* 43:49–65.

Hicks, Mary W., and Marilyn Platt. 1970. "Marital Happiness and Stability: A Review of Research in the Sixties." *Journal of Marriage and the Family* 32:553–74.

Hole, J., and E. Levine. 1971. *The Rebirth of Feminism*. New York: Quadrangle.

Johns-Heine, Patrick, and Hans Gerth. 1949. "Values in Mass Periodical Fiction, 1921–1940." *Public Opinion Quarterly* 13:105–13.

Kidd, Virginia. 1974. "Happy Ever After and Other Relationship Styles." Ph.D. Dissertation. Department of Speech, University of Minnesota.

———. 1975. "Happily Ever After and Other Relationship Styles: Advice on Interpersonal Relations in Popular Magazines, 1951–1973." *Quarterly Journal of Speech* 61:31–39.

Kohn, Melvin. 1969. *Class and Conformity: A Study in Values*. Homewood, Illinois: Dorsey Press.

Komarovsky, Mirra. 1962. *Blue-Collar Marriage*. New York: Random House.

Lasch, Christopher. 1977. *Haven in a Heartless World*. New York: Basic Books.

———. 1978. *The Culture of Narcissism: American Life in an Age of Diminishing Expectations*. New York: Norton.

Lebergott, Stanley. 1976. *The American Economy*. Princeton, New Jersey: Princeton University Press.

Lederer, William, and Don Jackson. 1974. "Do People Really Marry for Love?" *Reader's Digest*, January.

Luker, Kristin. 1984. *Abortion and the Politics of Motherhood*. Berkeley: University of California Press.

Lynd, Robert S., and Helen Lynd. 1937. *Middletown in Transition*. New York: Harcourt, Brace and Co.

Maslow, Abraham. 1970. *Motivation and Personality*. 2nd ed. New York: Harper and Row.

Mason, Karen; John Czajka; and Sara Arber. 1976. "Change in U.S. Women's Sex-Role Attitudes, 1969–1974." *American Sociological Review* 41:573–96.

Maurois, Andre. 1940. "The Art of Marriage." *Ladies' Home Journal*, April.

Miller, Ruth Scott. 1925. "Masterless Wives and Divorce." *Ladies' Home Journal*, January.

Newcomb, Theodore. 1937. "Recent Change in Attitudes Toward Sex and Marriage." *American Sociological Review* 1:659–67.

O'Neil, William. 1978. "Divorce in the Progressive Era." In M. Gordon (ed.), *The American Family in Social-Historical Perspective*, pp. 140–51. New York: St. Martin's Press.

Oppenheimer, Valerie Kincade. 1973. "Demographic Influence on Female Employment and the Status of Women." *American Journal of Sociology* 78:946–61.

Osmond, Marie W., and Patricia Y. Martin. 1975. "Sex and Sexism." *Journal of Marriage and the Family* 37:744–59.

Pahl, J. M., and R. E. Pahl. 1971. *Managers and Their Wives*. London: Allen Love and Penguin Press.

Parelius, Ann P. 1975. "Emerging Sex-Role Attitudes, Expectations and Strains among College Women." *Journal of Marriage and the Family* 37:146–54.

Pleck, Joseph. 1985. *Working Wives, Working Husbands*. New York: Sage.

Quinn, Naomi. 1982. "'Commitment' in American Marriage: A Cultural Analysis." *American Ethnologist* 9:775–98.

Roper, Brent S., and Emily Labeff. 1977. "Sex Roles and Feminism Revisited: An Intergenerational Attitude Comparison." *Journal of Marriage and the Family* 39:113–20.

Rothman, Sheila M. 1978. *Women's Proper Place: A History of Changing Ideals and Practices 1870 to the Present*. New York: Basic Books.

Rubin, Lillian. 1976. *Worlds of Pain*. New York: Basic Books.

Ryan, Mary. 1979. *Womanhood in America (From Colonial Times to the Present)*. 2nd ed. New York: New Viewpoints.

Swidler, Ann. 1982. "Ideologies of Love in Middle Class America." Paper read at Annual Meeting of Pacific Sociological Association, San Diego.

Thornton, Arland; Duane Alwin; and Donald Camburn. 1983. "Causes and Consequences of Sex-Role Attitudes and Attitude Change." *American Sociological Review* 48:211–27.

Turner, Ralph. 1976. "The Real Self: From Institution to Impulse." *American Journal of Sociology* 81:789–1016.

U.S. Bureau of the Census. 1976. *The Statistical History of the United States.* New York: Basic Books.

U.S. Bureau of the Census. 1982. Current Population Reports, Series P-20, No. 367 and No. 371.

Vahanian, Tilla, and Sally Olds. 1978. "How Good Is Your Marriage?" *Ladies' Home Journal,* January.

Veroff, Joseph; Elizabeth Douran; and Richard Kulka. 1981. *The Inner American: A Self-Portrait from 1957 to 1976.* New York: Basic Books.

Yankelovich, Daniel. 1974. *The New Morality.* New York: McGraw-Hill.

———. 1981. *New Rules.* New York: Random House.

Zaretsky, Eli. 1976. *Capitalism, the Family and Personal Life.* New York: Harper Colophon.

Zelnik, Melvin, and John Kantner. 1980. "Sexual Activity, Contraceptive Use and Pregnancy." *Family Planning Perspectives* 12:230–37.

Zube, Margaret. 1972. "Changing Concepts of Morality: 1948–1969." *Social Forces* 50:385–96.

CHAPTER 3

Reading 3-1

Berger, Joseph; Bernard P. Cohen; and Morris Zelditch, Jr. 1972. "Status Characteristics and Social Interaction." *American Sociological Review* 37:241–55.

Berger, Joseph; Thomas L. Conner; and M. Hamit Fisek, eds. 1974. *Expectation States Theory: A Theoretical Research Program.* Cambridge: Winthrop.

Berger, Joseph; M. Hamit Fisek; Robert Z. Norman; and Morris Zelditch, Jr. 1977. *Status Characteristics and Social Interaction: An Expectation States Approach.* New York: Elsevier.

Bernstein, Richard. 1986. "France Jails 2 in Odd Case of Espionage." *New York Times* (May 11).

Blackwood, Evelyn. 1984. "Sexuality and Gender in Certain Native American Tribes: The Case of Cross-Gender Females." *Signs: Journal of Women in Culture and Society* 10:27–42.

Bourne, Patricia G., and Norma J. Wikler. 1978. "Commitment and the Cultural Mandate: Women in Medicine." *Social Problems* 25:430–40.

Chodorow, Nancy. 1978. *The Reproduction of Mothering: Psychoanalysis and the Sociology of Gender.* Los Angeles: University of California Press.

Connell, R. W. 1983. *Which Way Is Up?* Sydney: Allen & Unwin.

———. 1985. "Theorizing Gender." *Sociology* 19: 260–72.

Cucchiari, Salvatore. 1981. "The Gender Revolution and the Transition from Bisexual Horde to Patrilocal Band: The Origins of Gender Hierarchy." Pp. 31–79 in *Sexual Meanings: The Cultural Construction of Gender and Sexuality,* edited by S. B. Ortner and H. Whitehead. New York: Cambridge.

Firestone, Shulamith. 1970. *The Dialectic of Sex: The Case for Feminist Revolution.* New York: William Morrow.

Fishman, Pamela. 1978. "Interaction: The Work Women Do." *Social Problems* 25:397–406.

Garfinkel, Harold. 1967. *Studies in Ethnomethodology.* Englewood Cliffs, NJ: Prentice Hall.

Gerson, Judith M., and Kathy Peiss. 1985. "Boundaries, Negotiation, Consciousness: Reconceptualizing Gender Relations." *Social Problems* 32:317–31.

Goffman, Erving. 1976. "Gender Display." *Studies in the Anthropology of Visual Communication* 3:69–77.

———. 1977. "The Arrangement Between the Sexes." *Theory and Society* 4:301–31.

Henley, Nancy M. 1985. "Psychology and Gender." *Signs: Journal of Women in Culture and Society* 11:101–119.

Heritage, John. 1984. *Garfinkel and Ethnomethodology.* Cambridge: Polity Press.

Hill, W. W. 1935. "The Status of the Hermaphrodite and Transvestite in Navaho Culture." *American Anthropologist* 37:273–79.

Hochschild, Arlie R. 1973. "A Review of Sex Roles Research." *American Journal of Sociology* 78: 1011–29.

Hughes, Everett C. 1945. "Dilemmas and Contradictions of Status." *American Journal of Sociology* 50:353–59.

Humphreys, Paul, and Joseph Berger. 1981. "Theoretical Consequences of the Status Characteristics Formulation." *American Journal of Sociology* 86:953–83.

Jaggar, Alison M. 1983. *Feminist Politics and Human Nature.* Totowa, NJ: Rowman & Allanheld.

Kessler, S.; D. J. Ashendon; R. W. Connell; and G. W. Dowsett. 1985. "Gender Relations in Secondary Schooling." *Sociology of Education* 58:34–48.

Kessler, Suzanne J., and Wendy McKenna. 1978. *Gender: An Ethnomethodological Approach.* New York: Wiley.

Kollock, Peter; Philip Blumstein; and Pepper Schwartz. 1985. "Sex and Power in Interaction." *American Sociological Review* 50:34–46.

Komarovsky, Mirra. 1946. "Cultural Contradictions and Sex Roles." *American Journal of Sociology* 52:184–89.

———. 1950. "Functional Analysis of Sex Roles." *American Sociological Review* 15:508–16.

Linton, Ralph. 1936. *The Study of Man.* New York: Appleton-Century.

Lopata, Helen Z., and Barrie Thorne. 1978. "On the Term 'Sex Roles.'" *Signs: Journal of Women in Culture and Society* 3:718–21.

Lorber, Judith. 1984. *Women Physicians: Careers, Status and Power.* New York: Tavistock.

———. 1986. "Dismantling Noah's Ark." *Sex Roles* 14:567–80.

Martin, M. Kay, and Barbara Voorheis. 1975. *Female of the Species.* New York: Columbia University Press.

Mead, Margaret. 1963. *Sex and Temperament.* New York: Dell.

———. 1968. *Male and Female.* New York: Dell.

Mithers, Carol L. 1982. "My Life as a Man." *The Village Voice* 27 (October 5):1ff.

Money, John. 1968. *Sex Errors of the Body.* Baltimore: Johns Hopkins.

———. 1974. "Prenatal Hormones and Postnatal Sexualization in Gender Identity Differentiation." Pp. 221–95 in *Nebraska Symposium on Motivation,* Vol. 21, edited by J. K. Cole and R. Dienstbier. Lincoln: University of Nebraska Press.

——— and John G. Brennan. 1968. "Sexual Dimorphism in the Psychology of Female Transsexuals." *Journal of Nervous and Mental Disease* 147:487–99.

——— and Anke A. Ehrhardt. 1972. *Man and Woman/Boy and Girl.* Baltimore: Johns Hopkins.

——— and Charles Ogunro. 1974. "Behavioral Sexology: Ten Cases of Genetic Male Intersexuality with Impaired Prenatal and Pubertal Androgenization." *Archives of Sexual Behavior* 3:181–206.

——— and Patricia Tucker. 1975. *Sexual Signatures.* Boston: Little, Brown.

Morris, Jan. 1974. *Conundrum.* New York: Harcourt Brace Jovanovich.

Parsons, Talcott. 1951. *The Social System.* New York: Free Press.

——— and Robert F. Bales. 1955. *Family, Socialization and Interaction Process.* New York: Free Press.

Raymond, Janice G. 1979. *The Transsexual Empire.* Boston: Beacon.

Richards, Renee (with John Ames). 1983. *Second Serve: The Renee Richards Story.* New York: Stein and Day.

Rossi, Alice. 1984. "Gender and Parenthood." *American Sociological Review* 49:1–19.

Rubin, Gayle. 1975. "The Traffic in Women: Notes on the 'Political Economy' of Sex." Pp. 157–210 in *Toward an Anthropology of Women,* edited by R. Reiter. New York: Monthly Review Press.

Sacks, Harvey. 1972. "On the Analyzability of Stories by Children." Pp. 325–45 in *Directions in Sociolinguistics,* edited by J. J. Gumperz and D. Hymes. New York: Holt, Rinehart & Winston.

Schutz, Alfred. 1943. "The Problem of Rationality in the Social World." *Economics* 10:130–49.

Stacey, Judith, and Barrie Thorne. 1985. "The Missing Feminist Revolution in Sociology." *Social Problems* 32:301–16.

Thorne, Barrie. 1980. "Gender . . . How Is It Best Conceptualized?" Unpublished manuscript.

Tresemer, David. 1975. "Assumptions Made About Gender Roles." Pp. 308–39 in *Another Voice: Feminist Perspectives on Social Life and Social Science,* edited by M. Millman and R. M. Kanter. New York: Anchor/Doubleday.

West, Candace. 1984. "When the Doctor Is a 'Lady': Power, Status and Gender in Physician-Patient Encounters." *Symbolic Interaction* 7:87–106.

——— and Bonita Iritani. 1985. "Gender Politics in Mate Selection: The Male-Older Norm." Paper presented at the Annual Meeting of the

American Sociological Association, August, Washington, DC.

———— and Don H. Zimmerman. 1983. "Small Insults: A Study of Interruptions in Conversations Between Unacquainted Persons." Pp. 102–17 in *Language, Gender, and Society*, edited by B. Thorne, C. Kramarae, and N. Henley. Rowley, MA: Newberry House.

Wieder, D. Lawrence. 1974. *Language and Social Reality: The Case of Telling the Convict Code*. The Hague: Mouton.

Williams, Walter L. 1986. *The Spirit and the Flesh: Sexual Diversity in American Indian Culture*. Boston: Beacon.

Wilson, Thomas P. 1970. "Conceptions of Interaction and Forms of Sociological Explanation." *American Sociological Review* 35:697–710.

Zimmerman, Don H., and D. Lawrence Wieder. 1970. "Ethnomethodology and the Problem of Order: Comment on Denzin." Pp. 287–95 in *Understanding Everyday Life*, edited by J. Denzin. Chicago: Aldine.

Reading 3–2

Allen, S. M., & Hawkins, A. J. (1999). Maternal Gatekeeping: Mothers' Beliefs and Behaviors That Inhibit Greater Father Involvement in Family Work. *Journal of Marriage and the Family, 61*, 199–221.

Beauvais, C. (2001). *Literature Review on Learning Through Recreation (Discussion Paper No. F-15)*. Ottawa: Canadian Policy Research Network.

Bird, S. R. (1996). Welcome to the Men's Club: Homosociality and the Maintenance of Hegemonic Masculinity. *Gender & Society, 19*(2), 120–32.

Brandth, B., & Kvande, E. (1998). Masculinity and Child Care: The Reconstruction of Fathering. *The Sociological Review, 46*(2), 293–313.

Burstyn, V. (1999). *The Rites of Men: Manhood, Politics, and the Culture of Sport*. Toronto: University of Toronto Press.

Chodorow, N. (1978). *The Reproduction of Mothering: Psychoanalysis and the Sociology of Gender*. Berkeley and Los Angeles: University of California Press.

Cole, E. B., & Coultrap-McQuin, S. (Eds.). (1992). *Explorations in Feminist Ethics: Theory and Practice*. Bloomington: Indiana University Press.

Coltrane, S. (1994). Theorizing Masculinities in Contemporary Social Science. In M. Kaufman (Ed.), *Theorizing Masculinities* (pp. 39–60). Thousand Oaks, CA: Sage.

Coltrane, S. (1996). *Family Man: Fatherhood, Housework, and Gender Equity*. New York and Oxford: Oxford University Press.

Connell, R. W. (1987). *Gender and Power*. Cambridge: Polity Press.

Connell, R. W. (1995). *Masculinities*. London: Polity Press.

Connell, R. W. (2000). *The Men and the Boys*. Berkeley: University of California Press.

Daly, K. (2002). Time, Gender, and the Negotiation of Family Schedules. *Symbolic Interaction, 25*(3), 323–42.

Dienhart, A. (1998). *Reshaping Fatherhood: The Social Construction of Shared Parenting*. London: Sage.

Doucet, A. (2000). "There's a Huge Difference Between Me as a Male Carer and Women": Gender, Domestic Responsibility, and the Community as an Institutional Arena. *Community Work and Family, 3*(2), 163–84.

Doucet, A. (2001). You See the Need Perhaps More Clearly than I Have: Exploring Gendered Processes of Domestic Responsibility. *Journal of Family Issues, 22*(3), 328–57.

Doucet, A. (2004). Fathers and the Responsibility for Children: A Puzzle and a Tension. *Atlantis: A Women's Studies Journal, 28*(2), 103–14.

Dowd, N. E. (2000). *Redefining Fatherhood*. New York: New York University Press.

Fisher, B., & Tronto, J. (1990). Towards a Feminist Theory of Caring. In M. K. Nelson (Ed.), *Circles of Care: Work and Identity in Women's Lives* (pp. 35–62). New York: State University of New York Press.

Gilligan, C. (1982). *In a Different Voice: Psychological Theory and Women's Development*. Cambridge, MA: Harvard University Press.

Gilligan, C. (1993). Reply to Critics. In M. J. Larabee (Ed.), *An Ethic of Care: Feminist and Interdisciplinary Perspectives* (pp. 207–214). London: Routledge.

Graham, H. (1983). Caring: A Labor of Love. In D. A. Groves (Ed.), *A Labor of Love: Women, Work, and Caring* (pp. 13–30). London: Routledge and Kegan Paul.

Jaggar, A. M. (1990). Sexual Difference and Sexual Equality. In D. L. Rhode (Ed.), *Theoretical Perspectives on Sexual Differences* (pp. 239–254). New Haven, CT: Yale University Press.

Johnson, M. M. (1988). *Strong Mothers, Weak Wives: The Search for Gender Equality.* Berkeley: University of California Press.

Kaufman, M. (1999). Men, Feminism, and Men's Contradictory Experiences of Power. In J. A. Kuypers (Ed.), *Men and Power* (pp. 59–83). Halifax: Fernwood Books.

Kimmel, M. S. (1994). Masculinity as Homophobia: Fear, Shame and Silence in the Construction of Gender Identity. In M. Kaufman (Ed.), *Theorizing Masculinities* (pp. 119–41). Thousand Oaks, CA: Sage.

Kremarik, F. (2000). Family Affair: Children's Participation in Sports. *Canadian Social Trends (Statistics Canada), Autumn 2000, 20–4*

Lamb, M. E. (Ed.). (1981). *The Role of the Father in Child Development.* New York: John Riley.

Lamb, M. E. (Ed.). (1987). *The Father's Role: Cross-Cultural Perspectives.* Hillsdale, NJ: Erlbaum.

Larrabee, M. J. (Ed.). (1993). *An Ethic of Care: Feminist and Interdisciplinary Perspectives.* New York and London: Routledge.

Lupton, D., & Barclay, L. (1997). *Constructing Fatherhood: Discourses and Experiences.* London: Sage.

Mac an Ghaill, M. (1994). *The Making of Men: Masculinities, Sexualities, and Schooling.* Buckingham: Open University Press.

Martin, P. Y. (2003). "Said and Done" Versus "Saying and Doing": Gendering Practices, Practicing Gender at Work. *Gender and Society, 17*(3), 342–66.

Messner, M. A. (1992). *Power at Play: Sports and the Problem of Masculinity.* Boston: Beacon Press.

Messner, M. A. (1997). *Politics of Masculinities: Men in Movements.* Thousand Oaks, CA: Sage.

Monaghan, L. F. (2002). Hard Men, Shop Boys and Others: Embodying Competence in a Masculinist Occupation. *The Sociological Review, 50*(3), 334–55.

Noddings, N. (2003). *Caring: A Feminine Approach to Ethics and Moral Education* (2nd ed.). Berkeley: University of California Press.

Parke, R. D. (1996). *Fatherhood.* Cambridge, MA: Harvard University Press.

Plantin, L., Sven-Axel, M., & Kearney, J. (2003). Talking and Doing Fatherhood: On Fatherhood and Masculinity in Sweden and England. *Fathering, 1*(1), 3–26.

Pleck, J. H. (1985). *Working Wives, Working Husbands.* London: Sage.

Pollak, W. (1998). *Real Boys: Rescuing Our Sons from the Myths of Boyhood.* New York: Owl Books.

Prendergast, S., & Forrest, S. (1998). "Shorties, Low-Lifers, Hardnuts and Kings": Boys, Emotions, and Embodiment in Schools. In S. J. Williams (Ed.), *Emotions in Social Life: Critical Themes and Contemporary Issues* (pp. 155–172). London: Routledge.

Pruett, K. (2000). *Fatherneed: Why Father Care Is As Essential As Mother Care for Your Child.* New York: Broadview Press.

Ruddick, S. (1995). *Maternal Thinking: Towards a Politics of Peace* (2nd ed.). Boston: Beacon.

Seidler, V. (1997). *Man Enough: Embodying Masculinities.* London: Sage.

Snarey, J. (1993). *How Fathers Care for the Next Generation: A Four-Decade Study.* Cambridge, MA: Harvard University Press.

Stueve, J. L., & Pleck, J. H. (2003). Fathers' Narratives of Arranging and Planning: Implications for Understanding Parental Responsibility. *Fathering, 1*(1), 51–70.

Thorne, B. (1993). *Gender Play: Girls and Boys in School.* Buckingham, UK: Open University Press.

Tronto, J. (1989). Women and Caring: What Can Feminists Learn about Morality from Caring? In S. Bordo (Ed.), *Gender/Body/Knowledge: Feminist Reconstructions of Being and Knowing* (pp. 172–87). New Brunswick and London: Rutgers University Press.

Tronto, J. (1993). *Moral Boundaries: A Political Argument for an Ethic of Care.* New York and London: Routledge.

Tronto, J. (1995). Care as a Basis for Radical Political Judgements (Symposium on Care and Justice). *Hypatia, 10*(2), 141–49.

Ungerson, C. (1990). The Language of Care: Crossing the Boundaries. In C. Ungerson (Ed.), *Gender and Caring: Work and Welfare in Britain and Scandinavia* (pp. 8–33). New York: Harvester Wheatsheaf.

Yogman, M. W., Cooley, J., & Kindlon, D. (1988). Fathers, Infants and Toddlers: A Developing

Relationship. In C. P. Cowan (Ed.), *Fatherhood Today: Men's Changing Role in the Family* (pp. 53–65). New York: Wiley.

CHAPTER 4

Reading 4-2

Aries, Philippe. 1962. *Centuries of Childhood: A Social History of the Family.* Translated by R. Baldick. London: Cape.

Bourdieu, Pierre. 1976. "Marriage Strategies as Strategies of Social Reproduction." Pp. 117–44 in *Family and Society,* edited by R. Forster and O. Ranum. Baltimore, MD: Johns Hopkins University Press.

———. 1984. *Distinction: A Social Critique of the Judgment of Taste.* Cambridge, MA: Harvard University Press.

———. 1986. "The Forms of Capital." Pp. 241–58 in *Handbook of Theory and Research for the Sociology of Education,* edited by J. C. Richardson. New York: Greenwood.

———. 1989. *The State Nobility: Elite Schools in the Field of Power.* Stanford, CA: Stanford University Press.

Bronfenbrenner, Urie. 1966. "Socialization and Social Class through Time and Space." Pp. 362–77 in *Class, Status and Power,* edited by R. Bendix and S. M. Lipset. New York: Free Press.

Burawoy, Michael; Alice Burton; Ann Arnett Ferguson; and Kathryn J. Fox, eds. 1991. *Ethnography Unbound: Power and Resistance in the Modern Metropolis.* Berkeley: University of California Press.

Chidekel, Dana. 2002. *Parents in Charge.* New York: Simon and Schuster.

Conley, Dalton. 1999. *Being Black, Living in the Red: Race, Wealth, and Social Policy in America.* Berkeley: University of California Press.

Corsaro, William A. 1997. *The Sociology of Childhood.* Thousand Oaks, CA: Pine Forge.

Donzelot, Jacques. 1979. *The Policing of Families.* Translated by R. Hurley. New York: Pantheon.

Epstein, Joyce. 2001. *Schools, Family, and Community Partnerships.* Boulder, CO: Westview.

Erikson, Robert, and John H. Goldthorpe. 1993. *The Constant Flux: A Study of Class Mobility in Industrial Societies.* Oxford, England: Clarendon.

Fordham, Signithia, and John U. Ogbu. 1986. "Black Students' School Success: Coping with the 'Burden of Acting White." *The Urban Review* 18:176–206.

Gordon, Linda. 1989. *Heroes of Their Own Lives: The Politics and History of Family Violence.* New York: Penguin.

Halbfinger, David M. 2002. "A Hockey Parent's Life: Time, Money, and Yes, Frustration." *New York Times,* January 12, p. 29.

Hart, Betty, and Todd Risley. 1995. *Meaningful Differences in the Everyday Experience of Young American Children.* Baltimore, MD: Paul Brooks.

Hays, Sharon. 1996. *The Cultural Contradictions of Motherhood.* New Haven, CT: Yale University Press.

Heimer, Carol A., and Lisa Staffen. 1998. *For the Sake of the Children: The Social Organization of Responsibility in the Hospital and at Home.* Chicago: University of Chicago Press.

Hochschild, Jennifer L. 1995. *Facing Up to the American Dream.* Princeton, NJ: Princeton University Press.

Kingston, Paul. 2000. *The Classless Society.* Stanford, CA: Stanford University Press.

Kohn, Melvin, and Carmi Schooler, eds. 1983. *Work and Personality: An Inquiry into the Impact of Social Stratification.* Norwood, NJ: Ablex.

Kropp, Paul. 2001. *I'll Be the Parent, You Be the Child.* New York: Fisher Books.

Lamont, Michele. 2000. *The Dignity of Working Men: Morality and the Boundaries of Race, Class, and Immigration.* Cambridge, MA: Harvard University Press.

Lareau, Annette. 2000. *Home Advantage: Social Class and Parental Intervention in Elementary Education.* 2d ed. Lanham, MD: Rowman and Littlefield.

———. 2002. "Doing Multi-Person, Multi-Site 'Ethnographic' Work: A Reflective, Critical Essay." Department of Sociology, Temple University, Philadelphia, PA. Unpublished manuscript.

———. 2003. *Unequal Childhood: Class, Race, and Family Life.* Berkeley: University of California Press.

Massey, Douglas, and Nancy Denton. 1993. *American Apartheid.* Cambridge, MA: Harvard University Press.

McLanahan, Sara, and Gary Sandefur. 1994. *Growing Up with a Single Parent: What Hurts, What Helps.* Cambridge, MA: Harvard University Press.

Newman, Kathleen. 1993. *Declining Fortunes: The Withering of the American Dream.* New York: Basic Books.

Pattillo-McCoy, Mary. 1999. *Black Picket Fences: Privilege and Peril among the Black Middle-Class.* Chicago: University of Chicago Press.

Sandberg, John F., and Sandra L. Hofferth. 2001. "Changes in Children's Time with Parents, U.S., 1981–1997." *Demography* 38:423–36.

Tatum, Beverly Daniel. 1997. *Why Are All the Black Kids Sitting Together in the Cafeteria? And Other Conversations about Race.* New York: Basic Books.

Van Ausdale, Debra, and Joe R. Feagin. 1996. "Using Racial and Ethnic Concepts: The Critical Case of Very Young Children." *American Sociological Review* 61:779–93.

Waters, Mary C. 1999. *Black Identities: West Indian Immigrant Dreams and American Realities.* New York: Russell Sage Foundation.

Wright, Erik Olin. 1997. *Class Counts: Comparative Studies in Class Analysis.* Cambridge: Cambridge University Press.

Wrigley, Julia. 1989. "Do Young Children Need Intellectual Stimulation? Experts' Advice to Parents, 1900–1985." *History of Education* 29:41–75.

Zelizer, Vivianna. 1985. *Pricing the Priceless Child: The Changing Social Value of Children.* New York: Basic Books.

CHAPTER 5

Reading 5-1

Blum, Linda, and Theresa Deussen. 1996. Negotiating independent motherhood: Working-class African American women talk about marriage and motherhood. *Gender & Society* 10:199–211.

Chang, Grace. 1994. Undocumented Latinas: Welfare burdens or beasts of burden? *Socialist Review* 23:151–85.

Collins, Patricia Hill. 1991. *Black feminist thought: Knowledge, consciousness, and the politics of empowerment.* New York: Routledge.

———. 1994. Shifting the center: Race, class, and feminist theorizing about motherhood. In *Mothering: Ideology, experience, and agency,* edited by Evelyn Nakano Glenn, Grace Chang, and Linda Rennie Forcey. New York: Routledge.

Dill, Bonnie Thornton. 1988. Our mothers' grief: Racial-ethnic women and the maintenance of families. *Journal of Family History* 13:415–31.

———. 1994. Fictive kin, paper sons and compadrazgo: Women of color and the struggle for family survival. In *Women of color in U.S. society,* edited by Maxine Baca Zinn and Bonnie Thornton Dill. Philadelphia: Temple University Press.

Gill, Lesley. 1994. *Precarious dependencies: Gender, class and domestic service in Bolivia.* New York: Columbia University Press.

Glenn, Evelyn Nakano. 1986. *Issei, Nisei, war-bride: Three generations of Japanese American women in domestic service.* Philadelphia: Temple University Press.

———. 1994. Social constructions of mothering: A thematic overview. In *Mothering: Ideology, experience, and agency,* edited by Evelyn Nakano Glenn, Grace Chang, and Linda Rennie Forcey. New York: Routledge.

Griswold del Castillo, Richard. 1984. *La Familia: Chicano families in the urban Southwest, 1848 to the present.* Notre Dame, IN: University of Notre Dame Press.

Hondagneu-Sotelo, Pierrette. 1995. Women and children first: New directions in anti-immigrant politics. *Socialist Review* 25:169–90.

Rollins, Judith. 1985. *Between women: Domestics and their employers.* Philadelphia: Temple University Press.

Romero, Mary. 1992. *Maid in the U.S.A.* New York: Routledge.

———. 1996. Life as the maid's daughter: An exploration of the everyday boundaries of race, class and gender. In *Feminisms in the academy: Rethinking the disciplines,* edited by Abigail J. Steward and Donna Stanon. Ann Arbor: University of Michigan Press.

Ruddick, Sara. 1989. *Maternal thinking: Toward a politics of peace.* Boston: Beacon.

Scheper-Hughes, Nancy. 1992. *Death without weeping: The violence of everyday life in Brazil.* Berkeley: University of California Press.

Segura, Denise A., and Jennifer L. Pierce. 1993. Chicana/o family structure and gender personality: Chodorow, familism, and psychoanalytic sociology revisited. *Signs: Journal of Women in Culture and Society* 19:62–79.

Skolnick, Arlene S. 1991. *Embattled paradise: The American family in an age of uncertainty.* New York: Basic Books.

Stacey, Judith. 1996. *In the name of the family: Rethinking family values in the postmodern age.* Boston: Beacon.

Stack, Carol B., and Linda M. Burton. 1994. Kinscripts: Reflections on family, generation, and culture. In *Mothering: Ideology, experience, and agency,* edited by Evelyn Nakano Glenn, Grace Chang, and Linda Rennie Forcey. New York: Routledge.

Wrigley, Julia. 1995. *Other people's children.* New York: Basic Books.

Zelizer, Viviana. 1994. *Pricing the priceless child: The social value of children.* Princeton, NJ: Princeton University Press.

CHAPTER 6

Reading 6-1

Blumstein, Philip, and Pepper Schwartz. 1983. *American Couples: Money, Work, Sex.* New York: William Morrow.

Buss, D. 1994. *The Evolution of Desire: Strategies of Human Mating.* New York: Basic Books.

———. 1995. "Psychological Sex Differences: Origins through Sexual Selection." *American Psychologist* 50:164–68.

D'Emilio, John, and Estelle B. Freedman. 1988. *Intimate Matters: A History of Sexuality in America.* New York: Harper and Row.

Dutton, D., and A. Aron. 1974. "Some Evidence for Heightened Sexual Attraction under Conditions of High Anxiety." *Journal of Personality and Social Psychology* 30:510–17.

Fisher, H. E. 1992. *Anatomy of Love: The Natural History of Monogamy, Adultery, and Divorce.* New York: Norton.

Foucault, M. 1978. *A History of Sexuality: Vol. 1. An Introduction.* New York: Pantheon.

Greenhalgh, S. 1977. "Hobbled Feet, Hobbled Lives: Women in Old China." *Frontiers* 2:7–21.

Malthus, T. R. [1798] 1929. *An Essay on the Principle of Population as It Affects the Future Improvement of Society.* New York and London: Macmillan.

Sexuality Information and Education Council of the United States. 1995. *A Report on Adolescent Sexuality.* New York: SIECUS.

Valins, S. 1966. "Cognitive Effects of False Heart-Rate Feedback." *Journal of Personality and Social Psychology* 4:400–8.

Reading 6-2

Aharons, C. R., and Rodgers, R. H. 1987. *Divorced Families: A Multidisciplinary Developmental View.* New York: Norton.

Befolkningsförändringar [Population Changes] (1968) Stockholm: Statistiska Central-byrån.

Befolkningsstatistik [Population Statistics] (1995) Stockholm: Statistiska Central-byrån.

Booth, A., and Amato, P. R. 2001. "Parental Pre-Divorce Relations and Offspring Post-Divorce Well-Being." *Journal of Marriage and Family* 63(1):197–212.

Caradec, V. 1996. "Les Formes de la vie conjugale des 'jeunes' couple 'âgés.' *Population* 51:897–928.

Furstenberg, F. F., and Kiernan, K. E. 2001. "Delayed Parental Divorce: How Much Do Children Benefit?" *Journal of Marriage and Family* 63(2):446–57.

Giddens, A. 1994. *Intimitetens forandring* [Intimacy in Change]. Copenhagen: Hans Reitzels forlag.

Heimdal, K. R., and Houseknecht, S. K. 2003. "Cohabiting and Married Couples' Income Organisation: Approaches in Sweden and the United States." *Journal of Marriage and Family* 65(3):539–49.

Historisk statistik (1967) Stockholm: Statistiska Central-byrån.

Hopper, J. 2001. "The Symbolic Origins of Conflict in Divorce." *Journal of Marriage and Family* 63(2):446–57.

Kamp Dush, C. M., Cohan, C. L., and Amato, P. R. 2003. "The Relationship Between Cohabitation and Marital Quality and Stability: Change Across Cohorts?" *Journal of Marriage and Family* 65(3):539–49.

Levin, I. 1993. "Family as Mapped Realities." *Journal of Family Issues* special issue "Rethinking Family as a Social Form" 14(1):82–91.

———. 1994. *Stefamilien—variasjon og mangfold.* Oslo: Aventura.

——— and Trost, J. 1992. "Understanding the Concept of Family." *Family Relations* 41:348–51.

——— and Trost, J. 1996. *Å forstå hverdagen—med et symbolsk interaksjonistisk perspektiv* [To Understand Everyday Life: With a Symbolic Interactionist Perspective]. Oslo: Tano Aschehoug.

——— and Trost, J. 1999. "Living Apart Together." *Community, Work and Family* 2(3):279–93.

———. 2001. "Barns perspektiv på skilsmisse—ett eller flere fenomen?" (Children's Perspective of Family—One or More Perspectives?) In K. Moxnes, I. Kvaran, H. Kaul, and I. Levin (eds.), *Skilsmissens mange ansikter.* Kristiansand: Norwegian Academic Press.

——— and Trost, J. 2003. *Særbo—ett par to hjem.* Oslo: Damm and Søn forlag.

Lewis, J., and Meredith, B. 1989. *Daughters Who Care.* London: Routledge.

Moxnes, K. 1990. *Kjernesprengning i familien.* Oslo: Universitetesforlaget.

———. 2001. "Skilsmissens virkning på barna." In K. Moxnes, I. Kvaran, H. Kaul, and I. Levin (eds.), *Skilsmissens mange ansikter,* pp. 17–32. Kristiansand: Norwegian Academic Press.

Schneider, N. F. 1996. "Partnerschaften mit getrennten Haushalten in den neuen und alten Bundesländern." In W. Bien (ed.), *Familie an der Schwelle zum neuen Jahrtausend,* pp. 88–97. Opladen: Leske und Budrich.

Sogner, S., and Dupâquir, J. 1981. "Marriage and Remarriage in Populations of the Past." *International Colloquium on Historical Demography 1979 in Kristiansand.* London: Academic Press.

Stryker, S. 1980. *Symbolic Interaction: A Social-Structural Version.* Menlo Park, CA: Cummings.

Sundt, E. 1975. *Om giftermaal i Norge.* Oslo: Gyldendal norsk forlag. (Orig. pub. 1855)

Trost, J. 1979. *Unmarried Cohabitation.* Västerås: International Library.

———. 1993. *Familjen i Sverige* [The Family in Sweden]. Stockholm: Liber.

———. 1995. "Ehen und andere dyadische Beziehungen." In B. Nauck and C. Onnen-Isemann (eds.), *Familie im Brennpunkt von Wissenschaft und Forschung,* pp. 343–56. Berlin: Luchterhand.

———. 1997. *Kvalitativa intervjuer* [Qualitative Interviews]. 2nd ed. Lund: Studentlitteratur.

———. 1998. "LAT Relationships Now and in the Future." In K. Matthijs (ed.), *The Family: Contemporary Perspectives and Challenges; Festschrift in Honor of Wilfried Dumon,* pp. 209–220. Leuven: Leuven University Press.

Wallerstein, J. S., and Kelly, J. B. 1980. *Surviving the Breakup.* New York: Basic Books.

Winfield, F. E. 1985. *Commuter Marriage: Living Together, Apart.* New York: Columbia University Press.

Reading 7-1

Bumpass, L., and Lu, H. 2000. Trends in cohabitation and implications for children's family contexts. *Population Studies* 54:29–41.

———, and Sweet, J. A. 2001. Marriage, divorce, and intergenerational relationships. In A. Thornton (ed.), *The well-being of children and families: Research and data needs* (pp. 295–313). Ann Arbor: University of Michigan Press.

Casper, L., and Bianchi, S. 2002. *Continuity and change in the American family.* Thousand Oaks, CA: Sage.

Cherlin, A. J. 2004. The deinstitutionalization of American marriage. *Journal of Marriage and Family* 66:848–61.

Clarkberg, M. E. 1999. The price of partnering: The role of economic well-being in young adults' first union experiences. *Social Forces* 77:945–68.

———, Stolzenberg, R. M., and Waite, L. J. 1995. Attitudes, values, and entrance into cohabitational versus marital unions. *Social Forces* 74:609–34.

Clark-Nicolas, P., and Gray-Little, B. 1991. Effect of economic resources on marital quality in African American married couples. *Journal of Marriage and Family* 53:645–55.

Conger, R. D., Elder, G., Lorenz, F., Conger, K., Simons, R., Whitbeck, L., Huck, S., and Melby, J. 1990. Linking economic hardship to marital quality and stability. *Journal of Marriage and Family* 52:643–56.

Edin, K. 2000. What do low-income single mothers say about marriage? *Social Problems* 47:112–33.

Ellwood, D., and Jencks, C. 2001. *The growing difference in family structure: What do we know? Where do we look for answers?* Retrieved June 8, 2005, from http://www.russellsage.org/programs/other/inequality/050221.100862/download

Fields, J., and Casper, L. 2001. *America's families and living arrangements: Population characteristics* (Current Population Reports No. P20-537). Washington, DC: U.S. Government Printing Office.

Fox, G. L., and Chancey, D. 1998. Sources of economic distress: Individual and family outcomes. *Journal of Family Issues* 19:725–49.

Furstenberg, F. F. 1995. Fathering in the inner city: Paternal participation and public policy. In

W. Marsiglio (ed.), *Fatherhood: Contemporary theory, research, and social policy* (pp. 119–47). Thousand Oaks, CA: Sage.

Gibson, C., Edin, K., and McLanahan, S. 2003. *High hopes but even higher expectations: The retreat from marriage among low income couples.* Center for Research on Child Wellbeing Working Paper 03-06-FF, Princeton, NJ.

Hughes, M. E. 2003. Home economics: Metropolitan labor and housing markets and domestic arrangements in young adulthood. *Social Forces* 81:1300–429.

Johnson, D., and Booth, A. 1990. Rural economic decline and marital quality: A panel study of farm marriages. *Family Relations* 39:159–65.

Landale, N. S., and Forste, R. 1991. Patterns of entry into cohabitation and marriage among mainland Puerto Rican women. *Demography* 28:587–607.

Lichter, D. T., Graefe, D. R., and Brown, J. B. 2003. Is marriage a panacea? Union formation among economically disadvantaged unwed mothers. *Social Problems* 50:60–86.

Lin, A. C. 1998. Bridging positivist and interpretivist approaches to qualitative methods. *Policy Studies Journal* 26:162–80.

Manning, W. 2002. The implications of cohabitation for children's well-being. In A. Booth and A. C. Crouter (eds.), *Just living together: Implications for children, families, and public policy* (pp. 121–52). Mahwah, NJ: Erlbaum.

Manning, W. D., and Smock, P. J. 1995. Why marry? Race and the transition to marriage among cohabitors. *Demography* 32:509–20.

Mead, G. H. 1934. *Mind, self, and society: From the standpoint of a social behaviorist.* Chicago: University of Chicago Press.

Oppenheimer, V. 2003. Cohabiting and marriage during young men's career development process. *Demography* 40:127–49.

Rubin, L. B. 1976. *Worlds of pain: Life in the working-class family.* New York: Basic Books.

Sassler, S. 2004. The process of entering into cohabiting unions. *Journal of Marriage and Family* 66:491–505.

——— and McNally, J. 2003. Cohabiting couples' economic circumstances and union transitions: A re-examination using multiple imputation techniques. *Social Science Research* 32:553–78.

Smock, P. J. 2004. The wax and wane of marriage: Prospects for marriage in the 21st century. *Journal of Marriage and Family* 66:966–73.

——— and Manning, W. D. 1997. Cohabiting partners' economic circumstances and marriage. *Demography* 34:331–41.

Stryker, S. 1972. Symbolic interaction theory: A review and some suggestions for comparative family research. *Journal of Comparative Family Studies* 3:17–32.

Thornton, A., Axinn, W., and Teachman, J. 1995. The influence of school enrollment and accumulation on cohabitation and marriage in early adulthood. *American Sociological Review* 60:762–74.

Thornton, A., Fricke, T., Axinn, W., and Alwin, D. 2001. Values and beliefs in the lives of children and families. In A. Thornton (ed.), *The well-being of children and families: Research and data needs* (pp. 215–43). Ann Arbor: University of Michigan Press.

Thornton, A., and Young-Demarco, L. 2001. Four decades of trends in attitudes toward family issues in the United States: The 1960s through the 1990s. *Journal of Marriage and Family* 63:1009–37.

Waite, L. 1995. Does marriage matter? *Demography* 32:483–507.

———. 2000. Trends in men's and women's well-being in marriage. In L. Waite, C. Bachrach, M. Hindin, E. Thomson, and A. Thornton (eds.), *The ties that bind: Perspectives on marriage and cohabitation* (pp. 368–92). New York: Aldine de Gruyter.

Weiss, R. S. 1994. *Learning from strangers: The art and method of qualitative interview studies.* New York: Free Press.

Weitzman, E. 1999. Analyzing qualitative data with computer software. *Health Services Research* 34:1241–63.

Xie, Y., Raymo, J., Goyette, K., and Thornton, A. 2003. Economic potential and entry into marriage and cohabitation. *Demography* 40:351–67.

CHAPTER 9

Reading 9-2

Badgett, M. V. Lee. 2001. *Money, Myths, and Change: The Economic Lives of Lesbians and Gay Men.* Chicago: University of Chicago Press.

Bech, Henning. 1997. *When Men Meet: Homosexuality and Modernity.* Chicago: University of Chicago Press.

Beck, Ulrich, and Elisabeth Beck-Gernsheim. 1995. *The Normal Chaos of Love.* London: Polity Press.

Beers, James Robert. 1996. "Desire to Parent in Gay Men." Unpublished Ph.D. dissertation, Columbia University, Teachers College, USA.

Bell, Alan P., and Martin S. Weinberg. 1978. *Homosexualities: A Study of Diversity among Men and Women.* New York: Simon & Schuster.

Bellafante, Ginia. 2004. "Two Fathers, with One Happy to Stay at Home." *New York Times,* January 12, pp. A1,12.

Bernstein, Robert A. 2005. *Families of Value: Personal Profiles of Pioneering Lesbian and Gay Parents.* New York: Marlowe & Company.

Bos, Henny. 2004. *Parenting in Planned Lesbian Families.* Amsterdam: Vossiuspers UvA.

Brodzinsky, David M., with the Staff of the Evan B. Donaldson Adoption Institute. 2003. "Adoption by Lesbians and Gays: A National Survey of Adoption Agency Policies, Practices, and Attitudes." Available on http://www.adoptioninstitute.org/whowe/Gay%20and%20Lesbian%20Adoptionl.html (accessed October 2005).

Elder, Sean. 2004. "Why My Wife Won't Sleep with Me: Confessions of a Dependent Male." *New York Magazine,* April 5, p. 43.

Furstenberg, Frank, Jr., and Andrew J. Cherlin. 1991. *Divided Families: What Happens to Children When Parents Part?* Cambridge, MA: Harvard University Press.

Gallagher, Maggie. 2003. "Silly Judges, Marriage Is for Kids." *New York Post,* November 28.

Giddens, Anthony. 1992. *The Transformation of Intimacy: Sexuality, Love and Eroticism in Modern Societies.* Stanford, CA: Stanford University Press.

Green, Jesse. 1999. *The Velveteen Father: An Unexpected Journey to Fatherhood.* New York: Villard.

Hertz, Rosanna, and Faith I. T. Ferguson. 1997. "Kinship Strategies and Self-Sufficiency among Single Mothers by Choice: Postmodern Family Ties." *Qualitative Sociology* 20:187–209.

Kapp, S. A., T. P. McDonald, and K. L. Diamond. 2001. "The Path to Adoption for Children of Color." *Child Abuse and Neglect* 25:215–29.

Kenny, Moira. 2001. *Mapping Gay L.A.: The Intersection of Place and Politics.* Philadelphia: Temple University Press.

Kipnis, Laura. 2003. *Against Love: A Polemic.* New York: Pantheon.

Laumann, Edward O., John H. Gagnon, Robert T. Michael, and Stuard Michaels. 2000. *The Social Organization of Sexuality: Sexual Practices in the United States.* Chicago: University of Chicago Press.

Miller, John C. 2001. "'My Daddy Loves Your Daddy': A Gay Father Encounters a Social Movement." In *Queer Families, Queer Politics Challenging Culture and the State,* edited by Mary Bernstein and Renate Reimann, pp. 221–30. New York: Columbia University Press.

PopLuckClub. 2002. *Newsletter,* August. Los Angeles.

Ryan-Flood, Róisín. 2005. "Contested Heteronormativities: Discourses of Fatherhood among Lesbian Parents in Sweden and Ireland." *Sexualities* 8(2):189–204.

Savage, Dan. 1999. *The Kid: An Adoption Story.* New York: Plume.

Sbordone, Albert. 1993. "Gay Men Choosing Fatherhood." Unpublished Ph.D. dissertation, City University of New York, USA.

Schacher, Stephanie Jill, Carl Auerbach, and Louise Silverstein. 2005. "Gay Fathers Expanding the Possibilities for All of Us." *Journal of GLBT Families Studies* 1(3):31–52.

Sears, Brad, and M. V. Lee Badgett. 2004. "Same-Sex Couples and Same-Sex Couples Raising Children in California: Data from Census 2000." Los Angeles: The Williams Project, UCLA School of Law.

Seidman, Steven. 1991. *Romantic Longings: Love in America 1830–1980.* New York: Routledge.

Shireman, Joan F. 1995. "Adoptions by Single Parents." *Marriage and Family Review* 20:367–87.

Simmons, Tavia, and Martin O'Connell. 2003. "Married-Couple and Unmarried-Partner Households: 2000." Washington, DC: U.S. Census Bureau, February.

Stacey, Judith. 1996. *In the Name of the Family: Rethinking Family Values in the Postmodern Age.* Boston, MA: Beacon Press.

———. 1998 [1990]. *Brave New Families: Stories of Domestic Upheaval in Late Twentieth Century America.* Berkeley: University of California Press.

————. 2004. "Toward Equal Regard for Marriages and Other Imperfect Intimate Affiliation." *Hofstra Law Review,* 32(1):331–48.

Stephens, Linda S. 1996. "Will Johnny See Daddy This Week? An Empirical Test of Three Theoretical Perspectives of Postdivorce Contact." *Journal of Family Issues* 17(4):466–94.

Strah, David, with Susanna Margolis. 2003. *Gay Dads.* New York: J. T. Tarcher/Putnam.

Townsend, Nicholas W. 2002. *The Package Deal: Marriage, Work and Fatherhood in Men's Lives.* Philadelphia: Temple University Press.

Turnbull, Lornet. 2004. "Family Is . . . Being Redefined All the Time." *The Seattle Times.* Republished in the *Indianapolis Star,* May 31, 2004.

U.S. Department of Health and Human Services, Administration for Children and Families, Administration on Children, Youth, and Families, Children's Bureau. 2003. *The AFCARS Report.* Available on (National) http://www.acf.hhs.gov/programs/cb/publications/afcars/report8.pdf; (California) http://www.acf.hhs.gov/programs/cb/dis/tables/race04.htm (both accessed October 2005).

Weeks, Jeffrey, Brian Heaphy, and Catherine Donovan. 2001. *Same-Sex Intimacies: Families of Choice and Other Life Experiments.* London: Routledge.

CHAPTER 10

Reading 10-1

Ahrons, C. R. 1994. *The good divorce.* New York: Harper Collins.

Amato, P., and Booth, A. 1997. *A generation at risk: Growing up in an era of family upheaval.* Cambridge, MA: Harvard University Press.

Bengtson, V. L. 1975. Generations and family effects in value socialization. *American Sociological Review* 40:358–71.

————. 1993. Is the "contract across generations" changing? Effects of population aging on obligations and expectations across age groups. In V. L. Bengtson and W. A. Achenbaum (eds.), *The changing contract across generations* (pp. 3–24). New York: Aldine de Gruyter.

————. 1996. Continuities and discontinuities in intergenerational relationships over time. In V. L. Bengtson (ed.), *Adulthood and aging: Research on continuities and discontinuities.* New York: Springer.

Bengtson, V. L., and Allen, K. R. (1993). The life course perspective applied to families over time. In P. Boss, W. Doherty, R. LaRossa, W. Schumm, and S. Steinmetz (eds.), *Sourcebook of family theories and methods: A contextual approach* (pp. 469–98). New York: Plenum Press.

Bengtson, V. L., Biblarz, T., Clarke, E., Giarrusso, R., Roberts, R. E. L., Richlin-Klonsky, J., and Silverstein, M. 2000. Intergenerational relationships and aging: Families, cohorts, and social change. In J. M. Claire and R. M. Allman (eds.), *The gerontological prism: Developing interdisciplinary bridges.* Amityville, NY: Baywood.

Bengtson, V. L., Biblarz, T. L., and Roberts, R. E. L. (2002). *How families still matter: A longitudinal study of youth in two generations.* New York: Cambridge University Press.

Bengtson, V. L., and Harootyan, R. (eds.). 1994. *Intergenerational linkages: Hidden connections in American society.* New York: Springer.

Bengtson, V. L., and Kuypers, J. A. 1971. Generational difference and the "developmental stake." *Aging and Human Development* 2:249–60.

Bengtson, V. L., and Mangen, D. J. 1988. Family intergenerational solidarity revisited. In D. J. Mangen, V. L. Bengtson, and P. H. Landry (eds.), *Measurement of intergenerational relations* (pp. 222–38). Newbury Park, CA: Sage.

Bengtson, V. L., and Putney, N. 2000. Who will care for the elderly? Consequences of population aging in East and West. In K. D. Kim, V. L. Bengtson, G. C. Meyers, and K. S. Eun (eds.), *Aging in East and West: Families, states and the elderly.* New York: Springer.

Bengtson, V. L., Rosenthal, C. J., and Burton, L. M. 1990. Families and aging: Diversity and heterogeneity. In R. Binstock and L. George (eds.), *Handbook of aging and the social sciences* (3rd ed., pp. 263–87). New York: Academic Press.

Bengtson, V. L., Rosenthal, C. J., and Burton, L. M. 1995. Paradoxes of families and aging. In R. H. Binstock and L. K. George (eds.), *Handbook of aging and the social sciences* (4th ed., pp. 253–82). San Diego, CA: Academic Press.

Bengtson, V. L., and Schrader, S. S. 1982. Parent-child relations. In D. Mangen and W. Peterson (eds.), *Handbook of research instruments in social gerontology* (Vol. 2, pp. 115–85). Minneapolis: University of Minnesota Press.

Bumpass, L. L., Sweet, J., and Martin, C. 1990. Changing patterns of remarriage. *Journal of Marriage and the Family* 52:747–56.

Burgess, E. W. 1916. *The function of socialization in social evolution.* Chicago: University of Chicago Press.

———. 1926. The family as a unity of interacting personalities. *The Family* 7:3–9.

Burton, L. 1995. Intergenerational patterns of providing care in African-American families with teenage childbearers: Emergent patterns in an ethnographic study. In V. L. Bengtson, K. W. Schaie, and L. M. Burton (eds.), *Adult intergenerational relations* (pp. 79–97). New York: Springer.

Burton, L. M., and Bengtson, V. L. 1985. Black grandmothers: Issues of timing and continuity in roles. In V. Bengtson and J. Robertson (eds.), *Grandparenthood* (pp. 304–38). Beverly Hills, CA: Sage.

Cherlin, A. J. 1992. *Marriage, divorce, remarriage* (rev. and enlarged ed.). Cambridge, MA: Harvard University Press.

———. 1999. *Public and private families.* Boston: McGraw-Hill.

Clarke, E., Preston, M., Raskin, J., and Bengtson, V. L. 1999. Types of conflicts and tensions between older parents and adult children. *Gerontologist* 39:261–70.

Collins, P. H. 1990. *Black feminist thought.* New York: Routledge.

Coontz, S. 1991. *The way we never were.* New York: Basic Books.

Davis, K. 1941. Family structure and functions. *American Sociological Review* 8:311–20.

Elder, G. H., Rudkin, L., and Conger, R. D. 1994. Intergenerational continuity and change in rural America. In K. W. Schaie, V. Bengtson, and L. Burton (eds.), *Societal impact on aging: Intergenerational perspectives.* New York: Springer.

Farkas, J., and Hogan, D. 1995. The demography of changing intergenerational relationships. In V. L. Bengtson, K. W. Schaie, and L. M. Burton (eds.), *Adult intergenerational relations: Effects of societal change* (pp. 1–19). New York: Springer.

Furstenberg, F., and Cherlin, A. 1991. *Divided families: What happens to children when parents part.* Cambridge, MA: Harvard University Press.

Giarrusso, R., Stallings, M., and Bengtson, V. L. 1995. The "intergenerational stake" hypothesis revisited: Parent-child differences in perceptions of relationships 20 years later. In V. L. Bengtson, K. W. Schaie, and L. M. Burton (eds.), *Adult intergenerational relations: Effects of societal change* (pp. 227–63). New York: Springer.

Goldscheider, F. K. 1990. The aging of the gender revolution: What do we know and what do we need to know? *Research on Aging* 12:531–45.

Goldscheider, F. K., and Goldscheider, C. 1993. *Leaving home before marriage: Ethnicity, familism, and generational relationships.* Madison: University of Wisconsin Press.

Hagestad, G. O. 1996. On-time, off-time, out of time? Reflections on continuity and discontinuity from an illness process. In V. L. Bengtson (ed.), *Adulthood and aging: Research on continuities and discontinuities* (pp. 204–22). New York: Springer.

Harris, S. C. 2000. *Grandmothers raising grandchildren: An ethnography of family life and life in "The System."* Dissertation in progress, University of Southern California, Los Angeles.

Harris, S. C., and Pedersen, H. L. 1997, October. *Grandparents who parent.* Paper presented at the American Association for Marriage and Family Therapists, Atlanta, GA.

Hayward, M. D., and Heron, M. 1999. Racial inequality in active life among adult Americans. *Demography* 36:77–91.

Johnson, C. L., and Barer, B. M. 1987. Marital instability and the changing kinship networks of grandparents. *Gerontologist* 27:330–35.

King, V. 1994. Variation in the consequences of nonresident father involvement for children's well-being. *Journal of Marriage and the Family* 56:963–72.

King, V., and Elder, G. H., Jr. 1997. The legacy of grandparenting: Childhood experiences with grandparents and current involvement with grandchildren. *Journal of Marriage and the Family* 59:848–59.

Kurdek, L. A., and Schmidt, J. P. 1987. Perceived emotional support from family and friends in members of homosexual, married, and heterosexual cohabiting couples. *Journal of Homosexuality* 14:57–68.

Laslett, P. 1976. Societal development and aging. In R. Binstock and E. Shanas (eds.), *Handbook of aging and the social sciences* (pp. 87–116). New York: Van Nostrand Reinhold.

Lee, G. R., Netzer, J. K., and Coward, R. T. 1994. Filial responsibility expectations and patterns of intergenerational assistance. *Journal of Marriage and the Family* 56:559–65.

Mangen, D. J., Bengtson, V. L., and Landry, P. H., Jr. (eds.). 1988. *The measurement of intergenerational relations.* Beverly Hills, CA: Sage.

Marshall, V. W., Matthews, S. H., and Rosenthal, C. J. 1993. Elusiveness of family life: A challenge for the sociology of aging. In G. L. Maddox and M. P. Lawton (eds.), *Kinship, aging, and social change. Annual review of gerontology and geriatrics, Vol. 13* (pp. 39–74). New York: Springer.

McGarry, K., and Schoeni, R. F. 1995. Transfer behavior in the health and retirement study. *Journal of Human Resources* 30 (Suppl.): S184–S226.

McLanahan, S. S. 1983. Family structure and stress: A longitudinal comparison of two-parent and female-headed families. *Journal of Marriage and the Family* 45:347–57.

———. 1994. The consequences of single motherhood. *American Prospect* 18:94–58.

McLanahan, S. S., and Sandefur, G. 1994. *Growing up with a single parent: What helps, what hurts.* Cambridge, MA: Harvard University Press.

Minkler, M., and Rowe, J. 1993. *Grandparents as caregivers.* Newbury Park, CA: Sage.

Myers, G. 1990. Demography of aging. In R. Binstock and L. George (eds.), *Handbook of aging and the social sciences* (3rd ed., pp. 19–44). New York: Academic Press.

Ogburn, W. F. 1932. The family and its functions. In W. F. Ogburn, *Recent social trends.* New York: McGraw-Hill.

Osmond, M. W., and Thorne, B. 1993. Feminist theories: The social construction of gender in families and society. In P. G. Boss, W. J. Doherty, R. La Rossa, W. R. Schumm, and S. K. Steinmetz, *Sourcebook of family methods and theories* (pp. 591–623). New York: Plenum Press.

Parsons, T. 1944. The social structure of the family. In R. N. Anshen (ed.), *The family: Its function and destiny* (pp. 173–201). New York: Harper.

Popenoe, D. 1993. American family decline, 1960–1990: A review and appraisal. *Journal of Marriage and the Family* 55:527–55.

———. 1996. *Life without father: Compelling new evidence that fatherhood and marriage are indispensable for the good of children and society.* New York: Free Press.

Riley, M. W., and Riley, J. W. 1993. Connections: Kin and cohort. In V. L. Bengtson & W. A. Achenbaum (eds.), *The changing contract across generations.* New York: Aldine de Gruyter.

Roberts, R. E. L., and Bengtson, V. L. 1990. Is intergenerational solidarity a unidimensional construct? A second test of a formal model. *Journal of Gerontology: Social Sciences* 45: S12–S20.

Roberts, R. E. L., Richards, L. N., and Bengtson, V. L. 1991. Intergenerational solidarity in families: Untangling the ties that bind. In S. K. Pfeifer and M. B. Sussman (eds.), *Marriage and Family Review, Vol. 16* (pp. 11–46). Binghamton, NY: Haworth Press.

Rossi, A., and Rossi, P. 1990. *Of human bonding: Parent-child relations across the life course.* New York: Aldine de Gruyter.

Silverstein, M., and Litwak, E. 1993. A task-specific typology of intergenerational family structure in later life. *Gerontologist* 33:256–64.

Silverstein, M., Giarrusso, R., and Bengtson, V. L., 1998. Intergenerational solidarity and the grandparent role. In M. Szinovacz (ed.), *Handbook on grandparenthood* (pp. 144–58). Westport, CT: Greenwood Press.

Silverstein, M., Parrott, T. M., and Bengtson, V. L. 1995. Factors that predispose middle-aged sons and daughters to provide social support to older parents. *Journal of Marriage and the Family* 57:465–75.

Skolnick, A. 1991. *Embattled paradise: The American family in an age of uncertainty.* New York: Basic Books.

Smock, P. J., and Manning, W. D. 1997. Nonresident parents' characteristics and child support. *Journal of Marriage and the Family* 59:798–808.

Soldo, B. J., and Hill, M. S. 1993. Intergenerational transfers: Economic, demographic, and social perspectives. *Annual Review of Gerontology and Geriatrics* 13:187–216.

Stacey, J. 1990. *Brave new families: Stories of domestic upheaval in late twentieth century America.* New York: Basic Books.

———. 1993. Is the sky falling? *Journal of Marriage and the Family* 55:555–59.

———. 1996. *In the name of the family: Rethinking family values in the postmodern age.* Boston: Beacon Press.

Stacey, J., and Biblarz, T. (2001). How does the sexual orientation of parents matter? *American Sociological Review* 66(2):159–83.

Stack, C. 1974. *All our kin: Strategies for survival in a Black community.* New York: Harper and Row.

Szinovacz, M. 1998. *Handbook on grandparenthood.* Westport, CT: Greenwood Press.

Thorne, B., and Yalom, M. 1992 *Rethinking the family: Some feminist questions.* Boston: Northeastern University Press.

Treas, J. 1995a. Commentary: Beanpole or beanstalk? Comments on "The Demography of Changing Intergenerational Relations." In V. L. Bengtson, K. W. Schaie, and L. M. Burton (eds.), *Adult intergenerational relations* (pp. 26–29). New York: Springer.

———. 1995b. Older Americans in the 1990s and beyond. *Population Bulletin* 50:2–46.

Uhlenberg, P. 1996. Mutual attraction: Demography and life-course analysis. *Gerontologist* 36:226–29.

Wachter, K. W. 1997. Kinship resources for the elderly. *Philosophical transactions of the Royal Society of London* 352:1811–17.

Walker, A. J., and McGraw, L. A. 2000. Who is responsible for responsible fathering? *Journal of Marriage and the Family* 62:563–69.

CHAPTER 11

Reading 11-2

American Civil Liberties Union. 2007. *Domestic Violence: Protective Orders and the Role of Police Enforcement.* http://www.aclu.org/womensrights/protectiveorders.pdf (last accessed 15 April 2007)

Avakame, Edem F. and James J. Fyfe. 2001. "Differential Police Treatment of Male-on-Female Spousal Violence: Additional Evidence on the Leniency Thesis." *Violence against Women* 7: 22–45.

Belknap, Joanne. 2001. *The Invisible Woman: Gender, Crime, and Justice* (2nd ed.). Belmont, CA: Wadsworth.

Belknap, Joanne and Jennifer L. Hartman. 2000. "Police Responses to Woman Battering: Victim Advocates' Reports." *International Review of Victimology* 1–3: 159–77.

Bohmer, Carol, Jennifer Brandt, Denise Bronson and Helen Hartnett. 2002. "Domestic Violence Law Reforms: Reactions from the Trenches." *Journal of Sociology and Social Welfare* 29: 71–87.

Buzawa, Eve S. and Thomas Austin. 1993. "Determining Police Response to Domestic Violence Victims: The Role of Victim Preference." *American Behavioral Scientist* 36: 610–23.

Catalano, Shannon. 2006. *Intimate Partner Violence in the United States.* Washington, DC: US Department of Justice, Bureau of Justice Statistics. http://www.ojp.usdoj.gov/bjs/intimate/ipv.htm (last accessed 15 April 2007)

Cho, Hyunkag and Dina J. Wilke. 2005. "How Has the Violence Against Women Act Affected the Response of the Criminal Justice System to Domestic Violence?" *Journal of Sociology and Social Welfare* 32: 125–39.

Crenshaw, Kimberle W. 1994. "Mapping the Margins: Intersectionality, Identity Politics, and Violence against Women of Color." Pp. 93–118 in *The Public Nature of Private Violence,* edited by Martha A. Fineman and Roxanne Mykitiuk. New York: Routledge.

Dasgupta, Shamita D. 2003. *Safety & Justice for All: Examining the Relationship between the Women's Anti-Violence Movement and the Criminal Legal System.* New York: Ms. Foundation. http://www.ms.foundation.org/user-assets/PDF/Program/safety_justice.pdf (last accessed 15 April 2007)

DeLeon-Granados, William, William Wells and Ruddyard Binsbacher. 2006. "Arresting Developments: Trends in Female Arrests for Domestic Violence and Proposed Explanations." *Violence against Women* 12: 355–71.

Epstein, Deborah. 1999. "Redefining the State's Response to Domestic Violence: Past Victories and Future Challenges." *Georgetown Journal of Gender and the Law* 1. 127–43.

Ferraro, Kathleen J. and Lucille Pope. 1993. "Irreconcilable Differences: Battered Women, Police and the Law." Pp. 96–123 in *Legal Responses to Wife Assault: Current Trends and Evaluations,* edited by N. Zoe Hilton. Newbury Park, CA: Sage Publications.

Finn, Mary A. and Pamela Bettis. 2006. "Punitive Action or Gentle Persuasion: Exploring Police Officers' Justifications for Using Dual Arrest in Domestic Violence Cases." *Violence against Women* 12: 268–87.

Ford, David A. 1991. "Prosecution as a Victim Power Resource: A Note on Empowering Women in Violent Conjugal Relationships." *Law and Society Review* 25: 313–34.

Gelles, Richard J. 1993. "Constraints Against Family Violence: How Well Do They Work?" *American Behavioral Scientist* 36: 575–85.

Gosselin, Denise K. 2000. *Heavy Hands: An Introduction to the Crimes of Family Violence* (2nd ed.). Upper Saddle River, NJ: Prentice Hall.

Hilton, N. Zoe. 1993. "Introduction." Pp. 3–8 in *Legal Responses to Wife Assault: Current Trends and Evaluations,* edited by N. Zoe Hilton. Newbury Park, CA: Sage Publications.

Hirschel, J. David and Eve Buzawa. 2002. "Understanding the Context of Dual Arrest with Directions for Future Research." *Violence against Women* 81: 1449–73.

Johnson, Michael P. 2005. "Domestic Violence: It's Not about Gender—Or Is It?" *Journal of Marriage and Family* 67: 1126–30.

Johnson, Michael P. 2006. "Conflict and Control: Gender Symmetry and Asymmetry in Domestic Violence." *Violence against Women* 12: 1003–18.

Johnson, Michael P. and Kathleen J. Ferraro. 2000. "Research on Domestic Violence in the 1990s: Making Distinctions." *Journal of Marriage and the Family* 62: 948–63.

Jones, Dana A. and Joanne Belknap. 1999. "Police Responses to Battering in a Progressive Pro-Arrest Jurisdiction." *Justice Quarterly* 16: 249–73.

Mahoney, Martha R. 1994. "Victimization or Oppression? Women's Lives, Violence, and Agency." Pp. 59–92 in *The Public Nature of Private Violence,* edited by Martha A. Fineman and Roxanne Mykitiuk. New York, NY: Routledge.

Maxwell, Christopher D., Joel H. Garner and Jeffrey Fagan. 2002. "The Preventive Effects of Arrest on Intimate Partner Violence: Research, Policy, and Theory." *Criminology and Public Policy* 2: 51–80.

McLeod, Maureen. 1983. "Victim Noncooperation in the Prosecution of Domestic Assault." *Criminology* 21: 395–416.

Mills, Linda G. 1996. "Empowering Women Transnationally: The Case for Postmodern Interventions." *Social Work* 41: 261–68.

Mills, Linda G. 2003. *Insult to Injury: Rethinking Our Responses to Intimate Abuse.* Princeton, NJ: Princeton University Press.

Miller, Susan L. 2001. "The Paradox of Women Arrested for Domestic Violence: Criminal Justice Professionals and Service Providers Respond." *Violence against Women* 7: 1339–76.

Osthoff, Sue. 2002. "But, Gertrude, I Beg to Differ, a Hit Is Not a Hit Is Not a Hit." *Violence against Women* 8: 1521–44.

Rajah, Valli, Victoria Frye and Mary Haviland. 2006. "Aren't I a Victim? Notes on Identity Challenges Relating to Police Action in a Mandatory Arrest Jurisdiction." *Violence against Women* 12: 897–916.

Schmidt, Janell D. and Lawrence W. Sherman. 1996. "Does Arrest Deter Domestic Violence?" Pp. 43–53 in *Do Arrests and Restraining Orders Work?* edited by Eve S. Buzawa and Carl G. Buzawa. Thousand Oaks, CA: Sage Publications.

Schneider, Elizabeth M. 2000. *Battered Women and Feminist Lawmaking.* New Haven, CT: Yale University Press.

Sherman, Lawrence W. 1992. *Policing Domestic Violence: Experiments and Dilemmas.* New York: Free Press.

Sherman, Lawrence W. and Richard A. Berk. 1984. "The Specific Deterrent Effects of Arrest for Domestic Assault." *American Sociological Review* 49: 261–72.

Simpson, Sally S., Leana Allen Bouffard, Joel Garner and Laura Hickman. 2006. "The Influence of Legal Reform on the Probability of Arrest in Domestic Violence Cases." *Justice Quarterly* 23: 297–316.

Smith, Alisa. 2001. "Domestic Violence Laws: The Voices of Battered Women." *Violence and Victims* 16: 91–111.

Sparks, Anne. 1997. "Feminists Negotiate the Executive Branch: The Policing of Male Violence." Pp. 35–52 in *Feminists Negotiate the State: The Politics of Domestic Violence,* edited by Cynthia R. Davies. Lanham, MD: University Press of America.

Stark, Evan. 1993. "Mandatory Arrest of Batterers: A Reply to Its Critics." *American Behavioral Scientist* 36: 651–79.

Stark, Evan. 2004. "Insults, Injury, and Injustice: Rethinking State Intervention in Domestic Violence Cases." *Violence against Women* 10: 1302–30.

Stephens, B. Joyce and Peter G. Sinden. 2000. "Victims' Voices: Domestic Assault Victim's Perceptions of Police Demeanor." *Journal of Interpersonal Violence* 15: 534–47.

Stewart, Anna. 2001. "Policing Domestic Violence: An Overview of Emerging Issues." *Police Practice and Research* 2: 447–59.

Wittner, Judith. 1998. "Reconceptualizing Agency in Domestic Violence Court." Pp. 81–104 in *Community Activism and Feminist Politics: Organizing Across Race, Class, and Gender,* edited by Nancy Naples. New York: Routledge.

CHAPTER 12

Reading 12-2

Amato, P. R. (1994). Life-span adjustment of children to their parents' divorce. *Future of Children: Children and Divorce, 4,* 143–164.

Amato, P. (1996). Explaining the intergenerational transmission of divorce. *Journal of Marriage and the Family, 58,* 628–640.

Amato, P. (1999). Children of divorced parents as young adults. In E. M. Hetherington (Ed.), *Coping with divorce, single parenting, and remarriage* (pp. 147–164). Mahwah, NJ: Erlbaum.

Amato, P. (2000). The consequences of divorce for adults and children. *Journal of Marriage and Family, 62,* 1269–1287.

Amato, P. R. (2001). Children of divorce in the 1990s: An update of the Amato and Keith (1991) meta-analysis. *Journal of Family Psychology, 15,* 355–370.

Amato, P., & Booth, A. (1996). A prospective study of divorce and parent-child relationships. *Journal of Marriage and the Family, 58,* 356–365.

Amato, P., & Gilbreth, J. (1999). Nonresident fathers and children's well-being: A meta-analysis. *Journal of Marriage and the Family, 61,* 557–573.

Amato, P., & Keith, B. (1991). Parental divorce and adult well-being: A meta-analysis. *Journal of Marriage and the Family, 53,* 43–58.

Amato, P. R., Loomis, L., & Booth, A. (1995). Parental divorce, parental marital conflict, and offspring well-being during early adulthood. *Social Forces, 73,* 895–916.

Amato, P. R., & Rezac, S. (1994). Contact with residential parents, interparental conflict, and children's behavior. *Journal of Family Issues, 12,* 578–599.

Bausermann, R. (2002). Child adjustment in joint-custody versus sole-custody arrangements: A meta-analytic review. *Journal of Family Psychology, 16,* 91–102.

Booth, A., & Amato, P. R. (2001). Parental predivorce relations and offspring postdivorce well-being. *Journal of Marriage and Family, 63,* 197–212.

Braver, S. L., & O'Connell, E. (1998). *Divorced dads: Shattering the myths.* New York: Tarcher, Putnam.

Bray, J. H. (1999). From marriage to remarriage and beyond: Findings from the Developmental Issues in StepFamilies research project. In E. M. Hetherington (Ed.), *Coping with divorce, single parenting, and remarriage: A risk and resiliency perspective* (pp. 253–272). Mahwah, NJ: Erlbaum.

Buchanan, C., Maccoby, E., & Dornbusch, S. (1991). Caught between parents: Adolescents' experience in divorced homes. *Child Development, 62,* 1008–1029.

Chase-Lansdale, P. L., Cherlin, A. J., & Kierman, K. E. (1995). The long-term effects of parental divorce on the mental health of young adults: A developmental perspective. *Child Development, 66,* 1614–1634.

Cummings, E., & Davies, P. (1994). *Children and marital conflict.* New York: Guilford Press.

Doherty, W. J. (1998). Responsible fathering: An overview and conceptual framework. *Journal of Marriage and the Family, 60,* 277–292.

Dunn, J., Davies, L., O'Connor, T., & Sturgess, W. (2001). Family lives and friendships: The perspectives of children in step-, single-parent, and nonstop families. *Journal of Family Psychology, 15,* 272–287.

Emery, R. E. (1999). *Marriage, divorce, and children's adjustment* (2nd ed.). Thousand Oaks, CA: Sage.

Emery, R. E., & Forehand, R. (1994). Parental divorce and children's well-being: A focus on resilience. In R. J. Haggerty, L. Sherred, N. Garmezy, & M. Rutter (Eds.), *Risk and resilience in children* (pp. 64–99). London: Cambridge University Press.

Emery, R. E., Kitzmann, K. M., & Waldron, M. (1999). Psychological interventions for separated and divorced families. In E. M. Hetherington (Ed.), *Coping with divorce, single parenting, and remarriage* (pp. 323–344). Mahwah, NJ: Erlbaum.

Fabricius, W. V. (2003). Listening to divorce: New findings that diverge from Wallerstein, Lewis, and Blakeslee. *Family Relations, 52,* 385–396.

Fabricius, W. V., Braver, S. L., & Deneau, K. (2003). Divorced parents' financial support of their children's college expenses. *Family Court Review, 41,* 224–241.

Fabricius, W. V., & Hall, J. (2000). Young adults' perspectives on divorce: Living arrangements. *Family and Conciliation Courts Review, 38,* 446–461.

Furstenberg, F. F., & Kiernan, K. E. (2001). Delayed parental divorce: How much do children benefit? *Journal of Marriage and Family, 63,* 446–457.

Hetherington, E. M. (1999). Should we stay together for the sake of the children? In E. M. Hetherington (Ed.), *Coping with divorce, single parenting, and remarriage* (pp. 93–116). Mahwah, NJ: Erlbaum.

Hetherington, E. M., & Kelly, J. (2002). *For better or for worse.* New York: Norton.

Johnston, J. R. (1995). Research update: Children's adjustment in sole custody compared to joint custody families and principles for custody decision making. *Family and Conciliation Courts Review, 33,* 415–425.

Johnston, J. R., & Campbell, L. (1988). *Impasses of divorce: The dynamics and resolution of family conflict.* New York: Free Press.

Johnston, J. R., & Roseby, V. (1997). *In the name of the child. A developmental approach to understanding and helping children of conflict and violent divorce.* New York: Free Press.

Kalter, N., Kloner, A., Schreiser, S., & Okla, K. (1989). Predictors of children's post-divorce adjustment. *American Journal of Orthopsychiatry, 59,* 605–618.

Keitner, G. I., & Miller, I. W. (1990). Family functioning and major depression: An overview. *American Journal of Psychiatry, 147,* 1128–1137.

Kelly, J. B. (2000). Children's adjustment in conflicted marriage and divorce: A decade review of research. *Journal of Child and Adolescent Psychiatry, 39,* 963–973.

Kelly, J. B. (2002). Psychological and legal interventions for parents and children in custody and access disputes: Current research and practice. *Virginia Journal of Social Policy and Law, 10,* 129–163.

King, V., & Heard, H. E. (1999). Nonresident father visitation, parental conflict, and mother's satisfaction: What's best for child well-being? *Journal of Marriage and the Family, 61,* 385–396.

Kline, M., Johnston, J., & Tschann, J. (1990). The long shadow of marital conflict: A model of children's postdivorce adjustment. *Journal of Marriage and the Family, 53,* 297–309.

Krishnakamur, A., & Buehler, C. (2000). Interparental conflict and parenting behaviors: A meta-analytic review. *Family Relations, 49,* 25–44.

Laumann-Billings, L., & Emery, R. E. (2000). Distress among young adults in divorced families. *Journal of Family Psychology, 14,* 671–687.

Lee, M.-Y. (2002). A model of children's postdivorce behavioral adjustment in maternal and dual-residence arrangements. *Journal of Family Issues, 23,* 672–697.

Maccoby, E., & Mnookin, R. (1992). *Dividing the child.* Cambridge, MA: Harvard University Press.

McIntosh, J. (2000). Child-inclusive divorce mediation: Report on a qualitative research study. *Mediation Quarterly, 18,* 55–70.

McLanahan, S. S. (1999). Father absence and children's welfare. In E. M. Hetherington (Ed.), *Coping with divorce, single parenting, and remarriage: A risk and resiliency perspective* (pp. 117–146). Mahwah, NJ: Erlbaum.

McLanahan, S. S., & Sandefur, G. (1994). *Growing up with a single parent.* Cambridge, MA: Harvard University Press.

Menning, C. L. (2002). Absent parents are more than money: The joint effects of activities and financial support on youths' educational attainment. *Journal of Family Issues, 23,* 648–671.

Neighbors, B., Forehand, R., & McVicar, D. (1993). Resilient adolescents and interparental conflict. *American Journal of Orthopsychiatry, 63,* 462–471.

Nord, C. W., Brimhall, D., & West, J. (1997). *Fathers' involvement in their children's schools.* Washington, DC: National Center for Education Statistics.

Pleck, J. H. (1997). Paternal involvement: Level, sources, and consequences. In M. E. Lamb (Ed.), *The role of the father in child development* (3rd ed.; pp. 66–103). New York: Wiley.

Pong, S.-L., & Ju, D.-B. (2000). The effects of change in family structure and income on dropping out of middle and high school. *Journal of Family Issues, 21,* 147–169.

Seltzer, J. (1991). Relationships between fathers and children who live apart: The father's role after separation. *Journal of Marriage and the Family, 53,* 79–101.

Seltzer, J. (1998). Father by law: Effects of joint legal custody on nonresident fathers' involvement with children. *Demography, 35,* 135–146.

Simons, R. L., & Associates (1996). *Understanding differences between divorced and intact families: Stress, interaction, and child outcome.* Thousand Oaks, CA: Sage.

Smart, C., & Neale, B. (2000). "It's my life too"—Children's perspectives on post-divorce parenting. *Family Law, 30,* 163–169.

Stewart, A., Copeland, A., Chester, N., Malley, J., & Barenbaum, N. (1997). *Separating together: How divorce transforms families.* New York: Guilford.

Sun, Y. (2001). Family environment and adolescents' well-being before and after parents' marital disruption: A longitudinal analysis. *Journal of Marriage and Family, 63,* 697–713.

Sun, Y., & Li, Y. (2001). Marital disruption, parental investment, and children's academic achievement. *Journal of Family Issues, 22,* 27–62.

Sun, Y., & Li, Y. (2002). Children's well-being during parents' marital disruption process: A pooled time-series analysis. *Journal of Marriage and Family, 64,* 472–488.

Vandewater, E., & Lansford, J. (1998). Influences of family structure and parental conflict on children's well-being. *Family Relations, 47,* 323–330.

Wallerstein, J. S., & Blakeslee. S. (1989). *Second chances: Men, women and children a decade after divorce.* New York: Ticknor & Fields.

Wallerstein, J. S., & Kelly, J. B. (1980). *Surviving the breakup: How children and parents cope with divorce.* New York: Basic Books.

Wallerstein, J. S., Lewis, J. M., & Blakeslee, S. (2000). *The unexpected legacy of divorce: A 25 year landmark study.* New York: Hyperion.

Whiteside, M. F., & Becker, B. J. (2000). Parental factors and young child's postdivorce adjustment: A meta-analysis with implications for parenting arrangements. *Journal of Family Psychology, 14,* 5–26.

Wolfinger, N. H. (2000). Beyond the intergenerational transmission of divorce: Do people replicate the patterns of marital instability they grew up with? *Journal of Family Issues, 21,* 1061–1086.

Zill, N. D. (1988). Behavior, achievement, and health problems among children in stepfamilies: Findings from a national survey of child health. In E. M. Hetherington & J. D. Arasteh (Eds.), *Impact of divorce, single parenting, and stepparenting on children* (pp. 325–363). Hillsdale, NJ: Erlbaum.

Zill, N., Morrison, D., & Coiro, M. (1993). Long-term effects of parental divorce on parent-child relationships, adjustment, and achievement in young adulthood. *Journal of Family Psychology, 7,* 91–103.

Zill, N., & Schoenborn, C. A. (1990). *Developmental, learning, and emotional problems: Health of our nation's children, United States, 1988.* Advance data from Vital and Health Statistics, No. 190. Washington, DC: National Center for Health Statistics.

CHAPTER 13

Reading 13-2

Bumpass, Larry, and R. Kelly Raley. 1995. "Redefining Single-Parent Families: Cohabitation and Changing Family Reality." *Demography* 32 (February): 97–109.

Dean Brick, Pat, Genevieve Kenney, Robin McCullough-Harlin, Shruti Rajan, Fritz Scheuren, Kevin Wang, J. Michael Brick, and Pat Cunningham. 1999. *1997 NSAF Survey Methods and Data Reliability.* Washington, D.C.: The Urban Institute. National Survey of America's Families Methodology Report No. 1.

Ehrle, Jennifer, and Kristen Anderson Moore. 1999. *Benchmarking Child and Family Well-Being Measures in the NSAF.* Washington, D.C.: The Urban Institute. National Survey of America's Families Methodology Report No. 6.

Manning, Wendy, and Daniel T. Lichter. 1996. "Parental Cohabitation and Children's Economic Well-Being." *Journal of Marriage and the Family* 58 (November): 998–1010.

McLanahan, Sara, and Gary Sandefur. 1994. *Growing Up with a Single Parent: What Hurts, What Helps.* Cambridge, MA: Harvard University Press.

Moore, Kristen Anderson, Juliet L. Hatcher, Sharon Vandivere, and Brett V. Brown. 2000. *Children's Behavior and Well-Being: Findings from the National Survey of America's Families.* Washington, D.C.: The Urban Institute. Snapshots of America's Families II.

Smock, Pamela J., and Wendy Manning. 1997. "Cohabiting Partners' Economic Circumstances and Marriage." *Demography* 34 (August): 331–341.